Tennessee Women

Tennessee Women

THEIR LIVES AND TIMES

Volume 1

EDITED BY

Sarah Wilkerson Freeman and

Beverly Greene Bond

Associate Editor, Laura Helper-Ferris

❀ ❀ ❀

The University of Georgia Press *Athens and London*

Athens, Georgia 30602

Set in Minion by Graphic Composition, Inc.
Printed and bound by Thomson-Shore
The paper in this book meets the guidelines for
permanence and durability of the Committee on
Production Guidelines for Book Longevity of the
Council on Library Resources.

Printed in the United States of America
13 12 11 10 09 C 5 4 3 2 1
13 12 11 10 09 P 5 4 3 2 1

Library of Congress Cataloging-in-Publication Data

Tennessee women : their lives and times / edited by Sarah Wilkerson
Freeman and Beverly Greene Bond ; associate editor, Laura Helper-Ferris.
p. cm.
Includes bibliographical references and index.
ISBN-13: 978-0-8203-2948-2 (v.1 : hardcover : alk. paper)
ISBN-10: 0-8203-2948-7 (v.1 : hardcover : alk. paper)
ISBN-13: 978-0-8203-2949-9 (v.1 : pbk. : alk. paper)
ISBN-10: 0-8203-2949-5 (v.1 : pbk. : alk. paper)
1. Women—Tennessee—Biography. 2. Women—Tennessee—History.
3. Tennessee—Biography. I. Freeman, Sarah Wilkerson, 1956–
II. Bond, Beverly G. III. Helper-Ferris, Laura.
CT3262.T2 T46 2009
920.72'09768—dc22
[B] 2008036509

British Library Cataloging-in-Publication Data available

Contents

Preface

SARAH WILKERSON FREEMAN

> A sense of one's place and of history makes distant places less strange and the past more pertinent to the present.
>
> WILMA DYKEMAN

Tennessee Women: Their Lives and Times examines women's private and public experiences within the context of more than two centuries of history and the South's richly diverse geography and cultures. These eighteen biographical chapters focus on women whose stories are familiar and others whose lives have remained in shadow, revealing a history that is often unexpected and complex. As historian Margaret Ripley Wolfe, author of *Daughters of Canaan: A Saga of Southern Women* (Lexington: University Press of Kentucky, 1995), observed, "Coming to terms with females below the Mason-Dixon line demands attention to the subtleties and nuances of women's private worlds of life and work in addition to the dynamics of the public arenas of their eras" (5). Envisioning these women in the times and spaces they inhabited inspires a heightened sense of place, a greater appreciation of the role of gender and race in the stories of our lives, and a clearer understanding of the uniqueness of Tennessee history.

The focus on women in Tennessee, a racially diverse mid-South state with a competitive political system and extraordinary musical cultures, sets this volume apart from more general studies of southern women. Likewise, the placement of women at the center of the historical stage, with Tennessee as a setting and backdrop, re-envisions the state's past. These women left intriguing footprints in Tennessee's history. While their biographies tend to heighten the significance of individual women, grouping these women's life stories in a single volume encourages a greater appreciation of women's history as an integral part of Tennessee's history.

These eighteen women reflect the state's three principal geographic regions and larger regional cultures. A defining characteristic of Tennessee is its vastness, as it stretches for five hundred miles, from North Carolina in the east to Arkansas in the west, sharing common borders with seven states. Kinship and community networks cross state lines and variously influence personal orientations. While some subjects knew and interacted with each other, others remained circumscribed and separated by great distances, thick forests, steep mountains, and wild rushing rivers—terrain that isolated even as it inspired.

Women living within the hollows and ridgelines of the Great Smoky Mountains of East Tennessee shared conditions experienced by mountain women of Kentucky, Virginia, and North Carolina to the north and east and South Carolina, Georgia, and Alabama to the south. Knoxville, located in the center of East Tennessee's Great Valley at the headwaters of the Tennessee River, became the urban center of this region as it drew migrants from nearby mountain counties to work in industries based on coal, lumber, marble, textiles, and energy generated by the Tennessee Valley Authority.

A much different landscape defined women's lives in West Tennessee, where proximity to the Mississippi River encouraged a more metropolitan orientation. River traffic between St. Louis and New Orleans, before and after the Louisiana Purchase, hastened the transformation of an ancient American Indian trading center into what became Memphis—a world capital for the cotton trade. As floods regularly inundated the delta, the bluffs on the Tennessee side of the river provided safe haven for people working the rich lowlands of Mississippi and Arkansas. The cultures, lifestyles, and skills of African Americans who migrated from these regions especially shaped Memphis, just thirty miles north of the Mississippi state line, into a unique southern city.

Middle Tennessee represents yet another geographically and culturally distinct region, defined by the Cumberland Plateau and the Cumberland River, which flows from eastern Kentucky into northern Tennessee then back into western Kentucky, where it joins the Ohio River. Middle Tennessee's natural resources (especially coal and mineral deposits) and transportation provided by the Cumberland and Tennessee rivers fueled the growth of Nashville. This key port along the Cumberland River became the region's commercial and industrial center. Influences from the north, especially from Kentucky and Ohio, helped establish educational institutions that gave Nashville its reputation as the "Athens of the South." Legislative battles in Nashville, the state capital, determined the laws and policies that shaped women's lives from the Great Smokies to the Mississippi River and provided common ground for Tennessee women across the distances.

The book begins with early tensions and interactions between ethnic groups, focusing specifically on Nan-ye-hi, the "Beloved Woman" of the Cherokee, and

Fanny Wright, founder of the abolitionist, feminist/egalitarian commune of Nashoba. As native women endured the relentless encroachment of Europeans, they also became part of emerging mixed-race societies of slave and free populations that extended their claims into Tennessee. Nan-ye-hi's vision of peaceful coexistence of native and new people, as interpreted by Cynthia Cumfer, reminds us also of the violent experiences and subjugation of the region's first inhabitants and the circumstances under which Tennessee, as a state within an evolving nation, began. Fanny Wright's biographer, Celia Morris, illuminates Wright's struggle to create new freedoms for women and people of color in the midst of patriarchal, racist, and slave-based societies and how important the land itself was in shaping her extraordinarily modern vision.

Beverly Greene Bond's treatment of Milly Swan Price, a free woman of color whose life spanned generations before and after the Civil War, emphasizes the difficulties of maintaining family connections in a society and legal system in rapid flux, especially where the rights and protections of African Americans were concerned. Cherisse Jones-Branch picks up on this theme in her portrait of Mary Church Terrell, a familiar historical figure. Jones-Branch invites us to revise our understanding of Terrell by seeing her in the context of a family and community, rooted in Tennessee, that fundamentally inspired Terrell's dedication to seeking justice even at the highest political levels.

These roots become even more meaningful in Linda T. Wynn's chapter on Diane Nash and the early civil rights activism of students at Fisk University in Nashville in the 1960s. Nash, whose grandparents migrated from Memphis to Chicago, represents the return of Tennessee's African Americans to challenge the southern roots of racism. Her willingness to stand up to Nashville's political authorities and to lead her fellow students to defy Jim Crow is an important part of the larger story of the modern civil rights movement. Nash's goal of peaceful coexistence, based on mutual respect and recognition of a common humanity regardless of race, seems an old and hauntingly familiar dream in the context of Tennessee history. Indeed, Melissa Checker finds a similar influence running deep within the generations of her subject, Doris Bradshaw, whose efforts to expose health hazards posed by toxic waste in African American communities began in the 1990s and continue today.

In a related theme of women's rights activism, several chapters focus on Tennessee women as feminists and political players. Tennessee's critical role as the thirty-sixth state to ratify the Nineteenth Amendment, which in 1920 granted women the right to vote, is well known. But two Tennessee women, Sue Shelton White and Charl Ormond Williams, have often been neglected or misunderstood in treatments of the woman suffrage and women's rights movements.

White and Williams seem at first to represent different locations on the feminist spectrum, but both eventually emerged as militant advocates for women's rights. Williams's strategy of attacking the inadequacies in public education in the South by working for federal support remains controversial. Her story reminds us of work that remains and of a Tennessee woman's potential to influence public policy, even if she has to go to Washington, D.C., to do it.

Connie L. Lester's portrait of Lucille Thornburgh, a lifelong labor organizer, shows the tremendous obstacles arrayed against working-class Tennesseans. Even as antiunion forces and gender discrimination threatened her efforts, Thornburgh kept organizing. Her political support of Estes Kefauver, a homegrown liberal politician and Democrat, seems to have helped protect her. Several of our subjects were deeply involved in Kefauver's three successful U.S. Senate campaigns (1948, 1954, and 1960) and in his unsuccessful vice presidential and presidential bids in the 1950s. Another subject, Martha Ragland, supported him in order to combat corruption and advance progressive agendas, such as birth control and anti–poll tax movements. The ideological evolutions of Thornburgh and Ragland illuminate feminist and labor activism during the 1940s and 1950s—a period ordinarily associated with progressive inactivity. The importance of Tennessee in the history of gender politics is illustrated further by Gail S. Murray's chapter on Jocelyn Dan Wurzburg, a civil rights and feminist organizer and pioneer in conflict mediation. It is due in part to Wurzburg's work on the Tennessee Commission on the Status of Women that the history of women in the state received some attention in the 1970s with the publication of *Tennessee Women: Past and Present*, written by Wilma Dykeman, edited by Carol Lynn Yellin, and sponsored by the commission (privately published, 1977). Melissa Walker gives us a fine portrait of a Tennessee woman in her chapter on Dykeman, whose beloved stories of Appalachian communities, mountains, rivers, and sacred natural spaces that call, comfort, and renew the soul touch a chord in many who abhor the environmental desecration and disappearing beauty of Tennessee.

This volume also emphasizes the importance of Tennessee women in creating phenomenal movements and trends in music. The cultural influence of Tennessee women has rocked the world, and their voices and performances receive particular attention here. Alberta Hunter, raised in Memphis, was part of a long line of extraordinarily talented blues women who migrated north. As Michelle R. Scott illustrates, Hunter found her voice and livelihood in the music of her Memphis childhood. Like Hunter, other powerfully creative Tennessee women not included in this collection—such as Chattanooga's Bessie Smith; Tina Turner, a native of Nutbush; and Dolly Parton, from the mountains of

Seiverville—are part of much more than Tennessee's musical heritage as their performances and compositions influenced music across the globe and generations. It is interesting that women from this state have in common a potency that is liberating and undeniable and that reaches across ideological, cultural, and racial divides.

This force spawned music industries that draw millions to Memphis, Nashville, and Appalachian hill towns, millions who hope to touch whatever is the source of that amazing music. Three of our authors give us new perspectives on how the industries evolved and the central roles women played in the music business—certainly one of Tennessee's unique legacies. Laura Helper-Ferris, in her essay on Bettye Berger, shows us the interracial side of the music business and club scenes in Memphis, as well as the activities of impresarios and entertainers like Sam Phillips, Elvis Presley, and Ivory Joe Hunter. Nashville's country music industry owes a tremendous debt to Sarah Colley Cannon (Minnie Pearl) and Jo Walker-Meador, who turned this genre of entertainment into a global force. Authors Kristine M. McCusker and Diane Pecknold illustrate the importance of combining feminist scholarship with the study of southern musical cultures.

This volume also examines two women who challenged traditional female stereotypes through demonstrations of remarkable physical talent and endurance. Phoebe Fairgrave Omlie, a record-breaking aviator and stunt woman, began in the 1920s to amaze the world with her piloting prowess, high-flying trapeze acts, and wing-walking techniques. Her skill and courage later proved invaluable when she tested new aircraft and trained pilots during World War II and the Cold War. Janann Sherman recounts how, in the dawning modern age, Omlie's dreams and beliefs in what women could do truly took flight. And yet, as Aram Goudsouzian's biography of Olympic track star Wilma Rudolph reveals, racism and sexism continued to permeate traditionally male-dominated fields in the 1960s. Even such a talented and determined African American woman, who broke records in the sports world with her explosive strength, could not break the back of Jim Crow.

The arrangement of these biographies is more or less chronological, based on the women's birth dates (all subjects were born prior to 1955) and some common themes. Many of the women lived long and active lives, so there is a good deal of temporal overlap. For example, the African American civil rights pioneer Mary Church Terrell began life in Shelby County in the age of slavery and died just months after the 1954 U.S. Supreme Court decision outlawed racial segregation in public accommodations. The white Shelby County education activist Charl Ormond Williams was born in 1885, as "lynching bees" swept the South, and died shortly after the assassination of Dr. Martin Luther King Jr. in Memphis in 1968. Both women worked in Washington, D.C., within blocks of each other, from the 1920s to the 1950s. While the authors treat their subjects individually, readers can imagine the women occupying the same world—perhaps literally crossing paths through time, space, and history.

Tennessee Women: Their Lives and Times explores a broad range of women's experiences gleaned from a great variety of public and private sources. Many of these have only recently been discovered or catalogued. Some common themes emerge, such as the formative power of the land itself in the development of the women's values, purposes, and opportunities. An appreciation of the environment as something sacred and fragile is a central part of many of these women's stories, linking across nearly three hundred years the lives of Nan-ye-hi, Wilma Dykeman, and Doris Bradshaw. Likewise, extending through colonial times, the modern civil rights movement, and the second wave of feminism, we find a common thread of heartache and uncertainty as women struggled to survive. But not found within these pages are accounts of the desperate and embattled lives of women during the Civil War. Our authors preferred to focus on the very long journey from slavery and slaveholding to a society that valued freedom in equal measure for all. Many women represented here dedicated themselves to righting inequity and injustice in order to protect future generations from unnecessary misery and deprivation—a struggle that continues in the new millennium.

This single volume does not provide a comprehensive treatment of Tennessee women's history but, instead, begins our efforts to reveal this past. With this collection, we hope to inspire new interest in sources and sites that are important to Tennessee women's history—evidence that is in our own backyards—and convey messages from the past that resonate, become "less strange," and reveal a history more "pertinent to the present."

Beverly and I wish to thank the eighteen contributors to this book for helping to make this the exciting, dynamic project we envisioned several years ago. Each of these persons, an expert in his or her own right, graciously consented to add this project to their already busy schedules. We also appreciate the generous support we have received from the history departments at our universities, the University of Memphis—which served as our institutional base—and Arkansas State University. We are particularly grateful for the assistance of Edwin Frank and the Special Collections staff at the University of Memphis, John Dougan and Vincent Clark at the Shelby County Archives, and the staff of the Memphis Room at the Memphis Public Library. They have helped us uncover little-known facts about Alberta Hunter, Milly Swan Price, Mary Church Terrell, and Charl

Ormond Williams, which we incorporated into our own essays or passed along to the other authors. Our contributors have also worked with archives, research libraries, and special collections throughout the country. These include the State Historical Society of Wisconsin; the Library of Congress; Harvard University's Houghton Library; the Theresa Wolfson Papers, Martin Catherwood Library, School of Labor and Industrial Relations, Cornell University; the National Archives and Records Administration; the Women's Studies Manuscript Collections, Charl Ormond Williams Papers, and Martha Ragland Papers at the Schlesinger Library, Radcliffe College; the Lucille Thornburgh Collection at Wayne State University's Walter P. Reuther Library; the Country Music Foundation Oral History Collection at the Country Music Hall of Fame and Museum Library; the Grand Ole Opry Museum Archives; and the Tennessee State University Special Collections.

We especially thank our associate editor, Laura Helper-Ferris, and Stephanie Gilmore, who both provided editorial assistance when this book was in its developmental stages. Lou Paris contributed additional editing assistance in the final stages of manuscript preparation. Elizabeth Anne Payne and Martha Swain have been guiding spirits in the conception and development of this work. The model and standards set by our sisters to the south in *Mississippi Women: Their Histories, Their Lives* (Athens: University of Georgia Press, 2003) inspired us to extend the torch of inquiry up and into Tennessee's challenging historical terrain. We are deeply appreciative of their example, encouragement, and advice, which helped make this book possible. Kriste Lindenmeyer and Kathleen Berkeley suggested authors and topics. We reserve special appreciation for Nancy Grayson, editor-and-chief of the University of Georgia Press, for providing priceless encouragement and guidance throughout this project, and for our husbands, Geraldus "Fuzz" Bond and Herschel Freeman, and our children—Christopher and Julia Bond Ellingboe, Amelia and Ingrid Ellingboe, and Ben David ("BD") and Molly Freeman—whose generosity, good natures, and assistance enhanced the personal value of this communal venture.

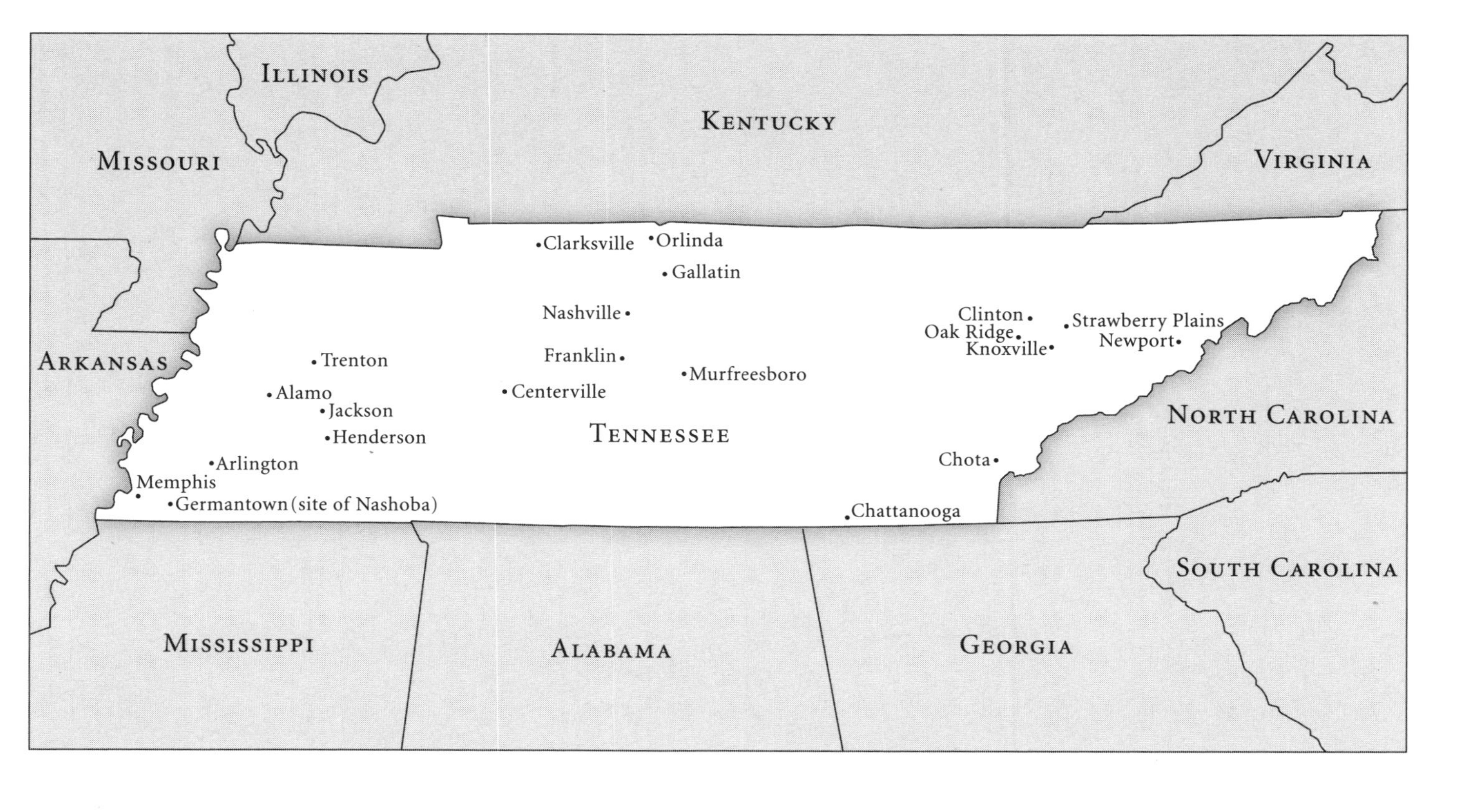

Illinois
Missouri
Kentucky
Virginia
Arkansas
Clarksville
Orlinda
Gallatin
Nashville
Franklin
Murfreesboro
Centerville
Trenton
Alamo
Jackson
Henderson
Arlington
Memphis
Germantown (site of Nashoba)
Tennessee
Clinton
Oak Ridge
Knoxville
Strawberry Plains
Newport
North Carolina
Chota
Chattanooga
South Carolina
Mississippi
Alabama
Georgia

Tennessee Women

Nan-ye-hi (Nancy Ward)

(c. 1730s–1824)

Diplomatic Mother

CYNTHIA CUMFER

❀ ❀ ❀

Called "the Pocahontas of her people," Nan-ye-hi, also known as Nancy Ward, is the most eulogized of the Cherokees. Authors portray her as an exceptional woman who was a friend to frontier people in the Tennessee region in the late eighteenth century, a woman who sought harmony between her nation and the settlers. Many stories position her as a peaceful foil to her more warlike "cousin" Tsi-yugunsini (Dragging Canoe). Writers are conflicted about her motives—some see her as peace loving while others claim that she embraced the more advanced white civilization or that she sought to placate the more militarily powerful whites.[1]

Growing evidence suggests that eighteenth-century Native American women in communities throughout the eastern woodlands of what is now the United States had an important voice in international affairs through marriage, adoption, and authority in decision making. In order to manage tensions about values, conquest, and nationhood that arose from American mistreatment of Native Americans, white mythologizers have constructed a narrative about some of these women that describes them as acting in remarkable ways to befriend white people. In these accounts, the recognition of white superiority by far-sighted Native American women implicitly confirms the white rationale for displacing indigenous peoples.[2] These stories often mask the motivations behind women's diplomacy, overlook the intricacies of clan and tribal relationships, and misconstrue the identities that the women constructed.[3] An exploration of Nan-ye-hi's life as a diplomat and as a member of the Wolf clan and the Women's Council allows us to understand more fully the role that Native American women played in foreign affairs during the Revolutionary and post-

Revolutionary period and how embedded their actions were in clan and communal connections. Reclaiming Nan-ye-hi as a Cherokee woman prompts us to probe more deeply into why authors create romanticized stories about powerful Native American women.

Very little is actually known about Nan-ye-hi; only a handful of contemporaneous sources mention her, and we are uncertain about most of the details of her life. Historians place Nan-ye-hi's birth at various dates between 1684 and 1739. More recent writers tend to put her birth date in the 1730s, and a later birth year is most likely correct, since she bore a child after 1755. No records establish her birthplace but some writers record that she was born in Chota, an Overhill town in what was then claimed by the colonists as the western region of North Carolina and is now eastern Tennessee. Many biographers state that Nan-ye-hi lived most of her adult life in Chota. These undocumented assertions are part of an argument that Nan-ye-hi devoted her life to peace, since Chota was important to Cherokee diplomacy and was known as the Beloved Town, a place of refuge where no violence was permitted. But contemporaneous sources indicate that she lived in Citico, a town about twelve miles from Chota, at least by the early 1770s and for many years thereafter.[4]

Nan-ye-hi was born into a society undergoing considerable change. At the beginning of the eighteenth century, the Cherokees lived in clusters of towns in present-day South Carolina, North Carolina, and eastern Tennessee. As the century progressed, white settlements pushed the Cherokee towns west into present-day Georgia and Alabama. The Overhill towns, those situated west of the Appalachians, were removed from early colonial settlements but engaged in considerable trade with South Carolina and Virginia. These towns were in a region that both the English and French, and later the Spanish, sought to control.[5]

At the time of Nan-ye-hi's birth, the Cherokees believed in a spiritual world in which the universe was composed of opposing forces, such as those between war and peace, animals and humans, and men and women. Harmony was achieved by balancing these forces. Women and men did not dominate, but complemented each other. Like men, women had considerable freedom, including the right to choose their husbands and to leave them if they were unhappy. Kinship was the nucleus of Cherokee society, which was structured around seven clans with equal rights, although some clans at times were more influential than others. Cherokee society was matrilineal, rooted in a cosmos in which all Cherokees were descendants of Selu, a corn goddess who was the first mother. The primary identity of each Cherokee was the clan of her or his mother. Because women did not marry within their clans the father was not related to his children. One of the mother's male kin, usually her oldest brother, formed the closest male parental relationship with them. Individuals without clan ties, whether they lived in Cherokee villages or were members of other nations, were considered strangers. Clan ties affected virtually all social and political arrangements in Cherokee society.

Spiritual principles dictated the economic relations of the Cherokees. They believed that the creator gave them their lands. They were attached to them because their ancestors were buried there and the spirits of the dead lingered in some localities. They owned their land in common, with occupants having rights to tenure. Women did most of the farming and child rearing while men hunted. Personal property was individually owned, but a strong ethic of reciprocity required that those who had goods shared with those who did not. With the growth in trade, some individuals increasingly owned more property than others during the last half of the century, including the ownership of black men and women as slaves. Merchants also brought disease, including a devastating smallpox epidemic in 1738–39 that killed approximately half of the Cherokee people.

Each town governed itself through councils. Although women and men had some separate areas of authority, they generally shared governance. Women could override the council on issues reserved for men—for example, the decision to go to war—through the Women's Council, a body composed of delegates from each of the seven clans chosen by the women of the clan. The Beloved Woman, the most prominent woman in the nation through whom the Great Spirit spoke, headed the Women's Council. She also had the authority to punish or pardon prisoners. Individuals who disagreed with the councils were not compelled to abide by their decisions. The English colonial authorities made efforts to organize the Cherokees by designating a male national chief, a practice continued by the Americans. These chiefs governed by influence, not compulsion, although over the course of the eighteenth century their access to treaty goods enhanced their powers.

Historians believe that Nan-ye-hi was a member of the Wolf clan. Through her mother, Tame Doe, Nan-ye-hi had important diplomatic clan connections. Her great-uncle was Kanagatucko (Old Hop), the leader of the Cherokee nation during the war between the French and English from 1756 to 1763. Her mother's brothers included Attakullakulla (the Little Carpenter) and Willinawaw (Great Eagle). In the Cherokee clan structure, these were the most important male clan figures to Nan-ye-hi. Attakullakulla traveled to England in 1730 and the British recognized him as one of the major peace chiefs of the Cherokees during the third quarter of the eighteenth century. Willinawaw was also involved in diplomatic affairs and by 1770 was one of the most important peace chiefs in the nation. Nan-ye-hi had one brother, Tuskegateehee (Long Fellow), who also became a chief and diplomat. Because of the relative unimportance of the father, who was not a clan member, the significant influences on Nan-ye-hi's life were from her Wolf clan relatives, so it is not unexpected that Nan-ye-hi's father is unknown.[6]

Like many Native American peoples, the Cherokees conducted diplomacy through two venues. Women commonly integrated traders and diplomats into tribal life and into the clan system by marrying or adopting them. Through these unions, the Cherokees gained access to material goods and at times to the loyalty of white merchants and diplomats. Traders spoke and often wrote English, making them valuable as scribes and translators. By midcentury, women and men considered women's alliances with merchants to have significance comparable to that of heroic war deeds. Women extolled their accomplishments in obtaining goods from the traders who loved them in the same councils in which warriors boasted of their exploits.[7]

To establish diplomatic connections with peoples who remained outside the clan structure, the Cherokees reconstituted foreign communities as diplomatic kin. This method of conducting foreign affairs centered on relationship and mutuality, in which the parties achieved harmony by a balance of obligations. The parties were careful to avoid blaming one another, since the atmosphere at peace talks and not the agreements reached were central. The parties maintained their relationships over time by frequent visits to one another.[8]

Around 1750 Nan-ye-hi married Kingfisher, a Cherokee man of the Deer clan. They had two children, a daughter, Ka-ti, also known as Catherine or Caty, and a son, Hiskyteehee, later known as Little Fellow or Fivekiller. According to accounts written generations later, Kingfisher fought in the war with the Creeks in the decisive battle at Taliwa in 1755. Nan-ye-hi accompanied her husband and chewed bullets to make them more destructive when he fired them. When Kingfisher was killed, Nan-ye-hi seized his gun and joined the fight, helping to defeat the Creeks. The victory ended a long war between the two nations and resulted in a large land cession to the Cherokees. Nan-ye-hi shared in the property seized by the Cherokees, including a slave, and earned the office of Beloved Woman.[9]

After Kingfisher's death, Nan-ye-hi responded to the growing importance of trade in Cherokee life by marrying an Irish trader, Bryan Ward, who had also participated in the battle at Taliwa. Through this marriage, Nan-ye-hi became known as Nancy Ward, and the couple had a daughter, Betsey. Responding to mistreatment by the British, the Cherokees attacked their former ally in 1760 during the period when the British were fighting the French. Bryan Ward left the Cherokee nation and joined the English army but returned to his wife and family after the Cherokee war was over in late 1761. By 1764 Nan-ye-hi and Bryan had separated and Bryan returned to South Carolina.[10]

The Cherokees recognized Great Britain as the governing authority for the eastern seaboard colonies, but it was a troubled alliance. After the defeat of the French in 1763, England attempted to strengthen the alliance by issuing the Proclamation of 1763, which forbade settlement west of the Appalachian Mountains, but migrants pressured Cherokees by settling on their land on the eastern slope of the mountains. The Cherokees were ambivalent about the newcomers, wanting trade but uncomfortable with the encroachments on their lands. To accommodate the new settlements, English negotiators, led by John Stuart, superintendent for the Southern Department, pressed for land cessions from the Cherokees from the mid-1760s until the early 1770s. The chiefs, including the primary chiefs of the Overhill Cherokees, Oconostota and Attakullakulla, and the Women's Council headed by Nan-ye-hi considered how to handle these new challenges. The Cherokee councilors initially agreed to sell property in return for British promises to provide trade at good prices and to establish firm boundary lines, a strategy that kept the peoples separate while allowing for commercial interaction. On each new marking of the line, in 1767, in 1769, and in the early 1770s, Cherokee women and men observed the surveying of the lines to ensure that they were accurate.[11]

By the time the parties marked the boundary in the early 1770s, settlers and their slaves were already moving onto Overhill Cherokee lands, which were on the western side of the Appalachians into what is now eastern Tennessee and Kentucky, lands claimed by North Carolina and Virginia. Nan-ye-hi and her daughters, Ka-ti and Betsey, and Ka-ti's husband, John Walker, resided in Citigo, a small village in this region. The trans-Appalachian settlements represented a different experience for the Overhill people. Traders previously lived in the Cherokee villages, married Cherokee women, were largely integrated into Cherokee life, and in significant measure were under Cherokee control. But the new settlements, involving larger numbers of whites governing themselves, threatened these arrangements.[12]

The Cherokees' greatest concern was the encroachment by immigrants on Cherokee lands. Many frontier people settled on Cherokee land, believing that as civilized white farmers they had superior land rights to those of savage natives who used large tracts of land for hunting. The most dramatic appropriation of Cherokee property occurred with Henderson's Treaty in 1775. William Henderson, a North Carolina speculator acting as a private party, asserted that he obtained deeds from the Cherokees conveying much of present-day Kentucky and Tennessee north of the Cumberland River. Although there is no documentation that Nan-ye-hi attended Henderson's treaty conference, it is likely that she was present. Attakullakulla, Oconostota, and Willinawaw were the primary chiefs present, and Ellis Harlan and Isaac Thomas, traders who were Nan-ye-hi's close associates, served as interpreters. The Cherokees believed that whites could only change boundary lines with the consent of the British government and contended for years afterward that they did not give up their lands. Along with the chiefs, the women almost certainly did not support a land cession. Oconostota's wife became very uneasy when a trader told her that the chiefs had signed a deed for the lands, and she went to talk to the chiefs about it.[13]

During the year after the conference, whites made it clear that they interpreted the deeds as land grants, and new settlers flooded into the region. Many of the Cherokee warriors and chiefs threatened war against the settlements at the same time that rebellious colonists on the east coast were declaring their independence from England. While British Indian superintendent John Stuart urged restraint by the Cherokees because he wanted to protect loyalist settlers, a delegation of Shawnees from the north came to a council in Chota in the summer of 1776 and called for war. The elderly Attakullakulla and Oconostota refused the war belts proffered by the Shawnees, and Nan-ye-hi responded coolly to the northern Indians. Attakullakulla's son, Tsi-yugunsini, and his followers accepted the belts. Led by Tsi-yugunsini, the warriors decided to drive the whites off of Cherokee lands.[14]

Many historians portray Tsi-yugunsini as Nan-ye-hi's cousin—casting the two as the major players in a family drama between a warrior who fought for his country and a woman whose main goal was peace. However, this characterization is misleading on two counts. In Cherokee terms, Tsi-yugunsini was not related to Nan-ye-hi. Attakullakulla was Tsi-yugunsini's father, but Tsi-yugunsini belonged to his mother's clan. Attakullakulla was related to Nan-ye-hi as her uncle because he was her mother's brother, making both of them members of the Wolf clan. Historians do not know which clan Tsi-yugunsini belonged to, but since Cherokees did not marry their own clan members at that time, he was not of the Wolf clan. The second problem with characterization is that both Tsi-yugunsini and Nan-ye-hi pursued similar goals. Both wanted to preserve Cherokee lands, and both sought trade relations that would benefit the Cherokees. But the two disagreed about the best strategy to realize their goals.[15]

Tsi-yugunsini's war plans ran counter to Nan-ye-hi's strategies of containment and alliance. The British, Attakullakulla, Nan-ye-hi, and the Women's Council saw the tramontane people as disobedient British subjects to be dealt with by the English, who would honor the boundary lines. Nan-ye-hi dispatched two traders, Isaac Thomas and William Fallin, to alert the settlers of Tsi-yugunsini's attack. This warning allowed many of the settlers to repel the warriors. Writers, particularly those who portray Tsi-yugunsini as a hero resisting white encroachment, explain Nan-ye-hi's actions as something other than betrayal by casting her as a woman of peace who sought friendship with the culturally or militarily superior white people.[16] However, Nan-ye-hi opposed the war not because she loved white people or thought them more advanced or stronger, but because she believed that conflict would weaken British efforts to control the encroachers and would destroy necessary commercial relations.

During the attack, the warriors took as a prisoner Lydia Bean, one of the oldest settlers, and condemned her to burn. Nan-ye-hi acted to avoid further bloodshed by exercising her prerogative as a Beloved Woman to free the captive. In contrast to the traditional custom, Nan-ye-hi did not adopt Bean, because Nan-ye-hi did not intend to incorporate her into the tribe. Rather she dispatched her brother and her son to return Bean to her home, where allegedly her husband gave Nan-ye-hi one hundred pounds sterling in gratitude.[17]

The Virginia, North Carolina, South Carolina, and Georgia militias responded to the Cherokee attacks by waging a new kind of war on the Cherokees—destroying towns, supplies, and homes. Approximately four hundred Cherokees attended a peace conference with North Carolina and Virginia commissioners at Long Island in the Overhill country in July 1777. The major chiefs present were Oconostota, Attakullakulla, Willinawaw, Onitossitah (Old Tassel), and Savanukeh (the Raven). Oconostota told the conference that because of his age he assigned his power to speak to Onitossitah and Savanukeh, who conducted all of the negotiations. The Women's Council did not concern itself with the conference, probably because it understood the purpose to be to make peace after the latest war, a task primarily for the warriors. To the surprise of the Cherokees, the North Carolina commissioners forced a land cession by threatening more military actions. Breaking with past custom, North Carolina refused to compensate the Cherokees.[18]

North Carolina's arrogant actions at the treaty negotiations alienated many important peace chiefs, and several, including Savanukeh and Nan-ye-hi's Wolf clan relatives Willinawaw and Tuskegateehee, joined Tsi-yugunsini, creating a realignment of power in the peace faction. After Savanukeh's defection, Onitossitah continued as the primary peace chief of the Upper Towns until his murder in 1788. Upon Attakullakulla's death around 1778, Nan-ye-hi became the most prominent diplomat in the Wolf clan and asserted a stronger role as the peace chief speaking for the women.[19]

By 1778 the Women's Council and the peace chiefs realized the implications of the spreading Revolutionary War—Britain no longer controlled its American subjects. Militias made war as a way to take land and to destroy towns. The Women's Council and the chiefs worked to establish a kinship with American officials who could control the immigrants in order to protect their lands and to sustain commerce. As head of the Women's Council, Nan-ye-hi used the diplomatic strategy of marriage, and Nan-ye-hi and other members of the Women's Council, for the first time, exerted their authority as matriarchs to speak at treaty conferences.

Cherokee women exercised power through the political influence of their kin, a route taken by Nan-ye-hi through the marriage of her daughters to important white traders and diplomats. Nan-ye-hi's older daughter, Ka-ti, married John Walker, a white trader who provided access to goods during the early years of white settlement, and later Ellis Harlan, a trader, interpreter, and emissary for Nan-ye-hi. Nan-ye-hi's younger daughter, Betsey, made the most influential match, marrying Joseph Martin, North Carolina and Virginia's Indian agent to the Cherokees. Following a common practice, Martin had a Virginia wife and children who were aware of the arrangement. The marriage probably took place in 1778, and the couple had dual residences—one home at Long Island near the white settlements in eastern Tennessee and another with or near Nan-ye-hi, Ka-ti, and Harlan at Citico. Their son, James, was born in Citico in 1780, and after that they had a daughter, Nanny. The Wolf clan recognized Martin as a relation—giving him connections to the most influential clan of the nation.[20]

Joseph Martin came to share many of Nan-ye-hi's goals for the Cherokees. He was an early settler in Tennessee who planned to speculate in land. Although he never abandoned his speculations, Martin came to see events from the Cherokee perspective and to view the Cherokees as a people entitled to fairness. Often reviled and occasionally threatened by the frontier people for his support of the Cherokees, Martin pleaded their case to the North Carolina legislature and to various Virginia and North Carolina governors. In response, Virginia governor Benjamin Harrison recognized Indian rights and equated their rights to those of white people. Martin also encountered opposition from the militant factions of the Cherokees and relied on the Wolf clan for protection.[21]

Nan-ye-hi, Onitossitah, and Martin faced a formidable task. By 1780 westering people established towns in the Cumberland region 150 miles to the west, around present-day Nashville. Angered by the new encroachers, the dissidents, now called Chickamaugans, increased their attacks. Led by Colonel Arthur Campbell from Virginia, the militias in late 1780 invaded the Overhill country.[22]

Nan-ye-hi and Martin struggled to maintain a connection with the frontier people that would temper the violence. As the war heated up, Savanukeh plotted to kill Nan-ye-hi's associate Isaac Thomas and some other American traders in Citico, men he believed supported the settlers. Nan-ye-hi and several other women aided the traders' escape from Citico on November 22, 1780. On December 24, 1780, Campbell took possession of Chota. Two days later Nan-ye-hi intervened as a diplomat—approaching him with information, overtures of peace from the friendly chiefs, and cattle for his hungry soldiers. Undaunted by Campbell's military force, Nan-ye-hi invited Campbell into a kinship in which he would be obligated to reciprocate with favorable treatment of the Cherokees. Campbell accepted the offer of food but deferred peace talks in order to destroy all the principal Overhill towns, including Chota and Citico. In spite of the destruction of her town, Nan-ye-hi honored her commitment by supplying the cattle. The militia took seventeen prisoners, including members of Nan-ye-hi's family who, according to Campbell, "for their good offices we considered in another light." Martin took the prisoners and Nan-ye-hi and her family to his house on Long Island where he lived with his wife, Betsey, and son, James. Martin persuaded Nan-ye-hi's brother, Tuskegateehee, to return from Chickamauga. The destruction by the militias and pressure from the peace faction convinced the Chickamaugans to relocate further from the white settlements over the next several years. They eventually settled around Muscle Shoals (in present-day southern Tennessee and northern Alabama) in communities that became known as the Lower Towns, in contrast to the Overhill Cherokees' Upper Towns.[23]

The devastation of the Overhill towns and the burning of Chota propelled the Women's Council to undertake a more visible diplomatic presence. Ignoring white men's denigration of women in diplomacy, Nan-ye-hi and other women pursued their diplomatic strategy by speaking publicly at several peace conferences in the 1780s. The women used matriarchal images to assert a common humanity between Cherokees and whites—a strategy that encouraged recognition of Cherokee land rights by white negotiators. In 1781 General Nathanael Greene, commander of the Continental Army in the South, convened peace talks with the Cherokees after the campaign of 1780–81. Described by Joseph Martin's white son, William, as "one of the most superior women I ever saw," Nan-ye-hi spoke through an interpreter for the first time to white negotiators at Greene's conference. Nan-ye-hi ignored the Cherokee custom in which diplomats avoided assigning blame in order to create an atmosphere conducive to peacemaking. Although most of her remarks are lost or illegible, what is preserved contradicts the mythology that Nan-ye-hi spoke for peace because she was a friend to the white people. Nan-ye-hi prefaced a plea for peace with an explicit indictment of white conduct that led to the war. "You came [*illegible*] and settled on our land and took it [*illegible*] by main force; therefore we call you [*illegible*]. Why then will you quarrel with us?" Invoking her considerable matriarchal authority, she chastised the Americans for breaking the 1777 Long Island treaty. "We [women] did never concern [ourselves with] the former treaty, which has been broken, but we do in this and on our account, who are your mothers, let it never be broken."[24]

Nan-ye-hi understood that settlers believed that white claims to land were superior to those of "savage" Indians. She crafted a web of fictive motherhood to challenge these assumptions: "You know women are always looked upon as nothing, but we are your mothers. You are our sons. Our cry is all for peace. Let it continue because we are your mothers. This peace must last forever. Let your women's sons be ours, and let our sons be yours."[25] Nan-ye-hi's metaphor extended beyond the linkage of motherhood with peace to suggest that native and white men should consider themselves to be the sons of both races—an image that dissolved racial and cultural boundaries in a vision of parity.

Five older women, almost certainly members of the Women's Council, affirmed this vision of universal humanity in their address to the council on behalf of women at the conclusion of the peace talks. They sought to bolster their authority by having a male chief, Scolacutta (Hanging Maw), whose wife was an important woman and probably on the Women's Council, accompany them. They whispered their speech to him, which he delivered to the assembled audience. A transcribed version of only part of their remarkable address survives in the Nathanael Greene Papers:

> We the women of the Cherokee nation now speak to you. We are mothers, and have many sons, some of them warriors and beloved men. We call you also our sons. We have a right to call you so, because you are the sons of mothers, and all descended from the same woman at first. We say you are our sons, because by women, you were brought forth into this world, nursed, suckled, and raised up to be men before you reached your present greatness. You are our sons. Why should there be any difference amongst us? We live on the same land with you, and our people are mixed with white blood: one third of our [people are] mixed with white blood.[26]

Building on Nan-ye-hi's construction, these women imagined a diplomatic motherhood, one they linked to Selu, the first woman and a powerful spiritual figure. They reminded white men of the importance of women. Responding to white notions of superiority, they stressed the similarities between Indians and settlers, pointing to the fact that all were descended from the same woman and occupied the land, and that the Cherokees were increasingly people with "white blood."

During negotiations, Colonel Arthur Campbell, now one of the American commissioners, pressed for a land cession from the Cherokees as compensation for their aggressions. Nan-ye-hi answered that such a transfer impaired Cherokee survival. "We know that the white people are more and stronger than us, but will you take everything from us and leave us to starve?" Coming shortly after her support of Campbell during his military campaign, her plea successfully invoked mutual obligations between diplomatic kin who shared a common humanity. The commissioners concluded the treaty without forcing a land cession. Although Nan-ye-hi prevented a property loss, negotiations about prisoner exchanges continued into the next year. Nan-ye-hi's influence was critical in ironing out this issue as well. A "great and beloved woman," almost certainly Nan-ye-hi, spurred Virginia Governor Benjamin Harrison to agree to a prisoner exchange in 1782.[27]

After the successful establishment of a kinship in the treaty proceedings of 1781, Nan-ye-hi and Martin engaged in a series of actions that encouraged a balance of mutuality between the Cherokee and American nations. Nan-ye-hi persuaded the Upper Towns to provide corn to the starving settlers in 1782, which allowed women in the Upper Towns to convert their traditional role as farmers for their community into relationships with whites that produced greater prosperity for the Cherokees and, at times, social bonds with white fictive kin. The settlers depended on the corn for survival. By 1785 the Upper Town settlements lived primarily on the strength of the sale of their crops to the new settlements. Nan-ye-hi participated in this market, supplying crops and cattle. During his tenure at Long Island, Martin also linked the two societies, feeding needy Cherokees who visited and concluding a peace treaty with the Lower Towns in 1783, an agreement that lasted until it was broken two years later by local whites.[28]

Upon the conclusion of the Revolutionary War in 1783, Congress moved to establish peace with the Indians throughout the extensive western territory now claimed by the United States. After making treaties with the northern tribes, U.S. Commissioners met with the Cherokees at Hopewell in November 1785. Because North Carolina had not ceded its claims to its western lands to the United States, North Carolina sent William Blount, a major speculator with lands in the Tennessee region, as a treaty commissioner to object to the proceedings.[29]

Onitossitah was the primary peace chief for the Cherokees. He sought payment for Cherokee lands taken illegally by settlers and refused to give up more lands. He then introduced "one of our beloved women . . . who has born and raised up warriors." Now about fifty years old, Nan-ye-hi followed Onitossitah's grievances with a vision of a matriarchal kinship:

> I am fond of hearing that there is a peace, and I hope you have now taken us by the hand in real friendship. I have a pipe and a little tobacco to give the commissioners to smoke in friendship. I look on you and the red people equally as my children. Your having determined on peace is most pleasing to me, for I have seen much trouble during the late war. I am old, but I hope yet to bear children, who will grow up and people our nation, as we are now to be under the protection of Congress, and shall have no more disturbance.
>
> The talk I have given, is from the young warriors I have raised in my town, as well as myself. They rejoice that we have peace, and we hope the chain of friendship will never more be broke.[30]

As she had in 1781, Nan-ye-hi suggested that the settlers had caused the disturbance because they did not abide by the rules of "real friendship," which required that they respect Cherokee land rights. She countered by casting red and white children as equal, then gathered both progeny into her clan. Moreover, her claim to speak for young warriors established that she had acquired authority beyond that traditionally bestowed on Beloved Women, who spoke only for the women. Nan-ye-hi and the other Cherokee negotiators persuaded the federal government to recognize the boundaries set in the 1777 treaty, except for some areas in Cumberland and in eastern Tennessee with numerous settlers, for which the Cherokees were paid, and to void claims to Cherokee lands made by North Carolina in 1783 and by settlers in eastern Tennessee in 1785. On behalf of North Carolina, William Blount protested the agreement.[31]

Because the United States had no authority in the Tennessee region, settlers continued to move onto Cherokee lands. The Chickamaugans allied with the Creeks and resumed their attacks. Angered by the murder of an encroacher's family in the French Broad area in May 1788, a militia company headed by local leader John Sevier lured Onitossitah and several other Upper Town chiefs to a peace conference the next month and murdered them. The Cherokee nation united in war against the eastern settlements, launching a major attack on Gillespie's Station in eastern Tennessee in October that killed a number of settlers. This time Nan-ye-hi did not warn the settlers. Fighting continued into the winter. Nan-ye-hi's ally Joseph Martin worked with the women and the friendly chiefs to protect them from the effects of the war. Martin provisioned his hometown of Citico with corn at his own expense, supplied salt to the women, and sent some Cherokees to his South Carolina and Georgia plantations to protect them from Sevier.[32]

In North Carolina, the United States and the Cherokees carried on peace talks from fall 1788 until May 1789. Although the Chickamaugans now exerted a strong diplomatic presence, the Women's Council also spoke in these talks, urging peace for the sake of the children. In a Grand Talk from the head men and warriors of the nation addressed to the Governor of North Carolina in 1789, the women made their voice explicit at the conclusion of the talk: "Now, this is our beloved women's talk; they say they have heard our great talks, and they hope to live at home in their houses in satisfaction, and they have told their warriors to be at peace from this time out, that they may raise their children in happiness." When North Carolina ceded its western lands to the United States in 1789, Congress organized these lands into the Southwest Territory. President George Washington rewarded North Carolina for its cession by appointing William Blount, the speculator who protested the 1785 treaty, as governor and as Indian commissioner, replacing Joseph Martin.[33] Washington's actions were a victory for the settlers seeking new lands and a setback for the Cherokees.

Upon losing his appointment, Martin returned to his family in Virginia, leaving Betsey Ward and his daughter in the Cherokee nation but taking their son with him to educate him so that when he was grown he might be useful to the Cherokee people. With Martin's departure and the growing power of the Chickamaugans in diplomacy, Nan-ye-hi no longer spoke at treaty conferences, but she maintained her position at the head of the Women's Council. As late as 1819 Indian agent Reuben Lewis related that Nan-ye-hi's "advice and council borders on supreme." Most of Nan-ye-hi's extended family lived with or near her, and Nan-ye-hi also exercised influence through her clan, primarily through her brother, Tuskegateehee, and her children, Ka-ti, Betsey, and Hiskyteehee, and their extended family connections.[34]

Operating under a new constitution, the United States signed its first treaty with the Cherokees in 1791 on the Holston River near Knoxville, where Governor Blount met a new coalition of Upper and Lower Town Cherokee headmen. The record does not reflect whether Nan-ye-hi was present. Her brother, Tuskegateehee, was one of the treaty signers. Chickamaugan diplomats conducted almost all of the negotiations on the Cherokee side and were joined by Scolacutta, now the primary Upper Town peace chief. The Chickamaugans advanced many of the points raised earlier by the Women's Council and the Upper Town chiefs. They pressed Governor Blount to agree that red people had the same right as any other human being to enjoy their property, and Blount agreed that the federal government considered Cherokees "as good as ourselves, not one better than the other." The conference notes taken by the secretary for the Southwest Territory, Daniel Smith, reflect that the Cherokees opposed a land cession but inexplicably reversed their position and agreed to the treaty.[35]

During the next several years, much of the nation united in war in opposition to the purported Holston land grant. Through her family, Nan-ye-hi sought to maintain a kinship with the federal government. Following the methods used by his sister, Tuskegateehee and other chiefs in 1792 warned John Sevier that six hundred troops were advancing toward the settlements. Tuskegateehee was part of the Cherokee delegation that arranged a peace mission to Congress in Philadelphia in 1793. Nan-ye-hi's daughter, Betsey Ward, was one of the diplomats gathered at Scolacutta's house to journey to Philadelphia when a Tennessee militia attacked the gathering, killed eight people including several chiefs, and wounded Scolacutta, his wife, and Betsey Ward. Samuel Candy, probably the son of Nan-ye-hi's daughter Ka-ti, was one of the interpreters chosen by the Cherokees at the December 1794 talks—one of several conferences that resulted in a lasting peace between the Cherokees and the United States.[36]

By the time of peace in 1795 the Cherokees inhabited a different world. The settler population in the region exploded. Newcomers vastly outnumbered native peoples and created strong pressures for more Indian land. The Cherokee people themselves disagreed about how to deal with the United States until 1809, during which time a cacophony of voices spoke for the Cherokees on international affairs. White agents took advantage of the divisions to pressure, and in some cases to bribe, the Cherokee negotiators to agree to more land sales. The Women's Council was concerned about the land sales but deferred to the chiefs' judgment about diplomacy in this chaotic period. Tuskegateehee was one of the representatives who agreed to cessions. In 1798, 1802, and 1805, Tuskegateehee signed treaties that ceded land to the United States. By 1806 the United States recognized Tuskegateehee as a chief in his region by giving him annuity money to be distributed to his district. In 1809, though, Tuskegateehee and a group of dissident chiefs, almost certainly supported by the Women's Council, unified the Cherokees to halt land sales.[37]

Although the Women's Council failed to press its agenda opposing land sales prior to 1809, women continued to advance the Cherokee notion of a relational peace that included reciprocal obligations by visiting governmental officials and by attending peace conferences. Women also insisted on the permanence of the Cherokee nation by marking treaty lines. Although white norms meant that federal government officials often ignored the presence and voice of the women, local officials took notice. When Governor John Sevier of Tennessee discussed the goods he needed for the upcoming treaty in 1808, he penned a rare acknowledgment of the women's authority. "The goods would have a pleasing and alluring effect on the Indians," he wrote, "particularly the females and young men, who have their weight and influence."[38]

With peace achieved after 1795, many women turned their attention to building a stronger economy that would support an independent nation and improve their own well-being. Women increasingly joined men in hunting. Women also supplied food, livestock, and cotton to the exploding immigrant population, bringing in considerable cash. Nan-ye-hi and her family continued the traditional practice of allying with white men who linked them to material resources. Visiting Bryan Ward and his family in South Carolina on numerous occasions, Nan-ye-hi and Betsey Ward maintained a connection with Ward that had economic advantages for all parties. By the 1790s Nan-ye-hi and Betsey were prosperous. Moravian missionaries who visited Betsey's residence in Wachowee on the Hiwassee River in 1799 described it as a "fine plantation" of four houses surrounded by high fences. She grew a number of crops, had livestock, spun cotton, and owned black slaves. Many of Nan-ye-hi's other female descendants married merchants.[39]

Nan-ye-hi's adoption of some American economic practices does not tell us how she incorporated them into her Cherokee identity. She may have accepted Euro-American ideas of self-interest, or she may have seen her increase in wealth as part of a process that benefited all Cherokee people. We do not know if she observed the traditional practices of redistribution. Although the federal government sought to "civilize" the Cherokees by encouraging them to farm rather than hunt, to accept white gender roles, and to convert to Christianity, Nan-ye-hi retained much of her Cherokee heritage. Unlike many Cherokees who welcomed white travelers, no travelers report visiting Nan-ye-hi in her village. Nan-ye-hi's active involvement in political affairs throughout her life defied American civilized gender expectations. While several other prominent Cherokee women converted to Christianity in the early part of the eighteenth century, there is no evidence that Nan-ye-hi or any of her close kin did, and they may have been opposed to it. When Moravian missionaries visited her daughter Betsey's home, in her absence they spoke to Betsey's "cousin" Walker, probably Ka-ti's son. Walker listened politely to their explanation about God but refused to convene the Cherokees so that the Moravians could spread their message about Christianity.[40]

After the War of 1812 the government again urged the Cherokees to sell or exchange their lands and to move across the Mississippi. Shortly after a secret meeting in 1817 between the federal Indian agent and some of the Lower Town chiefs who favored the move, Nan-ye-hi and twelve other women drafted a petition opposing the exchange of land for property across the Mississippi.

Nan-ye-hi made her last recorded appearance in May 1817 at the Cherokee Council of Amohee, where she submitted the petition to the council. Speaking now as mothers of the nation, the women implored the chiefs to refuse to agree to a land exchange:

> Our beloved children and head men of the Cherokee nation, we address you warriors in council. We have raised all of you on the land which we now have, which God gave us to inhabit and raise provisions. We know that our country has once been extensive but by repeated sales has become circumscribed to a small tract and never have thought it our duty to interfere in the disposition of it till now. . . . We do not wish to go to an unknown country which we have understood some of our children wish to go over the Mississippi but this act of our children would be like destroying your mothers. Your mothers your sisters ask and beg of you not to part with any more of our lands. We say . . . you are descendants and take pity on our request, but keep it for our growing children for it was the good will of our creator to place us here and you know our father the great president will not allow his white children to take our country away. Only keep your hands off of paper talks for it is our own country. . . .
>
> Nancy Ward to her children warriors to take pity and listen to the talks of your sisters. . . . I have great many grand children which I wish them to do well on our land.[41]

Five of the other twelve signers were related to or connected to Nan-ye-hi through her daughter Ka-ti. Ka-ti signed as Caty Harlan, her name after her marriage to Ellis Harlan. Signer Jenny Walker McIntosh was Nan-ye-hi's granddaughter by Ka-ti and her first husband, John Walker. Elizabeth Walker and Asty Walker, probably related to John Walker, were also petitioners. Jennie Walker McIntosh had previously been married to Charles Fox, who was likely related to Susanna Fox, another signer. The petition was successful—the Council of Amohee in 1817 adopted a new governmental structure designed to prevent further land cessions. Legend says that Nan-ye-hi sent a relative with her walking cane to vote at Amohee.[42]

In spite of the action at Amohee, federal agents pressured some of the chiefs into signing a vaguely worded treaty in July 1817 that the United States interpreted as granting large tracts of land in Georgia and Tennessee. After the treaty, Nan-ye-hi acted to secure land for her family by registering a piece of land on Mouse Creek and bequeathing it to her "beloved" granddaughter Jenny McIntosh and her heirs. In 1819 the government obtained another cession of much of the Overhill land under duress, forcing many Cherokees, including Nan-ye-hi, to move from their ancestral homelands.[43]

Later generations say that, after losing her home, Nan-ye-hi ran an inn at the Womankiller Ford of the Ocowee in eastern Tennessee. The traveling public called her Granny Ward. Nan-ye-hi died around 1824 at Womankiller Ford. Her great-grandson said that those attending her on her deathbed reported that she died at dawn and "when her breath left her the light that was in the room went out and a dim light was seen going out at the door." Twelve years after her death, the United States moved almost all the eastern Cherokees west of the Mississippi along the Trail of Tears. After the Cherokee removal, Nan-ye-hi's heirs filed suit for the land that Nan-ye-hi gave to her granddaughter Jenny in 1818, but the United States rejected their claim in 1847.[44]

In the end, what do we know about Nan-ye-hi? The evidence we have suggests that the mythology about Nan-ye-hi tells a misleading story. Nan-ye-hi did not act in exceptional ways to promote peace because she was a friend to white people, admired their civilization, or felt defeated by the militias. Rather she used her clan connections and acted in concert with other Cherokee women and peace chiefs to create diplomatic kinships in order to retain ancestral lands and to preserve Cherokee well-being. Nan-ye-hi challenged the idea that whites were superior and resisted most acculturation promoted by the United States—she exercised her considerable power as a Cherokee woman, lived most of her life within the Cherokee community, avoided American visitors until forced from her home, and refused to adopt Christianity. Nor did Americans reward her for her imagined role as a friendly Pocahontas. Although she had considerable success, she eventually lost her ancestral lands. Not long after her death, her people were removed and her granddaughter's heirs lost the land that Nan-ye-hi tried to retain for them.

If Nan-ye-hi's story is ultimately one of defeat, why do biographers rewrite the story of her life? Why do writers create a narrative in which she successfully sought peace rather than one in which she failed to preserve her homeland? The mythology about Nan-ye-hi serves several purposes. It allows those who are not indigenous to this continent to imagine an American history in which farsighted Native Americans acceded to white superiority rather than one that acknowledges the damage that newcomers caused the first peoples. This account also constructs Nan-ye-hi's biography to be a success story in a tradition that prefers to write American history as a chronicle of progress. In this retelling of Nan-ye-hi's life, authors in an era that promotes multiculturalism dream a world in which a concordant relationship between very different cultures is possible.

How would Nan-ye-hi tell her story? Perhaps she would not see it as one of disillusionment but a story of persistence—of a woman of the Wolf clan with many descendants and of a leader of a people who survive today. She might rue her losses but remember her life in a beautiful country—the home of her ancestors. She might believe that white people had irretrievably destroyed the kinship between Cherokees and whites, or she could have faith in the spiritual forces that she believed in as a Cherokee woman, hopeful that Cherokee and American women and men will someday restore balance between the Cherokees and their diplomatic kin.

NOTES

This chapter is drawn from *Separate Peoples, One Land: The Minds of Cherokees, Blacks, and Whites on the Tennessee Frontier* by Cynthia Cumfer. Copyright © 2007 by the University of North Carolina Press. Used by permission of the publisher. www.uncpress.unc.edu.

1. John Haywood, *The Civil and Political History of the State of Tennessee from Its Earliest Settlement Up to the Year 1796 Including the Boundaries of the State* (Knoxville, Tenn.: Heiskell and Brown, 1823), 47 (Pocahontas); Carolyn Thomas Foreman, *Indian Women Chiefs* (Muskogee, Okla.: Hoffman Printing, 1954), 7, 10–12, 73–86; Ben Harris McClary, "Nancy Ward: The Last Beloved Woman of the Cherokees," *Tennessee Historical Quarterly* 21 (December 1962): 352–64; Pat Alderman, *Nancy Ward: Cherokee Chieftainess* and *Dragging Canoe: Cherokee-Chickamauga War Chief* (Johnson City, Tenn.: Overmountain Press, 1978); Brent Yanusdi Cox, *Heart of the Eagle: Dragging Canoe and the Emergence of the Chickamauga Confederacy* (Milan, Tenn.: Chenanee Publishers, 1999).

2. On marriage in other cultures, see Lucy Eldersveld Murphy, *A Gathering of Rivers: Indians, Métis, and Mining in the Western Great Lakes, 1737–1832* (Lincoln: University of Nebraska Press, 2000), 19–76. On women's involvement in treaty making, see Greg O'Brien, "The Conqueror Meets the Unconquered: Negotiating Cultural Boundaries on the Post-Revolutionary Southern Frontier," *Journal of Southern History* 67 (February 2001): 39–72; and Richard A. Sattler, "Women's Status among the Muskogee and Cherokee," in *Women and Power in Native North America*, ed. Laura F. Klein and Lillian A. Acherman (Norman: University of Oklahoma Press, 1995), 222. On white mythological interpretation, see Susan Scheckel, *The Insistence of the Indian: Race and Nationalism in Nineteenth-Century American Culture* (Princeton, N.J.: Princeton University Press, 1998), 41–69; and McClary, "Nancy Ward."

3. Although scholars agree that clan was a central element in Cherokee life in the eighteenth century, few historians have attempted to articulate how specific clan connections informed Cherokee political or diplomatic ideas or actions in the last half of the eighteenth century. Circe Sturm, *Blood Politics: Race, Culture, and Identity in the Cherokee Nation of Oklahoma* (Berkeley: University of California Press, 2002), 27–51; Rennard Strickland, *Fire and the Spirits: Cherokee Law from Clan to Court* (Norman: University of Oklahoma Press, 1975), 22–25, 44; John Phillip Reid, *A Law of Blood: The Primitive Law of the Cherokee Nation* (New York: New York University Press, 1970), 147–51; Theda Perdue, "Clan and Court: Another Look at the Early Cherokee Republic," *American Indian Quarterly* 24 (Fall 2000): 562–69.

4. Her great-grandson claimed that Nan-ye-hi was 140 years old at her death, which would place her birth date in 1684 ("Some Recollections of Jack Hilderbrand as Dictated to Jack Williams Esq., M. O. Cate, at the Home of Hilderbrand in the Summer of 1908," Corn Collection, Cleveland Public (History) Library, Cleveland, Tennessee). Dr. Emmet Starr, who lived among the Cherokee in the early twentieth century, placed Nan-ye-hi's birthdate as 1695 (Emmet Starr, *Old Cherokee*

Families: Notes of Dr. Emmet Starr, ed. Jack D. Baker and David Keith Hampton, vol. 1, *Letter Books A–F* [Oklahoma City: Baker Publishing Co., 1988], 72). Ben Harris McClary picked 1738 (McClary, "Nancy Ward," 353). On Chota, see McClary, "Nancy Ward," 353; Cox, *Heart of the Eagle*, 65, 235; and Colin G. Calloway, *The American Revolution in Indian Country: Crisis and Diversity in Native American Communities* (Cambridge: Cambridge University Press, 1995), chap. 7.

5. The background in this and the following paragraphs is based on William G. McLoughlin, *Cherokee Renascence in the New Republic* (Princeton, N.J.: Princeton University Press, 1986); M. Thomas Hatley, *The Dividing Paths: Cherokees and South Carolinians through the Era of Revolution* (New York: Oxford University Press, 1993), 32–41; Theda Perdue, *Cherokee Women: Gender and Culture Change, 1700–1835* (Lincoln: University of Nebraska Press, 1998); John Phillip Reid, *A Better Kind of Hatchet: Law, Trade, and Diplomacy in the Cherokee Nation during the Early Years of European Contact* (University Park: Penn State University Press, 1976).

6. McClary, "Nancy Ward," 353; Foreman, *Indian Women Chiefs*, 73; Muriel Wright, *Springplace Moravian Mission*, quoted in Annie (Walker) Burns Bell, *Military and Genealogical Records of the Famous Indian Woman, Nancy Ward* (Washington, D.C.: n.p., 1958), 96; William Martin to Lyman Draper, 7 July 1842, Draper mss. (microfilm edition), State Historical Society of Wisconsin, 3XX4; Henry Timberlake, *Lieut. Henry Timberlake's Memoirs, 1756–1765*, annotated by Samuel Cole Williams (Marietta, Ga.: Continental Book Co., 1948), 39–40; "Journal of the Proceedings at Treaty of Lochaber," in *Virginia Treaties, 1723–1775*, ed. W. Stitt Robinson, vol. 5 of *Early American Documents: Treaties and Laws, 1607–1789* (Frederick, Md.: University Publications of America, 1983), 360–71; talk by Tuskegateehee, June 12, 1787, Cherokee Collection, Tennessee State Library and Archives, Nashville, Box 1, Folder 27.

7. Perdue, *Cherokee Women*, 74, 76; Rev. William Richardson's report, December 29, 1758, quoted in Samuel Cole Williams, *The Dawn of Tennessee Valley and Tennessee History* (Johnson City, Tenn.: Watauga Press, 1937), 221.

8. Reid, *A Law of Blood*, 201–7.

9. Starr, *Old Cherokee Families*, 72; Wright, *Springplace Moravian Mission*, quoted in Bell, *Military and Genealogical Records*, 96; James Mooney, *Myths of the Cherokee* (New York, 1995), 384–85; Timberlake, *Lieut. Henry Timberlake's Memoirs*, 93–94; McClary, "Nancy Ward," 354.

10. Mooney, *Myths of the Cherokee*, 384–85; Wright, *Springplace Moravian Mission*, quoted in Bell, *Military and Genealogical Records*, 96; William Martin to Lyman Draper, July 7, 1842, Draper mss., 3XX4.

11. John R. Finger, *Tennessee Frontiers: Three Regions in Transition* (Bloomington: Indiana University Press, 2001), 39–43; Williams, *Dawn of Tennessee*, 184; talk from the Headmen and Warriors of the Cherokee nation, October 20, 1765, in William L. Saunders, ed., *Colonial Records of North Carolina* (Raleigh, N.C.: P. M. Hale, 1890) [hereafter CRNC], 7:115–17; Governor Tryon's Cherokee Boundary Expedition in 1767, CRNC, 7:991–1008, esp. 997 and 999 for women; Report of Col. Lewis and Dr. Walker to Lord Botetourt, February 2, 1769, in "Virginia and the Cherokees, &c The Treaties of 1768 and 1770," *Virginia Historical Magazine* 13 (June 1906): 20–36, at 30; Draper mss., 30S345; "Journal of Proceedings at Treaty of Lochaber," 360–71.

12. Cynthia Cumfer, *Separate Peoples, One Land: The Minds of the Cherokees, Blacks and Whites on the Tennessee Frontier* (Chapel Hill: University of North Carolina Press, 2007), chap. 1; John Walker (from Citico) to William Preston, July 19, 1774, Draper mss., 3QQ65; Reid, *A Better Kind of Hatchet*, 88–95, 115–41.

13. Bethabara Diary, November 23, 1774, February 9, 1775, and Salem Diary and Marshall's Report, January 9, 1775, in *Records of the Moravians in North Carolina*, ed. Adelaide L. Fries (1925; repr., Raleigh, N.C.: State Dept of Archives and History, 1968), 2:835, 836, 863, 900, 901; J. G. M. Ramsey,

The Annals of Tennessee to the End of the Eighteenth Century (Charleston, S.C.: Walker and Jones, 1853; repr., Johnson City, Tenn.: Overmountain Press, 1999), 119–21. The reports by whites about the conference are wildly conflicting; see Deposition of Thomas Price, John Reid, Deposition of Isaac Shelby, Robertson Deposition, and Deposition of James Robinson, in Julian P. Boyd, ed., *The Papers of Thomas Jefferson, 1777–1779* (Princeton, N.J.: Princeton University Press, 1950), 2:72, 85–90; Stuart's Account, August 25, 1776, *CRNC*, 10:769–70.

14. Finger, *Tennessee Frontiers*, 53–64; Grace Steele Woodward, *The Cherokees* (Norman: University of Oklahoma Press, 1963), 92.

15. On historians, see Finger, *Tennessee Frontiers*, 98; Alderman, *Nancy Ward*, 6; Cox, *Heart of the Eagle*, 47–51. On different missions, see Cumfer, *Separate Peoples, One Land*, chap. 4.

16. William Christian to Governor of Virginia, n.d., quoted in Samuel Cole Williams, *Tennessee during the Revolutionary War* (Knoxville: University of Tennessee Press, 1994), 57–58; Foreman, *Indian Women Chiefs*, 73–86; McClary, "Nancy Ward"; Alderman, *Nancy Ward*.

17. Haywood, *Natural and Aboriginal History of Tennessee*, 260; Emmet Starr, *History of the Cherokee Indians and Their Legends and Folk Lore* (Oklahoma City: Wardman Company, 1921), 32, 468–69; Starr, *Old Cherokee Families*, 72.

18. Haywood, *History of Tennessee*, 52–55; April 1777 conference, Draper mss., 4QQ87–148; talk by Nan-ye-hi, July 28, 1781, Nathanael Greene Papers, Library of Congress, Ms. Div., Shelf No. 13,421, reel 2, 17; "Treaty at Long Island at Holston," *North Carolina Historical Review* 8 (January 1931): 55–116.

19. John P. Brown, *Old Frontiers: The Story of the Cherokee Indians from Earliest Times to the Date of Their Removal to the West* (Kingsport, Tenn.: Southern Publishers, 1938), 164; talk by Tuskegateehee, June 12, 1787, Cherokee Collection; William Fleming to Thomas Jefferson, January 19, 1781, Draper mss., 11S44–48; Starr, *History of the Cherokee Indians*, 26.

20. Raymond D. Fogelson, "Cherokee Notions of Power," in *The Anthropology of Power: Ethnographic Studies from Asia, Oceania, and the New World*, ed. Raymond D. Fogelson and Richard Adams (New York, 1977), 192; Starr, *History of the Cherokee Indians*, 350; Virginia Commission, November 3, 1777, Draper mss., 1XX29; William Martin to Lyman Draper, July 7, 1842, Draper mss., 3XX4; Steiner and Schweinitz's Report (November 10, 1799), in *Early Travels in the Tennessee Country 1540–1800*, ed. Samuel Cole Williams (Johnson City, Tenn.: Watauga Press, 1928), 465–66; "Brother Martin Schneider's Report of His Journey to the Upper Cherokee Towns," January 5, 1784, in *Early Travels in the Tennessee Country*, 258.

21. On early plans, see John Redd Papers, Draper mss., 10NN13. On unpopularity, see Brother Schneider's Report, December 31, 1783, in *Early Travels in the Tennessee Country*, 253; William Martin to Draper, February 13, 1843, Draper mss., 3XX12. On Martin's advocacy for the Cherokees, see Martin to Governor of Virginia, February 7, 1781, Draper mss., 11S24–26; Martin to Governor Harrison, May 3, 1782, Draper mss., 11S26–28; Harrison to Governor Martin, November 12, 1782, Draper mss., 10S87–90. On Cherokee protectors, see William Martin to Lyman Draper, July 7, 1842, Draper mss., 3XX4.

22. Finger, *Tennessee Frontiers*, 71–89.

23. William Springstone's deposition, January 19, 1781, Cherokee Collection, Tennessee State Library and Archives [hereafter TSLA], Mf. 815, Box 2, Folder 1, reel 1; Arthur Campbell to Gov. Thomas Jefferson, January 15, 1781, Draper mss., 10S163; William Martin to Lyman Draper, October 17, 1845, Draper mss., 3XX44; talk by Tuskegateehee, June 12, 1787, Cherokee Collection.

24. Talk by unnamed woman [Nan-ye-hi], July 28, 1781, Nathanael Greene Papers; Williams, *Tennessee during the Revolutionary War*, 201.

25. William Martin to Lyman Draper, July 7, 1842, Draper mss., 3XX4; talk by unnamed woman [Nan-ye-hi], July 28, 1781, Nathanael Greene Papers.

26. Talk by Cherokee women, July 31, 1781, Nathanael Greene Papers (quotation); report of Steiner and Schweinitz, November 10, 1799, in *Early Travels in the Tennessee Country*, 469–70. The 1781 treaty talks in the Nathanael Greene Papers are water-damaged and many pages are lost. The remainder of the women's talk is missing.

27. Arthur Campbell to Gov. Thomas Jefferson, January 15, 1781, Draper mss., 10S163; talk by unnamed woman [Nan-ye-hi], July 28, 1781, Nathanael Greene Papers (quotation); Campbell to Nathanael Greene, August 2, 1781, in *The Papers of General Nathanael Greene*, ed. Dennis M. Conrad et al. (Chapel Hill: University of North Carolina Press, 1997), 9:118–19; message from Benjamin Harrison to friendly Cherokee, 1782, Cherokee Collection, Mf. Ac. No. 815, Box 1, Folder 7.

28. Joseph Martin to Gov. Harrison, July 22, 1784, in *Calendar of Virginia State Papers and Other Manuscripts, 1652–1781*, ed. William P. Palmer (Richmond, Va.: R. F. Walker, 1875) [hereafter *VSP*], 3:601–2; letter from gentleman in Franklin to friend in Virginia, August 17, 1785, Draper mss., 3JJ208–10; William Christian to Gov. Harrison, December 16, 1782, *VSP*, 3:398–99; Cumfer, *Separate Peoples, One Land*, chap. 2.

29. Reginald Horsman, *Expansion and American Indian Policy, 1783–1812* (East Lansing: Michigan State University Press, 1967), 3–35, esp. 29; report of North Carolina House Committee on Indian Treaties and Indian Affairs, January 6, 1787, in Walter Clark, ed., *State Records of North Carolina* (New York: n.p., 1970) [hereafter *SRNC*], 18:462–64.

30. Talk by Onitossitah, November 23, 1785, in *American State Papers: Indian Affairs*, Class II (Washington, D.C.: Gales and Seaton, 1832) [hereafter *ASP*], 41. The quotation is the version of Nan-ye-hi's talk recorded by Joseph Martin, who was present as one of the federal commissioners. Martin's notes can be found in Draper mss., 14U24. The official version is found in the Talk by the War-woman of Chota, November 23, 1785, in *ASP*, 41. The difference is that Martin's account adds the word "equally."

31. Protest by William Blount, November 28, 1785, in *ASP*, 44.

32. Talk by Tuskegateehee, June 12, 1787, Cherokee Collection; Cumfer, *Separate Peoples, One Land*, chap. 2; Joseph Martin to Henry Knox, January 15, 1789, in *ASP*, 46–47.

33. Grand Talk, February 16, 1789, *SRNC*, 22:789 (quotation); William Martin to Lyman Draper, July 11, 1846, Draper mss., 3XX56.

34. Martin to Draper, July 7, 1842, Draper mss., 3XX4; L. T. Mason to Joseph Martin, June 30, 1795, Draper mss., 2XX47; Thomas Nuttall, *A Journal of Travels into the Arkansas Territory during the Year 1819* (Norman: University of Oklahoma Press, 1980), 145 (quotation from Nuttall); Cherokees to Return Meigs, January 8, 1808, Bureau of Indian Affairs, RG 75, Records of the Cherokee Indian Agency in Tennessee, 1801–1835, National Archives, Washington, 1952, M208 [hereafter, M208].

35. Treaty of Holston, 1791, Draper mss., 15U1–56; talk by chiefs and Blount, June 28, 1791, Draper mss., 15U43–46 (quotation); Cumfer, *Separate Peoples, One Land*, chap. 2.

36. John Sevier to Gov. William Blount, September 13, 1792, in *ASP*, 277; Conference at Henry's Station, February 6, 1793, in *ASP*, 447–48; Major King and Daniel Carmichael to Daniel Smith, June 12, 1793, in *ASP*, 459; talks at Tellico Blockhouse, December 28, 1794–January 3, 1795, in "Correspondence of Gen. James Robertson," *American Historical Magazine* 4 (January 1899): 66–96, at 82–94.

37. Cumfer, *Separate Peoples, One Land*, chap. 3 and 4; petition of the Cherokee women at Amoah Council, May 2, 1817, quoted in Foreman, *Indian Women Chiefs*, 79–80.

38. Historians generally conclude that women's influence in diplomacy and councils declined in the latter part of the eighteenth century; see Perdue, *Cherokee Women*, 103–8; and McLoughlin, *Cherokee Renascence*, 398. However, women remained involved in diplomacy through at least 1817. David Henley to John Chisholm, October 29, 1796, David Henley Papers, TSLA, Mf. Ac. No. 625; David Henley Waste Book, April 19, 1797, March 28, April 26, and May 17 and 24, 1798, McClung Library, CS 6–2; Freeman Survey Notes of 1802, August 21, 1802, M208; Samuel Riley to Meigs, March 22, 1808, M208; *Carthage Gazette*, January 23, 1809, 2; Bethania Diary, December 9, 1811, and February 29, 1812, in *Records of the Moravians*, 7:3160, 3184; Sevier to Robertson, May 20, 1808, in "Correspondence of Gen. James Robertson," *American Historical Magazine* 5 (July 1900): 255–56 (quotation).

39. Cumfer, *Separate Peoples, One Land*, chap. 4; William Martin to Lyman Draper, July 7, 1842, Draper mss., 3XX4; report of Steiner and Schweinitz, November 15, 1799, in *Early Travels in the Tennessee Country*, 490–91; Starr, *History of the Cherokee Indians*, 350; "Some Recollections of Jack Hilderbrand," 1.

40. Report of Steiner and Schweinitz, November 15, 1799, in *Early Travels in the Tennessee Country*, 490–91.

41. Journal of Brother Cyrus Kingsbury, February 13, 1817, in *The Brainerd Journal: A Mission to the Cherokees, 1817–1823*, ed. Joyce B. Phillips and Paul Gary Phillips (Lincoln: University of Nebraska Press, 1998), 29; petition of the Cherokee women at Amoah Council, May 2, 1817, reproduced in Foreman, *Indian Women Chiefs*, 79–80.

42. Starr, *History of the Cherokee Indians*, 350–51, 471; McLoughlin, *Cherokee Renascence*, 224–27.

43. McLoughlin, *Cherokee Renascence*, 228–31; registration of claim, National Archives, RG 75, reproduced in Bell, *Military and Genealogical Records*, 28–29.

44. Starr, *History of the Cherokee Indians*, 471; Hildebrand Recollections, 5; registration of claim, National Archives, RG 75, reproduced in Bell, *Military and Genealogical Records*, 29.

Fanny Wright

(1795–1852)

Battle against Slavery

CELIA MORRIS

It was early fall 1825 when Fanny Wright first rode into a little trading post in Tennessee called Memphis, and after a journey on horseback of more than four hundred miles, she must have been an astonishing sight. Nearly six feet tall and strong-featured like Minerva, she was a Scotswoman brought up in England to be a lady out of the pages of Jane Austen, and by now she was an ornament in the drawing rooms of the rich and famous on both sides of the Atlantic. Brilliantly educated even by the standards of the upper middle class among whom she was raised, she had recently spent a week with Thomas Jefferson at Monticello and shortly thereafter parted from her beloved friend and mentor, and possibly her lover, the Marquis de Lafayette. Emulating the pattern of his passionate involvement in the American Revolution and inspired by a bold vision of racial justice she was striking out in this, her second visit to the United States on her own.[1]

At thirty years old, Frances Wright was on the verge of becoming the first woman in America to act publicly to oppose slavery. After her initial two-year visit with her younger sister Camilla in 1818, when she was twenty-three, she published *Views of Society and Manners in America*, a panegyric to a republican experiment disdained by most Englishmen of her class. But she considered slavery both a blight and a menace to an otherwise superior social and political system. To take personal responsibility and address this evil directly, then, she had decided to establish a commune to discover how slaves could be responsibly educated and subsequently freed with no financial loss to those who owned them—an experiment that, if successful, could be emulated by people all through the South.[2]

FANNY WRIGHT

1881. John Chester Buttre, engraver.

Prints and Photographs Division, Library of Congress, Washington, D.C.

Her companion in this bold venture was an impressive and engaging square-jawed Englishman named George Flower, who had emigrated from Hertfordshire less than a decade earlier and, with a handful of compatriots, had founded a fiercely antislavery farming community in Albion, Illinois. She had met him at Harmonie, Indiana, a town on the Wabash River built by an evangelical German sect called the Rappites and labeled by some the "Wonder of the West." They were now leaving this, their first American home, for a new location outside Pittsburgh, and Harmonie had just been bought for $125,000 by the controversial Welshman Robert Owen to become New Harmony, the site for his New Moral World.

Early nineteenth-century America was dotted with intentional communities, and even before Fanny Wright got the idea, Flower, who was nine years older, had imagined that slaves could surely build a town and create a community like illiterate German peasants had at Harmonie in little more than a decade. Flower was at once a kindred spirit, a practical farmer, and a man who treated black people as peers, and soon Fanny had come to consider him an equal partner in this hugely ambitious undertaking.[3]

Tennessee had seemed a sympathetic site for their experiment, as the state had twenty antislavery societies by 1823, with a membership of about six hundred. So Fanny Wright and George Flower made a special trip to Nashville to see General Andrew Jackson, who tacitly approved their plan and directed them to a tract of land along the Wolf River on the Chickasaw Bluffs about fifteen miles inland. By late November 1825 Fanny had bought 320 acres there. The soil was second rate, but she thought the area relatively healthful, as it was back from the Mississippi River and away from the marshes. She continued to negotiate for other 320-acre sections and by 1828 owned about 1,800 acres. That fall she also bought ten slaves—six men and four women—in the markets of Nashville, and using the Chickasaw name for the little Wolf River, she called her commune Nashoba.

They then wrote a proposal, had it printed as an anonymous circular, and sent it to journals like *The Genius of Universal Emancipation* and to a number of people they considered sympathetic. Fanny had inherited a small fortune from an uncle who had owned valuable land in India, and she was plunging a substantial portion of it into Nashoba. George Flower would donate his time, skill, and experience, and others they had met along the way had seemed interested in joining them. To succeed they would need considerable help, for their goal was to create a model others could emulate. It was in the infinite extension of her plan that Fanny saw the doom of slavery, for when planters discovered that Nashoba's way of working was economically superior to the slave system, surely, she thought, they would be inspired to follow her example.

So in the fall of 1825 they were trolling for donations of money and slaves, proposing initially to put fifty to a hundred slaves to work on the equivalent of two sections of public land, and calculating that after five years, under the system they envisioned, a slave could repay his or her purchase price. To inspire the slaves to work sufficiently hard and purposefully, they would hold out the promise of liberty along with the liberty and education of their children.

The centerpiece of their proposal was a school where adult slaves could be educated in the hours after their work in the fields—a notion inspired by the evening study meetings where the nineteenth-century British working class fought so doggedly for its self-respect. At the same time, their children would learn in schools of industry similar to those Robert Owen had established in New Lanark, Scotland, and now proposed for New Harmony, Indiana. Informed by the most progressive educational methods of their day, the teachers would never push their students beyond their strengths but instead would blend their time to learn and their time to work.

Calculating that they could begin such an establishment with just over $40,000, they counted on making about $10,000 a year in cotton. They considered their proposal's details provisional and expected to improvise as they went, but essentially they were trying to do good by exploiting people's greed. Flower argued that the great obstacle to ending slavery was the amount of money bound up in slaves, so he reasoned that if Nashoba could make at least a 6 percent profit, which he thought a low estimate, they could persuade capitalists to invest in such institutions and make money.

Finally, they assured their potential donors that freed slaves would be colonized outside the United States. Though skeptical of colonization societies and a true egalitarian, Fanny had acquiesced to Jefferson's fears of a biracial society by tying her plan to colonization. She simply thought it politically necessary to do so.

Although for personal reasons Fanny refused the $8,000 Lafayette offered, he did what he could, sending copies of the proposal to such influential people as James Monroe and Chief Justice John Marshall and asking them to judge it candidly and to write him or Fanny with their suggestions. Monroe approved the project on the understanding that the slaves would be colonized. James Madison was highly skeptical, pointing out that the Harmonists and Shakers were inspired by a religious fervor for which Fanny could offer no substitute of remotely equal power. But Jefferson, though evasive, was by no means discouraging. Wondering too if "moral urgencies" were sufficient to prompt slaves to work hard, he nonetheless concluded on a positive note: "You are young, dear Madam, and have powers of mind which may do much in exciting others in this arduous task. I am confident they will be so exerted, and I pray to Heaven for their success, and that you may be rewarded with the blessings which such efforts merit."[4]

In mid-November 1825 Flower left Fanny in Memphis to supervise the building of cabins and the clearing of land, and in eleven winter days he rode the 370 miles to Albion, Illinois, where he expected to gather up his wife and three children, along with Fanny's sister Camilla, and return soon to Nashoba. Meanwhile, he wrote the Rappites in Pittsburgh to inquire about a steam engine that would run both a grist mill and a cotton gin, and he ordered glass, cotton shirting, linsey for jackets and trousers, nails, hoes, axes, and assorted farm equipment. By the first of December he had sent a flatboat laden with meal, corn flour, a yoke of oxen, a wagon, two horses, and "sundry furniture and implements of husbandry" down the Mississippi toward Memphis.

Fanny, in turn, wrote the Quaker merchant Jeremiah Thompson in New York that asking for money, albeit in a good cause, was a task for which she felt unsuited, but as she needed to establish a store to bypass merchants who made "exorbitant profits" on "a ruinous system of long credits," she commissioned him to send her stout domestic cotton for shirts and sheets, white and red flannels, heavy blankets of different sizes, printed calico, several dozen heavy wool men's socks, and sturdy shoes for men and boys. In response, Thompson donated goods worth $580 to begin the store, calling it, in his engaging Quaker way, "my mite in aid of thy good efforts."

And then their troubles really started.

The winter of 1825 was so cold that the Mississippi River froze over in places, and the flatboat Flower had sent from Illinois was stopped along the way and lost, apparently forever. Then, unexpectedly summoned to Memphis, Flower was seized by a violent fever some twenty miles south of New Harmony. Terrified of catching the plague, most people shunned him, and after a frenzied search, his wife, Eliza, found him alone in a cabin, filthy and on the verge of starvation. For days he lay near death, and more than a month passed before he began to mend.

Stuck in Albion due to the ice, Camilla discovered that Eliza Flower had no faith in Nashoba's chances for success, which may be one reason the Flowers would eventually settle in Memphis, some fifteen miles from the farm George expected to manage.

Benjamin Lundy, editor of *The Genius of Universal Emancipation*, found that many people dismissed Fanny's idea and more than a few were hostile. A number of antislavery papers refused to publish their proposal, and Lundy innocently printed misleading information, saying that Fanny had "ample funds at command, as several wealthy gentlemen have contributed largely." But nobody had.

Many had said they would send their slaves when Nashoba was flourishing, but the only contribution Fanny got was from one Robert Wilson of South Carolina, who had inherited a family of seven slaves—a pregnant mother and her six daughters—whom he had been directed by the deceased to educate and emancipate when they came of age. Revolted by slavery and unwilling to take on this huge responsibility himself, Wilson agreed to take them seven hundred miles to Nashoba. In February 1826, then, Fanny paid Wilson $446.76 for his expenses in bringing them and thereby took on seven people ludicrously unsuited to the brutal work of clearing forests, building fences, and raising cabins.

The only other person who joined her during that lonesome winter was James Richardson, a Scotsman who, when she met him, had been recovering in Memphis from a painful illness. In time, Robert Dale Owen, Robert Owen's eldest son, would describe him as "an upright, impractical, and acute metaphysician of the Thomas Brown school," but Fanny liked talking with him. She trusted him with Nashoba's bookkeeping and wrote that he "unites to the invaluable qualities of trust prudence and accurate attention to business a finely cultivated mind with every liberal and generous opinion and sentiment." Only one other person she would so radically misjudge would do her such deep and lasting harm.

Despite all these problems during that winter of 1826 Fanny was caught up in the thrill of a grand adventure that would call on all her strengths and resources—a possibility virtually unknown in the early nineteenth century to most white women of her class. Her contemporary Mary Shelley would be awed by the image she was creating for herself: "a woman, young rich & independent, quits the civilization of England for a life of hardship in the forests of America, that by so doing she may contribute to the happiness of her species." Within the limits of imagery, this was true, and though accustomed to command, she now practiced an unwonted patience. And she welcomed the drama: writing a friend in Paris, she talked of forests still full of bears, wolves, and panthers, and pictured herself galloping her white horse over rough, open country in forty-mile jaunts. At times she even slept in the open, with a bearskin for a bed and her saddle for a pillow.[5]

She made friends with Marcus Winchester, the first mayor of Memphis and son of one of Andrew Jackson's closest colleagues, and with his wife, Mary, a free woman of color. So close did the three of them become that the Winchesters named a daughter Frances Wright. At their general store, Fanny would learn, through the Indians and backwoodsmen who came to trade, as much as an English lady could about American frontier democracy. (More than a decade later,

Mary Winchester suffered a peculiarly American form of cruelty when she was barred by special ordinance from the city of Memphis because of her color.)

In mid-January the weather began to turn and the ice in the Mississippi River to melt, and after trying unsuccessfully to hail a steamboat, Camilla and the Flowers settled for a flatboat winding its way slowly toward the Gulf of Mexico. Once they were snagged on a protruding tree trunk, but at the end of February, they came finally to Memphis.

"After all of our perils disasters and delays," Fanny wrote, they were together at last, and on March 3, they officially broke ground. Eight of the ten slaves Fanny had bought in Nashville arrived, and the five men proved to be good workers. Still, they had to reorder their goods from Pennsylvania, and when they arrived in late April or May, they learned that the Rappites' new town of Economy was in full operation and "much superior to those we formerly had." Smarting from the painful contrast, Fanny realized that it would be at least two years before the farm at Nashoba would thrive and three before they could get a return on their investment.

However, in the letters they wrote to Lundy's *Genius*, they sketched what they were doing—the acreage they cleared, the apple orchard they started, the buildings they raised. By early summer their store could supply the neighborhood, and a small tavern accommodated visitors. They started regular Sunday evening classes for the slaves and built a room large enough for them to dance twice a week.

They had thought hard about how to persuade slaves to work, and shunning the myriad forms of brutality common in slave territory, they were determined to use coercion merely as a last resort. Only once, in fact, did they put a Nashville girl in solitary confinement on bread and water, and the strategy worked: after twenty-four hours, "her obduracy gave way" and they released her.

Treating the slaves as responsible men and women, they did not use the lash, nor did they have an overseer. According to Flower, the slaves were given three solid meals a day and all the necessary clothing: "Their work is conducted by themselves. Advice is given them to refrain from any bad habits they may have contracted." Nashoba's goal was to inspire "habitual industry voluntarily arising amongst the people themselves, induced by advice and example." Not even education was forced: "By slackening the hand of authority over them, until it is totally withdrawn," Flower wrote, "it is believed that they will not only be well disposed and industrious, but prudently managing, and wise."[6]

A letter from an outsider suggests what Fanny Wright and George Flower managed to accomplish: William Maclure, a cranky, millionaire genius who was Robert Owen's increasingly reluctant partner at New Harmony, visited for several days in December 1826 and wrote a colleague to say he was astonished that everything was proceeding so smoothly. Slaves worked hard without coercion—even without apparent direction. All the houses were kept in excellent order, and so quiet was it that he did not even hear a baby cry. Nashoba seemed popular in the vicinity, and he thought that by the next year the community would be able to feed and clothe itself and even make a small profit.[7]

As for the thrilling sense of companionship there among at least some of the whites, George Flower put it best: "Just to hear the sound of your voices and see the lines of your countenances whilst you are talking to me! So one comes to the heart of the matter and really begins to understand those remote, those secret springs of action.... That is the real pleasure. Then we feel an assurance that we have a glimmering of the truth which words plainly printed and messages conveyed second hand, can never give.... In silence, in secret and in twilight, in soft suppressed accents [the truth] is sometimes uttered." At last, Fanny Wright had begun to create her own home.[8]

Confident, then, that they were soundly on course, Fanny decided sometime in June 1826 that Nashoba could do without her for several weeks while she went upriver to see what was happening at New Harmony. Camilla and the Flowers had brought her tales of the community's tempestuous beginnings, and roughly every month the *New Harmony Gazette* had come to spell out its bewildering mixture of trouble and excitement.

After all, she and Robert Owen were both trying to establish a community without religious sanction—a proposition that may suggest how tone-deaf they were to the American mainstream—and Owen's principles, she would write, "have been mine ever since I learnt to think." Maclure, whom she had first met in Paris, had been trying to convince her to come teach in New Harmony—in fact, he offered to outfit a school with junior teachers for her if she would help—and he argued that her talents would be better used there than at Nashoba. At New Harmony the scale of good, as he put it, was much more extended.

Unlike the Rappites' Harmonie, the community that took its place was disorderly, cheerful, and irreverent, and Fanny clearly reveled in it. Camilla would later write that her sister's "talents and influence had no small share in settling many important matters relative to the interests of the School and Society there." And it was probably at this time that Fanny began to see herself as a public teacher. By now she had published two books and a play; she was at least bilingual (French); she had studied drama, history, political theory, philosophy, and slavery; she spoke so well that she had held her own with some of the most interesting people of her time. And having a large captive audience thrilled her.[9]

On July 4, 1826, Robert Owen gave his "Declaration of Mental Independence" in the New Harmony town square. A man of modest habits and tranquil demeanor, he was, philosophically speaking, very nearly an anarchist—announcing that he was ready to lead the war against three evils that had corrupted and confused human history: private property, absurd and irrational systems of religion, and the institution of marriage. Fanny loved it. She would write that Owen was to "influence the condition of mankind [more] than any individual that has ever existed," but his influence was one she would come to rue.[10]

At the time, however, Owen was the least of Wright's worries. She came back from New Harmony exhausted, and not long after throwing herself again into the business of Nashoba, she fell dangerously ill with a severe fever that Camilla said went to her brain. James Richardson proved to be a devoted nurse, without whose ministrations, Camilla wrote, "I am persuaded we [could] not have saved her invaluable life." After ten days' suffering, Fanny seemed on the mend, but two weeks later, Camilla was ill, and the strain of nursing her brought a recurrence of Fanny's fever that was far worse than the first round. For three months Fanny lay in imminent danger, and now Camilla thought they both owed their lives to Richardson's "unremitting care and admirable skill."[11]

Meanwhile Nashoba suffered a crippling loss: George Flower abandoned them and took his family back to Illinois. Camilla mourned his going but not his wife's, and her harsh words about Eliza suggest tensions among the whites that could not be suppressed. Nashoba had been George Flower's idea even before it was Fanny Wright's. As he had planned it with her and put his life at hazard for it, he must have known that his going probably doomed Nashoba—he was the only experienced farmer there, and at the same time he was a forceful man who helped translate her ideas and good intentions into ways of dealing effectively with slaves.

Rumors later circulated in Cincinnati that Fanny Wright and George Flower had had an affair, and though such tales initially seem preposterous, they ultimately are persuasive and appear more likely than not to be true. For Flower was a man whose susceptibility to women had already complicated his life—his marriage to Eliza Andrews, in fact, was bigamous, as he had left England to flee a wife he could not divorce despite the fact that their marriage had irretrievably foundered. An affair with Fanny would most likely have begun when they explored the Tennessee wilderness together to find the right place for Nashoba, and no doubt they tried to suppress their turbulent emotions. Still, even stronger, luckier people than they have failed at such a goal, and Eliza was too smart to be fooled. Although he and Fanny were soul mates in a way that he and Eliza were not, George Flower was not a man who could leave a wife and three small children merely because he had fallen in love with another woman.

Fanny had built her character on defiance. Orphaned at two and a half and girded for survival from childhood, she did not have the psychic luxury of self-knowledge in its subtler and less transparent forms. When in pain, she looked outside herself and armed for battle. She could not fight Eliza Flower and win, and so she prepared to take on evangelical religion. That the enemies she found were often worthy enemies is a measure of her intelligence, integrity, and ambition. That she saw the world and her relation to it in terms too simplistic is one measure of what became her personal tragedy.

In mid-December 1826, haunted by illness, Wright wrote a trust deed to clarify the legal and economic relationships that would prevail at Nashoba and named ten trustees, among them Lafayette, Maclure, Robert Owen and his eldest son, Robert Dale Owen, Camilla Wright, James Richardson, and Richesson Whitby—this last a man who had come from New Harmony to try to take George Flower's place on the farm. She set two conditions: a school for black children would always be maintained, and freed slaves must be colonized outside the United States. No distinction was to be made between black and white children in the schools, and neither group was to be privileged over the other. The children of slave owners would be taught to respect and accomplish physical labor; the children of slaves would be given an education that would "fit them for the station of a free people." When these children grew up, then, they would together enjoy "that complete equality of habits and knowledge alone consistent with the political institutions of the country." Tightening the requirements for full participation in Nashoba and making it clear that a husband's admission did not automatically mean his wife's, she then stipulated that no trustee could be expelled for any reason whatever.

In her moments of comparative lucidity after the Flowers left, Fanny also worked to finish an addendum to *A Few Days in Athens*, a book she had published more than five years earlier. The connection between the original and the addendum, however, is tenuous, for the latter constitutes the kind of broadside attack she had learned from Owen. On her trip to New Harmony, she had encountered what is called the Second Great Awakening, and in Fanny's view, this revival movement sweeping the Ohio River valley demeaned women and threatened the freedom of thought she found most hopeful in her adopted country. Revolted at the spectacle of women screaming and writhing on the ground, she despised evangelical preachers whom she saw preying on their emotions and destroying their dignity.

Wracked by acute personal pain, she lashed out on paper, calling religion not only "the poisoner of human felicity" but "the first link in the chain of evil." Deluded into thinking she could reason her listeners out of belief in a higher power, she invited warnings from an admirer regarding "the obstacles attached to her reputation as being without religious principles."

While honoring her belief that plain speaking was not only a right but a duty, Fanny had been even more inflammatory than Robert Owen. She had not only looked skeptically at the marriage tie and cast doubt on the efficacy of religion, but said that blacks and whites could live freely together if only they were brought up as equals. Two months later James Richardson tried to persuade newspapers in New Orleans to print Fanny's Deed of Trust, but all refused, and her appeal apparently gained her nothing but notoriety.

Nashoba had remained for the most part a dream on paper: they had cleared about one hundred acres of lightly timbered land and fashioned a rough square with two hundred feet on each side. They had a single and two double log cabins for the whites, a cabin for the slaves' dining room, along with a storeroom and several slave cabins on the outside rim of the square. The carpenter Fanny expected never came, and neither did the blacksmith or the bricklayer. They had no sawmill, steam engine, washhouse, bathhouse, or dairy. No cattle or oxen were on their way downriver from Illinois, and the school lived only as a distant hope. They had not made it to the good life.

In March 1829 Fanny went once more to New Harmony, where she discovered that Robert Owen had enjoyed little more success than she—the millennium he had confidently expected had not come. Late that month Robert Dale and William Owen published a joint editorial acknowledging defeat: "The experiment, to ascertain at once whether a mixed and unassorted population could successfully govern their own affairs as a community, was a bold and hazardous attempt, and, we think, a premature one." All was not lost, however, and Fanny's powers of persuasion were clearly still intact, for Robert Dale wrote his mother that at some indefinite time in the future he thought the community at Nashoba would be more congenial to a man of his sentiments and habits.[12]

Meanwhile Robert Dale's friendship with Fanny had blossomed, and he had decided to accompany her to Europe, where she was bent on going to improve her precarious health. She was still wretchedly ill, and staying in a problematic climate much longer seemed foolish. They set out downriver, but by the time they got to Memphis, Fanny's health had again deteriorated to the point that she had to be carried to Nashoba in a hammock slung in a covered wagon. Despite their mutual anxieties, she and Camilla, who dreaded the Atlantic crossing, decided that the latter would stay in Tennessee, for neither sister thought they should be gone at the same time.

In the course of a drizzly Sunday, the resident trustees discussed Nashoba, agreeing to a number of resolutions and settling "all matters regarding the negroes." A week later, in mid-May, Robert Dale and Fanny lumbered in a wagon back to Memphis, where they met Charlotte Larieu, a mulatto woman whom Richardson had hired in New Orleans to supervise the school at Nashoba. Sweltering in the muggy weather and tormented by mosquitoes, they took ship for New Orleans, where they found themselves at the mercy of an erratic sailing schedule. There they languished for more than three weeks before their ship pushed at last into the deeper waters of the Gulf of Mexico and headed for the tip of Florida and the Atlantic Ocean.

On July 28, the day after Fanny and Robert Dale arrived in Le Havre, France, *The Genius of Universal Emancipation* published excerpts from a log James Richardson had sent from Nashoba. The entries spanned a six-week period—the first two encompassed the ten days Fanny and Robert Dale had been there; the next month's described what happened in their absence. The publication of this appalling information destroyed the Nashoba Fanny had worked so hard to build:

- On May 20 Camilla had announced that the children would be taken from their parents and put into a school managed by Charlotte Larieu, called Lolotte. All future communication between parents and children would take place only by permission and in Lolotte's presence.
- On May 26 the slaves were told that they could receive no gifts or tokens, and if they did, such objects would be returned or destroyed. Further, they could eat only at public meals.
- On June 1 a woman asked to have a lock for her door to prevent a man from entering, as he had earlier, and "endeavoring, without her consent, to take liberties with her person." The lock was refused. "Our views of the sexual relation had been repeatedly given to the slaves," Richardson wrote. "Camilla Wright again stated it." Camilla had then added that their doctrine was stronger than a lock, and said the man should be flogged if he repeated his offensive behavior.
- On June 3 Richardson announced that all colors were equal in rank, and on the 17th, he wrote that he had informed the slaves that he had begun to live with "Mamselle Josephine," Lolotte's mixed-race daughter.

They had denied the claims of family—ruthlessly separating parents from their children, asserted white superiority by treating slaves as less than human to the point of dictating when they could and could not eat, refused to protect a woman from a man's lust, endorsed flogging, and announced that "free love" was the principle governing sexual relations at Nashoba.

It was of course the last entry that toppled Fanny Wright's world. The miscegenation horrified Lundy's readers, along with the open acknowledgment that

Nashoba not only countenanced but also preached sexual intercourse without marriage. One man wrote of his disgust "that an accomplished young English woman . . . apparently concurs . . . in giving a sanction to the formation of illicit sexual connexions, without the obligations of marriage" and called Nashoba "one great brothel, disgraceful to its institutors, and most reprehensible, as a public example, in the vicinity."[13]

An entry that Lundy did not publish indicated that Camilla had stood by while Richardson flogged two female slaves, "two dozen and one dozen on the bare back with a cowskin." Another reprimanded the cook for giving bread and meat to one of her own children. Had this not happened, it would seem a bad parody—while the slaves come off as vital, resilient people, their "managers" had been made monsters by theory.

What they had done was diametrically opposed to the way Fanny Wright and George Flower had worked with slaves, so the central question is how deeply Fanny was implicated in Richardson's sadism. Before she and Robert Dale left Nashoba, the resident trustees had discussed "the slave system," and although flogging violated every principle Fanny had ever defended, it seems unlikely that Camilla would endorse something to which she knew her sister irrevocably opposed.

If Fanny and George had been lovers, she must have been not only sick but deeply demoralized when he left her at Nashoba. When James Richardson talked about the "slave system," she must have seen it from a theoretical distance—she knew he would do things rather differently, but she couldn't afford to know exactly what that meant. Often she had railed against marriage, for it had blocked her chance to be happy. And she was a proud woman who would have found it hard to believe that something more than the law tied George Flower to his wife.

So Camilla and Richardson probably did not violate the letter of Fanny's law, but they had profoundly violated its leavening spirit. Theoretically she and Richardson agreed, but he was a petty tyrant and she was not. And he had run up a huge debt that she would have to pay.

This news took several weeks to reach Fanny in France, but when it did, she immediately canceled a proposed trip to Italy to study peasant communes and made plans to return after no more than three months. What Richardson had done was irrevocable; she believed herself indebted to him for life itself; and her Deed of Trust had made it impossible to remove a trustee for any reason whatever. As indignation would therefore have been beside the point, she wrote him a letter that was a model of restraint. "All principles are liable to misinterpretation," she wrote, "but none so much as ours." He had provoked "unnecessary hostility and misconception," and thereby undermined Nashoba: "Were our own happiness our sole object, it might be indifferent in what manner we addressed ourselves to this world we had left. . . . But surely Richardson, that is not our only objective—at least it is not mine."[14]

Fanny's friends in Europe were dumbfounded by the tawdry revelations, and many of them were deeply troubled that she had left Camilla in such a place alone. They were bewildered, furthermore, that the gentle Camilla would have said and done such things, and some of their closest friends and relatives believed the sisters to be irretrievably lost. More than a few blamed the nefarious Robert Owen—the sisters were "the dupes and the victims of the wretched sophisms . . . of a madman"—but Owen himself told Fanny's uncle James Mylne that her "folly cannot fail to obstruct the very objects of a philanthropical kind she has in view, and to bring ruin upon her project and disgrace upon herself." The one old friend whose loyalty held was Lafayette.[15]

The piling-on of bad news was shattering—Fanny's hair began to turn white, and she behaved so erratically that at least one observer thought her brain perhaps affected. Trying to calm herself, she spent a good deal of time at Lafayette's chateau LaGrange—most of it alone in her room or out walking by herself to calm her nerves.

Stubbornly contemplating new plans and rationales for Nashoba, however, she also sought out potential new recruits, among them Mary Shelley, daughter of Mary Wollstonecraft and William Godwin, widow to the poet Percy Bysshe Shelley, and author of *Frankenstein*. "We endeavour to undermine the slavery of colour existing in the North American Republic," Fanny wrote, at the same time calling Nashoba "an establishment where affection shall form the only marriage, kind feeling and kind action the only religion, respect for the feelings and liberties of others the only restraint, and union of interest the bond of peace and security." Bound to England by her son Percy, Mary declined, but she went to the docks to see the ship off and kept a lock of Fanny's hair all her life.[16]

Meanwhile, Fanny also wrote a circular describing yet another radical vision of Nashoba and had it printed and sent to friends and likely supporters. Everybody would have equal rights, whatever their sex or skin color. Moral pleasure would be their only compensation for badly thatched cabins, hard beds, and simple fare. The dirtiest work would have the greatest social value, and together they would discover how human beings ought properly to live, thereby setting "a first example of union and brotherhood."

Various people seemed to be interested—a medley of names crop up in the correspondence between Fanny and Robert Dale about potential recruits for Nashoba—but as the time for departure neared, the only person ready to join them was the redoubtable Frances Trollope, who called Fanny "the most interesting woman in Europe."[17]

At forty-seven, Frances Trollope was embarrassed by her husband's inability to support her in the style to which she preferred to be accustomed, and by spending a year or so at Nashoba, she expected to evade her creditors and possibly help repair the family fortunes. Leaving her son Anthony in school at Winchester and her husband at home in Harrow, then, she gathered her two daughters and a second son, a manservant, a maid, and émigré artist Auguste Hervieu, and met Fanny on November 3, 1827, at Tower Stairs, where they hastily boarded ship and took leave of England. Robert Dale was to sail ten days later from Liverpool and expected to bring more new settlers with him.

A sea voyage in good weather was a fine time to work, and Fanny used it to write her definitive answer to criticisms of Nashoba. She called her article "Explanatory Notes, Respecting the Nature and Objects of the Institution of Nashoba, and of the Principles upon Which It Is Founded." It was both the most powerful statement she ever wrote, and the most revealing. "The husbandman who supports us by the fruits of his labor, the artizan to whom we owe all the comforts and conveniences of life, are banished from what is termed intellectual society," Fanny wrote, and "too often condemned to the most severe physical privations and the grossest mental ignorance; while the soldier who lives by our crimes, the lawyer by our quarrels and our rapacity, and the priest by our credulity or our hypocrisy, are honored with public consideration and applause." Values so skewed, she thought, deserved contempt.[18]

At the psychological center of her treatise she put an affirmation of sexual experience that, in the nineteenth-century United States, only Walt Whitman would approach. Sexual passion was "the strongest and . . . noblest of the human passions," "the best source of human happiness." If ignored or abused, a force so powerful could lead to physical and mental disease and squalor. As it was, "ignorant laws, ignorant prejudices, ignorant codes of morals . . . condemn one portion of the female sex to vicious excess, another to as vicious restraint, and all to defenceless helplessness and slavery, and generally the whole of the male sex to debasing licentiousness, if not to loathsome brutality." At Nashoba, Tennessee state marriage laws would have no force, and no man could assert any rights over a woman beyond what he might exercise over her free and voluntary affections. The school would provide an alternative to the home itself, and to what was so often "the forcible union of unsuitable and unsuited parents."

Nashoba was to be a biracial community of equals, and the African Americans who joined them now would come only from "the free citizens of color." Drawing on her experience with Marcus and Mary Winchester, she wrote hopefully of miscegenation—the races were mixing, and "the only question is whether it shall take place in good taste and good feeling . . . or whether it shall proceed, as it now does, viciously and degradingly, mingling hatred and fear with the ties of blood." Nashoba would educate its black and white children together, "thus approaching their minds, tastes and occupations," and then they would "leave the affections of future generations to the dictates of free choice."

Repudiating both competition and religion, Fanny saw education as the lever that would move the world, and the cooperative system as the principal form education would take, being "the best means yet discovered for securing the one great end, that of human liberty, and equality."

All the community needed was a handful of like-minded people who were now scattered about the world, and in order to reach them, she asked that editors publish the "Explanatory Notes," honoring "the spirit of human inquiry and disinterested efforts." By carefully explaining her assumptions as well as her hopes, she had imposed a poignant trust in the American people. And so serene was she in her expectations that from the mouth of the Mississippi she wrote a European friend to offer Nashoba as a solace and home if ever she should need it: "if ought ever happen to thee to render a change of place desirable & friendship needful or but soothing to the heart, thou knowst where Nashoba lies & who dwell therein."[19]

When their ship docked, however, Fanny discovered that the Nashoba she had hastened to defend no longer existed. Camilla had married Richesson Whitby after discovering that living "in open violation of the civil institutions of the country" provoked general indignation. James Richardson had left Nashoba, going once more into what he called the sordid world of competition, because he had decided he could not live comfortably in the cooperative system. And when Frances Trollope saw Nashoba she wrote, "One glance sufficed to convince me that every idea I had formed of the place was as far as possible from the truth."[20]

There was nothing to drink there except rainwater; the only food included pork, rice, and a few potatoes they'd brought from Memphis, a little wheat bread and some inedible cornbread, but neither cheese nor butter. The bedroom Fanny and Frances shared had no ceiling; rain fell through the roof; and the chimney caught fire a dozen times a day. Camilla and Richesson looked like specters, and as she looked around, all Frances Trollope could see was desolation.

Fanny, on the other hand, seemed utterly indifferent to the things Frances Trollope looked on with dismay—an entirely different person, "in dress, looks, and manner," from the woman Mrs. Trollope had admired in Paris and London. Apparently she was "perfectly unconscious that her existence was deprived of all that makes life desirable": "I never heard or read of any enthusiasm approaching her's," she wrote, "except in some few instances, in ages past, of religious fanaticism." Frightened for her children in "the pestilential atmosphere," Fanny Trollope borrowed $300 from Nashoba and fled with her entourage to Memphis, where she would await a steamboat to take them to Cincinnati.

The *Memphis Advocate* apparently published Fanny's "Explanatory Notes" in late January, and about the same time the *New Harmony Gazette* began to publish it as well. Fanny's New Orleans agent pretended ignorance when a man sitting nearby observed loudly that one fine morning Miss Wright might find her throat cut. Virtually every close friend of hers denounced the threat, and the general outcry was deafening. James Madison wrote Lafayette that with her "rare talents & still rarer disinterestedness," Fanny had nonetheless created "insuperable obstacles to the good fruits of which they might be productive by her disregard or rather defiance of the most established opinion & vivid feelings."[21]

The last disappointment was perhaps the most bitter. When Robert Dale arrived, he brought along no more recruits, and Fanny had to accept Nashoba's failure both as an experiment to end slavery and as a community based on cooperative labor. She acknowledged in the Nashoba log that her methods of dealing with the slaves—and the methods of those she trusted—had failed. In the end, the slaves had become idle unless constantly watched, and so the trustees put them under the management of one John Gilliam—the conventional southern overseer system that Fanny Wright and George Flower had designed Nashoba to avoid had won out at last.

Fanny wrote yet another prospectus for yet another version of Nashoba, but it was merely an exercise on paper. Robert Dale left to go up to New Harmony, and not long after, Camilla and her husband followed, hoping that New Harmony would restore them to health. A handful of people stopped by, but after six weeks of solitude, when Robert Dale wrote that things in Indiana were better than he had expected and perhaps the theater group there could produce some of Fanny's plays, she was ready. By the first week of June she was on a steamboat heading upriver.

Years later, Fanny wrote that she had "bowed her spirit in humility before the omnipotence of collective Humanity. 'Man Species is alone capable of effecting what I, weak existence of an hour! have thought myself equal to attempt.'" The experience had given her an extraordinary amount of knowledge, however, which she was prepared to put to use in serving her fellow human beings in a different way. She now had "the information and the experience . . . to guide the efforts of a really efficient leader of the popular mind," and her goal was to restore America to its revolutionary ideals. She talked a while longer as though she would go back, but the stage was empty and the drama of Nashoba was done.[22]

On July 4, 1828, Fanny Wright became probably the first woman in America to be the main speaker on a public occasion to a large, "promiscuous" audience of men and women. She followed this a month later with a lecture at the Cincinnati Courthouse, where she spoke again the two following Sundays. Frances Trollope, who had little reason to be a friendly witness, marveled at her commanding presence. "I knew her extraordinary gift of eloquence, her almost unequalled command of words, and the wonderful power of her rich and thrilling voice . . . [but] all my expectations fell far short of the splendour, the brilliance, the overwhelming eloquence of this extraordinary orator. . . . Her tall and majestic figure, the deep and almost solemn expression of her eyes, the simple contour of her finely formed head . . . her garment of plain white muslin, which hung around her in folds that recalled the drapery of a Grecian statue, all contributed to produce an effect, unlike any thing I had ever seen before, or ever expect to see again."[23]

Lecturing as she made her way up the Mississippi, Fanny then crossed the Alleghenies, arriving in New York City at the beginning of 1829. The next two years would prove the most vital of her life, filled as they were with triumph and notoriety. As a lecturer and joint editor of the *New Harmony Gazette*, which she and Robert Dale moved that year to New York under the name the *Free Enquirer*, she was attacked shamelessly, labeled among other degrading things "the Red Harlot of Infidelity." At the same time, she was celebrated extravagantly: Walt Whitman would write, "We all loved her: fell down before her: her very appearance seemed to enthrall us." She was "sweeter, nobler, grander—multiplied by 20—than all who traduced her." John Stuart Mill would call her one of the most important women of her day.[24]

Late that winter, Fanny took time to fulfill a promise she had made when she founded Nashoba: opposed to colonization, she nonetheless felt a personal obligation to spare her own slaves the wretched life they could expect in this country. So she took her freed slaves to Haiti, a trip on which she was accompanied by William Phiquepal—a teacher whom William Maclure had brought to the United States—and, because he had lived in the West Indies, a man she expected to help her negotiate the difficulties of port cities. By the time she was on a ship headed back up the Atlantic coast to New York, she knew she was pregnant, and in July 1830, with the vaguest reasons given, she and Camilla sailed for England.

Her troubles multiplied. In Paris on February 8, 1831, Camilla died in Fanny's arms, and nothing for Fanny would ever be the same. For the next several years she essentially disappeared—everyone who caught a glimpse of her seems to have come away in confusion and dismay. Clearly understanding that an illegitimate child of hers would be given no quarter in the world, she married Phiquepal privately in June of that year after their daughter Sylva was born. She asked that her husband begin using his family name d'Arusmont, and then took it herself. When a second daughter died, she assigned her birthday to Sylva and maintained the lie all her life.[25] In the course of ten years, she destroyed every friendship that had mattered to her when Camilla was alive.

In the mid-1830s, Fanny returned to America and for almost two years tried to assume the role of a self-described leader of the public mind, but by then she had become one of the most notorious women in America. Riots erupted in the streets of New York City when she spoke, and the entire police force had to be called out to protect her and her followers. She was an oddity and her lectures were free, but gradually no more than a handful of people came to hear her, and finally she conceded defeat. A brief attempt in the 1840s to resurrect the old Fanny in London proved a disaster. Her audiences dwindled to shadows, she quarreled with ardent supporters, and critics accused her of having nothing lucid to say.

She kept on writing, however, certain that she would ultimately succeed in publishing a theoretical work that would illuminate all of human history. She continued to travel up and down the Ohio and the Mississippi between Cincinnati, where she built a house, and Nashoba, where she lived intermittently. She crossed the Atlantic several times, separated more often than not from her daughter and the husband whose insignificance had misled her into thinking that he could do her no irreparable harm.

In 1850 she finally sued Phiquepal for divorce in Shelby County. It was granted, but the following March she discovered that she had lost her daughter as well—Sylva filed suit to take Nashoba away from her mother, whom she even refused to see alone. Though Sylva was in Cincinnati in the winter of 1852 as her mother lay dying, she did not visit her. Becoming an ardent Christian, Sylva referred in old age to the "infidel trash" published in the *Free Enquirer*. But her final repudiation of her heritage may have come in 1874. Speaking at a congressional hearing "as the daughter of Frances Wright, whom the Female Suffragists are pleased to consider as having *opened* the door to their pretensions," Sylva begged the Speaker and committee members "to *shut* it forever, from the strongest convictions that they can only bring misery and degradation upon the whole sex, and thereby wreck human happiness in America!"[26]

Fanny Wright had had her share of human weaknesses—in her relentless high-mindedness she must have been a trying companion, and her arrogance became insufferable. She laughed too seldom and talked too much. She lived, for the last twenty years of her life, in a sort of emotional and intellectual isolation. She tried, it seems, to exorcize the ghosts of the past, and she ended up talking to herself.

But if she had the wound, she also had the bow. She scorned the obvious targets and ranged far beyond most people of her generation or any other to ask how to make life worth the having. Again and again she attacked the hard questions—about money, privilege, and power—and scoffed at those who contented themselves with the old excuses for misery and injustice. Her sympathy for black people and her deep desire for egalitarian relationships between the races are arguably still rare in this country. Her understanding of the keen importance of sexuality far preceded that of the cultures she lived in. She proved right in saying that later generations would know that she, and not those who attacked her, spoke for a sane and healthy morality. The issues she raised are vital still, while those who mocked her rank among the curiosities of history.

NOTES

1. The information in this essay comes from my book, *Fanny Wright: Rebel in America*, published initially by Harvard University Press in 1984 under the name Celia Morris Eckhardt. In 1992 the paperback edition was published by the University of Illinois Press under the name Celia Morris. The most pertinent chapters are 5 and 6, pages 108–67.

2. The most fruitful sources of information about the commune, in time named Nashoba, are the Garnett Letters at the Houghton Library at Harvard, given them by Cecilia Payne-Gaposchkin, Julia Garnett's great-granddaughter, and the serial *The Genius of Universal Emancipation* for 1825–28. The relevant parts of the Garnett Letters were published by Payne-Gaposchkin in "The Nashoba Plan for Removing the Evil of Slavery: Letters of Frances and Camilla Wright, 1820–1829," *Harvard Library Bulletin* 23 (July 1975): 221–51, (October 1975): 429–61.

3. See George Flower, *History of the English Settlement in Edwards County, Illinois* (Chicago: Fergus Printing Co., 1882).

4. *The Writings of Thomas Jefferson*, ed. Paul Leicester Ford (New York: Putnam's, 1895), 10:343–45.

5. Mary Shelley to Fanny Wright (hereafter FW), September 12, 1827, Garnett Letters.

6. George Flower to Benjamin Lundy, June 12, 1826, published in *The Genius of Universal Emancipation*, July 17, 1826.

7. William Maclure to Madame Marie Fretageot, December 19, 1826, Mss., Workingmen's Institute, New Harmony, Indiana.

8. Flower to FW, October 3, 1827, quoted in A. J. G. Perkins and Theresa Wolfson, *Frances Wright, Free Enquirer: The Study of a Temperament* (New York: Harper Bros., 1939), 156.

9. Camilla Wright to Julia Garnett, August 20, 1826, Garnett Letters.

10. Quoted in CW to JG, December 8, 1826, Garnett Letters.

11. Camilla Wright to Julia Garnett, August 20, 1826, Garnett Letters. The disease may have been dengue fever, which still menaces large parts of the world.

12. *New Harmony Gazette*, March 28, 1827.

13. *Genius of Universal Emancipation*, August 18, 1827.

14. FW to Richardson, August 18, 1827, Theresa Wolfson Papers, Martin Catherwood Library, School of Labor and Industrial Relations, Cornell University.

15. James Mylne to Julia Garnett, August 12, 1827, Garnett Letters.

16. *The Life and Letters of Mary Wollstonecraft Shelley*, ed. Mrs. Julian Marshall (1889; repr., New York: Haskell House, 1970), 2:168–71.

17. Frances Trollope to Julia Garnett, May 17, 1827; FT to Julia Garnett Pertz, October 7, 1827, Garnett Papers.

18. "Explanatory Notes on Nashoba," *New Harmony Gazette*, January 30, February 6 and 13, 1828.

19. FW to Julia Garnett Pertz, December 26, 1827, Garnett Letters.

20. Frances Trollope, *Domestic Manners of Americans* (1832; repr., Gloucester, Mass.: Peter Smith, 1974), 18–28.

21. *The Writings of James Madison*, ed. Gaillard Hunt (New York: G. P. Putnam's Sons, 1900–1910), 9:310–11.

22. FW, *Biography of Frances Wright D'Arusmont*, reprinted in *Life, Letters and Lectures, 1834–1844* (New York: Arno Press, 1972), 32–33.

23. Trollope, *Domestic Manners*, 70–73.

24. Horace Traubel, *With Walt Whitman in Camden* (New York: Appleton, 1908), 1:80.

25. Sylva d'Arusmont actually had her official birthday carved on her mother's tombstone in Cincinnati, Ohio.

26. Frances Sylva Guthrie d'Arusmont, *Memorial on Suffrage*, February 3, 1874, Wolfson Papers.

Milly Swan Price

(1824–c. 1880)

Freedom, Kinship, and Property

BEVERLY GREENE BOND

❀ ❀ ❀

On March 2, 1840, sixteen-year-old Milly Swan—along with her three brothers (Nick, eighteen; Jim, seven; and Addison, about three) and four sisters (Peggy, twelve; Charity, about eleven; Kitty, about four; and Sally Ann, about one)—was indentured to Tipton County planter Ellen C. "Nelly" Newman. Court records do not reveal the extent of their mother Anna Swan's involvement in this decision to "bind and put [the children] under the care and management" of Newman, but these sources, along with census data, suggest that the Swan children were already living with Newman and that their indenture only formalized a longstanding relationship and allowed Nelly Newman to keep the Swan children (and benefit from their labor) until each turned twenty-one years of age. Once free from her bondage, Anna Swan's oldest daughter, Milly, carved out a unique place for herself and her family on the West Tennessee frontier. Her story reveals how free black women negotiated racial, gender, and familial relationships in the antebellum and post–Civil War South.[1]

Although the particular events of their lives varied, most free black women struggled to act as autonomous beings in settings where race and gender were badges of subservience. They had some of the same rights as other free persons, but their social and economic activities were restricted by state statutes and local ordinances that regulated the behavior of African Americans, free and enslaved. And as women they were bound by the gender constraints of nineteenth-century society. Legal marriage also limited the influence of black and white women within their households since coverture laws allowed husbands to exercise control of property and to act as the public faces of their households. Despite these race- and gender-based restrictions, some free black women, through their own labor and/or social and economic associations with white residents, acquired and maintained control over property (including slaves). The intersection of property, race, and gender provides a useful framework for examining the lives of nineteenth-century African American women in Memphis and throughout the South.[2]

The nearly seventy-year period of Milly Swan's public life illustrates the convergence of property, race, and gender as well as the shifting domestic relationships within many African American households. Before the Civil War, Milly Swan represented herself and her household in her public role as a property owner. Although marriage to Bob Price led to some limitations on this public role, Bob's death restored some of Milly's public presence. After the Civil War, Milly faced new challenges brought on by the property claims of Bob's newly emancipated family as well as her own second marriage. Her struggles mirror those of other women, as African Americans constructed identities as free persons and redefined family roles and responsibilities, property rights, and ideas of proper gender relationships in the post–Civil War South.

Reconstructing Milly Swan's life is like piecing a quilt from fragments of larger fabrics. While the lives of nineteenth-century middle-class white women are revealed in paintings, journals, diaries, letters, or other correspondence, the lives of most poor white and black women come to us primarily through judicious reading of scattered public records. Court proceedings like the indenture of the Swan children, lists of free blacks maintained by county courts throughout Tennessee, marriage licenses, deeds, wills, business licenses, probate and civil litigation, tax records, and federal census reports are all that we have to re-create the lives of antebellum free black women like Milly Swan. Evidence of her post–Civil War experiences is as fragmentary as that for the antebellum years. Yet each fragment, when combined with the records of other black women, suggests the parameters of their lives. While I cannot enrich this narrative with Milly Swan's own thoughts and words, the public record provides an unexpected story of one woman's life on the West Tennessee frontier.

Although the experiences of free blacks were similar across the state of Tennessee and the Upper South, a plantation economy based on cotton and slavery, as well as the influence of Memphis as an urban center for western Tennessee and northern Mississippi, created a unique setting for Milly's life. Located in the southwestern corner of the state, Shelby County, Tennessee, was established in 1820. Bordered by the Mississippi River and the Arkansas territory on the west, the state of Mississippi on the south, and Fayette County on the east, Shelby County was carved out of lands that had once been the hunting grounds of the Chickasaw Indians. In 1823 the county lost part of its northern section to

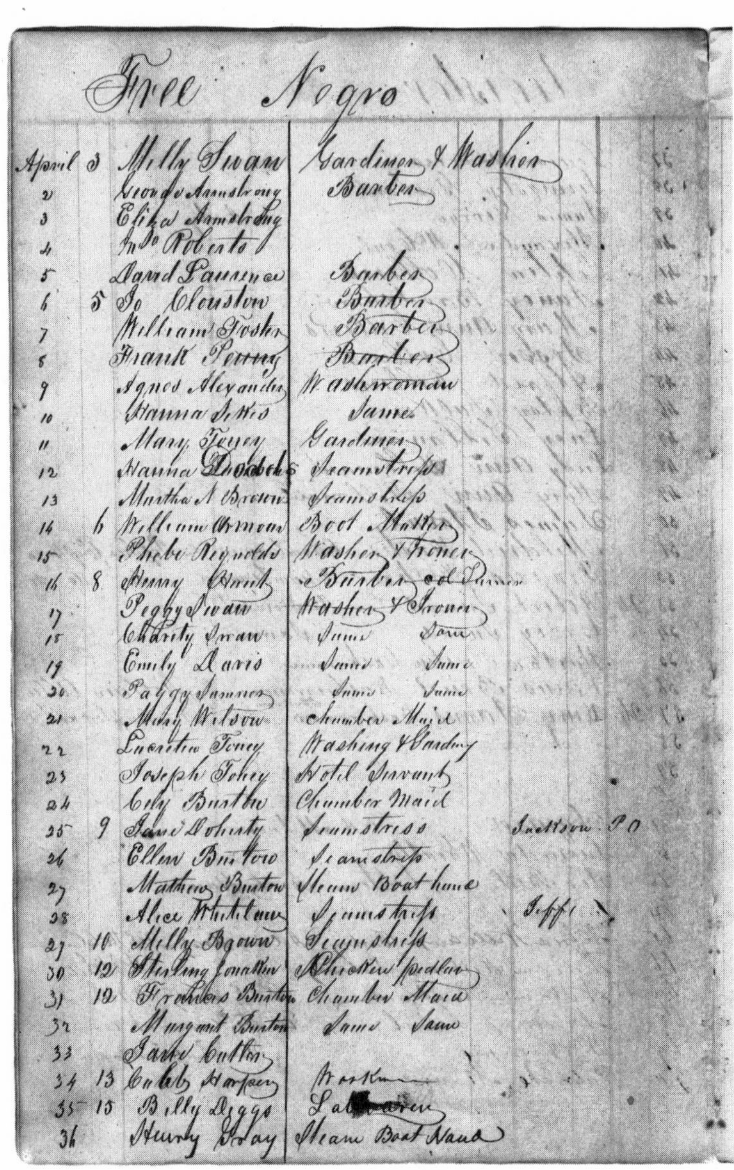

Free Negro

No.	Date	Name	Occupation	
April	3	Milly Swan	Gardiner & Washer	
2		George Armstrong	Barber	
3		Eliza Armstrong		
4		Jno Roberts		
5		David Laurence	Barber	
6	5	Jo Clouston	Barber	
7		William Foster	Barber	
8		Frank Perring	Barber	
9		Agnes Alexander	Washerwoman	
10		Hanna Sittes	Same	
11		Mary Toney	Gardiner	
12		Hanna Dodds	Seamstress	
13		Martha A Brown	Seamstress	
14	6	William Armour	Boot Maker	
15		Phebe Reynolds	Washer & Ironer	
16	8	Henry Hunt	Barber [illegible]	
17		Peggy Swan	Washer & Ironer	
18		Charity Swan	Same Same	
19		Emily Davis	Same Same	
20		Peggy Sumner	Same Same	
21		Mary Wilson	Chamber Maid	
22		Lucretia Toney	Washing & Gardening	
23		Joseph Toney	Hotel Servant	
24		Cely Burton	Chamber Maid	
25	9	Jane Doherty	Seamstress	Jackson P O
26		Ellen Burton	Seamstress	
27		Mathew Burton	Steam Boat hand	
28		Alice Whitlaw	Seamstress	Jeff
29	10	Milly Brown	Seamstress	
30	12	Sterling Jonathan	Chicken pedler	
31	12	Frances Burton	Chamber Maid	
32		Margaret Burton	Same Same	
33		Jack Cutter		
34	13	Caleb Harper	Workman	
35	15	Billy Diggs	Laborer	
36		Henry Gray	Steam Boat Hand	

MILLY SWAN PRICE

1853. Listed (top of page) in the

Shelby County *Free Negro Register*.

Shelby County Archives, Memphis, Tennessee.

a newly created Tipton County. In the 1820s and the 1830s both counties were rugged, sparsely populated areas; the principal towns—Randolph and Covington (both in Tipton County), Raleigh and Memphis (both in Shelby County)—competed for economic and political dominance. The main attraction of both Randolph and Memphis was their locations on the Second and Fourth Bluffs of the Mississippi River, but in the 1830s neither town was a seat of county government. Instead, Covington in Tipton County and Raleigh in Shelby County were the political centers of their respective counties.[3]

But trade flowed in and out of Randolph and Memphis. Farmers from other parts of rural western Tennessee (Tipton, Shelby, Fayette, Hardeman, Haywood, and Madison Counties), loaded cotton, corn, hogs, whiskey, tobacco, and other goods on crudely constructed barges or flatboats and maneuvered their boats down inland creeks and rivers to the Big Hatchie River at Randolph or the Wolf River at Memphis. Both rivers emptied into the Mississippi, allowing easy access south to the Gulf of Mexico or north to the Ohio River system. Regular mail service between Memphis or Randolph and other Tennessee towns and cities began in the 1830s. Travelers arriving in the two towns traded their goods and spent a few nights and many dollars in local inns and saloons. As historian Gerald Capers noted, "arriving in Memphis singly or in groups they completely controlled the settlement. . . . [T]hese transients ruled the town, refused to pay wharfage, and violated laws at their pleasure." Over the next thirty years, Memphis surpassed its rivals to become a commercial center that drew thousands of permanent settlers, including many blacks, to its environs.[4]

By 1860 there were approximately 4 million African Americans in the United States—only about 500,000 of them were free. About half of the nation's free black population lived in the slaveholding Upper South, but only 7,300 lived in Tennessee, most in East and Middle Tennessee. Few free blacks settled in western Tennessee. In 1830 only 62 of Shelby County's 5,648 residents were free blacks; 2,149 residents were slaves. Only 17 free blacks lived among neighboring Tipton County's 5,317 residents, of whom 1,731 were slaves. After 1830 the free black population as a percentage of the total population in western Tennessee declined as farmers and planters increased their dependence on slave labor. Antislavery activity essentially disappeared in the state in the aftermath of the 1831 Nat Turner rebellion and rumors of other insurrection plots, and constitutional changes made it more difficult to free a slave or for the newly freed to remain in the state. By 1860 it was clear that western Tennessee was a region that discouraged free black settlers. Only 788 of the state's 7,300 free blacks lived in this region.[5]

In general, free black populations were concentrated in Tennessee's towns and cities, particularly Knoxville, Nashville, and Memphis. As in other states of the Upper South, this free black population was made up of the descendants of free black settlers who had migrated from North Carolina, Virginia, or other states; the children of enslaved black men and free black, white, or Indian women; former slaves who had purchased their freedom or whose freedom had been purchased by family members or who had been freed by their owners; or "quasi-free" blacks who acted as though they were free but whose status had not been fully recognized by the state legislature or county courts. The largest population of free blacks was in Davidson County (about 17 percent of the total population). Shelby County's free black population was only the fifth-largest concentration in the state, and of the 276 free blacks in Shelby County in 1860, only 198 lived in Memphis. Women outnumbered men among the city's enslaved and free black populations.[6]

Like most nineteenth-century African American women, slave or free, Milly Swan's origins are shrouded in mystery. Census data and other public records suggest that she was born in 1824, but the month, date, and location of her birth are unclear. She was probably born in Tennessee or Alabama. Her mother may have been a free woman when Milly was born, but the status of Milly's father (or the fathers of her siblings) is unknown. While her parents may have been part of the 1820s "Trail of Tears" migration of Native American tribes, and the slaves or free blacks who lived with them, a more likely story is that the Swans accompanied the steady stream of black and white migrants who arrived in Tennessee in the late eighteenth and early nineteenth century from Virginia and North Carolina, by way of northern Alabama.

While there is no clear evidence of where Milly's parents came from or when and how they came to Tennessee, the white family to whom the Swan children were apprenticed was part of a prominent Virginia family who moved west in the late eighteenth or early nineteenth century. Ellen "Nelly" Newman was the daughter of Frances Taylor Madison, the youngest sister of President James Madison, and Robert Henry Rose II. Around the turn of the century, the Roses left Virginia for Alabama and later moved on to western Tennessee, where they eventually settled in newly formed Tipton County in 1823 or 1824. Ellen Rose married John F. Newman, and by 1830 the couple owned a farm in Tipton County. Their household included two young sons and one daughter, as well as fourteen free blacks—three adult women (twenty-four to thirty-six years of age), two younger adults (one male and one female, ten to twenty-four years of age) and nine children (ten and under)—and twelve slaves. Anna Swan's husband may have been one of the Newman slaves, or perhaps he was the lone free black male in the group.[7]

Milly Swan's public presence begins with her indenture to Ellen Newman. In exchange for food, clothing, shelter, and training in some craft or skill, indentured free black children, like their white counterparts, were bound by contracts (supervised by county courts) to serve their masters or mistresses for a specified period of time. Although their bondage was limited by these contracts, indentured servants frequently performed the same tasks as slaves. The Tennessee system of indenture or apprenticeship was based on that of North Carolina except that the role of churches in regulating the system in the latter state was replaced by that of the county courts. Indenture and apprenticeship as sources of labor were gradually replaced by black slavery throughout much of the South. But indenture or apprenticeship remained a viable system for managing the care of pauper orphans, or of children whose fathers were absent and whose mothers were considered unfit or unable to care for them, as well as for training young people in particular crafts or skills.[8]

An indentured servant's labor belonged to the master or mistress. A disobedient servant or one who attacked their master or mistress could receive twenty-one lashes. While the county courts acted in loco parentis for the indentured or apprenticed child, if the latter complained about his or her treatment and courts found no basis for these complaints, the period of service could be doubled. If a female servant became pregnant, she had an additional year added on to her bondage and her child might be bound out for a period of indenture, but the child was still "freeborn." County courts were responsible for maintaining the free status of indentured children; however, while the legal system protected the status of indentured free blacks, this quasi-bondage could also be a precarious prelude to reenslavement in antebellum communities where all African Americans were assumed to be enslaved not free.[9]

In the first four years of Milly's life, her family included Anna and (possibly) her husband, her brother Nick (who was two years older) and herself. Milly was four years old when her sister Peggy was born, followed a year later by another sister, Charity. Four other siblings—Jim, Kitty, Addison, and Sallie Ann—rounded out the family by 1838. Throughout her life, Milly did not seem to have the same close relationship with these younger siblings as she did with Nick, Peggy, and Charity, although Jim or Addison (referred to as "George" in court papers) was indentured to Milly in the 1850s. The young boy's indenture to his older sister guarded his free status in a decade of growing animosity toward free black men and women that resulted in the reenslavement of many. Some free blacks were kidnapped and enslaved, others lost the documents that proved their status. Indentured free black children faced a more gradual devolution of their status as memories—their own and those of the people to whom they were indentured or the communities in which they lived—of their free status faded after decades of bondage. This does not seem to have been true for Anna Swan's children, since all except the oldest, Nick, registered as free blacks with the Shelby County Court at one time or the other between 1846 and 1862.[10]

Milly's work and life on the Newman farm probably differed little from that of other free black indentured children or enslaved children. In fact, a federal census taken in 1840, when the Swan children were indentured, did not list any free blacks in the Newman household; the census taker probably included the Swan children among the thirty-six slaves on Newman's farm in 1840.[11] Although the terms of their indenture specified that they would receive adequate sustenance, the Swan children, like other indentured children, would have been unable to protect themselves from overwork or physical abuse. Unlike indenture contracts for white children, those for free blacks did not include requirements that the child be educated. And for sixteen-year-old Milly there were also additional concerns for the well-being of her younger siblings. How much of this burden would she have shared with her brother Nick? The eighteen-year-old boy's work assignments would have been similar to those of an adult male; his bondage, however, ended two years before Milly's.

In their indenture/apprenticeship contracts, masters and mistresses assumed responsibility for guarding the morals of their young servants. For example, when R. A. Collins of Shelby County apprenticed nine-year-old Catherine in 1845, he agreed to provide the child with food, clothing, and lodging until she was twenty-one and to "take care of her morals and treat her with humanity." Catherine was also to receive a good horse, saddle, and bridle in freedom dues at the end of her servitude. But these contractual arrangements offered no guarantees of protection. Physical or sexual abuse from a master or mistress was always a possibility for an apprentice—although county courts had the power to remove the child if this occurred.[12]

In August 1844, four years after the original indenture of the Swan children, the Tipton County Court reaffirmed the terms of their servitude. But Milly, in the last year of her indenture, was pregnant. It is not clear who fathered her child or whether the court added another year to Milly's service because of her pregnancy since, within the next two years, Milly left Newman's service with $7.50, a "good and sufficient suit of wearing apparel," and an infant daughter. Roxana Swan had been born on November 15, 1844, in Shelby rather than Tipton County. On February 2, 1846, Milly appeared before the Shelby County Court clerk, to register her fourteen-month-old daughter as a free child of color. The clerk noted that Roxana's "mother the said Milly Swan was a free woman of color at the time of said infant['s] birth and before that time and still is such free person," and described Roxana as "a negro of a rather yellow complection of ordinary stature."[13]

When Milly settled in Memphis, the town was already a commercial center for the Mid-South (western Tennessee, northern Mississippi, eastern Arkansas, and southern Missouri). But in 1845 fewer than one hundred of the town's three thousand residents were free blacks. Both slaves and free blacks provided the domestic and common labor that supported the city's social, political, and economic structure. Although white city residents valued the presence of slave laborers, some cautioned against allowing slaves to hire their own time or live apart from their owners. There was an undercurrent of suspicion concerning relationships between free blacks and slaves. As a writer to one local newspaper noted, "How long will our citizens quietly permit free negroes to remain among us, demoralizing and ruining our slaves and endangering the lives of our families. . . . The truth is, the free negroes do more to injure our slaves than all the abolitionists in the world."[14]

Despite such suspicions, Milly Swan and several other free black women and men managed to accumulate property in the town. In April 1846 Milly purchased her first lot and put it in her infant daughter Roxana's name. The 60-by-150-foot lot on Linden Street near St. Martin Avenue was purchased from Robertson Topp's South Memphis Company. Milly's neighbors included several other free black female property holders—Ellen Burton, Maria Batte and Agnes Alexander, Phebe Reynolds, (Martha) Ann Brown, and Harriet Penny. Ellen Burton and her children, Matthew, Mary, Celia, Frances, Martha, and Jane, had migrated to Memphis from Dyer County a few months after Milly and Roxana arrived in the city. Sources do not reveal the motivations of Ellen, Milly, or other free black women who migrated to Memphis. However, they obviously expected to find more economic opportunities in this developing commercial center than in small rural communities. Fourteen years earlier, Ellen Hilyer purchased her husband, Jacob Burton, and successfully petitioned the Tennessee General Assembly for a private emancipation act. The Burton family's decision to migrate to Memphis may have been a consequence of Jacob Burton's death in 1843 or 1844. Maria Batte and her sister Agnes Alexander also owned real estate near Milly Swan. Records do not indicate when they arrived in Memphis, but Batte (and possibly Alexander) was manumitted in the 1840 will of John Austin of Giles County. Washerwoman Phebe Reynolds "amassed, by her own exertions, a considerable amount of property" even before she was freed by Rueben Kay in 1848. Reynolds owned two lots that constituted the most extensive property holdings of any free black woman in South Memphis at that time.[15]

Like Milly Swan, seamstress Martha Ann Brown, the daughter of a free black woman—Elizabeth Larry from Bedford County in Middle Tennessee—migrated to Shelby County. Brown and Larry first petitioned the county court for permission to remain in 1843. Seven years later, (Martha) Ann Brown's household included her husband (John, a barber), a son, and a daughter (named Elizabeth, after Martha's mother). Harriet Penny, another free black woman, lived with her husband (Frank, a barber) and their five children in a house near Milly's. Sources do not reveal how the Pennys gained their freedom.[16]

Although records do not indicate how much Milly Swan or any of these other women paid Topp's company for their property, on the 1850 city tax rolls the two lots that Phebe Reynolds owned were valued at $1,600, while Milly's property was worth $1,000. Ellen Burton's lot was worth $500 in 1847–49 but only $200 in 1850, and Agnes Alexander's was worth $300 in 1847–49 but increased to $400 in 1850. Ann Brown had the least valuable real estate—hers was only worth $150 in 1850. The property holdings of Memphis's free black women were comparable to those of the average property holder in the city at the time. Although several white Memphians had more real estate and personal property, most property holders, like these women, owned just a lot or two on which they constructed small houses and/or kept subsistence gardens.[17]

Milly bought more land in the 1850s. In 1851 she paid $120 for another lot on St. Martin. She acquired this land as repayment for a loan she had made to another Memphis resident, Jim Williams. It is not clear whether Williams was a free black man or a white man, but in 1847, he borrowed $300 from Milly on a thirty-six-month note. He guaranteed the debt with his lot on St. Martin, and when he was unable to repay the loan, the land was sold at a public auction. Milly Swan was the highest bidder, paying $120 for the real estate.[18]

We can only speculate on how these free black women got the money to purchase land. Milly lived with and worked for the Rose/Newman family for over a decade before completing her indenture, receiving her "freedom dues," and coming to Memphis. She may have earned extra money by washing, ironing, and cooking for the Newmans. Once free, Milly put these skills to good use. In the 1850s she and her sister Charity purchased licenses to operate single and double horse drays (wagons). They may have used these wagons to sell vegetables from their gardens, or to deliver clothing that they washed in the yards of their little houses, to clients throughout the town; or they may have purchased the licenses for other free blacks or slaves. Several other free black women (Mary Matine, Alice Whitelaw, Mary Ann Shaw Hunt, Ellen Mayho, Adelia Burnett, and Agnes Alexander) also had licenses to operate drays.[19]

By 1850 Milly's neighbor Agnes Alexander still lived on the lot on St. Martin but her family now included her one-year-old daughter, Lucinda Alexander, and four-year-old daughter, Amanda Williams, along with her older sister, Maria Batte. While Agnes, Lucinda, and Amanda were listed in census records as "mulattos," Maria was considered "black." Alexander may have used a dray wagon to transport laundry to her clients, or the wagon may have been used by someone else, possibly an enslaved husband. Alice Whitelaw, emancipated when she was twenty-two years old, was thirty-two when she purchased her dray license. She owned a lot on Avery Street at the corner of Vance Avenue, also near Milly and Charity Swan, and listed her occupation as "seamstress" on the city's Free Negro Register. Mary Ann Shaw Hunt lived in the household of William Richardson Hunt on Beale and was married to one of Hunt's slaves. Adelia Barnett (also Delilah Burnett) rented a house near Milly's, where she lived with several of her siblings and her infant daughter Virginia. Little is known about Matine and Mayho. While other free black women worked as stewardesses and maids on the steamboats that plied the Mississippi River or as domestics or as washerwomen, only the Swans, Matine, Whitelaw, Hunt Shaw, Mayho, Burnett, and Alexander were prosperous enough to pay $15.00–$18.37 to purchase dray licenses.[20]

In 1850 Milly's household included her daughter Roxana and several members of her biological and fictive "family." That same year, George (Jim or Addison) Swan joined his sisters (Milly, Charity, and Peggy) in Memphis when he was apprenticed to Milly. Milly promised to train George in farming and to "constantly provide for him . . . sufficient diet, washing, lodging and apparel fitting for Apprentices with every necessity both in sickness and health." George provided extra help on Milly's farm. Milly also owned several slaves in the 1850s. The 1860 census identified three of her slaves as a "mulatto" male and a "mulatto" female, both about thirty years old, and a twenty-year-old black male. Since Milly only had one slave house on her property, her three slaves may have been related to each other, or one or more of them may have lived in her house or been hired out. Like other slaves who were owned by free blacks, some of Milly's slaves may have been related to her. Indeed, many free blacks chose to remain in the South in order to be near enslaved family members.[21]

Also in 1850 Milly emancipated one of her slaves, a ten-year-old girl named Harriet; and in 1853 Milly freed another, a man named Bob Price. (In subsequent documents, Bob acknowledged that he was Harriet's father.) Bob, described in his emancipation paper as "a negro of very dark complexion, aged about thirty-six years and six feet in height," had been living in Tennessee since 1834. Sources also suggest that Milly may have known Bob since the mid-1840s. In 1852 she purchased him from the estate of E. H. Price for $1,000 ("the proceeds of her own industry")—$500 in cash and the rest to be paid by January

1853. Milly then placed Bob Price with Memphis lawyer David Currin so that Currin could emancipate Price. Court papers described Bob Price as a black man who possessed "many good qualities, moral and industrious habits, and obedient and submissive deportment." He would be an asset to the community and, more importantly, not "give trouble or offence to white citizens of the county and the state."[22]

Bob Price's purchase and emancipation occurred during a turbulent period in his life—a period that illustrated the precarious nature of familial relationships among enslaved people. Slaves were considered property and could not enter into legally binding contracts like marriage agreements. But owners often encouraged their slaves to "marry" and create families, and slaves valued their family relationships. In 1841 or 1842 Bob and a slave woman, Eliza Smith, were "married" by Rev. Samuel Watson at the white Methodist Church in Memphis. Bob's owner, E. H. Price, a planter from Mississippi who maintained a residence in Memphis, and Eliza's owner, another Memphis resident named George Smith, agreed to this "marriage." Bob and Eliza had four children, but only one daughter, Bettie, survived. Ten years into their marriage, Eliza's owner decided to move his household to Arkansas. Bob pleaded with Smith to allow him to purchase and free Eliza and Bettie, but Smith refused, and Bob probably never saw his wife or daughter again. However, Bob Price created a new, more permanent "family" with Milly and Roxana Swan, and Harriet Swan (his daughter from a relationship that may have predated that with Eliza Smith). When Bob Price legally married Milly Swan in 1855, he created a family and began amassing property that would be more directly under his control. But her marriage to Bob Price also changed Milly's relationship to both family and property.[23]

The possession of property was important to the economic security of free blacks like Milly Swan and Bob Price. Four months after she purchased Bob (but one month before his emancipation petition), Milly sold the St. Martin Street lot she had purchased from Jim Williams to a white neighbor, Michael Magiveny (or Magevny). While the purchase price is not recorded, tax records indicate that the land was valued at $300, and improvements to it (house) were valued at $500. While Milly had been the sole owner of the lot since 1851, she and Bob were both listed as the sellers. Bob may have been involved in the 1851 purchase, but as a slave, he could not claim to legally own it. On the other hand, as an unmarried free woman in Memphis, Milly was recognized as a *femme sole*, a woman who had the authority to buy, sell, and control property. Although Bob's emancipation was not fully recognized when the land was sold, Bob Price was already enjoying the coveted status of "quasi-free." He and Milly had obviously agreed on his eventual emancipation, and all that remained was the acquiescence of the county court. In fact, Bob had actually been recognized as a Shelby County property holder as early as July 1852 (soon after Milly purchased him) when he was listed in tax assessment books as owning and paying taxes on two lots; and in April 1854 he purchased a third. But Milly continued to be listed as the owner of record for the Linden Avenue lot she had purchased for Roxana. This little piece of land represented Milly's claim to independence and perhaps security against the unwise financial judgment of a future husband, although this property was never officially recognized by the court as a "separate estate" or legally outside of her husband's control.[24]

Other free black women also used their property to guarantee their own and their family's security. When Ellen Burton drafted her will in 1850, she made it clear that her older children (Celia, Frances, Martha, and Matthew) were to "hold possession of the house and lot where I now live, pay taxes on the same, also to hold possession of my household and kitchen furniture but not have authority to sell any part or portion of the same individually or collectively until Jane [her youngest child] comes of age." Rutha Anna Maria Boyd left her two lots, horses, cows, wagons, furniture, personal possessions, and money to white merchant Adlai O. Harris. Harris was to use the proceeds from the sale of Boyd's property to purchase her son, Robert Boyd, and her husband, Simpson Bayliss. And if there was not enough to purchase both, Rutha Boyd directed Harris to purchase Robert and to keep the horses and wagons so that Simpson Bayliss could earn enough money to buy his own freedom.[25]

Legal marriage was another way for free black women to protect their families and, to some extent, their property. Although free black women like Rutha Anna Maria Boyd "married" enslaved men in religious or community ceremonies (or just by agreeing to live together), these marriages, as previously noted, had no legal standing. In fact, Rutha Boyd left her property to Adlai Harris because, as slaves, neither her son nor her husband could claim legal title to her possessions. On January 2, 1855, Milly and Bob were married by Rev. J. H. Gray, pastor of the Second Presbyterian Church. This marriage guaranteed that Bob Price would never have to watch the forced removal of his family by their owners.

But Milly Swan's legal identity as an independent person ended when she married Bob Price. By law, married women exercised control over their lives and property only in the absence, abandonment, physical or mental incapacity, or death of their husbands, or in cases where "separate estates" protected property a woman brought to a marriage. For Milly Swan Price, these coverture laws meant that Bob Price assumed control over most of the family's resources, including what she had acquired through her own labor.[26]

Despite the permanence of family that Bob Price gained as a result of his marriage to Milly, by the mid-1850s life was becoming more insecure for free black men and women in Memphis. And, although they were among the city's more prosperous and respected free blacks, Bob and Milly were not immune to this growing tide of opposition. City and state leaders strengthened the restrictive legislation of the 1830s and 1840s that required free blacks to register with county courts and to pay bonds guaranteeing their good behavior. In 1851 the Tennessee General Assembly ruled that free blacks who became disorderly could be hired out for one to five years, and sent to prison if they refused or tried to escape these punishments. The following year, the assembly required that manumitted slaves be transported to the west coast of Africa. If the slave was freed in a slaveholder's will, the former owner also had to provide enough money to transport the newly emancipated back to Africa, or the county court would hire the person out until sufficient money was raised. It also became more difficult for free blacks to support themselves when the assembly made it a misdemeanor for free blacks to engage in peddling or bartering of market products; and in 1857 free blacks in road districts were required to work on these roads just as any other slave laborer would be. Finally, a free black person who failed or refused to pay his or her residency bond after two months notice was subject to removal to Africa.

In Memphis, as in other Tennessee cities and towns, efforts to control the free black population centered on knowing who had a legal right to be in these urban settings and expelling all others. Identifying legal free blacks was made more difficult by the presence of thousands of domestic slaves who drove the familiar one- and two-horse drays, hauling, loading, and unloading merchandise, and the cooks and servants who accompanied their owners to urban centers from neighboring farms and plantations. African American riverboat workers—free and enslaved, male and female—joined these urban workers when their boats docked at Memphis's wharves. White residents searched every black face for signs of who was slave and who was free and resolved the difficulty of distinguishing slave from free by regulating both populations.

Controlling slaves—most of whom were women—involved bringing them more directly under the authority of their owners, employers, or municipal authorities; punishing any behavior that was offensive or threatening to white people; or eliminating opportunities to share information about the world beyond the slaveholding South. Slaves were also arrested by city police for violating pass laws, frequenting establishments that sold liquor, or just being "unruly." In 1853 a Memphis newspaper carried the story of a hired slave woman named Candace who was arrested for "strolling about and living away from the residence of her owner." Another woman, identified only as Cynthia, was sentenced to fifteen lashes for disorderly conduct and using "offensive language to white persons." In 1856 the city's Board of Mayor and Aldermen passed an ordinance eliminating Sabbath Schools operated by some churches where slaves and free blacks were taught to read the Bible because "letter instruction to slaves is dangerous in a high degree." As one writer noted, "however excellent a thing it may be for the slave to read the Bible, it is by no means probable that his reading will be confined to this."[27]

For free blacks, violations of similar local statutes, as well as residency requirements, could result in arrest, removal, or forced labor. In July 1853 a local newspaper reported that a free black man was arrested "under suspicious circumstances . . . with some property in his possession." Although the man was released, he was forced to leave the city until he could obtain the proper papers. Long-time free black residents sometimes challenged these interpretations of their "freedom." In an 1856 letter to the editors of the *Memphis Daily Appeal*, Hugh Lewis wrote of unsuccessful efforts to force him out of the city based on allegations that he had failed to renew his papers.

> Subsequently, various and insidious plans were laid to entrap me, and by a man, as I believe, who took offense at me without cause. Reports, also, highly injurious to me, were started and kept afloat. Those plans and reports . . . created suspicion and prejudice in the minds of some persons uninformed as to them and as to me; and, on last Tuesday, I was notified by the City Marshal to leave in twenty-four hours, and on Wednesday evening I was taken by him and two of the policemen to the jail, and kept there all night, without hearing, or knowing, what offense I had committed against the city or the peace and dignity of my native State. . . . The morning after my incarceration, the fact was published and I was characterized as a "suspicious character."[28]

Lewis noted that he was a good citizen with "highly respectable" friends in Memphis and other parts of the South, that he had substantial property, and that his neighbors had never complained about his character. "It may be my misfortune, but surely it is no fault of mine that I am a colored man; and I know that there are many here who do not sympathize with the oppressor." The editors of the *Daily Appeal* seemed to agree that he had a right to be heard and to defend himself in court, although they regretted publishing his letter. The following day, the newspaper published a letter from a "Citizen" who noted that every free black in the city had influential friends, in fact the "greater the scoundrel, the more friends such a negro has." "Citizen" even admitted that he had a free negro "attaché" who did him favors and that he couldn't help liking the man. But "Citizen" considered the man a "nuisance" whose presence in the neighborhood led to declining real estate values. Slaves and "disreputable white men" (of course, this group did not include "Citizen") congregated at the home of this free negro on Sundays and at night. "He plays the pimp, the spy, the emissary in all intrigues, and sometimes loans his special friends a little money. He receives, perhaps, stolen goods; waits on women of easy virtue, who may be seen about his residence at all hours of the night. But this is the cleverest free negro in Memphis; he has troops of friends, of whom I am one."[29]

Despite (or because of) these friendships, "Citizen" felt that the city would be better off if *all* free blacks were forced to leave, because their presence corrupted slaves and endangered the lives of white men, women, and children. "They do us no good here and nothing but harm. They never aid in any public spirited enterprise—they are never useful citizens in any capacity; but, on the contrary, are a gambling, drinking, corrupting class, who should be expelled at once from this city."[30]

In his letter, "Citizen" acknowledged that this forced removal might be harsh or unfair to some free blacks, and he specifically cited men like "Hugh [Lewis], Bob [Price], and Frank [Talley]." Two days later, the editors of the *Memphis Daily Appeal* called for an "energetic plan . . . to expel from the community, all free colored persons who have not done some signal service to the State or community." The Board of Mayor and Aldermen discussed but did not approve an ordinance calling for the removal of "all negroes, claiming to be free, from the city, within sixty days after notice is given." The alders did not want to confound "the good with the bad," nor did they think the city had the power to expel all free blacks, since state laws gave them the right to remain. A committee was appointed to study the issue of free black residency in the city.[31]

Although free black women were rarely mentioned in local newspapers, they were also affected by these repressive attitudes and actions. By the late 1850s Milly and her family had moved out of Memphis to a farm in Shelby County, but it is unlikely that the move was wholly by choice. In July 1856 Bob Price was summoned before the county court for an inquiry into his "character and conduct" and to "show cause why the privilege previously granted to him to remain and reside in said County and State should not be revoked." One of Price's neighbors, John Stephenson, charged that Bob had not renewed his residency bond since his emancipation on April 4, 1853, and that his "character and conduct . . . have not been and are not such as make it consistent with the interest of the public and the public peace and morals." Yet in a move that demonstrated the value of the relationships that "Citizen" had criticized, over one hundred white Memphians signed a counter-petition claiming that they had known Bob

Price before and since his emancipation, that he was "honest, industrious and a valuable man in our Community," and that Bob had done nothing to "change the good opinion we have heretofore entertained of him." The county court allowed Bob to renew his residency petition.[32]

However, seven months later Bob Price sold a three-acre plot (adjacent to John H. Stephenson's) for almost $16,000 to a group of buyers that included several of the men (including John H. Stephenson) who had supported the original charges against Price. Bob then paid $1,000 for a 114-acre farm about four miles outside of Memphis. Bob also paid $1,000 for another slave, a fourteen-year-old boy named Green. By 1860, Price's property holdings had expanded to 250 acres and were worth $6,000, with milk cows, pigs, oxen, and mules valued at $2,500. The farm, on which the Prices produced corn and potatoes as well as butter, bacon, and lard, was located close to the Mississippi River in an area of cypress, ash, hackberry, and gum trees.[33]

Two years before his death in 1860, Bob Price drafted a will dividing his estate between his wife, Milly, and his daughter Harriet. An inventory of the estate provides a rare glimpse into Milly's world on the eve of the Civil War. Household furnishings included bedsteads and bedroom furniture for six (probably some for the three slaves who lived on the farm); several wardrobes, bureaus, washstands, and tables; a dining room table and chairs; a sofa, divans, and ottomans; a mantel clock, mirror, and ornaments; rocking chairs, lamps, window curtains, pictures; a cedar chest; a set of "Queensware and Glassware" in a sideboard; and kitchenware, stone churns, andirons, and an ironing table. The inventory also included livestock (oxen, mules, cows, and hogs) and horses, two side saddles and a regular saddle, wagons, and a carriage.[34]

Price left the property to Milly and Harriet as "life estates" to be enjoyed by the women during their lifetimes, free of the debts of any future spouses, then to be divided either between Harriet and her children, if she survived Milly, or only among her children if she died before Milly. However, Bob Price did not clarify what was to become of Harriet's share of the property if she died childless. It is important to note that Bob's will was not designed to protect the women in his life, but rather to make sure that his property was distributed among his biological descendants. One additional provision in Price's will set aside funds to purchase and emancipate his brother John (Green), who still belonged to the estate of the late E. H. Price. (Milly had purchased Bob from this estate seven years earlier.) But Bob Price did not make similar provisions for his daughter Bettie (or her mother, Eliza Smith), who had been taken to Arkansas by their owner almost a decade before. Bettie later suggested (in court proceedings) that this was not because her father cared less for her than for Harriet, but simply because she was still the slave of an owner who refused to sell her and, as a slave, she could not inherit property.[35]

Milly and Harriet continued to live on the Bear Creek farm (or in the house on Linden Avenue) after Bob's death and throughout the Civil War. But Harriet's health was failing. She moved (or was taken) to a house occupied by her uncle John Green—emancipated as a result of Bob Price's bequest or the wartime self-emancipation of rural slaves. Available records do not indicate the reason for Harriet's removal from Milly's household, but Green may have been the reason for the end of the sixteen-year relationship. Alone or with his sisters, Janny and Virginia, and their families, Green was probably among the thousands of freedpeople who arrived in Memphis between 1862 and 1865. If, like other newly emancipated blacks, Green's concept of freedom was tied to gaining a measure of economic security and reuniting his family, he found both in the person of Harriet Price. But his reunion with his niece was short lived. Harriet Price left Milly's household on January 1, made her will on February 22, and died two days later.

In her will, probated two weeks after her death, Harriet Price left her entire estate to her uncle and her aunts. The document made no mention of Milly Swan—the woman who had helped Harriet's father protect her from the fate of her sister Bettie by arranging her purchase and subsequent emancipation, then become her stepmother and finally, her caregiver during the last six years of Harriet's life. On October 30, 1868, the court partitioned Bob Price's real estate, which Milly had controlled since his death—setting lease agreements, collecting rents, paying taxes. Milly retained her house and lot on Linden Avenue (she had owned these since the 1840s), but the farm on Bear Creek was now divided between Milly, John Green, and Green's sisters, Janny and Virginia, with Green controlling half of the original farm. Milly was caught in a web of "family" (Bob's, not hers) claims to real estate she had helped accumulate. But John Green's control was soon challenged not by Milly, but by Bettie Price. Bettie's claim to a share of her father's estate revealed the complexity of issues of slavery, freedom, family, and property in the post-emancipation South.[36]

Three years after Harriet's death, Bettie Price filed a lawsuit charging that the executor of Harriet's estate, William Foster, or her uncle and aunts had taken advantage of Harriet's poor health to influence her to make a will leaving them her share of Bob Price's property. Bettie also claimed that provisions of Bob Price's will made it impossible for Harriet to leave her property to her uncle and aunts. Bettie contended that her father clearly intended for his property to pass to his direct descendants and that Harriet's "life estate" ended with her death. Bettie charged that her father had always acknowledged her as his child, and he only left her out of his will because she was a slave and could not legally possess or inherit property. He had taken care of John Green by providing money for his purchase and emancipation, but he had never intended that his brother inherit any portion of property. Bettie Price argued that as Bob's only other child and only surviving direct descendant, she alone was entitled to his property.[37]

John Green responded that his brother had left his entire estate to Milly and Harriet, that Harriet had the full power to make a will leaving her portion of the estate to whomever she chose, and that Bettie had no right or interest in Harriet's share of Bob's estate. He also charged that the marriage between Bob and Bettie's mother was a "nullity" because of her status as a slave; that if it had ever had any legal standing, that standing was superseded by Bob's marriage to Milly; and that Milly was Bob's legal wife at the time of his death. Finally, he charged that Bettie was Bob's illegitimate daughter—in other words, never legally claimed, as was Harriet in Bob's will—and as such could not, under Tennessee law, inherit his property.

Green was drawing on post-emancipation state statutes concerning marriage, kinship, property, and inheritance rights for African Americans. In 1866 and 1870 the state assembly enacted legislation legitimizing slave marriages and allowing the children of these unions to inherit their parents' property. The assembly also provided that if the property of deceased free persons of color had not been paid out, their formerly enslaved children were entitled to inherit portions of the estates. So if Bob and Eliza Price had still been together at the time of his death, their marriage, Bettie's legitimacy, and her right to share in his estate would not have been questioned. In a sense, Bob's death and subsequent testamentary dispersal of his property constituted the "paying out" of his property. Slavery had destroyed Bob's first family relationship, just as it had ruined the relationships of countless other enslaved families. Because of a slaveholder's refusal to allow him to purchase his first wife, Bob (and possibly Eliza) had moved on to another relationship, and his marriage to Milly Swan made her his legitimate widow.[38]

The court finally ruled in John Green's favor in 1869, but Bettie immediately sought an injunction to prevent him from selling the property and, in 1871, appealed the case to the Tennessee Supreme Court. While existing records do not describe the higher court's final decision, it seems unlikely that they reversed the lower court's ruling. While Bettie's appeal moved through the Tennessee courts, John Green resided on half of the Bear Creek farm, claiming Harriet's share of the land. Milly's household included a thirteen-year-old child named Anna (after Milly's mother) Price and a fifty-six-year-old man, James Hill. Anna may have been Milly and Bob's daughter, since she would have been born after their 1855 marriage but before Bob's death. However, Bettie Price claimed (in 1868) that Bob and Milly's child was dead and Anna had not been listed in Milly's household in 1860. Whoever she was, Anna Price disappeared from Milly's public presence as quickly and mysteriously as she appeared. But Milly added another person to her household with her marriage on Christmas Day 1871 to George W. Dean. Just as Bob Price assumed public control of Milly's household in the 1850s, George Dean now exerted more and more control over her property. Like many other black families in this period, Milly and George Dean adopted a lifestyle that removed Milly from the public arena.[39]

In the early 1870s, after the final decree in Bettie's case awarded Harriet's share of Bob's land to Green and the Hunts, John Green sued Milly Dean for half of the rents and other monies she had collected on the property from the time of Bob's death in 1860 until the estate was formally partitioned in 1868. Milly's partner in this suit was her new husband, George W. Dean. Sources are not available on the lower court's ruling, but the case was appealed to the Tennessee Supreme Court. While this court would not disallow the monies that Milly (and not George) owed to the executor of Harriet's estate, they did allow Milly to recover ten dollars in monthly "wages" for the sixty-nine months (May 14, 1860, until January 1, 1866) she had cared for Harriet during her illness. The Supreme Court also demanded that Milly sell two parcels of the land on Bear Creek (totaling eighty-eight acres) she had received as her share of Bob's estate. The money was paid to John Green to settle his claims against the estate. Milly's land was sold at public auction on Christmas Eve in 1875; the highest bidder was Joseph Clouston, who had been one of Milly's antebellum free black neighbors. He may have bought Milly's land to help his old friend.[40]

The year before the sale of the Bear Creek property, Milly had nearly lost her Linden Avenue lot—one of the first pieces of real estate she had purchased when she came to Memphis in the 1840s—when Memphis city tax officials claimed that she had not paid her city taxes for the period of July 1, 1860, to July 1, 1861. Supposedly, the local sheriff had been unable to deliver the first two of three summonses to Milly at the Bear Creek farm because of "high water." Milly paid her delinquent taxes and secured her property, at least for a few more years. However, in 1877 she sold the Linden property for much less than it was worth. The sale of this property marked Milly's final act on the public stage. There are no further references to her—not even a death notice. She may have been among the thousands who died in the 1878 or 1879 yellow fever epidemics, or she may have died sometime in the 1880s. In 1895 George W. Dean used the remaining tract of land on Bear Creek as collateral for a twelve-month $120 loan from W. H. Cousins, but Dean was identified as a "single man," not as a married man or a widower. Three years later, when he used the same land as collateral for a six-month $85 loan from Cousins, Dean listed his status as "widower." He may have been unable to repay this last loan, since a September 1900 note on the loan identified Cousins as "the true and lawful holder" of the land.[41]

The events in Milly's life illustrate many of the issues that confronted African American women in the nineteenth century. As a free woman of color, Milly could never completely separate herself from her enslaved neighbors and relatives. She owned and emancipated some slaves (Harriet and Bob Price), but others remained her possessions until slavery ended during the Civil War. Bob's family relationships drew Milly into a web of claims and counterclaims to family legitimacy and property. As a single woman, Milly used her initiative and economic skills to acquire property and her status as a *femme sole* to control it. But she lost much of her economic authority and voice when she married first Bob Price and then George W. Dean. The legal challenges she faced in the 1870s grew out of the convergence of freedom, kinship, and property that confronted thousands of African Americans in the post–Civil War South. More than anything else, Milly Swan Price Dean was an example of the opportunities and the limitations of black women in nineteenth-century Tennessee.

NOTES

Some material from this chapter was based on an earlier essay, "The Extent of the Law: Free Women of Color in Antebellum Memphis, Tennessee," in *Negotiating Boundaries of Southern Womanhood: Dealing with the Powers That Be*, ed. Janet L. Coryell, Thomas H. Appleton Jr., Anastatia Sims, and Sandra Gioia Treadway (Columbia: University of Missouri Press, 2000).

1. For consistency, I have decided to call her "Milly" throughout this chapter, although the spelling of her name varied in court records, census, and other public documents from this spelling to "Melly" and even "Mittie." "Price" was also added to her name in the 1850s, even before her legal marriage to Bob Price. Milly married a second time in 1870, this time to George W. Dean. Shelby County Court records indicate that at least thirty-five free black children (ranging in age from four months to late teens), including the Swans, were indentured between 1830 and 1852; all but nine were orphans. The decision to indenture children ultimately rested with the county court, not the parent, especially when the children were orphaned paupers or the mother was destitute or declared unfit. Tennessee law allowed the involuntary indenture of indigent or orphaned white or free black children, even though this procedure might result in the gradual degradation of the "free" status of the latter. See Durwood Dunn, "Apprenticeship and Indentured Servitude in Tennessee before the Civil War," *West Tennessee Historical Society Papers* no. 36 (1982): 25–37.

2. Suzanne Lebsock, *Free Women of Petersburg: Status and Culture in a Southern Town, 1784–1860* (New York: W. W. Norton, 1984), 22–23, 87–111.

3. "Tipton County," *Goodspeed's History of Tennessee* (Nashville: Goodspeed Publishing Company, 1887), 810.

4. For a description of the city during this period, see John Harkins, *Metropolis of the American*

Nile: An Illustrated History of Memphis and Shelby County (Woodland Hills, Calif.: Windsor Publications, 1982), 48–50; and Gerald Capers, *The Biography of a River Town, Memphis: Its Heroic Age* (New Orleans: Tulane University, 1966), 50.

5. U.S. Bureau of the Census, Fifth Census of the United States (hereafter 5th Census), "Population Schedules," Shelby County, Tennessee, 1830, vol. 8 (Washington, D.C.: Duff Green, 1932), microfilm; U.S. Bureau of the Census, Sixth Census of the United States, "Population Schedules," Shelby County, Tennessee, 1840, vol. 8 (Washington, D.C.: Thomas Allen, 1941), microfilm (hereafter 6th Census); William Lloyd Imes, "The Legal Status of Free Negroes and Slaves in Tennessee," *Journal of Negro History* (1919): 254–72; Roger R. Van Dyke, "The Free Negro in Tennessee, 1790–1860" (Ph.D. diss, Florida State University, 1972); J. Merton England, "The Free Negro in Ante-Bellum Tennessee," *Journal of Southern History* (February 1943): 37–58.

6. Robert E. Corlew, *Tennessee: A Short History* (Knoxville: University of Tennessee Press, 1981), 218; Marius Carriere Jr., "Blacks in Pre–Civil War Memphis," *Tennessee Historical Quarterly* 43, no. 1 (1989): 4; J. Merton England, "The Free Negro in Ante-Bellum Tennessee," *Journal of Southern History* 9 (February 1943): 38; Van Dyke, "The Free Negro in Tennessee, 1790–1860," 12, 23–24, 27.

7. *Goodspeed's History of Tennessee*, chap. 20, 808, 815. One of Ellen Rose Newman's brothers, James Madison Rose, died at the Alamo in 1836; other siblings—Hugh F. Rose, Erasmus T. Rose, and Samuel Rose—also settled in West Tennessee. Drs. Hugh and Erasmus Rose were among the first physicians in Randolph. Erasmus Rose was also a surety on the indenture of the Swan children. See 6th Census; 5th Census, Tipton County, Tennessee, household of Nelly C. Newman, p. 277. Newman's household included seven white males between five and forty years of age; five white females ranging from thirty to under five years of age; thirty-six slaves (nineteen women and seventeen men); but no free blacks. Free blacks were listed in seven other households in Tipton County. See also http://ourworld.cs.com/christine4rose (accessed February 3, 2005) or Tipton County Archives for an affidavit establishing land bounty clams for heirs of James M. Rose to land in several Texas counties.

8. Dunn, "Apprenticeship and Indentured Servitude," 27–28. Indenture of the Swan Children, Minutes of Tipton County Court of Pleas and Quarterly Sessions, March Term 1840, Tipton County Archives (hereafter TCA); Affidavits from R. Munford, Clerk of Tipton County Court, and Wm. D. C. Jones, Chairman Tipton County Court, August 6, 1844, TCA; 5th Census, "Population Schedules," Tipton County.

9. Dunn, "Apprenticeship and Indentured Servitude," 25–37.

10. Anna Swan may have had other children during the four-year gap between Milly's birth and Peggy's, but they were not indentured or did not survive. There is a three-year gap between Jim and the youngest Swan siblings—Kitty, Addison, and Sally Ann. While there is no further reference to the oldest Swan sibling, Nick, in the public records examined for this paper, Charity owned property near Milly's in Memphis; and Charity, Peggy, Kitty, Sally Ann, and Addison are all listed in the Shelby County Free Negro Register. Jim may have been Milly's brother "George" who was apprenticed to her in 1850, and whose name appeared on the Free Negro Register in March 1862.

11. While Anna Swan remains a mystery, much more is known about Ellen C. Newman; 5th Census, Tipton County, Tennessee, 277.

12. Shelby County Probate Court Records (hereafter SCPCR), Apprenticeships and Indentures, Free Persons of Color—Esther Hall (January 6, 1846) and Catherine (February 3, 1845), loose papers, Shelby County Archives (hereafter SCA).

13. "Roxana Swan—Description of for Bob Price," February 2, 1846, Free Negro Papers, Milly Swan, Shelby County Quarterly Court (hereafter SCQC) Minute Book 5, p. 283, SCA.

14. "Fair Warning," *Memphis Weekly Eagle*, January 9, 1846; see also *Memphis Weekly Appeal*, October 27, 1843;

15. Shelby County Deeds (hereafter SCD), book OOV, p. 337, microfilm, SCA; Acts Passed by the (Nineteenth) General Assembly of the State of Tennessee, Private Acts, chap. 131 (Knoxville: Heiskell and Brown, 1832); Petitions to remain—Francis Burton, Ellen Burton (included Martha and Jane), Phebe Reynolds, Agnes Sikes, all on July 3, 1848, SCQC Minute Books 5 and 6, SCA; South Memphis Property Tax Assessments (hereafter SMPTA) Book, 1847–1849, 1850, microfilm, SCA; City of Memphis Recorder's Blotter, "Free Negro Register—April 3–October 4, 1853" (hereafter FNR), microfilm, SCA. In 1838 the area bordered by Union, Delaware, Walnut, and East Streets was incorporated by Robertson Topp as the town of South Memphis. Topp's South Memphis Company sold lots to any buyers, including free black women like Milly Swan. In 1845 Topp incorporated the town of South Memphis, but five years later it was annexed by its more prosperous neighbor, Memphis. See also Files of the Freedmen's Savings and Trust Company, Memphis Branch: Signature Books (1865–70)—#188 (Martha Burton) and #186 (Celia Burton Burris), microfilm, Benjamin L. Hooks Branch—Memphis Public Library (hereafter BLHMPL); U.S. Bureau of the Census, Seventh Census of the United States (hereafter 7th Census), "Population Schedules," Memphis, Tennessee, 1850, 6th Ward, household of Agnes Alexander, microfilm.

16. Petitions to remain, Elizabeth Larry and Martha Ann Brown, October 2, 1843, SCQC Records, loose papers—Petitions for Emancipation and Petitions of Free Negroes to Remain in Tennessee, SCA; SMPTA, 1850, microfilm, SCA; 7th Census, "Population Schedules," Memphis, Tennessee, 5th Ward, households of John Brown and Frank Penney.

17. SMPTA, 1847–1849, microfilm, SCA. Property ownership among free black women was not confined to the South Memphis area: Charlotte Brocard or Brocan, Hannah Rawlings, Milly Richmond, and Jane Cutler all owned lots on or near Commerce Street.

18. SCD Book 7, pp. 8–9, microfilm, Reel 337, SCA.

19. Other free black women received money or property when they were freed in the wills of white slave owners. When Matilda Mead(e) was freed in the 1850 will of Dr. Caesar Jones, Jones left $2,000 to be invested in state stock and held in trust for Mead(e) and her children. O. G. Kennedy also directed that any money left after the payment of his debts was to be given to Eliza Kennedy (whom he had freed earlier), and her children (who were freed in his will). Hannah Rawlings was granted a lifetime annuity when she and her children were freed in the 1839 will of Isaac Rawlings. She used this income to purchase land, which she owned until the early 1850s. Isaac Mercer left his property to Maria Mercer and her eight children with the stipulation that she choose whomever she thought was proper to help her manage the property. Maria Mercer sold the property a year later to Joseph Clouston, a free black man. See wills of Caesar A. Jones (#890) and O. G. Kennedy (#1380) in SCPCR; and Isaac Rawlings (book 1, pp. 138–140) and Isaac Mercer (book 2, p. 182) in Shelby County Will Books, microfilm, SCA. Other women, like Adeline Yeats (Robinson) did not own land but owned slaves or luxury items (Yeats owned a piano); see Shelby County Tax Book (hereafter SCTB), 1862–63, microfilm, SCA. For information on business licenses, see Register of Licenses Issued by the Corporation of City of Memphis (hereafter RLCCM), 1854–63, microfilm, SCA, and Record of City Licenses, Businesses and Privileges, RLCCM, July 1863–August 1864, July 1863–June 1866.

20. 7th Census, Memphis, Tennessee, households of Swan and Alexander, microfilm; U.S. Bureau of the Census, Eighth Census of the United States (hereafter 8th Census), "Population Schedules," Memphis, Tennessee, 1860, 6th and 7th Wards (Washington, D.C.: Government Printing Office, 1864), microfilm. See Charity Swan (December 5, 1855), Adelia Barnett (October 11, 1856), Agnes Alexander (October 3, 1859), Alice Whitelaw (August 1, 1855), Mary Matine (October 26, 1854), Ellen

Mayho (December 1, 1858), and Mary Ann Hunt (November 1, 1858) in RLCCM, 1854–67, SCA; Alice Whitelaw, in SCTB, 1856–57, p. 137, SCA; Alice Whitelaw, FNR, #28, SCA; Thomas Buchanan, *Life on the Mississippi: Slaves, Free Blacks, and the Western Steamboat World* (Chapel Hill: University of North Carolina Press, 2004), 10, 13, 188 n.35.

21. Since there are no deeds for the Swans' other slaves, they may actually have been hired slaves living in her household. See Indenture of George Swan, loose papers, SCQC, November 6, 1850, SCA; George Swan, Petition for Apprenticeship, November 6, 1850, SCQC Minute Book 6, p. 482, SCA; 8th Census, "Slave Census" for Fourth Civil District, Tennessee.

22. Harriet Swan, Petition to emancipate, SCQC Minute Book 6, no. 2, p. 318, January 1850, SCA; Deed for purchase of Bob Price, SCD Book 0011, p. 87, and 0019, p. 455 (deed for purchase of "Angellinia"), microfilm, SCA; David Currin petition to emancipate Bob Price, April 1853, Shelby County Chancery Court (hereafter SCCC) Minute Book, SCA. In 1836 E. H. Price and Co. operated a drug store in Memphis at the corner of Mississippi and Winchester streets. Bob's relationship to Harriet's mother had no legal standing in Tennessee or any other slave state, since both were slaves. However, Bob legitimized Harriet in his will, granting her status as his daughter and making her co-heir (with Milly) of his property. In 1855 Harriet Swan Price paid $800 for a slave woman named Angellinia, who was listed as her father's property in his will. Angellinia may have been Harriet's property, given the predilection of Swan and Price to purchase their relatives, but Harriet may have been unable to free her mother in the late 1850s because such an action would have required Angellinia's emigration to Africa.

23. SCCC, case #3563, *Bettie Price v. John Green, et al.*, SCA; Bob Price and Milly Swan, October 27, 1854, Shelby County Marriage Bonds and Licenses, 1850–1865, SCA.

24. Memphis Tax Assessment (hereafter MTA), 1852, p. 71; MTA, 1853, p. 46; MTA, 1854, p. 47; MTA, 1855, p. 52—all SCA; SCD Book 7, p. 8–9, microfilm, reel 337, SCA; Milly also purchased a lot in Winchester cemetery, possibly for Roxana, who disappears from public records in the early 1850s.

25. Will of Ellen Burton, SCPCR, #1005, January 6, 1851, SCA; Will of Rutha Anna Maria Boyd, SCPCR, #1210, October 29, 1852, SCA.

26. Bob Price and Milly Swan, Shelby County Marriage Books 1, p. 416, 1854, SCA; W. R. Smith to Milly Swan, SCD Book 0023, p. 141, microfilm, SCA; SCCC, case #3563, *Bettie Price v. John Green, et al.*, SCA. Tennessee did not alter married women's status until 1919, with Senate Bill No. 316 (passed April 15, 1919).

27. "Blank Deeds," *Memphis Daily Appeal*, July 25, 1853; "Recorder's Court," *Memphis Daily Appeal*, July 25, 1853; "From the St. Louis Republican, December 25," *Memphis Daily Appeal*, December 28, 1856.

28. "To the Editors of the Daily Appeal," *Memphis Daily Appeal*, December 27, 1856.

29. "To the Editors of the Daily Appeal," *Memphis Daily Appeal*, December 27, 1856; "A Word of Explantation" and "Free Negroes—Shall We Drive Them from the City," *Memphis Daily Appeal*, December 28, 1856.

30. "Free Negroes—Shall We Drive Them from the City," *Memphis Daily Appeal*, December 28, 1856.

31. "Free Negroes," *Memphis Daily Appeal*, December 30, 1856; Report on meeting of Board of Aldermen, January 7, 1857. The surnames of the three free black men "Citizen" identified were not given, but they were easily identifiable from the Free Negro Register, petitions to remain in the county, and their public activities. For example, Bob Price had a history of working at the county court, and in 1856 he was the focus of expulsion efforts. On the eve of the Civil War, the city was still trying to work out some measures for expelling free blacks. In December 1860, in one hour,

five hundred citizens signed petitions supporting the forcible expulsion of free blacks; although one writer noted that "it is understood that such negroes as have a constitutional right can remain upon sufficient security" ("Free Negroes," *Memphis Daily Appeal*, December 18, 1860).

32. *State of Tennessee in relation of John H. Stephenson v. Petition Bob Price*, #209, filed July 10, 1856, SCQC, microfilm, SCA. Stephenson was supported in his petition by six other white businessmen: Thomas James, L. J. Dupree, Arthur Beatty, W. C. Bradford, Isaac Blackwell, and Benjamin Haves.

33. Bob Price, SCPCR, Will #2081, microfilm, BLHMPL; SCD Book 28, p. 141, microfilm, SCA; SCD Book 31, p. 370–71, microfilm, SCA. The slave boy, Henry or Green, may have been related to Bob Price, possibly the son of Price's brother John. Price left instructions in his will that "a sufficient amount [of money] be appropriated to the purchase and emancipate my brother John, now a slave, and the property of the estate of the late E. H. Price." Later documents indicate that John's surname was Green. See SCPCR, "Inventory of the estate of the late Bob Price," microfilm, BLHMPL; SCCC, case #3563, *Bettie Price v. John Green, et al.*, "Inventory of the Personal estate of Robert Price," SCA; 8th Census, "Agriculture Schedule," Shelby County, Tennessee, 4th Civil District, microfilm, roll 77; U.S. Bureau of the Census, Ninth Census of the United States (hereafter 9th Census), "Agriculture Schedule," Shelby County, Tennessee, 17th Civil District, 1870 (Washington, D.C.: Government Printing Office, 1872), microfilm, BLHMPL.

34. Bob Price, SCPCR, Will #2081, microfilm, BLHMPL.

35. SCCC, case #3563, *Bettie Price v. John Green, et al.*, SCA.

36. Register of Deaths in the City of Memphis, "Harriet Price," #9062, microfilm, SCA; "The last Will and Testament of Harriet Price (Coloured Woman)," SCPCR, Will #1869, microfilm, BLHMPL; SCCC, case #588, New Minute Group 9, p. 3–7, *Harriet Price v. Milly Price et al.*, SCA; 8th Census, "Agriculture Schedule," Shelby County, Tennessee, 4th Civil District; Record Group 191, Tennessee Supreme Court Clerk's Records, 1810–1955, vol. 11, West Tennessee Supreme Court Minutes (hereafter WTSCM), June 1874–October 1875, p. 149, microfilm, Tennessee State Library and Archives (hereafter TSLA).

37. SCCC, case #3563, *Bettie Price v. John Green et al.*, SCA.

38. Seymour D. Thompson and Thomas M. Steger, *A Compilation of the Statute Laws of the State of Tennessee* (St. Louis: W. J. Gilbert, 1872), 2:1094–95.

39. SCCC, case #3563, *Bettie Price v. John Green et al.*, SCA.

40. Record Group 191, Tennessee Supreme Court Clerk's Records, 1810–1955, microfilm reel 47, vol. 11, WTSCM, June 1874–October 1875, pp. 148–52, 240, 241, 308, TSLA; Record Group 191, Tennessee Supreme Court Clerk's Records, 1810–1955, microfilm reel 48, vol. 13, WTSCM, December 1875–December 1876, pp. 466–68, 523–26, TSLA; "In Supreme Court at Jackson," *Memphis Public Ledger*, December 12, 1875, microfilm, BLHMPL.

41. SCCC, case #1429, *City of Memphis v. Milly Price*, SCA; SCPCR, Minute Book 27, p. 308, March 7, 1876, SCA; SCPCR, Minute Book 30, p. 471, SCA; SCD Book 0109, p. 466 (January 3, 1876), Book 119, p. 605 (September 15, 1877), Book 037, p. 119 (March 18, 1895), and Book 0255, p. 87 (September 26, 1900), SCA; MTA Book for 1877, p. 136–37, SCA.

Mary Church Terrell

(1863–1954)

Revisiting the Politics of Race, Class, and Gender

CHERISSE JONES-BRANCH

❦ ❦ ❦

Mary Church Terrell was a pioneer in America's civil rights struggle whose activism spanned the late nineteenth and early twentieth centuries. As the daughter of the South's first black millionaire and the first president of the National Association of Colored Women, Terrell recognized early in life that African Americans faced limitations in mainstream society solely because of their race. Her childhood in Memphis demonstrated clearly how African Americans were increasingly restricted to lives little better than what many had known as slaves. Furthermore, Terrell's personal and family experiences with racism and racial violence in the city left an indelible mark that necessitated and informed her lifelong activism.

Existing sources have cast Mary Church Terrell as a black woman activist whose family was a part of Memphis's black elite. Although this is true, these interpretations fall short of truly examining the early years of Terrell's life in Memphis and the impact they had on her later activism. Such limitations beg for closer analysis of Terrell as a national figure by examining her family's beginnings in Memphis, especially those of her parents, Robert and Louisa Ayres Church, who were slaves, and how such events as the 1866 race riots influenced them and other African Americans as they tried to make lives for themselves in post–Civil War Memphis. Included in my analysis is an exploration of the circumstances that created the family's wealth after the 1878–79 yellow fever epidemic and how, even after Terrell left Memphis, she was still influenced by and active in struggles against the racial injustices that plagued blacks in the South in the late nineteenth and early twentieth centuries.

Mary Church Terrell, "Mollie" as she was known to family and friends, was born in Memphis, in 1863, in the midst of the Civil War. Both of her parents had been slaves but dedicated themselves to suppressing any information about their experiences under the institution. Robert Reed Church, most commonly known as "Bob," was born in Holly Springs, Mississippi, in 1839. His mother, Emmeline, was a sixteen-year-old enslaved seamstress who lived with a family in Holly Springs; his father, Captain Charles Beckwith Church, was her master and a steamboat owner. Bob Church was not treated as most slaves were, but his father did not legally or publicly claim him. Bob was twelve years old when his mother died in 1851. He worked on his father's steamboats on runs between Memphis and New Orleans and eventually became a steward on the *Victoria*. He escaped unharmed when that vessel was captured by U.S. troops during the 1862 Battle of Memphis.[1]

Terrell's mother, Louisa, was born in Mississippi in the early 1840s. She was the slave of T. S. Ayres, an attorney. Louisa Ayres revealed few details about her life as a slave, but what is known shows quite a different experience from that of most enslaved blacks. She enjoyed a fairly privileged life as a household slave of the Ayres family. Her owner even taught her to read and write and provided her instruction in French. It is not known when or how she met young Bob Church, but in December 1862 the two, like many other slaves, agreed to live together as man and wife. At the time, Louisa was already pregnant with Mary. Her early experiences in the Ayres household suggest that she had assimilated the gender ideal of the southern elite—a fact that was borne out by her attempted suicide when she discovered her pregnancy. But Louisa Ayres was a slave, not a privileged daughter, and the issue of her pregnancy was soon resolved. Indeed, Ayres's legitimate white daughter even provided the bride with a trousseau from New York and a wedding reception. As slaves, Bob and Louisa's marriage was not legally binding until an 1866 Tennessee statute validated slave marriages (and legitimated the children of these unions) if the couple continued to live together after emancipation.[2]

After the Civil War, the family moved from Holly Springs to Memphis, where Bob Church opened several businesses, including Church's Hotel at South Second Street and Gayoso, a restaurant and saloon. But the family was far from wealthy. In 1868 Church opened a saloon and billiard room with a man named John Carnes. But Church was heavily in debt and unable to pay his rent or purchase the liquor he needed to operate his establishment. That same year, David H. Evans, a Memphis importer of wine, liquor, and cigars, sued Bob Church to recover a $250 debt. In response to Evans's accusation, Church claimed he had fallen on "hard times and heavy expenses" and was unable to make the saloon profitable enough to pay for itself. He had no available funds in his possession

MARY CHURCH TERRELL

Circa 1925. Photograph by Harris and Ewing.
Prints and Photographs Division, Library of Congress,
Washington, D.C., reproduction number LC-USZ62-92821.

or in the bank. Nor did Church have any funds invested in any other properties. Evans was unable to collect on the debt.[3]

Although Bob Church's business ventures and real estate purchases later became the source of much of the family's wealth, it was Louisa Church's skills as a hairdresser that provided much of the family's income. Indeed, in the late nineteenth and early twentieth centuries many members of the black elite became wealthy and obtained substantial land holdings through their occupations in such service trades as hairdressing, catering, barbering, and tailoring. Such occupations allowed them regular contact with white customers, and they often built their businesses solely on white patronage. Louisa Church learned the skill of "ladies hairdressing" while a slave in the Ayres household. She was the first black woman in Memphis to establish a hair salon for elite white women. Her former owner, T. S. Ayres, assisted her in setting up the salon. His financial support allowed her to rent a store at 56 Court Street, an exclusive business district in Memphis. Ayres also loaned or gave Louisa $800 for store goods. The salon was a "brilliant success," and Terrell's mother earned a reputation not only as a hairdresser but also as an artist. Wealthy white women in Memphis purchased their hair products from her store. Louisa Church's skills were in such demand that when Grand Duke Alexis of Russia visited Memphis in February 1872, several prominent white women who were invited to a ball honoring the duke arrived at Louisa's store at seven a.m. the day before the event to have their hair dressed. Terrell's mother worked until midnight to fill their particular hair care requests. The money she made from her business went toward the purchase of the Church family's first home and carriage.[4]

Although some sources purport that Bob and Louisa Church separated in 1867, the 1869 Memphis City directory and the 1870 census indicate that the two still shared a residence. Whatever the date of their separation, Louisa continued to operate her hair salon, probably to support her children, until 1878 or 1879, when she sold the business and moved to New York City. She established another successful hair salon on Sixth Avenue in that city. After the separation, but before the move to New York, Mary lived with her mother while her brother, Thomas, remained with Bob Church. This arrangement continued until the day a "hack" drove up to Louisa's house and deposited the boy, "bag and baggage," on the sidewalk. The Memphis court had refused Bob Church's request to keep Thomas and awarded custody to Louisa.[5]

The reasons for the separation are unclear, but some parts of Mary's autobiography are revealing. Although she chose to remember her father fondly, she also recognized that he was far from a saint. Bob Church had a violent temper and was prone to do anything during a fit of rage. Mary later suggested that these fits were the result of his early experiences as a slave or injuries suffered during the 1866 race riots. After the Civil War, much to the ire of local whites, but particularly to the consternation of poor Irish immigrants, rural blacks moved to Memphis in search of new opportunities. In this hostile environment, Irishmen claimed the privileges of their "whiteness," yet they still had to vie with blacks for the least desirable and lowest paying jobs. African Americans were further victimized by the mostly Irish Memphis police force, many of whom resented the presence of black uniformed soldiers who were stationed at Fort Pickering.[6]

In late April 1866 the United States Army mustered out the last of its black soldiers. However, on May 1, 1866, some of these soldiers decided to go to a south Memphis neighborhood, where a large number of black migrants had settled, to celebrate the Union's victory in the Civil War. While en route they encountered a number of white policemen. As the soldiers cheered "Old Abe Lincoln, the Great Emancipator," the policemen responded with insults to the assassinated leader. Two of the soldiers were arrested. These relatively minor disputes were followed by two days of rioting that left forty-six blacks and two whites dead and resulted in the destruction of approximately $110,000 of black property. The riots did not end until martial law was declared on May 3.[7]

Bob Church was a victim of this race riot. Having been warned by friends that he was one of those to be shot and despite Louisa's pleas, Bob still went to work at his saloon. Policemen broke into his saloon, drank all the whiskey, stole $250 from the cash register, and during the scuffle that ensued, Church was shot at approximately twelve to fifteen times. One bullet struck him in the head, and he was left for dead.

Church later testified before federal officials that, in addition to his injuries, he lost over $750 in cash and damages to his property. He identified one of the policemen who had shot him as Dave Roach, whom he saw "lounging about the streets yet." It is likely that in addition to resenting the increased number of African Americans pouring into Memphis, Irish policemen like Roach also resented the economic success of men like Bob Church. Mary was only a toddler during the riots, but she recalled that her father had a hole at the back of his head as a result of the shooting and that he suffered from headaches so severe that he often threatened to kill himself.[8]

Mary also learned other lessons about the power of bigotry when she accompanied her father on a train trip north. At the time, only a few years after the riots but before 1870, Tennessee had not codified separation of the races. Instead, in the post–Civil War South, racial (and class) segregation was defined by customary behavior. Blacks and people of low socioeconomic status were expected to defer to their "betters." On trains, blacks were expected to occupy separate coaches, such as "the smokers" where men went to enjoy cigars. However, Bob Church and other "self-respecting colored people did not go in the coach set apart for them." Mary later remembered that when she and her father boarded the train for this trip, Bob took her to the "best coach," then went to the smoking car to enjoy a break. Growing up in Memphis, Mary saw her father associate with white men of a similar social and economic class on a more or less equal footing, although she later recalled that it was "remarkable that in their relations to each other both the ex-masters and the ex-slaves could adjust themselves as quickly as they did in some instances to the new order of things."[9]

While her father was in the smoking car, a conductor confronted little Mary, telling her that she belonged in the coach set aside for blacks. He yanked her out of her seat and asked another man, "Whose little nigger is this?" The other passengers identified Mary to the conductor, and one went to the smoking car to get Bob, who defended his daughter's presence in the "best coach" (perhaps with a gun), but who would not explain to young Mary why the incident occurred in the first place. To Mary, the fact that she was properly coiffed and dressed and "behaving like a little lady" seemed to be enough to justify her presence in the company of other respectable black and white people. The incident on the train was her first experience with the racial prejudice and segregation that would confront her (and other African Americans) for decades. However, Mary's assumption that the accoutrements of her social and economic "class"—proper dress, impeccable manners, and ladylike behavior—should overcome this racism became a hallmark of her lifelong activism.[10]

Mary and Thomas moved to New York with their mother after her parents separated. Finding their way in this new environment may have been a little easier because of an unexplained "shift" in their racial identity. The 1880 census listed all three as white. Census takers may have assumed that the fair-skinned Church family members were, like others in their neighborhood, just another family of second- or third-generation Irish immigrants. Perhaps the presence of their Irish servant, Catherine Kusker, encouraged this assumption. Yet this situation also highlights how tenuous racial identification was in nineteenth-century America. Louisa Church, perhaps remembering the family's Memphis experiences, may have seen some advantages in this racial ambiguity. In any event, racial misidentification ("passing") was a strategy Mary Church would later use to avoid the inconveniences and discomforts of Jim Crow segregation. On several occasions throughout her life, particularly when traveling through the South, Mary allowed people to assume that she was white rather than face the humiliation of racial discrimination. She wrote in her diary of one such trip from Salisbury to Asheville, North Carolina, for a speaking engagement. "The colored maid in the station at Salisbury when I changed for Asheville took my dress suit case when I left the train and marched me straight into the white waiting room. I went up the street a short distance & took my breakfast at a white restaurant." On the return trip to Salisbury, Mary "traveled Jim Crow but after that I went into the white coach. (It is very exciting and interesting to be making such acrobatic leaps from the black to the white woman's role.)" But she, Louisa, and Thomas began practicing these "acrobatic leaps" as soon as they moved to New York.[11]

Thomas Church probably shared in these racial acrobatics, but neither he nor Mary could enjoy their ambiguous identity as easily when they visited their father in Memphis. In the early 1890s Thomas sometimes worked for his father as a barkeeper and clerk in his Memphis saloons. He was easily identified as Bob Church's son and could not hide his race. But later in life he apparently made a conscious decision to pass for white professionally and personally. He graduated from Marietta College in Ohio and Columbia Law School but had difficulty getting a position as a court clerk in any New York law firm. He often wrote his younger siblings in Memphis, particularly Robert R. Church Jr., asking for money or proposing business ventures. Thomas later married a white woman with whom he had a son, Thomas Jr., and practiced law in New York until his death in 1937.[12]

Louisa, Mary, and Thomas Church apparently left Memphis sometime after the 1878 yellow fever epidemic decimated the city's population. The city lacked an adequate infrastructure and hence the funds to provide even basic sanitation, garbage collection, and clean water—poor health conditions afflicted its residents. As a consequence, Memphis was besieged by yellow fever plagues several times between 1870 and 1880 as well as in earlier decades. The impact was so devastating that over the course of the 1870s the population dropped from 40,000 to 34,000. The city's water supply came from wells and cisterns that were often contaminated. Like other New South cities, inadequate trash removal resulted in streets that were filled with refuse from animals (and sometimes the carcasses of dead animals as well) and human beings alike. During and after the 1878 epidemic thousands of white Memphians who had the means to do so fled the city. But nearly 6,000 whites, many of whom were poor immigrants, remained in the city, and died in large numbers. About 14,000 African American residents stayed in the city, either to protect their property or because they had no means or opportunity to leave. Some may also have believed that blacks were less likely to die from the disease, since blacks contracted the disease at the same rates as whites but many fewer died of its symptoms. The yellow fever epidemic, as brutally unfortunate as it was, created unprecedented opportunities for African Americans. So many whites died or left Memphis that officials were forced to lower the color barrier and add blacks to the police force for the first time in the city's history.[13]

Although she spent considerable time visiting her father and grandmother after her parents' separation, Mary Church's education took her far away from Memphis. Schools for blacks had only been in existence since the Civil War, and an 1870 state law mandated that these facilities be segregated. About that same time, when Mary was six years old, Louisa took her to live with close family friends, the Hunsters, in Yellow Springs, Ohio. The Hunsters were a black couple who ran the town's only hotel and ice cream parlor. Mary attended the Antioch College Model School for her primary and secondary education.[14]

Mary Church had just graduated from high school in Ohio when the 1878 epidemic struck Memphis. She was visiting her father and grandmother in Memphis when another yellow fever epidemic struck the city in 1879. Mary later recalled the chaos in Memphis and the despair of its residents:

> Some claim that at least five thousand people rushed away from the city, while others declare there were more than that. The whole population seemed to be at the station trying to leave. Naturally, the trains were late starting and the confusion was indescribable. Those who were going were weeping and those who could not go were crying as though their hearts would break. Every now and then a defiant voice would shout aloud: "You all are trying to run away from death. You are leaving us poor folks behind to die. We haven't got enough money to get out of the city. But you had better look out. Death can find you where you are going just as easy as he can find us here with the yellow fever."[15]

Although she and her brother arrived in New York safely, Terrell herself was ill for several days with a high fever. Bob Church accompanied his children as far as Cincinnati, then returned to Memphis. Like many blacks in the city, he took advantage of the window of opportunity provided by the yellow fever epidemic to gain an economic foothold in the New South. Although many of his friends declared him insane, Church invested every penny he had in real estate all over the city. He used an inheritance from his father to purchase real estate below cost from white landowners who were fleeing the city. He was confident that Memphis would recover once the city had a more centralized form of government and had made sanitary improvements. By 1881 Church owned saloons and other properties all over Memphis. His real estate holdings were valued at

$17,000. He had an additional $4,000 in interest-bearing loans and $1,500 in the bank. By the mid-1880s, Bob Church had a fortune that neared $100,000, and he was widely recognized as one of the wealthiest black men in the South.[16]

Memphis was plagued with recurring disease epidemics, a deteriorating infrastructure, and municipal debt even before the yellow fever epidemics of 1878 and 1879.[17] The situation worsened as the health crises left behind a declining tax base. Memphis was left bankrupt and, in 1879, city leaders petitioned the Tennessee legislature to dissolve the charter. The resulting Taxing District Act, passed on January 29, 1879, revoked the power of taxation and created a Memphis Taxing District directly under the jurisdiction of the State of Tennessee. Six years later, when the city sold taxing district bonds to acquire capital to repay creditors, Bob Church was the first purchaser.[18]

In 1884 Mary Church received her A.B. degree from Oberlin College in Ohio. She had excelled as a student at Oberlin, confounding whites who thought blacks were not capable of comprehending a classical curriculum. Despite these racist assumptions, Mary recalled only one occasion where she felt she had been discriminated against while attending Oberlin and that was when a white male student, rather than Mary, was elected poet for the junior class exercises. She was convinced that her color had kept her from receiving the honor. She had been freshman class poet, was a member of the literary society, and the Aeolian Society Editor of the *Oberlin Review*.[19]

After graduation, Mary spent a year as her father's housekeeper, but she realized that she had a greater calling and a desire to return to public life. She wanted to teach in Memphis public schools, but like many middle-class women of the time was dissuaded from doing so by her father, who felt that a woman with her wealth and status should not work outside of the home and that she "would be taking the bread and butter out of the mouth of some girl who needed it."[20]

Bob Church married again in 1885. The bride, Anna Wright, had been born in Memphis before the Civil War and was part of the city's free black community that had also included Milly and Bob Price.[21] Anna was a graduate of Antioch College, a teacher in Memphis's black schools, and an accomplished pianist and trained vocalist who had studied at the Oberlin Conservatory of Music. She was considered "a belle in colored society." Anna also shared a long friendship with Louisa Ayers Church, a friendship that would continue after Anna became the second "Mrs. Church." Bob and Anna Church had two children, Robert Jr. and Annette. Although she was the ex-wife, Louisa Church remained a part of the fabric of the Church family. Bob Church sent his ex-wife money, sometimes at Mary's urging but on other occasions just because he knew she needed it; and when he, Anna, and the children were in New York, they often visited

Louisa. In fact, Mary's little sister Annette affectionately referred to Louisa as "Mama Lou."[22]

Mary relished the relationship she had with her family in Memphis. She and her stepmother, whom she called "Miss Anna," wrote each other often, and Anna sometimes shopped for formal attire that Mary wore on special occasions. For example, in February 1897, as the two women prepared to attend the inaugural festivities for President William McKinley, Mary received a letter from Anna letting her know that "Your dress has just been sent to the express office. I packed it very carefully and I hope it will not be crushed when you receive it. . . . I know you will like it. . . . I'll bring your cape with me—I shall leave here Monday night. Mr. Church can't leave on account of business."[23]

After her father's remarriage, Mary felt he no longer needed her, but she also believed it was wrong for her to "remain idle" in Memphis: "I could not be happy leading a purposeless existence. Situated as I was, I could not put the college education I had taken such pains to acquire to any good use. . . . All during my college course I had dreamed of the day when I could promote the welfare of my race. Therefore, after graduating from Oberlin I grew more and more restless and dissatisfied with the life I was leading in Memphis, as the year I remained there rolled by. . . . I left Memphis and engaged in the work I had prepared myself to do." Mary accepted a position as an instructor at Wilberforce College in Ohio, where she remained for two years. Her decision so angered her father that he refused to write to her for a year.[24]

Mary left Wilberforce in 1887 and moved to Washington, D.C., to accept a position at the M Street High School for Colored Youth. She had made connections in Washington while a student at Oberlin when she received an invitation to an inaugural ball from Mrs. Blanche K. Bruce of Mississippi, the wife of the second African American elected to the Senate and a good friend of her father's. It was her father's friendships with men like Bruce and Pinckney B. S. Pinchback, Louisiana's first black governor, that allowed her to entry into Washington's black elite. While in Washington, Mary also established a professional and personal relationship with Robert Heberton Terrell, a cum laude graduate of Harvard University and chairman of the language department at the M Street School, who later became her husband.[25]

At the end of her first year at M Street School, Mary decided to take a two-year leave of absence to travel and study in Europe on a grant from the Slater Fund. Like many fair-skinned blacks, Mary was able to move almost seamlessly between racial identities while in Europe. As a black woman with olive skin, almost straight hair, and a barely perceptible trace of African ancestry, she might have easily stayed in Europe, passed for white, and lived a life free of racial discrimination. She even had serious suitors who tried to convince her to stay. But Mary chose (with some prodding from her father) to return to the land of her birth.[26] As she later wrote: "I knew I would be much happier trying to promote the welfare of my race in my native land, working under certain hard conditions, than I would be living in a foreign land where I could enjoy freedom from prejudice, but where I would make no effort to do the work which I believed it was my duty to do. I doubted that I could respect myself if I shirked my responsibility and was recreant to my trust."[27]

Mary resumed her teaching position at the M Street School, but in 1891 she turned down a teaching position at Oberlin to marry Robert H. Terrell. She spent the summer before her wedding with her mother in New York preparing a trousseau (which her father paid for). Robert and Mary were married in an elaborate ceremony at her father's home in Memphis. The guests included prominent black Memphians like attorney Josiah Settles, his wife Fannie, and Charles and Julia Hooks. The wedding guests dined on turkey, roast pig, salad, ice cream, and wine. As a testament to the prestige of both her father and husband, the couple received gifts from T. Jefferson Coolidge, grandson of Thomas Jefferson and one of Robert Terrell's classmates. Although Louisa did not attend, the newlyweds later took a train to visit her in New York.[28]

By the late nineteenth century Terrell was fully entrenched in the world of the black elite in Washington, D.C., but she knew well the precarious economic position of the black middle class. Although she was the wife of a municipal judge, she often wrote to Memphis asking her father for money for clothing, travel expenses, and the like. Terrell never forgot her Memphis roots or the plight of African Americans less fortunate than herself. She kept up with happenings in the city and the South in general. In 1892 one Memphis tragedy in particular affected her profoundly. As Terrell and her husband were awaiting the birth of their third child (who died shortly after birth, as had their previous two children), she learned of the murder of one of her childhood friends, Tom Moss, a former postman and part owner of the Peoples' Grocery Store, located in south Memphis on the corner of Walker Avenue and Mississippi Boulevard. As blacks came from the rural areas to Memphis to shop they increasingly patronized the establishment, where prices were lower and black customers were treated with respect. But this growing competition angered William H. Barrett, a white grocer who ran a similar store across the street.

Relations between the two stores were contentious and often violent. The very idea of black men succeeding and the obvious financial losses were too much for the white merchant to bear. Barrett and other whites in the neighborhood plotted to destroy the black-owned business. After a minor disturbance, plain-clothed county deputies barged into the store late one evening as it was closing and shot at patrons and clerks, who returned fire. One deputy was seriously injured and dozens of black men, including Moss and two of the store's clerks, Calvin McDowell and William Stewart, were rounded up and placed in the Shelby County Jail. Four days later, a white mob broke into the jail; seized Moss, McDowell, and Stewart; took them to a ravine across from a brick yard a short distance north of the jail; and shot them to death. No one was held accountable for these murders.[29]

Mary Church Terrell reflected upon this tragedy, "Thus Tom Moss, who left a wife and several children, and two others were murdered, because they were succeeding too well. They were guilty of no crime but that."[30] This and other occurrences of racial violence throughout the South tested Terrell's Christian beliefs:

> I had read of such lynchings before and had been deeply stirred by them. A normal human being is always shocked when he reads that a man or a woman had been burned at the stake or shot to death, whether he is acquainted with the victim or not. But when a woman has been closely associated with the victim of the mob from childhood and knows him to be above reproach, the horror and anguish which rend her heart are indescribable. . . . For a time it came near to upsetting my faith in the Christian religion. I could not see how a crime like that could be perpetuated in a Christian country, while thousands of Christians sinfully winked at it by making no protest loud enough to be heard nor exerting any earnest effort to redress this terrible wrong.[31]

The 1892 Memphis murders politicized the lynching issue for Terrell and other black Memphians, including Ida B. Wells. Wells, who had once taught in the city's black schools, was (by 1892) editor of a newspaper, *The Free Speech*. She was acquainted with Bob and Anna Church, but probably did not know Mary well. The two women would continue along parallel roads of activism in causes like woman suffrage, the club women's movement, and antilynching campaigns, and they were even among the founders of the NAACP. But Wells's blunt, outspoken approach was very different from Terrell's "kid-glove" approach.

Wells used her writings and the platform provided by international antilynching activists and black club women to challenge racial violence. Terrell looked to the federal government to curb the increasing tide of lynchings. She sought the assistance of influential African American leaders like Frederick Douglass. Douglass had long been a Church family friend as well as a friend of Anna Wright Church's mother, Jane; Anna had known Douglass before she married Bob Church. In fact, whenever Douglass visited Memphis, he stayed in the Wright home. In 1893 Terrell accompanied Douglass when he visited President Benjamin Harrison to urge the president to speak out against lynching in his annual message to Congress. She later recalled that although President Harrison listened attentively, he declined to publicly condemn lynching.[32]

Even in her grief and frustration after the Moss lynching, Terrell threw herself into her commitment to improve conditions for African American women. Black women struggled against a popular image that portrayed them as inherently immoral and unable to properly care for their homes and families. A Memphis newspaper editor reflected these assumptions when he commented, "The truth of the matter is . . . the negro is corrupted at the source. When immorality is almost universal among the women of a race; its doom is sealed." Middle-class black women like Terrell, working in their clubs or in their churches, strove to improve the impoverished conditions in which many African American women found themselves and to "uplift the race." Cities with large black populations like Memphis, Washington, D.C., Boston, and New York were the loci for middle-class black women's social, cultural, and reform organizations. In Memphis, for example, Terrell's stepmother was a member of the Liszt-Mullard Club, the Live Oak Club, and the Whist Club (Annette Church was also a member).[33] Family friend Julia Hooks organized the Phillis Wheatley Union (a branch of the Woman's Union of New York) to uplift the "fallen humanity, regardless of race, color or nationality." Another Memphis group, the Coterie Migratory Assembly, focused on self-improvement and character building, and hosted lectures by suffrage leaders like Susan B. Anthony and Carrie Chapman Catt.[34]

In 1892 Terrell, along with Anna Julia Cooper and Mary Jane Patterson, founded the Colored Women's League of Washington, D.C., a coalition of several of that city's black women's organizations. Following this example, in 1894 middle-class black women in Boston, led by Josephine St. Pierre Ruffin, formed the Women's Era Club. Leaders from a coalition of black women's organizations established the National Federation of Afro American Women, which merged with the Colored Women's League to form the National Association of Colored Women (NACW) in 1896. The NACW galvanized the resources of educated middle-class black women who wanted to improve social and political conditions for African Americans in general and black women in particular. Terrell served as the NACW's first president, and the organization's 1897 meeting was held in Nashville. NACW provided a national platform to highlight the issues, concerns, and reform activities of African American women.[35]

The National Association of Colored Women also gave Mary Church Terrell a venue for her interest in improving conditions for all African Americans and grounded her participation in the struggle for women's suffrage. In 1901 Terrell was one of the speakers at the Thirty-second Annual Convention of the National American Woman Suffrage Association (NAWSA). Her speech, "The Justice of Woman's Suffrage," was the hit of the convention. Mary Seymour Howard was so impressed that she had a bust of her sister, Harriet Beecher Stowe, sent to Terrell.[36]

Always at the forefront of Terrell's activism were issues that African American women faced as a double minority. In 1904 Terrell was the only African American woman invited to the International Conference of Women in Berlin, Germany. Although she was eager to accept the invitation, her family's financial situation was prohibitive. After contacting her father for help, Terrell received $300 to help finance the trip. Terrell suggested, in a letter thanking her father, that she hoped to take her seventeen-year-old half-sister, Annette, to Germany with her, but records do not indicate whether this actually occurred. She wrote her father: "How can I find words to thank you for your great kindness in making it possible for me to attend the Congress of Women which meets in Berlin and at which I am to speak. I really do not know what to say, but you must realize how grateful I am to you for this wonderful opportunity. I have not yet written to Annette about it, for I wanted to see what you thought of the matter, but I shall write her immediately to urge her to go. What a fine time we would have together abroad. I do hope she will go."[37] At the conference in Berlin, addressing the delegation in English, French, and German, Terrell described the contributions of African Americans. In a speech entitled "The Progress and Problems of Colored Women," Terrell especially lauded the contributions of black women to "regenerate and elevate the race."[38]

In the early 1900s Mary Church Terrell was moving from a position of gender-based centralized community self-help, reflected in her activities in NACW, to one of promoting interracial understanding through education and dissemination of information, perhaps best reflected in her lectures on the Chautauqua circuit or her work with the International Conference of Women. Unfortunately, this was not enough to stem the tide of increasing violence toward African Americans in the post-Reconstruction years as whites reasserted their political and social dominance. In 1906, race riots in Atlanta, Georgia, and Brownsville, Texas, and in 1908 in Springfield, Illinois, encouraged many activists, black and white, to think that the time was ripe for the creation of national organizations that could respond to and counteract all forms of racialized terrorism.[39]

In February 1905 W. E. B. DuBois and twenty-nine other activists met at the Buffalo, New York, home of Mary Burnett Talbert, founder of Buffalo's Phillis Wheatley Club of Colored Women. The group adopted resolutions founding the Niagara Movement. The movement's men met from July 11 to 14, 1905, on the Canadian side of Niagara Falls to formally establish the first national organization of African Americans dedicated to aggressively demanding the same rights that other Americans enjoyed. Among the Niagara Movement's goals were demands to end antiblack violence and to counter the loss of black suffrage, and to promote black access to equal employment opportunities. Although Mary Talbert was present at the initial meeting, black women did not attend the July conference. They were, however, present at the Harper's Ferry conference in 1906. The Niagara Movement was a forerunner of the interracial NAACP, of which about one-third of the founders (in 1909) were women. These women included Mary White Ovington, who became the first white member of the Niagara Movement in 1908, her fellow settlement house activist Jane Addams, Mary Church Terrell, and Ida Wells-Barnett. In 1917 Terrell's half-sister, stepmother, and sister-in-law, Sarah Johnson Church, were the only women among the charter members of the Memphis chapter of the NAACP. The chapter, organized by Robert R. Church Jr., was the first one established in a southern city.[40]

Although Mary Church Terrell and Ida B. Wells-Barnett were both born just before the Civil War and had met in Memphis as young women, they approached activism from different perspectives. The two never became friends and, in fact, were bitter rivals despite their similar interests and involvement in the black women's club movement. This is quite likely attributable to their personality differences. As noted above, Wells-Barnett was aggressive and assertive when it came to lambasting American racism. Terrell's approach was decidedly more cosmopolitan and nonconfrontational.[41]

When Terrell joined the NAACP there were some who criticized her because the organization's actions and pronouncements often ran counter to those of Booker T. Washington. Terrell was certainly aware that her husband owed his appointment as a judge to Washington, the preeminent African American leader of the era who controlled federal patronage and private donations that could be channeled into black communities from politically and economically prominent whites. However, Terrell asserted that Washington's influence was not the sole factor in her husband's appointment: "If the leading citizens of the National Capital had not wanted my husband to occupy that position, he would have never been appointed by the president." Terrell was already becoming disaffected with Washington and his accommodationist policies years before she became a part of the NAACP. In Memphis, Bob Church also disagreed with Washington's philosophies, although the two remained lifelong friends. In fact, Washington visited Church whenever he was in Memphis and was one of the last persons to see Bob Church before his death in 1912. However, Mary Church Terrell's criticism of Washington rang clear, and her break with his camp was made complete in the aftermath of the Brownsville riot in 1906.[42]

Despite an impressive history of meritorious service, the arrival of companies B, C, and D of the all-black Twenty-fifth Infantry in Brownsville, Texas, in 1906 was less than welcoming. Local whites wrote to officials in Washington, D.C., demanding that the black soldiers be sent elsewhere. But Washington officials, including Secretary of War William Howard Taft, stood firm and refused to reassign the units. No friend to African Americans, Taft nonetheless acknowledged the bravery and contributions of the Twenty-fifth and other African American troops during the 1898 Spanish-American War. The Twenty-fifth had been ordered to reinforce the First Volunteer Cavalry, better known as Theodore Roosevelt's "Rough Riders," at El Caney, Cuba, in June 1898. In the course of three days of fighting, most of the black soldiers saw action and received praise from their white officers.[43]

But eight years later, when the Twenty-fifth Infantry arrived in Brownsville, stories of the units' bravery in battle were overshadowed by calls for their removal from service. It all began on August 13, 1906, around midnight, when approximately a dozen armed men were involved in a brief confrontation. Official records listed two casualties, a bartender and a policeman. The soldiers resented being quartered in segregated Brownsville and had been involved in at least three earlier skirmishes with local whites in which several of the soldiers had been physically assaulted for alleged impudence. On the day of the August confrontation, there was a complaint that a member of the Twenty-fifth had attempted to rape a white woman. Such rumors or allegations were common starting points for racial violence in turn-of-the-century America.[44]

Two days after the confrontation, Brownsville's Citizens' Committee sent a telegraph to President Roosevelt requesting that the Twenty-fifth be replaced with white troops. Roosevelt sent an inspector general to conduct an immediate investigation, the results of which tentatively confirmed the Twenty-fifth's guilt. However, it was difficult to implicate any individuals, and members of the Twenty-fifth maintained their innocence, even denying knowledge of the riot. As a result, the inspector general recommended that all members of the highly decorated Twenty-fifth Infantry be dishonorably discharged.[45]

Although President Roosevelt admitted that the majority of the men had done nothing wrong, he instructed Secretary of War Taft to carry out the recommendation for discharge. Like many whites of the time, Roosevelt believed that African Americans accused of crimes were guilty until proven innocent.

But the discharge order was not released to the public until after the 1906 midterm elections, enabling the Republican Party, with its African American supporters, to retain control of the House of Representatives.[46]

Mary Church Terrell, like many African American leaders, believed the soldiers' actions did not warrant wholesale discharge of the unit, especially from a president many had supported. In 1901 black leaders had praised President Roosevelt when he crossed the color line by inviting Booker T. Washington to lunch at the White House. The president also took his message to black audiences. He had given a speech at Church Park Auditorium when he visited Memphis in 1902. Although Booker T. Washington chose to make apologies for the president's action, Mary Church Terrell later noted that when she heard of the president's decision, "If my heart had been weak, I should have had an attack of heart failure right there and then." This difference in responses signified a growing ideological and political breach between Washington and Terrell—one that was so open that one of Washington's supporters suggested to Robert Terrell that his wife should be "muzzled."[47]

At the urging of John Milholland, a founder of the Constitutional League (of which Terrell was also a member), Terrell met with Taft to "urge him to suspend the [president's] order till an investigation can be made." But Taft was hesitant to do so since the president had already left the country on a trip to Panama. Terrell would not be denied. She asked Taft to delay the execution of the order until Roosevelt returned and the soldiers could be given a proper trial. She urged him to consider this because many of the soldiers had been in the army for years and had excellent service records. Terrell did not want them to be "sent forth branded as murderers." Terrell argued that black soldiers were a source of pride among African Americans because of their bravery in every war in which the United States was involved. She knew this to be true because of the soldiers who were stationed in Memphis after the Civil War whose very presence had sparked the 1866 race riots.[48]

Terrell was well aware of the racial climate of her time. She knew that even before the Twenty-fifth arrived at Fort Brown, local residents had asked Washington officials to have the unit's orders rescinded and the soldiers stationed elsewhere. But she had faith that "men of power and influence in national affairs" would be fair in their actions toward the troops, and she urged the Brownsville community to tolerate the soldiers' presence. Apparently, she was not the only one who recognized the stellar military records of the Twenty-fifth. After the president left for Panama, his office had been bombarded with complaints and protests about his decision. On the very same day that Terrell visited Taft, the Republican Party of New York sent a telegram to the War Department also requesting that the dismissal order be suspended temporarily. After meeting with Terrell, Taft sent a cable to President Roosevelt asking him to suspend the order. Newspapers across the country carried reports about her visit with Taft, praising her for convincing the Secretary of War to suspend the president's order.[49]

Terrell wasted little time in getting an appointment with Theodore Roosevelt after his return from Panama. Accompanied by Gilchrist Steward, a representative from the Constitutional League, she presented her case to the president. He assured the two that all of the evidence would be considered when the case was sent to the War Department. He further promised that the soldiers could reenlist if they provided enough information to convince the War Department of their innocence. However, this promise was not realized. At the root of Roosevelt's final decision to discharge the soldiers was his desire to appease southern whites and his ambivalence toward African Americans.[50]

Mary Church Terrell's political maneuvering in the Brownsville incident stemmed from her knowledge and understanding of the times in which she operated. In September 1906 she published an article entitled "Race Prejudice and Southern Progress" in the *Colored American Magazine.* Terrell not only discussed how racial prejudice made African Americans slaves to the South; she also noted that it had enslaved southern whites as well. She appealed to the conscience of southern whites declaring that there were many white men in the South who had been "blessed with splendid intellects, who are kind and tender of heart and who yearn to be true to their higher better natures." Yet they chose not to do so because they were so heavily influenced by public opinions that ostracized anyone who dissented from the views of the majority. It was no accident that the black soldiers were dishonorably discharged during a time of heightened tensions in American race relations. And indeed, contributing to this were increasing incidents of race riots and other forms of racial violence around the country.[51]

In another article, this time for the 1906 *Voice of the Negro*, entitled "The Disbanding of the Colored Soldiers," Terrell noted that the accusations against, and the subsequent disbanding of, the three companies of black soldiers seemed incredible for a number of reasons. First, Roosevelt's order affected patriotic career soldiers, many of whom had served for over thirty years. The president's order effectively wiped out their opportunities to retire on three-quarters pay and possibly live at the Soldiers Home. The dishonorable discharges also prevented those soldiers with shorter careers from ever reenlisting or being employed in any federal or military positions.[52]

Second, Terrell traced the tension between black soldiers and whites to the four decades of national racial drama that had followed the Civil War. During this time, blacks like her father had asserted their rights to first-class citizenship and equality. She recalled what had happened to Bob Church during the 1866 Memphis race riots; the lynching of men like Tom Moss, William Stewart, and Calvin McDowell; and the increasing racial violence as Jim Crow segregation manifested itself in American society. The presence of black men in the United States military undermined a racial status quo that demanded African American subordination. In fact, when writing to Secretary of War Taft, Major Augustus P. Blockson noted that whites in Brownsville thought black soldiers should be treated like laborers. He also commented that "the colored soldier is much more aggressive in his attitude on the social equality question than he used to be." Thus, the Brownsville riot was inevitable, although the absolute culpability of the Twenty-fifth was not. For Terrell, this was evidence that questions of social equality were, directly or indirectly, part of anything pertaining to African Americans.[53]

This was also proof that black male assertiveness was not well received in the late nineteenth or early twentieth century. In fact, alleged black male "impudence" was more often than not an excuse for white mob violence. Black women posed less of a threat to the racial status quo, and leaders like Mary Church Terrell and Ida B. Wells-Barnett, working through organizations like the NACW, assumed the reins in the struggle for racial progress.

What makes Mary Church Terrell's role in the Brownsville case all the more amazing is that black soldiers sought her out to explain their side of the story and to further assert their innocence and their patriotism. According to Terrell, the men of the Twenty-fifth believed that in the end, they would be vindicated. She assured some of the men she met that the Constitutional League of New York would do everything possible to obtain a hearing to reinstate them. Unfortunately their efforts were not enough to reverse President Roosevelt's decision.[54]

In the years following the Brownsville incident, Mary Church Terrell became involved in other activities. In 1914, for example, she was instrumental in the formation of Delta Sigma Theta Sorority at Howard University. Terrell also wrote the Delta Creed for the organization, which outlined a code of conduct for young black women. During World War I she worked as a clerk in the War Department until someone recognized her and she was sent to the department's all-black division. In 1919 she was a guest speaker at the Women's International League for Peace and Freedom Conference in Zurich.[55] Even through all of these activities, however, Mary Church Terrell retained her ties with the Republican Party. She was president of the Women's Republican League of Washington after the passage of the Nineteenth Amendment to the Constitution (which gave women the vote) and attended the Republican National Convention in New

York in 1920. Terrell was later appointed "director of work among the colored women of the East" during Herbert Hoover's 1932 presidential campaign. Although many African Americans defected from the Republican Party in the 1930s, Terrell, like other members of the Church family, still believed it to be the best hope for black enfranchisement and thus first-class citizenship.[56]

Mary Church Terrell's life as a black woman was as precarious as that of most other African Americans at the end of the nineteenth century. Although existing sources have paid little attention to her parents' slave origins and their lives in post–Civil War Memphis, Tennessee, these experiences informed their lives and Terrell's. While it is true that she was from a prestigious and socially connected family, both of Terrell's parents' very real experiences with slavery and racial discrimination left an indelible mark on their psyches and shaped how Terrell saw herself as a person of African descent and a woman. As an educated black woman in the late nineteenth century she understood her duty to include racial uplift in her repertoire of racial activism. Her family's wealth did not shield her from the miserable existence of most African Americans. Nor did it shield her personally from racial discrimination. In 1946, when she was eighty-three years old, she applied for membership in the all-white American Association of University Women. Despite her determination, it was three years before she and other black women were accepted into the organization. In 1950, when she was eighty-seven and walking with a cane, Terrell led a picket line in protest of Washington's segregated restaurants.[57] Such was her activism until her death at age ninety-one in Annapolis, Maryland, on July 24, 1954—just two months after the landmark *Brown v. Board of Education* decision.[58]

Mary Church Terrell began life as a child of privilege in Tennessee and later became a member of the black elite in Washington, D.C., with class advantages that set her apart from the mass of impoverished African Americans. But Terrell was not blind to the reality that all blacks were understood monolithically by whites and thus subject to unfair treatment. Terrell's personal experience with racism in Memphis, and those of her family, informed her activism nationally. Her recollection of her father's experiences during the 1866 race riots and of the lynching of her friend Tom Moss in 1892 continuously fed her awareness of and thus her activism against American racial injustice. During the Brownsville riots, Terrell's skills as a writer brought attention not only to the injustice the Twenty-fifth faced, but also that of all African Americans. When she visited Secretary of War Taft and President Roosevelt to ask that the order be suspended, it was as a representative of the Constitutional League and as a member of the Republican Party. And although her efforts failed, the political influence of this daughter of Memphis was nonetheless significant because it demonstrated her commitment to pounding at the doors of the powerful and influential for the sake of racial justice.

NOTES

1. U.S. House of Representatives, *Memphis Riots and Massacres,* report no. 101, 39th Cong., 1st sess. (July 25, 1866), 227, http://www.loc.gov (accessed April 24, 2006) (hereafter cited as *Memphis Riots and Massacres*); Lester C. Lamon, *Blacks in Tennessee, 1791–1970* (Knoxville: University of Tennessee Press, 1981), 75; Pamela Palmer, ed., *The Robert R. Church Family of Memphis: Guide to the Papers with Selected Facsimiles of Documents and Photographs* (Memphis: Memphis State University Press, 1979), 8; Robert Church, Ronald Walter, and Charles W. Crawford, eds., *Nineteenth Century Memphis Families of Color, 1850–1900* (Memphis: Murdock Printing Co., 1987), 16.

2. Louisa Ayres Church married again after she left Memphis with her children, Mary and Thomas, but it is not clear when the marriage took place. She is listed by the name Martell in the 1900 Washington, D.C., census; see U.S. Bureau of the Census, Twelfth Census of the United States, "Population Schedule," Washington City, Washington, D.C., 1900, digital scan of original records in the National Archives, Washington, D.C., roll T623, 183, http://www.ancestry.com (accessed April 14, 2006). Seymour D. Thompson and Thomas M. Steger, *A Compilation of the Statue Laws of the State of Tennessee,* vol. 2 (St. Louis: W. J. Gilbert, Law Book Publishers, 1872), 1094–95. Sources suggest that Bob Church fathered a daughter before Mary; see *Memphis Commercial Appeal,* November 16, 1928; R. R. Church to Professor Ogden, March 5, 1869, *American Missionary Association Manuscripts,* reel 2 (New Orleans: Amistad Research Center, Dillard University, 1869).

3. *David H. Evans v. Robert R. Church, Lou Church, and T. S. Ayres,* Chancery Court of Memphis, New Rule Docket, Number 2673, filed March 31, 1868, Shelby County Archives, Memphis, Tennessee (hereafter cited as *Evans v. Church*).

4. Willard B. Gatewood, *Aristocrats of Color* (Bloomington: Indiana University Press, 1990), 27; *Evans v. Church*; Mary Church Terrell, *A Colored Woman in a White World* (New York: G. K. Hall, 1980), xvii–xix, 9; *The Grand Duke Alexis in the United States of America,* (1872; repr., New York: Interland Publishing, 1972), 208–9.

5. U.S. Bureau of the Census, Ninth Census of the United States, "Population Schedule," Seventh Ward, Memphis, Shelby County, 1870, jpeg image (Online: The Generations Network, Inc., 2005), digital scan of original records in the National Archives, Washington, D.C., roll M593_1563, http://www.ancestry.com (accessed April 14, 2006);Terrell, *A Colored Woman in a White World,* 10.

6. James Gilbert Ryan, "The Memphis Riots of 1866: Terror in a Black Community during Reconstruction," *Journal of Negro History* 62, no. 3 (1977): 244, 243.

7. David T. Gleeson, *The Irish in the South, 1815–1877* (Chapel Hill: University of North Carolina Press, 2001), 177; Beverly Washington Jones, *Quest for Equality: The Life and Writings of Mary Eliza Church Terrell, 1863–1954* (Brooklyn: Carlson Publishing, Inc., 1990), 4; *Memphis Riots and Massacres.*

8. *Memphis Riots and Massacres*; Terrell, *A Colored Woman in a White World,* 7.

9. Terrell, *A Colored Woman in a White World,* 14.

10. Ibid.

11. See Noel Ignatiev, *How The Irish Became White* (New York: Routledge, 1996), for discussion of color, race, and ethnicity. U.S. Bureau of the Census, Tenth Census of the United States, "Population Schedule", Six Avenue, New York, State of New York, 1880, jpeg image (Online: The Generations

Network, Inc., 2005), digital scan of original records in the National Archives, Washington, D.C., roll T9_880, http://www.ancestry.com (accessed April 14, 2006). Terrell later had a German servant named Anna; see Terrell, *A Colored Woman in a White World*, 81; Mary Church Terrell Papers, reel 1, January 28 and 30, 1908, Ned McWherter Library, University of Memphis, Memphis, Tenn.

12. Terrell, *A Colored Woman in a White World*, 232–33; Thomas A. Church to Robert R. Church Jr., April 22, 1912, October 2, 1912, The Robert R. Church Papers (hereafter Church Papers), ser. 2, box 3, folder 8, Special Collections, Ned McWherter Library, University of Memphis, Memphis, Tenn.; *Dow's Memphis Directory*, 1890 and 1891 (Memphis: Dow's, 1890 and 1891) jpeg image (Online: The Generations Network, Inc., 2005), http://www.ancestry.com (accessed April 14, 2006), U.S. Bureau of Census, Thirteenth Census of the United States, "Population Schedule," Manhattan Borough, New York, New York, U.S. Bureau of Census, Fourteenth Census of the U.S., 1920, "Population Schedule," New York City, New York, 1910, jpeg image (Online: The Generations Network, Inc., 2005), digital scan of original records in the National Archives, Washington, D.C., rolls T624_1023 and T625_1224, http://www.ancestry.com (accessed April 14, 2006); New York City Directory, Manhattan and Bronx Residents, 1931, jpeg image (Online: The Generations Network, Inc., 2005), http://www.ancestry.com (accessed April 14, 2006); Terrell, *A Colored Woman in a White World*, 83, 402; Dorothy Sterling, *Black Foremothers* (Old Westbury, N.Y.: The Feminist Press, 1979), 133.

13. Dennis C. Rousey, "Yellow Fever and Black Policemen in Memphis: A Post-Reconstruction Anomaly," *Journal of Southern History* 51, no. 3. (1985): 361, 357; Gerald M. Capers Jr., "Yellow Fever in Memphis in the 1870s," *Mississippi Valley Historical Review* 24, no. 4 (1938): 484, 486; Lynette Boney Wrenn, *Crisis and Commission Government in Memphis* (Knoxville: University of Tennessee Press, 1998), 22.

14. Terrell, *A Colored Woman in a White World*, 18; Sterling, *Black Foremothers*, 123.

15. Terrell, *A Colored Woman in a White World*, 36.

16. Ibid., 38; Wrenn, *Crisis and Commission Government in Memphis*, 79; Fred L. Hutchins, "Beale Street As It Was," *West Tennessee Historical Society Papers* no. 26 (Nashville: West Tennessee Historical Society and Tennessee Historical Commission, 1972), 57; M. Sammye Miller, "Last Will and Testament of Robert Reed Church, Senior (1839–1912)," *Journal of Negro History* 65, no. 2 (1980): 156; Beverly G. Bond and Janann Sherman, *Memphis in Black and White* (Charleston, S.C.: Arcadia Publishing, 2003), 80; John E. Harkins, *Metropolis of the American Nile* (Woodland Hills, Calif.: Windsor Publications, Inc., 1982), 108; Annette E. Church and Roberta R. Church, *The Robert R. Churches of Memphis: A Father and Son Who Achieved in Spite of Race* (Ann Arbor, Mich.: Edward Brothers, 1974), 16; Carroll Van West, ed., "Robert Church, Sr." *The Tennessee Encyclopedia of History and Culture* (Nashville: Tennessee Historical Society, 1998), 161; Shields McIlwaine, *Memphis: Down in Dixie* (New York: E. P. Dutton, 1948), 323; "Last Will and Testament of R. R. Church," *Journal of Negro History* 65, no. 2 (1980): 159; Board of Health, Commission Government, City of Memphis, Burial Permit, 1912, Shelby County Archives, Memphis, Tennessee.

17. Wrenn, *Crisis and Commission Government in Memphis*, 14–15.

18. Ibid., 79; John Preston Young, *Standard History of Memphis, Tennessee* (Knoxville: H. W. Crew, 1912), 186; Wrenn, *Crisis and Commission Government in Memphis*, xv, 12.

19. Sterling, *Black Foremothers*, 127; W. E. Bigglestone, "Oberlin College and the Negro Student, 1865–1940," *Journal of Negro History* 56, no. 3 (1971): 199; Jones, *Quest for Equality*, 11; "Dr. Mary Church Terrell, 90, Dies," *Memphis Tri-State Defender*, July 31, 1954; "Mary Church Terrell," *Journal of Negro History* 39, no. 4 (1954): 335.

20. Terrell, *A Colored Woman in a White World*, 59.

21. See Beverly Greene Bond, "Milly Swan Price: Freedom, Kinship, and Property," this volume.

22. Shelby County Marriage Record, L., Shelby County Archives, Memphis, Tennessee; Church and Church, *The Robert R. Churches of Memphis*, 27, 30; Church, Walter, and Crawford, *Nineteenth Century Memphis Families of Color*; Terrell, *A Colored Woman in a White World*, 37, 58–59; Lou Church to Bob Church, January 7, 1904, December 15, 1907, Church Papers, ser. 1, box 1, folder 38.

23. Anna Church to Mary Church, February 27, 1897, box 22, folder 5; Robert Terrell to Robert R. Church, April 4, 1907, ser. 1, box 1, folder 2; R. H. Terrell to Mrs. Church, ser. 1, box 1, folder 8; letter to Robert R. Church, November 3, 1897, ser. 1, box 1, folder 26, Church Papers; Terrell, *A Colored Woman in a White World*, 58–59, 97, 111; Anna Church to Mollie Church, November 6, 1913, Mary Church Terrell Papers, reel 2–3, Ned McWherter Library, University of Memphis, Memphis, Tenn. Mary visited her Memphis family often. Bob Church also owned a house, next door to Mary and her husband (which they sometimes rented to writer and friend Paul Lawrence Dunbar), where the Memphis Churches stayed when they were in Washington.

24. Terrell, *A Colored Woman in a White World*, 59, 60, 62.

25. G. James Fleming, *Who's Who in Colored America: An Illustrated Biographical Directory of Notable Living Persons of African Descent in the United States*, 7th ed. (Yonkers-on-Hudson, N.Y.: Christian E. Burckel and Associates, 1950), 449; Joyce A. Hanson, *Mary McLeod Bethune and Black Women's Political Activism*, (Columbia: University of Missouri Press, 2003), 110; Gladys Byram Shepperd, *Mary Church Terrell, Respectable Person* (Baltimore: Human Relations Press, 1959), 23; P. B. S. Pinchback to Robert R. Church, January 12, 1885, Church Papers, ser. 1, box 1, folder 8. Terrell's daughter Phyllis later married into the Langston family, also a part of the Washington, D.C., black elite. See also, Lawrence Otis Graham, *The Senator and the Socialite: The True Story of America's First Black Dynasty* (New York: Harper Collins, 2006); Jones, *Quest for Equality*, 12.

26. Jones, *Quest for Equality*, 12; Terrell, *A Colored Woman in a White World*, 97–99.

27. Terrell, *A Colored Woman in a White World*, 99.

28. Miriam DeCosta-Willis, *The Memphis Diary of Ida B. Wells: An Intimate Portrait of the Activist as a Young Woman* (Boston: Beacon Press, 1995), 54; Terrell, *A Colored Woman in a White World*, 105, 113–15; Shepperd, *Mary Church Terrell*, 10; Ronald M. Johnson "From Romantic Suburb to Racial Enclave: LeDroit Park, Washington, D.C., 1880–1920," *Phylon* 45, no. 4 (1984): 266. Louisa Church Martell last appears in the 1910 census.

29. David M. Tucker, "Miss Ida B. Wells and Memphis Lynching," *Phylon* 32, no. 2 (1971): 115; Miriam DeCosta-Willis, *The Memphis Diary of Ida B. Wells*, 2;

30. Terrell, *A Colored Woman in a White World*, 105.

31. Ibid., 106.

32. Church and Church, *The Robert R. Churches of Memphis*, 42; Philip S. Foner, *The Life and Writings of Frederick Douglas*, vol. 4, *Reconstruction and After* (New York: International Publishers, 1955), 140; Terrell, *A Colored Woman in a White World*, 108, 409–10. See also Sterling, *Black Foremothers*, 133.

33. *Memphis Commercial Appeal*, August 2, 1901; Church, Walter, and Crawford, *Nineteenth Century Memphis Families of Color*, 43, 127, 132.

34. Dorothy Sterling, *We Are Your Sisters: Black Women in the Nineteenth Century* (New York: W. W. Norton, 1997), 131. On black women and reform see Beverly Greene Bond, "'Till Fair Aurora Rise': African American Women in Memphis, Tennessee 1840–1915", chap. 6 (Ph.D. diss., University of Memphis, 1996); Jacqueline Anne Rouse, *Lugenia Burns Hope: Black Southern Reformer* (Athens: University of Georgia Press, 1992); and Elizabeth Lasch Quinn, *Black Neighbors: Race and the Limits*

of Reform in the American Settlement House Movement, 1890–1945 (Chapel Hill: University of North Carolina Press, 1993).

35. Deborah Gray White, *Too Heavy a Load: Black Women in Defense of Themselves, 1894–1994* (New York: W. W. Norton, 1999), 27; Sharon Harley, "Mary Church Terrell: Genteel Militant," in *Black Leaders of the Nineteenth Century*, ed. Leon Litwack and August Meier (Urbana: University of Illinois Press, 1988), 312; "Dedication to Be Tribute to Late Mary Church Terrell," *Washington Evening Star*, November 24, 1966; Church Papers, ser. 6, box 22, folder 7; Sterling, *We Are Your Sisters*, 131; Darlene Clark Hine and Kathleen Thompson, *A Shining Thread of Hope: The History of Black Women in America* (New York: Broadway Books, 1998), 180.

36. The Thirty-second Annual Convention of the National American Woman Suffrage Association and newspaper clipping (date, title, and author unknown), from Church Papers, ser. 1, box 1, folder 9; Linda O. McMurry, *To Keep the Waters Troubled: The Life of Ida B. Wells* (New York: Oxford University Press, 1998), 307, 308. See also, Pat Schechter, *Ida B. Wells-Barnett and American Reform, 1880–1930* (Chapel Hill: University of North Carolina Press, 2001).

37. Terrell, *A Colored Woman in a White World*, 197; Church Papers, ser. 1, box 1, folder 26.

38. "She Fought for Rights of Women, Negroes," *Chicago Tribune*, September 29, 1966; Mary Church Terrell, "The International Congress of Women," *Voice of the Negro* 1, no. 10 (1904): 461, found in Church Papers, ser. 6, box 22, folder 11; Shepperd, *Mary Church Terrell*, 90.

39. Carroll Van West, ed., "Mary Eliza Church Terrell," *The Tennessee Encyclopedia of History and Culture* (Nashville: Tennessee Historical Society, 1998), 968; James L. Crouthamel, "The Springfield Race Riot of 1908," *Journal of Negro History* 45, no. 3 (1960): 164.

40. Elliott M. Rudwick, "The Niagara Movement," *Journal of Negro History* 42, no. 3 (1957): 177, 179; M. Sammy Miller, "Mary Church Terrell's Letters from Europe to her Father," *Negro History Bulletin* 39, no. 6 (1976): 618; Special Collections, University of Memphis, Memphis, Tenn.; "Saluting the Churches," *Memphis Tri State Defender*, February 20, 1993; Church, Walter, and Crawford, *Nineteenth Century Memphis Families of Color*, 14.

41. McMurry, *To Keep the Waters Troubled*, 47, 49, 135, 183–184; DeCosta-Willis, *The Memphis Diary of Ida B. Wells*, 6; Charles Flint Kellogg, *A History of The National Association for the Advancement of Colored People*, vol. 1, *1909–1920* (Baltimore: Johns Hopkins University Press, 1967), 19, 23, 26.

42. Terrell, *A Colored Woman in a White World*, 194; Church and Church, *The Robert R. Churches*, 43; Charles W. Crawford, "Robert Church Family of Memphis," interviews with Roberta Church and Annette E. Church, Oral History Research Office, Memphis State University, Memphis, Tenn., 1974, 7.

43. Ann J. Lane, *The Brownsville Affair: National Crisis and Black Reaction* (Port Washington, N.Y.: Kennikat Press, 1971), 14; John Hope Franklin, *From Slavery to Freedom: A History of African Americans*, 8th ed. (Boston: McGraw-Hill, 2000), 332; John D. Weaver, *The Senator and the Sharecropper's Son: Exoneration of the Brownsville Soldiers*, (College Station: Texas A&M University Press, 1997), 68.

44. James A. Tinsley, "Roosevelt, Foraker, and the Brownsville Affray," *Journal of Negro History* 41, no. 1 (1956): 44.

45. Emma Lou Thornbrough, "The Brownsville Episode and the Negro Vote," *Mississippi Valley Historical Review* 44, no. 3 (1957): 470; Anne J. Lane, *The Brownsville Affair: National Crisis and Black Reaction* (Port Washington, N.Y.: Kennikat Press, 1971), 19.

46. "Colored Soldiers Dishonorably Discharged," *Voice of the Negro* 3, no. 11 (1906): 466.

47. Terrell, *A Colored Woman in a White World*, 268; Beverly G. Bond, "Roberta Church: Race

and the Republican Party in the 1950s," in *Portraits of African American Life since 1865*, ed. Nina Mjagkij (Wilmington, Del.: Scholarly Resources Inc., 2003), 183; Paula Giddings, *When and Where I Enter: The Impact of Black Women on Race and Sex in America* (New York: William Morrow and Co., 1984), 46, 106; Mary Church Terrell, "The Disbanding of the Colored Soldiers," *Voice of the Negro* 3, no. 12 (1906): 558.

48. Weaver, *The Senator and the Sharecropper's Son*, 117; Lane, *The Brownsville Affair*, 25; Terrell, *A Colored Woman in a White World*, 270; "Secretary Taft and the Negro Soldiers," *New York Independent*, July 23, 1908, 189; "Appeal for Black Troops: Mrs. Mary Church Terrell Asks Suspension of Order," *Washington Post*, November 18, 1906.

49. Mary Church Terrell, "The Disbanding of the Colored Soldiers" *Voice of the Negro* 3, no. 1 (1906): 557; "Appeal for Black Troops"; "Taft's Bold Step: Possible Friction with President Over Troops," *Washington Post*, November 21, 1906; Terrell, *A Colored Woman in a White World*, 270, 272. In addition to the *Washington Post*, Terrell's plea was printed in the *Washington Evening Star* and the *St. Louis Globe Democrat*.

50. Lewis N. Wynne, "Brownsville: The Reaction of the Negro Press," *Phylon* 33, no. 2 (1972): 158; Kathleen Dalton, *Theodore Roosevelt: A Strenuous Life* (New York: Alfred A. Knopf, 2002), 322.

51. Mary Church Terrell, "Race Prejudice and Southern Progress," *Colored American Magazine* 2, no. 3 (1906): 188.

52. Terrell, "The Disbanding of the Colored Soldiers," 555.

53. Ibid., 556–557.

54. Terrell, *A Colored Woman in a White World*, 272–73.

55. Church, Walter, and Crawford, *Nineteenth Century Memphis Families of Color*, 92; Sterling, *Black Foremothers*, 144; This organization was originally called the International Committee of Women for Permanent Peace.

56. Terrell, *A Colored Woman in a White World*, 308, 309, 413; Western Union Telegram, September 22, 1920, E. F. Colladay to the Honorable Will H. Hays, Chairman of the Republican National Committee, September 13, 1920, Church Papers, ser. 6, box 22, folder 6. She also campaigned for President Calvin Coolidge.

57. Perre Magness, "Long Career Paved Way for Women, Blacks," *Memphis Commercial Appeal*, July 28, 1994, Church Papers, ser. 14, box 43, folder 4.

58. "Mary Church Terrell," *Journal of Negro History* 39, no. 4 (1954): 334.

Alberta Hunter

(1895–1984)

"She Had the World in a Jug, with the Stopper in Her Hand"

MICHELLE R. SCOTT

On October 6, 1978, the lights went up on the premiere of the Robert Altman film *Remember My Name* at the historic Orpheum Theater. The location was not Hollywood but Memphis, Tennessee. The over twenty-six hundred people gathered at the theater at the corner of Main and Beale Streets included print and broadcast journalists, producers, directors and actors, well-wishers, and a special visitor—a petite, self-assured elderly African American woman who, for many Memphians, was the real guest of honor. She was the composer of the movie's soundtrack and an icon in the music industry. The music that emanated from the theater's sound system was not the R&B or soul music for which 1970s Memphis was famous, but a remastered collection of classic blues. This was the music popularized by black female entertainers in the 1920s. On the soundtrack a powerful voice belted out "Downhearted Blues," a song about a woman who was "disgusted" with the man who mistreated her and who had resolved that her next suitor would have to come "under her command" to deserve a relationship. Listeners fifty years removed from the original venues of this blues song might wonder who could compose such timeless lyrics. But blues aficionados knew that this was the legendary Alberta Hunter. Hunter was making one of her infrequent visits to the hometown she had run away from six decades earlier to celebrate the opening of Altman's movie and to remind the public of its debt to another genre of Memphis music.[1]

Alberta Hunter rose to prominence in the early twentieth century as a blues vocalist and composer, and as an international cabaret entertainer. Between

ALBERTA HUNTER

Circa 1983. Press-Scimitar Photo/Special Collections/
University of Memphis Libraries.

1912 and 1957 Hunter's mezzo-soprano voice, often comic lyrics laced with classic double entendres, and spirited interactions with her band members and her audiences, attracted fans throughout the United States and Europe. She captivated crowds in Chicago nightclubs, recorded with jazz legends in New York, starred on Broadway, performed before royalty in France and Britain, and served her nation as a USO performer during World War II and the Korean War. Then she gave up the life she loved to pursue a twenty-year career as a hospital scrub nurse. When she returned to the stage in the late 1970s she brought her style of blues, with all its wit, rhythm, and subtleties, to a whole new audience of listeners; and these listeners, whether at the Cookery in New York or the Central City Opera House in Colorado, at Chicago's Cool Jazz Festival or the White House, knew that they were enjoying a national treasure. Hunter was very much a product of the times in which she lived, but her success can also be attributed to the sociocultural environment of her youth. Although she was not "born on Beale Street," as some writers have claimed, the "rough and ready" neighborhoods of black Memphis as well as her supportive, female-led family nurtured Alberta Hunter's thirst for fame, respectability, and economic security.[2]

The years of Hunter's infancy and childhood were ones of intense struggle in race relations and tentative hope for social and economic progress in urban and rural communities across the state. The turmoil of Civil War, emancipation, and Reconstruction were quickly replaced by new social, political, and economic conflicts. In 1882 Tennessee passed the nation's first Jim Crow law, one that segregated railway passengers traveling across the state. Local communities followed suit, passing laws allowing proprietors and service-providers to segregate the races in their establishments. These laws were challenged in local and state courts by women like the journalist Ida B. Wells and Julia Hooks.[3] But challenging the rising level of racial violence proved more difficult. Between 1882 and 1920 over two hundred men, women, and children were lynched statewide, the overwhelming majority of whom were African American. In an 1892 Memphis lynching, one of the victims was Tom Moss, a personal friend of Ida B. Wells, who was the godmother of Moss's young daughter. Wells launched an antilynching campaign in articles published in her newspaper, *Free Speech and Headlight*, and reprinted in other African American papers across the nation. Wells attacked southern racial hypocrisy, particularly the premise that these acts of racial violence were rooted in efforts to protect white women from the sexual assaults of black men. She encouraged Memphis blacks to leave a city that did not value their economic and social contributions. In response to her editorials, as many as four thousand black residents fled the city.[4]

Racial violence continued to plague the city and surrounding rural communities. In July 1893 a mob of more than a thousand whites took Lee Walker from the Shelby County jail in Memphis, hanged and shot him, then burned the body. Walker had been accused of assaulting a white woman. In late August 1894, eight months before Alberta Hunter's birth, six black men were murdered as they were being transported from Kerrville (in Tipton County just north of Shelby County) to the jail in Memphis. The victims of the "Big Creek Lynching," as it was called, had been accused of belonging to an organized "barn burning" ring in their rural Tipton community.[5] Wells's response to this continued racial violence was to suggest that a "Winchester rifle should have a place of honor in every black home and it should be used for that protection which the law refuses to give."[6]

Alberta's mother, Laura Peterson, was born in Knoxville and arrived in Memphis in about 1880 with her parents and siblings from Brownsville in Haywood County (about sixty miles east of Memphis). Laura's father, Henry Peterson, was a brick mason who by the 1890s was working for Memphis's Bluff City Brick and Manufacturing Company. His income made it possible for Hunter's grandmother, Nancy, to stay home, keeping house and raising her children and grandchildren. Laura Peterson married Charles Hunter, a Pullman porter, in 1890. They had two children before Alberta was born—a son, John, who died at birth, and a daughter, La Tosca, who was two years older than Alberta.[7]

In the fall of 1894, as the trial of the Big Creek lynchers progressed through the Memphis courts, Laura and Charles Hunter awaited the birth of their third child. At the time the couple lived with or near Henry and Nancy Peterson on High Street, which enabled Nancy Peterson to keep an eye on the young family. However, in late February 1895, about six weeks before Alberta's birth, Charles Hunter died of pneumonia. Weeks later Charles's attending physician, Dr. Albert S. J. Burchette, returned to the house on High Street to deliver Alberta. Alberta later suggested that she had been named for Dr. Burchette.[8] Laura made little effort to keep Charles's memory alive for his daughters. When Alberta Hunter was interviewed for the documentary on her life, *My Castle's Rockin'*, in the early 1980s, she said little about her father, which led many researchers to assume that Charles Hunter had simply abandoned his family. However, recently catalogued records of the Shelby County Register's office clearly indicate that Charles died shortly before Alberta's birth. Although we can never know for certain, Laura's silence may have been rooted in grief or anger, since Charles's death plunged the family into economic difficulties from which they never seemed to recover. Perhaps Laura Hunter tried to erase the pain of Charles's death from her consciousness by never speaking about him or fully explaining his absence to her daughters. Alberta Hunter assumed this was part of her mother's "coldness." "She never mourned anything," Alberta told her biographer, and that included the deaths of her first child and her husband.[9]

During her Memphis years, Alberta's primary economic and emotional support system was female. This pattern would continue throughout her life. After Charles Hunter's death, Laura lived with or near her mother's family until 1903, when she and her daughters rented a room in a house across the street from Beale Street Baptist Church. The family moved several more times over the next seven or eight years before finally settling in a house on Lane Street, "the last little house in Memphis" where Alberta would live before running away to Chicago. All of these locations—High, Robeson, Beale, Menager, Manassas, North Dunlap, and Lane—were in commercial or black working-class communities in the city, perhaps reflecting the economic instability of Laura's household.[10]

Laura surrounded herself with a community of women who in one way or another helped her raise her daughters. Alberta's grandfather, Henry Peterson, died in 1899, leaving Nancy and Laura as the primary providers for the household. Nancy took in laundry and cared for her grandchildren while Laura worked outside the home, possibly as a domestic. Alberta had close relationships with her grandmother and her mother, and these two women became the touchstones for Alberta's sense of home and safety, even after she left Memphis.[11] Nancy Peterson also took care of Alberta and La Tosca's religious training. Nancy attended Collins Chapel Colored Methodist Episcopal (CME) church, a pillar of the black Memphis community with a congregation dating back to the 1840s.[12] As Alberta recalled, "My grandmother would take me to the church. If the church opened at five o'clock in the morning my grandmother would have me there at five and I'd stay there 'til the church closed—all day long."[13] Churches provided black communities with more than spiritual guidance and stability. In a society where segregation and discrimination closed many other institutions to African Americans, churches functioned as social, educational, and political centers for their black congregants. At Collins Chapel, Alberta and La Tosca also received an education in social class norms. Collins Chapel was "the church of the teachers, doctors, lawyers, postal workers—the 'socially ambitious'—where the virtues of educating children, paying debts, and buying property were extolled over shouting the loudest on the amens."[14]

Alberta's religious education was probably reinforced by her mother's half-sister, Ella Campbell (Aunt Babe), whose husband Benjamin was a "minister of sorts." The female network also included another of Laura's half-sisters, Aunt Fletcher, and her children, and neighborhood women like Ann Deb ("Aunt Deb"), her mother's employers, brothel owners Emma and Myrtle Taylor, and a succession of black and white landladies (including Josie McCoy and Nellie Hunter). From the latter, Alberta learned the value of a dollar and the importance of a woman earning and keeping her own money.

The Memphis of Alberta Hunter's youth was fast becoming an economically and technologically progressive New South city. In 1892 the city celebrated the opening of the Great Mississippi River Bridge, an eight-thousand-foot span that was in its day the longest bridge in the United States, the third longest in the world, and the first bridge across the Mississippi River below St. Louis, Missouri. Memphis thought of itself as a progressive city, rapidly on the rise with new housing, expanding city transportation system (over one hundred miles of street railroads by 1900), and bustling commercial activity. Electric lights and telephone service had come to the city in the decades between the 1870s and the 1890s. City boosters touted an improved water system, courtesy of a system of underground artesian wells that provided the cleanest, safest, and best-tasting water in the region. The city's downtown district housed an ornate federal building, the Cossitt Library (opened two years before Alberta Hunter's birth), the eleven-story Continental Bank Building, and numerous hotels and theaters, including the Gayoso House, the Peabody Hotel, the Grand Opera House, and the Lyceum.

However, in the early 1900s most black and white Memphians lived in separate neighborhoods, belonged to separate churches and social organizations, and attended separate schools with all-white or all-black teaching staffs. If they shared the same social spaces in theaters or other public establishments, it was in separate seating areas. Although African Americans had served in Memphis government and on the police force from the 1870s through the 1890s, Lymus Wallace was the last black man to serve in city government until the 1960s, and when Dallas Lee retired in 1895 there would be no more blacks walking police beats in the city until 1948. Statewide poll taxes were instituted in the early 1890s, but blacks in Memphis continued to exercise their franchise. Influential black men and women in the city organized efforts to help those who could not afford to pay these taxes.[15]

Statewide streetcar segregation was instituted in 1905. Blacks were required to pay their fares in the front, get off the streetcar and reboard through the rear. Streetcar segregation aroused different levels of protest throughout the state, ranging from boycotts in Clarksville, Memphis, Knoxville, Chattanooga, and Nashville to court cases challenging the streetcar law (*Morrison v. State of Tennessee*, which originated in Memphis), to the formation by African Americans of their own separate transportation companies. Even ten-year-old Alberta Hunter felt the effects of segregation in the city, but as she later told her biographer, "I was always equal. I always felt I was good enough to do anything that anybody else could do, but I was not given a chance to do so." Alberta responded to streetcar segregation by taking down the sign marking where blacks and whites were supposed to sit, and sitting wherever she wanted to.[16]

However, racial contestation in the public arena of the streetcar was not the only discrimination facing African American children like Alberta Hunter. The effects of community-wide segregation laws affected the social and economic lives of all black Memphians, especially nonelites. Homes in the older downtown areas of the city where black residents like the Hunters lived often provided just the basic necessities of life, and mortality rates for blacks in Memphis were higher than for whites. As Memphis historian G. P. Hamilton noted in *The Bright Side of Memphis*, a compendium of information on the city's black population published in 1908, these high mortality rates were caused by "a lack of education and careful home training among the colored people," as well as poverty, which "is the cause of sickness, disease and death." Hamilton went on to note that it "cannot be denied that the circumstances of the colored people are not favorable when considered as a whole. Many are not able to provide for themselves the ordinary comforts of life." Hamilton was also concerned by the "alarming prevalence of consumption and other forms of pulmonary disease" that afflicted black Memphians—including Charles Hunter, who had succumbed to pneumonia just before Alberta's birth. "It is now predicted by some bearing the weight of medical authority," Hamilton revealed, "that it is merely a matter of time when the whole colored race will be destroyed by the great plagues of consumption. Furthermore it is advised that the general employment of colored people as household servants be, to a great extent, restricted, as their consumptive tendency is considered a menace to the health of the white race."[17]

Such dire warnings must have concerned Laura Hunter and Nancy Peterson since, like other working-class black women in the urban South, domestic work was their most likely livelihood. But their concerns were not simply about whether they would continue to find jobs. Laura Hunter and Nancy Peterson, like many other African American women, shared a deep concern for image and respectability. The suggestion that black women brought diseases into the houses that they tended implied that these women were unclean. Alberta later told her biographer that "Miss Laura kept their house clean as a pin," even though she couldn't force these same habits on her young daughter, who was nicknamed "Pig" because she "was always so dirty."

Color consciousness also plagued Alberta's family and community. The petite Alberta felt that her mother favored her older sister La Tosca, who was "tall and beautiful" with facial features that suggested the family's Native American heritage. La Tosca had "long, straight, shiny hair" and Alberta "went to sleep each night praying that she would awaken the next morning to find that her hair, too, had grown long and straight." Alberta also described Laura Hunter's half sister, "Aunt Fletcher" or "Aunt Mary," as a beautiful woman "very fair in complexion with straight black hair, 'like a white woman.'" Aunt Mary had two children by a white judge (identified in Alberta's biography only as Judge Bissel), a boy called Arthur and a girl named Kenneth. The latter looked "as if she were white and had chestnut brown hair." Another of Aunt Mary's children, Tom, was a "handsome boy" who "looked like an Indian." Alberta's stepfather, Theodore Beatty, "was fair-skinned and looked a bit like an Irishman." Alberta remembered that in turn-of-the-century Memphis, these differences in skin color and hair texture often translated into perceptions of superiority or privilege. "Aunt Deb" was "lighter-skinned than most of her neighbors. So she stayed pretty much to herself." Aunt Deb's granddaughter Daisey Topley, who "looked like a white child," was not allowed to play with darker-skinned children like Alberta.[18]

Regardless of skin color, life for African Americans in the segregated South was difficult. In Memphis, African American women like Laura Hunter and Nancy Peterson faced increasing competition for jobs and housing from rural migrants. Like other cities of the New South, including Atlanta and Nashville, Memphis was a beacon for rural southerners—black and white—who flocked to the city in the last quarter of the nineteenth century. The city's total population increased from 64,495 in 1890 to over 100,000 in 1900, and over 131,000 in 1910. By 1910 Memphis was thirty-seventh out of the one hundred most populous cities in the United States. Its closest southern rivals were Birmingham, Alabama, at number thirty-six with about fifteen hundred more residents; and Atlanta, Georgia, at number thirty-one with nearly twenty thousand more residents. By 1900 Memphis had moved ahead of Nashville as Tennessee's largest city. But the percentage of African Americans in the Memphis population declined from 48 percent in 1890, to 44 percent in 1900, and to 39 percent in 1910. As G. P. Hamilton also noted, "Both skilled and unskilled labor receive a scale of wages in some respects higher than in any other city in the South," but "everything in Memphis is high. House rent is high, provisions and clothing are high, water is high in the spring time and even pure air for breathing purposes is high."[19]

Memphis's black communities played a significant role in the development of the city. African Americans lived in all of the city's wards and districts, and as in other cities, Memphis's black population was socially, economically and politically diverse.[20] By the early 1900s forty black physicians and surgeons, seven dentists, and twelve lawyers practiced in Memphis. The city was home to two African American hospitals, two black cemeteries and four undertaking establishments, one black high school, seven black elementary schools, LeMoyne Normal School, and the University of West Tennessee, which offered programs in medicine, dentistry, pharmacy, law, and nursing. Businessman Robert R. Church organized the city's first black-owned bank, the Solvent Savings Bank and Trust Company. Like the families of other well-to-do businessmen and professionals, Church and his family lived in a stately mansion in the suburbs of downtown Memphis.

Despite the hardships of a primarily single-income household, Laura Hunter ensured that her children went to school for at least the basics of literacy. La Tosca and Alberta both attended Grant School, an African American elementary school on Auction Street.[21] Although many Memphis children from the working classes left school in their adolescent years to join the workforce and contribute to the family income, Hunter lived in a period where the city placed increasing importance on educating its young black and white children both, despite the persistence of racial segregation in all public institutions. By the first decade of the twentieth century, 80 percent of white children age six to fourteen attended school, while at least 60 percent of African American children in the same age bracket attended the seven schools in the city reserved for colored students.[22] Although formal education was not a consistent part of Alberta's childhood beyond elementary school, it played a role in her introduction to music. Hunter's love of music and her initial singing efforts began in elementary school. She later recalled that students and teachers noticed her musical talent in school singing programs and told her "she could sing, you know."[23]

But in spite of the models of middle-class respectability and Christian morality Laura Hunter and Nancy Peterson tried to present, Alberta's interest in music also attracted her to the underside of her Memphis community. At times, Laura Hunter worked as a domestic servant in a brothel in the center of a Memphis red light district—Gayoso Street, just off of Beale Street.[24] Although longtime Memphis resident and Beale Street historian George W. Lee's characterization of the constant activity of Gayoso came twenty years after Alberta Hunter left the city, the description was probably as fitting as it would have been earlier in the century:

> Gayoso "Street of Shame,"... had been aptly described as "red hot and low down." Its hundreds of lovely women—richly red brown like the glow of the sunset; white like the snow of an inaccessible mountain top, black and smooth like velvet with a soul—were brought to Gayosa [*sic*] each year to live in the twenty or more gaudy palaces of pleasure. There favors were offered to white men who were carefree and reckless in their spending.... These houses on Gayosa were gorgeously furnished;

> not even the castle of a baron could compare with them in grandeur. But the young women who went to Gayosa to live amid pleasure and hope invariably came out old and faded and broken, with bloodshot eyes.[25]

Lee's portrayal may have been somewhat romanticized, but the street was notorious as a center of criminal activity and was targeted for cleanup by progressive-era reformers.[26] Laura Hunter shielded her daughters from the activities occurring inside the houses of Gayoso. When Alberta and La Tosca visited their mother at work it was on the street in front of these brothels, not inside.[27] Young Alberta may not have understood that the young women living in these houses were prostitutes or that the ornate establishments were brothels. Yet she lived a life of contradictions, surrounded by excessive drinking, smoking, and young women who sold their bodies at her mother's workplace and the Christian virtues and middle-class ideals of her grandmother's church.

The most eminent dangers for young Alberta came not from the patrons of her mother's workplaces, but from the people who lived at or visited her home. She later described several instances of sexual abuse by a boyfriend of "Miss Nellie," the white landlady at a boardinghouse where Alberta lived with her mother and sister. Alberta was approximately thirteen years old at the time. According to Hunter the man "put his hands on me . . . he was a child molester, the dirty dog."[28] There was little recourse for black women and girls who suffered the sexual advances of white males. Hunter, fearful of her abuser and perhaps realizing that her accusations might not be believed and could cost her family even this semblance of a home, did not report the abuse to anyone, not even her mother. She was also sexually abused by the black principal of one of the local schools, whose wife ("Aunt Martha") was part of Hunter's female network. Aunt Martha was "the first person she remembers using a hot iron to straighten her hair." But her husband was "a dirty, stinking puppy," who Alberta claimed molested her and several other children in the neighborhood. She learned at an early age to dislike men. "I got so down on fellows that I hated to breathe the air that they breathed. 'Cause I thought they were taking advantage. I figured that if I told somebody those old men were doing this to me, they wouldn't believe me [because I was a child]."[29] She also felt she had lost her innocence and wanted to "just stay away from men" long after the abuse.

But the physical abuse of women was a constant aspect in her young life. Alberta's stepfather, Theodore Beatty, physically assaulted Laura, and Alberta would often be in the middle of these confrontations, attacking Beatty as he hit her mother.[30] Rampant domestic violence accompanied the poverty and racism that could be found in urban communities of the segregated South, and these early instances of abuse had a powerful effect on Alberta that lasted for the rest of her life.

Seeking refuge from sexual abuse and poverty, Alberta turned to the vibrant music scenes of Memphis. She had already absorbed the sacred hymns at Collins Chapel Church and the traditional secular music at Grant Elementary School. As she approached adolescence, Alberta turned her ear to the sounds of the popular music emanating from Beale Street. By the early 1900s the mile-long stretch of commercial and residential properties extended east from the wharf at the Mississippi River to Pigeon Roost Road.[31] Along the first three blocks, from the river to Hernando Street, Beale was lined with groceries, drugstores, restaurants, saloons, and rooming houses. Mansions that had been constructed by and still housed some of the city's wealthy white families were on either side of the street from Hernando to Pigeon Roost Road. But by the turn of the century, the Beale Street of Alberta Hunter's childhood was evolving into a black commercial district due in part to the efforts of the black entrepreneur Robert R. Church.[32] During the yellow fever epidemic of 1878, when nearly thirty thousand Memphians fled the city, Church, a saloon owner in the Beale Street area, purchased property at drastically reduced prices.[33] In 1899, when black Memphians could not use the city's public parks, Church built a recreational area for them. Church's Park, a landscaped six-acre site with picnic areas, playgrounds, and a bandstand, also housed an auditorium that seated twenty-two hundred people. At the time of his death in 1912 Church owned numerous commercial and residential properties along Beale, Gayoso, Second, Third, Fourth, and Pontotoc streets.[34]

Alberta Hunter always said that she never formally sang on Beale Street because it was not a respectable space for young black women who aspired to be middle class, given its associations with crime, violence, and vice.[35] Beale Street invited the rough-and-tumble behavior of riverboat workers eager to find temporary lodging at the street's rooming houses before spending their wages on alcohol, gambling, and sex in Beale's less savory establishments. In a two-week period in January 1910 many headlines in the Memphis paper the *Commercial Appeal* emphasized the violent behavior of African Americans near and around the Beale Street area, alerting the public to the activities of "big black brutes," "negro purse snatchers," and "bad negros [*sic*]" in general.[36] But these stereotyped descriptions masked Beale Street's more important role as one of Memphis's most significant black communities. Black churches and fraternal lodges, restaurants and theaters, as well as the offices of black businessmen and professionals, existed alongside (or above, in some cases) Beale Street's saloons, bordellos, and gambling houses.[37] In 1911 African American establishments like the Knights of Tabor Hall, Beale Street Baptist Church, the Star Printing Company, Church's Park and Auditorium, the Pastime Theater, the Lincoln Hotel, and the medical offices of Dr. F. M. Kneeland were all interspersed among the twenty African American residences, bars, and restaurants on Beale Street between Third and Fourth Streets. Beale Street was a true microcosm of African American life in the urban South.[38]

This was the early twentieth-century Beale Street that Alberta Hunter knew. She was attracted to the street not by the saloons or gamblers, but by music from the saloons, park bandstands, concert stages, and street corners. A burgeoning commercial blues music industry flourished in Memphis thanks to the arrival of African American composer and bandleader William Christopher (W. C.) Handy, the "Father of the Blues," who came to Memphis from Alabama in the early twentieth century. Handy, who specialized in brass band dance music, became an instructor for a band organized by the Memphis chapter of the Knights of Pythias, a fraternal organization. Handy took the blues melodies he heard from itinerant musicians when he lived in the Mississippi Delta and infused them into his dance band compositions in Memphis.[39] By the early 1900s his bands were some of the most sought-after musical ensembles in the city. In 1909 Handy wrote a campaign song for mayoral candidate E. H. Crump. The song became the first blues composition ever published when it was issued in 1911 as the "Memphis Blues." In 1913 Handy and his business partner, Harry Pace, opened Pace and Handy Music Company, a sheet music company that specialized in blues and popular African American music, at 386 Beale Street.[40]

In search of thematic inspiration to fuel his blues compositions, Handy spent much of his time in the saloons and entertainment institutions of Beale Street, both gathering ideas and testing out tunes with his various dance bands. Alberta Hunter was one of the adolescents who frequented the Handy bandstand in local Dixie Park on Florida Avenue; indeed, she and her friends spent much of their free time "stalking the Handy band."[41] While Hunter may have not sung a note on Beale Street in her teen years, her interest in the blues grew during the same period that Handy began composing the "Memphis Blues" and later the famed "St. Louis Blues."[42]

While W. C. Handy was making Beale Street a home for the blues, Alberta Hunter was growing weary of her Memphis home. She dropped out of school when she was around twelve or thirteen and began searching for ways to make her own money. In 1911 a petite sixteen-year-old Hunter used a child's railway pass and traveled with one of her former school teachers at Grant Elementary, Floyd Lillian Cummings, and Cummings's husband, to Chicago.[43]

The motives behind her move to Chicago echo those of the thousands of other African Americans who migrated to the urban North and West in the early twentieth century—hope for better economic opportunity and the desire to escape the racial violence of the South. Between 1910 and 1920, 56,442 African Americans flooded into Chicago alone, several thousand coming from Tennessee.[44] They saw the urban North, particularly New York, Detroit, and Chicago, as the promised land, and they hoped to trade the toil of sharecropping and domestic service for the higher wages of factory labor. Alberta's passion for music was only heightened by the stories she heard of singers earning ten dollars a week in Chicago.[45] In a society governed by racial and gender hierarchies, most African American women who worked outside of the home in the early 1900s South were limited to the tedious and strenuous labor of domestic service, child care, and laundry—occupations with which Alberta was already familiar through the labors of her mother, grandmother, and other women in Memphis. By the age of fifteen, Alberta was working as a laundress alongside others in her family to supplement the household income.[46] Laundresses earned as little as one dollar for an entire week's worth of washing, while domestic workers earned three to four dollars a week.[47] Food leftovers—or "service pans"—and cast-off clothing were often also part of a domestic's wages.[48] Hunter did not wish to be limited by the few work opportunities and paltry wages Memphis afforded a working-class black woman. She recalled, "There weren't any options for us colored girls. . . . I never knew what was going to happen to me, but I knew that something was going to happen, and I knew one of those days would be my day."[49] The promise of ten dollars a week doing something she had enjoyed as a pastime at school and church beckoned her to Chicago, and she hoped that her "day" would come after she fled the segregated South.

Once in Chicago, Hunter boarded with a family friend, Ellen Winston, in the common pattern of black female chain migration, in which single women relied on extended family or family friends who already lived in a new city. It was Winston who helped her find employment. But Hunter did not immediately find herself on the city's stages singing the blues. Instead, by day she did the same type of domestic work she had sought to escape in Memphis, and by night she visited saloons and after-hours clubs, hoping that owners would overlook her youth and give her an opportunity to sing. Hunter traded the often vice-filled corners of Memphis's Beale Street for the vibrant but often dangerous community of Chicago's Southside. The neighborhood in which Alberta struggled to succeed in Chicago was often plagued with pickpockets, bootleggers, and prostitutes. Yet Hunter survived because the women in the neighborhood watched over her.[50] Hunter told one biographer how prostitutes looked after the teenager by warning her about men who might try to entice her into the sex trade. The prostitutes "made the johns give her money," first for small domestic tasks and later as tips when Hunter finally got her chance to sing in Chicago saloons beginning in Dago Frank's, a small bar at the corner of Archer and State Streets that catered to pimps and prostitutes.[51]

In the period 1914 to 1921 Hunter rose to the top of the black music scene in Chicago. She initially lied about her age so that she would be allowed in bars and after-hours clubs. She began not by singing the blues, but by offering tentative renditions of popular tunes of the day such as "Where the River Shannon Flows."[52] Hunter progressed through Chicago's small venues performing at a black club called Hugh Hoskins, and a white club known as the Panama Café. All the while, Hunter worked to improve her voice, performance skills, and repertoire. She eventually reached Chicago's premiere club, the Dreamland Ballroom, where she was billed as the "Southside's Sweetheart."[53] Although she had left Memphis years before, Hunter brought the sounds of Beale Street to the North as she became one of the first singers to perform W. C. Handy's "St. Louis Blues" and "Beale Street Blues" in Chicago.

A typical Alberta Hunter performance was a sight to behold, and Chicago club regulars rarely missed her. In her early performances at bars on Archer and State Streets, prostitutes taught her how to wear makeup and select clothes that suited her small frame.[54] By the time she arrived at the Dreamland, Hunter was priding herself on being able to dress with sophistication and style. She wore beaded gowns with contrasting flowing scarves and with her hair coiffed in the latest style of the day.[55] She took requests from the audience and could croon popular love songs, belt out blues ballads, and deliver provocative double entendres. In "A Good Man Is Hard to Find," she sang about how a woman wanted to see her man "dead and in his grave" after finding him in "another chick's stall."[56] Hunter's very precise diction, a skill her mother had encouraged since childhood, meant that audiences need not miss any part of her songs. During the instrumental interludes, Alberta encouraged the bassist, pianist, or horn player to "play it" or "to lay it on me now, talk to me." To increase tips, Hunter walked through the ballroom and sang to individual tables, making select customers feel as if she were singing only to them. Hunter possessed a remarkable ability to make audiences feel at home by singing about emotions they all experienced at some point—love, joy, pain, laughter, and despair.

While Alberta was rising through the ranks in Chicago's music scene, she was sending money to her family in Memphis. In 1914 she relocated her mother to Chicago. She periodically shared an apartment with Laura while in Chicago and supported her mother the rest of her life. When Hunter briefly married waiter Willard Townsend in 1919 he joined his wife and mother-in-law in Alberta's

Chicago apartment. Hunter and Townsend soon separated and were divorced in 1923. In later interviews, Alberta blamed her divorce on her ineptitude at traditional domestic duties. Even with Laura's help, Alberta claimed that she just "wasn't the type to stay at home and see that the man's underwear is clean."[57] However, Hunter's biographer, Frank C. Taylor, maintains that Hunter's marriage failed because she was a lesbian and suggests that her sexuality stemmed in part from the repeated abuse she suffered at the hands of adult men as a little girl in Memphis.[58] Taylor depicted Hunter as very guarded about her sexuality. In Hunter's eyes, discussion of sexual relationships with anyone, male or female, was a mark of low-class behavior. According to Taylor, she looked down on other blues women when they had public arguments with their girlfriends and took great pains never to "share her private life with anybody in the world."[59] Hunter's veiled private life might have represented an effort to live up to her mother's image of respectability. As a black woman in the Jim Crow era, Hunter already had to fend off negative stereotypes about her integrity. As a blues singer in the heyday of the Jazz Age, she had to contend with disparaging critiques of her morality both from mainstream white society and middle-class African Americans who thought female entertainers were "loose" women who lived in society's margins because they were often financially independent, unmarried, and childless.[60] Although she never publicly admitted that she was a lesbian, she told Taylor that after she separated from Townsend, she met and became intimate friends with Lottie Tyler, the niece of legendary black vaudevillian Bert Williams. Alberta also developed a deep relationship and briefly lived with a black Chicago rooming house owner, Carrie Mae Ward.[61] The specific nature and details of Alberta's friendships with Tyler and Ward remain in shadow, yet Alberta stayed close to Tyler for several years, particularly after she left Chicago.

During Alberta's years in Chicago the new phonograph industry began to record African American female voices. Chicago's African American newspaper, the *Defender*, heralded the development: "Well, you've all heard the famous stars of the white race chirping their stuff on the different makes of phonograph records. [We've heard] Caruso . . . Tettrazini . . . Nora Bayes . . . but we have never—up to now—been able to hear one of our own ladies deliver the canned goods. . . . Okeh Phonograph company has initiated the idea by engaging the handsome, popular and capable vocalist, Mamie Gardner Smith."[62]

These first recordings of black vaudevillian Mamie Smith sold several thousand copies to a primarily African American market, ignited the "race record" boom, and furthered the classic blues music craze.[63] The classic or vaudeville blues performance often consisted of a female vocalist backed by bass, piano, drum, and brass instruments, and it reached the height of its popularity in the

1920s.[64] Popular classic blues artists included Mamie Smith, Ma Rainey, Trixie Smith, Ethel Waters, and Bessie Smith. Blues women sang about sexual desire, abuse, poverty, and unrequited love. Their music expressed the thoughts and experiences of working-class black women whose voices were often unheard outside of poor black neighborhoods. While middle-class African Americans had newspapers, pulpits, and organizations as platforms for their ideas, the concerns of laundresses, domestics, migrants, or day laborers might more readily be found in the lyrics of recordings such as "Chicago Bound Blues" or "Mistreated Blues." In 1921 Hunter traveled to New York and made her first recordings on Black Swan Records, the African American record label owned by Harry Pace, W. C. Handy's former business partner at Pace and Handy Music Company.[65] Hunter went on to record with jazz musicians like Fats Waller, Fletcher Henderson, Eubie Blake, and Louis Armstrong.

But Hunter avoided exclusive recording contracts that would have tied her to one record label and, instead, recorded under various names for several different companies, including Columbia, Okeh, Paramount, and Victor. On stage Hunter's soprano voice drew audiences into her tales of how "He's a Darned Good Man (to Have Hanging Around)" or how she had the "Daddy Blues," or the "Bleeding Hearted Blues." Not solely a vocalist, Hunter also wrote lyrics, and with pianist Lovie Austin had several hits, including "Down Hearted Blues" and "Chirpin' the Blues."[66] Her popularity in Chicago, in small venues and in the Dreamland Ballroom, encouraged her to seek even more recognition in New York City, specifically in Harlem—the 1920s "mecca of the New Negro."

Created by Alain Locke, a literature professor and one of the architects of the Harlem Renaissance, the term "New Negro" described urban African Americans in the post–World War I era. "New Negroes" challenged degrading stereotypes of African Americans that pervaded American society. Where negative images portrayed black people as lazy, oversexed, slow-witted, and eager to be subservient to white people, the "New Negro" was self-defined, determined, and ready to fight for social change.[67] According to Locke, a central goal of the "New Negro" and the Harlem Renaissance was to fight for acceptance and fuller integration into mainstream American society through cultural and artistic excellence.[68] Just how acceptable blues and jazz music were as examples of "black excellence" was a source of debate among middle-class and elite African Americans. By the mid-1920s hundreds of black visual, literary, and performance artists joined the thousands of southern black migrants who had made their home in Harlem. But the 1920s was the Jazz Age, and performers like Hunter and Smith were popular with black and white audiences alike. Hunter and her mother, Laura, were among the over sixty thousand African Americans who streamed into New York City during the decade.[69] Just as she had used her Memphis connections to make the trip to Chicago when she was a teenager, Hunter used her contacts at Black Swan Records to make this critical move to New York. There, she occasionally shared an apartment with her mother. But at other times she lived in a separate apartment with her Chicago friend, Lottie Tyler, who continued to be a pivotal part of Hunter's life in the early New York years.

In 1923 Hunter landed a part in the Broadway musical *How Come.* The part had been played by fellow Tennessee native (from Chattanooga) and blues woman Bessie Smith in the show's out-of-town runs.[70] The musical won rave reviews, and critics remarked that *How Come* "set a pace which it will be hard for most any of these new offerings to follow right through here."[71] The press lauded Hunter for infusing her personality into her compositions and noted that she was "the most advertised of present day singers."[72] Hunter continued to record in New York and travel throughout the East Coast after the musical closed. She also sought further performance opportunities outside the United States.

In the early twentieth century, Europe had provided African American entertainers with social acceptance and performance opportunities they were denied in the United States. This promise of greater income and social freedom drew Hunter to Paris and London in the late 1920s, and she remained throughout the Great Depression of the 1930s. In 1927 Hunter relocated to Paris's Montmartre district, famous for its artists and bohemian lifestyles. There she joined a community of African American expatriates that included Ada "Bricktop" Smith, Cora Green, Sidney Bechet, Florence Jones, and Josephine Baker.[73] Hunter won the part of Queenie in *Show Boat* at London's Drury Lane Theater in 1928. Alongside African American actor, activist, and vocalist Paul Robeson, Hunter performed in this show before European royalty and garnered international acclaim. "We had a ball [in Europe], it was a wonderful life, a great experience," she remembered.[74] She returned to New York in 1930 to perform in revues on Broadway, such as the musical *Change Your Luck* performed at the George M. Cohan Theater, and in off-Broadway follies at Greenwich Village's Cherry Lane Theatre.[75] But the relative freedom and escape from American race relations that Europe offered drew her back to Paris. She observed that "the Negro artists went to Europe because we were recognized and given a chance. . . . [P]eople in the United States would not have given us that chance."[76] Hunter's experiences in Paris stood in strict contrast to her upbringing in Memphis, where color and race defined where African Americans lived, worked, shopped, and worshiped. In editorials she sent to a black New York newspaper, *Amsterdam News*, Hunter told her fans in the United States, "I do not know when I will be home. . . . I am mad for the freedom of Paris. . . . [C]olor means nothing over here."[77]

This freedom influenced Hunter's selection of material and performance styles, and both expanded during her time abroad. She performed in such magnificent and exotic cities as Copenhagen, Cairo, Istanbul, and Athens, in addition to Paris, where she became fluent in French. She sang blues, ballads, popular songs, and folk songs from countries in which she performed, developing a repertoire of songs in Dutch, Italian, French, and German. Until 1939 Alberta made herself at home in the London and Paris entertainment scene, returning to the United States only occasionally for select engagements. But even as she traveled the world, Hunter used her earnings to provide for her mother in New York.

But not everywhere in Europe was there such an open atmosphere. As World War II loomed on the horizon, American embassies abroad advised United States citizens that they should return to the States for their own safety.[78] By the mid-1930s, countries that had turned to fascism, particularly Italy, adopted a whites-only entertainer policy in their cabarets and theaters.[79] Forced to permanently resettle in the United States when war officially commenced in 1939, Hunter was denied a renewal of her passport and was restricted to travel within the United States for the next few years.

In 1939 Hunter and Ethel Waters, a Philadelphia-born blues diva and actress who remained in New York during the 1930s, were both cast in the Broadway drama *Mamba's Daughters*. Hunter had met and performed on the same bill as Waters in New York in the 1920s, and Waters had been polite but distant. By the 1930s Waters, whose performances at Harlem's Cotton Club had brought her tremendous acclaim, did not want any female costar to outshine her, and Hunter was clearly an artistic rival. As Alberta remembered it, Waters "gave her a bad time" and treated her "like a dog," particularly when the audience applauded Hunter's performances.[80]

During the crises and uncertainty of World War II and the Korean War, Hunter entertained U.S. troops as part of the United Service Organizations (USO). She was one of the seven thousand USO performers in World War II and led one of the 126 entertainment units in the Korean War who entertained troops overseas at USO camp shows.[81] As the military was still segregated until 1948, Hunter initially was a member of the "all-Negro" units of the United States. Her engagement with the USO also brought her back to Memphis for a performance in the early 1950s.[82]

After her work with the USO in the 1950s, Alberta Hunter's performance and recording pace slowed considerably. She had traveled the world and performed and recorded with music legends while maintaining friendships and relationships and caring for her family. After over forty years in the entertainment industry, Hunter's blues and cabaret music style was not topping the charts. Dinah Washington, Ruth Brown, Big Mama Thornton, and Ella Fitzgerald were topping the R&B and jazz charts, and rock and roll was on the horizon.[83] Hunter wanted to retire from the industry while she was still remembered favorably at home and abroad. With Laura Hunter's death in January 1954 at the age of eighty-three, Alberta Hunter lost her desire to entertain. She had provided for her mother since she began singing professionally as a teenager and had written her weekly when she was on the road. Laura's absence pushed Alberta, now age fifty-eight, to reevaluate her own life and involvement in the music industry.

She slowly retreated from music in order "to serve humanity."[84] In 1954 shortly before her mother's death, Hunter began volunteering at the Joint Diseases Hospital in Harlem. She joined the Williams Institutional CME Church in New York City in 1954, the same denomination her grandmother had taken her to in Memphis.[85] In 1956 she began the next phase of her life. Hunter lied about her age again—claiming that she was only fifty years old, when she was in fact sixty-one—in order to enroll in a practical nursing course at the YMCA. After her graduation in 1957 she embarked on an entirely new career as a scrub nurse at Goldwater Hospital on Roosevelt Island in New York.[86] She came out of retirement briefly in the 1960s when record producer and blues music historian Chris Albertson asked her to record a classic blues retrospective with her former composing partner, Lovie Austin.[87] Otherwise, she generally refrained from involvement in the music industry throughout the tumultuous period of the 1960s, when the civil rights movement, antiwar protests, the rise of drug and countercultures, rock and roll, and the music of Motown and STAX artists eclipsed the work of classic blues and jazz performers. She pursued her second career, nursing, with her customary energy and only left this profession when the hospital administration forced her to retire in 1977, believing that she was seventy years old when she was really eighty-two.

But Hunter grew bored with retirement. After she sang at a private party in 1977, friend and singer Mabel Mercer and pianist Bobby Short convinced Hunter that she still had a powerful voice. Songwriter Charlie Bourgeois, who had attended the party, called club owner Barney Josephson to suggest that Hunter headline at Josephson's lounge, the Cookery in Greenwich Village, New York. Without an audition and based on her reputation alone, Josephson hired Alberta and she began singing at the Cookery.[88] She was eighty-two years old, but Hunter brought audiences back to the musical genres that had captivated listeners from Memphis to Paris in the first half of the twentieth century.

Between 1977 and 1984 Hunter performed in the United States, France, and Brazil, made television appearances, reissued some of her earlier recordings and compositions, and released a series of new live recordings that included "My Handy Man Ain't So Handy No More" and "A Good Man Is Hard to Find."[89] Alberta's mezzo-soprano voice had deepened with age to a husky tenor, and she continued to enchant audiences with tales of her ice delivery man, who "never lets her ice melt away, and gives her a nice, fresh piece everyday."[90] Her sexual double entendres were even more amusing when audiences observed a woman who appeared to be a kindly grandmother, wagging and snapping her fingers, tapping her feet, and winking as she spoke of how her man "strokes her fiddle." For Alberta, one of her most significant spectators during this period of her revival was President Jimmy Carter. On December 3, 1978, and again, at the closing of a governors' conference on February 27, 1979, the White House event staff asked Hunter to perform. The Carters were "amazed" and truly loved her performance, which Alberta called the pinnacle of her career, asking, "How much higher can you go . . . than to sing for your president?"[91]

Hunter's new efforts led her back to Memphis in 1978 for the opening of the Robert Altman film *Remember My Name* at the Orpheum Theater. The Orpheum, located at the corner of Beale and Main Streets, had hosted live shows fifty years earlier that featured performances by African American artists such as Duke Ellington and Cab Calloway; but at that time the venue was segregated.[92] To be acknowledged onstage at the Orpheum before an integrated audience seemed, to Alberta Hunter, a highly significant and monumental occurrence. But the Beale Street she came home to in 1978 was not the same community she had left in the early 1900s. Integration led some black Memphians to abandon former black neighborhoods for the suburbs. The violent racial confrontation that preceded and followed the 1968 assassination of Dr. Martin Luther King Jr. and, indeed, the assassination itself, tarnished the "land where the blues began."[93] The Beale Street Heritage Foundation used Alberta Hunter's 1978 visit to inject life into the crumbling district by recalling with new pride its historic musical past and international cultural importance. Hunter's extraordinary work and talent were part of this heritage. Mayor Wyeth Chandler gave her the key to the city and designated October 6, 1978, "Alberta Hunter Day."[94] But Hunter used her speech at the film's opening not to recount the importance of Memphis's place in blues history, but to chastise city leaders for not addressing the devastating effects of racism in the city and to ask them not "to let the city fall this way."[95]

Alberta's travels had come full circle, and she was determined not to allow racism and poverty, which had driven her away from Memphis in 1911, to be the city's primary legacy. Instead, she became an important ambassador for the preservation and reclamation of Memphis's heritage as "the home of the blues." When interviewed about her performance for President Carter, she told a reporter, "You tell them all, I'm up here keeping Memphis on the map. I'm holding it all up for them to see. And I'm letting the world know that Beale Street is still there and will again be the great street it used to be."[96]

Hunter returned to New York and resumed her singing engagements, many of which reached millions of new and old fans through her numerous appearances on television talk shows. In 1981 Hunter was included, along with anthropologist Margaret Mead; Congresswoman Eleanor Homes Norton; Supreme Court Justice Ruth Bader Ginsburg; activists Dorothy Height, Betty Friedan, and Gloria Steinem; tennis star Billie Jean King; and others, in the book *Particular Passions: Talks with Women Who Have Shaped Our Times*.[97] The volume provided role models for young women and future generations beyond the second wave of feminism.

By the 1980s she had been living alone in New York for thirty years and depended a great deal on the support of her friend and pianist Gerald Cook. In the last few months of her life, Cook and biographer Frank Taylor spent hours interviewing Hunter to ensure that her legacy would be preserved. Bolstered by a family of women, a fierce determination to succeed, and a unique gift for song and showmanship, Alberta Hunter had transformed herself from a poor black girl from Memphis into an internationally known and beloved vocalist, composer, and entertainer. She had been at the forefront of the blues music craze and among the first black female voices captured on record. Hunter's strength of mind, sense of adventure, and independent spirit took her from Memphis's Beale Street to Chicago and New York; to the cabarets of Paris, Cairo, Athens, and London; to the White House, and back again. Her life had mirrored the last lines of "Downhearted Blues." Her travels and achievements made her feel as if she really did "have the world in a jug, with the stopper in her hand."[98] Alberta Hunter used music to escape poverty and support her family, elude racial and gender hierarchies, and entertain listeners for much of the twentieth century. Perhaps the American entertainment audience truly did "come under her command."

Alberta Hunter died in New York City on October 17, 1984. A year later, the National Blues Awards Association named her top female singer in traditional blues at its ceremony in Memphis. Four years earlier, when she was nominated for a W. C. Handy Award but could not attend the ceremonies, she had given her birthplace an honor of its own. She would "be there in spirit," Alberta Hunter told a Memphis reporter who contacted her before the event, and "tell Memphis, I said, I'm still their child."[99]

NOTES

1. Jane Sanderson, "Alberta Hunter Is Her Name, Rhythm Her Game," *Memphis Commercial Appeal*, October 5, 1978; Edwin Howard, "'Contemporary Fable' to Open in Birthplace of the Blues," *Memphis Commercial Appeal*, October 6, 1978; Edwin Howard, "Three Women Triumph at World Premiere," *Memphis Commercial Appeal*, October 7, 1978; Alice Fulbright, "Homecoming for Alberta Hunter Opens with Tears of Joy at Changes," *Memphis Commercial Appeal*, October 7, 1978; "Night To Remember Is Witnessed by 2,600," *Memphis Commercial Appeal*, October 7, 1978; Bruce Cook, "Remember Her Name: The Lady, 83, Sings the Blues," *Washington Post*, October 22, 1978; Alberta Hunter, *Remember My Name*, CBS 25AP199, 1981.

2. Richard Harrington, "Singer Alberta Hunter, Made Comeback at 82," *Washington Post*, October 19, 1984; Joseph McLellan, "Back to the Blues; at 83, Alberta Hunter Wows Them Again," *Washington Post*, January 9, 1979; Onah Spencer, "Alberta Hunter, Born on Beale Street, Has Sung in 25 Countries," *Downbeat*, July 1994 (reprint of 1941 article).

3. Beverly G. Bond, "'Every Duty Incumbent Upon Them': African American Women in Nineteenth Century Memphis," *Trial and Triumph: Essays in Tennessee's African American History*, ed. Carroll Van West (Knoxville: University of Tennessee Press, 2002), 213–14.

4. Campbell Gibson and Kay Jung, Table 43: Tennessee in *Historical Census Statistics.* The lynching of Moss, McDowell, and Stewart, owners of People's Grocery Store on Walker Avenue, inspired Wells to lash out against the murder of her friends and systemically attack the pervasive myth that white mobs only murdered black men who had been accused of raping a white woman. See Ida B. Wells, *Southern Horrors. Lynch Law in All Its Phases* (New York: New York Age Print, 1892), 6; and David M. Tucker, *Black Pastors and Leaders: Memphis, 1819–1972* (Memphis: Memphis State University Press, 1975), 49–50.

5. Jacqueline Jones Royster, ed., *Southern Horrors and Other Writings: The Anti-Lynching Campaign of Ida B. Wells, 1892–1900* (Boston: Bedford/St. Martins, 1996), 112–17, 123, 132–34.

6. Ibid., 70.

7. Frank C. Taylor and Gerald Cook, *Alberta Hunter: A Celebration in Blues* (New York: McGraw-Hill, 1987), 4; Edwin Howard, "Alberta Hunter's Happily Coming Home," *Memphis Commercial Appeal*, September 26, 1978. Hunter told Edwin Howard of the *Memphis Commercial Appeal* that her mother was born in Knoxville. She also mentioned that she had used her sister Josephine Beatty's name on a record in 1924, because Hunter was under contract to Paramount and could not use her own name.

8. Shelby County Deaths, Charles Hunter, February 24, 1895, file 49763, Shelby County Archives; Taylor and Cook, *Alberta Hunter*, 1, 2.

9. *Alberta Hunter: My Castle's Rockin'*, directed by Stuart Goldman (Stuart Goldman Productions Inc., 1988); Taylor and Cook, *Alberta Hunter*, 4.

10. Taylor and Cook, *Alberta Hunter*, 1; R. L. Polk and Company, *Memphis City Directory* (1895); Shelby County Register of Deaths, March 9, 1899, Book #6, File (page) #52. Taylor states that Laura and her daughters moved to Josie McCoy's house at 170 Beale, across the street from Beale Street Baptist Church, but the actual address for the church is 379 Beale Street. Josie McCoy's house at 170

Beale would have been two blocks west of the church, especially if it were near Abraham Schwab's general store at 149 Beale. See also R. L. Polk and Company, *Memphis City Map*, 1909; *Goodspeed's General History of Tennessee* (Nashville: Goodspeed Publishing Co., 1887), 870; Robert A. Sigafoos, *Cotton Row to Beale Street: A Business History of Memphis* (Memphis: Memphis State University Press, 1979), 104.

11. McLellan, "Back to the Blues."

12. Sandra Mathias, "Together Again after 166 Years Collins Chapel and Memphis First," *Memphis Conference*, February 2, 2007, http://www.memphis-umc.org/reporter/2007/20070202web.pdf (accessed June 5, 2007).

13. Ibid.

14. Taylor and Cook, *Alberta Hunter*, 6–7.

15. "Colored Women Give Thanks," *Memphis Commercial Appeal*, September 22, 1894.

16. August Meier and Elliott Rudwick, "Negro Boycotts of Jim Crow Streetcars in Tennessee," *American Quarterly* 21, no. 4 (1969): 755–63; Taylor and Cook, *Alberta Hunter*, 12.

17. R. L. Polk and Company, *Memphis City Directory* (1907), 1; Beverly Bond and Janann Sherman, *Memphis in Black and White* (Charleston, S.C.: Arcadia Publishing, 2003), 66–73; G. P. Hamilton, *The Bright Side of Memphis* (1908; repr., Memphis: Burke's Book Store, [1978?]), 2–4. See also Tera Hunter, *To 'Joy My Freedom: Southern Black Women's Lives and Labors after the Civil War* (Cambridge, Mass.: Harvard University Press, 1997), chap. 9: "Tuberculosis Is the 'Negro Servants' Disease."

18. Taylor and Cook, *Alberta Hunter*, 4, 13, 16.

19. Taylor and Cook, *Alberta Hunter*, 3; Hamilton, *The Bright Side of Memphis*, 5.

20. See http://www.census.gov/population/www/documentation/twps0027.html; http://www2.census.gov/prod2/decennial/documents/36894832v3ch5.pdf.

21. Taylor and Cook, *Alberta Hunter*, 8; R. L. Polk and Company, *Memphis City Directory* (1902); Department of Commerce and Labor, Bureau of the Census, *Thirteenth Census of the United States: 1910—Population*, Memphis, Shelby County, Roll 1521, Book 1, 78a.

22. Sigafoos, *Cotton Row to Beale Street*, 131; R. L. Polk and Company, *Memphis City Directory* (1900).

23. *My Castle's Rockin'*.

24. Taylor and Cook, *Alberta Hunter*, 3; Bureau of the Census, *Thirteenth Census of the United States: 1910—Population*, Memphis, Shelby County, 78a.

25. George W. Lee, *Beale Street, Where the Blues Began* (New York: Robert O. Ballou, 1934), 104, 106.

26. Richard M. Raichelson, *Beale Street Talks: A Walking Tour down the Home of the Blues* (Memphis: Arcadia Records, 1999), 5; Sigafoos, *Cotton Row to Beale Street*, 128–30.

27. Taylor and Cook, *Alberta Hunter*, 3–4.

28. Ibid., 13–14.

29. Ibid., 14.

30. Ibid., 16.

31. Lee, *Beale Street*, 13; Raichelson, *Beale Street Talks*, 1; Margaret McKee and Fred Chisenhall, *Beale Street Black and Blue: Life and Music on Black America's Main Street* (Baton Rouge: Louisiana State University Press, 1981), 15.

32. Raichelson, *Beale Street Talks*, 2.

33. *Goodspeed's General History of Tennessee*, 876.

34. R. R. Church, L. M. Neely, and George Alban, "Last Will and Testament of R. R. Church,

January 14, 1911," *Journal of Negro History* 65, no. 2 (Spring 1980). See also Cherisse Jones-Branch, "Mary Church Terrell: Revisiting the Politics of Race, Class, and Gender," this volume.

35. Taylor and Cook, *Alberta Hunter*, 37.

36. "Bad Negro Shoots Police Officer," *Memphis Commercial Appeal*, January 3, 1910, "Girl Fights Negro Brute" *Memphis Commercial Appeal*, January 7, 1910; "Negro Battles with Officers," *Memphis Commercial Appeal*, January 17, 1910.

37. Taylor and Cook, *Alberta Hunter*, 9; Beverly G. Bond and Janann Sherman, *Images of America: Beale Street* (Charleston, S.C.: Arcadia Publishing Company, 2006).

38. R. L. Polk and Company, *Memphis City Directory*, 1911, 1534–35.

39. W. C. Handy, *Father of the Blues: An Autobiography* (New York: Macmillan Company, 1941), 93–94.

40. Ibid.; R. L. Polk and Company, *Memphis City Directory* (1911); W. C. Handy, Press Release Letter, Handy Brother Music Co. Inc., 1948 in W. C. Handy Collection, Archives Center, National Museum of American History, Smithsonian Institution; Raichelson, *Beale Street Talks*, 72, 78; Hamilton, *The Bright Side of Memphis*, 95; Bond and Sherman, *Memphis in Black and White*, 82–84. Handy's first residence, and the base for his orchestra, was on Ayers Street, but he later moved to Jennette Place. Both locations were in a working-class African American community.

41. R. L. Polk and Company, *Memphis City Directory* (1911); Taylor and Cook, *Alberta Hunter*, 17.

42. Handy, *Father of the Blues*, 102–21.

43. Taylor and Cook, *Alberta Hunter*, 21.

44. Appendix A: "Net Black Migration to Chicago, 1910–1920, by Age," in James R. Grossman, *Land of Hope: Chicago, Black Southerners and the Great Migration* (Chicago: University of Chicago Press, 1989).

45. Hubert Saal, "Rebirth of the Blues," *Newsweek*, October 31, 1977, 101; *My Castle's Rockin'*.

46. Bureau of the Census, *Thirteenth Census of the United States: 1910—Population*, Roll 1521, Book 1, 78a.

47. Susan Tucker, interview with Cecelia Gaudet in *Telling Memories among Southern Women: Domestic Workers and Their Employers in the Segregated South*, ed. Susan Tucker (Baton Rouge: Louisiana State University Press, 1988), 84. The average annual salary for a domestic worker in the United States in 1900 was $240 per year. See *Historical Statistics of the United States Colonial Times to 1970* (White Plains, N.Y.: Kraus International Publishers, 1989), 167.

48. For more on the social function of the service pan see Hunter, *To 'Joy My Freedom*, 60–61; and Stanley Lewis and Elizabeth Clark-Lewis, prod., *Freedom Bags*, videorecording (New York: Filmmakers Library, 1991).

49. Taylor and Cook, *Alberta Hunter*, 19.

50. *My Castle's Rockin'*.

51. Ibid.; Taylor and Cook, *Alberta Hunter*, 27–28.

52. Taylor and Cook, *Alberta Hunter*, 26.

53. Ibid. 33, 48; *My Castle's Rockin'*.

54. *My Castle's Rockin'*.

55. Taylor and Cook, *Alberta Hunter*, 40–41.

56. Eddie Green, "A Good Man Is Hard to Find," 1918.

57. Taylor and Cook, *Alberta Hunter*, 43.

58. Ibid., 42.

59. Ibid., 30.

60. Daphne Duval Harrison, *Black Pearls: Blues Queens of the 1920's* (New Brunswick, N.J.: Rutgers University Press, 1988), 30–31.

61. Taylor and Cook, *Alberta Hunter*, 34, 49.

62. "Making Records," *Chicago Defender*, March 18, 1920.

63. In order to capitalize on the growing interest for this "authentic" black music, record companies including Columbia and Okeh created a separate "Race Record" labeling system. For references on how blues prompted this system, see Harrison, *Black Pearls*, 44–61.

64. "Classic" blues by female performers were the first blues to be recorded, yet they were predated by the "country" or down-home blues. For in-depth discussion of the various styles of blues music see, William Barlow, *Looking Up and Down: The Emergence of Blues Culture* (Philadelphia: Temple University Press, 1989).

65. Taylor and Cook, *Alberta Hunter*, 50.

66. Alberta Hunter and Lovie Austin, "Chirpin' the Blues," sheet music in Samuel DeVincent Illustrated Sheet Music Collection, Archives Center, National Museum of American History, Smithsonian Institution.

67. Alain Locke, "The New Negro," in *The New Negro* (New York: Albert and Charles Boni, Inc., 1925), 5.

68. Ibid., 15.

69. Department of Commerce, *Negroes in the United States 1920–1932* (Washington, D.C.: Government Printing Office, 1935), 55.

70. Sidney Bechet, *Treat It Gentle* (New York: Hill and Wang, 1960), 134–36; "'How Come' in Town," *New York Amsterdam News*, March 24, 1923.

71. "New Show Opens at the Lafayette Monday Night," *New York Amsterdam News*, July 11, 1923.

72. James A. Jackson, "Recent Craze Bringing Another Big Publishing—House—to the Fore," *New York Amsterdam News*, July 11, 1923.

73. William Shack, *Harlem in Montmartre: A Paris Jazz Story between the Great Wars* (Berkeley: University of California Press, 2001), 41–47.

74. *My Castle's Rockin'*.

75. "'Change Your Luck' Has Nimble Dancers," *New York Times*, June 7, 1930; "New Revue in the Village," *New York Times*, June 30, 1930, 24.

76. Taylor and Cook, *Alberta Hunter*, 88.

77. Ibid., 91.

78. Shack, *Harlem in Montmartre*, 104.

79. Ibid., 101.

80. Taylor and Cook, *Alberta Hunter*, 146–47.

81. "USO Camp Shows," http://www.uso.mediaroom.com/index.php?s=pageB (accessed February 20, 2006).

82. Edwin Howard, "Alberta Hunter's Happily Coming Home," *Memphis Commercial Appeal*, September 26, 1978.

83. "Ten Top Songs of Each Year (1950–1969)," http://www.digitaldreamdoor.com/pages/best_songs50–69.html (accessed April 27, 2006).

84. John S. Wilson, "Alberta Hunter, 89, Cabaret Star Dies," *New York Times*, October 19, 1984.

85. Taylor and Cook, *Alberta Hunter*, 148.

86. McLellan, "Back to the Blues."

87. Alberta Hunter, *Chicago Living Legends: Alberta Hunter with Lovie Austin's Blues Serenaders*, Columbia Records, 1961.

88. Saal, "Rebirth of the Blues," 101.

89. Alberta Hunter, *Amtrak Blues*, CBS Inc., 1980.

90. Andy Razaf and Eubie Blake, "My Handy Man Ain't So Handy No More," 1930.

91. "Alberta Hunter's Triumph," *Memphis Commercial Appeal*, December 5, 1978; Taylor and Cook, *Alberta Hunter*, 237.

92. Raichelson, *Beale Street Talks*, 13–15.

93. McKee and Chisenhall, *Beale Street Black and Blue*, 5–10.

94. Cook, "Remember Her Name."

95. Taylor and Cook, *Alberta Hunter*, 249.

96. "Alberta Hunter's Triumph."

97. Lynn Gilbert and Gaylen Moore, *Particular Passions: Talks With Women Who Have Shaped Our Times* (New York: Clarkson N. Potter-Crown, 1981).

98. Cook, "Remember Her Name."

99. She was nominated for "Female Contemporary and Female Traditional Blues Artist of the Year" (Jane Sanderson, "Memphis' Famous 'Child' Salutes Handys," *Memphis Commercial Appeal*, November 14, 1980).

Phoebe Fairgrave Omlie

(1902–1975)

Wing Walker, Parachute Jumper, Air Racer

JANANN SHERMAN

Aviation pioneer Phoebe Fairgrave Omlie, a contemporary of women flyers like Amelia Earhart, Jacqueline Cochran, and Florence "Pancho" Barnes, brought Tennessee into the "air age"—a romance with the promise and possibilities of aviation that blossomed in the first few decades of the twentieth century.[1] And through her leadership, her adopted state led the nation in a host of innovations in aviation. After a thrilling career as a wing walker, parachutist, and air racer, she became one of the field's most ardent supporters and innovators, primarily through her work in aviation administration in the federal government. She was one of the most famous women in America in 1931, but she had long since faded into obscurity by the time she died in 1975.

Phoebe Jane Fairgrave was born in Des Moines, Iowa, in November 1902, the daughter of saloon keeper Andrew Fairgrave and his wife, Madge Traister. When Phoebe was twelve her family, including her fourteen-year-old brother Paul, moved to St. Paul, Minnesota.[2] According to family friends, she was a tomboy, always eager to join in games with neighborhood boys. She tinkered with cars and learned to drive at age twelve.[3] She attended Mechanic Arts High School, where she joined the literary society, acted in school plays, and announced her intention to study the law. These were heady days for young women, at the climax of the woman suffrage movement. Phoebe made quite a name for herself in her junior year when she was elected president of her class after the departure of the male president. The school newsletter noted, "She is the first girl to hold office as president of a Mechanic Arts class, but we felt that Phoebe was competent and had enough executive ability to manage the class successfully."[4]

PHOEBE FAIRGRAVE OMLIE

Circa 1922. Courtesy of Janann Sherman.

During her junior year, in September 1919, the president of the United States came to town. President Woodrow Wilson was on a national tour to mobilize public support for the Versailles Treaty and League of Nations.[5] Part of the celebration surrounding his visit was an air show featuring the Ruth Law Flying Circus, a three-plane troupe that amazed spectators by racing against cars, doing dozens of consecutive loops, and flying through fireworks.[6]

Phoebe was enchanted by the adventure of flying and inspired by the example of Ruth Law and likely that of the handful of other women who took to the skies during the early decades of the twentieth century. Their novelty ensured abundant publicity and inspired young girls to want to be like them.[7]

Phoebe began to haunt the local airfield, operated by the Curtiss Northwest Flying Company. The field was teeming with World War I veterans enamored with flying and trying to make a living in aviation. After some hesitation, veteran Ray Miller took her up for a ride, planning to give the girl "the works"—a few loops, maybe a nosedive or two—and get her good and sick. Then maybe she would leave them alone. But the pilot's efforts to discourage Phoebe were counterproductive. She enjoyed the thrills and resolved that she would fly.[8]

When she turned eighteen, Phoebe inherited a nest egg from her grandfather that she used to buy her own airplane, a war-surplus Curtiss JN-4D "Jenny."[9] On the same day that she spent $3,500 on the plane, she contracted with the Fox Film Corporation to do $3,500 worth of stunts for the movies.[10] The fledgling movie industry sought to tap into the romance, danger, and excitement of early aviation. During the 1920s and 1930s, approximately 250 major motion pictures featuring stunt flying were made. Fox also produced the Saturday matinee serial *The Perils of Pauline*, and Fox's Movietone News also carried aviation features.[11] There is little information available about stunt flying for the movies, except for those flyers specifically hired by Hollywood to work in Hollywood. These were all men. However, many freelancers with cameras haunted the barnstorming venues in the 1920s to gather additional footage.[12]

Phoebe was fearless and eagerly learned all the tricks: standing on her head on the top wing, dancing the Charleston on the top wing during touch-and-go landings, hanging by her teeth in the slipstream below the plane, changing from one plane to another in midair, and parachuting. Early parachuting was only for the fearless. The folded chute was held in a cloth duffle bag tied to a wing strut. The jumper had to crawl out on the wing in midflight, put on the harness, untie a string holding the bag closed, and then jump. The weight of the body falling away from the plane was supposed to pull the chute open. Most of the time it did. This was particularly risky for someone Phoebe's size, as she barely weighed ninety-five pounds.[13]

She planned her first parachute jump for April 9, 1921, but when she got to the field, "I found that Major Ray Miller, chief pilot for the company, did not wish to drop me off for fear of my getting killed. So on April 17, 1921, I engaged Lieut. V. C. Omlie, another pilot, to take me up to 1200 feet and let me jump." The parachute opened, but she struggled to control the swinging chute as she drifted towards a grove of trees. "Thus my first jump landed me unhurt but dangling from a tree top."[14]

Vernon Omlie, a twenty-five-year-old veteran of the Great War, had been a military flight instructor and dreamed of making his living in aviation. For the moment, the best he could do was fly for the Curtiss Company for twenty-five dollars a week. After working with Phoebe for a few weeks, while she perfected her wing walking and parachuting, Vernon quit his job with Curtiss to become Phoebe Fairgrave's personal pilot.[15]

Six months after her first plane ride and barely two months after her first jump, Phoebe decided to go for the world record in the parachute jump for women. Miss Mabel Cody had set the record at 11,000 feet in Chicago the previous summer. Now, on a blistering July 10, 1921, Phoebe climbed into a specially rigged high-performance Curtiss Oriole for the attempt, which was sanctioned by the Aero Club of America. Since the day was so hot, she dressed lightly, but because there were so many lakes in the vicinity and she couldn't swim, she wrapped an inflated inner tube around her body in case she should land in water.[16] The temperature dropped rapidly as the plane climbed to 12,000 feet; frost formed on her goggles and the motor started to miss from the cold. At 15,200 feet she climbed out onto the wing "with my hands numbed and my body shaking from the intense cold." She recalled,

> On account of the rarefied atmosphere I dropped like a bullet for about 500 feet, then the parachute started to quiver but did not open immediately. Finally the chute opened and I started a more gradual descent toward the earth. After reaching about 10,000 feet, I hit an air pocket. My chute nearly collapsed and [I] fell for about 1000 feet after which the chute again opened. I fell through several of these pockets in the course of my descent. . . . It took 20 minutes from the time my chute opened until I reached the ground, thus ending the biggest event in my career.[17]

She had handily broken the record. She had gotten sick on the way down, she told reporters, adding, "It was terrible; I never want to try it again."[18] But there were few things Phoebe would not try at least once. It is remarkable that she survived the 1920s, given the chances she took. During one early jump, the wind carried her into electric lines and she suffered serious burns on her arms, hands, and face. She was also involved in two serious plane crashes, both of them resulting in broken legs and multiple contusions, as well as numerous close calls and minor mishaps.[19]

After only a few short weeks of practice, the Phoebe Fairgrave Flying Circus took off, putting on shows and offering rides at county fairs and farmers' fields across the upper Midwest. The thrill show featured the daring Phoebe, wearing riding breeches, a silk shirt, a goggled leather helmet, and basketball shoes with suction soles.[20] Once airborne, she would climb to the top of the upper wing, the wind whipping her clothes, and stand there with her arms spread wide while Vernon put the plane through a couple of loops, landed on stubbled fields, and took off again. She told the press that wing walking wasn't much different from climbing up on a table: "You just shimmy up the strut, grab hold of something on the top wing, throw your knee up there, and climb up."[21] Phoebe had a special leather mouthpiece attached to the end of a rope that she gripped between her teeth as she dangled and twirled in the slipstream behind and beneath the plane while Vernon swooped low over the crowd.[22] The show stopper, though, was Phoebe's own invention—a double parachute drop.

In addition to the main parachute attached to the plane's wing, she carried a small reserve chute on her back. She would walk out on the wing wearing the harness and jump from the plane, which would open the first chute. Once free of the plane, she would cut the lines of her main chute and free fall. With the crowd holding its breath—thinking her chute had failed and she was headed for certain death—Phoebe would wait until the last possible minute, then pull the cord on the secret second chute just in time to slow her descent. The extra chute actually doubled the hazards, since the jumper had to depend on two chutes opening instead of just one. Phoebe interleaved the parachutes with newspapers to keep the lines from tangling. A safety precaution, it was also a crowd pleaser—the newspapers fluttering out like confetti.[23]

Barnstorming, for all its adventure, was a tough way to make a living. Many of the brave pilots who were trained in the war and came home to run flying circuses died in small heaps of wood and canvas. Most of the survivors went broke. Thousands would come out to see air shows, but it was difficult to ensure that all of them paid to see it, since one could watch from well beyond the paid infield.[24] The real money was made in encouraging the crowd to take rides at five or ten dollars a pop.

Phoebe and Vernon headed south at the end of 1921, hoping to stay one jump ahead of the coming winter weather. By December they had landed in Memphis, where the Claridge Hotel seized their luggage because of an unpaid bill.[25] Phoebe spent much of the winter speaking to various audiences around Memphis about her life in aviation and in the movies. One publicity poster featured a photograph of her standing spread-eagle on the top wing of a biplane in flight, with the announcement "Miss Phoebe Fairgrave, Movie Actress and Aviatrix, Will Appear in Person and Will Tell Her Experience in the Air at the Princess [Theater in Memphis] Tomorrow Night." She told her audience, "Doing high jumps and wing walking are lots of fun when once you get the hang of it."[26] In February 1922 Phoebe married her pilot and changed the name on the side of her plane to read the Phoebe Fairgrave Omlie Flying Circus. But they continued to struggle.

She and Vernon teamed up with an accomplished stunt flyer named Glenn Messer the following summer. Phoebe had ideas for newer and tougher stunts, one of which involved changing from plane to plane in midair. She talked Messer into working with her on it. They found a barn in Iowa that had a central runway from end to end. They rigged a trapeze bar and hung it from the rafters. Messer would hang by his knees from it and extend his hands. Phoebe stood on the seat of an old buggy, as Vernon piloted its team of horses. As Vernon drove the buggy through the barn, Phoebe would grasp Messer's hands and let him pull her up alongside him on the trapeze. Gradually they increased the speed of the horses to a fast trot until she could connect with Messer on every pass. When they thought they had it perfected, they alerted Fox to send along a camera crew to film it.

There were three planes: the upper plane carried Messer and the trapeze, Vernon flew the lower plane with Phoebe aboard, and the movie man was in the third, flying alongside.[27] Messer was hanging from the axle of the upper plane, hands down, ready to grasp Phoebe's hands, as the two pilots jockeyed into position, trying also to get in a good position for the camera. Suddenly the lower plane hit an updraft. Phoebe, standing near the right wing tip of the upper wing on the lower plane, with her toes hooked under two guy wires, saw the upper plane's propeller coming rapidly toward her. She dropped to her knees, reached under the leading edge of the wing, and grabbed a strut. Then she flipped forward and over the edge and shinnied down to the lower wing, safely out of the range of the whirling prop. The turbulent air continued for a few moments, and the propeller of the upper plane sliced into an aileron on the Omlie plane. Fortunately, Vernon was able to land safely and quickly patched it up. The movie people were still eager for the footage of the actual stunt, so they went up and did it all again, this time successfully. Talking it over later, they agreed to make the stunt a bit less dangerous. After that, Messer hung by his knees from the lowest rung of a twenty-foot rope ladder to grab Phoebe's hands, creating a margin of unoccupied air between the planes. The act became one of the most spectacular and exciting for the Messer-Fairgrave Flying Circus.[28]

But the partnership with Messer lasted only one summer. Vernon was eager to settle down and build himself a business around aviation. Memphis was warm and geographically central. Moreover, the city lacked aviation facilities, making it an auspicious place to build his new business. He set up operations first in the middle of the horse track at the Memphis Driving Park and began offering rides and lessons. He and Phoebe put on shows for the locals, including a thrilling automobile-to-plane transfer stunt. Pheobe would stand on the back seat as the car sped along the track. The plane would approach with a rope ladder extended. With one hand, she would grab the bottom rung and be lifted into the air.[29]

Gradually the Omlies attracted and trained a group of flying enthusiasts, many of them veterans of the Great War who had trained at Park Field in Millington, a military base just north of Memphis. Gathering together during the Armistice Day parade in 1925, they organized themselves into the Memphis Aero Club. A year later, again on Armistice Day, the Aero Club established Memphis's first real airport in Woodstock in north Shelby County, naming it Armstrong Field in honor of Lieutenant Guion Armstrong, a Memphis flyer who lost his life during the Great War.[30] Vernon opened Mid-South Airways at the field, offering flight instruction, cargo and passenger trips, and aerial photography. He taught hundreds to fly—including the author William Faulkner and his brother Dean, with whom Vernon formed a flying circus for a brief time. Faulkner wrote a novel called *Pylon*, loosely based on the Omlies and the barnstorming culture, published in 1935.[31] Mid-South Airways began the first scheduled air service in Memphis with a six-passenger Stinson Detroiter that flew three round trips a week to Chicago.[32]

On October 3, 1927, four months after his epic nonstop flight from New York to Paris, Charles Lindbergh landed his *Spirit of St. Louis* at Armstrong Field. He was midway through his tour of eighty-three cities to promote the airplane as a dependable mode of transportation. Memphis newspapers reported that "one hundred thousand people cheered him. . . . [A]ll Memphis fawned at his feet" as his motorcade passed on its way to Overton Park. There Lindbergh made a brief speech about the future of air travel. He even suggested that "Mud Island would be ideal for an airport."[33] Mayor Watkins Overton soon named an airport commission and leased 202 acres at the northeast corner of Winchester and Hollyford (now Airways) Roads for the area's first municipal airport.[34]

Vernon was happy to settle down. For him, barnstorming had been a stopgap measure to make money until he could establish a more stable career in aviation. But Phoebe still craved excitement and a career of her own. She gave up wing walking and took up piloting. In 1927 she became the first woman to receive a transport pilot's license, which allowed her to carry passengers. License number 199 was signed by Orville Wright and issued by the U.S. Department of Commerce, which had taken on the responsibility of licensing commercial pilots. She was also the first woman to earn an Aircraft and Engine Mechanics license. She believed this was essential to maintaining her independence in the air. Given the frequency of repairs early planes required, she did not want to have to depend on someone else to keep her flying.[35]

That same year, the Mississippi Delta adjoining Memphis was hit by a devastating flood that inundated some twenty-seven thousand square miles—an area "roughly equal to Massachusetts, Connecticut, New Hampshire and Vermont combined."[36] The Omlies leapt at the chance to help and to demonstrate that aviation was a serious and a publicly beneficial business. They flew daily patrols, spotting and reporting problems along the river's levees. They landed in precarious places to pick up stranded refugees and drop off medical personnel. They air-dropped hundreds of pounds of food and medical supplies all up and down the river. An aviation magazine later reported, "The Omlies were everywhere, flying above the ugly, yellow torrents, carrying photographers and newsmen, doctors, nurses, medicines, antitoxins and food. One of their planes had been equipped with pontoons, enabling them to land passengers, rescue marooned families and deliver nurses to fever-stricken homes. From Dorena, Missouri, to Vicksburg, Mississippi, they piloted their amphibian, and when a bridge washed away, they flew the mail from Memphis to Little Rock. 'It was eight weeks of tough work, with mighty little sleep,' says Mrs. Omlie, 'but it helped a lot to prove the usefulness of airplanes in disaster relief.'"[37]

In 1928, as Vernon was moving his management and charter operation to what would become the new Memphis Municipal Airport the following year, Phoebe was winning new fame. She had taken a position as a "consultant" with the Mono Aircraft Company of Illinois.[38] They built tiny (thirty-foot wingspan) single-wing two-seater Monocoupes. The company planned to market this consumer-friendly plane (so unlike the huge war surplus biplanes) to families and believed having a tiny woman demonstrate them would convince customers of their safety and practicality. Hoping to capitalize on the press's eager coverage of women in aviation, they provided the planes, and Phoebe provided the publicity.

In her first summer with the company, Phoebe decided to try to top the old altitude record of 20,800 feet held by Louise Thaden of Bentonville, Arkansas. Thaden had set the record the previous year in a specially equipped three-hundred-horsepower Beech Travel Air.[39] Phoebe took her little sixty-five-horsepower Monocoupe up to an astonishing 25,400 feet, but the attempt almost turned tragic. Later that evening, she gave an account of her experience to reporters:

> Everything went fine. I circled the field gaining altitude. It began to get pretty cold and I was glad I had plenty of warm clothes with me. At 19,000 feet it was winter and the atmosphere began to thin out. I put on the oxygen mask and turned the oxygen tanks on. I thought the oxygen would run out and cut down the flow and right there I made a mistake. I had it too thin and it began to tell on me. All the time I was watching my altimeter and thinking of Marvel Crosson, who holds the unofficial record of 24,000 feet, which she set in Los Angeles last May. At 24,000 feet, it was eight degrees above zero. When the altimeter reached 25,400 feet, my motor blew a spark plug. Almost at once the main oil line went bad and the oil began to spray back in my face. It blinded me and I was half dizzy from lack of sufficient oxygen. I nosed the ship down and started for earth. I guess I was pretty dizzy when I finally got down low enough to breathe well and peek out a little hole in the side of the cabin to see where I was heading. I managed to swing the plane around the field a couple of times and start side slipping and fish tailing in. The plane landed all right but I was groggy. I feel all right now. I can make the attempt again if I need to.

She didn't need to—she had set a new world altitude record for women and light aircraft.[40]

The late 1920s and early 1930s featured a series of transcontinental air races designed to demonstrate the safety and reliability of the era's new planes. Phoebe's work for Monocoupe shifted accordingly—from breaking records to air racing. She finished first or in the money most of the time. In 1928 she became "the first lady pilot in any air tour" when she joined the National Reliability Air Tour for the Edsel Ford trophy and $12,000 in prize money.[41] Twenty-seven planes departed Detroit on June 30 for a 5,304-mile journey that would take them through eighteen states over regions rough enough to test the stability of any plane and the skill of any pilot.[42] There were two Monocoupes in the race, flown by Phoebe and Jack Atkinson. These 55-horsepower planes were dwarfed by seventeen competitors in 225-horsepower planes and several others even higher rated.[43] Air race results were figured on a handicapping system that took horsepower and cubic inch displacement of the engines into account in order to allow planes of varying sizes to compete.

In her tiny black and orange Monocoupe, which she had named *Miss Memphis*, Phoebe traveled alone, taking neither navigator nor mechanic. She told reporters: "If I take a mechanic, they'll say that he flew the ship over the bad spots! No. I'll be my own mechanic and I'll fly my plane myself!"[44]

Reporters eagerly followed her progress. They seldom failed to mention that she was one of the few women who made her living flying, and they found her petite size and reputation for fearlessness charming. During the race, she became the first pilot to cross the Rockies in a light aircraft. She ground-looped and flipped the Monocoupe in Marfa, Texas, and went down again at Laguna Beach.[45] She finished the race in twenty-fourth place, but she did finish.[46] At the beginning of the National Air Tour, some questioned the feasibility of small planes handling the high altitudes and completing the tour's rigid schedule, but a Detroit reporter noted that "Mrs. Omlie's little plane carried her through the contest at an average speed of nearly seventy miles an hour, weathered sweltering heat over the desert in the southwest, soared over some of the highest peaks in the Rocky Mountains, maintained a more precise schedule than some of the higher powered and more expensive planes and completed the flight with an average of about fifteen miles on a gallon of gasoline."[47]

America staged its first "ladies' race" in 1929. The National Exchange Club, a men's service club, sponsored the All-Women's Air Derby from Santa Monica, California, to Cleveland, Ohio—a distance of 2,759 miles.[48] Of the seventy women who inquired about the race, only forty met the minimum requirements: a minimum of one hundred hours solo experience, twenty-five of which had to be cross-country flights of greater than forty miles from the starting point.[49] Phoebe was the senior pilot in the group, with an astonishing two thousand flying hours.[50] Twenty planes departed on August 17, 1929, and arrived nine days later, averaging just over three hundred miles a day.[51]

Press coverage of the race was predictably flippant. Will Rogers remarked that it looked "like a powder puff derby" to him, coining the perennial term.[52] The entrants were labeled "Petticoat Pilots," "Ladybirds," "Angels," even "Flying Flappers."[53] At every refueling stop and checkpoint, the "girls" were greeted by the press and expected to appear prettily attired for daily banquets and receptions. Though they flew in trousers or jodhpurs, the women carried dresses and cosmetics along for their public appearances. The festivities often stretched into late evening. Two hours sleep became the norm.[54] And the race itself was grueling. Heat over the desert Southwest hovered around 110 degrees, making gaining altitude with limited horsepower difficult. Hot air is thin air, creating less lift. Further, the heat sometimes caused extreme turbulence and dust storms. Thaden wrote of "violent updrafts followed by equally vicious downdrafts [that] threw the plane into awkward positions until it might have been a toy in giant hands flung about in devilish mischievous glee."[55] Because they had no information about winds aloft, dead reckoning (flying by compass heading) was unreliable.[56] The pilots, with maps propped on their knees (many of them in open cockpits) tried to follow roads and known landmarks. Over the desolate terrain, Thaden's imagination tortured her. "Through your mind's eye flashes a picture of a twisted mass of tangled wreckage, lying in a small crumpled heap far off the beaten track. You see yourself painfully crawling from between broken longerons [*sic*] and telescoped cowling, to lie gasping under the pitiless glare of the desert sun, helpless and alone."[57]

Wrecks were commonplace. Repairs were often done on the spot, especially during races. Sometimes crews followed, or airport personnel rallied to help racers. More often, racers helped themselves. Blanche Noyes was forced to land in a desolate area of Texas when she discovered that the back end of her plane was on fire. She landed, put out the fire, and took off again.[58] At Pecos, Texas, Pancho Barnes overshot the runway and hit a car, wrecking both it and her plane. She lost her way after returning to the race and made an unscheduled stop in Mexico. Amelia Earhart nosed her plane over on landing in Yuma and broke her propeller.[59] Worst of all, on the third leg, from Phoenix to Douglas, Marvel Crosson crashed and died in the desert. Editorial writers called for cancellation of the "ill-advised competition" as too hazardous for women. Amelia Earhart responded, "Marvel Crosson left a challenge to the women of the Derby and there is certainly no aftermath of fear among us." The women vowed to continue.[60] The race went smoothly for Phoebe, and she led in her CW class on every leg.[61]

Louise Thaden beat out Gladys O'Donnell and Amelia Earhart in the DW class, and Phoebe won the light plane division in *Miss Memphis*. She made the 2,723 miles in twenty-five hours ten minutes. Because judges used a complicated handicapping formula to determine the winner, the press erroneously reported Louise Thaden as the winner, since she had arrived at the destination field first. Phoebe Omlie actually won the race, 289.3 points to Thaden's 273.2. Then she won a closed-course (marked out by pylons on the ground) beat-the-clock event at 112.38 mph.[62]

At the completion of the competition at Cleveland, this small sorority of women welcomed the chance to share their experiences with one another. After they had all arrived, Phoebe Omlie, Louise Thaden, Amelia Earhart, Gladys O'Donnell, Ruth Nichols, and Blanche Noyes met under the grandstand. At Phoebe's suggestion, they decided to form an organization for women pilots for the purpose of "good fellowship, jobs and a central office and files on women in aviation." The women sent out solicitations to the 117 female pilots then licensed in the United States. Ninety-nine of them became charter members, so they named themselves the Ninety-Nines.[63] Louise Thaden led the group on an informal basis until they organized, then stepped aside to let Amelia Earhart lead as the Ninety-Nines' first president. Phoebe would value the friendship and collegiality of these women all of her life.

Phoebe continued to pursue air racing titles in *Miss Memphis*. Some thirty-five thousand spectators cheered her decisive win in the Women's Dixie Derby of 1930, a 1,575-mile race through the South that ended in Chicago with a spectacular air show. She took the $3,000 first place cash prize (equivalent to almost $35,000 in current dollars), an undetermined amount of lap money for closed-course races, and the Washington City Club trophy.[64] The next year, she was the overall winner in the 1931 Transcontinental Handicap Air Derby, a race from Santa Monica to Cleveland, besting fifty-five other entrants, including thirty-six male pilots. Back in Cleveland, she also won two "mad-dash" 30-mile closed course races. She took home another $3,000 in prize money and a brand-new Cord automobile. They draped a big horseshoe of roses around her neck and her picture was published around the nation.[65]

The money really helped. The Depression had hit Mid-South Airways hard. For a time, Vernon was forced to sell his controlling interest to the Curtiss-Wright Company, although he remained as president and manager of Mid-South.[66]

His wife was, in 1931, one of the most famous women in America. Then, as now, political candidates sought the endorsement of celebrities. Two weeks after her win in Cleveland, Phoebe received a telegram from the Democratic National Committee, signed by Eleanor Roosevelt. It read:

> AS ONE OF THE LEADING WOMEN FLYERS IN THE COUNTRY AND A SOUTHERNER WOULD YOU BE WILLING TO HELP US ON THE DEMOCRATIC CAMPAIGN STOP OUR IDEA WAS THAT IF YOU COULD POSSIBLY ARRANGE IT WE SHOULD LIKE TO HAVE YOU FLY TO NEW YORK MEET DEMOCRATIC OFFICIALS AS OUR GUEST RECEIVE DEMOCRATIC CAMPAIGN LITERATURE FROM THE NATIONAL COMMITTEE HERE AND FLY BACK WITH IT TO MEMPHIS WHERE YOU WOULD AGAIN BE MET BY A NATIONAL COMMITTEE WOMAN STOP NEEDLESS TO DAY IT WOULD BE SPLENDID PUBLICITY FOR THE DEMOCRATS AND WE SHOULD GREATLY APPRECIATE IT IF YOU COULD GET IN TOUCH WITH ME BY RETURN WIRE COLLECT ON THE MATTER I SHOULD BE GREATLY OBLIGED.[67]

Phoebe promptly flew to New York, met Committeewoman Sarah Fain, repainted the side of *Miss Memphis* to read "The Victory Pilots—Win with Roosevelt," and flew some twenty thousand miles in twelve different states to champion the candidacy of Franklin D. Roosevelt.[68]

The Roosevelt camp, in its success, was grateful. After the inauguration, Phoebe received an appropriate appointment—Special Advisor for Air Intelligence to the National Advisory Committee for Aeronautics (the research and development division). She was to act as liaison officer between the Bureau of Air Commerce and NACA, the predecessor of the National Aeronautics and Space Administration (NASA). Adding to her long list of firsts, Phoebe became the first woman in the federal government to hold an official post connected with aviation.

Over the next few years, she completed a survey of all airports and facilities throughout the United States for the Bureau of Air Commerce and the NACA. She helped with the development of tricycle landing gear at the NACA Langley Field Laboratories. Tricycle gear was developed in the early 1930s as a more stable landing platform for small aircraft. It was easier to handle than conventional gear (which had a wheel at the tail), much less susceptible to crosswinds, and easier to land. Phoebe also built a model and led a design contest that resulted in the development of the Hammond airplane. The Hammond was initially designed to be an "everyman's safe, low-cost, foolproof airplane." The notion of an airplane in every garage was an intriguing promotional idea of aviation enthusiasts in the 1930s, and one that has historically persisted. But neither the Hammond, nor any other plans for low-cost "foolproof" airplanes, proved practical because of engineering difficulties and price.[69]

Among Phoebe's most significant achievements was the air marking program that she conceived and initiated in 1935, driven no doubt by her own and her colleagues' cross-country experiences of flying over uncharted territory and struggling to hold a thumb on a map in an open cockpit. This navigational aid program called for twelve-foot black and orange letters to be painted on the roofs of barns, factories, warehouses, and water tanks. Visible from four thousand feet, each marker identified the locale, gave the northern bearing, and indicated by circle, arrow, and number the distance and direction of the nearest airport. The air markers were to be placed across the country at fifteen-square-mile intervals. Financed by the Works Progress Administration's $120 million airport and airway development program, air marking not only helped flyers but provided thousands of jobs for unemployed men as well as a handful of women pilots. Phoebe hired Blanche Noyes, Helen Richey, Louise Thaden, Nancy Harkness, and Helen McCloskey to establish and administer the program in all forty-eight states. The marker program was an unqualified success.[70] Within eighteen months some sixteen thousand markers were completed. Phoebe and her flying staff received well-deserved credit for both an innovative idea and effective execution. The program, however, was short-circuited by the war looming on the horizon. Panicky civil defense officials feared that the markers might help invading enemy airplanes find their targets, so they hired another set of workers to paint over all markers within 150 miles of coasts. The government revived the program after the war under the leadership of Blanche Noyes.[71]

In 1934 famous radio broadcaster Mary Margaret McBride named Phoebe one of twelve women who were then contributing most to American life.[72] In 1935 First Lady Eleanor Roosevelt honored Phoebe Omlie along with a host of women achievers, whom she said had been a constant inspiration to her and to the country and "whose achievements make it safe to say that the world is progressing."[73]

Unfortunately, personal tragedy soon overshadowed Phoebe's triumph. On August 5, 1936, Vernon Omlie and seven others died when *The City of Memphis*, a commercial airliner, crashed while trying to land in fog in St. Louis. The plane cartwheeled and blew apart. Vernon was dead at age forty.[74] A devastated Phoebe resigned her post with the NACA and rushed home to Memphis to bury her husband and flying partner. She did not return to Washington for several years, but she did not give up her aviation career nor her keen interest in politics. She promptly took to the sky again to campaign for Roosevelt. Along with Democratic committeewoman Izetta Jewell Miller and assistant attorney general Stella Akin of Georgia, Phoebe logged 10,000 miles, stopping in 150 towns in twenty-two states during the six-week campaign trip.[75]

In 1937, while living in Memphis, Phoebe coauthored the state's new aviation act with W. Percy MacDonald, chairman of the Tennessee Aviation Commission and one of the original members of the Memphis Aero Club. This established Tennessee as the first state to dedicate state funds for the training of aviators. The bill provided for an aviation fuel tax to be divided between maintenance and improvements to state airports and aviation education for Tennessee's youth. Under this program, Phoebe introduced the first vocational courses in aviation in public schools and set up ground schools at airports in Memphis, Nashville, Chattanooga, Knoxville, and the Tri-Cities. She taught the aviation classes in Memphis city schools herself; students receiving the highest scores were awarded flight scholarships.[76] The program lasted two years, during which sixty men and fifteen women completed the program and secured private pilot's licenses.[77] As the war overseas heated up, most of the male pilots went into the Army Air Corps, and the federal government took over the Tennessee schools. These became a model for the national Civilian Pilot Training Program. The women trainees were dismissed.[78]

Phoebe returned to Washington in 1941 as Senior Private Flying Specialist of the Civil Aeronautics Authority (CAA), to coordinate aviation activities for the WPA, the National Defense Commission, and the Department of Education.

During the first months of that year she traveled some twelve thousand miles, visiting more than seventy cities in twenty-two states. She established sixty-six aviation schools. One of these, in Tuskegee, Alabama, was the only school that trained black pilots.[79] Later that year, she visited more than two hundred airports throughout the country to choose those best suited for training ground crews to service military planes during the war.[80]

Early in 1942 she returned to Tennessee (on loan from the CAA) to establish a model program intended to alleviate an anticipated pilot shortage by training women as primary flight instructors for both the Army Air Forces and the Navy. The CAA anticipated training 200,000 military pilots per year. "To do that," said CAA administrator C. I. Stanton, "we shall need at least 5,000 women instructors."[81] Applicants for the Women's Flight and Ground School Experimental Training Program were required to be single, or if married, their husbands had to be in active military service. Each applicant had to hold a private license or better, with over 120 hours of flying time, and they had to agree to instruct wherever and whenever the bureau decided to place them. In return, the bureau promised each woman 62 hours of supervised flying, 216 hours of ground school instruction, 162 hours of flight instructors' ground school, and, at Phoebe's insistence, another 162 hours of mechanical training. From over a thousand applicants, Phoebe chose the top ten for the model program.[82] Their training was tough and Phoebe expected a lot. The training had to be rigorous, because in such nontraditional arenas, women had to be better schooled, better trained, better skilled than men, and beyond reproach. She kept the school deliberately spartan and resisted the press's attempts to talk about her women as glamour girls. Her ten graduates ultimately trained more than five hundred men. Phoebe had expected that the federal government would adopt the program. But the military was reluctant to use women flight instructors to train men, regardless of need, and disbanded the program.[83]

After the war, Phoebe continued to conduct aviation research involving a broad array of aviation issues and concerns. One was an extensive analysis of flight-training methods, and included the installation of photographic and sound-recording devices in training planes to record the stresses of students learning to fly. She did an exhaustive survey of fatal air accidents that resulted from the stall condition of aircraft. Another study provided economic information about the financial status of persons investing in aircraft. A third large project was to formulate plans to coordinate the activities of federal and state agencies and standardize practice for Air Search and Rescue.[84] But she was becoming increasingly unhappy about changes at the Civil Aeronautics Administration as President Truman appointed more non-aviation people to the hierarchy. She abruptly resigned in 1952, complaining about excessive regulations and federal interference in civil aviation.[85] Phoebe would remain out of aviation for the rest of her life.

Back home, she bought a cattle farm in Como, Mississippi, something she and Vernon had planned for retirement. Five years later she traded it for a hotel and cafe in Lambert, Mississippi. It was destroyed by a tornado in 1960. Phoebe lost everything. By 1961 she was broke, living with friends in Memphis, and in the early stages of lung cancer. She made a few public speeches, mostly to rail about excessive regulation of aviation and education, but mostly she was publicly invisible.[86]

In 1970 Phoebe checked into a fleabag hotel in Indianapolis and never checked out. She lived there for five years, a victim of poverty, lung cancer, alcoholism, and old age—too proud to let anyone see her in what she described in letters to friends as her deteriorated condition. She died on July 17, 1975, at age seventy-three. Her obituary in the *Indianapolis Star* paints a grim picture of her last days: "She wore silver wings on her lapel. She met acquaintances for good conversation at the YWCA or in a busy hotel lobby. Seldom did she invite guests to her $21 a week shabby room. She ate one full meal a day, and kept eggs, butter and milk in her window. Her small Social Security check and much smaller amount from her husband's pension sustained her. She would have no part of welfare or food stamps." The Ninety-Nines of Memphis brought her back for burial next to her husband in Forest Hill Cemetery.[87]

James T. Kacarides, editor of the *Memphis Flyer*, the publication of the Memphis Experimental Aircraft Association, began to lobby to get an aviation facility named for Phoebe Omlie in the 1970s. He first tried to get Shelby County Airport named for her, but it was instead named for Charles W. Baker, a former Millington mayor. Then he tried to get the Mud Island Downtown Airport named for her when it was relocated north of town; instead it was named for Brigadier General DeWitt Spain, an Air Force officer. Kacarides's suggestion that her name be included in the Memphis International Airport's designation was rejected by the Airport Authority. Undaunted, he persuaded members of Tennessee's congressional delegation to initiate a bill that would name the new Federal Aviation control tower at Memphis International for Phoebe Omlie.[88] He wrote, "Her place in the pages of aviation history is unchallenged. A woman of daring, courage, intelligence and devotion to the 'air age,' she ranks as one of the greatest participants in American progress."[89]

In 1982, sixty years after Phoebe and Vernon landed in Memphis and brought the city into the air age, President Ronald Reagan signed a bill designating the airport control tower as Omlie Tower. Unfortunately, no dedication ceremony was ever held; the commemorative plaque from the Federal Aviation Administration never arrived; the honor accorded Phoebe Omlie was never fulfilled.[90]

NOTES

1. "Air age" was in common usage following World War I; it sometimes functioned as a synonym for modern times.

2. Gene Slack Scharlau, "Phoebe: A Biography" (unpublished manuscript, in possession of the author, 1988), 1. Scharlau was a licensed pilot (1938), a contemporary of Phoebe's, and aviation editor for the Tennessee Bureau of Aeronautics and the *Nashville Tennessean*. Scharlau died while this manuscript was in process in the late 1980s.

3. Neighbors Harold E. Ruttenberg and Harold Dahlquist quoted in *St. Paul Pioneer Press*, July 10, 1967.

4. *The M* 7, no. 3 (1919): 60, in Minnesota Historical Society archives, St. Paul.

5. Wilson began his eight thousand mile tour on September 3, 1919, arriving in St. Paul on September 9. Itinerary from *Literary Digest*, September 15, 1919, reproduced at history.acusd.edu/gen/WW2Timeline/1919League2.html; Jean Adams and Margaret Kimball, *Heroines of the Sky* (Doubleday, Doran and Co., 1942), 69–70; Charles Lane Cullen, "There's No Stopping a Woman of Courage Like This," *The American Magazine*, August 1929, 28–29, 141–43.

6. On December 17, 1916, Ruth Law flew an aerial salute to President Wilson aboard his yacht, *Mayflower*, in New York harbor. She had mounted magnesium flares and an electric sign spelling "Liberty" on her plane's lower wing. Law's aviation career came to an abrupt halt in 1922 when her husband, fearing for her life, put an announcement of her retirement in the newspaper. She deferred to her husband's wishes. Charles E. Planck, *Women with Wings* (New York: Harper and Brothers, 1942), 52; Kathleen Brooks-Pazmany, *United States Women in Aviation, 1919–1929* (Washington, D.C.: Smithsonian Institution Press, 1991), 11; Bill Guston, ed., *Aviation Year by Year* (London: Dorling Kindersley Limited, 2001), 141.

7. A few women flew in France in the 1910s. Blanche Stuart Scott was declared the first American aviatrix by her mentor Glenn Curtiss in 1910; Katherine Stinson began flying exhibition aerobatics in 1914; her sister Majorie and brother Eddie were also pilots. Others in this early period included the first black woman flyer, Bessie Coleman, and Laura Bromwell, who set a record of 87 loop-the-loops over Mineola, New York, in 1920; she topped that with 199 consecutive loops in 1921, stopping only when she ran low on fuel. Lu Hollander, Gene Nora Jessen, and Verna West, *The Ninety-Nines: Yesterday, Today, Tomorrow* (Paducah, Ky.: Turner Publishing Company, 1996), 10; Brooks-Pazmany, *United States Women in Aviation*, 2–4.

8. Planck, *Women with Wings*, 52. Charles Planck was a personal friend of Phoebe's who worked with her in early aviation circles in Washington in the 1930s.

9. Cullen, "There's No Stopping a Woman," 142, indicated that Phoebe's inheritance was four thousand dollars. This source seems to be the best concerning much about Omlie's biography to 1929; when asked for biographical information about his wife for an encyclopedia article, Vernon referred the author to this article for details. Exchange in Phoebe Fairgrave Omlie Personnel File, Federal Records Center, St. Louis (hereafter cited as Personnel File).

10. This was an exchange of considerable money in 1920, the equivalent of $34,000 in 2005 dollars. Cullen, "There's No Stopping a Woman," 142; Planck, *Women with Wings*, 52.

11. *The Perils of Pauline* was a cliffhanger serial, released in weekly installments, featuring Pearl White as the adventurous heroine. Each episode would end with her in a life-threatening situation, from which she would be rescued at the beginning of the next.

12. See H. Hugh Wynne, *The Motion Picture Stunt Pilots and Hollywood's Classic Aviation Movies* (Missoula, Mont.: Pictorial Histories Publishing, 1987); Jim and Maxine Greenwood, *Stunt Flying in the Movies* (Blue Ridge Summit, Pa.: TAB Books, 1982); Don Dwiggins, *The Air Devils: The Story of Balloonists, Barnstormers, and Stunt Pilots* (New York: J. B. Lippincott Company, 1966).

13. Planck, *Women with Wings*, 53.

14. Phoebe Fairgrave, "Jumps I Have Made," *The M* 10, no. 3 (1922): 23–24.

15. Vernon Omlie's date book for Saturday, May 21, 1921, reads: "Started as pilot for Phoebe Fairgrave, quitting a position with the Curtiss N. W. Airplane Co. to do so." In possession of author.

16. Photo of her with inner tube around her waist in "She Made Record Drop," *Minneapolis Evening Tribune*, November 11, 1921.

17. Fairgrave, "Jumps I Have Made," 23–24.

18. "Breaks Parachute Drop Record for Women; Vows 'Never Again'" *Des Moines Evening Tribune*, July 11, 1921.

19. Cullen, "There's No Stopping a Woman," 144; Scharlau, "Phoebe," 56–57; Personnel File.

20. From article in "Phoebe Fairgrave Breaks World's Mark in 15,200-Foot 'Chute Jump," *St. Paul Pioneer Press*, July 11, 1921, quoted in "Daredevil Phoebe," *St. Paul Pioneer Press*, July 10, 1967.

21. "18-Year-Old Girl to Make 15,000 Foot Parachute Drop," *Minneapolis Morning Tribune*, July 10, 1921.

22. The actual bit she used is in the historical room at Memphis International Airport.

23. "Aerobatic Athlete of the Airways," *Memphis Press-Scimitar*, October 28, 1980.

24. A clipping from 1921 notes over a thousand people parked their cars along the road "refusing to pay admission" and hundreds of others also lined the fences, also refusing to pay admission ("Air Show Attracts 15,000," *Fairfield (Iowa) Daily Ledger–Journal*, August 5, 1921).

25. Paul R. Coppock, "Those Daring Young Aviators" *Memphis Commercial Appeal*, September 19, 1982.

26. "Actress and Aviatrix Phoebe Fairgrave," *Memphis News-Scimitar*, December 19, 1921. In early publicity posters she listed herself as "Movie Actress and Aviatrix." Princess Theater poster circa 1922 in File: Memphis-biography-Omlie, Phoebe Fairgrave, Memphis Room, Memphis/Shelby County Library.

27. Planck, *Women with Wings*, 53–55.

28. Ibid; *Fairfield (Iowa) Daily Ledger–Journal*, August 5, 1921.

29. Scharlau, "Phoebe," 49.

30. Harry Martin, "Aviation in Memphis . . . ," *Memphis Commercial Appeal*, June 11, 1933, Sunday magazine. Historical marker, created in 1987 by the Memphis–Shelby County Airport Authority and the Shelby County Historical Commission.

31. Relationship with Dean Faulkner noted in Vernon Omlie obituary, "Capt. Omlie Dared Death Many Times," *Memphis Press Scimitar*, August 6, 1936; David Dawson, "The Flying Omlies: A Barnstorming Legacy," *Memphis*, December 1980, 48; Gene Nora Jessen, *The Powder Puff Derby of 1929* (Naperville, Ill.: Sourcebooks, Inc., 2002), 239.

32. Helen M. Coppock and Charles W. Crawford, eds, *Paul R. Coppock's Mid-South*, vol. 4, 1979–1982 (Memphis: Paul R. Coppock Publication Trust, 1994), 169.

33. Memphis papers quoted by Vance Lauderdale, *Ask Vance* (Memphis: Bluff City Books, 2003), 82–83. See also Martin, "Aviation in Memphis."

34. Paul R. Coppock, "Those Daring Young Aviators," *Memphis Commercial Appeal*, September 19, 1982.

35. Omlie's Aircraft and Engine license, #422, was also issued in 1927 (Personnel File).

36. John M. Barry, *Rising Tide: The Great Mississippi Flood of 1927 and How It Changed America* (New York: Simon and Schuster, 1997), 285.

37. Cullen, "There's No Stopping a Woman," 28. Quoted by Max Stern, "Aviation's Nursemaid," *Today*, February 23, 1935, 5, 19.

38. She later listed herself as "Director of Public Relations, Test Pilot and Sales Representative" for Mono Aircraft Corp., Moline, for summers from 1928 through 1931 (Personnel File).

39. Louise Thaden, *High, Wide and Frightened* (New York: Stackpole Sons, 1938), 26–28.

40. "Phoebe Omlie Breaks Two Altitude Marks . . . ," *Memphis Commercial Appeal*, June 30, 1929.

41. A salesgirl in 1920 earned $8 a week. Conversion of the prize money to 2005 dollars yields $136,364.

42. The tour began and ended in Detroit, Michigan. The route took them over Ohio, Indiana, Illinois, Missouri, Kansas, Oklahoma, Texas, New Mexico, Arizona, California, Oregon, Washington, Idaho, Montana, North Dakota, Minnesota, and Wisconsin. See Lesley Forden, *The Ford Air Tours, 1925–1931* (New Brighton, Minn.: Aviation Foundation of America, 1973), 64–68.

43. Forden, *Ford Air Tours*, 84–85.

44. Scharlau, "Phoebe," 63.

45. A ground loop is a rapid and uncontrolled turn while the plane is on the ground caused by a sideways force on the landing gear. This causes the inside wing to go up and the outside wing to go down and scrape the ground. In severe cases, if the ground is soft, the tip digs in and cartwheels the plane. This can be fatal to the pilot. At the very least, it causes severe damage to the plane.

46. Forden, *Ford Air Tours*, 64–65.

47. James V. Piersol, "Detroit Writer Pays Tribute to Moline Airplane," *Moline Dispatch*, August 6, 1928.

48. The best source for the 1929 Women's International Air Race is Gene Nora Jessen, *The Powder Puff Derby of 1929* (Naperville, Ill.: Sourcebooks, Inc., 2002). Although it is peppered with made-up dialogue and has some facts and chronologies confused, it remains the best source for this event. Kathleen Brooks-Pazmany's short book seems more factual, but far less colorful. See her account in Brooks-Pazmany, *United States Women in Aviation*, 34–51. Louise Thaden, in *High, Wide and Frightened*, devotes a chapter to the derby, 67–90.

49. Brooks-Pazmany, *Women in Aviation*, 34.

50. Jessen, *Powder Puff Derby*, 26.

51. Ibid., 63.

52. Hollander, et al., *The Ninety-Nines*, 11; Jessen, *Powder Puff Derby*, 66.

53. Jessen, *Powder Puff Derby*, 59.

54. Thaden, *High, Wide and Frightened*, 67–90.

55. Ibid., 74.

56. Planes move through the air and are subject to the wind—they don't cut across wind, they move with it. When the wind blows, pilots must make mathematical calculations to estimate how far off compass heading they will drift.

57. Ibid.

58. Ibid., 47; Brooks-Pazmany, *Women in Aviation*, 46.

59. Hollander et al., *The Ninety-Nines*, 11; Jessen, *Powder Puff Derby*, 106–8; Thaden, *High, Wide and Frightened*, 75.

60. Jessen, *Powder Puff Derby*, 117–20, 128–29; Earhart quoted in Thaden, *High, Wide and Frightened*, 76.

61. CW class: less than 510-cubic-inch displacement; DW class: greater than 510 but not more than 800 cubic inches. See Brooks-Pazmany, *Women in Aviation*, 54.

62. The formula to determine the winner was based upon average speed divided by cubic inch piston replacement. Cleveland National Air Races Archives, Western Reserve Historical Society, Cleveland, Ohio.

63. Hollander, et al, *The Ninety-Nines*, 11–12.

64. "Moline Fliers Win Cheers and Prizes in Plane Races," *Moline (Ill.) Dispatch*, August 27, 1930, 1.

65. H. Glenn Buffington, "Phoebe Fairgrave Omlie: USA's First Woman Transport Pilot," *Journal of the American Aviation Historical Society* 13, no. 3 (1968): 187.

66. Scharlau, "Phoebe," 82.

67. Copy of telegram, dated September 12, 1931, in File: Memphis-biography-Omlie, Phoebe Fairgrave, Memphis Room, Memphis/Shelby County Library.

68. "Victory Fliers," *Washington Herald*, November 25, 1933; Claudia M. Oakes, *United States Women in Aviation 1930–1939* (Washington D.C.: Smithsonian Institution Press, 1985), 40.

69. Several Hammond planes were built, but few sold. A later hybrid, the Stearman Hammond, proved equally unsuccessful. One of these is owned by the Smithsonian National Air and Space Museum. Phoebe's activities on these projects are described in her personnel file. See "Woman Sees $700 Plane," *Washington Press-Herald*, August 23, 1934.

70. "Air Markers," *Time*, August 24, 1936, 48.

71. Jessen, *Powder Puff Derby*, 236.

72. Jean Adams, Margaret Kimball, and Jean Kimball, *Heroines of the Sky* (Garden City, N.Y.: Doubleday, Doran and Co., Inc., 1942), 81.

73. "First Lady Honors Mrs. Phoebe Omlie," *Memphis Commercial Appeal*, March 9, 1935.

74. "One of Those Things," *Time*, August 17, 1936.

75. "Taking the Air," *Democratic Digest* 13 (December 1936): 19.

76. Fifteen flight scholarships were awarded per school: twelve to men and three to women (Personnel File).

77. Eldon Roark, "Strolling with Eldon Roark," *Memphis Press-Scimitar*, February 14, 1962.

78. Phoebe Omlie vertical file, Tennessee Bureau of Aeronautics History Collection, Tennessee Department of Transportation, Office of Aeronautics, Tennessee State Library and Archives.

79. "Ends Long Aerial Tour," *Memphis Commercial Appeal*, May 28, 1941.

80. Personnel File.

81. Quoted in Gene Slack, "Tennessee's Airwomen," *Flying*, May 1943, 46.

82. Ibid., 128.

83. Personnel File; "Ten Women Pilot Instructors Seen First of Nationwide Move," *Nashville Tennessean*, February 4, 1943.

84. Personnel File.

85. "Phoebe Omlie Quits CAA Post," *Memphis Commercial Appeal*, March 30, 1952.

86. She was living on Agnes Place in Memphis in 1962; she was living on Delafield Place NW in Washington, D.C., in 1967. Roark, "Strolling with Eldon Roark"; Mary E., "Between You and Me" (column), *St. Paul Pioneer Press*, July 24, 1967; Dawson, "The Flying Omlies," 48.

87. "A Great Lady Passes By," *Indianapolis Star*, July 23, 1975.

88. Orville Hancock, "Proposal to Name Control Tower for Barnstorming Pilot Is Getting Off the Ground," *Memphis Press Scimitar*, March 5, 1981.

89. Letter to the editor from James T. Kacarides, quoted in "Memorial Suggested in Honor of the Omlies," *Memphis Press Scimitar*, December 4, 1980.

90. "Omlie Tower Ceremony," *Memphis Press Scimitar*, August 31, 1982. This article indicates that they were still awaiting the commemorative plaque from the FAA so no dedication ceremony was planned. According to James Kacarides (interview with author, Memphis, October 2004), the plaque never arrived and the official dedication did not happen.

Sue Shelton White

(1887–1943)

Lady Warrior

BETTY SPARKS HUEHLS AND BEVERLY GREENE BOND

On February 9, 1919, in front of a crowd of sister suffragists, curious onlookers, newspaper reporters, and Washington policemen, Sue Shelton White burned an effigy of Woodrow Wilson. The policemen, fire extinguishers in hand, rushed forward in an attempt to rescue what they assumed to be a straw dummy of the president. But the effigy White burned was made of paper—a cartoon of Wilson delivering one of his "freedom-for-everybody" speeches with a woman's head chained to his belt. The effigy had barely turned to ashes before police arrested White and thirty-eight other demonstrators from the National Woman's Party (NWP). The next day, White and twenty-seven of her associates were sentenced to five days in jail, during which time the militants launched a hunger strike to protest the denial of their right to vote.[1]

After they were released, the protesters boarded a train, the "Prison Special," which White nicknamed the "Democracy Limited," and began a twenty-six-day cross-country speaking tour from South Carolina to California, traveling back to New York City by a northern route. Their tour garnered tremendous publicity, most of it favorable, for the suffrage movement. As White later noted, their purpose was "to get action before the adjournment of the 65th congress." The Suffrage Amendment had passed the House and needed only one more vote to pass the Senate. However, although they carried the message "from the prison to the people," the women did not get the needed vote.[2]

Sue Shelton White was born and reared in Henderson, Tennessee. Her life spanned nearly six decades of American female activism, from the revitalization of the feminist movement and the dramatic struggle for woman suffrage through the growing political involvement of women in the 1920s and 1930s.

SUE SHELTON WHITE

June 1920, Chicago. Left to right: Abby Scott Baker, Florence Taylor Marsh, Sue Shelton White, Elsie Hill, and Betty Gram. *Women of Protest: Photographs from the Records of the National Woman's Party,* Manuscript Division, Library of Congress, Washington, D.C.

White was a court reporter, lawyer, bureaucrat, suffragist, reformer and equal rights advocate, practical idealist, intrepid feminist, and savvy politician. Extensive primary sources reveal that White, orphaned at age fourteen, sought and achieved an excellent education, became a radical suffragist and a New Deal liberal, and simultaneously championed causes that ran the gamut from equal rights for women to the peace movement. During the 1920 battle for woman suffrage White maneuvered behind the scenes to get a successful vote in Tennessee. She was one of Tennessee's first female court reporters, a principal attorney, and, from 1935 to 1943, assistant to the general counsel at the federal Social Security Board. White, a master politician, expanded political patronage for women, especially southern women, during the Roosevelt years. From 1930 to 1932, she successfully crafted the foundation for a women's faction within the Democratic Party—a faction that contributed to Franklin D. Roosevelt's winning political coalition in 1932. But although she recognized the inequities that confronted African Americans during these years, Sue Shelton White was ambivalent on pushing for changes in race relations, perhaps fearing the repercussions activism in this area might bring to other programs she advocated. Having sensed early in her life that blacks were discriminated against and that this discrimination needed to be addressed, she wavered in her efforts to counteract this unequal situation.

Jack B. Tate, a fellow Tennessean and general counsel for the federal Social Security Board, described White as a "lady warrior"—a southern gentlewoman and a fighter. White made outstanding and unique contributions to the woman's movement during the early decades of the twentieth century.[3] After eight years of involvement and leadership within the woman suffrage movement, White played a pivotal part in securing Tennessee's ratification of the Nineteenth Amendment in August 1920. Her behind-the-scenes political maneuvering on her home ground during that special session of the General Assembly made it possible for Tennessee to become the thirty-sixth state to ratify, thus making the amendment part of our Constitution.[4]

Loyal to the Democratic Party, White began preparing for its comeback shortly after the 1928 Republican victory. In early 1930 she parlayed herself into the executive secretary's position of the Woman's Division of the Democratic National Committee based in Washington, D.C. For the next two and a half years, while her boss Nellie Tayloe Ross toured the country speaking on behalf of the Democratic Party, White used her skills of communication and organization to forge a grassroots foundation of support among women within the Democratic Party. This was the foundation that the Women's Division of Democratic National Campaign Committee (WD/DNCC) was built upon.

White filled an important and distinctive position within the women's political leadership of the Democratic Party. Eleanor Roosevelt, Molly Dewson, Nellie Tayloe Ross, and Sue Shelton White formed the initial top echelon of national women leaders who maneuvered to get Franklin D. Roosevelt elected in 1932 and then fought to get patronage for deserving women within the party. Of these four women, White was the only one who came from a common rather than an elite background. She was also the only southerner. Another difference that existed between White and the majority of women Democratic leaders (including Roosevelt and Dewson) was that White, as an advocate of the Equal Rights Amendment (ERA), belonged to the minority when it came to the main disagreement among women during the 1920s and 1930s. This disagreement centered on the battle between proponents of the ERA and champions of protective legislation for women. White was adept at hurdling this philosophical and intellectual chasm. According to Jack Tate, she "knew politics from the inside and from the outside" and had acquired an arsenal of political weapons—verbal and literary abilities, networking, compassion and common sense, wisdom and wit. She knew how to use these skills effectively in fighting for the causes she believed in—woman suffrage, peace, ERA, the Democratic Party, and the advancement of woman.[5]

Much of White's effectiveness as an activist and an adept politician—her success as a "lady warrior"—was rooted in her southern background. Her parents, James Shelton White and Mary Calistia Swain, reflected the diversity of white family life in the South. Before the Civil War, James White's family had been well-to-do slaveholders in Wilson County, Tennessee. The family traced their lineage to the Marshalls and the Jeffersons of Virginia. On the other hand, Mary Swain was a Kentuckian from "'immigrant,' non-slaveholding stock." James served in the Confederate Army during the Civil War and suffered a leg wound that left him permanently lame. James and Mary met about 1870 at a school near Mary's home in McCracken County, Kentucky. The eighteen-year-old Mary was old enough to marry, but postponed the union for five years, during which time she taught school. Although it was unusual for a woman of her time, she continued to teach even after her marriage. Economic need, as much as her own innate independence, may have influenced Mary's decision to continue working.[6]

James White was a Methodist minister as well as a teacher, but although Mary attended the churches her husband pastored, worked alongside him in Sunday School, and took their children to services, she remained a staunch Baptist. In the "rabidly intolerant southern Methodist community" where James ministered, church members "baited and harassed" his wife over her refusal to join the church. In 1879 the presiding elder confronted James White and demanded that Mary become a Methodist. But in the heated disagreement that followed the elder's comment, Preacher White "smote" the elder's cheek and lost his position. Sue White later commented that her father "might have slapped his wife rather than his presiding elder and thus held on to his frock." James White was expelled from the Methodist Episcopal Church and the ministry, and he lost his position as principal of the Methodist-sponsored Jackson District High School in Montezuma, Tennessee.[7]

The Whites moved six miles away, to Henderson, where Sue Shelton White was born on May 24, 1887. She was the fourth of six children—four sons and two daughters. Henderson, Tennessee, got its beginning in 1857 when the Mobile and Ohio Railroad extended its line from nearby Jackson south to Mobile, Alabama. The railroad linked Henderson, a small rural community dependent on cotton farming, to northern markets and brought needed manufactured products into the town. Henderson developed around the railroad and its depot. By 1879 it was the county seat of newly established Chester County—and by 1900 it boasted a population of one thousand. Retail businesses, professional offices, hotels and rooming houses, livery stables, banks, schools, churches, and residences surrounded the busy railroad area. James White planned to settle his family near the physical center of the town, but they actually lived in what Sue Shelton White referred to as a "twilight zone" between the main part of town and a segregated black community, referred to as "Jaybird." To Sue, this physical isolation symbolized her family's marginal social status.[8]

Yet James White was deeply involved in the growth and development of the new county seat. In the summer of 1882 he served as a magistrate on the first county court and appeared as a solicitor before the chancery court. He also worked as superintendent of Chester County schools in the 1880s. The school system authorized him to keep records, make reports, visit schools, encourage teacher institutes, conduct teachers' examinations, and issue teaching certificates, but he did not control school financing or the employment of teachers. The meagerness of his own salary led his daughter to define the family's economic status as poor.[9]

Sue and her siblings attended Henderson's public schools, where she studied reading, writing, and arithmetic along with spelling, history, physiology, and geography. Recalling her school experiences, she later remarked that so much of her early studying was done at home that she had limited opportunities to make comparisons between her own abilities and those of others. But in the classroom, she quickly discovered that there were "degrees of intelligence lower than my own" and understood that she could perform as well or better than most boys. Sue's mother encouraged literacy and achievement in her children.

The children read everything from *Arabian Nights* to William Shakespeare, Thomas Carlyle, Thomas Paine, Victor Hugo, and George Eliot. Mary White made a point of telling Sue that the latter "was really a woman named Mary Ann Evans."[10]

In Henderson, Sue Shelton White also learned lessons about the racial divide in Tennessee and throughout the South. By the 1890s the South's brief flirtation with racial equality had ended. Democratic redeemers reigned and Tennessee, like much of the region, had become solidly Democratic—and just as solidly committed to maintaining white supremacy and black inferiority. Southern whites imposed a rigid system of legal disfranchisement and segregation, and relegated the majority of blacks to menial low-paying jobs to keep African Americans in their "place." If all else failed, whites were not above using violence, including lynch mobs, to instill the social, political, and economic order. *Plessy v. Ferguson* (1896) and *Williams v. Mississippi* (1898) provided the legal imprimatur of the nation's highest court to "separate but equal" and disfranchisement. As an adult, Sue Shelton White recalled that during her childhood Henderson provided no schools for black students. By the end of the nineteenth century, in communities across Tennessee, racial segregation extended to churches, housing, restaurants and saloons, parks and sporting events, hospitals and prisons, funeral homes and cemeteries. The final plank in this ladder of separatism was Tennessee's 1905 streetcar segregation law.[11]

Enmeshed in the South's segregated, white supremacist society, but living close to over a hundred African Americans in a small community, Sue Shelton White noted that her parents were Democrats and "consistent in a moderate Southernism." They rejected the extreme racism of Democrats on the right as well as the egalitarian beliefs of those on the left. They also rejected the semi-integrationist Populist ideology. Their moderate stance indicated that they favored Democratic home rule, racial paternalism, noblesse oblige, and, like the minority of well-educated middle- to upper-class southerners in the party, they probably accepted black subordination but not the humiliating behaviors required by segregation. But what exactly did White mean by her reference to her family's behavior as "consistent in a moderate Southernism"? In light of her discussions of her parents' independent thinking and their resistance to certain southern mores, it is clear that she found them less conservative and racist than most of their white neighbors, yet proud to claim their southern roots. They were, however, less broad-minded than Sue White would later become when she sought social justice through expanding opportunities for all segments of society.[12]

The White family had a history of compassionate and maternalistic behavior toward black people. Before the Civil War, Sue White's paternal aunt Sue defied custom and law to teach reading to the slaves living on her father's Middle Tennessee plantation. She considered it her "Christian duty." The elder Sue White traced her abolitionist leanings to her awareness of the work of Susan B. Anthony, but when her young niece asked if she were an abolitionist, Aunt Sue equivocated with, "I wasn't, and yet I was." She had "compromised" by not openly declaring her antislavery beliefs, since she did not want to embarrass her father in their proslavery community.[13]

Similarly, half a century later, Sue's mother risked ostracism by teaching black children in Henderson to read, sew, and play the piano. Usually her black pupils or their parents paid Mrs. White with their labor by milking the Whites' cows, doing the washing, or cooking for the family. But in giving piano lessons to black children, Mary White was subtly rebelling against the white superiority/black inferiority caste system. She was, in a sense, recognizing the possibility that African Americans were capable of the same level of intellectual and creative achievement as whites. Sue White and her sister Lucy emulated the behavior of their aunt Sue and their mother by giving school lessons and music instruction from hymn books to "certain little Negro girls." As Sue later wrote, "I . . . began, early in life, to observe the black and the white and to note some differences in their lives." She could see the contrasts between the "Jaybird" community and the "white town" of Henderson—the "little huts" that blacks lived in and the "houses" of the whites; the fact that blacks had no schools while education was accessible to white children and that most black women were servants of the white "ladies." Blacks were jostled "off the side-walks into the mud," black women were called "Aunt" but never "Mrs."; and there were the constant rumors of certain "white gentlemen" visiting specific "Negro cabins" after dark.[14]

Sue White's awareness of gender proscriptions and of her parents' (especially her mother's) willingness to step beyond these norms also came at an early age. Mary White did not draw strict traditional gender lines between expected roles and behaviors for her sons and her daughters. The boys cooked and did domestic chores, and Sue "ran, jumped, climbed and, not infrequently, fought." Sue took over more household chores after her older brothers joined the army in 1898. She carried water from the well, brought in coal and wood, chopped kindling, started fires, gardened, and learned to use carpentry tools. Mary White, widowed five years earlier, struggled to support her family. Although she was an educated woman and an experienced teacher who owned her home, she found it difficult to find a job. She taught piano, gave voice lessons, and wrote articles for a local newspaper, but these tasks provided only minimal support for a family of six. As Sue White later wrote, "Between these activities she

[Mary] supervised our studies, our reading, our behavior, our work; nursed her neighbors, laid out the dead, helped their children with school essays, and was kind to the Negroes who lived in the little huts nearby."[15]

Mary White's struggle to provide for her family strengthened her resolve that her own daughters had to prepare for their own economic independence. "She fed our ambitions," Sue White recalled. "I have never classed my mother a feminist, but I suspect she was one. Life would have made her one in the end if she had not been one in the beginning. . . . In her narrow, almost primitive field, she held her position as an unusual, if sometimes a troublesome woman—always tolerated and sometimes acclaimed."[16]

Mary White's death in 1901 left Sue an orphan at age fourteen. She rejected the idea of moving to her father's hometown of Lebanon, Tennessee, to live with her aunt, Sue White Tarver. In the Tarver house, Sue would have "belonged" to a female circle of "genteel" ladies. Sue Tarver was the wife of a judge, active in the local Daughters of the American Revolution, the Women's Christian Temperance Union, and the Methodist Women's Missionary Society. Sue Shelton White also resisted her mother's chosen field, teaching, which was considered the most respectable public work available to a southern woman in financial distress. Instead, she decided to build on her innate intelligence by pursuing a practical education with career possibilities. Along with her sister Lucy and brother Marshall, she entered Georgie Robertson Christian College, a normal or teacher training school that offered stenographic courses for young women. Sue also spent time at a private school in Hernando, Mississippi, and a year at the West Tennessee Business School in Dyer. When she completed her education in 1905, she joined the ranks of twentieth-century "new women"—women who earned their own money and lived independently.[17]

In 1905 an eighteen-year-old Sue White moved from Henderson to Jackson, Tennessee, to work as a stenographer and clerk for the Southern Engine and Boiler Works, the largest factory of its kind in the South. She typed specifications and, curious about what they meant, studied catalogues and asked questions about the business. But her employers discouraged her interest, and the foreman rebuffed her when she requested a tour through the workshops. When she suggested that a correspondence course in mechanical engineering might also help her to better understand her job her employer gave her a fatherly lecture on women's "sphere." On the other hand, the office boy was encouraged to "learn the business."[18]

Two years later, when Lucy White gave up her job as court reporter for the Tennessee Supreme Court in Jackson, Sue was more than ready to replace her sister. Sue also opened her own public stenographers' agency where she employed at least one other stenographer, possibly more. Although the lawyers complimented her on her skills as a court reporter, they discouraged her when she talked about becoming a lawyer. Sue White was seen as an "impractical and visionary" young woman while "young men were encouraged to 'read.' They were taken into offices, into the trial cases, sponsored, even fed sometimes, by the older members of the bar; the banks would extend them credit while they were struggling."[19]

One judge did attempt to help White achieve her legal and political ambitions by suggesting her for a job as secretary to one of Tennessee's newly elected United States senators, Democrat Kenneth D. McKellar. However, McKellar refused to hire her because she was a woman. White continued to work for the state court of appeals as well as the federal court in Jackson, developing important contacts with influential lawyers and politicians—including McKellar. He, along with Governor Tom C. Rye, Supreme Court Justice Grafton Green, and Tennessee Court of Appeals Judge Hu C. Anderson were instrumental in White's later political activities.[20]

Meanwhile White became involved in one of the formative activities of her life—the woman suffrage movement. She began her suffrage activities as the movement gathered momentum in the 1910s. In late December 1912 she and about thirty other women from Jackson met at the local library and, under the guidance of Mrs. Perkins Baxter and Mrs. Guilford (Anne Dallas) Dudley of the Nashville League, organized the Jackson Equal Suffrage League (JESL). Both the Nashville and Jackson suffrage organizations affiliated with the National American Woman's Suffrage Association (NAWSA), as did the five other Tennessee leagues (two from Memphis and one each in Morristown, Chattanooga, and Knoxville). The membership of these combined groups totaled five hundred. The JESL chose White to represent them at the Tennessee Equal Suffrage Association annual convention in Nashville on January 6, 1913. The JESL, in line with Tennessee NAWSA's program of educating citizens about suffrage in order to convert them to the cause, participated in the revival of Jackson's dormant Fourth of July celebrations. At these patriotic events, Jackson suffragists prompted other groups to become involved, organized parades, gave prosuffrage speeches, and handed out suffrage literature. They also sponsored high school essay contests about woman suffrage and encouraged the inclusion of women on the school board. In 1915 they participated in a special "Suffrage Day" at the West Tennessee Fair in Memphis, sponsored a luncheon, held a rally at Jackson's Marlowe Theater, and hosted TESA's annual convention.[21]

Sue Shelton White rose quickly to leadership positions in the state organization. Members of the executive board made her acting recording secretary of

TESA—a position that TESA members made permanent in 1913, and which White held for five years. During her tenure as recording secretary, she was involved in the conflicts that mirrored the middle, eastern, and western regional factionalism common in Tennessee's politics. In May 1914 TESA's executive board, after a heated debate, decided to hold NAWSA's annual convention in Nashville rather than Chattanooga. The decision "provoked much discussion among Tennessee suffragists," and White, as recording secretary of the executive board, was one of the "storm centers" around which the conflict swirled. The controversy continued when TESA met the following October in Knoxville. Members requested that White read the minutes of the May executive board meeting. Then Mrs. J. D. Allen from Memphis asked and was given permission for Vice-President-at-Large Eleanor McCormack, the other "storm center" for this controversy, to read her version of the events. Despite efforts to adjourn the session, the arguments raged on as advocates of the Chattanooga site pressed their contention that the decision in favor of Nashville was unfair. The next day Lizzie Crozier French, president of TESA, arrived to find that her vice president, Eleanor McCormack, had already called the meeting to order. French and her followers, including Sue Shelton White, moved to the rear of the meeting hall where they, too, held a meeting. Each faction elected a president with McCormack heading one group and French the other. Each blamed the other for "bolting" and claimed to be the "regular" TESA. The separation was made permanent with the French faction becoming the Tennessee Equal Suffrage Association, Incorporated (TESA, Inc.) and the McCormack group retaining the original name, TESA. White continued as recording secretary for TESA, Inc., the group that dominated Tennessee's suffrage efforts.[22]

White later speculated that this rift was "probably not as unfortunate as it seemed at the time. . . . One thing it did was to create a spirit of rivalry between two irreconcilable groups each of which attempted to out do the other in the strengthening of its organization." Members of both factions cooperated with each other, so the rivalry appeared friendly. Nevertheless, the official separation lasted three and a half years. During that time NAWSA officials and Tennessee leaders, White included, attempted to keep the peace, reconcile these organizations, and strengthen the statewide movement for woman suffrage. White spoke at numerous gatherings, wrote articles for the newspapers, and compiled and published the *Handbook of the Tennessee Equal Suffrage Association: Proceedings of the Eight and Ninth Annual Conventions Held at Knoxville, 1914, Jackson 1915*. In late 1915, shortly after Anne Dallas Dudley became president of TESA, Inc., White took a month off from her stenographic/court reporter business to organize the state headquarters in Nashville.[23]

White also tried to effect a conciliation of Tennessee suffragists. On May 17, 1915, she participated in a "Harmony Meeting" at Tullahoma, where seventeen suffragists organized the Campaign Committee, independent of either of the TESAS. Sponsored by suffragists from Memphis, Nashville, Chattanooga, Murfreesboro, and Jackson, the "Harmony Meeting" included McCormack supporters, French supporters, and neutral women. Attendees at the "Harmony Meeting" felt that the suffrage cause itself was more important than any individual suffrage organization. They met, according to White, in order to "evolve some working plan whereby the women who were tired of strife and contention could work together, unhampered by factional differences." The Campaign Committee followed the congressional district plan suggested by NAWSA. The seventeen-member coordinating committee included joint chairwomen, one from each faction—Mrs. Henry J. Kelso originally represented TESA but was soon replaced by Abby Crawford Milton, while Catherine Talty Kenny represented TESA, Inc. As one of the ten district chairwomen, White headed the Eighth Congressional District in West Tennessee. She appointed county chairwomen who, in turn, appointed civil district chairwomen within their respective counties. In this way the Campaign Committee organized the entire state for the growth of the suffrage movement. In seven months the committee organized 32 leagues, added 9,600 members, printed and distributed over 75,000 pieces of literature, and spent over $4,000. More importantly, the Campaign Committee reduced regional conflict. White's friend and president of the Jackson suffrage league, Mary Ellis Butler, summed up Tennesseans' changing attitudes when she declared, "Hostility in 1913, ridicule in 1914, tolerance in 1915, and frank approval in 1916."[24]

White's work with the Campaign Committee involved her in parades and rallies. She gave speeches and organized leagues in several Tennessee towns including Tullahoma, Humbolt, Huntingdon, and Bolivar. In 1917 White lobbied for a proposed Tennessee law granting women the right to vote in municipal and presidential elections, although it did not pass the General Assembly until 1919. White quickly adapted techniques she observed at national conventions to the cause in Tennessee. For example, after seeing the effectiveness of street speaking at the 1916 NAWSA Atlantic City convention, she and four other women brought the strategy to Tennessee. In 1917 they took to the stump in Jackson and Memphis. Although many southerners considered this activity "unladylike," it worked and soon spread across the state. The following summer, at the Tennessee State Fair, "a group of these women spoke eight or ten times a day, being rewarded with many enrollments."[25]

Early efforts by national and state leaders to reconcile the incorporated and unincorporated TESAs were unsuccessful. NAWSA presidents Anna Howard Shaw and Carrie Chapman Catt, in 1915 and 1916 respectively, devised plans to reunite these organizations, but without success. Finally, circumstances in late 1917 and early 1918 made a merger possible. Just as White had been in the midst of the "storm" that caused the split, she helped repair the damage. At a conference in December 1917 White and Lulu Reese of Memphis developed a successful plan. White later wrote that "within a few weeks it was accomplished . . . [when the] presidents of the two old organizations [who resigned] were succeeded by Mrs. [Katherine Burch] Warner." On March 24, 1918, the executive committees of both TESA and TESA, Inc., met in Memphis, where they formed a new organization, the Tennessee Woman Suffrage Association (TWSA).[26]

As she worked for woman suffrage Sue Shelton White built an influential network of state and national contacts. Tennessee suffrage leaders included the socially prominent Nashvillian Anne Dallas Dudley, TESA, Inc., president and NAWSA third vice president; Eleanor McCormack, TESA president and activist; Lizzie Crozier French, Knoxville educator, TESA and TESA, Inc., president who later served as chair of the Tennessee branch of the NWP; Abby Crawford Milton, Campaign Committee cochair and the first president of the League of Women Voters in Tennessee; Catherine Talty Kenny, Campaign Committee cochair and Democratic political activist who later became chair of the Ratification Committee of the Tennessee League of Women Voters; Katherine Burch Warner, Tennessee Woman Suffrage Association (TWSA) president; and Lulu Colyar Reese, a noted Memphis civic reformer who later managed to maintain loyalty to both NAWSA and the NWP.[27]

At the 1914 NAWSA convention in Nashville, where Tennessee Governor Ben W. Hooper welcomed the delegates, White had ample opportunities to meet and add national suffrage leaders to her suffrage network. They included Dr. Anna Howard Shaw, president of NAWSA; Jane Addams, founder of Chicago's Hull House; Rose Schneiderman, president of the New York City Women's Trade Union League; and Senator Luke Lea, a prosuffrage Democrat from Tennessee. White's network also included NAWSA president Carrie Chapman Catt (1916–1920) as well as NWP leaders Alice Paul and Lucy Burns. These contacts drew her into the national struggle for woman suffrage.[28]

On April 6, 1917, the United States entered the Great War, World War I. NAWSA president Carrie Chapman Catt called upon members to divert part of their energies away from suffrage and toward the war effort. White, like hundreds of other women, complied with this request. Following the example of former NAWSA president Anna Howard Shaw, who became head of the Woman's Council of National Defense, White accepted the voluntary position of Chairman of Registration for the Tennessee Woman's Committee of the Council of National Defense. She used the skills and strategies she had acquired during her Campaign Committee days to register Tennessee women for the war effort. In six weeks White organized the state by counties to promote Registration Day (October 13, 1917). She contacted women all over the state and succeeded in registering over fifty thousand to aid the war effort. The Council of National Defense encouraged women to substitute for male workers and thereby free them for military service, to plant "victory gardens," to farm, to conserve food, to serve as nurses, and to sell Liberty Bonds.[29]

In their preaching and practicing of patriotism, White believed American women amply demonstrated their right to equal suffrage. But White went a step further and called attention to racial as well as gender inequity. In a letter to Rose Young, head of NAWSA's press department, White provided information on draft registration guidelines in a "typical southern town [Jackson] of about 20,000." She intended to refute the "overworked arguments" presented by some southern opponents to equal suffrage. These arguments were based on the assumption that all southerners believed that women should remain in the home or risk losing their femininity and that white women would somehow be defiled by contact with black women and men.[30]

White's information related to the willingness of both black and white women to volunteer and to serve in a wide variety of capacities. For example, white women left their homes to act as official registrars in each of Jackson's four wards. Women also offered their services under the auspices of the Association of Commerce and the United Daughters of the Confederacy (UDC). The white registrars and white female volunteers interacted with black women and men in all four wards. After the women volunteers, some suffragists and some not, distributed posters publicizing registration for the draft all over town, including the black sections, White, in a tongue-in-cheek manner, commented that these women "showed no evidence of having lost any womanly graces." She also expressed her pleasant surprise at the cooperation of the UDC with black women in presenting a badge of national colors to each man who registered. White wrote, "On June 5th . . . there will be found at least four registration booths . . . south of the Mason and Dixon Line, white men and women and negro [*sic*] men and women engaged in a public duty; no race riot will result, no presumption of denial [of] equality will follow, no woman will be insulted, none will be contaminated. . . . [I]f any revolution comes it will be only a change of heart and mind upon the question of how far women can safely exercise the duties of citizenship."[31]

But White's story of southern interracial cooperation was not published in NAWSA's official journal, *Woman Citizen*. The theme did not enhance NAWSA's policy of excluding black women. Beginning in the 1890s, when the white leadership of NAWSA started courting the support of southern white women, it became politically "expedient" for them to reject the support and involvement of black women and men. Many southern white women refused to associate with black women in social or civic activities. NAWSA and NWP leaders publicly argued that granting black women the vote would not affect white supremacy in the South, since white women outnumbered black women. In addition, the black woman's vote could be controlled as effectively as the black man's through poll taxes and literacy tests. Nonetheless, black women continued to work for woman suffrage. Black female leaders like Ida B. Wells-Barnett and Mary Church Terrell either formed their own suffrage organizations or worked through suffrage departments in existing segregated clubs under the auspices of the National Association of Colored Women. Black men tended to support black women in their suffrage efforts.[32]

Although NAWSA and NWP leadership, as well as the majority of white southern suffragists, rejected racial cooperation, a few mavericks refused to conform. For example, two of Sue Shelton White's closest friends—wealthy white suffragists Lulu Colyar Reese of Memphis and Catherine Talty Kenny of Nashville—collaborated with black female suffragists in their cities to get out the vote in 1919 and 1920. Reese and Kenny attended meetings with black women and spoke in black churches and meeting houses. Reese, while serving as president of a Memphis women's club, had even invited White to a meeting with the president of a black women's club. The three women discussed civic matters in Reese's living room.[33]

Considering White's maverick inclinations, her shared ideology with Reese, and her later writings on her racial activities, it is no great leap to assert that White personally believed that all women—black and white—should vote. She explained her racial interactions in an unpublished response to a *Harper's Monthly Magazine* article, "The Crumbling Color Line." White described the many occasions she had spoken to black audiences, including a women's club meeting in Washington, D.C. After speaking informally for her "cause," White had broken an unwritten rule of racial etiquette by dining, socializing, and even discussing current racial issues with the black women. She also talked about her emotional response to seeing a white election official "brow-beat and insult an old black woman," which culminated in the election official telling the woman to "get the hell out of here." Although White declared that she "wanted her to vote," she did not seem to have done anything to publicly confront the official.[34]

Suffrage may have been White's passion, but she still had to support herself. In January 1918 she moved to Nashville to become executive secretary of the newly organized Tennessee Commission for the Blind. Her service on Tennessee's Woman's Committee for the Council of National Defense, her work as a court reporter, and her suffrage activities had come to the attention of Tennessee's prosuffrage governor, Tom C. Rye. In this paid position White planned and administered Tennessee's progressive reform programs for the prevention of blindness and services to the blind. She conducted a survey of Tennessee industries in an effort to discover new employment opportunities, proposed that schools for the blind be used to instruct adults who had recently lost their sight, and wrote articles about her work for social service magazines. But White resigned her position after a year because new commissioners rejected her innovative progressive programs and returned to "old methods and attitudes."[35]

In the midst of this job crisis White became embroiled in a suffrage dispute that propelled her away from the NAWSA and into the NWP. Although her actual involvement spanned only eight months, from November 1917 to June 1918, the context of this acrimonious situation developed much earlier and involved complex national suffrage events. Between 1913 and 1916 factions within the NAWSA disagreed over suffrage aims and methods to be used in acquiring the vote. Under the direction of Alice Paul and Lucy Burns, NAWSA's moribund Congressional Committee, charged with lobbying Congress for a federal suffrage amendment and raising its own funds to do so, came to life. As its first project, the committee sponsored a suffrage parade in Washington on March 3, 1913, the day before Woodrow Wilson's presidential inauguration. A near riot developed when spectators along Pennsylvania Avenue laughed, jeered, and physically threatened the five thousand marching suffragists. Public outrage over this uncivil treatment and the lack of police protection provided the catalyst for the revival of the Susan B. Anthony Amendment. Tapping into this upsurge of interest, Alice Paul organized pilgrimages to Washington, petition campaigns, auto processions, and delegations to meet with Congress and to meet with President Wilson. Independent of NAWSA, Paul and her followers also formed the Congressional Union (CU), whose aims were to work for the federal woman suffrage amendment and to raise money. According to historian Eleanor Flexner, NAWSA leaders welcomed this groundswell of interest in the Anthony amendment but felt they had "released a force they would have difficulty in controlling."[36]

A growing rift over goals, methods, and power between the Congressional Committee and NAWSA erupted into an open fight during the 1914 national suffrage convention. The difficulty stemmed from Paul's demand that all suffrage work be focused on pressuring Congress and the president to pass the Anthony amendment. NAWSA board member Carrie Chapman Catt called for continued work on both state and federal suffrage and for the national organization's right to limit the policies and activities of the Congressional Committee. After much discussion and negotiation, the majority of delegates sided with Catt. Paul's faction, under the auspices of the Congressional Union, broke with NAWSA.[37]

Retaining most of its membership as well as leadership, NAWSA continued to support both state and federal suffrage efforts. It favored persuasion and nonpartisanship, thus supporting all politicians who backed suffrage. In 1916, after she replaced Anna Howard Shaw as the national president, Catt outlined her "Winning Plan" to the state chairwomen. Envisioning success within six years, Catt asked for at least thirty-six of the forty-eight state associations to sign a compact "to go after the [federal amendment] with a will." But before sending the proposed amendment to Congress, Catt wanted to win suffrage in several more states in order to strengthen the cause.[38]

By mid-1916, under Alice Paul's leadership, the Congressional Union reorganized and changed its name to the National Women's Party (NWP). Unlike NAWSA, the NWP concentrated all its efforts on the Anthony amendment. Following the example of British suffragists, the NWP advocated holding the political party in power, the Democrats, responsible for women not gaining the vote. The NWP recruited members and established state branches, among them a small group of suffragists in East Tennessee. These women had organized under the chairmanship of Mrs. Hugh Lawson White (no relation to Sue White). Sue Shelton White later noted that the NWP "had friends among suffragists throughout Tennessee and a number of these sympathizers became members." The NWP also refused to divert any of its energies toward the war effort. To NWP members America's involvement in the war, with the avowed ideal of making "the world safe for democracy," seemed a sham because women did not possess the basic right of a democracy—the vote. NWP members began picketing the White House on January 10, 1917, and continued after the United States formally entered the war. But instead of being an amusing news story or a curiosity for Washington visitors, the "picketers" were now viewed by many Americans as traitors. On June 22, 1917, Washington police began arresting the demonstrators on the spurious charge of obstructing traffic.[39]

Sue Shelton White's views on holding the party in power responsible for the status of the Anthony amendment and the validity of the NWP pickets differed from the official NAWSA policy of nonpartisanship. As recording secretary of TESA, Inc., White wrote a newspaper article in which she contended that "southern women . . . although strongly inclined toward the Democratic Party, were disappointed in Wilson's speech given at the 1916 NAWSA convention where he failed to specifically endorse the national suffrage amendment as Republican candidate Charles Evans Hughes had done." Rather, Wilson had sidestepped the issue by stating that "in the end we would not quarrel over the method," apparently referring to whether suffrage would be acquired through congressional or state legislation. White asked: "Will Congress help President Wilson to fight with us, without quarreling over the method?" For decades the majority of southern Democratic congressmen had opposed the Anthony amendment on the basis of states' rights. Yet, state legislators failed to enfranchise southern women through either referendums or state constitutional amendments. White felt that "if our (southern) Governors and political Masters will not grant the vote then we will have to 'accept freedom' from the federal government."[40] White set forth a hypothetical defense of the picketing suffragists. "I would not undertake to defend them, but in trying to guess by what logic they would defend themselves, I see a determination to emphasize, at whatever cost, the length to which women, who have no voice in their own government, must submit to authority in a nation entering a world war upon the declaration [of President Wilson]: 'we shall fight for the things we always held nearest our hearts, for democracy, for the right of those who submit to authority to have a voice in their own government.'"[41] White clearly criticized political leaders who proposed to fight for democracy for Europeans while half the population of their own country—women—submitted to authority without a voice in their own government.

The catalyst that caused White's final break with NAWSA came in November 1917, with the visit to Tennessee of NWP speaker and organizer Maud Younger. Younger explained the actions of the Washington picketers, gained publicity for the suffrage cause, and attempted to win the votes of southern congressmen for the Anthony amendment. But in Memphis she received a less than cordial welcome from civic groups, political officials, and NAWSA suffragists. She was accused of being "disloyal, pro-German and un-American" because of NWP's refusal to support the war, and she could not find a place to speak. Realizing they needed some local political clout to overcome this opposition, NWP advance agent Rebecca Hourwich Reyher telephoned Sue Shelton White. White rushed to Memphis to investigate the charges. She defended the NWP members as loyal Americans and called the charges against them "base political slander." Nevertheless, she was still unable to arrange a speaking site in Memphis for Younger. White later recalled, "I determined then that if the same thing occurred throughout the state, I would have to join the pickets at the White House gates, not so much for equal suffrage as for freedom of speech."[42]

White accompanied Younger to four other Tennessee cities (Jackson, Nashville, Lebanon, and Gallatin), where she vouched for the picketers' loyalty but not their policies. White quieted a hostile audience in Jackson, reminding them that "we had all been strangers at the gate once, and the South, with its great tradition of liberty-loving people[,] owed us [NWP organizers and speakers] every courtesy and a friendly welcome." The Jackson audience responded with courtesy and enthusiasm. However, Nashvillians refused to allow Younger to speak even with Governor Rye's apparent approval and published endorsements signed by White and other leading citizens of Jackson. But Reyher later recalled that White's name seemed to open doors with people like Governor Rye, who proclaimed, "Anyone who is a friend of Miss Sue's, is a friend of ours." White's name, Reyher noted, "was magic, everyone respected and loved her." Although this "magic" did not work in Nashville, it secured speaking places and respectful audiences in Lebanon and Gallatin. White did not accompany the NWP tour to Knoxville and Chattanooga, but audiences in those cities were more receptive to Maud Younger's message.[43]

However, White's troubles did not subside. An editorial criticizing White and the picketers, based on an interview with TESA, Inc., president Anne Dallas Dudley, appeared in the *Nashville Tennesseean.* White offered to resign her position in TESA, Inc., but Dudley refused to accept her resignation, perhaps because of their longstanding friendship. A Memphis newspaper expressed the disapproval of the Memphis Equal Suffrage League of White and the NWP. These mainstream suffragists were "neither in sympathy nor harmony with the picketers," and they questioned how White "could possibly belong to two parties so far asunder in their views as the woman's party [*sic*] and the National American Woman Suffrage Association."[44]

In late April 1918 Carrie Chapman Catt, in a curt letter to TWSA's newly elected president Katherine Burch Warner, reprimanded White for cooperating with NWP members during the Tennessee Dixie Tour. White later commented that Catt had not wanted to deal with the "turncoat" herself, so she asked Warner to tell White that there would be no giving of help or NAWSA's strategies to NWP members. Specifically, Catt was concerned that White would reveal "the plan for Congressional [*sic*] work in case the amendment does not pass and the plans of ratification if it does pass." White was insulted that Catt thought she would give away NAWSA's strategy, but her response indicated that she was not overawed by the powerful NAWSA president. She replied with a lengthy and strongly worded letter of her own. She informed Catt that she needed no intermediary (Warner), but could and would answer for herself. White outlined her past work and dedication to NAWSA, assured Catt that she had no intention of revealing NAWSA "secrets," and described her involvement with Younger and the NWP Dixie Tour. White also emphasized her belief that "free speech" was a basic right and that no organization, not even the conservative NAWSA, could survive without it. White repeated several times that she had not vouched for the policies of the picketers, only for their loyalty to America. Furthermore, White made it clear that she would not apologize for her actions; rather she declared that "the only apology I have is in behalf of my state, that such intolerance could have existed within its border."[45]

During the next two months, White and Catt engaged in a letter debate based on their opposing views. Central to their disagreement was the position of NAWSA concerning work to be done in the southern states in general and Tennessee in particular. Although Catt stated that the national organization would help the "fighting states," including Tennessee, White questioned this intent. White understood, however, that the assistance was "not for the Amendment, only for ratification" after the amendment passed Congress. But White wanted "Southern [congressional] votes for the Amendment." Southern white women wanted their own representatives to enfranchise them. In fact, because of their belief in states' rights and white supremacy and their fear of giving the vote to black women, many of the southern women leaders favored state amendments or referendums. White, on the other hand, supported the federal amendment. This was something that Catt just could not or would not understand.[46]

Gradually, the tone of White's letters to Catt changed—she began to say more and more about what the NWP was doing in Tennessee. Organizers were active in the state, and Mrs. Samuel G. Shields, sister-in-law of antisuffrage Senator John K. Shields (Democrat from Tennessee), was NWP state chairperson. In addition, White wrote that the NWP was "strengthening the public sentiment for the [federal] amendment." White also commented to Catt that the April edition of NAWSA's *Woman Citizen* reported and praised a resolution sent to Congress encouraging passage of the Anthony amendment. With just a note of sarcasm, White declared that the resolution had been sponsored by "a little group of willful women" in Knoxville, Tennessee, who just happened to belong to the NWP. To White, it followed that if NAWSA's official journal could make use of the work of the NWP, then "members of the N.A.W.S.A. would be justified in following suit." Catt finally delivered an ultimatum, asking White "to get the data and think the matter out to a conclusion and then make your stand fair and square, one side or the other." In doing this, White in all likelihood considered many different aspects of the "data," weighing the positives and negatives of both organizations.[47]

Sue Shelton White admired and respected Carrie Chapman Catt and Alice Paul, as well as the Tennessee leaders of both groups. White had five years invested in suffrage experiences that were tied to NAWSA's Tennessee affiliates where she had made numerous friends. Although NWP struggled for approval in the state, White thought NWP members she met were "splendid young women," admired their "courage," and loved their "zeal." White also took into account that NAWSA's national organization had done next to nothing in Tennessee toward acquiring passage of the federal amendment. White did not expect NAWSA to change unless the amendment passed Congress and NAWSA needed Tennessee's ratification. On the other hand, the NWP had sent organizers and speakers to Tennessee in the fall of 1917 and in the spring of 1918, and planned to send more in the future. In meetings, petitions, and resolutions, NWP organizers pressured antisuffragist Tennessee politicians, especially Senator Shields, to support the suffrage amendment.[48]

But on a more personal level, White was stung by the criticism she had received for trying to secure speaking forums for NWP speaker Maud Younger and felt that she was "playing a lone hand." Even so, she knew that many Tennessee suffragists wanted to give her moral support, although it was a quiet support. She received no criticism from NWP. The organization's journal, *The Suffragist*, praised White, Rebecca Reyher exhibited pride because she had "discovered" White, and Alice Paul "badgered" White to join the NWP and come to Washington. Perhaps White sensed change in the air even before Catt's reprimand. In March 1918, when the "amalgamation" of the two TESAs occurred, White had not sought a place of leadership in the new TWSA. Also, in early April, she pledged and donated money to the NWP.[49]

Sue Shelton White's indecisiveness ended in June 1918, when she "took her stand" with the NWP by accepting the Tennessee chairmanship. Her correspondence with Catt ended without malice. Catt magnanimously declared that "I know you are doing the best you can and beyond that no one can make demands upon you. . . . you are able and strong and splendid." White responded with an affirmation of her loyalty to Catt and to the cause. White's trench training ended as she embarked on the radical portion of her "suffrage first" journey. She had chosen the militant faction, the one that seemed to her the most passionate about woman suffrage and the most likely to succeed.

NOTES

1. Sue Shelton White, "'Militants,' Suffragists and What They Have Done to Win," *Montgomery Times*, September 12 and 16, 1919; Sue Shelton White to *International Suffrage News* (London), May 17, 1919, as found in James P. Louis, "Sue Shelton White and the Woman Suffrage Movement in Tennessee, 1913–20," *Tennessee Historical Quarterly* 22 (June 1963): 186; Louisiane W. Havemeyer, "The Prison Special," *Scribner's Magazine* (June 1922): 661–76.

2. White, "'Militants'"; Havemeyer, "Prison Special," 661–76; Inez Haynes Irwin, *Up Hill with Banners Flying* (Penobscot, Maine: Traversity Press, 1964), 416–17, originally published as *The Story of the Woman's Party* (New York: Harcourt, Brace, 1921); National Woman's Party press release, February 18, 1919, National Woman's Party Papers, Library of Congress, [on microfilm] National Woman's Party Papers, "Suffrage Years, 1913–1920," Microfilming Corporation of America, 1982; Lucy Somerville Howorth interview by Betty Huehls, tape recording, August 8, 1996, Cleveland, Miss.; Sally Swing Shelley interview by Betty Huehls, tape recording, Easton, Conn., May 29, 1999.

3. Although there is no dearth of sources on White's life she has, like other Tennessee women, failed to make it into traditional history textbooks. Secondary sources like James P. Louis's biographical sketch in *Notable American Women* and article "Sue Shelton White and the Woman Suffrage Movement in Tennessee, 1913–1920" in the *Tennessee Historical Quarterly* (1963); Inez Haynes Irwin's *The Story of the Woman's Party* and Doris Stevens's *Jailed for Freedom* provide a framework for examining White's life. White's papers and an autobiography written for Elaine Showalter's *These Modern Women: Autobiographical Essays from the Twenties*, as well as Susan Ware's *Beyond Suffrage: Women in the New Deal* (Cambridge, Mass.: Harvard University Press, 1981) add to this basic information. (Unless noted, these sources are all cited in full below.) Other sources on White's public activities include the National Woman's Party Papers at the Library of Congress in Washington, D.C., the collections at the Franklin D. Roosevelt Library in Hyde Park, New York, the papers of Senator Kenneth D. McKellar at the Benjamin L. Hooks Memphis Public Library. But White's private life was more difficult to document since she kept only a few personal letters. However, some aspects of her personal life are revealed in the papers of her contemporaries as well as in interviews with Lucy Somerville Howorth, one of White's allies in the suffrage struggle and in the Democratic Party. Although she was 101 years old when interviewed, Howorth was open, lucid, and candid about White's political and personal life. Sally Swing Shelley also was interviewed about the woman she affectionately called "Aunt Sookie." Shelley, the daughter of Betty Gram Swing, allowed access to her mother's papers, which supplied information concerning the friendship between White and Swing.

4. Jack B. Tate, "Sue White: An Appreciation," in *Women's Studies Manuscript Collections from the Schlesinger Library, Radcliffe College. Series 2, Women in National Politics*, part A, "Democrats," Research Collections in Women's Studies, ed. Anne Firor Scott and Randolph Boehm [hereinafter WNP], microfilm reel 12 (Bethesda, Md.: University Publications of America, 1992).

5. Tate, "Sue White."

6. Sue Shelton White, "Mother's Daughter," in *These Modern Women: Autobiographical Essays from the Twenties*, ed. Elaine Showalter (1979; repr., New York: Feminist Press, 1989), 45–51; Marshall K. White to Florence A. Armstrong, November 1, 1958, WNP, reel 12; Doris Stevens, *Jailed for Freedom* (New York: Liveright Publishing Corporation, 1920), 370; Anne Firor Scott, *The Southern Lady: From Pedestal to Politics, 1830–1930* (Chicago: University of Chicago Press, 1970), 3–21.

7. White, "Mother's Daughter," 46–47; Florence Armstrong, "Recollections," in WNP, reel 12; Marshall K. White to Florence Armstrong, November 2, 1958 in WNP, reel 12; *Minutes of Memphis Conference of the Methodist Episcopal Church (South), Fortieth Session held in Mayfield, Kentucky, November 19–25, 1879* (Memphis: Wills and Wildberger Printers, 1880), 7; "Journal of S. B. Love," 1879 entry, unpublished (in possession of Lambuth University, Jackson, Tennessee).

8. James Williams and Lewis Jones, eds. *Reflections* (Henderson, Tenn.: First State Bank, 1979), 29; White, "Mother's Daughter," 48.

9. Andrew David Holt, *The Struggle for a State System of Public Schools in Tennessee, 1903–1913* (New York: Bureau of Publications, Teachers College, Columbia University, 1938), viii, 5–20; White, "Mother's Daughter," 47.

10. Goodspeed Brothers, *History of Tennessee* (Columbia, Tenn.: Woodward and Stinson, 1971), 810–12; Williams, *Reflections*, 31–32; White, "Mother's Daughter," 47–49.

11. C. Vann Woodward, *Origins of the New South, 1877–1913*, 2nd ed. (Baton Rouge: Louisiana State University Press, 1951, 1974), 4, 22–29; John Egerton, *Speak Now Against the Day: The Generation Before the Civil Rights Movement in the South* (New York: Alfred A. Knopf, 1994), 34–35; C. Vann Woodward, *The Strange Career of Jim Crow*, 3rd ed. (New York: Oxford University Press, 1974), vii, 4–7, 52–53, 71, 97–102, 114–15; Lester C. Lamon, *Blacks in Tennessee, 1791–1970* (Knoxville: University of Tennessee Press, 1981), 67; Sue Shelton White, draft to editor of *Harper's Magazine*, August 1929, cited in WNP, reel 13.

12. White, "Mother's Daughter," 47; Woodward, *Strange Career*, 45–69.

13. White to *Harper's*, cited in WNP, reel 13; Janet Duitsman Cornelius, *"When I Could Read My Title Clear": Literacy, Slavery, and Religion in the Antebellum South* (Columbia: University of South Carolina Press, 1992), 1–10; United States Department of Commerce, *Historical Statistics of the United States: From Colonial Times to 1970*, Bicentennial Edition (Washington, D.C.: Government Printing House, 1975), 382.

14. White, "Mother's Daughter," 45–52; White to *Harper's*, cited in WNP, reel 13.

15. White, "Mother's Daughter," 49–50.

16. Ibid, 49.

17. Ibid, 48–50; Scott, *The Southern Lady*, 124, 133; Margery W. Davies, *Woman's Place Is at the Typewriter: Office Work and Office Workers, 1870–1930* (Philadelphia: Temple University Press, 1982), 51–78; *Georgie Robertson Christian College: The Henderson Normal, 1902–1903* (Henderson, Tenn.: n.p., n.d.); Sue White's Application for United States Civil Service Commission, June 1939, WNP, reel 14; James P. Louis, "White, Sue Shelton, 1913 to 1920," in *Notable American Women, 1607–1950: A Biographical Dictionary*, ed. Edward T. James et al., 590–92 (Cambridge, Mass.: Belknap Press, 1971).

18. Emma Inman Williams, *Historic Madison: The Story of Jackson and Madison County, Tennessee* (Jackson, Tenn.: Madison County Historical Society), 152, 227–36, 289, 330–32, 358, 360–64, 368, 378, 526–27, 532; Charles R. Warren, comp., *City Directory of Jackson, Tennessee, 1906* (Jackson, Tenn.: McCowat-Mercer, n.d.), 277; Charles M. Samson, comp., *City Directory of Jackson, Tennessee, 1910* (Jackson, Tenn.: McCowat-Mercer, n.d.), 312; Williams, *Historic Madison*, 364–65; White's Application for Civil Service, WNP, reel 14; White, "Mother's Daughter," 50–51.

19. White, "Mother's Daughter," 51; Rebecca Hourwich Reyher interview by Amelia Fry and Fern Ingersoll, 1917, "Search and Struggle for Equality and Independence," transcript, in Suffragists Oral History Project, University of California at Berkeley (hereafter SOHP), 57; Samuel C. Williams, *Phases of the History of the Supreme Court of Tennessee* (Johnson City, Tenn.: Watuaga Press, 1944), 77–78.

20. *The Suffragist* 6 (April 20, 1918): 6; White, "Mother's Daughter," 51; Robert Dean Pope, "Senatorial Baron: The Long Political Career of Kenneth D. McKellar" (PhD diss., Yale University, 1976), 140–44; *Memphis Commercial Appeal*, May 2, 1915; Anne Leslie Owens, "Rye, Thomas Clark," in *The Tennessee Encyclopedia of History and Culture*, ed. Carroll Van West et al. (Nashville: Rutledge Hill Press, 1998), 820; Rebecca [Hourwich] Reyher to Florence Armstrong, September 26, 1958, WNP, reel 12; Ward DeWitt Jr., "Tennessee Supreme Court," in *Tennessee Encyclopedia*, 956–57; *Jackson (Tennessee) Sun*, May 8, 1933; Mary Dewson to Franklin [D. Roosevelt], October 30, 1933, Official File 300, box 44, Franklin D. Roosevelt Library, Hyde Park, New York.

21. Louis, "White, Sue Shelton"; A. Elizabeth Taylor, *The Woman Suffrage Movement in Tennessee* (New York: Bookman Associates, 1957), 36; *Jackson Jacksonian*, January 1, 1913; WNP, reel

12; "Equal Suffrage Conference and Some of the Workers," *Nashville Tennessean*, January 5, 1913; Sue Shelton White, comp., *Handbook of the Tennessee Equal Suffrage Association: Proceedings of the Eight and Ninth Annual Conventions Held at Knoxville, 1914, Jackson 1915* (Jackson, Tenn., n.p., 1915), 16, 55–56.

22. Taylor, *The Woman Suffrage Movement*, 59–62; White, *Handbook of* TESA, 7–15; Ida Husted Harper, ed., *The History of Woman Suffrage* (n.p.: National American Woman Suffrage Association, 1922), 6:598, 601; Sue Shelton White to Elizabeth Hoyt, April 3, 1931, *WNP*, reel 13.

23. White to Hoyt, April 3, 1931; Taylor, *The Woman Suffrage Movement*, 61–62; Wilma Dykeman, *Tennessee Women: Past and Present* (Memphis: Brunner, Inc., 1977), 28; White, *Handbook of* TESA, 6; Harper, *History of Woman Suffrage*, 4:598.

24. White, *Handbook of* TESA, 5, 6, 19, 56; Harper, *History of Woman Suffrage*, 4:598, 601; Sue Shelton White to Elizabeth Holt, April 3, 1931, *WNP*, reel 13.

25. Harper, *History of Woman Suffrage*, 6:601; Careen Rich, "Brief History of the Suffrage Movement in Tennessee," *Nashville Tennessean*, September 6, 1920.

26. Sue S. White to Elizabeth Hoyt, April 3, 1931, *WNP*, reel 13; Taylor, *The Woman Suffrage Movement*, 68.

27. Carole Stanford Bucy, "Dudley, Anne Dallas," in *Tennessee Encyclopedia*, 263–64; Taylor, *The Woman Suffrage Movement*, 59–62; Jayne Crumpler DeFiore, "French, Lizzie Crozier," in *Tennessee Encyclopedia*, 344; Anita Shafer Goodstein, "A Rare Alliance: African American and White Women in the Tennessee Election of 1919 and 1920," *Journal of Southern History* 64 (May 1968): 219–46; Anastasia Sims, "'Powers that Pray' and 'Powers that Prey': Tennessee and the Fight for Woman Suffrage," *Tennessee Historical Quarterly* 50 (Winter 1991): 221.

28. Dykeman, *Tennessee Women*, 28; Taylor, *The Woman Suffrage Movement*, 62–66; Sue S. White to Carrie Chapman Catt, April 27, 1918, and Carrie Chapman Catt to Sue S. White, May 6, 1918, *WNP*, reel 12; Sue S. White to Alice Paul, July 11, 1919, and Lucy Burns to Sue S. White, February 3, 1919, National Woman's Party Papers, Library of Congress, [microfilm] National Woman's Party, Suffrage Years, 1913–1920, Microfilming Corporation of America, 1982.

29. Carrie Chapman Catt and Nettie Rogers Shuler, *Women Suffrage and Politics: The Inner Story of the Suffrage Movement* (Seattle: University of Washington Press, 1923), 323; Sue S. White to Mrs. C. J. Jerman, September 27, 1917, *WNP*, reel 13; Carrie Chapman Catt et al., *Victory: How Women Won It* (New York: H. W. Wilson, 1940), 123–24; List of Tennessee counties dated September 27, 1917, *WNP*, reel 13; Inez Haynes Irwin, *The Story of the Woman's Party* (New York: Harcourt, Brace, 1921; reprinted as *Up Hill with Banners Flying* [Penobscot, Maine: Traversity Press, 1964]), 303; Eleanor Flexner, *Century of Struggle: The Woman's Rights Movement in the United States* (New York: Atheneum, 1968), 289.

30. Flexner, *Century of Struggle*, 295–305; Sue S. White to Rose Young, June 1, 1917, *WNP*, reel 12.

31. Sue S. White to Rose Young, June 1, 1917, *WNP*, reel 12.

32. Alice Paul, interview with Amelia R. Fry, 1976, "Conversations with Alice Paul; Woman Suffrage and the Equal Rights Amendment," transcript, in SOHP, 5; Rosalyn Terborg-Penn, "African American Women and the Vote: An Overview," in *African American Women and the Vote, 1837–1965*, ed. Ann D. Gordon, 11–23 (Amherst: University of Massachusetts Press, 1997); Carol Lynn Yellin and Janann Sherman, *The Perfect 36: Tennessee Delivers Woman Suffrage* (Memphis: Wilson Graphics, 1998), 67–73; Rosalyn Terborg-Penn, *African-American Women in the Struggle for the Vote, 1850–1920* (Bloomington: Indiana University Press, 1998), 107–35.

33. Goodstein, "A Rare Alliance"; White to *Harper's*, in *WNP*, reel 13.

34. White to *Harper's*, in WNP, reel 13.

35. Application form, United States Civil Service Commission, June 1939, WNP, reel 14; Sue S. White to S. M. Green, May 31, 1919, WNP, reel 13; "Miss White Has Done Excellent Work for Blind," *Montgomery Times*, August 13, 1919.

36. Sue S. White to Elizabeth Hoyt, April 3, 1931, WNP, reel 13; Sue S. White to Carrie Chapman Catt, April 27, 1918, and Carrie Chapman Catt to Sue S. White, July 20, 1918, WNP, reel 12; Flexner, *Century of Struggle*, 263–65.

37. Flexner, *Century of Struggle*, 165–66.

38. Harper, *History of Woman Suffrage*, 5:675–77.

39. Irwin, *The Story*, 38, 48–49, 152–153; Sue S. White to Elizabeth Hoyt, April 3, 1931, WNP, reel 13; Inez Haynes Irwin, *Angels and Amazons: A Hundred Years of American Women* (Garden City, N.Y.: Doubleday, Doran and Company, 1933), 374–75, 380–82.

40. Taylor, *The Woman Suffrage Movement*, 56–57; *Woman Citizen* (July 7, 1917): 107; Sue S. White to Carrie Chapman Catt, April 27, 1918, WNP, reel 12; Sue Shelton White, "Democratic Party May Lose Support: Southern Suffragist Says Patiences [*sic*] of Women is Tried to the Limit," *Patriot Phalanx*, an undated article in WNP, reel 13; Elizabeth Hoyt to Sue Shelton White, April 13, 1931, WNP, reel 13.

41. White, "Democratic Party May Lose Support."

42. Sue S. White to Elizabeth Hoyt, April 3, 1931, WNP, reel 13; Sue S. White to Carrie Chapman Catt, April 27, 1918, WNP, reel 12; Irwin, *The Story*, 302–6; Rebecca Hourwich Reyher to Florence Armstrong, September 26, 1958, WNP, reel 12.

43. Sue S. White to Elizabeth Hoyt, April 3, 1931, WNP, reel 13; Sue S. White to Carrie Chapman Catt, April 27, 1918, WNP, reel 12; Rebecca Hourwich Reyher to Florence Armstrong, September 26, 1958, WNP, reel 12; Irwin, *The Story*, 302–6.

44. Sue S. White to Elizabeth Hoyt, April 3, 1931, WNP, reel 13; the Memphis newspaper article is without title, author, or date, WNP, reel 13.

45. Sue S. White to Carrie Chapman Catt, April 27, 1918, WNP, reel 12.

46. Carrie Chapman Catt to Sue S. White, May 6, 1918, WNP, reel 12; Marjorie Spruill Wheeler, *New Women of the New South: The Leaders of the Woman Suffrage Movement in the Southern States* (New York: Oxford University Press, 1993), 171.

47. Sue S. White to Carrie Chapman Catt, May 9 and 16, 1918; Carrie Chapman Catt to Sue S. White, May 6, 1918, WNP, reel 12.

48. Sue S. White to Carrie Chapman Catt, April 1918, WNP, reel 12; Sue S. White to Elizabeth Hoyt, April 3, 1931, WNP, reel 13.

49. Ibid; "Nation-Wide Tour Closes in Washington," *The Suffragist* 5 (8 December 1917): 11; Rebecca Hourwich Reyher to Florence Armstrong, September 26, 1958, WNP, reel 12.

Charl Ormond Williams

(1885–1969)

Feminist Politics and Education for Equality

SARAH WILKERSON FREEMAN

❀ ❀ ❀

In June 1920 Charl Ormond Williams, Superintendent of Shelby County (Tennessee) Public Schools, became the national Democratic Party's first female vice-chair—a remarkable feat considering that she, and millions of other women, did not yet possess full suffrage rights. Woman suffragists and antisuffragists were at that moment in a white-hot battle over the proposed Nineteenth Amendment to the Constitution. Ratification by one more state would give millions of southern women, whose state governments had failed to enfranchise them, a federally guaranteed right to vote. When this fight came to Tennessee in August 1920 Charl Williams earned an eternal footnote in the annals of women's history for her efforts in that final battle that made women's suffrage the law of the land.

Ironically, Williams was no great fighter for the cause before that donnybrook in Nashville, but she was nationally known as an activist for the "equalization of education." She believed that all children in the southern countryside, regardless of race, should have access to quality public education of the same caliber provided children in some southern cities and many places outside the South. To realize this vision, Charl focused her considerable energies on women who she believed would, if given the chance, exert their influence at the ballot box to fulfill this dream. Her women's rights activism stemmed from that belief.

For Charl Williams, eliminating gender discrimination, especially in politics and the workplace, and improving public education were codependent causes. From the Progressive Era to the dawning of the modern civil rights movement, Williams stayed remarkably dedicated to this two-front offensive, serving as president of the National Education Association (NEA) in 1921–22 and as the organization's chief lobbyist for federal aid for public education from

CHARL ORMOND WILLIAMS
Portrait located at the Shelby County
Board of Education, Memphis, Tennessee.
Reprinted with the permission of David Pickler,
Superintendent of Schools.

1922 to 1949. With forceful speech, decisive thinking, and a "brusque" manner "softened by the pleasing accent of her native state Tennessee," Williams fiercely campaigned for higher salaries and tenure systems for public school teachers—who were overwhelmingly female—and for the rights of married women in the work force.[1] During the Great Depression, when married women were condemned for working while men remained unemployed, Williams was elected president of the National Federation of Business and Professional Women's clubs (NFBPW), an organization that severely criticized New Deal policies that discriminated against women. In 1937, on Williams's watch, the NFBPW endorsed the Equal Rights Amendment, an event that marked a turning point in feminist history. She simultaneously cultivated a close relationship with the First Lady, Eleanor Roosevelt, whose anti-ERA sentiments were well known. Through this relationship, Williams elicited from President Franklin Roosevelt a historic endorsement of federal aid for the equalization of public education for black and white children and a pledge to include women in postwar policy-making decisions and the United Nations.

In spite of this remarkable and historic career, surprisingly little has been written about Charl Ormond Williams. This is due in part to the fact that the historical record available to scholars prior to 2004 revealed only a very professional and officious side of Williams, a carefully controlled version of her life, work, and relationships. Unsatisfied with this cold account, the author unearthed a significant vein of Williams's more personal papers in Arlington and Memphis, Tennessee. These letters, photos, and scrapbooks reveal how a country girl from Shelby County, inspired to develop and pursue her vision of a better, more humane and just world, was initially guided to that path by similarly dedicated women very close to home.

Williams was born in 1885 in Arlington, Tennessee, a "village," as Charl called it (five to seven hundred residents populated it throughout her life), located forty miles east of Memphis in Shelby County. Her family was not wealthy but thrived nonetheless. The children—Mabel, Merle, Charl, Mary, Hartwell, and Lawrence—grew up within the village's insular society and strove to be respected as individuals and as a family. Their father, Crittenden, a carpenter born in Tennessee in 1856, built their rambling home and the Methodist church where they worshiped. Raised by his mother and stepfather in Shelby County, Crittenden worked the family farm, cared for his younger half-siblings, and received little formal schooling, although he loved books. Crittenden's mother, a Virginian, lived with her son's family while the children were growing up. Charl's mother, Minnie Lawrence Thomas, born in nearby Fayette County in 1858, descended from North Carolina families that settled in West Tennessee before the 1830s. A decisive figure in the household, Minnie encouraged her children, boys and girls alike, to pursue life's opportunities far beyond Shelby County. Charl and her sisters were raised to be ladylike in appearance but also independent, resourceful, and articulate. Close ties to home, family, and community were crucial to the directions Williams's life and work would take.[2]

Charl was particularly inspired by the fact that women regularly served as superintendents of Shelby County schools, beginning with Mrs. W. H. Horton, who held the position from 1882 to 1886.[3] Five other women, including Charl's sister Mabel, occupied this office prior to Charl. They oversaw personnel and informed the county board of education of the needs of school-aged children outside the Memphis corporate limit and into the surrounding countryside. Superintendent Maude Moor signed Charl's teaching certificate in 1902 after she graduated from the eleven-grade Arlington school.[4] At age seventeen, Charl became eligible for her first teaching job at a one-room school in Bartlett. It is important to note that Shelby County, and Tennessee in general, was remarkably ahead of its time in hiring women to serve as county school superintendents, as very few public offices were available to women in the late nineteenth century.

A strong and dedicated local circle of Methodist women also provided unusual female role models in this period. In Arlington the Williams sisters came under the powerful and direct personal influence of Elizabeth Claiborne, a uniquely inspiring member of their Methodist church. Before Elizabeth was born in June 1878 (during the yellow fever epidemic), her mother dedicated her unborn child to missionary work in China. Local Methodist women, influential in the Memphis Conference of the Methodist Church, established a high school in Arlington in 1884. Claiborne and the Williams children attended this school, which became part of the Shelby County public school system in 1895.[5] All of the Williams girls became teachers soon after graduating. Claiborne kept her mother's promise and attended Scaritt College, then located in Kansas City, before sailing to Shanghai, where she taught for nearly thirty years as a Methodist missionary and principal of the McTyiere School for Girls. Charl corresponded with Elizabeth, who encouraged her to get involved in social welfare causes.[6] In 1908 Elizabeth sent postcards of Chinese peasant life to Charl, then a seventh-grade teacher and principal at the white Germantown school, to share with her students.[7]

The Williams sisters came into the profession during a period of tremendous change in education for white and black children in the South. In the 1880s and '90s Booker T. Washington, a graduate of the Hampton Normal and Agricultural Institute and founder of Tuskegee Institute in Alabama, popularized a model of industrial education for African Americans that attracted support from northern philanthropists and elite southern whites. The 1896 *Plessy v. Ferguson* decision, which gave federal sanction to the "separate but equal" doctrine, encouraged the establishment of racially segregated public school systems. For the most part, greater resources were allocated for the education of white children than nonwhite children, but in the rural South both groups faired badly as farm work, family responsibilities, poverty, and great distances impeded efforts to provide even minimal education. Laws requiring two sets of schools (white and black) and notoriously regressive systems of funding (such as poll tax systems designed to discourage payments and, thereby, suppress voting) made improvements in the quality of education in the region extremely difficult and controversial. In response to the crisis in rural southern education, especially for African American children, philanthropies, notably the Peabody, Slater, and Jeanes Funds, the General Education Board, and the Southern Education Board, worked closely with Booker T. Washington and privately funded rural schools with significant agricultural and industrial training components. In the toxic racial climate, characterized by the lynching of black men and the rapid spread of Jim Crow statutes into new sectors of life and commerce, efforts to improve education for black children in the South would be met with resistance, enmity, suspicion, and contempt by many white southerners. As historian Louis Harlan has demonstrated, even otherwise powerful philanthropists accommodated Jim Crow to advance what little progress in black education would be tolerated by southern whites. Race, class, and region clearly determined the form and quality of education children received.[8]

The Williams sisters joined the ranks of classroom teachers as the inequalities of Jim Crow education and gender-based wage discrimination expanded in Shelby County during the Progressive Era. Southern state governments had established white public teachers' colleges, and large numbers of female graduates taught in severely underfunded public schools for low wages. But many young women, especially in rural areas, received teaching certificates without the benefit of formal teacher training. To create more uniform standards, summer teachers' institutes were established. In the summer of 1908 the Shelby County Board of Education implemented a nominally "progressive" policy (though arguably regressive, paternalistic, and misogynistic) that shaped Charl's life. After much debate, and against Superintendent Elizabeth Messick's wishes, board members voted for a policy "forbidding the employment of married women as teachers."[9] The board considered this a constructive reform on par with a new policy that all teachers attend the summer teachers' institute. It seemed that the all-male board believed that to conform to new educational requirements for female teachers, the women had to be free of marital and domestic responsibilities. The unfairness and cruelty of this policy upset many in the community.

That summer, at age twenty-three, Charl Williams looked forward to her third year as principal of Germantown's white high school. She proudly worked for a living and had not become a teacher with the expectation of remaining single. She had been popular as a young woman and had close relationships with a couple of young men. Nearly thirty years later her feminist ideals and outspoken opposition to discrimination against married women in the work force placed her at the head of one the nation's most powerful women's organizations, the NFBPW. Her movement in that direction seemed to begin with the anger and frustration she felt at the hands of male policy makers who thoughtlessly relegated female teachers to lives without husbands and children. The only possible advantage was that teachers' salaries would have to be raised to a living wage and pensions instated since female educators could not, by law, be supported by husbands.

The following year, Mabel Williams, Charl's older sister, succeeded Messick as superintendent of Shelby County Schools and continued reforms started by her predecessor, especially rural school consolidation. Messick, the first student to enroll at and graduate from the University of Chicago, had already established a cooperative relationship with Dr. James H. Dillard, president and director of the Negro Rural School Fund (later known as the Jeanes Fund), and through this private initiative supported agricultural education for the county's African American students. As the board allocated public resources to racially segregated schools, black schools were unequally created and poorly maintained. Private efforts to redress this imbalance were a double-edged sword. Public white school boards in the South often used the existence of this private funding as an excuse for withholding public moneys from black schools and generally neglecting black education. During Mabel's administration, tension arose between the board and African American parents over the length of their children's school terms, which were erratically scheduled and rarely totaled more than six months.[10] In 1911 the intense outcry from black parents, teachers, and leaders moved the board to extend a term an additional month.[11] That same year, the board voted unanimously for a nine-month term for all white schools.[12] Black teachers also protested their low salaries and the difficulty of doing their jobs when the board voted to open and close black schools with almost no advance notice. When the board closed the Manassas school, which had been established with little public assistance by local African Americans, black community leaders sued the board. The suit failed, but to calm racial tension and keep the school viable, Mabel Williams offered Cora Price Taylor, a respected local black educator, the position of principal at Manassas.[13]

Mabel Williams's achievements and model for public service greatly influenced her younger sister. Mabel set a standard for expanding rural education using newly available federal funds and aggressively lobbied state legislators to pass a bill establishing several co-ed white-only normal schools. She succeeded in locating one of the schools in Memphis (now the University of Memphis) by leading West Tennessee women's organizations in a fight for the cause. Charl joined the founding faculty as a mathematics assistant in 1913, in part because the board now required principals of schools with two hundred or more students to have an A.B. degree from a four-year college, which Charl did not have. Mabel opened another door for Charl when she became engaged to marry in 1914 and resigned from her Shelby County post. Thirty-year-old Charl was chosen to succeed her sister as county school superintendent, a position she would hold for seven years. Following in Mabel's footsteps, she focused on improving teaching standards, elevating the status of teachers, and working closely with parents, local politicians, legislators, and national leaders in education. Charl also worked closely with Cora Price Taylor and other black educators, and took the expansion of black schools to a new level. In 1913 Mabel persuaded the board to allocate two hundred dollars to send a group of the county's black teachers to attend a short course at the Tuskeegee Institute. In April 1920 Charl herself would attend a meeting at Tuskeegee, with her expenses paid by the board.[14]

Although Mabel's energies were now channeled into creating a home for her husband and two boys, her executive talents, knowledge, and commitment to improving public education were expressed in parent-teacher organizations. In 1922 she came before the board in her new role as Mrs. Lawrence H. Hughes to request that a twelfth grade be added to "their high school" in Arlington. The motion carried. The influence of the sisters' personal and professional alliance grew as Tennessee's normal school graduates began teaching, formed organizations, and looked for leaders who understood their needs, goals, and concerns.

In her new office, Charl felt a particularly feminist responsibility to demonstrate what women, when given the chance, could accomplish. She eagerly solicited new federal funds for agricultural and vocational education and coordinated these with private and local initiatives. Within months of taking office, she submitted a plan to use aid from the private Jeanes Fund to turn the new black Woodstock school into "a model school for negroes." She explained to the board that with a comparatively small outlay of public funds the school could be equipped with modern cooking and agricultural departments. She created a new position, Home Economics and County Agent, to oversee tomato and poultry clubs and domestic science programs in the schools and used federal funds to pay a portion of the agent's salary.[15] Charl hired increasing numbers of qualified women, black and white, to staff programs and assist her. She joined professional organizations, such as the National Education Association, and attended national conferences where she was exposed to new ideas and met (and impressed) leaders in education. For Charl, the smallest mite of opportunity was ripe with possibility. The challenge was to build something substantial out of very little and to spin each meeting into a web of useful relationships in ever-rising circles of influence and power.[16]

Her increasingly ambitious vision for improving the quality of education for Shelby County children required long-term funding commitments that local governments in the rural South were unlikely to provide. She was convinced that the majority of southern rural children, black and white, were destined to be trapped in ignorance and poverty unless specific allocations of federal funds, extracted from prosperous regions and industries, were channeled into raising academic standards in rural schools. The disparity between the quality of public education found in wealthy and urban districts compared to the quality in rural communities was, Charl believed, undemocratic, unfair, and unnecessary. In 1916 as President Woodrow Wilson, a southern Democrat, sought reelection, she pinned her hopes on the Democratic Party to provide more federal aid for educating rural children, especially after Tennessee's Democratic senator Cordell Hull succeeded in his fight for the federal income tax amendment. She demonstrated her partisan interests by accepting an appointment to chair the education committee for the women's bureau of the 1916 Democratic Convention. This first taste of national political power unleashed a drive within her to dream large dreams, and for the next fifty years she never stopped believing that southern children, black and white, could have equal opportunities for quality education. For Charl, partisan politics, and her work for Wilson's victory, was another means to that end.

Back in Tennessee, Charl continued to grapple with inadequate and regressive methods of funding schools and began to devise new fiscal strategies that challenged the traditional system of funding education through poll taxes, a notoriously unpredictable source. When poll tax revenues fell short of covering the board's expenses in 1916, Williams worked for months on a bold alternative that required tremendous political savvy and vision.[17] In February 1917, after consulting with the chairman of the County Commission and the mayor, she invited local politicians to the "most important meeting of the year" and tried to convince the board to support a bond issue to repair or rebuild county schools. Many Shelby County schools were firetraps, she argued. The Bartlett school had caught fire three times. Teachers at Germantown's Mabel Williams School suffered from chronic throat complaints due to bad heating and ventilation systems. And those were white schools. Black schools had been so neglected, she insisted, that they had to be improved or closed. Indeed, African Americans had become increasingly vocal in the spring of 1916 about overcrowding and numerous unmet needs of black school children. Williams calculated that $300,000 was needed to rectify the situation. The board submitted the bond issue, the state legislature passed it in April, and a boom in the building, repair, and expansion of black and white schools followed.[18] National leaders in education took notice.

On the heels of this victory, Charl pressed further. She persuaded the board to change the hiring system by offering contracts in May so teachers could "make plans for summer work."[19] What she did not share with the board was her own deeply held belief that the uncertainty of employment for female teachers was a debilitating problem. Job security was crucial for the improvement of education and the quality of life for female teachers, and she believed these two issues were inseparable. She also criticized the top-down method of determining school policies and proposed that public officials confer with people in neighborhoods, black and white, before deciding on school terms. After the board voted yet again to hold classes in the black schools for only six months, Charl extended the summer term an additional two weeks and asked the board's permission after the fact.[20]

At the national level, momentous changes were on the horizon as President Wilson, soon after winning his second term in 1916, began preparing the nation to enter the First World War. For the first time, federal IQ tests were used to determine fitness for military service, and results indicated that thousands of prospective doughboys were illiterate, malnourished, and woefully lacking in basic education. The pattern was clear—poor regions produced poorly educated, unhealthy children. Because of the crisis, support for federal aid for home economics and infant and maternal care programs escalated. The passage of the Smith-Hughes Act in 1917, which allocated federal funds for agricultural and home economics training, validated Charl's faith in the Democrats. She felt a heightened sense of mission during this period, inspired in part by her own personal fears. Her brother, Hartwell—whom Mabel and Charl helped support—awaited deployment in his ROTC barracks in New York.[21]

In 1917, at the NEA convention in Portland, Oregon, Charl arrived as a nationally recognized leader in education, and her star was only just beginning to rise. Largely a bastion of white male education administrators since its establishment in 1857, the NEA had not functioned as a democratic organization for female teachers. But in the "democratic upsurge" of woman suffrage campaigns, fueled by the prodemocracy rhetoric of the war, female teachers agitated to play a real part in the NEA's operations.[22] At that convention, female teachers exerted their strength and elected three women to serve as president, vice president, and second vice president, ensuring a long run of female executive power. Charl was elected third vice president, a victory that put her on track to becoming the youngest president of the NEA in 1921. In those four years the organization hired business managers, established a research division and a systematic program for legislation, and opened a headquarters in Washington, D.C., indicating that political lobbying would be a central part of operations.[23] NEA membership grew exponentially as female teachers joined in droves, and Charl's popularity among this group became her springboard into ever-higher circles of influence, propelling her into the woman suffrage crusade and the women's movement within the Democratic Party.[24]

In September 1919 the Democratic National Committee [DNC] voted to elect national committeewomen, and Senator Cordell Hull of Tennessee, the DNC's chair and a woman suffrage supporter, chose Charl as Tennessee's first associate committeewoman. Her substantial influence among female teachers made Charl a good choice for the Democrats. In return, Charl hoped that the party's platform would bear the stamp of the NEA. At the Democratic convention in Oakland, California, Charl told a female reporter that her principal purpose was to secure an NEA-sponsored plank endorsing the creation of a Department of Education with its executive in the president's cabinet. As the interview warmed up, Charl confessed "that she likes to dance—although Tennessee looks with disfavor upon school teachers indulging in that pastime—she likes to ride horseback, to swim, to tramp in the country—but that her one ambition is to help be the means of giving an equal opportunity for education to every child—black and white—in the United States."[25] The all-male, all-white platform committee did not accept the NEA plank, but it did endorse federal aid to combat illiteracy and raise teachers' salaries. Charl saw some victory in this.

But the most compelling issue of the 1920 Democratic and Republican conventions was woman suffrage. Tennessee had not yet ratified the Nineteenth Amendment, and Senator Hull wanted Democrats to be able to take credit for enfranchising millions of new women voters. At the Democratic convention, Tennessee's female delegates engaged in deadly serious debates over when to bring the amendment to the floor of the state legislature. Charl had confided to the Oakland reporter that she had "never been a suffrage leader, although she ha[d] always believed in it and taught that belief in school."[26] Nonetheless, she led a faction of delegates who wanted the governor to wait until after the summer primaries to call a special legislative session to vote on ratification. As she gravely cautioned her sister delegates, "We can't make one false step now. Not alone our interests are at stake, but the interests of all American women."[27] Her leadership skills attracted attention, and political commentators speculated that Charl was among a handful of women who could be considered presidential timber. Recognizing an important ally, Hull chose Charl to serve as the DNC's first female vice-chair, making her the first woman in either of the two major political parties to hold such a high position.

Even greater tests of her political ability came as woman suffrage activists and their opponents all converged on Nashville for the special legislative session in August after the summer primaries. Tennessee's woman suffragists had formed competing organizations and passed state legislation for municipal and presidential suffrage in 1919. Some suffragists, notably Sue Shelton White, who had been jailed for setting fire to a portion of President Wilson's speeches about liberty and democracy, supported the militant National Woman's Party. Factions of state and local suffrage organizations disagreed on who should lead the critical battle in Nashville. To "restore harmony among the suffragists," Governor Albert Roberts appointed Charl, a reliable Democratic operative, to chair the Women's Steering Committee for the ratification of the amendment.[28]

After one of the dirtiest political fights the nation ever witnessed, Tennessee ratified the Nineteenth Amendment. Immediately after ratification, thirty-six anti–woman suffrage legislators tried to rescind the measure by challenging the validity of the vote and then fleeing to Alabama to prevent a quorum. Learning of their flight, Williams, at two o'clock in the morning, knocked on the hotel room door of Joseph Hanover, the young prosuffrage state representative heading the House steering committee, and alerted him to the threat. Carrie Chapman Catt, president of the National American Woman Suffrage Association, had the room next to Hanover, and in the early morning hours, Charl, Catt, and Hanover, who called together his forces, conducted a strategy session to subvert the antis' efforts to sabotage Tennessee's ratification.[29] When the law stood, Catt gave credit to Williams for the victory. Charl became a celebrity among suffragists and feminists, and within a year delegates at the NEA national convention unanimously elected her president.

But as Charl toured the country for the NEA, she worried that her highly partisan Democratic profile could be a problem, especially since the Republicans controlled the White House with the election of Warren G. Harding. In December 1922 she resigned from the DNC but kept her party loyalties clear by accepting Carrie Chapman Catt's request that she serve as the Tennessee state chair of the women's committees of the Woodrow Wilson Foundation. Against a backdrop of increasing isolationism, the women organized to perpetuate Wilson's ideals of peaceful international relations and the League of Nations. Under Charl's leadership the NEA organized an international conference of educators in 1922. "Education is the best possible preparation for wars if wars must come," Williams stated in an address before the National Council of Education; "it is the only sure preparation for universal brotherhood and world peace."[30] That same year, she campaigned as a "Female Spellbinder" for the Democrats.

Throughout those momentous years, Charl remained superintendent of Shelby County schools. By 1922 she had hired a biracial supervisory force of thirteen men and women, quadrupled the county school budget to a million dollars, developed an efficient clerical system, and—over a seven-year period—spent three-quarters of a million dollars building new schools. But she also had become an indispensable leader in the NEA. As her presidency ended, the organization's executive secretary offered Williams a job as director of field service to carry on the national campaign for equalization of education. She resigned her Shelby County post to accept the job in Washington.[31] Before leaving Tennessee, Charl invited Mr. S. L. Smith to her farewell board meeting. Smith, the southern states' representative for the Rosenwald Fund, had worked with Charl for six years and praised her work for African American rural schools accomplished through the support of the General Education Board, and the Jeanes, Slater, and Rosenwald Funds. Smith explained to the board that Charl had personally directed funds to support summer schools for black teachers, pay black teachers and supervisors, extend the term of the "Homemakers Club Fund" supervisor, and supported the black County Training School at Woodstock by building teacher housing, a workshop, and a barn, and by purchasing equipment for industrial training and furniture for the girls' dorm. Agents who inspected the Woodstock School pronounced it "one of the very best of its kind they have seen in the whole South." Furthermore, Smith reported, "Shelby County has led the South in the number of Rosenwald schools built." Charl had accomplished this work by meeting with black teachers at their schools and out of the board's view.[32] Stealth tactics helped shield her from critics who might have felt threatened had the extent of her work for black education been more publicized.[33] Now that she had gained a national stature and was leaving Tennessee, Charl clearly wanted her efforts entered into the county's official public record.

Another secret to her success in this period (and for the next nineteen years) was her secretary, Callie S. Waldran, a 1920 graduate of George Washington University and former Shelby County schoolteacher, whom Williams hired in 1921. Waldran relocated with Charl to D.C. and continued to work as her first lieutenant in the NEA. They shared a home, which Charl purchased, on Connecticut Avenue. Waldran became an important part of the Williams family circle as she provided companionship and emotional support for Charl, who had no intention of returning home to Tennessee once she accepted the NEA position.[34] Callie kept the family informed and took care of them when they visited. She also kept Charl organized and centered by holding the household together while Charl traveled thousands of miles each year lobbying for legislation and speaking to educators and women's organizations on behalf of the NEA.

The women moved to Washington at the same moment conservative Republicans ascended to power and maintained their control through alliances with evangelical fundamentalist Christians and prohibitionists. Racism, parading under the banner of states' rights, was intensifying during the Harding, Coolidge, and Hoover administrations. Southern racial conservatives and white supremacists, who detested the idea of "equalization" of black and white education, accused Charl and the NEA of seeking federal control of local schools through the backdoor of aid. Meanwhile, Catholic organizations argued that parochial schools would suffer if public schools received federal assistance. Both factions lobbied hard to defeat the NEA education bills. Charl developed a seething distaste for Catholic Church officials and strengthened her resolve to preserve the Jeffersonian "wall of separation between the church and state"—a principle she had embraced when she denied ministers access to Shelby County's public schools. Charl was forced into a defensive mode as she insisted, rather disingenuously, that improved public schools would not compete with parochial schools and that federally funded programs, administered by a Department of Education and a cabinet-level secretary, would not impinge on states' rights or "interfere" with local school administrations. In truth, she knew that federal funds could help put controversial programs over at the local level. She also wanted public schools to be of such a high caliber as to compete with private and parochial schools. But resistance to her efforts came from no less than the U.S. Commissioner of Education, John J. Tigert, a Tennessee native from a prominent southern Methodist missionary family, who was appointed by Harding and Coolidge. Tigert did not support the establishment of a Department of Education with a cabinet-level executive.[35]

With these battle lines drawn, Charl turned to women's organizations for support. During this reactionary period Charl downplayed her feminist ideology and goals and instead deployed more subtle "stealth feminist" tactics, crafted to ease the fears of antifeminists and conservatives. It is interesting that Charl, a woman who diligently pursued a professional career, told Wisconsin audiences that, "Marriage—the home—is the greatest career a woman can follow. Alone, a woman can have only one career. Married, she has a career to her credit for each of her children. . . . Men and woman [*sic*] never get as much satisfaction out of their own successes as they get out of the successes of their children."[36] In truth, she did not believe that women should have to choose between marriage (the maternal careers) and careers in the public sector. At the same time, she recognized the growing political influence of mothers, such as her sister and staunchest ally, Mabel. The sisters' alliance grew more powerful when Charl joined the Board of Managers of the National Parent and Teachers Association (PTA) in 1923.

At the 1924 Democratic convention she participated in the first women's advisory platform committee, representing twenty-five women's organizations and chaired by Eleanor Roosevelt. The women solidly supported Charl's plank but disagreed on almost every other issue: Prohibition, U.S. participation in the League of Nations, the anti–Ku Klux Klan proposal (which the women only "recommended" for adoption), and the protection of women in industry. Most damagingly, the National Woman's Party opposed protective legislation based on sex but supported a plank for an equal rights amendment. This move split women's rights advocates and enabled the all-male platform committee to discount the women's efforts altogether—a humiliating blow.[37]

After five years of failing to pass the NEA's bills, Charl looked to her sister Mabel and the southern Methodist's Woman's Missionary Council (MWMC) for help. Mabel, an officer in the MWMC's Memphis organization, approached the southern MWMC's superintendent, Mrs. W. A. (Bertha) Newell, in fall 1927 about her sister's efforts. Newell responded that, as an "old normal school teacher," she had supported the equalization legislation for some time and offered to send a leaflet of endorsement to each missionary society of all the local churches. These stacks of endorsement fliers helped offset the influence of conservative Southern Baptists, who opposed the bill. At the next Democratic Convention, in 1928, delegates endorsed a compromise education plank that affirmed the "sovereign right" of each state "in all matters pertaining to education" and its control of the "expenditure of the moneys collected by taxation for the support of its schools." The plank also stated that the federal government "should offer to the states such counsel, advice, results of research and aid as may be made available through the federal agencies for the general improvement of our schools in view of our national needs." Charl wrote Eleanor Roosevelt (ER), "The plank is not as outspoken as I should have wished but it does indorse [*sic*] the principle for which we stand and as a Democrat I am devoutly grateful for that." Exactly which "principle" she meant was left for ER to discern. Charl was far more disheartened that year by her party's choice of a presidential candidate, the Irish Catholic New York governor, Al Smith, but she nonetheless assisted ER's efforts to elect him and mourned when Herbert Hoover defeated Smith with the help of southern religious conservatives.[38]

As hard times deepened, the economic vulnerability of working women and female teachers increased precipitously. With millions of men unemployed in Europe and the United States, criticism of married women who earned paychecks intensified. Charl's feminist ideals moved her to help organize the first international meeting of business and professional women. In 1930, as chair of the NFBPW's education committee, she headed the "Geneva Special," a contingent of members who toured France, Belgium, and Germany, ending their trip at the international conference in Switzerland.[39] Their purpose was to combat employment discrimination against married women. Nonetheless, in 1932 the U.S. National Economy Act included Section 213, which prohibited spouses from simultaneously working in federal civil service. NFBPW members loudly protested and lobbied for repeal.

Even though Charl celebrated the routing of Hoover and supported the election of FDR in 1932, white male Democratic leaders proved resistant to her reforms. FDR needed southern Democrats to vote for New Deal legislation, but some southern politicians feared that expanded federal programs would threaten states' rights and antagonize white racially conservative constituents. FDR also needed the support of Catholic leaders. This racial and political climate made the NEA's reforms difficult for many politicians to endorse. But the economic crisis hit teachers and school systems particularly hard, and the administration's unwillingness to grant federal aid outright to public schools hurt FDR's popularity among female teachers especially. In the September 1935 *Journal of the NEA*, the organization's executive secretary, Willard E. Givens, published an editorial entitled "New Deal a Raw Deal for Public Schools."[40]

By 1935 Charl had earned even greater recognition among the nation's education activists and feminists, and she was extremely well positioned to take advantage of FDR's insecurities. She was a vice president in the national PTA throughout the 1930s and edited *Our Public Schools*, published by the PTA in 1934. After a heated contest in July 1935 Charl was elected president of the national NFBPW for a two-year term and made NFBPW history by keeping her NEA job while fighting simultaneously for both organizations' causes—which she said differed very little. With "Women Unite for Effective Democracy!" as her presidential slogan, Charl told audiences around the country that more women needed to be in state legislatures and in Congress, and it was time to "demand a greater contribution from women to government." She also opposed "special protection for women in the same manner she oppose[d] special discrimination against them because of their sex."[41] Her brand of feminist rhetoric resonated with ERA advocates, but in other venues she avoided this controversial issue, which had driven a wedge between women's rights activists. The First Lady opposed the ERA, and Charl needed FDR just as he needed to mend fences with teachers. Aware of this dynamic, ER appointed Charl to her 1935 National Women's Committee for the Mobilization of Human Needs.[42]

While other New Dealers focused on job creation, Charl focused on job security for already employed women. Newspapers across the country printed Charl's pointed responses to those who argued that women should leave the workforce, as was the policy in fascist Germany. "[I]f men displaced women in the working world," she countered, "the most immediate result will be that men will have a great many more women to support than they have now. For the woman who gives up her job to live at home has to have a home to go to, and if she can't pay for it herself someone else must; and if the men bounce the ladies out of offices and factories, that's a little matter they won't be able to overlook. . . . The working woman pays her own way in this world. The men ought to be the last people on earth to want to see her made a dependent again."[43]

She delivered this message to the nation's most influential professional women's organizations as she crossed the country on a speaking tour.[44] But the drum beat for women to leave the labor force continued. During a March 17, 1936, radio broadcast, Williams launched a two-pronged offensive that combined her militant defense of women's employment with a call for women's greater political power. She targeted new voters and called upon local women's organizations to study state election laws, find out more about elected officials, "and see if they measure up to the highest standard."[45] She called on women to imagine flexing their collective power, as she sarcastically mused, "Suppose that the women of the United States should stay home next Monday for a sort of feminine day of rest—I would not dream, of course, of suggesting that women go on strike. . . . The possibilities opened up are so upsetting that I think we should all consider how to avoid them."[46] Without the services of the nation's ten million working women, the "wheels of business and industry in this country would cease," she insisted, but perhaps women needed "to prove to cynical males that women are indispensable to the welfare of the nation."

The next day's headlines blared, "Charl O. Williams Is Women's Champion." If the Republicans had been in the White House, she probably would have kept her white gloves on and continued to understate her feminist ideals, but with ER (an active member of the New York chapter of the NFBPW) by her side, Charl crashed forward into unknown territory. Some male staff members at the NEA questioned her tactics, and she dismissed them as fools if they could not see how her defense of working women, especially married teachers, and the political empowerment of women advanced the NEA's cause.

Charl's relationship with the Roosevelts became rather complicated as ER strongly supported Charl but FDR remained distant. In a ten-minute radio program with ER called "Women's Responsibility for Effective Democracy," broadcast live from the White House via NBC stations, the women did not back down one iota from Charl's call for working women to keep their jobs and exercise more political power. Charl explained that gender discrimination dragged down public education and mocked democratic principles. Women were at the heart of public education, they insisted, and by standing up for themselves, women also stood for a more democratic society and, they insisted, the greater good of all. Charl had conducted a similar discussion with a Republican congresswoman from California on NBC's *Let's Talk It Over* program.[47] In April, with the 1936 election approaching, FDR's advisors invited a handful of prominent educators to meet with the president about teachers' negative attitudes toward him. After the meeting a source confidentially informed Charl that FDR had "committed himself on the matter of a Department of Education to the extent of stating that he would be in favor of a Department of Education and Welfare."[48] Perhaps to impress upon the president the high expectations of the feminists she represented, she wrote FDR that the NFBPW had endorsed a bill to carve the face of Susan B. Anthony into Mount Rushmore.

As she basked in national attention that summer, Charl returned to Shelby County to receive an honorary Doctor of Literature degree from Southwestern College, the first given by the school to a woman.[49] While she began to use the title "Doctor," Charl remained painfully aware that she lacked a college diploma, much less a real doctorate. This, she knew, greatly curtailed her professional and political opportunities and obstructed her efforts to directly implement policies based on the principle of equalization of education. Her personal frustrations turned into highly publicized complaints about how few women, regardless of their qualifications, held positions of power. While she was gratified that FDR was reelected in 1936, she expressed her disappointment that "only a handful of women are holding office when there are 50,000 offices" they could fill. Only five women had been elected to the House of Representatives, only one to the Senate, and none as a governor.[50] By this time, the NFBPW was the largest national businesswomen's organization in the world, with 1,500 clubs holding 65,000 members, and many of these women were lawyers. Surely some of these women could hold public office. She launched a letter-writing campaign to the president of the American Bar Association, urging him and presidents of the state bar associations to advocate the appointment of qualified women lawyers to judicial office. Again, her efforts received national attention.[51]

Her feminist campaign continued through the spring. In another NBC broadcast, she presided over a debate called "The Pros and Cons of the Equal Rights Amendment." Her role, though ostensibly neutral, brought the issue further into the limelight.[52] Polls continued to indicate that many Americans considered it unethical for married women to be employed during the depression. Charl responded, "It seems to be chiefly based on the assumption that the number of jobs is strictly limited and that every time a married woman occupies one of them she excludes from it somebody who needs it worse."[53] She observed that women's status had declined in regions under fascist rule, drawing a connection between antifeminism and antidemocratic fascist ideology. But discrimination against married women remained government policy, and Charl was reduced to making public appeals to the WPA not to discharge married women first as it trimmed its personnel.[54]

At the end of her presidency, and during the 1937 NFBPW convention in Atlantic City, Congress repealed Section 213 of the National Economy Act, which discriminated against married working women. Charl persuaded ER to send a personal message to the convention celebrating the repeal and condemning gender discrimination that Charl proudly read, in her Tennessee accent, to the sea of women assembled. In the meeting's final moments, the NFBPW made feminist history and endorsed the ERA.[55] Knowing the NFBPW's endorsement of the ERA unnerved ER, Charl wrote to explain that the endorsement had slipped through after most delegates had left. But considering Charl's tremendous influence, it seems unlikely that she could not have prevented the endorsement had she wanted to. ER did not intend to be part of that cause, but Charl stealthily eased her closer to the feminists' campfire. Even though the First Lady still avoided the "feminist" label associated with ERA advocates, by early 1938 Charl had begun to refer publicly to ER as "an ardent feminist."[56] Through such maneuvers, the old antagonisms within the women's movement began to melt.

Her work as a feminist activist and NEA lobbyist came together in 1938 when she returned to Tennessee, fairly safe territory for her, to organize a new initiative, the Institutes on Professional and Public Relations, at George Peabody College for Teachers (now part of Vanderbilt University) in Nashville. The purpose of the institute was to empower classroom teachers by opening lines of communication to administrators and policy makers. This professional forum created new space where teachers, who were overwhelmingly female, and administrators, who were overwhelmingly male, could come together on fairly level ground. The institute was so successful that it continues to the present day.[57]

That same summer, Charl also convinced FDR to address the NEA meeting at the New York World's Fair Grounds. On June 30, 1938, ER introduced her husband, something the president could not recall happening before. Federal aid for public education had increased substantially during the New Deal through National Youth Administration student assistance programs for black and white students, the Civilian Conservation Corps, and Works Projects Administration education and school lunch programs. FDR's Advisory Committee on Education proposed a bill that would grant federal aid to support public schools through cooperative arrangements with states, and the president called upon the NEA to support the legislation. This historic moment marked the first time that a U.S. president supported "the principle of federal aid to education in the various states, based on an equalization program."[58] For Charl this was real progress in her fight to give poor rural school children an equal opportunity. She followed this victory by editing *Schools for Democracy*, a compilation of essays by education experts and published by the PTA, which made the case for federal aid to equalize education. ER promoted it in her "My Day" column.

In early 1940 ER also announced that the DNC had passed resolutions to give women "an equal voice in the affairs of the Democratic Party" in state Democratic committees.[59] Months later, leading southern women issued the "Statement of One Hundred Women," read on the floor of Congress, in which they asked members to eliminate the poll tax in federal elections. Charl's sister Mabel was among the illustrious signers.[60]

But just as women were poised to exert more political influence, FDR's administration turned its attention to war mobilization. Many women who entered government through the New Deal's domestic programs lost their jobs, angering and alarming leading Democratic women, including Charl, who had labored so hard to place more women in government. Personal tragedy also took a toll. In the summer of 1943, Mabel's son, a pilot, was killed in a training exercise. Grieving together at the family homestead in Arlington, Charl and her sisters could not recall the last time they all had been together, as Charl had not taken a vacation in three years.

The following winter, a bad fall put Charl in the hospital for weeks with two broken vertebrae and a broken ankle. As she convalesced, Charl read a report from the southern Methodist women who had helped her in 1927. They continued to endorse "Federal Aid to public education provided the administration of school remains under local supervision and that Federal funds be used without discrimination." But their report also noted that "The treatment of minorities in America has been a constant embarrassment to the United States in the present world conflict," and they condemned the poll tax and white primary system. One leader, Dorothy Rogers Tilly, had been a member of the Commission on Interracial Cooperation since 1930, as well as the Southern Regional Council in Atlanta. She was also an antilynching activist.[61] From her hospital bed, Charl wrote ER that she wanted to arrange a special meeting of select women from the Division of Christian Service of the Board of Missions and Church Extension of the Methodist Church, including her childhood friend, Elizabeth Claiborne (back in the United States since the late 1920s), Tilly (head of the United Church Women in the South), and Bertha Newell (superintendent of the southern Methodist's Woman's Missionary Council). The result was an April "Spend-the-Night-Party" with ER at the White House. Charl was back on her feet for the occasion. During the sleepover, Tilly invited ER to speak to the two thousand southern Methodist women who would assemble that summer at Lake Junaluska, North Carolina, and ER accepted.[62]

That same night, Charl persuaded ER to host a White House conference to pressure FDR and government officials to appoint women to positions of power and influence in postwar policy making. On June 14 two hundred of the nation's leading professional and club women, including a handful of black women, arrived at the White House to demonstrate their dissatisfaction with the sexist disregard of women and begin to generate a list of women qualified for high-level government service. But as Charl publicized the event, ER sent a note informing her that FDR wanted the list of qualified women kept confidential. Charl felt betrayed but had to comply in order for the conference to go forward.

The conference received tremendous publicity, more than anything Charl had been associated with since the passage of the Nineteenth Amendment. She was further vindicated when delegates at the Democratic Convention, held immediately after her conference, embraced a platform favoring "legislation assuring equal pay for equal work, regardless of sex" and recommended "to Congress the submission of a Constitutional amendment on equal rights for women." Even more gratifying was this plank: "We favor Federal aid to education administered by the states without interference by the Federal Government." Charl, in the midst of the convention, was surprised when the DNC chairman began to read the platform. "I got a copy just as he was beginning to read," she wrote a friend, "so I raced to my seat and found the federal aid plank before he got to it. I could hardly believe my eyes."[63]

Shortly afterward, FDR signed the Serviceman's Readjustment Act (GI Bill) which provided millions in federal funds for education. But the GI Bill focused on adult (and overwhelmingly male) veterans, and NEA experts argued that rural schools had been particularly hard hit since the war. Charl felt that FDR owed her for going along with his request to keep the list of 260 qualified women confidential, so she pressed ER to allow her to organize another White House conference. In early October, as the 1944 election neared, Charl and ER invited two hundred black and white educators and experts to "The First White House Conference on Rural Education." This conference was financed by the NEA's War and Peace Fund in collaboration with the White House. It focused on specific problems and included a special committee on minority students. The participants drafted a ten-year plan for improving the nation's rural schools. ER participated and at one point received vigorous applause for standing up for teacher tenure against a conservative and domineering Farm Bureau official. The group produced "A Charter of Education for Rural Children," which stated that every rural child had the right to satisfactory modern elementary and secondary education in schools open no less than nine months a year for twelve years. Education should bridge the gaps between home, school, adult, and community life and culture, and it should include health services, educational and vocational guidance, modern buildings and library facilities, recreational activities, school lunches (where needed), and pupil transportation at public expense. Every rural child had the "right to have the tax resources of his community, State and Nation used to guarantee him an American standard of educational opportunity." In large, bold, italicized letters at the bottom of the charter was the declaration, "These are the Rights of the Rural Child because they are the Rights of Every Child regardless of Race, or Color, or Situation, wherever he may live under the United States Flag."

FDR informally addressed the conference and stated that "the raising of educational and health standards in this country is a Federal task and should receive Federal aid." Those unaware of his 1938 speech before the NEA marked this as the historic moment when the first U.S. president publicly supported "federal aid for public schools." But this meeting did have greater significance for another reason: the inclusion of African Americans, and the charter's explicit statements, indicated that federal power and funds should be used to equalize education for black children as well as all others. FDR's remarks particularly impressed African American participants who publicized this as a breakthrough in the fight for racial equality.[64]

In February 1945, as FDR began his fourth term, Charl boldly lobbied for the position of U.S. commissioner of education. She emphasized her Shelby County experience and her work for black education.[65] "No man" in education would think to recommend a woman for the job, she stated, but they would support her if she were appointed. But her hopes died with FDR's death in April and ER's exit from the White House. In later years Charl bitterly recounted how Truman and his staff ignored her overtures. Many formerly influential Democratic women, including Charl's sister Mabel, who was elected national president of the PTA in this period, found Truman and his staff decidedly cold. And yet, Truman became the first president to request federal aid outright for public education. A Republican-controlled Congress rejected the measure in 1948.

Like many Democrats, Charl worried that Truman's unpopularity would return the Republicans to the White House. He had also embraced a civil rights program advanced by a coalition of black and white southerners that included Dorothy Tilly. Charl was not surprised by the Dixiecrat revolt. When conservative southern politicians walked out of the Democratic Convention, she sternly warned Democratic leaders it was "no laughing matter." She was somewhat surprised and greatly relieved by Truman's victory.[66]

By this time, at the age of sixty-four, it was clear that Williams's career had reached its highest mark. On December 1, 1949, after twenty-eight years of service, Charl officially retired but continued as a member of the NEA's board of directors. Mabel Williams, however, returned to public service in Shelby County when she was elected in 1951 to the lower house of the Tennessee legislature. "Boss" Crump, whose political machine was waning, asked her to run, and she held the office for six terms.

In 1952 Republicans, with the assistance of some former Dixiecrats, took back the White House. It must have been bittersweet for Charl when President Eisenhower established a cabinet-level Department of Health, Education, and Welfare in 1953 under the direction of a Texas woman and former Democrat, Oveta Culp Hobby. It would be Hobby's duty to deal with the 1954 U.S. Supreme Court ruling that the "separate but equal" doctrine violated the Constitution and the mandate that public schools desegregate with all deliberate speed. Charl wrote her old friend Eleanor Roosevelt, "At long last the Supreme Court has made its decision against segregation of the public schools. Some people will curse you for that, for indeed you did have something to do with bringing it about through the years." Even though she fervently longed for the promise of equal education to be fulfilled, she had long warned that white southerners would not tolerate racial integration of the schools. From her years as an education advocate she knew well the depth of prejudices that prevented federal, state, and local white politicians from providing quality education to the rural poor, black and white, in the South. Although her influence had waned, she tried to soften resistance to school desegregation in the South. "I have talked to leaders in Virginia and South Carolina," she wrote ER, "and I told them in no uncertain terms that abolishing the public schools and turning them into private schools would be an asinine procedure."[67] She was especially appalled as reactionary forces took hold in the South and used religion-based private white schools to preserve segregated education. She considered this to be a dangerous breach of Jefferson's "wall of separation between church and state" and was deeply troubled that nominally religious Protestant institutions would be fronts for forestalling the advance of civil rights. She was revolted by the perversion of Protestant church authority in the hands of white southern segregationists and frustrated by anti–public education forces in the Catholic Church. Her opinions about these forces were so strong that after her death, per her request, much of her estate was used to create the Charl Ormond Williams Foundation dedicated to the separation of church and state. She died in Washington, D.C., in 1969.

The story of Charl Williams's life illustrates the degree to which America's post–Civil War promises of equal education, justice, and opportunity remained so elusive that a woman could spend her entire life trying to realize some small part of those promises. Though she herself had little more than a high school education, Williams traveled tens of thousands of miles every year for nearly thirty years to battle in the highest circles of politics for those living in the remotest corners of the nation. In her lifetime, Charl influenced millions through her work for public education and women's rights, but her extraordinarily single-minded pursuit of a more truly democratic government that would dedicate its power and resources to serve equally all its citizens began in a country village in Tennessee. Today, portraits of her and her sister hang at the entrance of the main administration building of Shelby County's public schools, though few know the service record of these women. The Institutes on Professional and Public Relations still meet at Vanderbilt, and the fight to improve public education in the South continues.

NOTES

1. "Miss Williams Named Chief of Business Women," *Helena (Mont.) Independent*, July 20, 1935. I would like to thank Arkansas State University for generously supporting my research for this chapter.

2. This history was derived from U.S. Census schedules, a family Bible, and correspondence found in the former Crittenden Williams home in Arlington, Tennessee. To distinguish these materials from other Charl Ormond Williams Papers, located at the Library of Congress and Schlesinger Library, these papers will be referred to as the Charl Ormond Williams Family Papers (hereinafter, COWFP), currently in the possession of the author.

3. In May 1882 Tennessee made history when Julia A. Doak, a twenty-four-year-old from Greene County, was appointed State Superintendent of Public Instruction, succeeding her father, who died before completing his term. Doak was the first woman in U.S. history to hold such a post. Many women in Tennessee served as county superintendents from that time forward. In Shelby County alone, the following women held this public office: Mrs. W. H. Horton (1882–86), Nellie O'Donnell (1891–96), Lida Thomas (1896–1901), Maude Moor (1901–4), Elizabeth Messick (1904–8), Mabel

Williams (1909–14), Charl Williams (1915–22), and Sue Power (1922–50). Superintendents served for two-year terms (lengthened to four years during Charl Williams's administration) and were not voting members of the board until 1912 (during Mabel Williams's administration). This list was derived from records located at the Shelby County Board of Education, Memphis, Tennessee.

4. Teaching certificate of Charl Ormond Williams, COWFP.

5. Rachel H. K. Burrow, *Arlington: A Short Historical Writing of the Town* (Memphis: E. H. Clarke and Brother, 1962), 29, 41.

6. "Memorandum for Conference with Mrs. Roosevelt," December 18, 1943, File Eleanor Roosevelt (hereinafter ER), General Correspondence (June 11, 1940–April 20, 1945), box 2, Charl Ormond Williams Papers, Library of Congress, Washington, D.C. (hereinafter, CWPLC).

7. Postcard collection, COWFP.

8. For a nuanced examination of the difficulties education reformers faced in this period in the South, see Louis R. Harlan, "The Southern Education Board and the Race Issue in Public Education," *Journal of Southern History* 23, no. 2 (1957): 189–202.

9. F. E. Miller to the Honorable County Board of Education, Shelby County Board of Education Minutes (hereinafter SCBEM), August 31, 1908.

10. The Board's Minutes read as follows: "Motion made that all negro schools be closed at the end of six months. Carried" (SCBEM, March 6, 1911).

11. SCBEM, March 16, 1911.

12. SCBEM, September 4, 1911.

13. Mabel Williams hired at least two African American women, Iola Wimbs and Cora Price Taylor, to serve as supervisors of agricultural programs in Shelby County's black schools. For more on the work of these women, see *Biennial Report of the State Superintendent of Public Instruction of Tennessee for the Scholastic Years Ending June 30, 1915–1916* (Nashville: Baird-Ward Printing Company, 1916), 288; and "Special Report of Work Done by Negro Home Demonstration Agent, Tennessee, 1921," filed by Mattie L. Barr Keith, et al., *Extension Service Annual Reports: Tennessee*, T-889, roll 5, quoted in Mary S. Hoffschwelle, "'Better Homes on Better Farms': Domestic Reform in Rural Tennessee," *Frontiers: A Journal of Women Studies* 22, no. 1 (2001): 62.

14. SCBEM, April 7, 1913, and April 8, 1920.

15. During the Progressive Era in the South, girls' tomato clubs were organized, through cooperation between home demonstration agencies and departments of education, to promote efficient and modern ways of processing and marketing home-grown produce and to instill in young women a sense of self-sufficiency that could benefit them, their families, and their communities.

16. SCBEM, April 9, 1916. For more on network strategies and the feminist politics of southern female educators and social workers, see Sarah Wilkerson-Freeman, "The Creation of a Subversive Feminist Dominion: Interracialist Social Workers and the Georgia New Deal," *Journal of Women's History* 13, no. 4 (2002): 132–54, and "Pauline Van De Graaf Orr (1861–1955): Feminist Education in Mississippi," in *Mississippi Women: Their Histories, Their Lives*, ed. Martha Swain, Elizabeth Anne Payne, and Marjorie Julian Spruill, 1:72–93 (Athens: University of Georgia Press, 2003).

17. SCBEM, November 18, 1916.

18. SCBEM, April 19, September 6 and 20, and November 1, 1917.

19. SCBEM, April 30, 1917.

20. SCBEM, September 6, 1917.

21. Hartwell Williams to Mabel Williams Hughes, May 24, 1917, COWFP.

22. Ella Flagg Young, the NEA's first female president, was nominated from the floor in 1912. From that point on, female educators sought greater influence. In 1917 the organization gave vot-

ing delegate status to chapters of teachers' associations that joined the NEA, greatly increasing the power of female teachers. Female delegates were instrumental in the election of three female state superintendents of schools, Mary C. C. Bradford (president) of Washington state, Josephine Corliss Preston (vice president) of Colorado, and Williams (third vice president). Together, the women formulated a plan to more fully represent female classroom teachers in the organization. Bradford also initiated the NEA's quest for a federal Department of Education headed by a Cabinet-level secretary. "Poincare Greets U.S. Educators," *Washington Post*, July 11, 1917; and "She May Head Educators," *Washington Post*, July 13, 1917.

23. *Peabody Journal of Education* 17, no. 2 (1939): 89.

24. The NEA's recently privatized archives were not made available for research for this chapter in spite of repeated efforts on the part of the author to access these materials. Information included here was gleaned from secondary sources, NEA official publications, newspapers, and Charl Williams's letters in the COWFP. Scholarship on the history of U.S. education in this period is voluminous. For specific treatments of the NEA, see Wayne J. Urban, *Gender, Race, and the National Education Association: Professionalism and Its Limitations* (New York: Routledge Falmer, 2000), and Lynn Dumenil, "'The Insatiable Maw of Bureaucracy': Antistatism and Education Reform in the 1920s," *Journal of American History* 77, no. 2 (1990): 499–524.

25. Georgia G. Bordwell, "Women to Demand 50–50 on Committees and Cabinet Officer to Direct National Education," *Oakland Tribune*, June 21, 1920.

26. Boardwell, "Women to Demand 50–50."

27. "Delegates Face Fight by Women for Early Vote," *Oakland Tribune*, July 1, 1920. See also Jo Freeman, *A Room At a Time: How Women Entered Party Politics* (Lanham, Md.: Rowan and Littlefield, 1999), 113.

28. Williams announced to the press in August 1920 that she had received a telegram from the Democratic presidential nominee, Governor Cox, urging support for ratification. "Suffrage Holds Stage in Tenn.," *Decatur (Ill.) Review*, August 10, 1920.

29. Grace Elizabeth Prescott, "The Woman Suffrage Movement in Memphis: Its Place in the State, Sectional, and National Movements" (M.A. thesis, Memphis State University, 1963), 170, 182–84. A. Elizabeth Taylor also explored Williams's part in the historic Nashville fight in her book *The Woman Suffrage Movement in Tennessee* (New York: Bookman, 1957), 116. More recent scholarship inexplicably ignores or erases Williams's role. Anastasia Sims's chapter "Armageddon in Tennessee" (published in *One Woman, One Vote* [the companion volume to a popular documentary on the U.S. woman suffrage movement], ed. Marjorie Spruill Wheeler [Troutdale, Ore.: NewSage Press, 1995]), mistakenly names another woman as the individual selected by Governor Roberts to head up the ratification committee (see page 338). The documentary also ignores Williams.

30. "U.S. Education Blemished," *Lima (Ohio) News*, February 27, 1922.

31. Résumé of Dr. Charl Ormond Williams (given to President Harry Truman), circa 1950, file Harry S. Truman, White House Correspondence (September 19, 1945–May 17, 1945), Box 6, CWPLC.

32. SCBEM, October 19, 1922.

33. For more on "stealth feminism" and southern Democratic women, see Sarah Wilkerson-Freeman, "Stealth in the Political Arsenal of Southern Women: A Retrospective for the Millennium," in *Southern Women at the Millennium: A Historical Perspective*, ed. Melissa Walker, Jeanette Dunn, and Joe Dunn, 42–82 (Columbia: University of Missouri Press, 2003).

34. Williams's response to the Institute for Research in Social Sciences, project title: "Distinguished Southerners Outside the South," confidential serial number 1930, COWFP. In response to

the question: "When you first left the Southeast, did you expect to return in a short time to live and work there?" Williams checked "No" and wrote: "I uprooted myself from the Southeast to work through the National Education Association for the advancement of rural education in the Southeast as well as in the nation. That was a long time job, so I made no plans to return to the Southeast" (Williams to Howard Odum, July 3, 1946, COWFP).

35. Charles Stewart, "What's What in Washington," *Zanesville (Ohio) Times Recorder*, August 22, 1928.

36. "Marriage as a Career," *Appleton (Wis.) Post Crescent*, July 13, 1922.

37. Freeman, *A Room At a Time*, 204.

38. Mrs. W. A. (Bertha) Newell, superintendent of the Woman's Missionary Council, to Mabel Williams Hughes, September 3, 1927, COWFP. Three years later, the Bureau of Social Services of the Woman's Missionary Council of the Methodist Episcopal Church, South (M.E. Church, South) became the Bureau of Christian Social Relations with commissions on industrial relations, interracial cooperation, and rural development under the leadership of Bertha Newell. Subsequently, Newell became involved with the Southern White Women's Association for the Prevention of Lynching. For more on the importance of the Methodist women in social justice movements, see John Patrick McDowell, *The Social Gospel in the South: The Woman's Home Mission Movement in the Methodist Episcopal Church, South, 1886–1939* (Baton Rouge: Louisiana State University Press, 1982), and Jacquelyn Dowd Hall, *Revolt against Chivalry: Jesse Daniel Ames and the Women's Campaign against Lynching* (1979; repr., New York: Columbia University Press, 1993). Charl Williams (hereafter CW) to ER, August 4, 1928, General Correspondence (March 3, 1924–June 6, 1940), box 2, CWPLC.

39. "Leads European Tour," *Elyria (Ohio) Chronicle Telegram*, June 2, and "Europe to See Two-Job Wife of Americans," *Elyria (Ohio) Chronicle Telegram*, July 12, 1930.

40. Willard E. Givens, "New Deal a Raw Deal for Public Schools," *Journal of the National Education Association* 24 (January–December 1935): 198. While the New Deal directed millions of federal dollars to education programs and provided jobs for unemployed teachers, NEA leaders severely criticized the administration's refusal to coordinate its educational initiatives through a central Department of Education or to allocate funds to directly subsidize public schools.

41. "Greater Representation for Women in Politics South," *Sheboygan (Wis.) Press*, August 16, 1935.

42. "Business Women's Club," *Indiana (Pa.) Evening Gazette*, October 16, 1935.

43. "Have to Be Supported," *Ironwood (Mich.) Daily Globe*, December 6, 1935.

44. "National President Turns Columnist," *Elyria (Ohio) Chronicle Telegram*, January 29, 1936.

45. "Issues Challenge to 60,000 Members to 'Elect Qualified Candidates,'" *Elyria (Ohio) Chronicle Telegram*, March 17, 1936.

46. "If Women Quit Jobs for a Day?" *Oshkosh (Wis.) Northwestern*, March 17, 1936.

47. "Would Industry Be Halted on Feminine Day of Rest," *Sheboygan (Wis.) Press*, March 17, 1936.

48. Joseph Rosie to CW, May 4, 1936, file Franklin D. Roosevelt, Group Conference of Committee of Educators with President (April 30, 1936), box 4, CWPLC.

49. "Mrs. Maud F. Dominick is Reno's Busiest Woman," *(Reno) Nevada State Journal*, June 7, 1936.

50. "Only Few Women in Office thru Nation," *Helena (Mont.) Independent*, December 20, 1936.

51. *Elyria (Ohio) Chronicle Telegram*, January 27, 1936.

52. *Elyria (Ohio) Chronicle Telegram*, March 16, 1937.

53. "Business Women's Week Preface," *Helena (Mont.) Independent*, March 24, 1937.

54. "Appeal for Married Women," *Helena (Mont.) Independent*, July 19, 1937.

55. ER's message to the NFBPW delegates read as follows: "I congratulate you on this achievement which you have been a factor in bringing about (stop) It means much to every woman as any discrimination against woman working except as an emergency measure seems to me unwise (stop) I am happy to see us go back to our old respect for work of all kinds by all people now that we are returning to more normal times I have read the reports of your meetings with great interest (stop) Congratulations on all your successes." See ER to CW, July 23, 1937, telegram, and CW to ER, August 4, 1937, file Eleanor Roosevelt, General Corres. (March 3–June 6, 1940), box 2, CWPLC.

56. February 22, 1938, quoted from Charl Ormond Williams's biographical portrait of ER for the annual meeting of the Kansas Women's Woodrow Wilson Luncheon Club, Topeka, Kansas, COWFP.

57. Williams's Institutes on Professional and Public Relations (IPPR) initiative spread rapidly as educators in other states hosted their own IPPRs. The 1940 IPPR at Peabody College in Nashville focused on discrimination and inequality (rural-urban, political, gender and marital discrimination) in the profession. By 1942 over sixty institutes were being held each year around the country. These increasingly focused on achieving more democratic school programs and creating more egalitarian relationships between administrators, classroom teachers, students and the public. For information on the origin of the IPPR see "Our Professional Relations," Reuben T. Shaw, *Peabody Journal of Education* 16, no. 2 (1938): 103.

58. "Progress Toward Federal Aid," *NEA Journal* 28, no. 4 (1939): 109.

59. Eleanor Roosevelt, "My Day," *(Reno) Nevada State Journal*, February 11, 1940.

60. Ruth Anne Thompson, "After Suffrage: Women, Law, and Policy in Tennessee, 1920–1980" (Ph.D. dissertation, Vanderbilt University, 1994), 121–22 n. 23.

61. In 1946 Tilly served on President Truman's committee on civil rights, and she risked her life in the 1950s working for desegregation in Atlanta and Birmingham. See Alice G. Knotts, *Fellowship of Love: Methodist Women Changing American Racial Attitudes, 1920–1968* (Nashville: Kingswood Books, 1996); Edith Holbrook Riehm, "Dorothy Tilly and the Fellowship of the Concerned," in *Throwing Off the Cloak of Privilege: White Southern Women Activists in the Civil Rights Era*, ed. Gail S. Murray (Gainesville: University Press of Florida, 2004).

62. For more on southern women and their efforts to liberalize the Democratic Party, see Sarah Wilkerson-Freeman, "The 'Second Battle' for Woman Suffrage: Southern White Women, the Poll Tax, and V. O. Key's Master Narrative of Southern Politics," *Journal of Southern History* 68 (May 2002): 333–74, "Stealth in the Political Arsenal," and "From Clubs to Parties: North Carolina Women in the Advancement of the New Deal," *North Carolina Historical Review* 68 (July 1991): 320–39.

63. CW to Irving Pearson, Executive Secretary of the Illinois Education Association, August 3, 1944, file White House Conference on Rural Education, Initial Steps, box 6, CWPLC.

64. Alethea H. Washington, "Rural Education—Wartime 1944–1945: The White House Conference on Rural Education," *Journal of Negro Education* 14, no. 1 (Winter 1945), 101.

65. CW to ER, February 11, 1945, typed draft, March 1, 1945, file ER General Correspondence (June 11, 1940–April 20, 1945), box 2, CWPLC.

66. CW to ER, March 24, 1948, and December 19, 1947, April 11, 1947–May 2, 1948, box 3, CWPLC.

67. CW to ER, May 18, 1954, file ER Correspondence (February 13–December 14, 1954), box 3, CWPLC.

Lucille Thornburgh
(1908–1998)

"I Had to Be Right Pushy"

CONNIE L. LESTER

Lucille Thornburgh was always proud of her militancy, and her long life afforded her many opportunities to demonstrate her tendency to be "right pushy." She organized Knoxville's Cherokee Mill workers in the General Textile Strike of 1934, was identified as a "red" while employed at Tennessee Valley Authority (TVA) in the 1940s, served on the board of the Highlander Folk Center in the 1950s, became a civil rights activist in the 1960s, edited the *East Tennessee Labor News* (ETLN) for twenty-six years, and championed economic and social justice for the elderly during her "retirement." Thornburgh triumphed within a social structure that seldom tolerated "pushy" women. Bright and articulate, she rose through the ranks of the male-dominated American Federation of Labor (AFL) in the antilabor South, campaigned for an antimachine Democrat in Republican East Tennessee, and promoted social justice through her work with the Highlander Folk School, the Unitarian Church, and the National Council of Senior Citizens.

Thornburgh's militancy challenges traditional histories of the southern labor movement. Her years of labor activism raise questions about the regional exceptionalism that supposedly prevented unionization of the region's workers, and her decades-long commitment to social justice verifies the presence of a southern progressivism that has been largely ignored. At the same time, Thornburgh's insider view of the southern labor movement illuminates the barriers for the advancement of women that existed within the union organization. Her "pushy" independence was apparent long before she became involved with unionism—the agitator was not created by crisis or outside influence. This

LUCILLE THORNBURGH

Courtesy of Knoxville–Knox County
Community Action Committee Transportation Program,
Knoxville, Tennessee.

fierce advocate for workers' rights and social justice drew on the support of family and community in the Appalachian South to sustain her activities.

Born in 1908 to Thomas and Harriet Swaggerty Thornburgh, Lucille grew up in Rolling Hills, a crossroads community two miles west of Strawberry Plains in East Tennessee.[1] A "very politically minded" Republican, Thomas Thornburgh operated a country store and served as justice of the peace for more than thirty-five years. The store was the center of community life, the place where local families collected their mail, purchased manufactured goods, sold agricultural products, and swapped stories. With a large family of six children (five girls and one boy), Harriet managed the household and family garden. As the fourth child, Lucille enjoyed more independence than her older siblings, and she recalled, "I liked outside work. I didn't care much for housework. But I would rather stay at the store, and milk and work in the garden as anything else. And that made it pretty nice because my sisters would do the other things."[2]

Thornburgh grew up in a region marked by economic and social paradoxes. East Tennessee was the site of the state's only white land-grant university, the center of what remained of subsistence farming, and the most industrialized of the state's three grand divisions. Coal and iron mines, railroads and machine shops, and canneries and textile mills accounted for most of the nonfarm employment of the region's men and women. On the farms that dotted the valleys and straggled up the hillsides, East Tennesseans produced milk and butter for local consumption, beans and peas for the canneries, and burley tobacco for the cigarette manufacturers. The community that surrounded Thornburgh's store typified the agricultural and mining heritage of the area. Lucille remembered that her grandfather "raised what the family would eat . . . [and] made his money on his hogs and bees." The white families around Rolling Hills were "mostly farmers," but "many of the black men worked at the Mascot Zinc Mines and on the railroad as 'section hands.'"[3]

For the middle daughter of the local merchant, life revolved around family, school, and church. Lucille played ball, pitched horseshoes, and cut paper dolls from the Sears-Roebuck catalog. Her formal education began when, at age four, she followed her siblings to school. The teacher "didn't mind me staying," she explained. "The school wasn't filled anyway."[4] Like most families in Jefferson County, the Thornburghs worshiped in the Baptist Church, where Harriet and the Swaggertys were pillars of the congregation. Baptist churches of the day were fiercely independent and preached a doctrine critical of personal self-aggrandizement as a trait that destroyed the communal spirit that sustained poor communities. Having imbibed the lessons of independence and communal support, Thornburgh would become a founding member of Knoxville's socially activist Tennessee Valley Unitarian congregation in her adulthood.

By the time of Lucille's childhood, women in Tennessee, as elsewhere, enjoyed some freedoms that their mothers had not—a loosening of social and physical restraints that included changes in clothing styles, a recognition of their needs for exercise of the body and the mind, and opportunities to earn money in the mills and offices that marked the American transition into modern industrialization.[5] Tennessee women were on the cusp of a renewed, and ultimately successful, effort to gain woman suffrage. One of Lucille's recollections offers tantalizing evidence that she was aware of these political and social transformations. Thomas subscribed to the *Knoxville Journal and Tribune*, and Lucille recalled that when the newspaper arrived, "all the men would gather at the store . . . and I would read it to them." Lucille's lifelong interest in politics and her future social activism suggest that she might have followed the efforts of Anne Dallas Dudley and the Tennessee Equal Suffrage Association in their successful 1920 pursuit of the franchise.[6]

When Lucille was fourteen years old, her father sold the farm and store and moved the family to Dayton, Tennessee, in order to provide what he believed to be better educational opportunities for his children. Like many Tennessee families, her parents had only a modest education: Harriet's schooling had ended with the fifth grade, and Thomas finished the eighth grade. Perhaps they were influenced in their decision to provide a better education for Lucille by the high school movement that swept the country and by the opportunities for employment that promised greater economic independence for the "new women" of the 1920s. Country families allocated educational resources to maximize opportunities for boys and girls. Many families thought practical experience in farming best prepared boys for their future. For girls, whose work on the farm was less critical, high school seemed a better choice; with a family of five girls, the Thornburghs made a substantial sacrifice for education.[7]

As she struggled with high school math and grammar, Lucille envisioned a future beyond her small town and dreamed of an independent life of office work in New York City and the opportunity to travel abroad. She traced the inspiration for her daydreams to the periodic buying trips to Knoxville that she and her father took. There she saw women working in offices, typing, filing, and entering accounts in ledger books—"the most glamorous job[s] in the world"—and determined that she would work in an office one day.[8] Though poorly compensated, office employment offered a clean work environment with all the trappings of middle-class upward mobility. For countless young women, the lure was irresistible.[9]

Lucille finished high school in three years, graduating from Rhea County High School in 1924, one year before the Scopes Trial put the school and Dayton on the map.[10] Shortly after her graduation, Thomas's butcher business failed and the family moved to Knoxville. Settling into a house on Ailor Avenue, the Thornburghs struggled. Thomas opened a small grocery nearby, and the adult children, including Lucille, obtained employment in the nearby textile mills, adding their wages to the family economy. After a three-month employment, and with the blessings of her family, Lucille left the mills and Knoxville and headed west.

From 1926 through 1931, she moved across the country, working in a variety of jobs that included magazine sales, window decorating, and general office activities that ranged from mail clerk to stenographer. While living in Denver she took an important step in furthering her dreams and completed courses at the local business college. In the spring of 1930 she moved to Detroit, where she soon encountered the employment problems associated with the Great Depression, so she "came home" and once again found work in the local textile mills.[11]

The depression had caught the Knoxville business community by surprise, and a number of businesses declared bankruptcy. Unemployment rose steadily, as did other statistical indicators of misery: lengthening soup and bread lines, rising homicide and crime rates. The city attracted fewer migrants from the countryside, and some Knoxvillians sought "employment in other cities or retrace[d] their once-hopeful steps back to the hills and hollows of the surrounding hinterland." Whatever expectations Knoxville's leaders and its working class harbored for the industrial growth of the city were shattered as factories and mills closed and mines remained idle.[12]

Knoxvillians, like other Americans, listened eagerly in 1933 as the newly inaugurated President Franklin D. Roosevelt declared his primary task to be that of putting "the people to work." Out of a flurry of legislative activity, two federal acts—Tennessee Valley Authority Act and the National Industrial Recovery Act (NIRA)—promised important changes for East Tennessee. TVA immediately employed idle men to construct dams that would generate electric power for the region, provide flood control, and improve navigation on the Tennessee River. NIRA, with its Section 7(a), offered the first federal protection for organized labor and the legal right to bargain collectively, free from outside influence or coercion.[13] The two acts provided Lucille Thornburgh with the opportunities to channel her independence into social action.

The promise of federal protection of workers' rights coincided with a general return to work in the Appalachian textile mills. Generally southern industrialization had developed in isolated mill towns, where the manufacturer owned the mill as well as the stores, schools, churches, and homes. Mill workers risked loss of employment and homelessness if they advocated unionism—threats that were thought to have undermined previous efforts to organize southern textile workers. The events of 1934 suggested that the union leaders may have underestimated southern labor radicalism.

With the passage of NIRA, AFL organizers launched a drive to organize the region and press for union recognition, higher wages, and better working conditions. The accumulation of grievances made the southern textile mills ripe for organizing activities once federal legislation provided protection for workers' rights. Throughout the winter and spring of 1933–34, AFL organizers fanned out across the South, signing up new members and pressing industry managers to recognize local unions and sign contracts.[14]

By the end of the summer of 1934, enthusiasm for unionization and the expectation of immediate improvements in wages and working conditions had reached a fever pitch. At the center of events, as they unfolded in the Knoxville mills, Lucille Thornburgh found her life's work.

In later interviews, Thornburgh described her experiences as a winding machine operator at Cherokee Mills. The "terrible conditions" she encountered mirrored the experiences mill operatives across the South described in letters to President Roosevelt and in later interviews with historians. Cotton lint filled the air. At times, she complained, "you couldn't see your machine very well the [cotton] lint was so thick." At the end of their shifts, workers emerged from the plant "snow-white with that cotton," a condition that earned them the derogatory nickname "lint-head." She also recalled the unbearable summer heat, made worse by the fact that operatives were not permitted to open the windows because breezes would blow the lint around the room.[15]

Work hours were long, and pay was low. The standard work week for textile workers was fifty hours, for which spinners (the most common job for women) received $7.20. However, in 1934, the lingering effects of the depression forced many mills to operate on a reduced work schedule, and Thornburgh reported that her wages rarely exceeded $4.00 per week. Higher-paying jobs ($16–$17 per week), including that of weaver and "fixer" (machine repairer), were reserved for men. Many women, including Thornburgh, had acquired the necessary skills for the higher-paying jobs, but they were only permitted to work on the weaving machines temporarily or make minor repairs to their own machines; they never received the status or the wages associated with the permanent jobs of weaver or fixer. Looking back on the gendered allocation of jobs, Thornburgh recognized it "was out-in-out sex discrimination—but it was accepted and people weren't conscious of it then."[16]

In many places, including Cherokee Spinning Mill, workers took matters into their own hands and organized without official AFL sanction. With little knowledge about the AFL or unionization tactics, Thornburgh and six other Cherokee employees organized the mill. A local boilermaker named Sam Godfrey explained the steps for obtaining an AFL charter. Thornburgh and her fellow organizers chipped in one dollar apiece to cover the registration fees, obtained a charter, and began organizing workers. Although Knoxville workers did not live in company housing, the city was not large enough to offer them anonymity. Fearful that their activities would cost them their jobs, the would-be organizers swore the new union members to secrecy and met clandestinely in individual homes and at a nearby Moose Lodge. Within weeks, Thornburgh claimed that all six hundred employees had joined the union.[17]

In January, long before the events associated with the General Textile Strike of 1934, Cherokee workers presented mill managers with a list of grievances and entered into negotiations to satisfy their demands for "decent restrooms," additional water fountains, higher wages, abolition of the "stretch-out," and implementation of a seniority system for layoffs and firings. The stretch-out had troubled mill workers since the earliest days of textile manufacturing. A highly competitive industry with a low profit margin, textile manufacturing traditionally cut costs through draconian labor management practices. Stretch-out and speed-up reduced the number of laborers and increased productivity by requiring workers to attend more machines. The fledgling union demanded an end to such practices and sought to protect jobs through a seniority clause that would operate during any period of work reduction, whether temporary layoffs or permanent loss of jobs.[18]

Thornburgh always defended the demands as just, but she admitted that the 1934 showdown between Cherokee workers and management was ill conceived, poorly implemented, and doomed to failure. The fledgling union entered into negotiations with the managers of Cherokee Mills just as the national AFL announced plans for a general strike of southern textile workers for the summer of 1934. Optimistic that they would achieve concessions through negotiation and fearful of the consequences of a strike, the Cherokee local initially voted against a walkout. When informed by AFL's national headquarters that they had to strike or lose their charter, the mill workers abandoned their machines and established a picket line. Organized less than six months, the Cherokee union stood alone. As Thornburgh recalled, "When we came out on strike even the [Knoxville] Central Labor Council, with its old time conservative unionists were against us . . . the neighborhoods were against us, the churches were against us, the newspapers were against us, and the people were against us."[19]

During the first days of the strike, workers participated enthusiastically, and as the strike dragged on, men and women on the picket line bolstered their resolve with stories, songs, and assurances of their ultimate triumph. Nevertheless, the doomed strike ended after three weeks. A combination of lack of community support and family pressures to provide a paycheck took its toll, but an unexpected death signaled the demise of the strike effort. After two weeks of picketing, the president of Cherokee Spinning Mill died, apparently of a heart attack. Many workers blamed themselves, assuming that the stress of the strike had caused the death. Although union leaders reassured workers that their actions played no role in the death, the strike ended a week later. Workers returned to their jobs with nothing to show for their efforts, and the local union disappeared. Although mill managers assured returning workers that there would be no reprisals, union leaders, including Thornburgh, were denied re-employment and were blacklisted throughout the industry. Proud of her actions, Thornburgh nevertheless considered the General Textile Strike of 1934 "the biggest mistake the labor movement ever made."[20]

Without a job, Thornburgh applied for employment with the one place tolerant of unionization—the Tennessee Valley Authority (TVA). TVA had entered the region both as economic "savior" and as social disrupter. The federal agency addressed the region's most intractable problems in a one-size-fits-all plan that spawned both admirers and detractors. Admirers pointed to the potential to lift the region out of its habitual poverty by providing much needed jobs and attracting modern industrial development. Detractors quickly labeled the agency "socialist" in its intent and actions and mounted a decades-long campaign to destroy it.[21]

Thornburgh obtained a position as file clerk in the mail section of TVA's Knoxville office. Her TVA employment file documents the work record of a diligent and conscientious employee who received regular promotions and pay raises, eventually attaining the position of assistant head of the Mail and File Section. On the surface, Thornburgh's tenure at TVA seems unremarkable, but the agency's own political problems and her continuing activities on behalf of the AFL made her a minor target in the anticommunist probes of the 1940s and 1950s.[22]

Thornburgh's name first surfaced as a suspected "red" in the House Un-American Activities Committee hearings undertaken by Texas congressman Martin Dies in 1942. Five years later, when TVA chair David Lilienthal appeared before a senate committee in response to his nomination as the head of the new Atomic Energy Commission, Thornburgh's name surfaced during questioning about the socialist or communist tendencies among TVA employees. Lilienthal's congressional appearance provided an opportunity for Kenneth McKellar, Tennessee's senior senator, to attack TVA and the chair. Although the Dies investigations had produced evidence of only three communists employed by the agency, one of whom was described as a gullible youth, McKellar hammered Lilienthal about his personal relations with the three low-level employees and his knowledge of TVA's hiring and promotion practices. All three of the named communists had been employed in the agency's mail and stenographic divisions, the same areas where Thornburgh worked.[23]

The Federal Bureau of Investigation (FBI) maintained a file on her throughout the period. Although she "was not the subject of an investigation by the FBI," her employment in an agency suspected of leftist, if not communist, sympathies and her labor activism targeted her as a person worth watching.[24] Despite the implications of being named with others suspected of communist tendencies, the FBI concluded that Thornburgh "was not a communist but was required to 'closely associate' with Communist Party (CP) members employed by TVA in order for her to keep her position with the agency." FBI records further stated that she admitted to attending a meeting in the fall of 1936 that she suspected was a meeting of the TVA cell of the Communist Party.[25] Although her name did not generate a lengthy discussion during the hearings, the presence of a "red" in Knoxville created a local stir that followed Thornburgh for years.[26]

An accusation of communist leanings could have enormous consequences, and even years later Thornburgh still felt the need to address her brush with the Red Scare and provide the public with assurances of her loyalty. In repeated interviews she told a humorous story, either real or apocryphal, in which she claimed that a woman accused her of having communist sympathies. She asked her accuser what a communist was. Upon being told that a communist was a person from Russia, Thornburgh laughingly replied that the definition eliminated her because she was from Strawberry Plains.[27] In typical Thornburgh fashion, the story addressed an issue she knew from experience would be on the minds of readers, while defusing the accusation with country humor that validated her claim of being an ordinary East Tennessean.

Thornburgh was, of course, more than her country humor suggested. As a TVA file clerk she joined the American Federation of Government Employees, but she did not engage in union activism on the job, believing, as she said, that "TVA could take care of itself." Locally, she maintained her association with the Central Labor Union and volunteered as an organizer among Knoxville's bakery and laundry workers. Visiting nonunion workers in their homes, she preached organization as the only mechanism for protecting their rights. As her activities continued, Thornburgh became known outside Knoxville labor circles. Usually the only female among local labor leaders, Thornburgh became the first woman in Tennessee to hold a statewide office in the AFL when she was elected vice president of the state organization in 1937.[28]

In 1939 TVA promoted Thornburgh to a supervisory position and transferred her to the Wilson Dam site in northern Alabama, where she continued her organizing activities. She became so vital to the local AFL that the president of Alabama's Tri-Cities Labor Union, Morton E. Crist, protested her transfer back to Knoxville in March 1942. Armed with a resolution from the Tri-Cities organization, he pleaded with TVA's personnel director to keep Thornburgh in Alabama. The union, he explained, "feels that in all probability the Tennessee Valley Authority could find someone to fill the position now open in Knoxville . . . without depriving the Tri-Cities Central Labor Union of [her] services."[29] The transfer was completed, however, and Thornburgh remained in Knoxville from April 1942 until she left TVA four months later to take a position with the War Department at Fort Belvoir, Virginia.[30]

Thornburgh soon discovered her distaste for the regimented "military" life and resigned her position. Although in leaving Fort Belvoir, she had given up the best paying job she had ever had, the decision proved to have been a good one. Thornburgh began what would be a thirty-year employment with the AFL and soon realized one of her childhood dreams. For the duration of the war, she served as one of four regional directors for the AFL's Labor League for Human Rights. The league acted as a liaison between unions and charitable organizations such as the Red Cross and Community Chest to coordinate worker donations for war relief efforts. From Thornburgh's perspective, the opportunity to make a valuable war contribution carried a bonus—the chance to live in New York City.[31] She fondly recalled her hotel apartment off Broadway and her access to tickets to theater productions and charity dinners, "exciting" events for a "Tennessee ridge-runner."[32] Apparently, she also became quite serious about an unnamed man during this period, but finally rejected marriage. Although Thornburgh was never entirely forthcoming about personal matters, she suggested that her own desire for independence was not conducive to marriage.

When the war ended, Thornburgh returned to Knoxville and the life of an AFL organizer and associate editor of the *East Tennessee Labor News*. The *Labor News*, a weekly union newspaper, had first appeared in 1932 as a publication by local railroad workers. At the time Thornburgh assumed a position on the paper, the Central Labor Council was the publisher. On the surface, her activities suggested a gender equality that closer analysis does not support. Thornburgh admitted that her "ambition" had taken her higher in the AFL than most women, but she chafed under a male-dominated system that stymied her advancement as a journalist and as an organizer. The conservative building trades controlled the Knoxville Labor Council and blocked changes to the paper that they considered too radical. Although she edited the local labor newspaper, she was officially listed as associate editor until 1962, when the council finally recognized her as the primary editor and conferred the title.[33] Thornburgh attributed the misleading titles to the unwillingness of the local organization to pay her more than John Essary, the managing editor. Indeed, the gender discrimination was so blatant that the local office workers' union intervened on Thornburgh's behalf several times to help her gain small salary increases. The AFL's sex and wage discrimination within its own ranks produced a final irony in Thornburgh's work history: when she retired in 1972, she had no pension for her thirty-plus years of service to the organization.[34]

In 1946, while working as a union organizer in Georgia, Thornburgh noticed an advertisement in a labor newspaper inviting applications for a scholarship to Ruskin College in Oxford, England. She filled out the form, and as she disingenuously explained, "forgot about it." When the Knoxville newspapers announced her selection for the honor, there was no hint of the "manipulating and politikin'" that Thornburgh had exerted to obtain the scholarship. Later she revealed that the awards committee had balked at giving the scholarship to a thirty-seven-year-old woman; at the time, the local newspaper characterized the recipient as a vivacious "girl." Thornburgh granted celebratory interviews in which she contrasted her future and her recent past. "It'll be a change to be an Oxford student," she enthused, "after being erroneously labeled a radical, a pink and even a Red." She hoped Senator McKellar would "please note!" her new status, but observed, "maybe he'll be glad to have me out of the country."[35]

The opportunity to travel to England and study at Ruskin College was part of a larger effort between working-class women and higher education and progressive women's organizations that had a long history. By 1947 women's colleges had developed a number of programs designed to "train working women for union leadership roles." The best-known of the programs was the Bryn Mawr summer school for female industrial workers. Established in 1921 in conjunction with the Women's Trade Union League (WTUL), the programs empowered some women but according to one historian, "had little impact on the average woman industrial worker." For Lucille Thornburgh, however, the scholarship represented the "opportunity of a lifetime."[36]

Out of the public eye, Thornburgh faced a personal crisis that overshadowed her excitement about the scholarship. As she prepared for the voyage to England, her father was gravely ill. Although they both realized that probably he would die before she returned, Thomas encouraged his daughter to accept the award. This "broadminded" man and his independent daughter parted for the last time in September 1947; he died in May 1948, several months before she returned. Thornburgh seldom spoke of her personal pain in any context, and when she described her leave-taking from Knoxville she did so with a more humorous story about an aborted romance.

Interviewers always inquired about Thornburgh's marital status and wondered if she had ever considered marriage. Although she usually attributed her rise in the labor movement to her unmarried status—a condition that gave her the flexibility to travel—she once offered a more humorous explanation that tied her scholarship to her previously noted wartime romance. "I was going with a fella and I was tired of traveling, so I thought I might settle down," she told a reporter in 1995. "But then this scholarship [to Ruskin College] came along and I felt there are a lot of men out there, but only one scholarship," she explained.[37]

Ruskin College, founded in 1899, operated under the mandate of providing an educational experience for working-class students who had few opportunities for university admission. Founded in memory of John Ruskin, an eccentric and gifted artist and writer of the nineteenth century, the school offered courses in labor studies and economics.[38] Thornburgh's scholarship came through a joint effort between the AFL and Sarah Lawrence College. While in England, she learned firsthand the problems that English workers faced in the postwar era—food shortages played a prominent role in her reports to the Knoxville newspapers.[39] She found the British trade union movement far ahead of American efforts. She attributed their progress to generations of union membership that had instilled a sense of camaraderie that the American movement lacked. The year at Ruskin College did not radicalize Thornburgh—she was already committed to a life in pursuit of social justice—but she admitted that she "came back from over there more militant."[40]

Knoxville and the nation had changed during Thornburgh's absence. The Cold War stalemate between the United States and the Soviet Union was in its early years. The nation had become more conservative in its social and political life: women settled into a domestic life of housework and childbearing, social conformity produced "cookie cutter" communities, and social policy retreated from the New Deal's support for labor. Fearful of offending advertisers or encouraging the organizing efforts of the more militant Congress of Industrial Organizations (CIO), the always conservative Knoxville Labor Council pressured Thornburgh to rein in her radicalism in the pages of the *ETLN*.[41] However, if her editorial comments conformed to local AFL demands, her personal commitments did not. In the late 1940s, Thornburgh became active in the Unitarian Church, the Highlander Folk Center, and the Democratic Party.

Like many union members, Thornburgh believed that churches could provide a natural home for unions if properly mobilized. She told labor historian Perry Cotham that "We had some Bible-thumping fundamentalists in our union and they make good leaders, because they were such good speakers." She knew that Local 173 of Knoxville's marbleworkers conducted "their meetings . . . like religious services," calling "each other 'brother' and [including] a lot of preaching." Even when they quarreled among themselves, "they'd close every union meeting by joining hands and singing 'Bless be the tie that binds.'"[42] She also knew that a number of ministers supported the status quo and advised their congregants to vote against unions.

The Unitarian Church embraced the labor movement and provided a spiritual home for Thornburgh. She always explained her move to Unitarianism by claiming that the local worshipers needed one more member to establish a congregation. But one suspects a deeper motive, and certainly the religious and personal support she received through her fellowship with other social activists helped to sustain her enthusiasm over the decades. When the Reverend Daniel M. Welch (1951–55) left the Tennessee Valley Unitarian Fellowship to lead the Asheville, North Carolina, congregation, Thornburgh noted that he had been "keenly interested in the labor movement and has many friends among trade unionists in Knoxville. Having been a worker himself [in the coal mines at Soddy, Tennessee], he understands the problems which confront the working men and women."[43] In the Unitarian fellowship Thornburgh found a minister sympathetic to her labor unionism and a community of women and men who encouraged her social activism at the Highlander Folk School and in the civil rights movement.[44]

Thornburgh first became acquainted with Myles Horton and the Highlander Folk School in 1934, when Horton and his wife, Zilphia, arrived in Knoxville to educate striking workers in "trade unionism and labor economics." A native Tennessean and a student of the theologian Reinhold Niebuhr, Horton and Don West established their folk school in Monteagle in 1932. Highlander advocated adult education based on experience and collective action as a mechanism for establishing a "more democratic and humane society."[45] In the 1930s and 1940s Highlander was associated with the CIO organizing operations in the South and conducted workshops to educate workers in unionization. In the 1950s, however, as Highlander moved more clearly toward civil rights as its focus, the CIO distanced itself from the center. After a split with the CIO over policy differences, Highlander initiated workshops on desegregation.

Thornburgh had "always been in sympathy with Highlander," but the Knoxville unions considered it a "red communist school." As the only local labor leader associated with the school, Thornburgh did not advertise her relationship with Highlander, believing that the revelation that she worked with an integrated organization would reduce her effectiveness with the labor movement. She saw Highlander as an opportunity to "work out some of [her] militant feelings" and served as a board member until the AFL forced her to choose between labor unionism and the school in the wake of Highlander's increasing notoriety in the civil rights era.[46]

In the early 1960s Thornburgh participated in the civil rights movement to integrate Knoxville's lunch counters and restaurants, but her activism grew out of her association with the Unitarian Church, not as a labor leader.[47] Knoxville's racial history was complex, and Thornburgh's activities on behalf of civil rights illuminated both the strengths and weaknesses of labor's voice in the matter of race. East Tennessee's black population was historically the smallest in the state, never exceeding 10.5 percent in the twentieth century.[48] Indeed, by 1960 blacks accounted for a mere 7 percent of the population in the eastern Grand Division. Although East Tennesseans had rejected the Confederacy in the Civil War era and embraced the Republican Party after the war, African Americans enjoyed no respite from Jim Crow segregation. Thus, the changes promised by the U.S. Supreme Court decision in *Brown v. Board of Education* excited Knoxville's black community as much as it did those in the Deep South. In 1960, when black college students took matters into their own hands and staged peaceful sit-ins at lunch counters across the South, students at Knoxville College joined the protest. By June 1960, with the assistance of Knoxville mayor John Duncan, the city's lunch counters had been integrated, but many whites refused to sit beside blacks. Every day, Thornburgh ate her lunch at local variety and drug stores, taking a seat at the lunch counter beside a black patron in order to demonstrate her support for integration. She also purchased movie tickets for blacks to facilitate integration of the theaters. Thornburgh minimized her role in the civil rights movement, but her activities demonstrated her commitment to social justice and her unwillingness to be cowed by more conservative labor leaders.[49]

The demands of blacks went beyond the integration of lunch counters, and labor unions played an ambiguous role in the conflict over civil rights. As members of Knoxville's black community explained in a newspaper advertisement, African Americans could not obtain jobs as city bus drivers, they could not receive medical care at local hospitals, and they had no representation on the city council or the various governing agencies.[50] Regardless of educational qualifications, blacks worked at the lowest paying and least prestigious jobs. As late as 1967 a forty-seven-year-old black man noted that his status as a college graduate and a war veteran with a good work record gained him a job as a porter.[51]

The racial record of labor unions was mixed. The AFL gave lip service to organizing black workers, but its status as a federation of craft unions made its claims problematic, and Thornburgh privately maintained that Knoxville's conservative unions prevented integration. The CIO's somewhat better record can be attributed to its industrial rather than craft organization. Once the AFL and CIO merged in 1954, the combined organization publicly stated its commitment to racial equality, and the *ETLN* routinely printed national evidence of that commitment as a spur to local action. Though the *ETLN* highlighted sporadic local examples of integration, few African American workers found a home in East Tennessee's unions because most blacks labored in nonunion jobs.[52]

Thornburgh's activities soon drew her into politics. She loved a good political battle and once confessed, "We like politics and would wade a tar river to get to a political rally."[53] She first became active in Tennessee's 1948 Senate campaign. The contest pitted Estes Kefauver against the powerful Crump political machine and drew national attention. It was the kind of fight certain to engage a "militant" like Thornburgh. As a U.S. Senator, Kefauver's Democratic credentials and strong advocacy for the rights of working Americans endeared him to Thornburgh.[54] In 1955, when workers struck against the L&N Railroad after management refused to accept the negotiated agreement, Kefauver defended the strikers on the Senate floor. Thornburgh reported his actions, saying that "Senator Kefauver has really proven himself to be labor's friend in this situation" in explaining "the efforts that have been made by labor to avoid this walkout and the hollowness of the management position."[55] Thornburgh headed a "Kefauver for President" move in Knox County in 1956, and her disappointment in the senator's failure to win the nomination was palpable in her editorials and commentaries.[56] Following his death on the senate floor in 1963, she wrote, "it was encouraging and comforting to us to know that no matter how minute our problem was, we could take it to our friend Estes Kefauver and get an attentive ear, a warm handshake and a big understanding smile."[57] Likewise, she saw Eleanor Roosevelt as "an ardent advocate of labor's basic tenets" and mourned her death two months after that of Kefauver.[58]

Thornburgh's Democratic Party membership did not blind her to the perils of partisanship, and she worried that labor would become an appendage of the party, valued for the votes unions could deliver but denied full access to the party's decisions.[59] She viewed every election as important and exhorted union members to vote by reminding them, "WHAT WE GAIN AT THE BARGAINING TABLE CAN BE TAKEN AWAY FROM US IN THE LEGISLATIVE HALLS."[60] In the 1950s the Taft-Hartley Act, the subsequent state-sponsored "right to work" laws, and the Landrum-Griffin Act threatened to undo all the gains labor had made in the 1930s and 1940s. But in Thornburgh's mind, "The danger facing Organized Labor today is not the Taft-Hartley Law, the Open Shop Law nor the Unemployment situation—it is the complacency of our members."[61] Workers who were not informed on political issues and did not vote undermined the benefits unions won through collective bargaining.

Thornburgh admitted that she enjoyed writing about politics, and she presented complex legislative matters in a manner that demonstrated her knowledge of the issues and her understanding of the *ETLN* readers. In 1959 labor unions and their congressional supporters engaged in an unsuccessful fight to prevent the passage of the Landrum-Griffin bill. The measure established financial reporting requirements and standards for the election of union officers. Although it was presented as a measure for promoting democratic procedures, union officials saw it as government interference. When President Dwight Eisenhower publicly supported the bill, Thornburgh asked her readers to consider the conflict between their political loyalties and their self-interest as southern Appalachian union members: "Folks sitting back in their living rooms, with their TV operating on TVA power, remembered he's the very boy who said it was creeping socialism. They looked at the shaky roof and warped floors and remembered it was none other than this self-styled 'working man's friend' who vetoed desperately needed housing legislation. As the youngsters romped through the house they recalled that this is the same President Ike who just gave half-hearted, watered down support to the crying needs of education. They couldn't forget that he's the daddy of the 'tight money policy.'"[62] In her folksy, front porch style, she was asking the old labor question "which side are you on?"

Thornburgh made good use of the political boilerplate material that originated with the AFL, and she added comments of her own to focus reader attention on the implications of events for them as workers. Throughout the 1960s Thornburgh's own concerns about a rising radical conservatism crept into the pages of the *ETLN*. Generally she used the words of prominent labor leaders or moderate Republicans to nudge Knoxville's Republican union members toward more centrist positions or at least compel them to question the views of the far right. In 1963 she featured an article on Nelson Rockefeller's warning to the Republican Party that "vociferous, extremists are embarked on a determined and ruthless effort to take over the party, its platform, and its candidates on their own terms."[63] That same year, when Walter P. Reuther, president of the United Auto Workers union, predicted that the conservative plan of action included the admission of China to the United Nations and the rehabilitation of Richard M. Nixon for a renewed run for the presidency, Thornburgh gave the article a prominent place in the ETLN.[64] "The radical right," she wrote in an earlier issue, "is every bit as dangerous to American principles and American institutions as the radical left."[65]

By the late 1960s, as the Vietnam War, feminism, and civil rights roiled the nation, Thornburgh's liberal views were increasingly out of step with those of her readers. In November 1970, after a particularly bitter election that witnessed the triumph of the new conservatism, the ETLN admitted defeat and shut down its presses. Thornburgh avoided a discussion of the changing political climate and attributed the decline in readership to "ever rising costs, inflation, and increasing unemployment, all results of the prolonged stagnation of the economy." Sadly, she proclaimed, "we have weathered many storms and crossed many hurdles during the past 37 years [of the paper's publication], but there comes a time when the storm is too rough and the hurdles unsurmountable [*sic*]—that time has come for us."[66]

Thornburgh anticipated a quiet life, but "after I mopped the same floor every day for two or three weeks, I decided that was a real bore." Although she continued to be a regular visitor at the Central Labor Union offices and an active Democrat, Thornburgh focused her energies on the problems of aging, joining the ranks of the National Council of Senior Citizens (NCSC) and the Knoxville Community Action Committee (CAC) to fight for social services and health care benefits for the elderly. In 1981 she represented Knoxville as a delegate to the White House Conference on Aging. Assigned to the private sector committee, Thornburgh complained that the Republicans "stacked the 14 committees in their favor to prevent passage of any resolution strongly at variance with the Reagan Administration aims."[67] Making the best of her situation, she made a modest proposal to encourage public-private cooperation to provide jobs for the elderly, a seemingly nonpartisan suggestion that was defeated in committee. Defeats at the national level only encouraged Lucille to organize from the grassroots.

Concerned over rising energy costs, Thornburgh joined other Knoxville seniors to form the Tennessee Valley Energy Coalition (TVEC) and lobby against TVA's planned rate hikes to finance the construction of nuclear power plants. Worried that many on fixed incomes would face the dilemma of heating or eating, Thornburgh and her cohorts packed public hearings and marshaled a cadre of energy experts to offer alternatives to the rate hikes. To the amazement of TVA officials, the practical suggestions made sense; with their implementation utility rates stabilized.[68]

Operating under the premise that seniors had to "demonstrate and embarrass somebody before we can get anything done," Thornburgh tackled the American health care system, with somewhat less success. Seniors pressed for local doctors to "accept assignment" of Medicare payments—that is, accept the fee Medicare paid for service (80 percent) as the full fee. The seniors published a list of all Knoxville physicians who accepted the Medicare payments as full fees, an act that clearly irritated the members of the Knoxville Academy of Medicine. TVEC offered a number of suggestions for containing rising healthcare costs, including the establishment of national rate-setting commissions to monitor fee increases and a committee to approve hospital expansions.

In her seventies Thornburgh helped organize Solutions to Issues of Concern to Knoxvillians (SICK), which tackled such issues as Tennessee's sales tax on food. In order to pressure the state legislature, the seniors organized voter-registration drives and were promptly condemned as a "front for the Democratic Party." When the Knox County law director placed the government cheese lines off-limits for voter registration, the seniors challenged his ruling in federal court and had the order declared unconstitutional. SICK members campaigned for improved indigent health care, marched to prevent the closing of six Knoxville fire halls, campaigned against telephone rate hikes, and lobbied for state tax reform.[69] For her many efforts on behalf of the elderly and the poor, the CAC named Lucille Thornburgh Knox County's 1982 Senior Citizen of the Year.[70] Lucille Thornburgh continued to be "right pushy" until her death at age ninety in 1998.[71]

Through decades of activism, Thornburgh challenged the assumptions held by those in positions of social, political, and economic power. She fought for workers' rights on the picket lines and in the press—and then fought for her own rights as a woman within the labor organization. She embraced politics as the expression of democracy, though she never conceded the importance of grassroots organization to the hierarchies of power. In her mind ordinary people could find solutions to their problems through cooperative action. Her first and most enduring experiences in cooperativism developed through union activities, but over time, she moved into new areas of organization, including civil rights and senior rights.

Thornburgh's long activism, like that of other southern female labor unionists, including Lucy Randolph Macon and Eula McGill, challenges the assumptions of historians as well.[72] Contrary to conventional interpretations of southern labor history, Thornburgh was not wrested from a conservative, antilabor background by the events of 1934. She was already an independent woman who seized the opportunity provided by national events to join with her fellow workers and improve their condition. Setbacks and failures did not deter her—she found another way. Her persistence and commitment to social justice encourage a reassessment of southern labor history.

NOTES

1. Transcript of Oral History Interview with Lucille Thornburgh by June Rostan, 1978, in the Thornburgh Collection, box OH, "The Twentieth-Century Trade Union Woman: Vehicle for Social Change Oral History Project," Walter P. Reuther Library, Wayne State University (hereafter cited as Thornburgh Oral History). Thornburgh's birth year is 1909 in this collection, but is listed as 1908 in her TVA file and in other interviews. Dates are frequently inconsistent in the various interviews Thornburgh granted. The author has used the most consistent dates and those that can be verified in official files. Thornburgh generally told interviewers that she was a native of Strawberry Plains, a slight variation that required fewer explanations. For a description of Strawberry Plains, see Connie S. Campbell, *Coming Home to Strawberry Plains: A History of Strawberry Plains* (n.p.: n.p., 1986).

2. Thornburgh Oral History, 3, 7

3. Ibid., 1, 5.

4. Ibid., 4.

5. See Sheila M. Rothman, *Woman's Proper Place: A History of Changing Ideals and Practices, 1870 to the Present* (New York: Basic Books, 1978), and Jurgen Kocka, *White Collar Workers in America, 1890–1940: A Social History in International Perspective* (London: Sage Publications, 1980).

6. Thornburgh Oral History, 5. See Marjorie Spruill Wheeler, ed., *Votes for Women! The Woman Suffrage Movement in Tennessee, the South, and the Nation* (Knoxville: University of Tennessee Press, 1995).

7. Jeanette Keith, *Country People in the New South: Tennessee's Upper Cumberland* (Chapel Hill: University of North Carolina Press, 1995), 138–41.

8. Thornburgh Oral History, 12.

9. Alice Kessler-Harris, *Out to Work: A History of Wage-Earning Women in the United States* (New York: Oxford University Press, 1982), 213–14; Olivier Zunz, *Making America Corporate, 1870–1920* (Chicago: University of Chicago Press, 1990), chapter 5, "The Collar Line."

10. For the best and most recent discussion of the Scopes Trial, see Edward Larson, *Summer for the Gods: The Scopes Trial and American's Continuing Debate Over Science and Religion* (New York: Basic Books, 1997).

11. Kessler-Harris, *Out of Work*; Zunz, *Making America Corporate*. For descriptions of the Great Depression, see Roger Biles, *A New Deal for the American People* (DeKalb: Northern Illinois University Press, 1991); Anthony J. Badger, *The New Deal: The Depression Years, 1933–1940* (New York: Hill and Wang, 1989; Chicago: Ivan R. Dee, 2002); William E. Leuchtenburg, *Franklin D. Roosevelt and the New Deal* (New York: Harper and Row, 1963); and Robert S. McElvaine, *The Great Depression: America, 1929–1941* (New York: Times Books, 1984).

12. Michael J. McDonald and William Bruce Wheeler, *Knoxville, Tennessee: Continuity and Change in an Appalachian City* (Knoxville: University of Tennessee Press, 1983), 61–63.

13. See Perry C. Cotham, *Toil, Turmoil and Triumph: A Portrait of the Tennessee Labor Movement* (Franklin, Tenn.: Hillsboro Press, 1995), 126–37.

14. There is an extensive literature on southern textiles, labor, and the New Deal, including Lizabeth Cohen, *Making the New Deal: Industrial Workers in Chicago, 1919–1939* (New York: Cambridge University Press, 1990); James A. Hodges, *New Deal Labor Policy and the Southern Cotton Textile Industry, 1933–1941* (Knoxville: University of Tennessee Press, 1986); Janet Irons, *Testing the New Deal: The General Textile Strike of 1934 in the American South* (Urbana: University of Illinois Press, 2000); John A. Salmond, *The General Textile Strike of 1934: From Maine to Alabama* (Columbia: University of Missouri Press, 2002).

15. Cotham, *Toil, Turmoil and Triumph*, 131–32. For further discussion on the working conditions for female cotton workers, see Victoria Byerly, *Hard Times Cotton Mill Girls: Personal Histories of Womanhood and Poverty in the South* (Ithaca, N.Y.: Cornell University Press, 1986); and Jacquelyn Dowd Hall, James Leloudis, Robert Korstad, Mary Murphy, Lu Ann Jones, and Christopher B. Daly, *Like a Family: The Making of a Southern Cotton Mill World* (Chapel Hill: University of North Carolina Press, 1987).

16. Cotham, *Toil, Turmoil and Triumph*, 132.

17. Thornburgh Oral History, 20.

18. Ibid., 18, 19.

19. Ibid., 22. The Central Labor Council was made up of delegates from each of the city's unions. Thornburgh was the only female officer in her local, and the only female member of the Central Labor Council.

20. Lucille Thornburgh referred to the strike in every interview she gave, suggesting its importance in shaping her future as an AFL organizer. Blacklisting was a common antiunion tactic. Manufacturers distributed lists of names of union activists in order to prevent their employment at other factories. Despite this practice, Thornburgh asserted that "a lot of our blacklisted people here went to North Carolina and scabbed on the people over there." She defended their actions as the result of ignorance and the need for employment to feed their families (Thornburgh Oral History, 23). Also see Cotham, *Toil, Turmoil and Triumph*, 135, 136; "Octogenarian Action," *Knoxville Metro Pulse*, June 8–15, 1995; Jack Neely, "Lucille Thornburgh, 1908–1998," *Knoxville Metro Pulse*, November 12–19, 1998; and in *Knoxville News-Sentinel*: "Associate Labor News Editor Wins Scholarship at Oxford," September 9, 1947; Richard Powelson, "Knoxvillian Doubts Success of Seminar," December 3, 1981; Kaye Franklin Veal, "Lucille Picked a Fine Time . . . and She's Kept on Going," December 26, 1982; Mike Flannigan, "Organizer of '33," July 29, 1995; and "'No. 1 Lady of Community' Dies at 90," December 3, 1998. Janet Irons concluded in her study of the strike that "if there is a regional explanation for the failure of the '34 strike, it rests in the different position of southern workers in regional and national politics" (Irons, *Testing the New Deal*, 176).

21. In addition to its national and regional consequences, TVA interrupted local life by removing farmers from the land and destroying longstanding communities in order to construct the dams. See Michael J. McDonald and John Muldowny, *TVA and the Dispossessed: The Resettlement of Population in the Norris Dam Area* (Knoxville: University of Tennessee Press, 1981); Wilmon Henry Droze, *High Dams and Slack Waters: TVA Builds a River* (Baton Rouge: Louisiana State University Press, 1965); Thomas K. McCraw, *TVA and the Power Fight, 1933–1939* (Philadelphia: Lippincott, 1971); Michael L. Brookshire and Michael D. Rogers, *Collective Bargaining in Public Employment: The TVA Experience* (Lexington, Mass.: Lexington Books, 1977); and North Callahan, *TVA: Bridge Over Troubled Waters* (South Brunswick, N.J.: A. S. Barnes, 1980). Several of the early directors of TVA wrote their own histories, including David Eli Lilienthal, *TVA: Democracy on the March* (New York: Harper, 1944); Arthur Ernest Morgan, *The Making of TVA* (Buffalo, N.Y.: Prometheus Books,

1974); and Gordon R. Clapp, *The TVA: An Approach to the Development of a Region* (Chicago: Russell and Russell, 1971).

22. Lucille Thornburgh, TVA Personnel File, 1934–1942, accessed through Freedom of Information Act (hereinafter, FOIA).

23. Joint Committee on Atomic Energy, *Confirmation of Atomic Energy Commission and General Manager*, 80th Cong., January–March 1947.

24. FBI file on Lucille Thornburgh, FOIA.

25. FBI file on Lucille Thornburgh, FOIA.

26. *Knoxville News-Sentinel*, February 16, 1947; Cotham, *Toil, Turmoil and Triumph*, 138.

27. *Knoxville News-Sentinel*, December 26, 1982.

28. Thornburgh Oral History, 25, 26; Cotham, *Toil, Turmoil and Triumph*, 137.

29. "A Resolution," adopted by the Tri-Cities Central Labor Union, March 17, 1942, in Thornburgh, TVA Personnel File.

30. "Request for Certification, War Department," July 8, 1942 and "United States Civil Service Commission, Authority for Transfer," July 9, 1942 in Thornburgh, TVA Personnel File.

31. Thornburgh Oral History, 27, 28.

32. Ibid., 29.

33. Thornburgh's tenure with the *ETLN* lasted from 1946 to 1970. She was listed as "Editor" from 1962 to 1970. Earlier, John Essary, the managing editor, was listed as Editor. The council gave Thornburgh the title of Editor only after Essary left the paper to accept a position with the city of Knoxville and to run for political office (Thornburgh Oral History, 40–41).

34. Thornburgh Oral History, 30, 37, 40–41; Thornburgh, "Good Night *Labor News*," *ETLN*, November 27, 1970. Thornburgh believed that the decision to accept advertising from area businesses as a means to finance the newspaper also tempered the potential radicalism of the *ETLN*. Thornburgh also complained that the Central Labor Council limited her organizing activities to factories that were "female." She compared the gender attitudes of the AFL with those of the CIO, where her sister, a member of the Amalgamated Clothing Workers, was an organizer.

35. Thornburgh Oral History, 30; "Associate Labor News Editor Wins Scholarship at Oxford," *Knoxville News-Sentinel*, September 6, 1947.

36. Thornburgh quote from "Associate Labor News Editor Wins." For information on efforts to educate working-class women, see Nancy Woloch, *Women and the American Experience, A Concise History* (Boston: McGraw-Hill, 2002), 264–65; Margaret Ripley Wolfe, *Daughters of Canaan: A Saga of Southern Women* (Lexington: University of Kentucky Press, 1995), 163–67; Doris Cohen Brody, "American Labor Education Service, 1927–1962: An Organization in Workers' Education" (Ph.D. diss., Cornell University, 1973).

37. Mike Flannagan, "Organizer of '33: Knoxville Woman Launched Strike at Textile Mill," *Knoxville News-Sentinel*, July 29, 1995.

38. See http://www.ruskin.ac.uk and http://www.victorianweb.org/authors/ruskin.

39. "Knoxville Girl Labor Leader Visits Buckingham Palace," *Knoxville News-Sentinel*, October 26, 1947.

40. Thornburgh Oral History, 35.

41. Ibid., 37–38.

42. Cotham, *Toil, Turmoil and Triumph*, 137–38.

43. Lucille Thornburgh, *ETLN*, July 1, 1955. The recognition that churches held potential as allies for unions was more than a southern phenomenon. In 1959 George Meany asserted that "labor has

a natural ally in the churches in combating the 'tremendous opposition of big business'" (*ETLN*, October 8, 1959).

44. Interview with Pat Bing, member of the Tennessee Valley Unitarian Universalist congregation, 2006.

45. John M. Glen, "Highlander Folk School" in *Tennessee Encyclopedia of History and Culture*, ed. Carroll Van West (Nashville: Tennessee Historical Society, 1998), 423. The most complete study of the Highlander Folk School is John M. Glen, *Highlander, No Ordinary School, 1932–1962* (Lexington: University Press of Kentucky, 1988).

46. Thornburgh Oral History, 38–40.

47. "Octogenarian Action"; Thornburgh Oral History, 66–67.

48. Lester C. Lamon, *Blacks in Tennessee, 1791–1970* (Knoxville: University of Tennessee Press, 1981), appendix.

49. McDonald and Wheeler, *Knoxville, Tennessee*, 129–30, 137; Lamon, *Blacks in Tennessee*, 99–115; Thornburgh Oral History, 67.

50. Lamon, *Blacks in Tennessee*, 107–8.

51. Ibid., 111; Thornburgh Oral History, 39.

52. *ETLN* articles included Thornburgh, "Tobacco Workers Union Integrates All Locals," December 26, 1963; Thornburgh, "A Look at Last Week's City Elections," November 28, 1963; Thornburgh, "Segregation Is Costing Knoxville Thousands of Dollars," May 9, 1963; George Simmons, "Local 55 Salutes a Member," December 27, 1962; and Justin Griffin, "Letter to the Editor," April 25, 1968. Letters to the editor are always suspect: Thornburgh admitted that she sometimes wrote the letters under a fictitious name to stimulate discussion.

53. Thornburgh, "The Ramp Festival," *ETLN*, April 29, 1955.

54. Charles Fontenay, *Estes Kefauver, a Biography* (Knoxville: University of Tennessee Press, 1980); http://bioguide.congress.gov; Cotham, *Toil, Turmoil and Triumph*, 291–95.

55. Thornburgh, "High Spirits as L&N Men Hold Picket Line," *ETLN*, April 1, 1955.

56. "Miss Thornburgh Seeks Demo Post," *Knoxville News-Sentinel*, June 20, 1954; Cotham, *Toil, Turmoil and Triumph*, 139.

57. Thornburgh, "Estes Kefauver," *ETLN*, August 15, 1963.

58. Thornburgh, "She Was One of Us," *ETLN*, October 24, 1963.

59. Thornburgh Oral History, 64.

60. Thornburgh, "Stay in Your Own Field, Mrs. Ferguson," *ETLN*, August 12, 1955. Emphasis original to the document. Thornburgh's efforts to get out the vote were remembered long after she retired from the *ETLN*. See "Like It or Not, You're in Politics," *Mountain Laurel Review*, February 9, 1999, http://www.mlrmag.com/archive/99_spring/publishers_page40.html (accessed February 22, 2006).

61. Thornburgh, "Do You Attend Your Union Meetings," *ETLN*, August 5, 1955.

62. Thornburgh, "Eisenhower Badly Miscast as Friend of the Workingman," *ETLN*, August 20, 1959.

63. "Report on the Right Wing," *ETLN*, August 15, 1963.

64. Ibid.

65. Thornburgh, "Rockefeller Service," *ETLN*, July 25, 1963. Rockefeller's prediction of Nixon's rehabilitation proved prophetic. Despite the efforts of union leaders, Nixon won the 1968 election over his labor-friendly opponent, Hubert Humphrey. As Lyndon Johnson left office, the newspaper published a cartoon showing an AFL-CIO worker painting the letters LBJ. The caption reads "No

President has done more for the poor, the homeless, the elderly; no President has achieved more in the fields of education, civil rights, or health care" (ETLN, January 28, 1969).

66. Thornburgh, "Good Night *Labor News*."

67. Richard Powelson, "Knoxvillian Doubts Success of Seminar," *Knoxville News-Sentinel*, December 3, 1981.

68. Jack Neely, "Tennesseans Fight for Social Justice: Grassroots Power," *Southern Exposure*, March–June 1985, 40–41.

69. Ibid., 43–45.

70. Kaye Franklin Veal, "Lucille Picked a Fine Time . . . and She's Kept on Going," *Knoxville News-Sentinel*, December 26, 1982.

71. "No. 1 Lady of Community Dies at 90," *Knoxville News-Sentinel*, November 10, 1998.

72. See John A. Salmond, *Miss Lucy of the CIO: The Life and Times of Lucy Randolph Macon, 1882–1959* (Athens: University of Georgia Press, 1988); Lucy Macon Randolph, *To Win These Rights: A Personal Story of the CIO in the South* (New York: Harper and Brothers, 1952).

Martha Ragland

(1906–1996)

The Evolution of a Political Feminist

CAROLE BUCY

❀ ❀ ❀

During the years between the woman suffrage–era first wave of feminism in the 1910s and 1920s and the second wave of feminism of the 1960s, women struggled to define what their role in politics should be. Martha Ragland of Tennessee came of age in that time. As a woman who was unwilling to accept the status quo, her work—as well as the work of many other unnamed southern women—paved the way for that second wave. In a letter to Jane McMichael at the Schlesinger Library, Ragland described herself as "a life-long feminist; action-oriented and politically minded."[1] Her actions in the birth control campaign of the 1930s, in the movement to abolish the poll tax in the 1940s and 1950s, and with the Democratic Party provided Ragland and other women with important experiences whose results were not often seen until the 1960s. Gender, class, and race issues often intersected in these campaigns. From her experiences in numerous women's voluntary associations, Ragland realized that women must have greater participation in the political process: as voters, as campaign workers, and finally as candidates. As a product of the first wave of feminism, Ragland reflected the changes that occurred in the women's movement during the era of abeyance prior to the second wave of feminism. Ragland became what historian Sarah Wilkerson Freeman called a "stealth feminist," one who, using the guise of women's traditional roles, challenged the status quo to correct inequities throughout society.[2]

In 1950, when Senator Estes Kefauver, a first-term senator from Tennessee, opened investigative hearings in New York on organized crime, television cameras for the first time brought the entire congressional process into the living rooms of America. Kefauver, a rising star in the ranks of the national Demo-

MARTHA RAGLAND

Circa 1952. Jack Norman, Martha Ragland, and Estes Kefauver.

Courtesy of the *Tennessean*, Nashville, Tennessee.

cratic Party, suddenly became a nationally known political figure, particularly among white, middle-class American women who watched the hearings while performing their household chores. Women liked what they saw.[3] As Kefauver's popularity increased, the popularity of President Harry S. Truman declined to all-time lows. Because of the perception that Kefauver represented a break with the past, he quickly became a contender for the Democratic nomination for U.S. president. Could he capitalize on his appeal to women during the hearings to get the nomination without the support of President Truman?

Martha Ragland was among Kefauver's inner circle of supporters. Ragland, a Tennessee homemaker with a master's degree in economics, resigned a position on the national board of the League of Women Voters (LWV) in 1948 to head the women's division of Kefauver's campaign for the Democratic nomination for the U.S. Senate.[4] She was convinced that women would vote for Kefauver if they understood the issues and that if women voted in higher numbers, Kefauver would win. To achieve this, she created a grassroots network of women and appealed to them in their accepted roles as wives and mothers. When Kefauver won his Senate election in 1948 he credited his victory to Martha Ragland and the women who worked in his campaign.[5]

But in Kefauver's two national presidential campaigns of 1952 and 1956 Ragland discovered that despite her previous success she was unable to translate her grassroots organization of reform-minded women into a national victory over the party establishment for Kefauver. A small group of white male political operatives controlled the national Democratic Party, and they resisted the inclusion of women in the decision-making process. In Ragland's opinion, if women had been involved at *all levels* of the Democratic Party, Kefauver would have received the nomination. Her frustrations with party machinery during the 1952 and 1956 elections moved her from the position of a female party activist working for reform-minded male candidates to that of a political feminist working for women's equality.

When Martha Ragland entered politics in 1948 her views on the role of women reflected her Progressive Era roots in the League of Women Voters. Ragland interpreted Kefauver's inability to secure the presidential nomination as a defeat, but her experiences marked an important transition from a period in which women worked in politics as an extension of their domestic roles as wives and mothers to a later era when women served as politicians in their own right and as individuals.

Education was the centerpiece of Martha Ragland's life and work. Whether she was educating women about birth control, the general public about the unfairness of the poll tax, voters about Estes Kefauver, or politicians about the inequities of segregation, everything that she did involved a significant educational component. Martha Ragland was born to parents who valued education for women and rural southerners. Her mother, Vita Jane Troutt Ragsdale, a graduate of Kentucky Western College, and her father, Joseph Senter Ragsdale, a graduate of the University of Chicago, were lifelong educators. Joseph Ragsdale founded the Kentucky Western School in Lone Oak, Kentucky, a small town just south of Paducah, and the Ragsdales were teaching there when Martha was born in 1906. Joseph, a celebrated primary school teacher, had founded the school to provide education beyond the eighth grade. In 1910 he founded Heath High School near Paducah and served as principal. Vita taught history at the school. Martha graduated from Heath in 1923, and her family then moved to Russellville, Kentucky, where her father became the dean of Logan College for Young Women, a two-year school, and her mother became the principal of a local high school. Martha graduated from Logan College in 1925, winning top honors in her class, and was named the school's "Logan Girl," its highest honor. She then enrolled at Vanderbilt University in Nashville as a junior.[6]

As a student at Vanderbilt, Martha was drawn to public policy issues, especially world population problems. She majored in economics and earned her B.A. degree in 1927 and M.A. in economics in 1928.[7] Her thesis, privately published under the title *The National Origins Plan of Immigration Restrictions*, attracted national attention. During the first three decades of the twentieth century, Congress passed several bills to limit immigration. The Immigration Plan of 1924 was to go into effect on July 1, 1927, shortly after Martha's undergraduate graduation from Vanderbilt, but the outcry from the public about the unfairness of the quotas threatened its implementation. Acting under great pressure from numerous special interest groups, Congress passed a resolution in March 1927 to postpone enactment of the law for one year. Ragland's graduate advisor and thesis director, Roy L. Garis, had published a comprehensive study, *Immigration Restriction: A Study of the Opposition to and the Regulation of Immigration in the United States*, in 1927, as Martha was completing her own thesis. Congress again passed a resolution delaying the law's implementation another year, since 1928 was a presidential election year. Ragland's thesis analyzed the processes involved in making U.S. immigration policy, and she concluded that agitation by special interest groups made it difficult for members of Congress to consider what was in the best interest of the country. She called for Congress to act more independently on the immigration plan as well as other matters.[8]

After graduation, Martha moved to Washington, D.C., where she worked at the National Records Council Committee on Biological Genealogy gathering and tabulating data for Ellsworth Huntington, a Yale geographer known for his research and writing in the new field of eugenics and climatic determinism. Huntington's project focused on the education, occupations, and material status of descendants of two to three thousand Puritan families (including his own) who had settled in New England by 1633.[9] While working in this position, Martha first observed the national political scene up close, and particularly noted the limits of the Republican response to the national crisis when the stock market crashed in 1929. She felt that the federal government needed to do more to reduce the effects of the Depression.[10]

Although Ragland had already determined that she was going to marry Tom Ragland before she left Tennessee for Washington, she postponed her marriage to pursue her career for a few years and declined to have a traditional engagement. "I knew I wanted to marry Tom," she recalled a few months before her death. "I just didn't want to marry him then."[11] Ragland's decision to postpone marriage for a career was indeed unusual for a southern woman. As evidence of her "feminist instincts," she recalled that she refused to accept a wedding ring, the traditional symbol of marriage: "I told him I didn't want a wedding ring. It seemed to me to be a symbol of bondage."[12]

When she married Tom Ragland and returned to Tennessee at the height of the Depression in 1932, she replaced her career as a professional economist with social and political activism through a variety of women's voluntary associations. Tom Ragland's family owned a successful wholesale grocery business with distribution centers across the state as well as other business interests, which included supplying wheat flour to the Chattanooga company that made Moon Pies. Tom Ragland worked for the family business, but his work forced the family to move several times during the first ten years of their marriage. Martha Ragland's work in a variety of organizations allowed her to continue doing research on public policy issues and provided a platform from which she could voice her opinions. Living in Knoxville her interest in economics and immigration soon led her to consider the need for birth control as a means of population management. Her previous research gave her an understanding of the problems that poor women faced in this country. She quickly realized that an understanding of birth control could alleviate some of these women's difficulties. Working in Tennessee's nascent birth control movement, her activities went well beyond the accepted roles for elite white women living in the South. In Knoxville, Ragland was able to join forces with other like-minded women, many of whom had moved to town in the 1930s as wives of Tennessee Valley Authority engineers. Ragland and her Knoxville associates were educated women, most of whom had experiences outside the state of Tennessee.[13]

Ragland and her allies became active in the Birth Control League, founded by

Margaret Sanger to promote federal birth control legislation. It was through the campaign for state-supported birth control clinics that she met birth control pioneer Edna Rankin McKinnon, who established a birth control clinic in Knoxville. These women quickly became political allies.[14] "We wanted birth control included in the public health services of Tennessee," Ragland recalled. By 1937 Knoxville and Nashville had birth control clinics, but developing a statewide network proved to be difficult. The following year, there was a temporary setback in plans to establish birth control clinics across the state when a field representative of the Child Welfare Division of the Children's Bureau visited Tennessee and advised against public dissemination of birth control information in public health clinics. When the state public health department announced it was abandoning its birth control program because of this criticism, Martha Ragland, now a member of the state Planned Parenthood Federation Executive Committee, initiated a campaign to challenge the Children's Bureau position. Ragland wrote numerous letters to the bureau and traveled to Washington to protest. At Ragland's urging, the Children's Bureau held hearings about birth control at which Margaret Sanger testified. The Children's Bureau then issued a confidential statement, retracting their earlier position.[15]

At this time, contraception was still illegal in Tennessee and much of the South. In 1938 Ragland, the Tennessee representative to the National Birth Control Clinical Research Bureau meeting in Fishkill, New York, met Margaret Sanger. Ragland promptly invited Sanger to come to Tennessee to help get birth control education in public health clinics across the state. The year before, North Carolina had opened fifty-eight birth control clinics.[16] Ragland wanted Tennessee to do the same thing. Sanger, accompanied by Martha Ragland and Anne Dallas Dudley, a leading Tennessee suffragist, embarked on a statewide speaking tour to provide Tennessee women with factual information about birth control. They encountered protests along the way from religious leaders who opposed providing women with such information.[17] Some conservatives linked Sanger and the birth control movement to radical politics in Tennessee. In Nashville, Sanger addressed the African American student body and faculty at Meharry Medical School, one of the leading training institutions for African American doctors. In Memphis, she spoke at a public meeting for African Americans held at the Metropolitan Baptist Church.[18] Attending these meetings with Sanger helped Ragland to see the needs of African Americans in the South and planted ideas in her for interracial cooperation, particularly among women.

Dorothy Stafford became one of Ragland's closest political allies in Knoxville. After working together on several public policy issues, they decided to revive the Tennessee League of Women Voters, which had died out in the late 1920s.

When Ragland and her husband moved from Knoxville to Chattanooga in 1940, she continued her activities in support of birth control and joined the newly established Chattanooga League of Women Voters. Even though the attention of the country was focused on war, through the LWV Ragland was able to work on a variety of local public health issues as an extension of her long-standing interest in population problems and health issues of women and children. Because she was willing to challenge the political power structure even if it meant alienating those in the system who disagreed with her views, she quickly became a lightning rod for reform. In response to Ragland's outspoken views that women had a right to basic information about reproduction, for example, a state representative introduced a bill in the Tennessee General Assembly to prohibit the distribution of any information associated with birth control. Ragland's association with the LWV provided her with important grassroots organizational skills that she later applied to partisan politics. Her experiences in the LWV also allowed her to develop a public voice. There she was able to extend her areas of interest beyond public health issues into broader areas of public policy.

In 1941 Ragland was elected president of the Chattanooga–Hamilton County League of Women Voters. In spite of the fact that the nation's attention was focused on the war effort, under Ragland's leadership the LWV began to tackle important local issues, and its visibility in the local newspapers dramatically increased. When her presidency began, the LWV focused on issues of particular interest to women, but during her two-year term she gradually expanded the LWV's efforts to study a variety of issues related to local public policy, including public tuberculosis hospitals, the Tennessee Valley Authority, laws requiring milk to be pasteurized, and the need for the United Nations. Through her LWV work, she demonstrated her abilities as a coalition builder by bringing together like-minded women's groups to work collectively on issues of mutual interest.[19] Ragland and the LWV were shaping public policy through their influence on the legislative process. The next step would be direct involvement in the election process, working in campaigns and then running for office. She would later apply what she described as the "League technique" to partisan politics in the national arena—"Get the facts, then present them, together with recommendations, to the proper public officials and to the public. And keep after it. It is really democracy at work." She called on women to get involved, "to make participating in government a part of life along with going to church, tending the children, or playing bridge." She reminded women that "Being an active citizen interested in government does not necessarily constitute being 'mixed up in politics.'"[20] Here she stopped short of calling for women to run for office, but she would soon give up the activities of the nonpartisan LWV and become an active Democrat.

The poll tax dominated Tennessee political debate throughout the 1940s. The anti–poll tax campaign became for southern women what one historian has aptly called "the second battle for woman suffrage." Like the issue of birth control, the anti–poll tax fight intersected the civil rights movement. Ragland recognized that the lack of birth control information held women back and was particularly harmful to poor women and African American women. The poll tax worked in much the same way. It was poor women of all races who could not pay the tax in order to vote. Ragland understood "the suppressive effects of the poll tax" on women.[21] When the national League of Women Voters issued a "Statement of One Hundred Southern Women" calling for Congress to abolish the poll tax on the twentieth anniversary of the ratification of the suffrage amendment, Martha Ragland was among the signatories.[22]

The poll tax repeal campaign in Tennessee began when Silliman Evans, an ardent New Dealer from Texas, moved to Nashville to take over the *Tennessean*, Nashville's morning newspaper, which he had purchased out of bankruptcy receivership. Evans immediately challenged the "Boss Crump" political machine for power. Edward Crump, the West Tennessee political boss, had controlled Tennessee politics since the 1920s, and the poll tax enabled his machine to control elections. Even though the League of Women Voters secured pledges of support for various anti–poll tax initiatives when the legislature was not in session, each time the General Assembly convened, the LWV's support among lawmakers dissipated. The politicians could not easily give up the control of elections that the poll tax provided. Since the LWV in 1941 had only two local organizations in Tennessee (Knoxville and Chattanooga), Ragland and Stafford organized a coalition of organizations that included numerous civic, labor, and religious groups such as the Farm Bureau and the YWCA, which was called the Committee for Majority Rule. When the women discovered in early January 1941 that the state Senate Elections Committee was meeting in a room at the Hermitage Hotel behind locked doors, they went to the hotel and demanded open hearings on bills to repeal the poll tax. They were not admitted to the meeting. However, committee officials announced after the meeting ended that the committee had rejected three repeal bills.[23] Ragland and her LWV allies did not give up the fight. They continued to campaign against the tax. In 1943, at their urging, the Tennessee General Assembly removed the poll tax as a voting prerequisite. When a county sheriff quickly filed a lawsuit challenging the constitutionality of the bill, Ragland and Stafford realized that they were in for a long fight. The Tennessee Supreme Court declared the repeal to be unconstitutional. In the years that followed, the LWV's poll tax repeal bills were introduced each session, but none passed until 1949.[24]

In the midst of this fight, and as World War II ended in 1945, Ragland became the state LWV president. In this position, she identified state constitutional reform as a critical issue for the LWV, as it seemed that an amendment to the state constitution was the only effective way to repeal the poll tax. Ragland rallied women from across the state to pressure Tennessee's governor, James Nance McCord, to appoint a commission to study the state constitution. When the recommendations of the governor's commission fell short of the LWV's expectations for extensive reform, Ragland wrote her own assessment of the constitution, which the LWV published in a 1946 pamphlet entitled "Tennessee Needs a New Constitution." This pamphlet demonstrated her vision as well as the depth of her thinking. Ragland called for a unicameral state legislature, longer terms for representatives and the governor, and abolition of the poll tax. Although Tennessee did not implement constitutional revision until 1953, the National Municipal League, a good-government organization that produced models for state and local governments, correctly recognized that the League of Women Voters deserved credit when change took place.[25] Under Ragland's leadership, the League of Women Voters became a distinct voice in Tennessee politics for the first time. Her ability to identify issues and to propose solutions made the League of Women Voters a leader among Tennessee women's organizations in promoting reform. The people that she met through the networks that she created also served her well when she left the nonpartisan activities of the LWV and entered partisan politics.[26]

In 1946 Martha Ragland was elected to the board of the national League of Women Voters. While lobbying on the floor of the U.S. House of Representatives (an activity national board members regularly engaged in at the time of board meetings) she became personally acquainted with Tennessee's third-district congressman, Estes Kefauver. He had been elected to the House of Representatives in 1939 as a New Dealer, and he supported federal aid to education, legislative reorganization, civil rights, and abolition of the poll tax. While these issues were important to LWV members and feminists, many southern and Tennessee congressmen ignored or opposed them. Kefauver quickly became identified as a progressive congressman outside the mainstream of southern politicians.[27] A longtime admirer of Kefauver, Ragland introduced herself to the congressman and told him that she would work in his campaign should he ever run for higher office.[28]

A few months later, Estes Kefauver asked Martha Ragland to head the women's division of his campaign for the Democratic nomination for the U.S. Senate. By accepting this job, she joined the inner political circle of his campaign team. He would face incumbent senator Tom Stewart in the August 1948 state Democratic primary. Stewart served in the Senate with the support of Boss Crump. As Ragland saw the race, voters had a choice between a new liberal politician committed to reform or the continuation of twenty years of machine-controlled politics. Since LWV board members at all levels were prohibited from working in political campaigns, she resigned from the board to join Kefauver's campaign. When Ragland's appointment as chair of the campaign's women's division was announced, she told reporters, "I believe it is every woman's duty to be an active citizen. Otherwise, she is neglecting her responsibility to her home and family. War and depression can shatter overnight all the bright plans we have for our children's future. This year we must elect government officials with the ability, imagination and courage that the critical world situation demands. The old-style politician does not fit into today's stern picture. That is why I want to help send Estes Kefauver to the United States Senate, and why I believe the women of Tennessee will overwhelmingly support him."[29]

At this time, Ragland was the mother of two elementary school–age children. Her work for birth control clinics and the abolition of the poll tax had prepared her for organizing a statewide political campaign. Her view of the task at hand was straightforward and direct: bring the issues to the attention of the public across the state and convince women, in particular, to vote for Kefauver. Ragland reasoned that women, as wives and mothers, would be eager to "clean up" Tennessee politics and release it from the hold of the Crump machine that had dominated the state throughout the Depression and the difficult war and postwar years. Her letters to the women of Tennessee demonstrated her understanding of what would make women vote on election day. "Here it is spring again, and the jonquils are in bloom, and no one seems to be thinking much about politics. But I have two children and am very much interested in the worsening world situation."[30] Although feminist rhetoric was absent in her correspondence during the 1948 campaign, she clearly demonstrated that she was interested in tapping women's potential political power.

In the Kefauver campaign Ragland applied the methods and processes of the League of Women Voters by organizing a "school for politics" for Democratic Tennessee women that she recruited to work in the campaign. Following LWV principles, she held that women must be trained to be effective campaign workers. She traveled across the state holding local "schools for politics" in an effort to persuade women that the strong, fresh leadership Kefauver could provide was critical in Tennessee at this particular time. Each session began with an overview of the problems and challenges facing the United States in the post–World War II era. She emphasized the importance of supporting the United Nations to prevent the outbreak of another war and the need for leadership in preventing another depression. Her schools focused on national security, rising prices, and education, areas of particular concern to women. She emphasized the contribution each woman could make and the significance of the women's vote in this election, appealing to them as wives and mothers to vote for Kefauver out of concern for their children. When Kefauver made political capital out of Boss Crump's accusations that Kefauver had been a "pet coon" of the Communist Party, and photos of Kefauver wearing a coonskin cap appeared on the front pages of newspapers across the state, Ragland continued to focus on the issues, reminding women that a vote for Kefauver would protect their homes and families from the threat of another depression or war. By July, with the primary only a month away, Kefauver saw the results of the tireless work of Martha Ragland's women's division in the size of the crowds that came to his rallies.[31]

On the eve of the election, Ragland predicted a Kefauver victory, which she also interpreted as a defeat of Crump. Newspapers across the state carried her predictions. "The day of boss-rule in Tennessee is over," said Ragland in a radio address carried over local station WSM.[32] The *Chattanooga Times* ran a front-page photograph of Kefauver and Ragland and an article that described Kefauver's appreciation of Ragland and her efforts on his behalf. With Kefauver directly challenging Crump's candidate, and with record voter turnouts predicted on election day, this election was among the most exciting races in Tennessee political history.[33] When Kefauver and Gordon Browning, who ran against Crump's gubernatorial candidate, won impressive victories in the primary, many political observers hailed this as the "beginning of a new era in Tennessee politics."[34] In victory speeches, Kefauver reiterated his belief that the women's efforts had made the difference in the outcome of the election. *Chattanooga Times* publisher Martin Ochs described one such speech—"Highest in the winner's esteem was Mrs. Ragland, who as state manager of women for Kefauver strategy, launched a women's vote probably unprecedented in Tennessee history." The following week the *Christian Science Monitor* ran an article describing Kefauver's victory and crediting Ragland's organizational efforts as being a determining factor in the campaign.[35] Ragland saw Kefauver's victory as a great victory for women over machine politics. In her mind, it was the women now acting as informed citizens and full participants in the political process that had defeated Crump.

As Gordon Browning and Estes Kefauver joined forces to campaign for the November elections, the state Democratic Party appointed Martha Ragland to chair the women's division in the fall campaign. At the campaign schools that she organized across the state, Ragland continued to appeal to women, whom she believed to be naturally progressive. From the stump, she told workers at a Knoxville event that "Tennessee women are interested in the TVA, vitally concerned with peace and high prices, and anxious to improve voting laws and adoption proceedings. The best way we can do something about this interest is to become active instead of passive. We want to roll up a landslide vote to give these two men a mandate through a clear-cut majority so that they will know Tennesseans want progressive government."[36] Furthermore, she stated, "Tennessee women are doing things about today's problems and not just talking about them."

Together with her vice-chair, Pauline Gore, wife of Tennessee's fourth district congressman, Albert Gore Sr., she created a detailed network of campaign workers on county-by-county and precinct-by-precinct levels who were trained at the campaign schools. Poll watching was added to the training to ensure that a fair election was held. Poll watching had been a technique developed by the LWV to have women monitor the activities at each polling place throughout election day and then remain at the poll while the ballots were counted to make certain that there were no discrepancies or irregularities in the procedures. When women in other states learned of the success of these schools, they asked the Tennessee committee for instructions on how to organize a get-out-the-vote campaign.[37]

Although Boss Crump ultimately supported Dixiecrat candidate Strom Thurmond in the presidential race over Harry Truman, Crump reluctantly gave Kefauver his support in the general election to avoid a split in the state Democratic party.[38] Kefauver, Browning, and other Democratic candidates carried the state by a large margin. Kefauver's victory in November was no surprise to Ragland. In spite of the money that the Republican campaign spent on the senatorial race—the third highest in the country—B. Carroll Reece, the Republican candidate, did not enjoy the grassroots support that Ragland generated for Kefauver. As in the August primary, Kefauver publicly expressed his belief that the women's vote was a significant factor in his victory. Kefauver expressed his appreciation to Ragland in a letter saying, "It would not be my privilege to serve the people of Tennessee in my present capacity had it not been for the loyal and unselfish support of the women under your courageous leadership. You are a real pioneer."[39]

After the election, Ragland maintained close ties with Senator Kefauver as well as Pauline Gore, and she followed the actions of Congress with great interest. Gore and Ragland corresponded frequently concerning issues related to women in the Democratic Party. They wanted to have women equally represented on all state and county Democratic executive committees. Although in 1949 Hamilton County (Chattanooga) was the only county in which this goal had been achieved, the following year, Gore noted some improvement in the status of women throughout Tennessee politics. There were now more women in visible positions in local as well as state party machinery.[40] As Gore wrote to Ragland, "The truth is that men are waking up or beginning to, to just what women can and have done. One school of thought in Tennessee has been reluctant to accept the fact. Estes subscribed to the other school of thought and got so far ahead of them that they are waking up belatedly and just like all men—if it is a good idea, it was mine in the beginning. It is now their idea that women should get into politics. Well, I agree with you, they are just a little behind."[41]

Gore and Ragland agreed that Estes Kefauver's election signaled a new era for women but were able to laugh about the way the process worked. Both understood that Kefauver's willingness to give women so much credit for his election was a rare thing in Tennessee politics.

During the four years that followed Kefauver's election to the Senate, Martha Ragland refocused on her earlier interests in public health and children. To these she now brought her clout as well as that of Pauline Gore as the leading women among Tennessee Democrats. Governor Gordon Browning demonstrated his appreciation for her efforts by appointing her to a newly created Tennessee Children's Commission to address problems facing Tennessee's youth. Committee members elected Nashvillian Ora Mann, a Ragland ally in the birth control movement and state director of the Planned Parenthood Federation, as the chair of the commission. Ragland was elected vice-chair.[42]

In 1949 Ragland organized the Tennessee Citizens Committee for a Limited Constitutional Convention, a statewide coalition of organizations dedicated to the reform of Tennessee's constitution. The organization and activities of this committee bore a striking resemblance to Ragland's earlier efforts: the commission wrote and distributed pamphlets, organized county-by-county training sessions, and recruited local supporters from across the state.[43] Since this technique had worked so well in past campaigns, Martha Ragland had reason to believe that this strategy could be applied to any political campaign at any level of government.

Ragland campaigned again for Gordon Browning's reelection in 1950. The campaign provided her with numerous opportunities to speak to women's groups across the state and to focus on the meaning of increasing women's voice in state politics. For Ragland, the presence of women in politics would make government better because public policy would reflect the will of the people for the first time in history. "Women are concerned about good schools, good health for their children—things close to the heart. So now, you find them completely ignoring that old 'you shouldn't get mixed up in politics' idea and proudly 'taking part in government,'" she told a Memphis audience. "We can't have war and inflation without affecting every home and family."

Ragland viewed political activity as a vital outlet for women to maintain and uphold responsibilities at home and in the community. Women's organizations such as the League of Women Voters had also begun to see the potential of women in the political process. Ragland pointed out that the LWV at one time "seemed to be merely passing resolutions. But we know now they were helping women change their minds."[44]

Believing that Kefauver would win the party nomination for president in 1952, Ragland announced her candidacy for the position of national Democratic committeewoman from Tennessee. She believed that the job would give her a much better position from which to help direct his national campaign. Like Kefauver, however, Ragland had managed to alienate important state party officials in her bid.[45] One member of the state Democratic executive committee that would choose the national Democratic committeewoman informed Ragland that she could not support Ragland's candidacy because she had not "gone about it in the right way." When Ragland asked her "What is the right way?" the executive committeewoman responded, "You wait for the men to decide who they want."[46] For the first time, Ragland had crossed the boundary of accepted behavior of women in politics and alienated many political operatives in the process.

Until 1952 the Tennessee national Democratic committeewoman had been elected by the state party convention that also selected the delegates to the national convention. Since a Kefauver presidential bid seemed assured, the state Democratic executive committee announced that it would choose the national committeeman and committeewoman. Ragland took this decision as an attack on her, an attempt to prevent her from gaining the position—and with some reason. The executive committee, which had been elected two years earlier, still bore the stamp of Boss Crump's influence. Committee members might not support a Ragland candidacy because of her ties to Kefauver. She finally gained the position, however, when Kefauver intervened on her behalf.[47]

On January 23, 1952, after months of speculation, Kefauver formally announced that he was running in the New Hampshire primary, the first primary of the year that added a presidential preference to its delegate selection primary. Although Truman publicly expressed his displeasure with Kefauver's announcement, Truman refused to confirm that he would run for reelection. With little more than a month to go before the primary, set for March 11, President Truman announced that he would withdraw his name from the New Hampshire ballot.

Although his decision would in no way affect the votes for convention delegates, Truman's supporters in New Hampshire felt his withdrawal from the race had a negative impact on their efforts. Truman's supporters were convinced that a decisive victory in the New Hampshire primary would be a step toward securing the Democratic nomination. They put so much pressure on the president that he reversed his decision the following week and announced that his name would remain on the ballot.

Using many of the same organizational strategies that had served him well during the 1948 senatorial campaign in Tennessee, Kefauver immediately began an intensive grassroots campaign in New Hampshire during the month of February. He made an effort to meet as many voters as possible and was frequently photographed wearing his coonskin cap. From the Kefauver-for-President Headquarters in Nashville, Martha Ragland worked on Kefauver's presidential campaign even as she worked on her own campaign for Democratic committeewoman. She organized Tennessee women to write letters to women in New Hampshire and other states on behalf of Kefauver. She organized Kefauver-for-President clubs in ninety-three of Tennessee's ninety-five counties and set fundraising goals for each county. Although national political analysts predicted a Truman victory, Ragland's great faith in her candidate's ability to win the primary never wavered. For her, women would again make the difference—women interested in good government and reform would vote for Kefauver.[48]

Ragland's efforts attracted national attention, not all of it positive. Reporters frequently trivialized the substance of her remarks by describing her apparel and appearance. For example, a Knoxville reporter began an article about the presidential campaign by saying, "A very pretty Tennessee woman in a pink spring hat today told a lot of other Tennessee women what she wants for Tennessee. She wants Estes Kefauver elected President, and she wants herself elected Tennessee National democratic committeewoman."[49] Ragland accepted this as part of the price of participation. She later advised a Nashville woman running for office to "dress like a woman, but fight like a man."[50]

When the New Hampshire votes were counted, Kefauver had won a major victory over the president. Ragland triumphantly told reporters that "the old type of political leader" was "going out." For her, Kefauver's defeat of Boss Crump in 1948 and of President Truman in 1952 signaled the end of "boss-ism" in politics at all levels, and she believed that women had made the difference. Even Ragland was surprised by the margin of Kefauver's win. With this victory, she believed that Estes Kefauver again had demonstrated that he could successfully defeat the party machinery. Ragland downplayed her role in his victory, however, describing herself as "another amateur supporting Senator Estes Kefauver's bid for the Democratic presidential nomination" and emphasized the grassroots support of the candidate as the determining factor. She wanted the attention focused on the candidate rather than herself.

Within six weeks of announcing his run in the New Hampshire primary election, Kefauver led the race for the Democratic presidential nomination. He had defeated the incumbent president, and two weeks after the primary, Truman announced his plans to retire at the end of his term. With no significant organized opposition to Kefauver's campaign, he now won primary after primary. When the Republican convention nominated General Dwight D. Eisenhower as its nominee, Kefauver began to campaign against Eisenhower.

Despite his success, however, Kefauver still had no support from national party leaders. Kefauver's organized crime hearings offended the president because the Pendergast machine, which had helped launch Truman's political career in Missouri, was implicated. Truman worked behind the scenes trying to persuade other Democrats to get into the race. Nonetheless, Kefauver seemed to have the nomination wrapped up with 340 delegates assured as the Chicago convention approached. Ragland expressed her disappointment in the president's refusal to endorse Kefauver: "I have always been a Truman supporter, but I am disappointed that he failed to recognize the strength Estes could bring to the party."[51]

As Martha Ragland prepared to attend the Democratic national convention in Chicago in 1952, she gave little thought to Truman's opposition. But many years later, in correspondence with Joseph Bruce Gorman, a Kefauver biographer, she reluctantly admitted that most of Kefauver's support in terms of money and workers came from Tennessee. None of the national party machinery converted to Kefauver during the primaries. Convention delegates for a particular candidate were not bound by the primary vote, and the national organization of each party continued to have significant influence in determining the party's nominee. Illinois governor Adlai Stevenson had not campaigned in the primaries, but he received his party's nomination when a "Draft Stevenson" movement at the convention moved his name forward.[52]

As a convention delegate, Ragland watched the events that followed the opening of the convention with disbelief. Kefauver was in the lead for the first two ballots. When Governor Stevenson, under great pressure from President Truman, finally agreed to accept the party nomination if chosen, the third ballot and the party nomination went to Stevenson. The next day, the convention further rejected Kefauver when it chose Alabama senator John Sparkman, a former Dixiecrat, to be Stevenson's running mate. Martha Ragland, Kefauver, and the loyal supporters believed that Truman and the party had stolen the nomination from Kefauver. Ragland further concluded that the party bosses were able to wield such extraordinary control over the party because women were not adequately represented in the party machinery and that for significant change to occur on a national level, women would have to become more involved at the highest levels. The experience of the 1952 Democratic convention became a turning point in the political life of Martha Ragland.

Ragland returned to Tennessee knowing that, as the national Democratic committeewoman, she would have to work in the fall campaign for the Stevenson-Sparkman ticket. Governor Browning was defeated in Tennessee's August primary by Frank Clement, so Ragland also devoted her energies to the U.S. Senate campaign of Representative Albert Gore Sr., who in the August Democratic primary had defeated Kenneth McKellar, a thirty-five-year Senate veteran and a longtime ally of Boss Crump. With the Democrats so divided on the national and state level, it came as no surprise to Ragland when the Democrats lost the White House in 1952.

In the months that followed the November election Ragland turned her attention to the problems inside the national Democratic Party that had been responsible for Kefauver's defeat on the floor of the convention. Dedicated to eradicating "the bosses" and increasing the presence and number of women at the highest levels of decision making, Ragland began to criticize the national Democratic Party publicly. In an article that ran in the *Tennessean* under the headline "Nashville Woman Gives Party Tips for Comeback," Ragland reiterated her belief that women had been denied a voice in the convention actions. Ragland also admonished DNC chair and Stevenson supporter Stephen Mitchell for abolishing the Women's Department of the national Democratic Party, another example of an effort on the part of party bosses to exclude women.[53] Fighting the Democratic Party establishment would be a difficult battle for Ragland and one that she would wage at some level for the remainder of her life.

In spite of Ragland's view of the need for reform in the national Democratic Party, her speeches after the 1952 elections continued to make the case that political activity was simply an extension of traditionally prescribed roles for women. This rhetorical ploy failed to convince the antifeminist men who axed the Women's Department in 1953. Addressing a statewide League of Women Voters meeting, she told her audience, "While we may not agree on parties, Mrs. Elder [the Republican women's chair] and I both agree on one thing—the role of women in party politics. We both believe that if women take a more active part in the parties we will have better government." She continued, "The parties choose the major candidates, write the platforms, name the president's cabinets, and appoint major public officials such as the chairman of TVA, but a great many people overlook this. That is why they have been so surprised that they voted for Eisenhower and got McCarthy." In response to some who believed that women did not want to become involved in politics because women saw politics as "dirty," she argued that women would have to be able to "mesh party work with their other activities" and "work to make party politics as respectable as the Girl Scouts."[54]

Ragland began to criticize women, including those in the League of Women Voters, who wanted to identify themselves as independents or nonpartisans: "The machinery through which the individual voter can work most effectively for the improvement of politics is that of political parties." "Politics is a place for women because they are natural organizers," she told her audience. "If we can just get them into it, they take to it like a duck to water."[55] But nowhere in speeches, letters, and interviews written after the 1952 election did Ragland suggest that women should be running for office. "The traditional role of woman as mother and homemaker has been enlarged," she told a Knoxville audience. "More and more women are realizing that they must help elect honest and intelligent public officials, that they must take part in opinion-making processes, to properly fulfill their responsibility, not only as a citizen, but specifically as a homemaker."[56] She emphasized the importance of women becoming involved in the operations of political parties rather than running as candidates. Perhaps Ragland realized that women had to gain power in the party machinery before they could be successful in running for office. She devoted the last years of her life to working tirelessly to help women run for office and get elected.

Ragland did achieve one small victory in the days that followed the 1952 elections. In 1953 she finally won her long campaign for constitutional revision in Tennessee when a limited constitutional convention—Tennessee's first since 1807—passed eight amendments to the state constitution, including the final abolition of the poll tax. Many of the reforms that Ragland had advocated in 1946 in the League of Women Voters booklet on the state constitution were realized. The amendments lengthened the governor's term from two years to four years without the right of immediate succession, gave the governor a line-item veto, and provided for optional home rule for cities.[57]

As the 1956 elections approached, Ragland publicly criticized the national Democratic Party for trying to reconcile in 1952 with the Dixiecrats, who had walked out of the 1948 convention over Truman's stand on civil rights. She believed that this effort to recreate the New Deal coalition in 1952 had had a negative effect on the party. In spite of the fact that John Sparkman, himself a Dixiecrat, was on the Democratic ticket as Stevenson's 1952 running mate, many of the Dixiecrats did not support the Democratic ticket in 1952. In 1954 newspapers reported on a meeting attended by former President Truman, DNC national chair Stephen Mitchell, Adlai Stevenson, and other prominent Democrats at which party leadership was discussed. The newspapers claimed that it was the consensus of the group "to get someone acceptable to Southerners so as to maintain the unity built up since 1952 and avoid hurting again those upset by the 'loyalty pledge.'" This "loyalty pledge" was a reference to an effort at the 1952 convention to restore party unity by reconciling with the Dixiecrats. In a speech delivered at the 1954 Democratic National Committee meeting in Indianapolis, Ragland responded to these reports, adamantly opposing reconciliation with the Dixiecrats by what she termed "appeasement."[58] By this time, the political impact of the Supreme Court's decision in *Brown v. the Board of Education of Topeka*, handed down in the spring of 1954, was beginning to be seen. Ragland feared that the national Democratic Party would respond to the decision by taking some action in opposition to the decision in order to keep outraged southerners from again bolting the party. Since the Dixiecrats were segregationists who opposed changes in the racial status quo of the South, it was assumed by many that southern Democratic politicians would demand that the party denounce the high court's decision.

When Ragland's remarks were made public in Tennessee, Mary French Caldwell, a founder of the first Democratic woman's club in Tennessee, expressed her outrage over Ragland's approval of efforts "to drive Southern states out of the Democratic party." Caldwell's entire letter to Ragland was printed in the *Nashville Banner*, the city's afternoon newspaper. "I regret that you, Tennessee's national committeewoman, have publicly expressed approval of the disgraceful attempt of the left-wing element of the Chicago convention to drive Virginia, South Carolina and other Southern states out of the Democratic Party," she wrote to Ragland. Caldwell described herself as "a conservative, states-rights Democrat" and portrayed Ragland as a liberal.[59]

Ragland defended herself by responding to Caldwell in a letter published in the *Nashville Banner* the following day, but the issue continued to be debated among Tennessee Democrats. Articles running under such headlines as "Mrs. Ragland Takes Issues Over 'Dixiecrats in Party'" and "Mrs. Ragland Protests Appeasement," kept the story alive.[60] Crump had personally supported the Dixiecrat walkout in 1948. Even after his death in 1954, many Tennessee Democrats still supported his views. Ragland's criticism of the Dixiecrats, which included Crump, reflected the deep divisions within the state party. As the Ragland-Caldwell feud suggested, Tennessee Democrats were badly divided. Reporters kept this division alive throughout 1955, and Ragland maintained her position that those who walked out of the 1948 convention were "turncoats." She told *Tennessean* reporter Thomas L. Stokes that she opposed any efforts on the part of the national chairman to "kiss and make up" with the Dixiecrats, stating that the issue had already affected the ability of Democratic members of Congress to function freely because "committees were carefully selected so as not to upset vested interests that are the darlings of the Dixiecrats." She went further, telling him that to "counsel deference to the Dixiecrats, the Eisencrats and the Walk Softlies, at this point in history, is a disservice to the party and to the country; and because it is prompted by a mistaken estimate of the South, it does a disservice to the South."[61] Ragland believed that the party was operating under a policy of "unity at any price" that condoned any concession necessary to keep the Dixiecrats from staging another walkout, even if it meant the acceptance of a racist, anti–civil rights agenda. Ragland refused to accept this.[62]

As the 1956 election approached, newspapers and magazines across the country speculated on who the Democrats would pick to take on President Eisenhower in the general election. Writing in the *New Republic*, Frederic W. Collins proposed a plan by which Adlai Stevenson could become the leader of the party in fact as well as in name. *New Republic* editor Michael Straight sent Ragland an advance copy of the article and asked for her comments. Straight specifically posed the following question to Ragland and five male party activists from across the country: "Is the fact that in our present party system the titular leader of the Opposition has no control over party policy between elections a matter of concern?" On August 8, 1955, Ragland's response appeared in the *New Republic*, claiming that she was astonished by Collins's proposal, which she called "contrary to fundamental principles of democratic politics." She also disputed Collins's claim that the national party was weak, citing the fact that Democrats had picked up additional seats in Congress in the 1954 elections. In language reminiscent of her fight with Boss Crump, she criticized Collins's call for "a tight rein." She did not want Stevenson to receive the nomination again in 1956. "Stevenson was a good choice in 1952, but both he and the party suffered from the nature of his nomination. Since he already has this handicap of having been a handpicked choice in 1952, it is unfortunate for him that Mr. Collins proposes this 'Stevenson system' that is so contrary to the American political tradition and so congenitally uncongenial to the freewheeling Democratic Party."[63] Although Ragland was careful not to criticize Adlai Stevenson personally, nor to mention Kefauver's name in her response, she alluded to what she saw as problems with the outcome of the 1952 Democratic national convention.

In spite of Ragland's frustrations with the Democratic Party, she attended the regular national meeting of Democratic women in Chicago in November 1955. Her name was among three drawn at the meeting to address the entire group, which included in the audience former President Harry Truman. In her speech, Ragland called for a "clearer definition" of the political issues between the parties, which she believed Roosevelt and Truman had achieved in the 1940s. Returning to her unwavering belief in the power of grassroots politics, she told her audience that "the people are concerned about major problems" even though she felt that the Democratic Party had not been able to "translate this into political awareness." She reiterated her stance that informed female voters would inevitably support the Democratic Party: "If the people really understand the issues they will vote Democratic. Women everywhere are interested in a stable economy, world conditions, and the farm problem, but these issues have not been translated to them politically." Ragland recommended that local Democratic women's clubs create discussion groups to study the issues as the League of Women Voters did because "there must be a genuine understanding of the serious issues before us. Canvassers must be able to explain issues point by point to each person."[64]

Ragland continued to support Estes Kefauver and held out hopes that he would be the party nominee in 1956. When Kefauver was not asked to speak at a national Democratic women's event in Miami, Ragland wrote to Clara Shirpser, the Democratic national committeewoman from California, to announce that she would boycott the meeting solely because Kefauver was not on the program: "It seems to me that in view of Estes' record in the state primaries and the convention vote (until steam-rollered) that he is a top-ranking Democrat, with the confidence of millions of Democratic voters. What this does is underline and continue the feeling that millions of viewers of the convention had that the Democratic Party is, in the last analysis, controlled and manipulated by a little inner circle."[65]

At the same time that national newspapers carried this story on the women's pages, the front pages ran headlines that Kefauver would challenge Stevenson for the nomination. With Kefauver attempting to win the 1956 Democratic nomination, Martha Ragland again focused her energies on his campaign. Anticipating another fight, Ragland called for more women delegates to the Democratic national convention. She believed that increasing the number of female convention delegates was the best way to secure a win for Kefauver. But as the August convention approached, Ragland's hopes for Kefauver's nomination evaporated when he withdrew from the race and announced his support for Stevenson. After securing the nomination, however, Stevenson stunned the convention with a decision to allow the delegates to name his running mate. In what some observers described as "the most exciting session of a national political convention ever held," candidates quickly worked to gain support among the delegates. Ragland expressed hope that Governor Clement, now in control of the Tennessee party and its convention delegates, might be able to convince the convention to nominate Kefauver for vice president.[66] In the running were Kefauver, John F. Kennedy, Albert Gore Sr., Robert Wagner Jr., and Hubert Humphrey. Now energized by the prospect that Kefauver could become the vice-presidential nominee, Ragland worked the hall on Kefauver's behalf. Although Kefauver was the favorite and led the first ballot, he did not have the majority required to win.

When Kefauver lost the second ballot, Ragland began to press Senator Gore to withdraw from nomination. Gore responded to her first plea by telling her that he was "in this ballgame to stay."[67] Since Governor Clement was supporting Gore, Ragland tried to persuade Clement to withdraw his support of Gore in favor of Kefauver. Clement declined to intervene on Kefauver's behalf, and Ragland continued to go back and forth between Clement and Gore in a feverish effort to persuade Gore to withdraw. Finally, she told Gore, "You can't win, Albert. If you keep a native son from winning, you will be ruined politically." A short time later, Gore reluctantly went to the microphone and announced his withdrawal from the race. The final vote was Kefauver, 755.5; Kennedy, 589. *Newsweek* perhaps summed it up best: "It was a small, pert Nashville housewife who turned the tide. While most of her fellow Tennesseans worked for Senator Albert Gore, Mrs. Martha Ragland, her state's national committeewoman, still thought that Senator Estes Kefauver had the best chance." Although this victory did not give Ragland the satisfaction that Kefauver's win in 1948 had given her, she did enjoy the short-lived publicity that came from her efforts.[68]

The Stevenson-Kefauver Campaign named Martha Ragland vice-chair of the national Volunteers for the Stevenson-Kefauver Committee. She devoted much of her time during the campaign to recruiting volunteer workers at the neighborhood level to work for the election of Stevenson and Kefauver. All of her efforts to get Estes Kefauver elected vice president, as well as her efforts to retain her position as Democratic national committeewoman from Tennessee, ultimately proved to be futile. The Stevenson-Kefauver ticket lost the general election in 1956 to Eisenhower-Nixon. Kefauver returned to the Senate, but Martha Ragland was denied a second term as state Democratic committeewoman. She had alienated too many of the Frank Clement faction of the state Democratic Party and was not reelected.

The 1956 campaign marked the last time that Martha Ragland was directly involved in partisan politics. In 1957 Senator Kefauver, knowing of her support for civil rights, recommended to President Eisenhower that he appoint Ragland to the bipartisan U.S. Civil Rights Commission. Eisenhower passed over

Kefauver's recommendation and later appointed her instead to the Tennessee Advisory Committee to the Commission, a committee that would merely make recommendations to the national commission. Ragland regarded this as a distinct step down. She noted, "[I]t was the only government position I ever really went after, that I was not appointed [to]."[69]

In 1963, with the Democratic president John F. Kennedy now in the White House, Kefauver did succeed in getting Ragland appointed to the Federal Advisory Council on Employment Security chaired by Secretary of Labor Willard Wirtz. She did not enjoy her service on this committee and felt that her comments were not taken seriously because she was a woman. She voiced her frustrations to Kefauver and asked him how he could "stand it being up here all the time where there seems to be more effort to stop movement than to get things going." Kefauver replied, "Sometimes, I don't think I can." Ten days later, on August 10, 1963, Estes Kefauver died after suffering a massive heart attack on the Senate floor.[70]

For the remainder of her life, Martha Ragland worked to change the Democratic Party and get more women involved in politics. In 1971 she founded the Nashville Women's Political Caucus, which was designed to have women equally represented at all levels of the party. She wholeheartedly embraced the mission of the National Organization for Women and the second wave of feminism. She encouraged women to run for office and to become part of the party machinery rather than to function on the fringes of the establishment by merely encouraging women to express their opinions with their votes. Her strong support of women candidates made her a mentor for a new generation of women who wanted to become political activists. Writing to Jayne Ann Woods, a Nashville attorney, in 1977 she tried to convince Woods to oppose Howard Baker in 1978:

> I think you ought to plan to run against Baker. I realize fully that it would be a David and Goliath contest. But the mere audacity of it would work in your favor. I believe 'the men' plan to give Baker a free run. I doubt if a single male politician, initially, would encourage you to do this. But I also think that they never will. You probably wouldn't win. But you would win next time against Jim [Sasser]. I could give a lot of examples of that pattern. But I am not ruling out your winning against Baker. If you were in there you would be in a position to take advantage of the breaks. He is not invulnerable. His Watergate record has been tarnished, for one thing. None of the men really know how to organize. I would recommend for you a political handbook campaign, organized to the last precinct. Jayne Ann, I wouldn't throw you to the wolves. I think you can do it.[71]

Woods declined to run despite Ragland's encouragement. Shortly before Ragland died in 1996, she expressed her disappointment that more women were not running for office at that time. She believed that her efforts had not achieved her primary goal: women at every level of politics as a means to improve the process.[72]

In the decade that followed World War II, women remained on the periphery of the establishment of the national political parties in spite of substantial gains made by women during the New Deal and the war. Women were very visible as campaign workers, but had little influence at the highest levels of the national party machinery. During the years of Martha Ragland's most intense political activism on behalf of Estes Kefauver, reporters kept her name alive with descriptions of her that reflected the limits of female political activism in the 1950s. She was described as "pert," "a very pretty woman from Tennessee wearing a pink spring hat," or "a little housewife." Kathryn Stone, a legislator from Virginia, described Martha Ragland as "the best individual woman campaigner that I have ever met. She's completely feminine."[73] Ragland saw no distinction between being feminine and a feminist.[74]

At bottom, Martha Ragland came to believe that a change in the role of women was needed. Women had to overcome their marginalization within the national political parties. For women to really make a difference in politics, they would have to become part of the process rather than remain unequal outsiders attempting to exert influence on decision making. Although Ragland in her later years saw herself as a "life-long feminist" rather than as a female activist, her feminist philosophy evolved from her experiences and frustrations with the Democratic Party. Although much of her earlier work had been directed toward issues related to women, it was her personal political experiences that caused her ultimately to speak out against discrimination and to call for equality for women. The clean-up of government that Ragland believed would occur as a result of women becoming involved in politics as a function within conventional boundaries of behavior in normative roles as wives and mothers did not happen. Throughout the 1950s Martha Ragland defined herself exclusively as a wife and mother and saw her political activism as a direct outgrowth of her responsibilities in the home. Her background and experiences should have made her an ideal candidate to run for office herself, but as a product of "the feminine mystique," she was unable to step from the level of political supporter to politician. Ragland and her female political allies of the 1950s were confined by the times in which they lived. She was among those women whose efforts in the political arena were behind the scenes and largely invisible. Women, however, had begun to make some important, if tentative, steps into the political realm. Across the country, women's experiences in the 1950s caused them to become involved in grassroots politics with at least limited success.[75] Gradually, a new generation of women began to heed Ragland's advice and become more involved. In spite of the frustrations and disappointments of such women as Martha Ragland, their efforts provided a base from which the second wave of feminism could be launched in the 1960s. Martha Ragland's experiences convinced her that, for a woman, functioning within the confines of prescribed feminine behavior was not enough. In order for politics to be truly transformed, the role of women in politics would have to change. In the process, Martha Ragland moved from a post–Progressive Era female political activist to a modern political feminist.

NOTES

1. Martha Ragland to Jane McMichael, April 24, 1978, Martha Ragland Papers, box 1, folder 1, Schlesinger Library, Radcliffe (hereafter cited as Ragland Papers).

2. Leila J. Rupp and Verta Taylor, *Survival in the Doldrums: The American Women's Rights Movement, 1945 to the 1960s* (New York: Oxford University Press, 1987), 85–111; Cynthia Harrison, *Prelude to Feminism: Women's Organizations, the Federal Government and the Rise of the Women's Movement 1942 to 1968* (Ann Arbor, Mich.: University Microfilms, 1982); Sarah Wilkerson-Freeman, "Stealth in the Political Arsenal of Southern Women," in *Southern Women at the Millennium: A Historical Perspective*, ed. Melissa Walker, Jeanette R. Dunn, and Joe P. Dunn, 42–82 (Columbia: University of Missouri Press, 2003). Susan Ware, *Beyond Suffrage: Women in the New Deal* (Cambridge, Mass.: Harvard University Press, 1987).

3. David Halberstam, *The Fifties* (New York: Villard Books, 1993), 188–93.

4. Linda Quigley, "Rebels and Reformers: A Retrospective Exhibit Recounts the Efforts of Women Activists like Martha Ragland," *Nashville Tennessean*, July 20, 1995.

5. Martha Ragland to the women of Tennessee, April 10, 1948, Ragland Papers, box 1, folder 3.

6. Sandra R. Demson, Ragland's daughter, e-mail to author, June 18, 2007, in possession of the author.

7. Martha Ragsdale's parents were Joseph Senter Ragsdale and Viva Jane Troutt Ragsdale. Her father served as president of Athens College in Athens, Alabama, a Methodist coeducational institution. Her mother taught history there.

8. Martha Ragsdale, *The National Origins Plan of Immigration Restriction* (Nashville, privately printed, 1928) 59.

9. While it is difficult today to understand the extent to which the scientific and scholarly community embraced the study of eugenics, it must be remembered that the idea of scientific management was imbedded in progressivism. Eugenics was a respected field of science until the atrocities of Adolf Hitler's Third Reich discredited it. See Garland E. Allen. "The Ideology of Elimination: American and German Eugenics, 1900–1945," in *Medicine and Medical Ethics in Nazi Germany*, ed. Francis R. Nicosia and Jonathan Huener, 13–39 (New York: Berghahn Books, 2002); Ellsworth Huntington and Martha Ragsdale, *After Three Centuries: A Typical New England Family* (Baltimore: Williams and Wilkins Co, 1935). In the preface, Huntington writes, "This book belongs to the new

science which deals with the growth and qualities of a population. It is a combination of sociology, economics, eugenics, geography, and history" (iii–iv).

10. Interview with Martha Ragland by author, July 12, 1995. Demson to author. Demson described her mother as being different from her friends' mothers. "She was different, she worked very hard all day on the telephone, or at her typewriter, or at meetings (only during the day, NEVER at night), and we had live-in help which made it possible. I always thought she was a wonderful mother; the only thing I remember complaining about was her talking on the telephone! I never remember Daddy ever complaining about or criticizing what she did. . . . In her life, she showed you could be a strong, really revolutionary, feminist and still have a nurturing and loving family life." Demson went on to discuss her parents' last years. When poor health forced the family to move Tom Ragland to a nursing home, Martha Ragland visited him every day. During the last months of her life, she herself moved to the same nursing home, and her husband came and sat by her side every day. Tom Ragland died in 1996, five months after Martha. "I think it tells us that being a feminist does not preclude a strong and durable marriage relationship," wrote Demson. Demson was told by the nursing home staff that on the last day of his life, throughout the entire day, he repeatedly called out, "Martha, Martha."

11. Interview with Ragland by author.

12. Linda Quigley, "Rebels and Reformers: A Retrospective Exhibit Recounts the Efforts of Women Activists like Martha Ragland," *Nashville Tennessean*, July 30, 1995.

13. Demson to author.

14. In a letter to McKinnon's daughter, Dorothy McKinnon Brown, after the death of Edna Rankin McKinnon, Ragland wrote, "She was tremendously influential in my life, in big and little ways, that have greatly enriched it." Ragland convinced her friend Wilma Dykeman to write a biography of McKinnon, *Too Many People, Too Little Love*, which was published in 1974. Martha Ragland to Dorothy Brown McKinnon, April 5, 1978, Ragland Papers, box 2, folder 18.

15. Gwendolyn Pamenter Aseltine, "The Planned Parenthood Association of Nashville," Ph.D. dissertation, George Peabody College, 1977.

16. "South Offers Greatest Field for Birth Control Development, Says Mrs. Sanger Here for Talk," *Nashville Tennessean*, October 19, 1938.

17. Quigley, "Rebels and Reformers." Esther Katz, ed. *Selected Papers of Margaret Sanger*, vol. 2, *Birth Control Comes of Age, 1928–1939* (Urbana: University of Illinois Press, 2006), 466–67.

18. William B. Turner, "Class, Controversy, and Contraceptives: Birth Control Advocacy in Nashville, 1932–1944," *Tennessee Historical Quarterly* 53, no. 3 (1994): 166–79.

19. See *Chattanooga News-Free Press*, May 9, 1941; *Chattanooga Times*, May 9, 1941; *Chattanooga Evening Times*, November 5, 1941; *Chattanooga Evening Times*, March 24, 1942; *Chattanooga News-Free Press*, March 25, 1942; *Chattanooga Evening Times*, April 3, 1942.

20. "Mrs. Ragland Asks Woman Activities," *Chattanooga Times*, April 22, 1943.

21. Sarah Wilkerson-Freeman, "The Second Battle for Woman Suffrage: Alabama White Women, the Poll Tax, and V. O. Key's Master Narrative of Southern Politics," *Journal of Southern History* 68, no. 2 (2002): 333–74.

22. "Statement of One Hundred Southern Women on the Twentieth Anniversary of the Nineteenth Amendment to the Constitution of the United States," August 26, 1940, found in files of the League of Women Voters office in Washington, D.C.

23. Jennings Perry, *Democracy Begins at Home: The Tennessee Fight on the Poll Tax* (Philadelphia: J. B. Lippincott Company, 1944), 124.

24. Frederic D. Ogden, *The Poll Tax in the South* (Tuscaloosa: University of Alabama Press, 1948), 193–99.

25. "We Salute," National Municipal League, 1948, Ragland Papers, box 1, folder 3.

26. JoAnn Bennett, speech at League of Women Voters of Tennessee biennial meeting, Nashville, Hermitage Hotel, April 22, 1995.

27. Theodore Brown Jr., "Carey Estes Kefauver," *Tennessee Encyclopedia of History and Culture* (Nashville: Tennessee Historical Society/Rutledge Hill Press, 1998), 498.

28. Interview with Ragland by author.

29. Undated article from the *Chattanooga Times*, Ragland Papers, box 1, folder 3.

30. Martha Ragland to the women of Tennessee, April 10, 1948, Ragland Papers, box 1, folder 3.

31. "The Kefauver 1948 Primary Campaign," typed memo by Martha Ragland written January 13, 1977, Ragland Papers, box 1, folder 3, 130–36; "If You Believe in Democracy, Help Restore It in Tennessee. Vote for Estes Kefauver for U.S. Senator," pamphlet, Ragland Papers, box 1, folder 4; Charles L. Fonteney, *Estes Kefauver: A Biography* (Knoxville: University of Tennessee Press, 1980), 133–44. Estes Kefauver to Martha Ragland, postcard, postmarked from Linden, Tennessee, July 3, 1948, Ragland Papers, box 1, folder 4; "A Fright for Crump," *Time Magazine*, July 19, 1948.

32. Martin Ochs, "Kefauver Greeted by 500 on Return," *Chattanooga Times*, August 7, 1948.

33. Joseph Bruce Gorman, *Kefauver: A Political Biography* (New York: Oxford University Press, 1971), 59–60.

34. Ibid.

35. "Boss Defeat Seen by Mrs. Ragland," *Chattanooga Times*, August 4, 1948; Ochs, "Kefauver Greeted by 500"; "Man Who Toppled Crump Rides Tide in Tennessee," *Christian Science Monitor*, August 14, 1948.

36. "Chairman Says Demo Women Doing Things in Politics," *Knoxville News-Sentinel*, September 30, 1948.

37. Vivian Browne, "State Recreational Growth Keynote Here of Browning," *Chattanooga Times*, October 2, 1948.

38. William D. Miller, *Mr. Crump of Memphis* (Baton Rouge: Louisiana State University Press, 1964), 334; Wayne Dowdy, *Mayor Crump Don't Like It: Machine Politics in Memphis* (Oxford: University of Mississippi Press, 2006).

39. Estes Kefauver to Martha Ragland, June 15, 1950, Ragland Papers, box 1, folder 9.

40. Pauline Gore to Martha Ragland, January 28, 1949, and Martha Ragland to Pauline Gore, April 12, 1949, both in Ragland Papers, box 2, folder 14.

41. Pauline Gore to Martha Ragland, June 27, 1950, Ragland Papers, box 2, folder 14.

42. "Mrs. Mann to Head Child Commission," *Chattanooga Times*, August 16, 1949.

43. Mrs. Tom Ragland, "Constitution a Durable One," *Chattanooga Times*, August 16, 1949; *Chattanooga Times*, September 25, 1949. *Speakers Handbook in Behalf of Limited Constitutional Convention for Tennessee*, booklet published by Tennessee Citizens Committee for a Limited Constitutional Convention, 1949, Ragland Papers, box 1, folder 4.

44. "Ladies Day at the Polls," *Memphis Press-Scimitar*, July 26, 1950.

45. Estes Kefauver was holding congressional hearings on organized crime at that time. The rise in the number of televisions in households across the country transformed Kefauver into what writer David Halberstam has called America's "first political star." Women across the country watched these hearings, and many of them came to see Kefauver as a break from old-style politicians. Ragland recalled that "the ironing was done in the living room so as not to miss anything on

television. But one result was that millions of women had a new understanding of what courageous and firm leadership means." The hearings, however, proved to have a negative effect on Kefauver's relations with many elected officials, because his investigation uncovered ties between organized crime and Democratic political machines across the country. President Truman, who continued to have some allegiance to the Pendergast machine of St. Louis, saw Kefauver's actions as divisive and disloyal to the party. Martha Ragland, "Remarks at the Ryman Auditorium Rally Launching the 1952 Campaign of Senator Estes Kefauver for the Democratic Nomination for President of the United States," undated, Ragland Papers, box 1, folder 4, 113. David Halberstam, *The Fifties* (New York: Villard Books, 1993), 188–93.

46. Martha Ragland, handwritten note found on a *Nashville Tennessean* clipping in files dated February 28, 1952, Ragland Papers, box 1, folder 4.

47. "Governor Gordon Browning," typed summary of Ragland's relationship with Gordon Browning, December 30, 1976, Ragland Papers, box 1, folder 4.

48. Memo by Martha Ragland on memories from the 1952 campaign, October 26, 1977, Ragland Papers, box 1, folder 4.

49. Margaret Ragsdale, "Tennessee Can Do It, Mrs. Ragland Tells Women Backers of Kefauver," *Knoxville News-Sentinel*, March 7, 1952.

50. Comments made by Jane Eskind at the National Women's Conference in Houston in 1977. Luncheon held on the occasion of the opening of the League of Women Voters' Rebels and Reformers exhibit at the Tennessee State Museum, August 3, 1995.

51. Undated and unidentified newspaper clipping, Ragland Papers, box 1, folder 4.

52. Gorman, *Kefauver*, 149–50.

53. Joe Hatcher, "Nashville Woman Gives Party Tips for Comeback," *Nashville Tennessean*, 3 May 1953.

54. Joan Link, "Woman's Place Held in Politics—and Home," *Nashville Tennessean*, May 27, 1954.

55. Ibid.

56. Martha Ragland, "The Issues of the Coming Campaign," speech delivered at the University of Tennessee Law School, July 26, 1956, Ragland Papers, box 3, folder 47.

57. Martha Ragland, *Tennessee Needs a New Constitution* (Knoxville: The League of Women Voters of Tennessee, 1946).

58. "Comments by Mrs. Martha Ragland, Democratic National Committeewoman from Tennessee Prepared for Delivery 17 September 1954, Indianapolis, Indiana, Democratic National Committee Meeting," Ragland Papers, box 1, folder 5.

59. "Mrs. Caldwell Denounces Move to Destroy South Democrats," *Nashville Banner*, July 15, 1954.

60. Martha Ragland, letter to the editor, *Nashville Banner*, July 16, 1954; "Mrs. Ragland Takes Issue Over 'Dixiecrats in Party,'" *Nashville Tennessean*, May 7, 1955; "Mrs. Ragland Protests Appeasement," *Nashville Tennessean*, June 1, 1955.

61. Thomas L. Stokes, "A Nashville Lady Democrat Won't Embrace Party Turncoats," *Nashville Tennessean*, June 1, 1955; "State Democratic Leader Rebels over Appeasement of Dixiecrats," *Knoxville News-Sentinel*, May 30, 1955.

62. Demson to author. When the sit-ins began in Nashville in 1960, Ragland's friend Molly Todd became involved in supporting integration throughout the city. Ragland joined Todd and a group of white women one afternoon to integrate a movie theater. This was particularly unusual since

Martha Ragland rarely went to the theater. To demonstrate that some whites believed integrated seating acceptable, the women went in to the theater and sat down around the African American young people so that they would not be taunted by the crowd.

63. Michael Straight to Martha Ragland, July 20, 1955, Ragland Papers; Frederic W. Collins, "How Adlai Can Lead the Democrats," *New Republic*, July 25, 1955; Gerald W. Johnson, Paul T. David, Mrs. Martha Ragland, Henry S. Reuss, Richard Dilworth, Jonathan Daniels, and Oscar Ewing, "Adlai Stevenson's Role," *New Republic*, August 8, 1955.

64. "Mrs. Ragland Wins Prize, a Chance to Address Democratic Breakfast," *Chattanooga Times*, November 20, 1955; Shirley Lowry, "Adlai, Senator Kefauver Condemn Ike's Regime: 'Get Tough' Drive for Votes Set by Women," *Chicago Sunday Tribune* November 20, 1955.

65. Letter from Martha Ragland to Clara Shirpser, Democratic National Committee woman, February 21, 1954, Ragland Papers.

66. "Segregation Won't Be an Issue, Debaters Agree," *Knoxville News-Sentinel*, July 27, 1956.

67. "For Vice President: 'Housework' for Estes,'" *Newsweek*, August 27, 1956, 28.

68. Ibid., 28–29; Fred Travis, "Gore, Kefauver, Clement Figure in Highest Drama," *Chattanooga Times*, August 18, 1956; George Plimpton, *American Journey: The Times of Robert Kennedy, Interviews by Jean Stein* (New York: Harcourt, Brace, Jovanovich, 1970), 64–65.

69. Martha Ragland, handwritten note, n.d., Ragland Papers, box 1, folder 5. Ragland served for ten years on the board of the Southern Regional Council and made numerous speeches on the subject of racial injustice in the South. She also chaired the Tennessee Human Rights Commission.

70. Martha Ragland, Federal Advisory Council on Employment Security (1963–1969), typed memo, Ragland Papers, box 1, folder 5.

71. Martha Ragland to Jayne Ann Woods, March 22, 1977, Ragland Papers, box 3, folder 27.

72. Interview with Martha Ragland by author, July 12, 1995.

73. Nancy Bradsher, "Arlington's Newly Elected Woman Legislator Stops in at Conference Here to See Friends," *Richmond Times-Dispatch*, November 11, 1953.

74. Martha Ragland to Jane McMichael, Ragland Papers, box 1, folder 1.

75. Eugenia Kaledin, *Mothers and More: American Women in the 1950s* (Boston: Twayne Publishers, 1984), 83–91.

Wilma Dykeman

(1920–2006)

The Hearth and the Map

MELISSA WALKER

❁ ❁ ❁

In 2002 an interviewer asked why Tennessee writer Wilma Dykeman chose to stay in her native Appalachia. She said, "I think I could have lived a number of places, but . . . having a sense of place, a place that you know in an intimate way, is really necessary. When I say 'know it intimately,' I mean you know it with all your senses: you know it with your memory; you know it with your skin; you know the way it smells and sounds, a snowy morning, or the azaleas bursting into bloom. All of that is really important. It gives you a sense of what life is all about and influences all the choices you make along the way."[1]

Even as she relied on an intimate knowledge of her Appalachian home to root her writing, Dykeman never forgot her connections to a wider world, and she often reflected on the tension between the two kinds of place that had shaped her work, the local and the distant. She opened a collection of her newspaper columns with a description of the room where she wrote, a book-lined study, warmed by a fireplace, decorated with large wall maps. As she put it, "The books are other worlds, instant transport outside the prison of my own flesh and time. . . . There is a tug-of-war between the hearth and the map, the books and the woods, two kinds of exploration."[2]

Understanding the woman behind Dykeman's work is not an easy task. She died in December 2006. Her papers have not yet been placed in an archive so that they might be accessible to scholars, and only a few of her letters to others are currently available in repositories. Although she granted literary critic Patricia Gantt extensive interviews in the early 1990s, she declined my request for an interview ten years later, saying that she wanted to focus her energies on her own autobiographical writing. By the time of her death she had given

WILMA DYKEMAN

Courtesy of Dykeman Stokely,
Newport, Tennessee.

dozens of interviews to reporters and literary critics, and she had also written widely about the craft of writing and about her own work. Her newspaper columns often contained autobiographical reflections, as did her interviews. Yet, like most of us, Dykeman developed a life story that obscures as much as it reveals. She talked extensively about her parents' influence on her life, but less about her relationship with her husband and sons. She wrote a great deal about racial injustice; yet we know little about her personal interactions with African Americans. Her work featured strong women characters, and she combined a career with marriage and child rearing, but we know little about how she balanced these demanding roles or about her reactions to the second wave of the women's rights movement, an event that coincided with her middle years. This work, then, is necessarily a partial portrait of an extraordinary writer. Perhaps her papers will eventually be archived and made available to authors, providing us with a clearer picture of the woman behind the writer.

Born in the mountains of western North Carolina to parents who encouraged her intellectual curiosity, Dykeman's childhood memories were filled with the natural world of her isolated mountain community and with the wider world she encountered in books. Exposure to both worlds shaped her work as a writer. As Dykeman put it, "the world's best literature is regional, in the largest sense of that word. Discovering all that is unique to a place, or a person, and relating it to the universals of human experience may be old-fashioned, but I feel it is one of the challenges of writing."[3] Dykeman's work sought to do just that—to link the local and the unique with what she understood to be the universals of human experience—including the challenges of coping with loss, injustice, and change. Dykeman showed readers that "larger" issues are grounded in particular places. Although she wrote about the American South and most often about southern Appalachia, she sometimes bristled when critics pigeonholed her as an Appalachian author, believing that such categorization served to marginalize her work. She saw herself as an author who set her stories in a particular place, but one who explored a wide range of issues relating to the human condition.

To argue that place molds the contours of a southern writer's work verges on cliché. Literary scholars have long examined the links between southern landscapes and cultures and the work of the region's writers.[4] Yet few literary figures have embraced as many genres in their exploration of the American South, its varied landscape, and the struggles for social justice that took place there. Dykeman produced novels, journalistic accounts, reflective essays, newspaper columns, biographies, and general histories to explore her beloved Tennessee and North Carolina mountains, the larger South, and the universal human themes that engaged her attention. Moreover, Dykeman was seized by what scholar Fred

Hobson has called "the rage to explain," a compulsion to interpret the South for the wider world.[5] She was as troubled by many reporters' one-dimensional and often inaccurate portraits of the American South as she was by the region's oppressive racial, class, and gender hierarchies. She once complained, "Many people writing about the South were what we called 'the three-week experts.' You know, they stayed three weeks, and they went to Atlanta. . . . The writers didn't know who to approach—in three weeks—they didn't know who to see to find out who was thinking what about the South."[6] Dykeman employed her pen to add diversity and texture to the literary portrait of the former Confederate states. Dykeman's writings about southern Appalachia and the wider American South are marked by a remarkable commitment to activism via the written word, an activism that was anchored by her strong sense of place.

Dykeman's remarkable range of writings prove hard to categorize. All explore several broad themes—the waste of human or natural resources, the persistence of the past in the present, and the challenges and choices faced by ordinary people confronting extraordinary change. Yet most of her books are situated in a particular place—the mountain South—during the twentieth century. Dykeman wrote eighteen fiction and nonfiction books, including three with husband James Stokely, and one with each of her sons. Her first book, *The French Broad* (1955), published in the Rivers of America series, exposed the damage that industrial pollution did to river systems. The book earned her a Guggenheim fellowship in 1956. As a journalist she frequently collaborated with her husband to cover the civil rights movement for the *Nation* and the *New York Times Magazine*. Together Dykeman and Stokely wrote a volume of personal reflections on southern race relations entitled *Neither Black nor White* (1957). In this book they interpreted the meaning of the African American freedom movement for the South and the nation as a whole. Working alone Dykeman also wrote dozens of short stories, articles, and essays, including a regular column for the *Knoxville News-Sentinel* from 1962 to 1999. Her novels, starting with *The Tall Woman* (1962), traced the lives of individuals coping with rapid social, economic, and environmental change. These fictional works featured strong female characters who lived beyond the prescriptive boundaries that circumscribed southern women's lives. Dykeman also developed a reputation as a fine teacher and as a historian of her adopted state of Tennessee. She taught writing at the University of Tennessee from 1975 to 1995 and became a regular on the lecture circuit. She also engaged in environmental activism, testifying before local, state, and national legislative bodies on behalf of efforts to force corporations to end destructive mining practices and the dumping of toxic waste into the French Broad River. Later in her career, she turned to writing history for general audiences. Her historical accounts demonstrated her skill as a storyteller and synthesizer of historical scholarship.

Wilma Dykeman was born May 20, 1920, in Asheville, North Carolina. Her father, Willard J. Dykeman, was a transplanted New Yorker. While visiting western North Carolina, he had fallen in love with both the mountains and with Bonnie J. Cole, a highland girl thirty-five years his junior. Dykeman told a reporter that although her parents' courtship and May–December romance sounded "rather like a bad paperback," the couple shared a love for the mountains, history, language, and books. Of her parents, Dykeman wrote, "In the beginning there were the two of them. Then there was the place; the woods and wild azalea and rhododendron thickets, the spirited creek, the moss-backed boulders; where they made their nest, which was as personal and sturdy as any nest built by thrush or eagle. It was the relationship between my father and mother and the ways in which they related to the world around them that shaped, in varying degrees, everything I have written."[7] Indeed the Dykemans instilled their passion for the southern Appalachian Mountains in Wilma from her birth. Her father took her for long walks in the woods, where he taught her about trees, wildflowers, and animal life.

Her parents also encouraged her curiosity about the world beyond her mountains. Among Dykeman's sharpest memories of childhood were the hours spent hearing her mother read aloud about distant places. She recalled that "Frances Hodgson Burnett's *The Secret Garden* sent me into a delirium of Christmas joy. A child's abridged Charles Dickens overwhelmed me with pain." She remembered the hours that her parents spent in two great oak-and-leather Stickley chairs reading adult books aloud. Dykeman said, "I usually understood little about this adult reading. What I did understand was that books connected us to the world. From this little mountain cove we could reach out across space and time to know strange people and places and the intertwined evil and good that awaited our innocence and our choices."[8]

The Dykemans also encouraged young Wilma to write, and she was creating her own stories, poems, and plays by the time she was in elementary school. These early efforts kindled larger ambitions. She explained that she had pored over the monthly issues of *National Geographic*, which inspired her to think about "how satisfying it would be to travel to unfamiliar corners of the world—and write about the journey!"[9] Dykeman recounted that going to the mailbox was one of her favorite childhood rituals because "the mailman might leave messages from distant places, but he always left the *New York Herald Tribune* with its bold headlines and big city smell of newsprint." She also loved family visits to northern relatives each summer, with stops along the way at historic sites in North Carolina, Virginia, Pennsylvania, and the Hudson River Valley.[10] Her parents' broad interests helped Wilma see herself as part of a world beyond the one in which she lived from day to day.

Wilma's beloved father died when she was fourteen, but not before he taught her explicitly about the connections between her isolated mountain home and the larger world. Many years later, Dykeman recalled a walk beside the creek near their home. Her father explained how the familiar stream flowed into a river that flowed into another river and another and eventually into the ocean. "It was . . . my first lesson in globalization," she said. "I lived in a mountain valley that might seem to strangers to be remote from the rest of the world, but was in fact, connected to all the world."[11]

Dykeman attended Biltmore Junior College (an institution that has since become part of the University of North Carolina at Asheville) and then went on to earn a B.A., Phi Beta Kappa, in speech at Northwestern University in Evanston, Illinois. The summer after her graduation, as she prepared to move to New York for a job in the emerging field of television, her "life branched out in unexpected ways," as she later put it.[12] The sister of Asheville-born writer Thomas Wolfe introduced Dykeman to two brothers from the Stokely family of Newport, Tennessee. The Stokelys had built a vegetable canning empire in the heart of the Great Smoky Mountains. Mabel Wolfe Wheaton arranged for Wilma and another friend to double-date the brothers; Wilma's date was Ben Stokely. Though interested in Ben's tales of his recent African safari, she later recalled that she was not exactly swept away by his charms. Ben's brother, Jim, however, caught her interest, and apparently she his. The next day, he arrived at her door to invite her for a drive and dinner. Over the course of their courtship, she learned that Jim Stokely had rejected a career in the family business to pursue his interests in poetry and orchard work. He owned and operated an apple orchard near his family home in Tennessee. As they drove the winding roads around Asheville, Wilma and Jim discovered a shared love for books and classical music.[13] The couple married two months later, in October 1940, in her mother's garden. They settled near Jim's orchard in East Tennessee and soon had two sons, Dykeman and James III.[14]

Marriage derailed Wilma's ambitions for a television career, but she soon returned to her childhood passion for the written word, and it was Jim Stokely who opened Dykeman's eyes to many of the issues that she explored through her writing. In 2001 she told an audience at the North Caroliniana Society that her first visit to Jim Stokely's hometown of Newport, Tennessee, raised her consciousness about the environmental and social problems that later fueled her pen:

> First, as we crossed the Pigeon River to climb the hill to his family home, [James] slowed the car so that I might witness the choking, stinking, shocking pollution of that river, water that was clear and swift and sparkling at its headwaters in North Carolina. I had never witnessed such degradation. . . .
>
> Second, James took me to the other side of town to meet some of the black community. I found that James had a variety of friends there. . . . The most memorable was a doctor, over half of whose patients were white. . . .
>
> Our threatened environment. Our racial divide. These challenged my sense of place.[15]

Dykeman, who always published under her maiden name, and her husband developed careers as writers with a strong sense of place. The two often collaborated, conducting research for her books together, and the work became something of a family affair as the couple took their sons along on research trips. At home, Dykeman carved out hours for writing while the boys attended school.[16]

Her first book, *The French Broad,* cataloged the river, its flora and fauna, and the diverse peoples of southern Appalachia. In the pages of *The French Broad,* Dykeman sought to dispel persistent stereotypes of the region, even as she focused on the natural world in which the mountaineers lived. The book emphasized human dependence on the river in elegant prose that captured the cadences of local speech patterns, painted the spectacular beauty of the river, and chronicled the tragic destruction of that river by urban and industrial pollution.

The French Broad was the first book in the Rivers of America series to discuss the consequences of pollution.[17] In fact, Dykeman's awareness of environmental damage as the product of a long-term process shaped her story of the river. She dated the beginning of damage to the entire French Broad watershed to the arrival of Scotch-Irish, English, and German immigrants to the highlands of Tennessee and North Carolina:

> Tired and eager, they found their place, each his own cove or mountain slope or river field, and faced their first tremendous task: that of destroying the most precious resource on the continent. With all the vigor and recklessness of necessity which had been behind their forward push to this very place, they attacked the forests of primeval pine and poplar, walnut and oak, chestnut and maples. . . . The bitterest irony of all the years of settlement is in this process by which a people so frugal they utilized every element of nature, animal, vegetable, and mineral, to its least portion, made every scrap count, scraped and pinched and survived only by

> the closest economy, could waste, with prodigal abandon, the vast harvest of centuries as if it were not only useless but actually an enemy.[18]

Thus in this first book Dykeman displayed the keen awareness of links between past and present that are a hallmark of her work.

Dykeman was equally sensitive to the complexities of human history that fueled the ongoing degradation of the river. In a chapter entitled "Who Killed the French Broad?"—the one her editors found most controversial because it indicted unnamed industries for the bulk of the damage—Dykeman chronicled the gradual pollution of the river. She traced the history of riparian rights, the economic and industrial development of the region, and the biological forces that led to the river's defilement. To Dykeman, the destruction of the French Broad exemplified a paradox common to most instances of environmental damage; people destroyed the very qualities that drew them to the mountains and the river. The pure water and beautiful natural surroundings of the region lured industrialists to establish paper plants and mica mines in the mountains, but the industrial processes then destroyed those very streams and surroundings. Seven years before biologist Rachel Carson published her environmental clarion call *Silent Spring*, and long before a broad awareness of the impact of environmental damage on human health fueled a grassroots environmental movement in the United States, Dykeman called on her fellow mountain citizens to engage in activism to defend the river.[19] She stated, when "we realize what our apathy is costing us, we will realize it is too expensive a luxury and exchange it for enlightened self-concern and public concern. We would realize that we had rather raise our own voices to cleanse our own evils than to wait until emergency has brought other pressures to bear."[20]

Literary critic Elizabeth S. D. Engelhardt has argued that in *The French Broad*, Dykeman was participating in a tradition of "working-class . . . local activism by women in the southern Appalachian mountains."[21] Although Dykeman was hardly working class, her work does follow the lead of such mountain women as Emma Bell Miles, Grace MacGowan Cooke, and Maristan Chapman, all of whom wrote about environmental degradation and called for local action to prevent it.[22] Like these authors, it was the experience of living in the mountains that nourished Dykeman's insights. The childhood hours spent wandering with her father in the watershed, the adult hours sitting on the front porches of mountain cabins listening to the "simple stories" of local residents, and the "beauty of its water and the splendor of its mountains" all guided her storytelling.[23]

Although *The French Broad* is her most explicitly environmentalist book, many of Dykeman's books return to the theme of environmental degradation and the complex choices mountain people faced in trying to wrest a living from a beautiful but harsh environment. Lydia McQueen, the main character in the novel *The Tall Woman*, dies of typhoid fever after drinking from a mountain spring contaminated by runoff from a sawmill. Dykeman explained that she chose this fate for McQueen "as a symbol of the waste of natural resources." *The Far Family* charts the deforestation of an entire mountain by Lydia's descendants as they struggle to earn a living. In newspaper columns written during the later years of her career and her public appearances, Dykeman persistently explored environmental concerns, calling for clean water and a reduction in urban sprawl.[24]

After completing *The French Broad*, Dykeman turned her attention to the other social issue raised in the early visit to her husband's hometown—the problem of southern race relations. In 1982 she described her second book, *Neither Black nor White* (which she wrote with James), as the logical progression from her research for *The French Broad*. In the process of researching the natural history of the river, she became concerned about the waste of natural resources because of "greed and selfishness and apathy." The next step was to see and to write about "that waste of racial potential and talent both among the white and the Black races because we limit ourselves by our prejudices, by our narrow shutting out of each other from the fullness of opportunity. . . . [A]ll of these things—one sort of grows from another, as the pebble put in the water."[25] To Dykeman, wasting human resources through oppression and injustice was just another point along a continuum of unnecessary and profligate destruction. As she put it, "Race, sex, nationality, class—any condition that limits an individual's fulfillment of total potential is of concern to me, as a person, as a writer."[26] She told a somewhat different story about the book's origins in a 2002 interview, however, implying that the book grew out of her husband's long interest in civil rights issues. "He was against injustice and discrimination and inequity when it was not a popular subject," she explained. "I couldn't have written it without James."[27]

Whatever the genesis of the book, *Neither Black nor White* explored race relations from Dykeman and Stokely's positions as southern insiders. Historian Morton Sosna has argued that many southern liberals such as Dykeman and Stokely "felt a strong need to explain the South to outsiders."[28] David L. Chappell, another historian of white involvement in the civil rights movement, agreed, noting that white southerners who spoke out in favor of civil rights "saw themselves as defending, not attacking, the best of southern tradition. Though opposed to southern racism, that is, they were still southern: they could exploit their familiarity with other white southerners for purposes of persuasion or espionage. Their being white southerners was perhaps more important than their being white liberals."[29] These historians could be describing Dykeman and Stokely's research methodology. In a 2001 speech to the North Caroliniana Society, Dykeman explained, "We proposed a book of exploration across our region (messages from the front, as it were, and the front was everywhere) by two Southerners who had no title or commitments or hidden agenda beyond a deep desire to see our region come to grips with its history."[30]

To write *Neither Black nor White*, the couple traveled the South from Charleston to Houston, conversing with their fellow southerners of both races—state officials, business leaders, bankers, farmers. Along the way they happened on a Ku Klux Klan gathering in a country churchyard and attended the legendary 1955 Southern Historical Association meeting. At this conference, in a controversial integrated session at the Peabody Hotel, white author William Faulkner and white attorney Cecil Sims shared the platform with Benjamin Mays, the African American president of Morehouse College, to discuss the recent Supreme Court ruling in the *Brown v. Board* school desegregation case. The session was organized by a group of young progressive historians who challenged the politics of the segregationists' policies and the politics of the racial apologists who dominated the SHA's founding generation. Historians of both races, including respected African American historian John Hope Franklin and the equally respected white historian Thomas Clark, attended the event. That evening, Faulkner challenged the organization to take a public stand on issues of racial justice, and Dykeman and Stokely included a chapter on the historic meeting in *Neither Black nor White*.[31]

Dykeman later explained that they did not "go in [to the South] as reporters. We'd say, 'Look, we're Southerners and we're writing about the South.'" She noted that most people just assumed that Dykeman and Stokely agreed with them, although the two never indicated their own views. Dykeman later told an interviewer that they would listen "and then go to the car and write like mad on legal pads, both of us recording everything we could remember about the conversations, little bits of language, stories we'd heard. When we got home, we would compare notes." Dykeman drafted the initial text, then Stokely made revisions.[32] The result was a work that demonstrates an understanding of the complexities of southern history. The couple presented a remarkably astute analysis of the interlocking and reinforcing hierarchies of race, class, and gender combined with economic forces that shaped a South that shared an "irreverence for life," a tradition that included the abuse of the environment as well as slavery and racial violence.[33] The book received the prestigious Hillman Award for its contributions to world peace, race relations, and civil liberties.

Another Dykeman and Stokely collaboration, an essay on civil rights in Hoke Norris's collection *We Dissent*, reflected their vision of themselves as interpreters of the South to the rest of the nation. In the introduction to the collection, Norris asserted that all the essays in it were written by "Southern-born, Southern-raised, white Protestants."[34] Dykeman and Stokely's essay displayed a finely honed sense of the nuances of southern history and of the ways that geography shaped this history. "Let us begin at the beginning, with the land," they wrote. They outlined the exploration, colonization, and settlement of the South, arguing that the South's climate and soil proved favorable to staple-crop agriculture. This type of market-oriented farming required intensive labor. Thus, they noted, "the great single-crop kingdoms [of] . . . tobacco, rice, sugar, and cotton" could not have "come into being or flourished without . . . the human resources of Africa and the extension of African slavery that followed the opening of the New World."[35]

Dykeman and Stokely acknowledged that "many Southern people never held slaves," a reference to poor white southerners who shared few common interests with plantation owners, but they did not engage in a sustained critique of southern class relations in *We Dissent*. They noted that the agrarian way of life had persisted longer in the South than in any other region of the country and suggested that southerners' persistent attachment to life on the land "has complicated our entrance into the industrial age."[36] Most of all, they indicted the "myths that have gained currency throughout the region and helped paralyze us in a time calling for action." The most powerful of these myths was the myth of silence, a myth "designed to quell disagreement with the majority—or a vocal and often ruthless minority. It labels Southerners who wish to discuss their racial situation as 'trouble-makers,' disturbers of the peace. . . . This, of course, is somewhat like saying that the diagnostician who pronounces his patient ill of cancer is a trouble-maker."[37]

Dykeman and Stokely asserted that "What we have to fear in the South, and the world, today is not dispute—but silence."[38] They called for a new approach to race relations that would bring equality, freedom, and full participation in democracy to African Americans. "Change in the South is no longer debatable," they wrote. "It is already a demonstrable fact, reshaping the face of the region, refashioning the life of every person in it."[39] Dykeman and Stokely pursued a personal mission to nudge the South from the inside out toward accepting change, even as they sought to help the rest of the nation understand their homeland.

Even before the publication of *Neither Black nor White* and *We Dissent*, editors of the *Nation* and the *New York Times Magazine* accepted Dykeman and Stokely as balanced interpreters of the unrest in the South, publishing the couple's accounts of the end of segregated seating on Montgomery city buses; the bombing of the high school in Clinton, Tennessee, in the aftermath of its desegregation; and other landmark events in the Civil Rights Movement.[40] Moreover, their article, "Montgomery Morning," was honored by the National Conference of Christians and Jews with a certificate of recognition for excellence in reporting on social justice issues.[41]

Later, Dykeman and Stokely continued their efforts to explain their South and promote civil rights through their writing with biographies of white southern civil rights activists. Together they wrote *Seeds of Southern Change,* a biography of white civil rights activist and executive director of the Commission on Interracial Cooperation (CIC) Will Alexander. Dykeman also wrote the biography of W. D. Weatherford, a founder of the CIC.[42] In both books, the authors explore the critical role of place in shaping the white civil rights leaders. For example, Dykeman explored how Weatherford's childhood on a Texas farm and adolescence in a small town, and his observation of the poverty of the rural Jim Crow South heightened his awareness of class and racial injustice.

If concerns with issues of environmental degradation, racial segregation, and discrimination were at center stage of much of Dykeman's work, so was concern about the role of women in society. Although she did not call herself a feminist nor openly participate in the second wave of the women's movement, her work reflected her belief that women, too, were important human resources who contributed to the good of the larger society. Perhaps this consciousness is the result of her position as the pampered child of parents who valued education and helped her develop a strong sense of autonomy. Or perhaps the example of her mother, who lived a full and vibrant life after Dykeman's father's death, helped her view women as independent actors. Whatever the reason, Dykeman's ideas about the wide range of roles for women and about gender strictures in southern society placed her ahead of her time. She created autonomous fictional female characters and chronicled the lives of real-life women who embraced broader cultural roles than those endorsed by the larger society.

Dykeman created her earliest strong female characters in her high school years. She told an interviewer, "I dreamed up the idea that the women in *Julius Caesar* should be in the play." With the full approval of their teacher, Dykeman and some of her friends wrote additional scenes for Shakespeare's play that fully explored the lives of the women around Caesar. "[W]e got sheets [for costumes] from our mothers, and we . . . performed these extra scenes. . . . [L]ooking back on it, it's interesting that I even thought about the women in that play."[43] Her earliest published works were peopled with women who lived on their own terms. *The French Broad* featured a number of strong women—her husband's grandmother, Anna Stokely, a widow who founded a vegetable cannery on her rich river-bottom farm in East Tennessee; Maggie Jones, an African American moonshiner who repeatedly outwitted the Buncombe County, North Carolina, sheriff's efforts to catch her with illegal liquor; and the five Walker sisters, self-sufficient East Tennessee mountain farmers.[44] Likewise, Lydia McQueen, the fictional protagonist of *The Tall Woman*, defied stereotypes of mountain women cowed by patriarchal family structures. Dykeman said she based McQueen on real women: "[O]ften in the mountain family, . . . [the women's role] was the role of leadership, the women helping establish and keep going the churches . . . [and] the schools." She added that journalists and scholars who had studied the southern Appalachian region up to that time had overlooked the role of women because they did not know the region and its people well enough to understand its subtleties and nuances.[45]

Much of Dykeman's nonfiction work focused on women who made significant contributions to the worlds in which they lived. She ventured into writing about women's history when the subdiscipline was in its infancy with a 1974 biography of birth control advocate and peace activist Edna Rankin MacKinnon, the sister of Montana congresswoman Jeannette Rankin.[46] MacKinnon not only lobbied Congress for laws that protected women's right to practice birth control, but she also established a set of family planning clinics in the mountains of Tennessee and Kentucky and in the cities of New York and California. By the time Dykeman wrote MacKinnon's biography, *Too Many People, Too Little Love*, late twentieth-century changes in the economic and political roles of women had begun to influence her work, something she implies in the preface to the book: "There were three central reasons why I finally chose to write this book. First, Edna Rankin MacKinnon's life incorporates three of the major issues of our twentieth-century life—the population explosion, the changing status of women, and the imperative for peace. Second, it is a good story. It casts complex social issues in a human framework of fallibility and humor, shows idealism sustained by common sense and incredibly hard work. Third, it demonstrates the effectiveness of the individual."[47]

In 1977 Dykeman further explored the effectiveness of individual women when she wrote a volume, edited and with additional material by Carol Lynn Yellin, entitled *Tennessee Women: Past and Present*. The book included brief biographical sketches of dozens of women important to the state's history, ranging from Cherokee Beloved Woman Nancy Ward to opera singer Grace Moore, from white suffragist and club woman Lizzie Crozier French to African American suffragist and club woman Mary Church Terrell. In 1993 historian Carole

Bucy rediscovered the slender, little-known volume when she was researching a teacher's guide for incorporating women into Tennessee's social studies curriculum. She convinced Dykeman to update and expand the book. The revised version was published by her son Dykeman Stokely's Wakestone Books in 1993.[48]

Dykeman did not limit herself to exploring the work and lives of fictional or real-life women, however. She also theorized about the nature of southern restrictions on women and the way those restrictions intertwined with the racial hierarchies of the South. Like Lillian Smith, she recognized that white supremacist claims that segregation protected the flower of southern womanhood served to justify segregation and control women.[49] In *Neither Black nor White*, Dykman reflected on how this process worked. "The legend and myth of Southern womanhood was, is, inextricably interwoven with the legend and reality of the Negro," she wrote in 1957. In a chapter entitled "Sugar and Spice and Plenty of Backbone," she noted,

> Crinolines-among-the-camellias or calicos-in-the-cotton-patch, Southern [white] women have been in part overwhelmed by their romantic idealization. It is another of the ironies of history that during those decades when our foremothers were supposed to be occupying their proudest pedestals, many of them were, in reality, pushing the family plow. . . . For generations, like the Negro, [southern white women] had "their place," and they were kept in that place by many devices. The Negro's place was in the muck beneath the white man's, the [white] woman's was in the ethereal realms above—but both positions served the same purpose of keeping them out of the marketplace. . . . Southern [white] women have had many burdens to bear, but none more wearisome than being used as the buffer between the Negro and justice.[50]

Such a sophisticated understanding of the interconnections between racial and gender oppression grew directly out of Dykeman's observations of the twentieth-century South.

Dykeman continued to write into her eighth decade, producing a regular column for the *Knoxville News-Sentinel*. She also continued her travel, teaching, and activism. In the early 1970s she joined a group of American writers on one of the first tours of China after President Nixon normalized relations with that nation. She influenced a new generation of Appalachian writers, including novelist Sharyn McCrumb and poet and novelist Robert Morgan. In fact, Morgan noted that his interest in writing about his native Appalachia blossomed after he read *The French Broad*. In 2004 *Knoxville News-Sentinel* columnist Fred Brown called Dykeman "the grand dame of Appalachian letters."[51]

Dykeman died December 22, 2006, at the age of eighty-six, after suffering complications from a hip fracture she had sustained two months earlier. Her obituaries universally praised her literary and civic legacy. Novelist Sharyn McCrumb called her important because "she was someone from the region, talking about the region." McCrumb asserted that Dykeman's work fell into neither the local color romanticism of many early chroniclers of Appalachia nor the "we were so poor" style of Erskine Caldwell in his 1932 novel *Tobacco Road*. Rather, McCrumb said, Dykeman "was trying to present a realistic view" of the region.[52]

The environmentally ravaged southern mountains, the stark conflicts that marked the Civil Rights–era South, women's struggles to maintain independence and achieve equality, and even the teachings of her intellectually adventurous parents found expression again and again when Dykeman put pen to paper. The hearth and the map were apt metaphors for her enduring themes. Yet in the end, she seemed to believe that most of all, writing was a tool for exploring herself and for exploring our common humanity. In 1992 the North Carolina Writers Conference paid tribute to her at their annual meeting. Dykeman's response was a wandering reflection on the writers she had known, on her experiences researching her work, and on the meaning of the writing life. She told the audience, "I think of all the people you'll know as a writer, perhaps the one you get to know best is yourself. You discover that pettiness and generosity and nobility and grandeur, the creative and the trivial are all inside us, inside myself, inside yourself. And they are always in a struggle and you are each of them and you're all of them."[53] Wilma Dykeman animated this struggle in each of her written works.

NOTES

The author is grateful to John Lane and to the editors of this volume for their comments on an earlier version of this essay.

1. "Interview with Wilma Dykeman," *Appalachian Journal* 29, no. 4 (2002): 458.

2. Wilma Dykeman, *Explorations* (Newport, Tenn.: Wakestone Books, 1984), 1–2.

3. Wilma Dykeman, "Sidelights," *Contemporary Authors Online* (The Gale Group, 2001), http://galenet.galegroup.com.

4. For examples of scholarship that considers the role of place in shaping the work of southern writers, see Suzanne Marrs, *One Writer's Imagination: The Fiction of Eudora Welty* (Baton Rouge: Louisiana State University Press, 2002); Elizabeth Jane Harrison, *Female Pastoral: Women Writers Re-Visioning the American South* (Knoxville: University of Tennessee Press, 1991); and Louise Hutchings Westling, *Sacred Groves and Ravaged Gardens: The Fiction of Eudora Welty, Carson McCullers, and Flannery O'Connor* (Athens: University of Georgia Press, 1985). For examples of other southern writers' reflections on the role of place in her own and others' work, see Eudora Welty,

"Place and Time: The Southern Writer's Inheritance," *Mississippi Quarterly* 50 (Fall 1997): 545–47; and Joyce Dyer, ed., *Bloodroot: Reflections on Place by Appalachian Women Writers* (Lexington: University Press of Kentucky, 1998).

5. Fred C. Hobson, *Tell About the South: The Southern Rage to Explain* (Baton Rouge: Louisiana State University Press, 1983).

6. "Interview with Wilma Dykeman," 450.

7. "Wilma Dykeman," in *The Complete Marquis Who's Who*, 2003, reproduced in *Biography Resource Center* (Farmington Hills, Mich.: The Gale Group, 2004), http://galenet.galegroup.com/servlet/BioRC; Ina Hughes, "Natural Woman," *Knoxville News-Sentinel*, August 25, 2002, A1, 3; "Wilma Dykeman," http://www.ncwriters.org/wdykeman.htm; Wilma Dykeman, "'The Past Is Never Dead. It's Not Even Past,'" in *Bloodroot: Reflections on Place by Appalachian Women Writers*, ed. Joyce Dyer (Lexington: University Press of Kentucky, 1998), 106.

8. Dykeman, "The Past Is Never Dead," 108, 109.

9. Ibid., 109.

10. Wilma Dykeman, *Roots and Branches* (Chapel Hill: North Caroliniana Society, Inc. and North Carolina Collection, 2001), 5–6.

11. Hughes, "Natural Woman," A3.

12. Dykeman, *Roots and Branches*, 6.

13. Sam B. Smith, "Wilma Dykeman and James Stokely," *An Encyclopedia of East Tennessee*, ed. Jim Stokely and Jeff D. Johnson (Oak Ridge, Tenn.: Children's Museum, 1981), 163–65.

14. "Wilma Dykeman," http://www.ncwriters.org/wdykeman.htm; Hughes, "Natural Woman," A3; "Interview with Wilma Dykeman," 447.

15. Dykeman, *Roots and Branches*, 7.

16. "Interview with Wilma Dykeman," 456.

17. Chris Sinacola, "Rivers Spark Human Spirit," *Worcester Telegram and Gazette*, July 2, 2000, www.telegram.com/static/crosscurrents/july02b/html; Barbara Bryant, "Rivers of America: Library Celebrates 60th Anniversary of Landmark Series," *Library of Congress Information Bulletin*, June 9, 1997, http://www.loc.gov/lcib; Patricia M. Gantt, "'A Mutual Journey': Wilma Dykeman and Appalachian Regionalism," in *Breaking Boundaries: New Perspectives on Women's Regional Writing*, ed. Sherrie A. Inness and Diana Royer (Iowa City: University of Iowa Press, 1997), 211.

18. Gantt, "'A Mutual Journey,'" 211; Wilma Dykeman, *The French Broad* (1955; repr., Newport, Tenn.: Wakestone Books, 1992), 51.

19. Rachel Carson, *Silent Spring* (New York: Fawcett Crest, 1962).

20. Dykeman, *The French Broad*, chap. 18, quote on p. 292.

21. Elizabeth S. D. Engelhardt, "Wilma Dykeman and the Women of Appalachia: The Ecology of Mid-Century Environmental Activism," *Women's Studies Quarterly* 1 and 2 (2001), 156.

22. See Emma Bell Miles, *The Spirit of the Mountains* (1905; repr., Knoxville: University of Tennessee Press, 1975); Grace MacGowan Cooke, *The Power and the Glory* (New York: Doubleday, Page, 1910); and Maristan Chapman, *Glen Hazard* (New York: A. A. Knopf, 1933). Maristan Chapman was actually a husband and wife novelist team, Mary and John Stanton Higham, and the pseudonym is a combination of their names. Mary Chapman Higham was the primary writer of the couple.

23. Dykeman, *The French Broad*, 6.

24. Morgan Simmons, "Effort Launched to Clean Up Area's Waters: Business, Civil Leaders Join in Push by Izaak Walton League," *Knoxville News-Sentinel*, September 4, 1999, A4; Wilma Dykeman, "Biodiversity Truly an Ancient Concept," *Knoxville News-Sentinel*, July 11, 1999, H3, "Now There's a

Guide through the Sprawl," *Knoxville News-Sentinel*, August 29, 1999, H3, and "Safeguarding Water Is Key to Survival," *Knoxville News-Sentinel*, October 31, 1999, H3.

25. Danny Miller, "A MELUS Interview: Wilma Dykeman," *MELUS: Society for the Study of Multi-Ethnic Literature in the United States* 9 (Autumn 1982): 57.

26. "Wilma Dykeman," *Contemporary Authors*, New Revision Series, vol. 1 (Detroit: Gale Research Co., 1981), 171–72.

27. "Interview with Wilma Dykeman," 449, 451.

28. Morton Sosna, *In Search of the Silent South: Southern Liberals and the Race Issue* (New York: Columbia University Press, 1977), 200.

29. David L. Chappell, *Inside Agitators: White Southerners in the Civil Rights Movement* (Baltimore: Johns Hopkins University Press, 1994), xxii.

30. Dykeman, *Roots and Branches*, 9.

31. Dykeman, *Roots and Branches*, 9. For more on the 1955 Southern Historical Association meeting, see Fred A. Bailey, "The Southern Historical Association and the Quest for Racial Justice, 1954–1963," *Journal of Southern History* 71 (November 2005): 833–53, as well as comments from Thomas D. Clark, John Hope Franklin, and Anne Firor Scot in that issue.

32. "Interview with Wilma Dykeman," 450, 448.

33. Wilma Dykeman and James Stokely, *Neither Black nor White* (New York: Holt, Rinehart, and Winston, 1957), 5–6.

34. Hoke Norris, introduction to *We Dissent*, ed. Hoke Norris (New York: St. Martin's, 1962), v.

35. Dykeman and Stokely, "Our Changing South: A Challenge," in *We Dissent*, 3, 4.

36. Ibid., 7.

37. Ibid., 7–8.

38. Ibid., 8.

39. Ibid., 7.

40. See for example, all by Wilma Dykeman and James Stokely, "Courage in Action in Clinton, Tennessee," *Nation*, December 22, 1956, 531–33; "Montgomery Morning," *Nation*, January 5, 1957, 11–13; "Failure of a Hate Mission," *Nation*, April 20, 1957, 342–44; "Integration: Third and Critical Phase," *New York Times Magazine*, November 27, 1960, 24–25; and "The Big Cure for Segregation," *New York Times Magazine*, September 5, 1962, 30.

41. Wilma Dykeman and James Stokely, "Battlefield of Human Rights," *Nation*, March 1, 1958, 186.

42. Wilma Dykeman and James Stokely, *Seeds of Southern Change: The Life of Will Alexander* (Chicago: University of Chicago Press, 1962); Wilma Dykeman, *Prophet of Plenty: The First Ninety Years of W. D. Weatherford* (Knoxville: University of Tennessee Press, 1966).

43. "Interview with Wilma Dykeman," 451.

44. Dykeman, *The French Broad*, 195–209, 303–4, 61–62. For more on the history of the Stokely canning operation, see Ruth Webb O'Dell, *Over the Misty Blue Hills: The Story of Cocke County, Tennessee* (Easley, S.C.: Southern Historical Press, 1982), 205–6.

45. Miller, "A MELUS Interview," 51.

46. Dykeman's work on MacKinnon brought her into contact with Martha Ragsdale Ragland, the Tennessee political, civic, and women's rights activist. Ragland, a Planned Parenthood organizer, helped Dykeman raise money to underwrite the publication of *Too Many People, Too Little Love*. See correspondence in the Papers of Martha Ragland, Schlesinger Library, Radcliffe Institute for Advanced Study, Harvard University, Cambridge, Mass.

47. Wilma Dykeman, *Too Many People, Too Little Love: Edna Rankin MacKinnon, Pioneer for Birth Control* (New York: Holt, 1974), viii–ix.

48. Wilma Dykeman, *Tennessee Women: Past and Present*, ed. Carol Lynn Yellin (n.p.: n.p., 1977), and *Tennessee Women: An Infinite Variety* (Newport, Tenn.: Wakestone Books, 1993).

49. Lillian Smith, *Killers of the Dream* (1949; repr., New York: W. W. Norton, 1994), 138–55.

50. Dykeman and Stokely, *Neither Black nor White*, 134, 143–45.

51. Fred Brown, "Appalachian Journal: Author Captures Land's Grace on Paper," *Knoxville News Sentinel*, April 18, 2004; Robert Morgan interview with *Asheville Citizen-Times*, December 24, 2006, podcast on *Asheville Citizen-Times* Web site at www.citizen-times.com/cpps/pbcs.dll./article?AID200661223045.

52. "Dykeman Leaves Tall Literary, Civic Legacy," *Asheville Citizen-Times*, December 24, 2006; "Columnist and Author Dykeman Dies at 86," *Knoxville News-Sentinel*, December 24, 2006; Margalit Fox, "Wilma Dykeman, 86, A Writer on the Environment and Race, Dies," *New York Times*, December 29, 2006.

53. *Tributes to Wilma Dykeman*, privately published pamphlet (n.p.: North Carolina Writers Conference, 1992).

Sarah Colley Cannon (Minnie Pearl)

(1912–1996)

Gossiping about Grinder's Switch—The Grand Ole Opry and the Modernization of Tennessee

KRISTINE M. MCCUSKER

In 1970, Sarah Colley Cannon capitalized on her fame as the Grand Ole Opry's Minnie Pearl by publishing a cookbook entitled *Minnie Pearl Cooks*. In the preface, Sarah wrote, "Ever since I became two people, Minnie Pearl and Sarah Ophelia Cannon, I've been faced with the problem of when to be Minnie and when to be Sarah Ophelia. In creating this book I've decided to be both."[1] And both she was. The front cover pictured Sarah in her Minnie Pearl costume—gingham dress, black Mary Jane shoes, and a flowered hat with the price tag dangling. The back cover featured Mrs. Henry Cannon, Nashville socialite and trendsetter, elegant hostess, and wealthy matron. Photographs inside the book depicted Minnie Pearl laughing with her Opry friends Roy Acuff and Grandpa Jones while an elegant and refined Sarah Cannon poured tea from a silver tea service given her by her mother-in-law.[2]

Sarah's career being two people (as she put it, "to be both") began well before she wrote her cookbook. Encapsulated in the oft-used phrase, "Sarah Colley Cannon, better known as Minnie Pearl," her decision "to be both" was in response to the Opry's evolution from local programming to a nationally broadcast radio show just as World War II broke out, which meant its new national audience promised special challenges for Sarah and other Opry performers. Indeed, to attract the broadest number of fans from across the country, Sarah incorporated what she perceived to be her audience's diverse ideas of gender

SARAH COLLEY CANNON (MINNIE PEARL)

Late 1940s. Courtesy of Grand Ole Opry Museum.

into her act, providing multiple characters to cater to a variety of tastes. Thus, "to be both" required a multilayered stage performance that included a brash and brazen spinster, a sly and witty comic, and a southern matron—a performance that was second nature to her by the time her cookbook came out.

Sarah's performance of two people came at an important moment in Tennessee's history, too. In the 1930s New Deal programs had modernized Tennessee's (and the South's) infrastructure, in particular building roads and electrical grids that were immediately put to good use during World War II in the manufacturing of munitions. National broadcasts of the Grand Ole Opry enticed listeners and capitalists nationwide to visit the newly modern state after the war and invest their dollars there. Among the first industries to appear was an obvious one: the country and western music industry moved from Chicago, Los Angeles, Cincinnati, and other places to coalesce in Nashville in the 1940s and 1950s. By 1957 country and western music was a $50 million a year business.[3] Tourists flocked to Nashville to visit the Opry, patronize the stars' commercial outlets (e.g., Minnie Pearl's Chicken Shop), and travel on buses to see stars' homes. By the early 1960s the Opry was popular enough to perform at Carnegie Hall, where promoters noted: "Over 7,000,000 people have traveled to Nashville to WSM's live Saturday night radio show, Tennessee's largest tourist attraction. Some one has said, 'More people go to more trouble to see the "Grand Ole Opry" than any other show in the world.'"[4] Sarah's popularity was thus both a catalyst to—and an example of—these changes.

Tennessee's modernization required that social structures evolve as well, particularly racial hierarchies. Whereas a rural South depended on the cheap, exploitable labor of blacks, this modern South required a more flexible labor force that could cross what once seemed to be impermeable racial lines. Some white southerners were still determined to keep segregated boundaries between blacks and whites as a way to preserve their place in society. But rather than side with either integrationists (who wished for an interracial labor force) or segregationists (who wished strict divisions, usually unequal between blacks and whites), the Opry, and by extension, Sarah, opted for a third option: they embraced racially exclusive stages (a first for the Opry) on which whites performed and blacks were invisible, a legacy inherited from northern barn dance programs that the Opry had modeled itself on. Thus, its modern world would be one that was all white; racial problems simply did not exist because on the Opry's stage blacks rarely, if ever, appeared on the air after 1941, until Charley Pride broke the color barrier in the mid-1960s. Sarah's promotion of a racially exclusive world was not without contradictions, however, especially when she advocated for states' rights candidates like Alabama governor George Wallace.

Thus, the Opry may have embraced an all-white world, but ironically, Sarah and Wallace acknowledged an interracial one, albeit one where black men and women were segregated at the margins of southern society rather than an integrated New South that the civil rights workers desired.

There was little in her upbringing that suggested Sarah would eventually become one of the Opry's beloved characters. Her parents, Thomas and Fannie (House) Colley, were part of the New South expansion into rural areas in the 1880s and 1890s as Tennesseans attempted to industrialize the state by establishing small businesses in areas like Sarah's hometown, Centerville (approximately fifty miles west of Nashville). The move from the Colleys' hometown—aristocratic Franklin—to Centerville could not have been more dramatic. A Nashville finishing school made her mother an acknowledged belle of Franklin society; her wedding announcement in 1897 read, "The bride has had a ladyhood of pronounced social success, her charm of person and varied accomplishments rendering her exceedingly popular."[5] Sarah's father was a gentleman, she recalled, albeit a "gentleman of the woods."[6] Thus, he was the right kind of man for her socialite mother, but he was also a man willing to search out new places to establish his lumber enterprise. Thomas's business prospered in Centerville, providing a comfortable, upper-middle-class life for his family—a large and expensive house, a piano, Havilland china, Japanese teacups, and Russian tea for the cultural circles his wife hosted in their home. Sarah recalled, "I think it made him proud to spoil [her mother]."[7] The wives of Thomas's laborers, both black and white, provided domestic labor for the family so Fannie could pursue civic duties and volunteer work. She played organ in Centerville's Methodist Church, organized a chapter of the Women's Missionary Society, a Chautauqua Circle (a book club movement emanating from Chautauqua, New York), and an Eastern Star Chapter, all of which made her one of the "social leaders of Centerville."[8] In short, she embraced Victorian women's clubs that were indicative of the more conservative parts of the Progressive movement. She tried to reform her "wild" hometown by bringing cultural activities and religious organizations that would provide residents a modicum of civilization (activities that also marked her as southern, white, and elite), but she did not pursue Progressive Era activities that were considered more radical, such as woman suffrage.

When Sarah was born in 1912 to her "proud, conventional Southern parents," her mother was thirty-seven years old and her father was fifty-five. There were six years between Sarah and her next youngest sister, and her oldest sister was fourteen years her senior. The difference in ages, Sarah thought, marked her as different from the rest of the family.[9] She looked different, too, which reinforced her perception that she was unique and unconventional. She remembered, "I knew I wasn't pretty then—I had freckles, a knobby little body and straight, reddish blond hair."[10] Her desire to act also set Sarah off from her conventional family. She knew from an early age she wanted to be an actress and longed to follow in the footsteps of her idol, Katharine Hepburn. Family members called her by a Shakespearian nickname, Ophelia, and she took "expression" lessons—an early term for acting lessons—from a young age. She then pursued theatrical training at Nashville's Ward-Belmont College, "the most fabulous finishing school in the state," she said. But the Great Depression had severely damaged the family's finances (Thomas Colley eventually lost his lumber business, although he was still able to pay for Sarah's college education). Sarah's initial days at Ward-Belmont were difficult as she encountered young women whose families had not suffered these economic hardships.[11] She recalled going to her Ward-Belmont dormitory for the first time: "Even before I found my way to my room I was terrified. I had never seen so many well-dressed girls in one place in my life. Everything about them—clothes, haircuts, vocabulary, even the way they walked—reeked of money. It was hard to believe that just a few miles away, in downtown Nashville, people were actually standing in breadlines. The Depression apparently had not hit families of Ward-Belmont students. But then, of course, only the very wealthy could afford to send their daughters to Ward-Belmont. Very *few* were there because their parents had scraped to send them, as mine had."[12] Sarah soon found a place for herself at Ward-Belmont, however, as her gregarious personality and natural showmanship soon made her a standout among her classmates, who adored her dramatic flair.

After graduation, Sarah realized "that no long-lost rich uncle was going to provide the money I needed to continue my education in dramatics."[13] She taught acting, piano, and dancing in Centerville until she turned twenty-one (her parents would not let her leave home until then), after which she joined the Wayne P. Sewell Production Company in 1934. A unique organization based in Atlanta, the Sewell Company produced vaudeville shows written by Sewell's wife, a former vaudevillian, for civic organizations (chambers of commerce, for example) across the South. Sewell sent pretty young women he called "winsome directors" to those southern communities to produce the plays featuring local citizens.[14] Sewell and the organization then divided ticket-sale profits after the show.

As a "winsome director," Sarah traveled from town to town throughout the South, isolated from the women she trained with in Atlanta. And even though women kept their jobs in greater numbers in general than men did in the Great Depression, Sarah still felt she operated outside conventional female boundaries by working outside of the home—boundaries established by her mother and sisters.[15] Her reported shyness at various Sewell events may have been an implicit recognition of her transgression of those boundaries. She began to construct a character who would greet people in each new town, a gentle and ladylike mountain girl whose friendliness hid Sarah's doubts about her status.[16] The character Minnie Pearl thus began to appear when Sarah felt shy. In new towns she metamorphosed into this personality, saying to her various audiences: "I'd like to give you my impression of a mountain girl, Minnie Pearl (and then in a soft drawl said), 'Howdy. I'm just so proud to be here.'"[17] This initially gentle salutation eventually evolved into a boisterous shout that would greet listeners from the Opry's stage, but in its earliest incarnation, it depicted Minnie as a demure country girl.

Her shyness provided one reason for creating Minnie Pearl. Another factor was a seventy-year-old North Alabama farm woman who helped give shape to Minnie Pearl. On a trip for the Sewell Company, Sarah stayed with the woman, who charmed Sarah with her folksy sayings, such as "I've had sixteen young'uns and never failed to make a crop." Sarah began gathering more stories, jokes, and sayings from northern Alabama, eastern Tennessee, and western North Carolina to bring the mountain girl to life.[18] The jokes she told entertained locals, and she found that "it was a lot easier than [standing up there] as Ophelia Cannon, and the people really seemed to enjoy her."[19]

Jokes and sayings were the first step; costuming was the second. In 1939 Sarah began dressing in clothing she thought a country girl might wear to town on a Saturday afternoon outing: an old, cheap, yellow organdy dress; a hat with flowers on it (the price tag came later); and white shoes with cotton stockings. When she appeared in costume, she remembered, "It was the first time that I had really had a sense of being somebody else."[20] At other performances, dressed in full regalia, Sarah felt herself "moving out of Sarah Ophelia Colley into Minnie Pearl. I felt more uninhibited than I ever had felt doing her before, but it was more than that. I *became* the character. It was the first time I had ever really changed places with her, and it gave me a wonderful sense of freedom I hadn't had before."[21] Because Sarah recognized that dress transformed her into a woman who was not modern or urbane, she immediately changed into fashionable clothing that suited Sarah Colley. Changing clothes after a performance thus marked an important step in delineating her off-stage self from the Minnie Pearl character.

As Sarah traveled the South in the 1930s, the New Deal was transforming it from a rural region that had toyed with modern development into a modern industrial area, ripe and ready for economic expansion. For example, by the 1920s Murfreesboro, a small town thirty miles south of Nashville, had already begun to evolve from a sleepy agricultural town into a regional center by attracting new industries, particularly textile mills and cedar-bucket factories, and by incorporating new national industries (like movie theaters) into its economy. But it had expanded on a shaky infrastructure. Roads from Murfreesboro to surrounding areas were practically nonexistent. Tennessee itself was known as a "detour state" to automobile enthusiasts because its roads were so bad. Electricity was available only to some urban residents and remained expensive, and infrastructure, like sewer systems, remained a pipe dream.[22] Tennessee benefited significantly from New Deal largesse, thanks to southern Democrats who helped elect Franklin Roosevelt president in 1932, and Murfreesboro used New Deal money to build, for example, that badly needed sewer system.[23] Most important to the state's development, however, were the farm-to-market road building programs and the Tennessee Valley Authority (TVA). Road building modernized the state, initially allowing farmers to haul their goods to market expeditiously; those same roads later allowed war industries to develop while making it easier for people to transport goods through the state.[24] Roads were not the only infrastructure modernized. So, too, was the Tennessee electrical grid, thanks to the TVA, which provided cheap electricity to urban and rural dwellers alike. The TVA's effect was nothing short of revolutionary; where only one in ten rural dwellers had electricity before the TVA, after it and the Rural Electrification Administration were finished, now nine in ten rural dwellers had it. Finally, the New Deal program (in this case, the Works Progress Administration) employed Sarah after the Sewell Company disbanded in 1940, paying her fifty dollars per month to run an after-school program for children in Centerville.

Even with the WPA's help, financial problems still plagued Sarah, who was now financially responsible for her mother after her father's death in 1937. Minnie Pearl became a godsend, providing extra money that Sarah used to support herself and her mother. This time in her life seems to have been a desperate one. Her four sisters all had families (Sarah remained unmarried until after World War II and never had children) and were not able to help their mother out financially. Thus, it was left to Sarah. But her desperation was not simply due to her multiple responsibilities but her age and marital status: "I had left home in a burst of optimism, and returned broke, an old maid, a *failure*."[25]

It was at a side job that Opry personnel discovered her, and she was hired in November 1940, an important time in the Opry's evolution. The show was an early example of the barn dance radio genre, in which programs modeled themselves on a rural tradition, the Saturday night dance party. Programs initially appeared in the 1920s in urban centers like Chicago (WLS's National Barn Dance started there), and catered to southern migrants longing for home. By the 1930s, however, the barn dance radio genre had emerged as a national phenomenon (there were some five hundred shows nationwide by 1939) that offered refuge from the Great Depression to primarily middle-class audiences.[26] Broadcasters intended string band music (typically guitars, fiddles, and banjos) and jokes about barnyards and city living to be a haven for that middle class from a complicated and miserable industrial world. One writer wrote of barn dance star Cousin Emmy, for example, that "Every morning the notoriously noxious air of St. Louis is purified by the natural twang of real mountaineer goings on."[27]

Stressed listeners were also soothed by a common stage image: Appalachian mothers who crooned to their babes as they wove homespun, a constructed image that lauded women's preservation of the mountain South's oral culture. On the radio, however, women crooned in soft voices to their radio children rather than to their families.[28] Many characters were some version of the Appalachian mother, for example, the Little Sunbonnet Girl, who wore sunbonnets and sang sweet songs she learned from her own mountain mother. The southern gossip was another important character on barn dance stages because she reinforced social ties among constituent members through her "sociable" interactions, thereby sustaining the community itself. Gossips used the ritual nature of radio (barn dance shows tended to appear at the same time with the same personnel) to build warm, friendly relationships with their audiences, even though listeners could be thousands of miles away and not able to respond in a meaningful way.[29] Yet even as they built friendly relationships between performers and listeners, gossips also made their characters funny by simultaneously making themselves spinsters and widows. It is unclear when that juxtaposition became popular, but spinsters and widows tended to be suspect characters in a genre that lauded married mothers. Because she posed a threat to the genre's very foundation, the link between the gossip and the old maid promised that, although a joke-cracking old maid might wink at tradition, ultimately the gossip respected and even reinforced old-time communities by promoting social interaction. Indeed, what came to be funny was the old maid's ultimate inability to be married or fit within barn dance radio's traditional community.[30]

The Grand Ole Opry was still a regional program when these images and formats became standard. Originating from radio station WSM Nashville in 1925, the show mimicked some—but not all—of the practices of the barn dance genre that had had significant success in Chicago and other northern cities.[31] It deviated somewhat from the norm by featuring performers like Uncle Dave Macon and the Fruit Jar Drinkers, who were earthier, inclined to discuss alcohol on stage (some rural southerners drank alcohol from fruit jars), and not inclined toward a polite, middle-class atmosphere. The Opry also included black performers, especially harmonica player DeFord Bailey, which was an implicit recognition of the influence of black performers on white musicians' musical development in the South. It was also an implicit recognition that black men and women were common in early country music audiences. Opry broadcasters tended to finesse Bailey's appearances; at times they hid his race, especially when he performed on the air, but he also appeared at local concerts around the South at which there was no question what race he was. Moreover, listeners from outside Tennessee knew he was black. For example, Missourian Nelda Underwood's father woke her at 11:30 p.m. every Saturday night so she could hear Bailey play his harmonica.[32] In either case, he kept appearing on stage because of his overwhelming popularity with listeners.[33] Moreover, Dave Macon, a former vaudevillian and expert banjo player, was considered by some to be black because his banjo style (called "frailing") was a distinctly black sound, acknowledging black techniques in explicit ways.[34]

The gossip–old maid character appeared alongside Bailey in the comedy stylings of Sarie and Sallie, who performed on the Opry from 1934 to 1939 and who gossiped about a variety of topics ranging from fellow performers to the Tennessee Valley Authority to a local women's club and its tendency to hold snuff-chewing contests. They spiced their dialogue with a dialect familiar to local Opry audiences, complete with homey phrases like "a man of words and not of deeds is the same as a garden full of weeds." What little remains of their act (no Opry scripts exist from the 1930s because no one ever formally wrote down shows) suggests that their topics and style mimicked daily life in the middle South that furthered the Opry's supposed authenticity.[35]

In 1939 the Grand Ole Opry, now sponsored by the R. J. Reynolds's product Prince Albert Tobacco, became part of the Saturday night lineup on the National Broadcast Corporation (NBC). Now a new group of listeners from any of NBC's 151 stations nationwide could tune in, including audiences in New York City, Boston, and Seattle—listeners who might not have been familiar with the Opry's particular charms. As a consequence, "network" men, typically New York advertisers who paid performers' salaries and therefore demanded a say in show content, mandated new rules to make the Opry palatable to this broad audience. Race was one immediate issue; show management fired DeFord Bailey since other barn dance shows did not feature black performers. Those new producers assumed, of course, that only whites tuned in, and the Opry was more than willing to buy into this pure white version of the genre, by reducing the appearance time of white performers like Dave Macon who "sounded black." The emphasis on whiteness mimicked barn dance radio's culture; Chicago WLS's National Barn

Dance and other barn dance programs had erased black and ethnic characters from the radio in the 1930s as broadcasters presented rural music and characters that were considered wholesome and moral. That wholesomeness came in part from the so-called purity of rural music, free as it was from the taint of blacks or immigrants—or so broadcasters told audiences.[36]

Jokesters were another, special target of sponsor interference. Their ad-libbing frightened advertisers, because of the risk that they would portray a product in a potentially negative light. Because sponsors demanded to see what performers—especially comedians—would say on stage before broadcast time, broadcasters scripted every on-air moment, and sponsors "cleared" or approved each script. Thus, scripts for the Grand Ole Opry from the mid-1940s do exist. Moreover, NBC broadcasters served as the intermediaries between the sponsor and a program, issuing "continuity changes," or requests to rewrite jokes because they were in "poor taste." A March 29, 1947, continuity change, for example, deleted the following joke, probably from the Duke of Paducah, Whitey Ford: "I'll never forget the April Fools day party we had last year. It's imprinted in my memory. And that ain't all. Somebody pushed me backwards, and I sat down on the hot kitchen stove and that was the seat of my troubles."[37] Sponsors and broadcasters, unsure of who exactly tuned in to their programs, tended to err on the conservative side, and thus any joke that could offend a listener (like a reference to Ford's rear end) was sanitized or axed.

Traveling units were another change, also sponsored by R. J. Reynolds. Most of the Opry performers, including Sarah, had already taken their show on the road. But no longer did they perform for local and regional audiences in town halls, school houses, or movie theaters around Tennessee, where the admission price was as likely to be dropped into a passed hat as was a ticket bought at the door. Now the goals were to pack as many people as possible into a venue, to cover the new broadcast region, and to find new, professional venues—first tent shows, county and state fairs, and theater circuits like Loews; then military camps in the United States, Panama and Germany; and eventually, Carnegie Hall and Las Vegas showrooms. The effect was to boost the Opry's popularity nationwide. Simultaneously, it exposed performers like Sarah to new audiences—and some of them had different expectations of women on stage than those in Nashville.

Using a variety of props such as clothing, her trademark greeting, and (eventually) the hat with the dangling price tag, Sarah developed Minnie into a full-fledged character on the Grand Ole Opry as these changes occurred. Typically, both she and her sister Dixie wrote her jokes, and both seem to have turned especially to the legacy of vaudevillians who defined comedy and comediennes as masculine. Sarah's comment that the first thing a comedienne gave up was her sex appeal was a conscious acknowledgment of this legacy. She then made Minnie seem like a relic, like the mountain mother, in order to fit barn dance radio's gendered foundation. Minnie seemed to be unchangeable and enduring, like those mountain mothers (albeit without having children); she was constant even though the world around her had changed. Couching the character in traditional terms, Sarah said, "She has withstood the rigors of time because she's no threat to anybody. She's not pretty. She's not sexy. She's not smart and people just sort of think they're safe with her."[38] The perception of female stability was a cherished component of barn dance tradition even as remarkable changes occurred inside and outside radio studios.

Still, Minnie did evolve as Sarah became more comfortable with the character and as her popularity grew. More and more, Minnie Pearl changed from a gentle mountain girl into a diverse and varied character who would cater to a diverse audience. The most prominent new feature was her trademark slogan—instead of saluting her audience with a shy "Howdy," the new and improved Minnie Pearl shouted out at them. "Howdee! I'm jes so proud t'be here." She then expected them to holler "Howdee!" back. She also joked about herself as an oddity (unmarried, old, ugly) and as a traditional comic figure (the "gossip" of a fictitious southern town, Grinder's Switch). Her sexuality was a prime site for jokes. In later years, Minnie was known to comment, for example, that she wore a hat so that people could tell that she was not Dolly Parton.[39] Her age was another running joke on stage. On one 1947 show, for example, she joked, "Somebody asked me my age and I said when I got to be 21 I stopped counting my age and they said, yes, but your face didn't."[40]

Displaying Minnie Pearl as an oddity was important, but focusing on her traditional community was even more so. Without a rural home place, a cast of fictitious characters, and a philosophy, she would have been meaningless to an audience who expected to hear the trials and tribulations of a familiar group of people. If Minnie was odd, she was still a stalwart in an old-time rural community. Grinder's Switch served as her primary link to the traditional past that barn dances sought to sell. A variety of rural characters peopled Grinder's Switch, more than two hundred characters that seemed to live and work in ways similar to their colonial ancestors. All of these white characters lived in that fictional world without bothersome blacks intruding on their morals and values. Hezzie (her boyfriend who never proposed to her), Aunt Ambrosy, Uncle Nabob, Brother, Unicorn Buttelscut, and a host of other characters who had "no truck with modern things" appeared regularly in Sarah's "homespun" humor. Neighborliness continued to exist in Minnie's fictitious world, where residents still played "Pin the Tail on the Donkey," pulled candy, and dipped for apples.

Catering in part to ad executives' own stereotypes of the rural South—they sometimes wrote jokes for her that featured stereotypical hillbillies—Sarah played with southern clichés in her act. If her regional audience was familiar with her characters from everyday life, her new national audiences would have been more aware of the stereotypes through Li'l Abner and other hillbilly characters. Her cast included the fictitious Brother (who was arrested once, Minnie said slyly, for driving while ignorant) and Mrs. Orson Tugwell who had "23 young'uns"—presumably evidence of their mother's rampant sexuality. Sarah juxtaposed these negative assumptions about southern life with ideas about southern rural simplicity, making the stereotypes the center of her comedy. Thus, in Sarah's world, Minnie's friends and neighbors were not only examples of wholesome behavior, but could be caricatures as well.[41]

While negative stereotypes did creep into her comedy, in keeping with the barn dance radio tradition, her emphasis remained on rural southern life as clean and wholesome, with residents who lived better, more honest lives than those who lived in cities. Indeed, some of her characters may have been sexually promiscuous hillbillies, but the majority of her characters were good moral people whose racial purity and ability to withstand constant changes made them good role models for the audience. Sarah incorporated these two assumptions into her act. No black characters ever peopled Grinder's Switch (even though it was based on a railroad switchyard near her hometown that was most definitely integrated). She also reminded audiences that modern technology was not necessarily a good thing. In one instance, she reminded her audiences that good parenting was not achieved by the latest technology, but by sound reasoning: "Link Shank's wife says she don't have no truck with modern ways o' raisin' kids. She sez she don't need no thermometers or gadgets to tell 'er how to give the young-uns a bath. She sez if they turn red, the water's too hot. If they turn blue, the water's too cold . . . and if they turn white, they sure needed a bath!"[42] In this case, rural folk offered a kind of practical wisdom that urban folk had forgotten.

In one sense, Sarah agreed with much of barn dance radio's conventional wisdom: women should be married, have families, and be pretty. Evolving into a character that challenged those conventions so explicitly caused her ultimately to construct an off-stage character, Sarah Colley Cannon, who would embrace exactly that which Minnie seemed to give up, a process intended to soothe herself (she struggled at first with becoming Minnie Pearl) as well as her audience.[43] Moreover, the Camel Caravan shows she did during World War II showed that her new national audience had multiple opinions regarding women on stage. On December 8, 1941, for example, she was heckled by drunk, scared soldiers at Randolph Field in San Antonio, Texas. The soldiers wanted to see the sexy women ("glamorous" Kay Carlisle and the all "girl" trio the Camelettes, who appeared on stage before her), not a staid, uptight old maid who told jokes about marriage. To be successful in those soldiers' eyes, Sarah had to make fun of their ideas of sexy and glamorous. One of her jokes was a testament to a lesson well-learned: "I felt so at home [coming onto the military base]. In fact, one fella told me I was the homeliest woman he'd ever seen. They had fellers to meet us at the gate and they was so cordial and so pleasant. They had my name on their sleeve. MP—Minnie Pearl. They got on the bus and searched every car until they found me."[44] The joke became so popular that it followed her from camp to camp. Soldiers yelled out, "Tell us about the MPs," and in some places, the military police rushed the stage to grab her, while others gave her their badges.[45]

The Sarah Colley Cannon character was nearly an opposite picture of Minnie Pearl. While Minnie was a rural bumpkin who could not get a man, Sarah Colley was an educated modern woman who embraced conventional roles and reassured her audiences that Minnie's challenges to tradition were merely jokes. Media showcased that dichotomy, featuring such elements as her upper-class background, her attendance at Ward-Belmont, and her job with the Sewell Company; after her marriage, the phrase "Sarah Colley Cannon, better known as Minnie Pearl," introduced her in most articles about her.[46] Both personas appeared in magazines and newspapers soon after the Opry hired her in November 1940. In a 1941 *Radio Varieties* article, for example, the author noted that Sarah was from a "family [with] above the average means," and mentioned her time at Ward-Belmont College, described as a "superb finishing school." A *Record Roundup* article published in 1947 remarked that a "College Graduate Scores on 'Opry' as Girl Hillbilly."[47]

Most importantly, the dual personality began to pay off—literally—for Sarah in terms of financial remuneration. Although it was unlikely that she ever had a Scarlett O'Hara moment where she swore she would never be hungry again, her time at Ward-Belmont influenced her definitions of "real" wealth, while her difficulties during the Great Depression solidified her desire to be financially secure. As Sarah once remarked, Minnie Pearl was a commodity to her, nothing more than a jar of peanut butter in that Minnie was something to sell. And the profits seemed endless to Sarah, whose superstar status made her quite wealthy. Sarah's mother, Fannie, also liked the stream of money that allowed Sarah to purchase "little luxuries" for her mother.[48] She recalled, "I think Mama would have liked Minnie anyway, but she certainly liked the fact that this 'country girl' had brought us the means to live more comfortably than we ever could have otherwise."[49] National fame and celebrity followed on the heels of financial success with her trademark greeting becoming part of America's political lexicon in 1948 when vice presidential nominee Alben Barkley began his nomination acceptance speech with, "Well, as Minnie Pearl would say, 'I'm just so *proud* to be here!'" Cannon later attended Barkley's inauguration as a personal guest.[50]

Two factors beyond her acting ability also contributed to her international fame. The first was her marriage to Henry Cannon in 1947. Henry came from an elite family from Franklin, Tennessee (he was descended from a former Tennessee governor), and was a graduate of Battle Ground Academy, a private school for young men in Franklin. Henry's upper-crust status was reinforced by his World War II record as a fighter pilot. Pilots were considered the elite corps during the war, and for some men becoming a pilot made it possible to shift their class status up in postwar America.[51] As Sarah recalled upon seeing her future husband in his leather flight jacket, "[D]uring World War II all the girls had become enamored of the image of the pilot—brace and steady in the air, rough and ready on the ground, *sexy*! I just melted."[52] Sarah and Henry were quietly married on February 23, 1947 (Sarah's tour schedule precluded a large wedding and more than two people at the ceremony itself). Henry quickly took over Sarah's business responsibilities, which she did not mind since she thought she lacked a business mind. She also liked the fact that Henry took charge. She wrote in her autobiography, "[T]here was never any question as to who wore the pants in our family. . . . to this day [Henry] is the unchallenged head of our household."[53]

The second factor that contributed to her fame was the emergence of Nashville as the center of the country and western music industry in the 1940s and 1950s. As historian Diane Pecknold has argued, country music began to emerge in that era as a self-conscious cultural institution with Nashville as the center of its musical, economic, and cultural production. The Grand Ole Opry and Acuff-Rose Publications, a music-publishing firm founded in 1942 and operated by Fred Rose and Opry star Roy Acuff, attracted more music industry executives to the city. The industry men who moved to the city included A&R (Artist and Record) representatives like Chet Atkins and Owen Bradley, who were local representatives of New York and Los Angeles record companies and who guided country music greats like Patsy Cline and Loretta Lynn in the 1950s and 1960s. Insider magazines such as *Pickin' and Singin' News* publicized the burgeoning industry and provided information to deejays, music industry executives, and artists alike.[54] By the late 1950s enough professionals had moved to Nashville to make a professional organization necessary; the Country Music Association became that professional organization, and its charge was to promote country and western music.

The industry included a substantial tourist business based on sites associated with the Opry, the Ryman Auditorium (the site of Opry performances from 1943 to 1974), and other country music venues such as the Country Music Hall of Fame and the Minnie Pearl and Roy Acuff Museums. Tourist-based businesses required the entrepreneurial spirit of stars who started businesses ranging from photography studios to chicken shops (Sarah's cookbook, published in 1970, was indicative of this spirit). Eventually, Nashville was branded "Music City U.S.A.," a center not only known for its country music productions, but for its vibrant tourist industry that catered to people fascinated by country music stars.[55] The effect of music tourism would be felt statewide as other music venues like Elvis Presley's home, Graceland (in Memphis), and country music star Dolly Parton's music and amusement park, Dollywood (in eastern Tennessee), became popular tourist destinations as well, making Tennessee "Music State, U.S.A." Moreover, country stars (as Dollywood suggests) ventured out from Nashville's center and built new homesteads/music venues for themselves throughout the state. Loretta Lynn's Ranch in Hurricane Mills (in western Tennessee), for example, eventually included a stage, a museum devoted to Lynn, a simulated coal mine and replica of her Butcher Holler (Kentucky) homestead, and a full service recreational vehicle (RV) park.[56]

But Sarah's ability to sell the Opry and Tennessee to outsiders had other consequences, especially when she used Minnie to promote her political views. Very little evidence remains as to what those beliefs were in specific terms, but there is some indication that Cannon was a states' rights advocate (meaning a strict segregationist with no federal intervention in states' ability to separate blacks and whites), and she certainly supported political candidates who opposed civil rights. She had a paternalistic attitude toward black men and women, believing, as many white southerners did, that African Americans were childlike and in need of a white person's firm hand to guide them. Moreover, as a southern matron, she benefited (as her mother had) from working-class black labor, both literally and symbolically. For example, Mary Cannon (no relation, as most articles about the two women pointed out quickly) was a black woman who worked for Sarah for approximately thirty years. Mary, who enjoyed some fame because she was Sarah's housekeeper, did the housework and buttressed Sarah's status as a wealthy Nashville matron, the hallmark of which was the ability to afford full-time black help.

Those beliefs fed into Sarah's contribution to states' rights candidate George Wallace's first two gubernatorial primary campaigns, yet that contribution seems to have been a last attempt at maintaining an older form of racial segregation rather than an attempt to apply the Opry's racial exclusivity offstage. Pro-segregationist forces never wished for racial exclusivity; instead, they promoted degrading positions for blacks, a view that implicitly assumed that blacks still had a place in southern culture, albeit one where their labor could be exploited exclusively for white southerners' benefit.[57] Wallace had been a racial moderate until *Brown v. Board of Education* (May 1954) and the Montgomery Bus Boycott (December 1955 to December 1956) hardened the boundaries between integrationist and segregationist forces in Alabama specifically, and in the South generally. Then, Wallace used Sarah as many southern politicians traditionally had used musicians and comedians—to lend her celebrity to his candidacy as a way of saying to voters that he was the right candidate for the job.[58] Certainly, Sarah implied, if a home-folks type character like Minnie Pearl thought he was a good candidate, then voters should cast their votes for Wallace. Thus, dressed as Minnie Pearl, she announced, "I'm as happy as a dead pig in the sunshine to introduce your next governor, George Wallace," and was pictured next to a political sign saying, "Win with Wallace."[59]

To complicate the story, Sarah earned three thousand dollars for her first Wallace appearance, and northern newspapers at least considered the Minnie Pearl character "political dynamite" for Wallace in 1958. The *Wall Street Journal* reported that the Alabama gubernatorial candidates were so similar in their segregationist beliefs (at least to a newspaper situated in New York City) that an endorsement from Minnie could be key to winning the election.[60] While this did not prove true in Wallace's first run, Minnie Pearl (and six other country music acts, all of whom were most likely paid) campaigned once again in 1962 to promote his candidacy and most likely heard his infamous segregationist statement that "I shall refuse to abide by any such illegal federal court order even to the point of standing at the schoolhouse door."[61] There is little information, of course, as to whether Sarah's politics mimicked Wallace's, although she did help Wallace once again in 1962. Being the smart woman she was, Cannon probably learned that any explicit support of segregation or integration in the media in the 1960s would not have helped her fame (or her pocketbook), so she stayed mute in public. One might also wonder if she approved of the nation's rightward political shift after Ronald Reagan's election to the presidency in 1980. Except for Reagan presenting her with the American Cancer Society's Courage Award in 1987, recognizing her unflagging support of the organization, there is no evidence they ever met. Sarah remained circumspect about her political beliefs, at least in public, into the 1980s, since to be explicit could ruin her bank account. Indeed, she owned the mansion next door to the Tennessee governor's mansion and stated that she had had good relationships with all of the governors who lived there, whether Democrat or Republican.

As it was, in the late 1960s, Sarah found a new venue to focus her attention, one that showcased her country comedy: the television show *Hee Haw*. While performing on *Hee Haw*, at the Opry, and at personal appearances in the United States and Europe, Sarah continued to promote good causes, especially breast cancer awareness. Sarah, who lost her beloved sister Dixie to breast cancer in 1967, was successfully treated for the disease herself and established the Minnie Pearl Cancer Foundation for research. She was also elected to the Country Music Hall of Fame in 1975 and continued to perform, but she began to slow down in the 1980s. In 1991 she suffered a stroke that made her a recluse until her death on March 4, 1996. The *Nashville Tennessean* fashioned an appropriate obituary: on its editorial page, the cartoon featured a halo with a price tag dangling that read "Priceless."[62]

Sarah's life as "Sarah Colley Cannon, better known as Minnie Pearl" provides us with a remarkable opportunity to examine the transformation of mass media in the 1940s and 1950s. As a performer, she was an innovator who found ways to entertain multiple audiences who would hear, watch, and enjoy her over many decades. By invoking a rural past (albeit a modern one spruced up for modern times), she brought new customers and new businesses to an evolving modern southern state previously known for rural back roads and primitive accommodations. Sarah and Minnie made indelible and enduring impressions on Tennessee's cultural landscape. When an interviewer questioned her about her two names, she laughingly said, "Well, a lot of people are two people. They just don't have a name for the other one!"[63]

NOTES

1. This is an article about a woman who performed multiple roles, and it is hard sometimes to say which person went where. Sarah named some of her roles, had multiple nicknames, and changed her name to reflect her marital status. To ease the way for the reader, when I refer to the person who controlled this process offstage, I refer to her as "Sarah." Sarah Colley (after her marriage in 1947, Sarah Colley Cannon) is the media offstage character; Minnie Pearl is the onstage character.

2. Minnie Pearl, *Minnie Pearl Cooks* (Nashville: Aurora Publishers, Inc., 1970, rev. ed. 1971), 2. Pictures of Cannon with Acuff and Jones are not paginated. Cannon's autobiography, Minnie Pearl [Sarah Colley Cannon] with Joan Dew, *Minnie Pearl: An Autobiography* (New York: Simon and Schuster, 1980), has a similar back cover. Cannon is pictured there as Mrs. Henry Cannon, "Minnie Pearl"; Sarah Colley Cannon, interview tapes, Grand Ole Opry Museum Archives, Gaylord Entertainment, Nashville (hereinafter referred to as Cannon interview tape); Clipping, Michael McCall, "How-dee!" *Nashville Banner*, November 1, 1990, C1, Minnie Pearl File, Country Music Hall of Fame (hereinafter MPF); Clipping, Bob Allen, "The Two Faces of Sarah Cannon," *Nashville! Magazine* 8, no. 7 (1980): MPF.

3. Diane Pecknold, "The Selling Sound of Country Music: Class, Culture, and the Early Radio

Marketing Strategy of the Country Music Association," in *Country Music Annual 2002*, ed. Charles K. Wolfe and James Akenson (Lexington: University of Kentucky Press, 2002), 54.

4. Ellis Nassour, *Patsy Cline: An Intimate Biography* (New York: Tower Books, 1981), 294.

5. Pearl, *Minnie Pearl*, 7.

6. Ibid., 6.

7. Ibid., 13, 16.

8. Clipping, "Rites Conducted for Mrs. T. K. Colley, 88," *The Hickman County Chronicle*, August 29, 1963, SCC.

9. Pearl, *Minnie Pearl*, 1, 11.

10. Ibid., 43.

11. Ibid., 42, 73.

12. Ibid. (italics in original), 81.

13. Ibid., 97.

14. Ibid., 96.

15. Ruth Milkman, *Gender at Work: The Dynamics of Job Segregation by Sex during World War II* (Urbana: University of Illinois Press, 1987).

16. Allen, "The Two Faces of Sarah Cannon"; Pearl, *Minnie Pearl*, 122; *Minnie Pearl: Old Times*, Video produced by Opryland USA, 1988.

17. Clipping, Sarah Cannon, "Minnie of the Early Opry Days Had a Softer, More Gentle Voice," MPF.

18. Pearl, *Minnie Pearl*, 119.

19. Clipping, Sarah Cannon, "An Alabama Country Woman Was the Model for 'Minnie,'" MPF; Pearl, *Minnie Pearl*, 122.

20. *Minnie Pearl: Old Times.*

21. Cannon interview tape, #4; Pearl, *Minnie Pearl* (italics in original), 120–30.

22. Leslie N. Sharp, "Down South to Dixie: The Development of the Dixie Highway from Nashville to Chattanooga, 1915–1940" (M.A. thesis, Middle Tennessee State University, 1993).

23. Tennessee State Library and Archives, WPA Cards.

24. A. D. Morrell, Project Control Division, to Mr. S. Tate Pease, State Work Projects Administrator, March 24, 1942, National Archives, Washington D.C., for the building of Bradyville Pike.

25. Pearl, *Minnie Pearl* (italics in original), 146.

26. My research contradicts the long-standing presumption in country music historiography that the music is primarily a soundtrack for the working class. See, for example, Bill C. Malone, *Don't Get above Your Raisin': Country Music and the Southern Working Class* (Urbana: University of Illinois Press, 2002). See Kristine M. McCusker, "Dear Radio Friend: Listener Mail and the National Barn Dance, 1931–1941," *American Studies* 39, no. 2 (1998): 173–95.

27. No author, "Cousin Emmy," *Time*, December 6, 1943, 62.

28. Jack Temple Kirby, "The Southern Exodus, 1910–1960," *Journal of Southern History* 49 (November 1983): 585, 597; Kristine M. McCusker, "Bury Me Beneath the Willow: Linda Parker and Definitions of Tradition on the National Barn Dance, 1932–1935," *Southern Folklore* 56, no. 3 (1999): 223–44.

29. Alexander Rysman, "How the 'Gossip' Became a Woman," *Journal of Communication* 27, no. 1 (1977): 176–80; Sally Yerkovich, "Gossiping as a Way of Speaking," *Journal of Communication* 27, no. 1 (1977): 192–96; McCusker, "Dear Radio Friend."

30. Virginia Foster, "The Emancipation of Pure, White Southern Womanhood," *New South* 26,

no. 1 (1971): 46–54; WSM *Family Album*, [ca. 1938], Country Music Foundation; No author, "Over the Cracker Barrel," *Rural Radio* 1, no. 6 (1938): 6, CMF.

31. See Kristine M. McCusker, *Lonesome Cowgirls and Honky Tonk Angels: The Women of Barn Dance Radio* (Urbana: University of Illinois Press, forthcoming), for a discussion of the Grand Ole Opry's northern roots.

32. Jane Smith, oral interview with author, July 20, 2005.

33. Charles Wolfe, *A Good Natured Riot: The Birth of the Grand Ole Opry* (Nashville: The Country Music Foundation and Vanderbilt University Press, 1999), 119–28.

34. Elijah Wald, *Escaping the Delta: Robert Johnson and the Invention of the Blues* (New York: Amistad, 2005), 48.

35. Ibid., 112, 230–37, quote is on page 236.

36. James Kovach to Mr. Harry T. Floyd, January 17, 1949, NBC Network Order, December 9, 1949, NBC Network Order, November 30, 1948; all in Box 360, Folder 9, NBC Papers, State Historical Society of Wisconsin, Madison, Wis. (hereinafter NBC Papers).

37. Continuity Changes, Program Department, Grand Ole Opry, March 27, 1947, February 27, 1947, March 21, 1947, February 13, 1947, February 6, 1947, NBC Papers; Wolfe, *A Good Natured Riot*, 25.

38. Ibid; "Pearls of Wisdom."

39. Ibid.

40. Minnie Pearl Joke Collection, SCC.

41. Radio Script, Prince Albert Tobacco's Grand Ole Opry, January 14, 1950, May 6, 1950, Rod Brasfield Scripts, Country Music Foundation; Radio Script, Prince Albert Tobacco's Grand Ole Opry, February 1, 1947, Minnie Pearl Scripts, Gaylord Entertainment.

42. Radio Script, Prince Albert Tobacco's Grand Ole Opry, June 17, 1950, Rod Brasfield Scripts.

43. Cannon interview tape, #6.

44. Ibid.

45. Ibid.

46. Paul Bryant, "The Belle of Grinder's Switch," *The Mountain Broadcast and Prairie Recorder* (October 1946): 5–9, 34, SCC; Minnie Pearl, "My Religion of Laughter," *Together* (August 1957): SCC.

47. Clipping, "Minnie Pearl: The Girl with the Big Future," *Radio Varieties* (January 1941): 19, SCC; Clipping, "Eight Thousand Enlisted Men (Camel Caravan Makes a Big Hit) Pack Ft. Sam Houston Service Club," *The Military News Service*, December 12, 1941, 18, MPF; Clipping, "College Graduate Scores on 'Opry' as Girl Hillbilly," *Record Roundup* (1947): MPF.

48. Pearl, *Minnie Pearl*, 225.

49. Ibid., 224.

50. Ibid. (italics in original), 249.

51. See, for example, the Dana Andrews character in the movie *The Best Years of Our Lives* (1946), which won Best Picture that year.

52. Pearl, *Minnie Pearl* (italics in original), 220–21.

53. Ibid., 232.

54. Diane Pecknold, "The Selling Sound: Country Music, Commercialism, and the Politics of Popular Culture, 1920–1974" (Ph.D. diss., Indiana University, 2002) 93–143.

55. Pecknold, "The Selling Sound," 93–94.

56. http://www.lorettalynn.com/ranch/ (accessed June 12, 2007).

57. Howard Rabinowitz, *Race Relations in the Urban South, 1865–1890* (Urbana: University of Illinois Press, 1980).

58. Dan T. Carter, *The Politics of Rage: George Wallace, the Origins of the New Conservatism, and the Transformation of American Politics* (New York: Simon and Schuster, 1995), 68–109.

59. Clipping, Eleanor Nance Hamilton, "That Minnie Pearl Is Political Dynamite," n.d., no source, SCC.

60. Clipping, Ed Cony, "Alabama Hoedown: Few Issues Split Them so Governor Candidates Lean on Hillbilly Music," *Wall Street Journal*, May 6, 1958, SCC.

61. Five photographs, SCC; Carter, *The Politics of Rage*, 90, 105.

62. *Nashville Tennessean*, March 6, 1996, 8.

63. Allen, "The Two Faces of Sarah Cannon."

Diane Judith Nash

(1938–)

A Mission for Equality, Justice, and Social Change

LINDA T. WYNN

This chapter examines the life and activism of Diane Judith Nash, a Chicago-born Fisk University student known for her leadership in the Nashville sit-in and desegregation movements of the early 1960s. Nash, a quiet college student from a black middle-class background, publicly challenged Nashville mayor Ben West and other city leaders to desegregate downtown lunch counters and, in time, became a force in the larger civil rights movement of the mid-twentieth century. She was a founding member and active participant in the Student Nonviolent Coordinating Committee (SNCC). She was also involved in a desegregation movement in Rock Hill, South Carolina, and was an architect of the 1961 Freedom Rides. While Mississippi's Freedom Summer project is attributed to SNCC activist Robert "Bob" Moses and Allard Lowenstein, its roots can be traced to Diane Nash and James Bevel, who together devised a plan for a "nonviolent army" to help Alabama blacks fight for voting rights. While the plan was unsuccessful in Alabama, Freedom Summer organizers implemented it a year later, when almost seventeen thousand African American residents of Mississippi tried to vote. Local registrars accepted only sixteen hundred of their completed applications. The gross inequities uncovered in the course of the summer highlighted the need for federal voting-rights legislation as was later enacted during the Johnson administration. It was Nash's experiences during her student years in Nashville that launched her lifelong mission for equality, justice, and social change.

Diane Nash entered the dangerous and uncertain arena of the modern civil

DIANE JUDITH NASH

April 19, 1960. Diane Nash and Reverend Kelly Smith.

Gerald Holly, photographer.

Courtesy of the *Tennessean*, Nashville, Tennessee.

rights movement, called the "Second Reconstruction" by some historians, at a crucial moment. In 1954 *Brown v. Board of Education* struck down segregated schooling, but 1960 can be considered the beginning of the end for America's system of racial segregation. It was in that year that African American college students demonstrated that nonviolence could be an effective weapon in the arsenal of the movement against calcified racial intolerance and discrimination.[1]

Although Nash was born in Chicago, she was a granddaughter of Tennessee who found her way back to her ancestral home and worked to change it into the kind of society women like Mary Church Terrell dreamed it could be.[2] Nash's maternal great-grandmother, Jane Anderson, had migrated from Mississippi to Tennessee in the late 1800s. Jane's daughter, Carrie, was born in Memphis and reared in the city during the post-Reconstruction era when black Americans lost many of the civil rights they had gained in the aftermath of the Civil War. Carrie Anderson married William H. Bolton, a courthouse porter, and the two were the parents of four children, including Diane's mother, Dorothy. Carrie worked as a seamstress for a wealthy white doctor. In his family, she observed the seemingly effortless and refined lifestyles, culture, and gentility of elite white southerners. Carrie's employers took a special interest in their seamstress because of her youth and intelligence, and perhaps also because of her fair skin. They encouraged her to see herself as special and different from other African Americans.[3]

The Boltons left Memphis in the 1920s. Like thousands of other black southerners, they migrated to Chicago to escape southern racism and in search of more economic opportunity. Carrie Bolton seemed to prefer what middle-class whites had and the way they conducted their lives. She taught her family that manners, hard work, and making a good first impression were of prime importance. Moreover, she adhered to the era's destructive stereotypes about both races: she believed that whiteness was a benefit and blackness a handicap.[4]

She was also a very strong influence in the household. When Diane was born to Leon Nash and Dorothy Bolton Nash on May 15, 1938, Bolton took care of her granddaughter and instilled in Diane a sense of her own self-worth through a game that they played almost daily. Bolton would take Diane into her arms, and say, "You're more precious to me than anything in the world."

"More precious than one hundred dollars?" Nash would ask.

"That isn't even close," Bolton would reply.

"Two hundred dollars?" the girl would say.

"Not even close," Bolton would say.

"More precious than five hundred dollars?"

"Not even close."

In the end, Diane Nash was more precious to her grandmother than all of the money in the world. Through this game, Nash learned the underlying lesson that she was of value and loved, and that she should never let anyone mistreat her.[5]

Nash's parents divorced a year or so after her birth, and her mother later married John Baker, who worked as a Pullman car waiter—one of the few prestigious and relatively lucrative careers open to African American men. Baker's income provided the family a comfortable living among Chicago's black middle class. His job also afforded him membership in one of the country's most powerful and influential black unions, the Brotherhood of Sleeping Car Porters. During World War II her stepfather and two uncles served in the military, and an aunt served in the Women's Army Corps. Yet while they fought against the ethnic intolerance of Nazi Germany during the war, Nash's family seemed to ignore their own country's racial evils. Perceiving themselves as models of black achievement, they identified as "Americans," albeit Negro Americans. They lifted themselves up through the Protestant work ethic and the moral standards, attitudes, and conduct of middle-class white Americans. However, unlike most middle-class white women, Dorothy Baker worked during the day, and Diane's maternal grandmother, Carrie Bolton, cared for the little girl during the first seven years of her life.[6] Eventually the family could afford for Dorothy to stay home and take care of the family.

Carrie Anderson Bolton was a stabilizing force in Diane Nash's young life. During these formative years, Diane repeatedly faced racial discrimination in 1940s Chicago. When she was five years old and attending St. Anselm Roman Catholic School, which was staffed by the Sisters of the Blessed Sacrament—an order that only taught people of African descent and Native Americans—one nun nonchalantly said to her, "You know that we love God in our order, because we deal with the least of God's people."

Nash attended Hyde Park High School, a public school in the midst of a racial transition. Hyde Park had a reputation as an excellent educational academy that prepared students to enter postsecondary education. It consistently placed in the highest tier in state math and Latin competitions. Diane was an honor student at Hyde Park, a member of the student council, the Girl's Athletic Association, president of the drama club, a yearbook writer, and an English tutor. But these accomplishments did not shield her from racism.

While in high school, Nash answered an advertisement for a charm school. She called the school and spoke with a man who first expressed interest in her application. However, his attitude changed when she gave her home address. Recognizing that she lived in the predominantly black section of Chicago, the interviewer asked whether she was "colored." When Nash replied that she was, he told her, "We don't have a facility for colored students." Remembering her grandmother's teachings about self-worth, Nash did not let rejections like these restrict her dreams and aspirations or define her as a person. During her high school years she was voted Senior Girl and was the recipient of the Sigma Epsilon Honors Award.[7]

After graduating from Hyde Park High School in 1956, Diane Nash entered Howard University in Washington, D.C. She enjoyed the freedom of window shopping and dining with friends at restaurants in the city. These latter facilities had been desegregated only three years earlier as a result of court challenges lodged by longtime activist Mary Church Terrell. But Diane did not enjoy these luxuries for very long. In her junior year, financial difficulties forced her to transfer to Fisk University in Nashville.

In the 1950s Nashville had a national reputation as a racially progressive community. Black Nashvillians voted and served on the police force, the fire department, city council, and board of education. Both of Tennessee's United States senators, Estes Kefauver and Albert Gore Sr., along with its U.S. congressman, J. Percy Priest, refused to sign the 1956 Southern Manifesto. The manifesto, signed by nineteen senators and seventy-seven representatives, rejected the 1954 Supreme Court decision in *Brown v. Board of Education* two years earlier. But segregation was still widespread in Tennessee, including in its "progressive" capital city.[8]

When Diane Nash arrived in her grandmother's home state she, like many other African Americans, was well aware of the violence endemic to black life in the segregated South. Nash later recalled her anger in 1955 when she saw photographs of Emmett Till, the brutally murdered fourteen-year-old youth from Chicago, in *Jet* magazine. She remembered sympathizing in 1957 with the nine young black students who were harassed as they desegregated Central High School in Little Rock, Arkansas. The students were almost the same age as she. Nashville, considered a place of refinement and culture, a regional center for education and religion, and the "Athens of the South," would become her testing ground as she entered the struggle for racial justice.[9]

In 1959, shortly after her arrival at Fisk, Nash went with a date to the Tennessee State Fair. As she later recalled, "[this] was the first time that I had encountered the blatant segregation that exists in the South. . . . signs designating 'white' or 'colored' . . . had a tremendous psychological impact on me. To begin with, I didn't agree with the premise that I was inferior, and I had a difficult time complying with it." Nash framed her experience in religious as well as political terms. For her, these signs were symbols of a sin affecting society as a whole.

She did not limit this sinfulness to specific practices or behaviors; rather, it was the nature of life in a society where mutual respect between people was ignored. The flawed nature of social life, duplicitous relationships, the emotional duality of oppressed persons; all were present in Nashville. To Nash's way of thinking, both black and white citizens were sinning every day that they allowed this evil system to exist without doing what they could to change it.[10]

However, in contrast to her response to the fair's segregated facilities, Nash recalled that her date, a southerner, did not seem taken aback or insulted. She surmised that the man "knew his place" and accepted southern racial codes. In fact, the young man questioned whether "she was truly serious about her anger." She assured him she was. Nash questioned other students at the university, only to discover that many, like her date, did not share her sense of racial injustice. However, others questioned the democratic principles of freedom, equality, and justice, or the lack thereof for black Americans. Like Diane Nash, they had come of age and been influenced by popular culture and the political pronouncements of John Kenneth Galbraith's Affluent Society; they expected to share in the American Dream, regardless of race.[11]

Nash was intensely aware of how "segregation reach[ed] into every aspect of life to oppress the Negro and rob him of his dignity in the South." It restricted public and private relationships between blacks and whites in theaters, restaurants, hotels, parks, and other public accommodations. Nash's own personal encounters with Jim Crow made her increasingly impatient for change and openly critical of the status quo, and she questioned whether anyone was really attempting to change the system.[12]

But she was not alone in her eagerness for change in the city's racial climate. In early 1958 the Reverend Kelly Miller Smith, pastor of Nashville's First Baptist Church, and other local black leaders formed the Nashville Christian Leadership Conference (NCLC), an affiliate of the Southern Christian Leadership Conference (SCLC). SCLC had been founded in 1957 by Dr. Martin Luther King Jr. and other black ministers in the aftermath of the Montgomery bus boycott. The NCLC represented many religious denominations in Nashville and was mainly concerned with combating discrimination and racial injustice in the city. Ministers felt that the organization would be more effective if it included laypersons who shared their beliefs. The NCLC developed plans for challenging the social, political, and economic problems of black Nashvillians within a Christian framework, laying a foundation for using nonviolence as a way of confronting racial segregation. Another minister, James M. Lawson, became active in the NCLC, and Smith appointed him chairman of the organization's project committee. Lawson was responsible for training NCLC supporters in the tactics of nonviolent direct protest.[13]

The 1950s was not the first time that black Nashvillians had struggled against racism. In fact, traditions of resistance dated back to the earliest contacts between blacks and whites in the town. From the establishment of Fort Nashborough in the late eighteenth century to the city's mid-twentieth-century embodiment of a New South Mecca on the banks of the Cumberland River, the struggles for racial equality had involved a variety of strategies. Through direct resistance, escape and earned manumission prior to the Civil War, and protests and petitions challenging disenfranchisement, boycotts of Jim Crow streetcars, and the creation of civil rights organizations after the war, black Nashvillians sought greater freedom. Just after the *Brown v. Board of Education* decision, Nashville attorneys Z. Alexander Looby and Avon N. Williams Jr. had filed *Robert W. Kelly et al. v. Nashville Board of Education* challenging segregation in Nashville schools. By the mid-1950s, African Americans in Tennessee in general, and Nashville in particular, were actually in what some historians consider the third phase of their movement to secure civil and human rights.[14]

From the 1950s through the 1970s the four historically black colleges and universities in the city—Fisk University, Meharry Medical College, American Baptist Theological Seminary, and Tennessee A&I State University—would play major roles in this frontal assault on Jim Crow. In the fall of 1959 a cadre of students from these institutions joined Lawson's workshops. Diane Nash joined the group after being told of the workshops by Paul LaPrad, a white exchange student at Fisk. The workshops focused on how nonviolent confrontation could overcome evil and transform a community's social order through love and forgiveness. Lawson prepared participants for direct action campaigns. Participants pretended they were sitting at lunch counters, confronting angry whites, and protecting their bodies during severe beatings. They learned how to distribute the violence across their bodies to prevent serious injury. They also learned that if nonviolence was to work, they had to be unconditionally committed to "turning the other cheek."[15]

To some student activists, including Diane Nash, Lawson's lessons seemed too idealistic. Even after attending several sessions, she was not sure of the applicability of the beliefs, concepts, and attitudes from the classroom to scenes of direct confrontation. However, as Nash later noted, "it was the only game in town." She believed her options were "either to do nothing about segregation or work with them." She was attracted to Lawson's argument that to be effective, participants had to overcome self-hatred and the sense of inferiority. Nash, whose grandmother had downplayed her black heritage, now found herself surrounded by people who were "suddenly proud to be called 'black.'" But Carrie Bolton had also taught her granddaughter to love and respect herself, and now Diane had the means to reconcile those contradictory lessons of racial ambivalence and, as she later noted, the "realization of our own worth."[16]

Early in 1959 the NCLC decided that it was time to confront the segregation of Nashville's downtown restaurants. The NCLC first attempted to negotiate desegregation with representatives of the two larger department stores, Cain-Sloan and Harvey's, but store management feared losing white customers and chose to maintain the racially segregated eating facilities. Although negotiations failed, NCLC leaders felt that the meeting had laid a foundation for future conversations, but they also felt that direct action was needed to test the stores' governing principle of racial segregation.[17]

In the fall of 1959 students attending Lawson's workshops on nonviolent direct action formed a student decision-making committee within the NCLC. Later, this student committee became the NCLC's Student Central Committee. The clarity of Nash's thought, her dedication to nonviolent direct action, and her leadership skills captured the attention of her peers, who elected her to the central committee. Two days after Thanksgiving, on Saturday, November 28, the activists met at Harvey's Department Store. The group's plan was straightforward: enter the store, make a purchase, then proceed to the designated lunch counter and request service. If, or when, they were denied service they were to leave. When a server told the demonstrators that the store did not serve blacks, Nash asked to see the manager, who explained that "it is our policy not to serve colored people here." On December 5, as Christmas shoppers crowded into the downtown stores, another group of students targeted the more upscale Cain-Sloan department store. The students, including Diane Nash, purchased goods, attempted to sit down at the lunch counters, but encountered the same response.[18]

Lawson's workshops on nonviolent protest continued while the NCLC, based on their findings in November and December, planned to begin full-scale sit-ins in early 1960. However, on February 1, 1960, before the Nashville students could initiate their demonstrations, four students from North Carolina Agricultural and Technical College—with no plan or preparation—drew national media attention by staging a sit-in in Greensboro. NCLC leaders wanted the Nashville students to wait to begin their own action until they had arranged for lawyers, medical personnel, and money for bailing students out of jail. But twelve days after Greensboro, 124 student demonstrators entered three Nashville five-and-dime stores (Kress's, McClellan's, and Woolworth's).[19]

When the students entered the stores, they were composed, well mannered, well dressed, and respectful. Nash later noted that although they gave no apparent indication of being afraid, many were indeed frightened. They also struggled to keep from laughing at the stunned, panicky reaction of white store employees and customers who acted "as if these well-dressed young people were 'some dreadful monster(s) . . . about to devour them all.'" Nash described how "waitresses dropped dishes, cashiers broke down in tears, an elderly white woman almost had a seizure when she opened the door of a store's 'white' ladies room and found two young black women inside. Throwing up her hands, she screamed, 'Oh! Nigras everywhere!'" Although the students were not served, no one attacked, and they left without incident. Soon after the February 13 sit-in, students selected a leader for their NCLC committee. The leader acted as liaison between adult leaders and the students.[20]

Nash demonstrated strong leadership skills in the early sit-ins. She seemed tireless and intrepid, but this masked her fears and concerns for her own safety and that of the other demonstrators. After her election to the central committee, she said to herself, "this is Tennessee and white people down here are mean. We are going to be coming up against men who are white Southern men who are forty . . . fifty and sixty years old, who are politicians, and judges, and owners of businesses, and I am twenty-two years old. What am I doing! And how is this little group of students my age going to stand up to these powerful people?"[21]

The youthful protesters elected Nash as the chair of the NCLC's Student Central Committee. Her ascent to a position of leadership within the Nashville movement was atypical for a woman, considering the overall prevalence of patriarchal leadership models in American society. Traditionally, whether in business, politics, religion, or other associated affiliations, including civil rights organizations, men led while women served in supporting roles. For example, in Montgomery, Alabama, Jo Ann Robinson, president of the Women's Political Council (WPC), played a central role at the start of the 1955 bus boycott. The WPC produced the leaflets that spread information about the protest. Yet Robinson and the WPC were soon relegated to the margins of leadership while ministers such as Dr. Martin Luther King Jr. were thrust into more visible positions. Longtime activist Ella Baker was a key figure in the NAACP and SCLC from the 1940s through the 1950s, but she disapproved of top-down models of leadership. She eventually broke with the SCLC in favor of more grassroots organizational structures. In several other instances, women were influential leaders in the civil rights struggle. The NAACP's Daisy Bates was instrumental in organizing and implementing the 1957 Little Rock school desegregation. Septima Clark worked with the NAACP, YWCA, Community Chest, women's clubs, and Tennessee's Highlander Folk School. Clark's citizenship education programs at Highlander were attended by other female activists like Rosa Parks and Fannie Lou Hamer. Ruby Doris Smith-Robinson worked with Diane Nash in demonstrations in Rock Hill, South Carolina, and went on to leadership positions in SNCC. Historian Belinda Robnett notes that although she had no formal title, Smith-Robinson was in charge of "hiring and firing volunteers and signing checks for dispersal to various SNCC projects." All of these women were on the front line of the movement in their respective locales; however, the organizations followed the prevailing social paradigms of gender roles and gave little public recognition to their activities.[22]

On February 18, five days after Nashville's first real sit-in, approximately two hundred students, including Nash, held the second sit-in. Again, they met no violent resistance. But there were other reactions. Store owners inundated city officials with complaints that the demonstrations were causing white customers to stay away from the retail district. Officials asked the students to discontinue their protests and threatened to no longer respond moderately. Mayor Ben West had promised the merchants that some arrests would be allowed if the students failed to desist. Nine days later, in the midst of a snowstorm, the students staged a third sit-in. More than four hundred students took seats at the various lunch counters in downtown stores. This time they were beaten with fists and clubs, repeatedly knocked down, stomped, spit on, and burned with cigarettes. The passive resisters were at the mercy of their attackers, and Nashville had become, according to David Halberstam (at the time a young reporter), "A Good City Gone Ugly."[23]

Nashville police officers focused their attention on the demonstrators, not the whites who attacked them. One policeman shouted, "Okay, all you nigras, get up from the lunch counter or we're going to arrest you." When no student responded, the police arrested all of them for disorderly conduct. They were paraded through a crowd of hostile whites to waiting paddy wagons. But as police removed the protesters, others immediately took their places at the lunch counters. Another policeman approached Nash and politely requested that she and those with her leave their seats. They all refused. "All right, all right," he said. "That's it! You've been warned! You're all under arrest!" This was the first time Nash had been arrested; with eighty-one companions she faced humiliating physical searches, fingerprinting, and confinement. But Nash's fear turned to anger when the two white policemen who were fingerprinting her made disparaging remarks about her fellow protestors. She later recalled asking herself, "Who were they to judge her and her friends because they attempted to eat a crummy Woolworth's hamburger?" She completed the booking process and walked away with a clearer understanding of what she was doing and why she was participating in civil rights struggle. Like other students arrested, Nash was released on bail that evening.[24]

Trials for the students began the following Monday, February 29. More than twenty-five hundred observers gathered in and outside of the Nashville courthouse as attorneys from the black community defended the demonstrators. They were found guilty and each was fined fifty dollars, which they refused to pay because, as Diane Nash told the judge, "if we pay these fines we would be contributing to and supporting the injustice and immoral practices that have been performed in the arrest and convictions of the defendants." The demonstrators, including Nash, were sentenced to thirty days in jail, and city officials put them to work shoveling snow, cleaning city streets, and cleaning the courthouse.[25]

But jailing the students failed to quash the protests. Mayor Ben West, a Democrat and a political moderate who had courted black votes in the 1958 election, proposed a compromise: if the demonstrations ceased, he would release the jailed students and appoint a biracial committee to consider steps to desegregate the downtown stores' lunch counters. Nash and the other students agreed to the proposal and were released. A committee formed on March 3 held discussions with leaders from Fisk, Tennessee A&I State, and American Baptist Theological Seminary. Students from these institutions agreed unofficially to call off the sit-ins and give the committee a chance to work.[26]

In spite of the agreement, Nash and her cadre of students were not content to wait for the committee's findings. After her release she and other students sat in at the lunch counter at Nashville's Greyhound bus terminal. As in the previous sit-ins, the young protestors met resistance and were arrested. But this time they were booked on state charges of conspiracy to obstruct trade and commerce—more serious than the local disorderly conduct charges. On Wednesday, March 16, four students from Fisk University entered the segregated Post House Restaurant in the Greyhound bus terminal, took seats, and placed orders. A waitress served the students, but the group was beaten by angry white bystanders.[27]

Demonstrations and protest marches resumed on March 25 and continued amid increasing violence and racial strife. Nothing illustrated the unrest in the city more than the April 19 bombing of the home of black city councilman Z. Alexander Looby, the students' attorney. Immediately after the early morning attack, Nash and other angry demonstrators organized a mass march to City Hall and sent a telegram to the mayor asking for a meeting. Mayor West met the three thousand black and white citizens on the steps of City Hall. The Reverend C. T. Vivian read a statement in which he passionately articulated the outrage of the community about the bombing. When West attempted to reply, Vivian admonished him about the evils of segregation. Pleading for peace, the mayor said, "You all have the power to destroy this city. So let's not have any mobs." He further stated that he would enforce the laws without prejudice, but that he had no authority to force restaurant owners to serve anyone they did not want to. "We are all Christians together. Let us pray together." One student quickly rejoined, "How about eating together?"[28]

At that point, Diane Nash stepped forward with a list of questions for the mayor. She and the others wanted to know if he would use the standing of his office "to appeal to the citizens to stop racial discrimination." He replied, "I appeal to all citizens to end discrimination, to have no bigotry, no bias, no hatred." Nash asked, "Do you mean that to include lunch counters?" Infuriated at her persistence, he disparagingly replied, "Little lady, I stopped segregation seven years ago at the airport when I first took office, and there has been no trouble since." Nash stood her ground as the mayor told the crowd all that had been done for Nashville's black community. She asked, "Mayor West, do you feel it is wrong to discriminate against a person solely on the basis of their race or color? Do you recommend that lunch counters be desegregated?" West responded, "Yes."[29]

The front-page headline in the *Nashville Tennessean* the following morning read, "Integrate Lunch Counters—Mayor." The same day, Dr. Martin Luther King Jr. came to Nashville and spoke at Fisk University, where he addressed an over-capacity crowd. King called the Nashville movement "the best organized and the most disciplined in the Southland." He praised Nash, Bernard LaFayette Jr., James Bevel, John Lewis, and others for their work. "I came to Nashville not to bring inspiration," King said, "but to gain inspiration from the great movement that has taken place in this community."[30]

But the student sit-ins were not the only catalysts for change in Nashville. Economic realities were also at work. Fisk University professor Vivian Henderson estimated that blacks in Nashville poured approximately $50 million a year into the coffers of white businesses. As white customers moved to the suburbs, downtown merchants became more dependent on black customers. In April 1960 Rev. Smith and Professor Henderson organized a boycott of downtown merchants just before Easter, one of the busiest shopping seasons. If they were successful, there would be "No Fashions for Easter." Black Nashvillians mobilized the boycott in a forceful display of unity with the students. They sustained it for almost seven weeks. By the beginning of that April Nashville department stores were virtually empty, as fearful whites also stayed away. Other blacks also joined in what Henderson called an "economic withdrawal," as a show of support for the student demonstrators. Some sympathetic white women mounted their own form of protest by going to their favorite stores and turning in their credit cards. As he looked at the deserted downtown streets, one store merchant commented that "You could roll a bowling ball down Church Street and not hit anyone these days." Downtown retail merchants lost approximately 20 percent of their business. Empty downtown streets and empty cash registers caused merchants to consider dismantling segregation in Nashville's retail district. "No Fashions for Easter" had achieved its goal.[31]

As the student sit-ins and the Easter boycott continued, Nashville businessmen met to discuss their predicament. *Time* magazine described most of the store owners as "pocket book integrationists," more committed to their economic bottom line than they were to the city's proscriptive system of racial segregation. They did not want to become catalysts for social change, but the disruption of business and the April boycott made it economically unsound for them to carry on business as usual. So they reluctantly negotiated with leaders from the black community—the Student Central Committee. Diane Nash, who chaired the committee, was chosen to be one of the negotiators. Together they worked out a plan to begin the desegregation of Nashville's lunch counters. Only small groups of black customers at a time would ask for service at the lunch counters, and store employees would serve them. Plainclothes policemen would be on hand to take care of any trouble that might develop, and a corps of white United Church Women would mingle with those seeking service to give an "appearance of normalcy" to other shoppers and onlookers. The plan unfolded as written, and Nashville became the first major southern city to desegregate its downtown lunch counters.[32]

The sit-ins in Nashville, Greensboro, and other southern college towns fired the imagination of older civil rights organizers. Ella Baker, the SCLC's acting director and a longtime community activist, called students together from all of the sit-in movements to coordinate their actions, broaden their efforts to cover all forms of segregation, and give them a stronger voice in the struggle. The student activists met at Shaw University in Raleigh, North Carolina, over the Easter weekend (April 15–16, 1960). The result was the creation of SNCC. Because of the success of the students in the Nashville movement, their understanding of the direct nonviolent philosophy, discipline, and command of the language of nonviolence, many thought the elected leader for the organization should come from Nashville. Nash had been the spokesperson for Nashville's Student Central Committee, had worked with the overall leadership in the Nashville movement, and had demonstrated leadership skills. She was considered a favorite as the election drew near. However, when the votes were tallied, her fellow Fisk graduate Marion Barry was elected to lead the organization. Gender discrimination seemed to be a key factor in denying Nash the opportunity to head this new student-centered civil rights organization. As John Lewis, a member of the Nashville student group, later noted, "Diane was a devoted leader . . . but she was the wrong sex . . . [at a time when there] was a desire to emphasize and showcase black manhood."[33]

With the exception of her leadership role in 1960, the issue of gender discrimination was Nash's constant companion during her participation with both SNCC and the SCLC. However, she headed several SNCC initiatives over the next few years. She developed a reputation that made it impossible for men in SNCC not to acknowledge her leadership and take her seriously. A steadfast advocate of nonviolent direct action, Nash took its tenets of truth and love seriously. Male leaders at first tolerated Nash but, as she became more assertive—especially during the Freedom Rides—and interacted with others in the movement, including Dr. King and SCLC, these same leaders began to trivialize her role.[34] The Reverend Andrew Young later compared Nash's contributions to those of a pastor's wife: "No small measure of what we saw as Jim's [James Bevel, Diane's husband] brilliance was due to Diane's rational thinking and influence. The preachers of SCLC were not advocates for women's equality at this stage of our moral and political development. . . . As in the traditional church structure, a preacher's wife might direct the choir, run the Sunday school, and chair the women's fellowship. . . . It is not to our credit that we followed that model with Diane."[35]

In February of 1961 Nash was among a group of SNCC students who participated in a Rock Hill, South Carolina, protest for desegregation. After being arrested, Nash and the other students refused to pay bail, and the Nashville phrase "jail—no bail" became the national movement's rallying cry. Sentenced to thirty days in the York County jail, Nash reaffirmed her commitment to the tenets of nonviolence. In a March 8, 1961, correspondence from the jail that was published as a letter to the editor of the *Rock Hill Herald*, Nash wrote, "We are trying to help focus attention on a moral question . . . the principle of racial inferiority has been challenged . . . let us truly love one another, and under God, move toward a 'redeemed community.'"[36]

Reflecting her belief that one participates in redeeming society as a religious responsibility, Nash asserted that the purpose of any nonviolent demonstration was to show people how evil segregation was in order to change their hearts. This change would ultimately bring about a climate in which all people were treated as people, in which there was an appreciation of the dignity of humanity, and in which each individual was free to grow and produce to his fullest capacity.[37]

After her release from the York County jail, Nash contemplated whether or not to return to her studies. Her experiences had sharpened her perception of the difference between the world outside of academia and the more sterile academic environment that seemed to acquiesce to segregation. To Nash's way of thinking, higher education was more about seeking degrees and titles than learning about humanity and ethics. Soon after the South Carolina demonstrations, she decided to leave Fisk to work in the movement full-time. She earned twenty-five dollars a week working for both SNCC and SCLC, and rented a room at the Nashville YWCA.[38]

Although no longer attending the university, Nash remained a staunch supporter and leader of the students who were the heart of the Nashville movement. She was one of the chief architects of the "stand-in" protests in Nashville's segregated movie theaters. But in the early 1960s Nash shifted from the Nashville student movement to a position of leadership in the struggle to desegregate southern bus terminals, and finally into full-time civil rights work with SNCC. She realized that the movement in which she had played an integral part represented more than giving African Americans the right to eat a hamburger, enter a theater, or occupy a seat on its main floor. Nash recognized that she and the other student activists were challenging the lack of respect and dignity accorded African Americans as human beings.[39]

Two months after Nash returned to Nashville from South Carolina, James Farmer, director of the Congress of Racial Equality (CORE), launched a "Freedom Ride" modeled after CORE's 1947 Journey of Reconciliation. During the Journey of Reconciliation an interracial group of men had traveled on buses throughout the upper South to test the 1946 *Morgan v. Virginia* Supreme Court decision, which mandated desegregation of interstate buses. Fourteen years after the Journey of Reconciliation, CORE's Freedom Riders tested the court's decision in *Boynton v. Virginia* (1960), which extended the court's earlier decision to include all interstate transportation facilities—terminals, waiting rooms, restaurants, and other amenities. As many southern states ignored these Supreme Court decisions, Farmer and CORE were resolute in making both the South and the new Kennedy administration recognize that the Court's decision in the *Boynton* case could not be disregarded.[40]

Although not involved in the initial planning or execution of the southern "Freedom Rides," Diane Nash became a driving force in these protests. On May 4, 1961, CORE sent an interracial group of thirteen demonstrators (seven black men, three white men, and three white women) on a two-week trip through the South from Washington, D.C., to New Orleans to test the integration of the region's buses. CORE officials notified the United States Justice Department and the Federal Bureau of Investigation (FBI) of their schedule. The FBI transmitted this information to the local police forces in Alabama, who then shared it with the Ku Klux Klan.[41] The CORE group encountered only a few problems during their first week of travel. But when they reached Anniston, Alabama, on May 14, the Freedom Riders were attacked by a mob of more than one hundred angry whites. The demonstrators were beaten and their bus firebombed. They were attacked again when they reached Birmingham.[42]

Violent attacks on the Freedom Riders focused national and international attention on the brutality of segregation. When Nash heard about the assaults and that CORE leader James Farmer was being pressured by the Kennedy administration to stop the protests, she decided it was time to act. Farmer and others—including Rev. Fred Shuttlesworth, John Seigenthaler from the Justice Department, and Assistant Attorney General Burke Marshall—warned her of the dangers of continuing the "Freedom Rides," but Nash concluded that the protests had to continue.[43]

Diane Nash felt that the civil rights movement had reached a critical point, and that a decision to discontinue protests in the face of escalating racial violence would determine the future effectiveness of the movement and slow the pace of change for years to come. The Nashville movement had been her proving ground and had convinced her of the power of nonviolence over violence. But the violence in Alabama tested the resolve of all civil rights activists: while they professed belief in a nonviolent struggle, did they have the capacity, fortitude, resilience, and commitment to put their lives on the line? For Nash, the answer was a determined "yes." Nash contacted Farmer to see if he objected to some of the Nashville students going to Birmingham to continue the Freedom Rides. Although he cautioned her about the dangers the students would face and warned her that a bloodbath was probable in Birmingham, Nash would not let violence undermine the nonviolent struggle. James Farmer finally gave in to her pressure, and Nash and her group of activists joined the Freedom Riders.[44]

Nash also phoned Dr. Martin Luther King Jr. and urged him to join the Freedom Riders. She even drove to Atlanta with Rodney Powell, who had served with her on the Nashville Negotiating committee, in an attempt to convince King that he had to participate. But King refused to become involved. His advisors felt that angry white segregationists, who had already targeted him, might make good on their threats. On May 17, 1961, the seventh anniversary of the *Brown* decision, recruits left Nashville, Tennessee, for Birmingham, Alabama.

Nash, who had been chosen to head the Freedom Ride Coordinating Committee, stayed behind to organize the protests. Her first order of business was to secure funds to support the student project. She and other students met with members of the NCLC who, like Farmer, at first tried to persuade them to abandon the project. Then, realizing the students were committed to the Freedom Rides, he reluctantly provided the money they needed. Ten students—two whites and eight blacks—were chosen to participate.[45]

After the students boarded an early morning Greyhound bus, Nash called SNCC and SCLC leaders in Atlanta and her contacts in the Justice Department to inform them that the students from Nashville were continuing the ride. Federal officials anxiously sought a way to rein in Nash and the Freedom Riders. But, feeling no allegiance to the Kennedy administration, Nash refused to alter her position. When she was warned again about the dangers the group faced, she responded, "Then others will follow them."[46]

Although Nash would not be deterred from continuing the Freedom Rides, she was troubled by the possibility that the students, many of whom were her close friends, might be injured or even killed in Birmingham. In preparation for their journey, the group had even made out their wills and, as Nash later recounted, "A few . . . gave me sealed letters to be mailed if they were killed." When the Nashville students arrived in the Birmingham Greyhound bus station, the city's commissioner of public safety, Eugene "Bull" Conner, ordered them taken to the Birmingham jail. Nash called Assistant Attorney General Burke Marshall in Washington to ask why the Birmingham police were holding the Freedom Riders in custody. The following night, Conner released them at the Alabama state line. The students notified Nash of their whereabouts, and she sent sit-in leader Leo (known today as Kwame) Lillard to pick them up and transport them back to Birmingham. Within days, more Freedom Riders boarded buses, undeterred by mob assaults in Birmingham or the violence that probably awaited them at Montgomery's bus terminal.[47]

In Montgomery, the Freedom Riders were confronted by the Ku Klux Klan. Dr. King, who had refused Nash's initial request to join the Freedom Riders, and James Farmer flew to Montgomery from Atlanta, and Nash came from Nashville as soon as she knew the whereabouts of all of the students. Nash, King, Farmer, and other local and national movement leaders met at the Reverend Ralph Abernathy's First Baptist Church. From the meeting, King spoke on the phone to Attorney General Robert F. Kennedy, who asked him to end the rides so that the administration could gain time to resolve the crisis. Although King agreed, when Farmer consulted Nash, her answer was an unequivocal "No." "We can't stop it now," she responded, "right after we've been clobbered." Bolstered by her resolve, Farmer asked King to "please tell the attorney general that we have been cooling off for 350 years. If we cool off any more, we will be in a deep freeze. The Freedom Ride will go on."[48] Although thankful that King conveyed Farmer's unequivocal message that the Freedom Ride would continue, Nash mused about what might have taken place had the decision been left to the movement's male leadership.[49]

In early June 1961 Nash and others on the Coordinating Committee went to Washington to meet with Attorney General Kennedy and Assistant Attorney General Marshall. Kennedy told the students that the Freedom Rides were not accomplishing their desired outcomes and that if they wanted to desegregate the South, they should change their tactics and move from direct action protests to black voter registration. The administration would lend its support and protection, and thousands of dollars from charitable foundations interested in upholding civil rights would be forthcoming. Government officials also promised to make sure that male students working on voter registration would be exempt from the draft.[50] But Nash was skeptical of the administration's intent. As she later explained: "It was direct action that got us to the point where we had the country's as well as the Kennedys' attention. The Kennedy administration had done their best to try to stop us from continuing the Freedom Ride. It was quite obvious to us that if we allowed SNCC to become dependent on the money that the Kennedys would make available to us that we would be ceding a great deal of control of the movement to them, an entity far less committed than we to ending segregation."[51]

The Freedom Rides continued for the next four months with Diane Nash in the forefront. She and the tightly knit group of trained student activists were determined, and they finally forced the national government into action. On September 22, 1961, the Interstate Commerce Commission formulated regulations implementing *Boynton v. Virginia*, the Supreme Court decision prohibiting racial segregation in train and bus terminals.

Nash became chair of SNCC's direct action division. Flush with victory, SNCC tackled voter registration on its own terms in Mississippi, the most racially segregated state in America. Nash and fellow activist James Bevel also became romantically involved, and in the fall of 1961 the two married and moved to Jackson, Mississippi. They were effective organizers of the movement in the Deep South. But no one was prepared for the viciousness of Mississippi's response. Segregationists in the "Magnolia State" fought with every weapon in their arsenal—from physical and verbal attacks and incarcerations to burnings and killings.

Nash helped organize the Ruleville meeting where activist Fannie Lou Hamer joined the Mississippi movement for civil rights, and Nash was instrumental in teaching nonviolent direct action to high school students in Mississippi. In May 1962 Nash was arrested for these actions and charged with contributing to the delinquency of minors. Although she was pregnant with her first child, Nash was convicted and sentenced to two years in prison. In keeping with the student movement's "jail—no bail" principle, she opted to serve her prison sentence. "This will be a black baby born in Mississippi; whether I am in jail or not, he will be in prison. . . . I believe that if I go to jail now it may help hasten the day when my child and all children will be free—not only on the day of their birth but for all of their lives." Widely circulated in the black press, Nash's pronouncements stunned those involved in the movement as well as Mississippi judicial authorities. In an attempt to keep her from becoming one of the movement's martyrs, Hinds County Judge Russell Moore refused to execute his earlier two-year sentence, and instead jailed Nash for ten days for failure to move from the "white side" of the courtroom.

On August 5, 1962, Nash gave birth to her first child, daughter Sherrilynn. Two years later, on May 15, she gave birth to her son Douglass. Now a mother, Diane Nash Bevel was caught between caring for her young children and continuing to be active in the civil rights movement. She eventually left her public leadership roles for a new role as a full-time mother. For her, there could be no great personal achievement if she gave herself over to the movement and two children suffered because of her absence.[52]

But Diane Nash remained an astute, behind-the-scenes tactician. Along with her husband, Nash conceptualized and planned the initial strategy for the 1965 Selma, Alabama, Right-to-Vote campaign that helped bring about the Voting Rights Act of 1965. Reacting to the murder of Jimmy Lee Jackson during a voting rights demonstration in Marion, Alabama, Nash and Bevel proposed a protest march from Selma to Montgomery to confront Governor George Wallace. They envisioned a statewide campaign of protests, voter education, voter registration drives, and mock elections. Through a carefully orchestrated series of events, they planned to draw attention to the brutal forces of repression—notably Selma's Sheriff Jim Clark—thereby pushing the new president, Lyndon Johnson, to introduce new voting rights legislation. As her husband coordinated the escalating demonstrations, Nash oversaw the day-to-day work of canvassing the black communities for support and volunteers.[53]

Diane Nash also participated in the antiwar, antiapartheid, and feminist movements. Her focus in all of these domains remained consistent—for the human rights of equality, dignity, and self-determination. Disturbed by the "suffering of innocent people who were being killed," she believed the Vietnam

War was not only immoral but racist. In 1966 she was part of a small group of American women who spent a month in North Vietnam. The group hoped that the tactics employed by the antiwar movement could bring some relief to the war zone. But Nash's marriage was crumbling as her activism continued, and she made the decision to end the marriage. The couple divorced in 1968, and Nash became a single parent rearing two children, ages seven and five, with little or no financial resources.[54]

"There was a part of me that was terrified," she said later. "But there was a part of me that told myself, yes you can do it because you have to do it! Because your kids have to eat." She supported herself and her children through a number of jobs in community service organizations, lectures on college campuses across the country, and employment in real estate. While Nash remained committed to the goals of the civil rights movement and believed that its methodology could be applied to other human rights movements, she understood that she had a more important role on the world stage—that of being parent and provider for her two young children. Though apprehensive, Nash summoned the same tenacity and inner resolve to this personal crisis that she had used to confront racism and violence during civil rights demonstrations.[55]

Diane Nash continued advocating for political, social, and economic justice even after she formally left the leadership of the civil rights movement. As she noted in a 2005 interview, "There is still a great deal of racism in this country. . . . Blacks are still far from being on par with whites in education, employment, income level, housing, and access to preventative health care." She has been an advocate for tenants' rights, housing and welfare reform, feminism, and antiwar movements. She has also lectured in classrooms and other forums, and her experiences have been recounted in books and documentaries. Like many veterans of the twentieth-century civil rights struggles, Nash continues to comment on the movement's legacy and the applicability of its values and strategies to twenty-first-century issues. In January 2007, Nash and fellow activists John Lewis, James Lawson, and C. T. Vivian joined John Seigenthaler, an aide to Attorney General Kennedy in the early 1960s, on a journey retracing segments of the 1961 Freedom Ride. The group accompanied a caravan of four buses carrying one hundred students, historians, and college administrators from Nashville area colleges and universities from Nashville to Montgomery and on to Birmingham. In many ways this third "Journey for Reconciliation" (forty years after CORE's first journey) brought together past and present—to help a new generation of students understand what motivated young people like Diane Nash to accept the burden of leadership.

Five months later, on May 7, 2007, Fisk University awarded Diane Judith Nash an Honorary Doctorate in Humane Letters in recognition of the contributions and personal sacrifices she made in the struggles for racial justice. An unshakeable sense of self-worth given her by her grandmother, and an abiding religious faith, were at the center of Nash's activism. As she later recalled, "I felt that all of God's people should be treated with respect and dignity, and that segregation was disrespectable." For Nash, the essence of the problem of racism was the failure of white Americans to acknowledge their mutual humanity with black Americans. If America was truly to be a great democratic nation, relegating black Americans to second-class citizenship had to be resisted with courage and contested with moral authority. Although young and scared when she participated in the sit-ins, freedom rides, and voting rights campaigns, Nash met violence with nonviolence and hate with love on her mission for equality, justice, and social change.

NOTES

1. The modern civil rights movement refers to that period beginning with the 1954 decision by the United States Supreme Court in *Brown v. Board of Education* and waning after Congress passed the 1957 Civil Rights Act. According to Alton Hornsby Jr., this ten-year period was a resurgence of the progress aborted by the end of Reconstruction in the 1870s and 1880s. The attainments and the advancements that emerged were so consequential that numerous people believed that the period could be termed the "Second Reconstruction." See Alton Hornsby Jr., *African American History: Significant Events and People from 1619 to the Present* (Detroit: Gale Research, 1991), xxxiv–xxxv; C. Van Woodward states, "This historic movement falls into two fairly distinctive periods divided by the Supreme Court decisions of 1954 and 1955 on segregation in public schools. In the first period, the executive and judicial branches of government took initiative in inaugurating reform, while Congress and public opinion remained largely unresponsive. In the second period, Civil Groups responded with direct action that eventually aroused public support and stirred Congress into unprecedented and effective action." See C. Van Woodward, *The Strange Career of Jim Crow* (New York: Oxford University Press, 1955), 135.

2. For more on Mary Church Terrell, see in this volume Cherisse Jones-Branch, "Mary Church Terrell: Revisiting the Politics of Race, Class, and Gender."

3. David Halberstam, *The Children* (New York: Random House, 1998), 146–48.

4. A poignant depiction of this color-based social hierarchy is presented in the classic 1959 motion picture and social drama *Imitation of Life*. The first version was released in 1934 and was based on a best-selling novel by Fannie Hurst.

5. Rosetta E. Ross, *Witnessing and Testifying: Black Women, Religion, and Civil Rights* (Minneapolis: Fortress Press, 2003), 166.

6. Diane Nash, interview with author, Nashville, January 10, 2005; Darlene Clark Hine, Elsa Barkley Brown, and Roslyn Terborg-Penn, eds., *Black Women in America: An Historical Encyclopedia* (Bloomington: Indiana University Press, 1994), 834; Halberstam, *The Children*, 146–47; Ross, *Witnessing and Testifying*, 165; Reavis Mitchell and Jessie Carney Smith, "Diane Nash: Civil Rights Activist, Educator," in *Notable Black American Women*, ed. Jessie Carney Smith (Detroit: Gale Pub-

lishing, 1992), 796; Lynn Olson, *Freedom's Daughters: The Unsung Heroines of the Civil Rights Movement from 1830 to 1970* (New York: Scribner's, 2001), 153.

7. Nash interview, January 10, 2005; Halberstam, *The Children*, 147–48.

8. *District of Columbia v. Thompson Co.*, 346 U.S. 100 (1953); Kyle Longley, *Senator Albert Gore, Sr., Tennessee Maverick* (Baton Rouge: Louisiana State University Press, 2004), 123–24.

9. Fred Powledge, *Free At Last? The Civil Rights Movement and the People Who Made It* (Boston: Little Brown, 1991), 207.

10. Henry Hampton and Steve Fayer, with Sarah Flynn, *Voice of Freedom: An Oral History of the Civil Rights Movement from the 1950s through the 1980s* (New York: Bantam, 1990), 55; Diane Nash, "Inside the Sit-ins and the Freedom Rides: Testimony of a Southern Student," in *The New Negro*, ed. Mathew H. Ahmann (Notre Dame, Ind.: Fides, 1961), 49; Powledge, *Free At Last?* 208: Ross, *Witnessing and Testifying*, 168, 187.

11. Powledge, *Free At Last?* 208.

12. Nash, "Inside the Sit-ins and the Freedom Rides," 4.

13. Guy Carawan, "The Nashville Sit-in Story," Folkways Records (New York, 1960), album notes provided by the Reverend Kelly Miller Smith Sr.

14. The lawsuit filed by several African American families in 1955 to desegregate the Nashville public schools dramatically changed education patterns and produced much heated discussion. The longest running case in Tennessee history, *Kelly v. Board of Education* was prompted by the U.S. Supreme Court decision in *Brown v. Board of Education*, which outlawed the separate system of white and black schools nationally. Z. Alexander Looby and his partner Avon N. Williams Jr. litigated most of the civil rights cases in Tennessee. According to Bobby L. Lovett's *The Civil Rights Movement in Tennessee: A Narrative* (Knoxville: University of Tennessee Press, 2005), African Americans in Tennessee were in the third phase of a civil rights movement that had begun around 1935.

15. John Lewis and Michael D'Orso, *Walking with the Wind: A Memoir of the Movement* (New York: Simon and Schuster, 1998), 74–78.

16. Powledge, *Free At Last?* 208; Olson, *Freedom's Daughters*, 155.

17. Carawan, "The Nashville Sit-in Story"; Don Doyle, *Nashville since the 1920s* (Knoxville: University of Tennessee Press, 1985), 245; Lewis, *Walking with the Wind*, 88–89.

18. Lewis, *Walking with the Wind*, 88–89.

19. According to a study by the Southern Regional Council, between February 1 and March 31, 1960, major sit-ins, protests, and activity of a similar nature occurred in sixty-nine cities. See *Southern School News*, Southern Regional Council, April 1, 1960. "Phone Call Sparked Sit-ins, Says Lawson," *Nashville Tennessean*, March 21, 1960; Jim Sessions and Sue Thrasher, "A New Day Begun: An Interview with John Lewis," *Southern Exposure* 4 (Fall 1976): 19; Aldon Morris, *The Origins of the Civil Rights Movement: Black Communities Organizing for Change* (New York: Free Press, 1984), 205–6; Taylor Branch, *Parting the Waters: America During the King Years, 1954–1963* (New York: Simon and Schuster, 1988), 274.

20. Olson, *Freedom's Daughters*, 156; Ross, *Witnessing and Testifying*, 170.

21. Powledge, *Free At Last?* 208–9.

22. For information on the involvement of African American women in the civil rights movement see Olson, *Freedom's Daughter*; Belinda Robnett, *How Long? How Long?: African-American Women in the Struggle for Civil Rights* (New York: Oxford University Press, 1997) 103–8; Barbara Ransby, *Ella Baker and the Black Freedom Movement: A Radical Democratic Vision* (Chapel Hill: The University of North Carolina Press, 2003); Chana Kai Lee, *For Freedom's Sake: The Life of Fannie Lou*

Hamer (Urbana: University of Illinois Press, 1999); Darlene Clark Hine and Kathleen Thompson, *A Shining Thread of Hope: The History of Black Women in America* (New York: Broadway Books, 1998), chap. 11.

23. David Halberstam, "A Good City Gone Ugly," *The Reporter*, March 31, 1960.

24. Olson, *Freedom's Daughters*, 157; Linda T. Wynn, "The Dawning of a New Day: The Nashville Sit-Ins, 13 February–10 May 1960," *Tennessee Historical Quarterly* 50 (1991), 46; David Halberstam. *The Children*, 133–34. Of the eighty-one students arrested on February 27, 1960, seventy-seven were black and four were white. None of their attackers were arrested. All quotations from Wynn, "The Dawning of a New Day" are reprinted by permission of the Tennessee Historical Society.

25. Olson, *Freedom's Daughters*, 158; Wynn, "The Dawning of a New Day," 46.

26. David Halberstam, "Halt Predicted to Sit-in Here: Leaders Hope Mayor's Committee Can Work in Calm," *Nashville Tennessean*, March 6, 1960; "Tennessee," *Southern School News*, April 1960, 5, 16.

27. Julia Moore, "Letter to Alumni," *Fisk News* (Spring 1960), 17; "Sit-in: Advisable to Lawyers," *Nashville Banner*, March 4, 1960; "Bi-Racial Meetings Continue," *Nashville Banner*, March 17, 1960; Don Doyle, *Nashville since the 1920s*, 248.

28. Lewis, *Walking with the Wind*, 109–10.

29. "Tennessee," *Southern School News*, May 1960, 5–6; David Halberstam, "Integrate Counters—Mayor," *Nashville Tennessean*, April 20, 1960; Halberstam, *The Children*, 234.

30. Halberstam, "Integrate Counters—Mayor"; Garry Fullerton, "Clear the Hall . . . King Delayed by Bomb Scare," *Nashville Tennessean*, April 21, 1960; Lewis, *Walking with the Wind*, 109–10.

31. David Halberstam, "Negroes' Job Lag Rapped," *Nashville Tennessean*, April 24, 1960; Doyle, *Nashville since the 1920s*, 230–34; Louis E. Lomax, *The Negro Revolt* (New York: Harper and Collins, 1962), 142.

32. "The Nashville Lesson," *Time Magazine*, May 26, 1961, 17; Wallace Westfeldt, "Settling a Sit-In," *A Report Prepared for the Nashville Community Relations Conference* (Nashville: n.p, n.d.), 4; Wynn, "The Dawning of a New Day," 51.

33. Halberstam, *The Children*, 218–19; Olson, *Freedom's Daughters*, 160.

34. Ross, *Witnessing and Testifying*, 189–90; Lovett, *The Civil Rights Movement in Tennessee*, 138; Robnett, *How Long? How Long?* 102.

35. Andrew Young, *An Easy Burden: The Civil Rights Movement and the Transformation of America*, (New York: Harper Collins, 1997), 342.

36. Diane Nash, letter to the editor, *Rock Hill Herald*, March 8, 1961. The "redeemed community" was Nash's interpretation of the "beloved community," a term that was first coined in the early days of the twentieth century by the philosopher-theologian Josiah Royce, who founded the Fellowship of Reconciliation. However, it was the Reverend Martin Luther King Jr. who gave it a deeper meaning in the modern movement for freedom. As early as 1956, after the Supreme Court's ruling in the Montgomery bus desegregation case, he spoke of the beloved community as the end goal of nonviolent boycotts. The end represented reconciliation, redemption, and ultimately the creation of the beloved community, which resonated with movement participants. See Martin Luther King Jr., *Stride Toward Freedom: The Montgomery Story* (New York: Harper and Row, 1958).

37. Nash, "Inside the Sit-ins and the Freedom Rides," 45; Ross, *Witnessing and Testifying*, 189–90.

38. Nash interview, January 10, 2005; Halberstam, *The Children*, 269.

39. Halberstam, *The Children*, 269.

40. Olson, *Freedom's Daughters*, 182.

41. Branch, *Parting the Waters*, 413–24; Olson, *Freedom's Daughters*, 183–84; Halberstam, *The Children*, 258–60.

42. Olson, *Freedom's Daughters*, 182–84.

43. Ibid.,185.

44. Raymond Arsenault, *Freedom Riders: 1961 and the Struggle for Racial Justice* (New York: Oxford University Press, 2006), 180.

45. The ten students selected were: Jim Zwerg and Salynn McCollum (white) and John Lewis, William Barbee, Paul Brooks, Charles Butler, Allen Cason, Bill Harbour, Catherine Burks, and Lucretia Collins. Three were from American Baptist Theological Seminary, one was from Fisk and George Peabody College, and five were from Tennessee A&I State University. See Arsenault, *Freedom Riders*, 185.

46. Arsenault, *Freedom Riders*, 284, 286; Olson, *Freedom Daughters*, 185. Richard Reeves, *President Kennedy: Profile of Power* (New York: Simon and Schuster, 1993), 123; Mary L. Dudziak. *Cold War Civil Rights: Race and the Image of American Democracy* (Princeton: Princeton University Press, 2000), 158–59; Harris Wofford, *Of Kennedys and Kings: Making Sense of the Sixties* (New York: Farrar, Straus and Giroux, 1980), 125.

47. Nash interview, January 10, 2005; Leo "Kwame" Lillard, interview with author, Nashville, February 9, 2005.

48. Olson, *Freedom Daughters*, 188.

49. James Farmer, *Lay Bear the Heart: An Autobiography of the Civil Rights Movement* (New York: New American Library, 1985) 206–95; Olson, *Freedom Daughters*, 188–89; Diane McWhorter, *Carry Me Home: Birmingham, Alabama: The Climactic Battle of the Civil Rights Revolution* (New York: Simon and Schuster, 2001), 233; Arsenault, *Freedom Riders*, 235.

50. Olson, *Freedom Daughters*, 188; Branch, *Parting the Waters*, 480.

51. Olson, *Freedom Daughters*, 188; Nash interview, January 10, 2005.

52. Olson, *Freedom Daughters*, 212; Nash interview, January 10, 2005.

53. Clayborne Carson, Emma J. Lapsansky-Werner, and Gary B. Nash, *African American Lives: The Struggle for Freedom* (New York: Pearson Longman, 2005), 472–73; Olson, *Freedom Daughters*, 339.

54. Nash interview, January 10, 2005; Olson, *Freedom Daughters*, 403.

55. Halberstam, *The Children*, 601; Ross, *Witnessing and Testifying*, 183–84; Nash interview, January 10, 2005.

Wilma Rudolph

(1940–1994)

Running for Freedom

ARAM GOUDSOUZIAN

Gray skies hung over the sixty thousand spectators at Rome's Stadio Olimpico, but all eyes looked down upon a shining star—a black woman of athletic brilliance. The date was September 8, 1960, and the event was the Olympic finals for the 400-meter relay. The crowd murmured in anticipation. Then the starting gun was fired, and off went the six competing teams. Martha Hudson burst off the blocks and rounded the turn, then handed the baton to Barbara Jones, who passed it on to Lucinda Williams. The roars built as the American women took the lead. They ran with poetic precision, never breaking stride on the hand-offs. These women, representing a nation, all hailed from the same small, historically black, poorly funded university in Nashville, Tennessee. Already the world's best, they had broken the world and Olympic records in the semifinal heat. Now, in the final, the roars rumbled toward a crescendo. Victory seemed assured, because the runner for the Americans' final leg was the darling of the 1960 Summer Olympics, the Tennessee A&I teammate of Hudson and Williams and Jones, the gold medal winner for the 100- and 200-meter dashes, the fastest woman in the world—Wilma Rudolph.

Then Williams and Rudolph fumbled their exchange. The fans collectively gasped. For one crucial second, Rudolph had to stop and juggle the baton. The United Team of Germany's Jutta Heine surged ahead.

Rudolph had often struggled with slow starts, and now a world-class competitor had a two-stride lead and running momentum. Rudolph pumped her fists, churned her legs, and built speed. Still, Heine led. Then Rudolph glided into high gear. Her long strides gracefully unfolded, swallowing up the space between her and Heine. And as she ran, Rudolph reinforced her own conse-

WILMA RUDOLPH

Courtesy of Special Collections, Tennessee State University, Nashville, Tennessee.

quence, her own meaning to the world. She ran as a woman, shattering stereotypes of female athletes and building her sport's legitimacy. She ran as an African American, suggesting new racial possibilities in an arena of Cold War athletic competition. And she ran as Wilma Rudolph, the poor sick girl from Clarksville, Tennessee, who found her own personal freedom as she sped down a track. She ran, and she caught Heine, and she broke the tape.

The crowd exploded. It was so tumultuous that one spectator had to ask a nearby French photographer who won. "La Gazelle, naturellement," he replied. "'La Chattanooga Choo Choo.'" Wilma Rudolph was the first American woman to win three gold medals in one Olympics. "Vilma! Vilma! Vilma!" chanted the Italian fans. The Tennessee women accepted their medals, the "Star Spangled Banner" played, and a mob of well-wishers and reporters and photographers crowded around Rudolph. "Wilma," an American official said, "life will never be the same for you again."[1]

That was true. She had become an international icon, a triple gold medal winner, an athletic celebrity who would negotiate the constraints of her race and gender with sweet aplomb. But in life, as in sport, Wilma Rudolph only achieved glory after overcoming a slow start.

The story of Rudolph's childhood is the stuff of hokey Hollywood melodrama, the type of triumph-against-all-odds tale often found in sappy fiction. Her biggest demon was her own persistent infirmity. Rudolph was born on June 23, 1940, in St. Bethlehem, Tennessee. She arrived prematurely at only four and a half pounds. When only six weeks old, she fell off her aunt's lap, spurring worries that she would develop slowly. She was frail, thin, and sickly. Common colds lasted for weeks. She caught the measles, chicken pox, and whooping cough. She barely ate, and she did not toddle until she was four. That year, double pneumonia and scarlet fever almost killed her, and they partially paralyzed her left leg and twisted it outward. When she was six, doctors outfitted her with a special brace that allowed a halting walk.[2]

The handicap placed enormous burdens on the Rudolph family, which already bore the weights of poverty and race. Soon after Wilma's birth her father, Ed, a railroad porter, and her mother, Blanche, a domestic, had moved the family to a rental cottage on Kellogg Street in Clarksville, the county seat, fifty miles northwest of Nashville. Remarkably, Wilma was the twentieth of twenty-two children sired by Ed; Blanche was his second wife. Few kids shared the cottage during Wilma's childhood, however, as most had grown up and married.[3]

Clarksville adhered to the patterns of racial segregation that tainted the entire South; the Rudolph kids attended dilapidated, second-class, all-black Cobb Elementary School, the local rubber tire factory resisted hiring blacks, and only one public restaurant served black customers. Wilma and her mother rode a segregated bus to Nashville's Meharry Medical College, the black hospital where Wilma received therapeutic massages for her leg. Blanche also treated Wilma with folk remedies such as hot toddies and mountains of blankets, and Wilma's sisters learned how to give her leg massages.[4]

Wilma bore psychological pains, too. "The only thing I ever really wanted when I was a child was to be normal," she recalled. "To be able to run, jump, play and do all the things the other kids did in my neighborhood." She could not attend school until she was eight, when doctors replaced the brace with a high-top orthopedic shoe. Limping around school, she endured her fellow second-graders' stares and teasing. She countered their meanness with sweetness, compensating for her physical incapacities with gregarious charm. She was also determined to participate in the same activities as her friends. Wilma practiced basketball with patient obsession, wheeling around on her bulky shoe. Her drive to become a champion was first forged in her backyard, shooting at a peach basket on a pole. Sport provided both discipline and freedom.[5]

Wilma's life changed as she entered the seventh grade at Burt High School. Her leg had healed with time and treatment, and she could now wear normal shoes. Though barely free from her brace, she joined the girls' basketball team. She buzzed around the court with pesky enthusiasm. "I called her Skeeter, short for mosquito," said Coach Clinton Gray, and it would become her lifelong nickname. During her first few seasons, she practiced herself into an accomplished player. The sport fulfilled her. In one game during tenth grade, she scored thirty-two points in front of a packed gym, and for the first time in her life, she felt like someone important. She further reveled in the team's camaraderie, cracking jokes from the back of the bus during road trips. Basketball soothed the sting of her childhood exclusion.[6]

Coach Gray also established a girls' track team, mostly to keep his basketball players in shape after the season. As with most women's track and field teams from that era, practices consisted only of jogging and impromptu races. Instead of meets they staged "Play Days," informal competitions that mixed participants from various teams and awarded ribbons to the winners. The races were not on tracks but in open fields. Still, the competition gave young women opportunities to participate in sports.[7]

But the Play Day model also reinforced assumptions of female difference. According to prevailing thought, sport imposed strains inappropriate for women's delicate reproductive organs. Well into the 1950s, competitive sports remained a male domain, an arena of male socialization and male strength. Sport also molded ambition and single-mindedness, traits associated with the masculine, working world. Sportswriter Paul Gallico once famously described competitive woman athletes as "Muscle Molls." Play Days supposedly saved women from such a stigma.[8]

Whatever the nature of the competition, Rudolph exhibited a natural gift. She had a perfect sprinter's body, standing five feet, eleven inches with long legs on a thin frame. At every Play Day, she won every race and every ribbon. Ed Temple, the women's track coach at Tennessee A&I University in Nashville, often scouted new talent while working part time as a basketball referee. He often recruited "poor country girls" who knew that his track team might be their "only chance to get something extra out of life." He saw Rudolph's vast potential, and he also saw her ambition. After her sophomore year, he invited Rudolph to participate in his summer program for high school athletes.[9]

Opened on the grounds of an old plantation in 1912, Tennessee A&I—by then also known as Tennessee State—was a product of Jim Crow and the state's one designated black university. It survived on the crumbs of the state's higher education funds. When Temple started coaching track in 1950, he had an annual budget of sixty-four dollars. The cinder track bypassed the agricultural department's pigpen, which in the summer heat emitted a crippling stench. Temple raked and lined the track himself. (He also taught sociology and administered the university post office.) The school could not offer athletic scholarships, and the team could travel to meets only at Tuskegee Institute and Alabama State University.[10]

Yet the Tennessee State program created a realm of athletic possibility unique to black women. By the 1940s white women had essentially abandoned competitive track and field. Though some middle-class African Americans also considered the sport unfeminine, competitive track bore less of a stigma for black women. Victorian notions of sports participation meant little to working-class black women, who had historically assumed myriad responsibilities in domestic life, the working world, and the broader black community. In turn, black colleges, which often imagined sports as a means of racial uplift, often encouraged female athletes. The Tuskegee Institute, for example, won eleven of twelve American Athletic Union (AAU) championships in women's track between 1937 and 1948.[11]

By 1956 Temple had, improbably, built a similar dynasty at Tennessee State. His summer clinic for high school runners established a pipeline of athletes. When Rudolph first arrived in Nashville, Temple drove the girls on arduous cross-country runs. Then they began daily triple sessions of sprints, including practice bursting from the starting blocks, mastering footwork, and establishing proper posture. Rudolph, according to Temple, "ran straight up and down. I taught her how to lean forward. Then she ran leaned forward so far she couldn't raise those long legs all the way."[12]

Ultimately, Rudolph learned not only running technique, but also a structure for success. Temple demanded promptness. He organized a precise schedule for every practice. He delivered motivational speeches. He instructed his athletes on how to talk, how to dress, how to act. He warned the young women to watch their weight for both athletic and cosmetic reasons, insisting that track enhanced their femininity. "We want foxes, not oxes," he would say, trying to crush stereotypes of mannish female athletes. His patriarchal discipline extended to his runners' personal lives: he warned them against steady boyfriends. At the time, the girls resented the intrusion, but Temple became an influential father figure.[13]

Rudolph quickly developed into a world-class sprinter. Temple entered her relay team in national competitions, though the girls were still in high school, and the Tennessee State club won its first AAU championship in August 1956. The club drove to Philadelphia for the meet in a caravan of station wagons. The city's skyscrapers and fast pace were a world away from Clarksville, but the Tennessee women ruled the competition, winning most events in both the senior and junior categories. On top of all of this, Rudolph met Jackie Robinson, the star second baseman of the Brooklyn Dodgers who had integrated major league baseball in 1947. "Jackie Robinson, after that day," she recalled, "was my first black hero." Four years later, Rudolph would become a female equivalent to Robinson—an icon of black achievement in a time of racial upheaval.[14]

Rudolph's journey to that status began in earnest one week after the Philadelphia meet, during the cross-country drive to Seattle for the Olympic trials. Up to this point, and for all Rudolph's success, coaches and teammates thought she was holding back on the track. As a child, she had compensated for her disability with sweetness, and perhaps she was still deferring to others in order to fit in. But Mae Faggs, a 1952 Olympic champion eight years her senior, counseled Rudolph to push herself to her individual limits. In Seattle, Rudolph did just that. In the 200-meter final, the two shared first place. Sixteen-year-old Wilma Rudolph was going to the Olympics.[15]

The Olympic Games have long embodied a paradoxical mythology. Since their 1896 inception, the quadrennial festivals have promulgated the ideals of international cooperation, envisioning sport as a vehicle of social harmony. But this global spectacle becomes compelling only through national competition, with sport an instrument to demonstrate political supremacy. The 1956 Olympics in Melbourne, Australia, are a prime example of this contradiction. Egypt, Lebanon, and Iraq boycotted the games after the International Olympic Committee (IOC) refused to ban France, Great Britain, and Israel in punishment for a planned invasion of Egypt. Communist China withdrew over the separate inclusion of athletes from Taiwan. And the Committee welcomed the Soviet Union, although just weeks before the games, the Red Army had crushed an incipient rebellion against the Soviet occupation of Hungary.[16]

At the same time, the Cold War was actually boosting the standing of female athletes. As the Eastern Bloc entered international competition following World War II, their well-financed athletic programs produced world-class athletes. Soviet women dominated the 1952 Olympics. The American press tried dismissing them as "molls" and "Amazons," but women's and men's events weighed equally in the medal counts, the unofficial arbiters of international sporting supremacy. For proof of American primacy, the United States needed gold medals from all its athletes, male and female.[17]

Given the lack of white female participation, black women track stars served as vital representatives of American track. Alice Coachman won the high jump at the 1948 London Olympics, becoming the first African American woman to capture the gold. Mae Faggs led the American women to gold in the 400-meter relay at the Helsinki Games in 1952. The Tennessee State club provided six of the seventeen women for the Melbourne team, the most ever from one institution. Rudolph and her teammates were carrying the torch of Cold War America.[18]

But Rudolph would remember these Olympics with disappointment. "The thing that stands out in 1956," she later recalled, "was how naïve I was. I was sure I was going to win a gold medal." She qualified to advance in her preliminary heat for the 200 meters, but she finished third in the semifinal heat. Only the top two advanced. When she lost, she cried long, heaving sobs. She feared that she would be judged a failure, reflecting her tenuous hold on her emerging status.[19]

Her spirits improved, however, with the 400-meter relay competition. Although the experts had predicted that the American women were overmatched, Rudolph, Faggs, Margaret Matthews, and Isabelle Daniels ran a perfect race, besting the world record mark. Unfortunately, the Australians and British beat the record, too. The United States finished third, making Rudolph and her teammates bronze medalists.[20]

After a trip to Sydney for the British Empire Games, Rudolph came home. Tennessee State feted the team, and Burt High School honored Rudolph at a special assembly. She starred on the state champion basketball team, and dated football and basketball captain Robert Eldridge. She was Clarksville's "It Girl." Other sprinters dropped out of Play Day races rather than be embarrassed by an Olympian. Rudolph still trained with Ed Temple's junior squad, and at the

Tennessee State Relays and Tuskegee Relays in May 1957, she won three races in each meet's junior division. For all the barriers imposed upon a poor black teenage girl in the South, Rudolph seemed destined for a college education and another Olympic Games.[21]

Those hopes and possibilities crashed in late 1957, when Rudolph learned that she was pregnant. "I was mortified," she recalled. She and Robert had started having sex, but neither knew much about birth control. Now their immaturity threatened her future. Settling into domestic life meant a host of lost opportunities. But Ed Temple ignored his own rule against taking mothers onto his track team. Aware of her prodigious talent, he recruited her for the college team, even though she was missing her final high school track season. Rudolph graduated seven months pregnant, and in July 1958 she gave birth to a girl that she named Yolanda.[22]

Six weeks later, Rudolph enrolled at Tennessee State. Her sister Yvonne, who lived in St. Louis with her husband and child, agreed to take care of Yolanda while Wilma balanced a hectic schedule. She worked in Temple's post office in exchange for room, board, and tuition while maintaining a C average in her academic courses. Track ate up the day. Temple drilled the fundamentals. Through the summer heat and into the fall, they trained on the cinder track. During the winter they ran sprints in a hallway outside the basketball gym, locking the door at the end of the hallway to keep from bursting out of the building. While building camaraderie with her teammates and coach, Rudolph honed the sharp muscle memory a sprinter needs: the surge out of the starting gate, the gradual straightening of posture, the exact steps that covered each stretch, and the lean into the tape. She had once arrived at the summer clinic as a gangly, raw recruit. Now, Temple instructed young runners to "watch how Rudolph does it."[23]

Still, she missed Yolanda, a trial exacerbated by her sister's growing attachment to the baby. When Yvonne insisted upon adopting the child, Wilma panicked. During her three-day Christmas break, she and Robert drove to St. Louis, snuck into Yvonne's house, and took Yolanda back to Clarksville. Wilma's father raged when he learned of this subterfuge, especially because it involved Robert, whom he blamed for Wilma's pregnancy. But both grandparents melted in Yolanda's presence. They cared for the baby while Wilma returned to school in Nashville.[24]

Rudolph quickly became the lynchpin of the Tennessee State track dynasty. In January 1959 the team captured its fifth straight AAU indoor team title, and Rudolph won the 50-yard dash. In June the team captured its fifth straight AAU outdoor title, and Rudolph won the 100-meter dash. Besides the AAU meets, however, the team had only dual meets with Tuskegee. "If they want our girls to be as good as the Russian women," said the coach, "they'll have to give us more meets to compete in."[25]

The impending Olympiad only heightened such concerns. That July the U.S. and Soviet track teams met at Franklin Field in Philadelphia. The previous summer, the American men had outscored the Soviets 126–109 (calculated with three points for gold, two for silver, and one for bronze), while the Soviet women prevailed 63–44. Although the meets were technically separate, the Soviets had infuriated the American press by claiming the overall title, 172–170. The 1959 meet attracted huge, enthusiastic crowds despite searing heat and violent rainstorms. Again, the U.S. men won. But the Soviet women also won again, earning the USSR the unofficial overall title, 175–167. With the Olympics a year away, women's track seemed a weapon in the Cold War battle of athletic propaganda.[26]

Rudolph struggled, too. In Philadelphia and in that September's Pan-Am Games, she failed to capture a gold medal. Back at Tennessee State, Rudolph kept losing to fellow Tigerbelles Barbara Jones, Lucinda Williams, and Martha Hudson. "You've got the physical equipment and style," said Coach Temple. "You should be winning. What's wrong, Skeeter?" Rudolph remained mystified until November 1959, when her tonsils painfully swelled. According to her doctor, her infected tonsils had been debilitating her for years. Now, after an emergency tonsillectomy and three weeks rest, she was completely healthy for the first time ever.[27]

By the spring of 1960 Rudolph was peaking. In Chicago that April she led Tennessee State to its sixth straight AAU national indoor title. She won the 50-yard dash, set an American record in the 100-yard dash, and then set another in the 220-yard dash. In Cleveland that June, she set American records for the outdoor 100- and 220-yard dashes.[28]

Her success continued in August at two key Texas meets preceding the Olympics. At the women's AAU championships in Corpus Christi, Rudolph tied the American record in the 100-meter dash. She finished the 200-meter finals in 22.9 seconds—a world record, topping the old mark set by Betty Cuthbert at the Melbourne Games. One week later at the final Olympic trials in Abilene, Rudolph again won the 100- and 200-meter dashes.[29]

As Rudolph solidified her perch atop the women's track pantheon, political intrigue swirled, suggesting some potential ramifications for the upcoming Olympics. Olga Fitokova, the 1956 Olympic discus champion from Czechoslovakia, had qualified for the 1960 Games as a U.S. citizen, but in Texas she criticized the substandard accommodations and food, contrasting the lack of institutional attention to women's sports with the gender equality of Eastern

Bloc athletics. Meanwhile, rumors surfaced that segregation rules separated the athletes in Corpus Christi and Abilene. Those rumors proved unfounded, though Rudolph remembered that one driver walked off the bus rather than shuttle an integrated group to the track.[30]

Nine of the thirteen women representing the United States at the Olympics were African American. Thanks to Tennessee State's success, Ed Temple landed a position as the only black coach for the United States. In this atmosphere of struggles for gender equality, questions of racial justice, and competition structured by the Cold War, Wilma Rudolph led the American women's track team to Rome.[31]

Rudolph arrived in Italy brimming with enthusiasm. During the one-month training period in Emporia, Kansas, Temple had worked his charges with typical vigor, but he scaled back Rudolph's workouts for the final two weeks to avoid burnout. Rudolph believed that she possessed a legitimate shot at three gold medals. Temple exercised more caution, grudgingly allowing that if Rudolph "can sprint among the first three in the Olympic final I'll be happy."[32]

Rome was a chaotic feast of sensations, a whirl of honking cabs and historic sights and excited Italians. The American women drank in the experience. Rudolph was photographed arm-in-arm with basketball center Walt Bellamy and linked romantically to the great sprinter Ray Norton. One night, the women had spent hours dancing the jitterbug, to the delight of athletes on both sides of the Iron Curtain. Whatever the international fascination with African American culture, Temple laid down the law: no more dancing. "I wouldn't have minded if the girls had done a little light dancing and then gone to bed," the coach explained. "But my girls are regular hepcats."[33]

Rudolph was approaching her athletic pinnacle at the perfect moment. She practiced the 100-meter dash in 11.1 seconds, unofficially breaking the world record. But on the day before her first heat, Temple held a loose, informal workout designed only to limber up the muscles. At the end, the team cooled off with a romp through some sprinklers. Rudolph took one last hop over a sprinkler and landed in a hole. Her left ankle popped. She sobbed as her teammates crowded around her swollen, purple ankle. That evening the team watched the boxing matches, and Temple bought Rudolph a cold Coca-Cola to press against the swollen ankle. The next morning, she took a nervous step. The ankle held. She had sprained it, but she could run straight distances without pain.[34]

In the Stadio Olimpico tunnel before her first 100-meter heat, a calm seemed to come over Rudolph. She lay down on a bench with her feet propped up until race time. Then she serenely carried out her routine, taking a single practice start and walking around with hands on hips. She won her preliminary heat, tying the Olympic mark of 11.5 seconds, and prevailed in subsequent heats, tying the world record of 11.3 seconds in the semifinal. She also won all her heats for the 200 meters. "She has perfect control of her body," marveled track legend Jesse Owens. "Wilma could be one of the greatest woman sprinters of all time." The Italian fans loved her. They chanted "Vilma! Vilma! Vilma!" before and after every Rudolph triumph.[35]

As Rudolph cruised through her heats, American track fans fretted over other races. Commentators labeled September 1, 1960 "Black Thursday" and the "Darkest Day in U.S. Track History." Heavy favorite John Thomas fell third to two Soviets in the high jump, and sprinter Ray Norton finished last in the 100-meter dash. The Soviets controlled the overall medal standings. To no small relief, American athletes recaptured the spotlight on "Bright Friday." Ralph Boston set an Olympic record in the broad jump, and Glenn Davis led an American sweep in the 400-meter hurdles.[36]

But Wilma Rudolph stole the show that Friday. Germany's Jutta Heine had also won all of her heats, setting up an anticipated duel. Rudolph nevertheless maintained her uncanny calm, even napping on the rubdown table one hour before the race. As the other runners fidgeted by the starting blocks, she calmly wiped the cinders off her fingers and entered her starting stance. The starting gun fired, and she trailed the pack for about twenty meters. Then her long legs stretched into full, fluid strides, and she soared past her challengers. With forty meters left, victory was assured. A gold medal! Her time of 11 seconds flat crushed the world record, though not officially because there had been significant wind at her back. Rudolph leapt into the arms of teammate Earlene Brown, and then scooted under a parasol while Barbara Jones found a comb and brush. The gold medal winner took the stand in feminine style.[37]

Three days later, Rudolph won the 200-meter final. Heavy rains had turned her inside lane soggy, so she ran a slow time of twenty-four seconds. But she became the first American woman to win two gold medals since Babe Didrikson at the 1932 Olympics, and her victory inspired a patriotic outpouring as Rudolph stepped onto the medal stand, carrying her trademark straw hat. The "Star Spangled Banner" stopped after "rockets' red glare," but the American fans sang the entire anthem. Again the chants of "Vilma!" coursed through Stadio Olimpico. Rudolph had won both national and international affection.[38]

On September 8, Rudolph anchored the 400-meter relay final, dramatically overtook Jutta Heine after a faulty baton handoff, and became the first American woman to win three gold medals in one Olympic Games. Without the fumbled exchange, the United States might have surpassed its own world record of 44.4 seconds, which the team had set in the semifinal heat. "The greatest strain has been on Rudolph," marveled Ed Temple. "This was her tenth race of the Olympics—four 100-meter heats, three in the 200s, and these two relays. She won all of them. The remarkable thing is that she's stayed so sound and ever-sharp."[39]

Then Rudolph heard some bad news: Ray Norton had disqualified the American men in the 400-meter relay by receiving the baton outside the passing zone. In the midst of her triple triumph, she felt sick. Few had expected Rudolph to win three gold medals, but many had predicted that Norton would. Instead, he finished last in the 100-meter final, last in the 200-meter final, and disqualified his team in the 400-meter relay. He claimed no injury but just felt "tied up like a knot inside." Rudolph and Norton had been dating during the Olympics. When she had tried to console him after the 200-meter final, he sulked away. "I can't do anything right," he moaned after the relay fiasco. "First I run too slow. Then I run too fast. So what happens? I become the goat of the Olympics."[40]

Norton embodied the larger American failures in the international track spotlight. John Thomas lost the high jump, world record holders Hal Connolly and Bill Alley failed to medal in the hammer throw and javelin, and the United States men won only seven gold medals—half their tally from Melbourne.

Rudolph emerged as the most popular, engaging American track hero from the 1960 Olympics. Not only had she accomplished a historic feat, but she also possessed conventional feminine beauty. The media almost never celebrated black female beauty, but *Time* noted, "In a field of female endeavor in which the greatest stars have often been characterized by overdeveloped muscles and underdeveloped glands, Wilma ("Skeeter") Rudolph had long legs and a pert charm that caused an admiring Italian press to dub her the 'the Black Pearl.'" Rudolph acquired a host of other nicknames: the French called her "the Black Gazelle," the Russians "the Queen of the Olympics," and others "the Chattanooga Choo Choo" or "the Tennessee Tornado." *Life* remarked that "the quintessence of Olympian effort was expressed in the lissome, straining figure of this 20 year-old American girl as she sprinted across the finish line." Media profiles noted her affection for reading and sleeping, along with her popularity among potential suitors.[41]

Rudolph would remember the Rome Olympics as her life's greatest thrill—the ecstasy of victory, the rapture of hearing eighty thousand fans chant her name, the honor of meeting Pope John XXIII. But her newfound fame brought enormous burdens, too. "I can't go anywhere, I can't do anything," she mourned while in Rome. Fans asked her to pose for pictures and sign autograph books, programs, and newspaper scraps. Even before the closing ceremony, Rudolph felt overwhelmed. "I sure am glad to be getting away from here," she told her hometown newspaper.[42]

Before returning to Nashville, however, Rudolph fulfilled the obligations of an international tour, which both burnished her eminence and inflamed her anxieties. After the Olympics, fifteen nations invited Rudolph and her teammates to competitions. Temple settled on meets in Athens, London, Cologne, Frankfurt, and Berlin. Rudolph kept winning races and charming audiences. Mounted police restrained crowds in Cologne, and admirers in Berlin shook her bus until she smiled and waved. This adoration for Rudolph stimulated jealousy among some of her teammates, who stopped speaking to her, played petty tricks such as hiding her hair curlers, and even ran purposely slow legs during relay races. A sensitive young woman who had found acceptance through sport, Rudolph ached at this turn of events.[43]

The whirlwind of excitement and angst only intensified upon her return to American shores. In New York City she received a citation from Mayor Robert Wagner and an award from Tennessee State alumni. Similar banquets, honors, speeches, and handshakes followed in Detroit and Chicago. Reporters speculated about her plans, including the 1964 Olympics and marriage. Rudolph wore down under the public crush. She could not shake a persistent cold, and her old insecurities surfaced in frequent worries about her appearance. The pressures of her growing celebrity often drove her to tears.[44]

By the time she returned to Tennessee, a coughing, sniffling Rudolph felt grumpy and aloof. "I don't want a big welcome," she said in Detroit. "I've seen enough people for a while." Yet she handled the celebrations with consummate grace. One thousand people roared with delight when Rudolph shyly emerged from the plane in Nashville. That night Tennessee State held a rally for its Olympians, including the relay team, hurdlers Joan Terry and Shirley Crowder, and broad-jumper Ralph Boston. They accepted merit certificates from Nashville's mayor and gold watches from the university president.[45]

Rudolph had a triumphant homecoming in Clarksville the next day. A motorcade of bands, civic groups, and representatives from the 101st Airborne Division began two miles outside the city. Schools let out at noon, local businesses displayed flags and pictures, Clarksville's mayor presented a bouquet of roses, and the paratroopers put on a demonstration. That night eleven hundred people attended a banquet—the first racially integrated banquet in Clarksville history. Rudolph pledged "to use my physical talents to the glory of God and the honor of womanhood." County Judge William Hudson captured the day's sentiment with a paean to racial amity. "If you want to get good music out of a piano," he proclaimed, "you have to play both white and black keys."[46]

The Tennessee State administration immediately sent the Olympic hero back on the rubber chicken circuit. Rudolph's visits in the fall of 1960 included charity fundraisers in Youngstown, Ohio, and Louisville, Kentucky, an award from the Pigskin Club in Washington D.C., a citation from the Philadelphia Cotillion Society, and the annual dinner for the NAACP Freedom Fund. At every stop she charmed her audiences with modest grace. As the year drew to a close she received the UPI Athlete of the Year award in Europe and the AP Athlete of the Year in America, along with a host of honors from newspapers and athletic organizations. Though they awarded golfer Arnold Palmer "Sportsman of the Year," *Sports Illustrated* gave her honorable mention: "With her lissome grace and warm smile, Wilma was not only a winner, she was delightfully American as well." She also finished second to decathlete Rafer Johnson for the prestigious Sullivan Award, the AAU's honor for the year's outstanding amateur athlete.[47]

In the wake of the Olympics, Rudolph embodied both achievement and integrity, particularly salient impressions given the black political upheaval of 1960. The year had witnessed unprecedented surges of grassroots protest in much of the South. Students from Tennessee State and Fisk had launched a sit-in movement in Nashville that February, desegregating lunch counters and helping spark demonstrations throughout the South. So Rudolph's athletic glories and public adoration adopted extra significance: to many Americans, she represented new possibilities for African American progress.[48]

Politicians could thus bask in Rudolph's glow and celebrate the myth of racial democracy. Richard Nixon, campaigning for the presidency, sought to keep the African American vote within the Republican Party. He invited the Tennessee State track stars to his rally in downtown Nashville. Later in the campaign, Nixon called for giving black people more opportunities to make important contributions to American life, citing such black icons as Booker T. Washington and Rafer Johnson. "How about my girl?" interjected Nixon's wife, Pat, in a rare public display of personality. "Of course," Nixon said. "And Wilma Rudolph."[49]

Nixon lost the election to John F. Kennedy, who soon met Rudolph himself. In April 1961 Tennessee State alumnus Bobby Logan arranged a meeting with Vice President Lyndon Johnson for Rudolph, her mother, and Ed Temple. The vice president thought that Kennedy would want to meet Rudolph, so they called on the Oval Office. Kennedy, exhibiting his trademark breezy charm, invited them to sit down. But the president absentmindedly went to sit down, missed his rocking chair, and crashed to the floor. To Rudolph's relief, Kennedy cracked up laughing, and everyone soon joined in. They then enjoyed a pleasant conversation about sports, and Rudolph grew impressed with the new president.[50]

Rudolph had become an emblem of racial and gender democracy. In a letter to the editor of the *Chicago Defender*, an Arkansas author named Ralph Creger refuted segregationists' claim of black biological inferiority, citing Rudolph as evidence of black achievement. The NAACP protested when the AAU accepted an invitation from apartheid South Africa's track federation, citing the absurdity of not inviting Rafer Johnson or Rudolph; the trip was snuffed. Ed Temple called for more opportunities for America's women athletes, because "there are a lot of Wilma Rudolphs around, but they have never been given a chance."[51]

Rudolph captured the world's fancy by successfully negotiating a delicate balance. Though a matchless athlete, she sidestepped any direct threat to masculine power in sport, insisting that she would never race men. "I'm a young lady," she explained. She wore skirts, jewelry, and high heels. Reporters often noted her stylish outfits, and they called her "willowy," "very feminine," and "lissome." With her high cheekbones, engaging smile, and graceful figure, she was incontrovertibly pretty. In his 1963 book *Negro Firsts in Sports*, a commemoration of black athletes as ambassadors of racial progress, journalist Doc Young celebrated Rudolph as "*the first Negro woman to draw worldwide praise for her beauty*." This, he added, "is indisputable proof that 'things are getting better' for Negroes!"[52]

Given the nation's deep racial prejudices at the dawn of the civil rights era, it is remarkable that Rudolph became the sweetheart of American sports. One explanation is that the United States had no white rival to Rudolph—women's track was a black world. She also possessed an unassuming, smiling magnetism, which countered age-old stereotypes of black women as bossy mammies or seductive jezebels. Her teenage pregnancy and baby Yolanda stayed out of the public eye. She received countless requests for public appearances, autographs, and her hand in marriage. Despite romances with high-profile track stars such as Ray Norton and Ralph Boston, she responded coyly to questions about her personal life.[53]

Meanwhile, Rudolph shattered barriers for American women in track. Meet organizers begged for her after the Olympics. Some added women's races for the first time, and others installed additional events. Throughout 1961 the national track circuit featured Rudolph as the star attraction. At the Los Angeles Invitational, a sellout crowd of 13,622—including fans paying 300 percent markups for scalped tickets—watched her set a world record in the indoor 60-yard dash. She later tied that record in front of 14,500 in Madison Square Garden at the Millrose Games. At every stop a swarm of fans begged for autographs, a crush of reporters asked the same banal questions, and pressures to win another race weighed heavily. Yet Rudolph radiated a consistent demure affability. The burden finally overwhelmed her in March at the AAU indoor championships in

Columbus, Ohio. After three consecutive races, she collapsed. She spent a few days in the hospital. Temple tried masking her exhaustion by calling it an upset stomach.[54]

Rudolph recovered quickly enough to win the 100-yard dash at the Drake Relays in April, and she won the same race at the AAU outdoor championships that July. But she was beating lesser competition and still recovering from illness. She finally recaptured peak form during a European tour that summer. The American women lost all their meets against the Soviet Union, West Germany, England, and Poland, but Rudolph won every race that she entered. In Stuttgart she ran the hundred in 11.2 seconds, a new world record.[55]

After the European tour, Rudolph stopped competing so that she could finish her degree in elementary education. She nevertheless captured another round of awards, including another AP Female Athlete of the Year. To her greatest delight, she also won the AAU's esteemed Sullivan Award. Rudolph also confirmed a spreading rumor: she was married. On October 14, 1961, she had secretly wed William Ward, who also ran track for Tennessee State. For all the attention to such suitors as Norton and Boston, Ward had successfully stayed off the media's radar screen.[56]

The marriage was a mistake. By May 1962 Rudolph had moved out of their Clarksville home and into a college dormitory. When she filed for divorce in January 1963, she charged her husband with "cruel and inhuman treatment." The hasty marriage seemed a consequence of the upheavals that followed her gold medals. She had tried to cope with the attention, the pressure, and the questions about her future by retreating into domesticity, and the experiment failed.[57]

In the meantime, Rudolph had mostly retired from competition. She did run in the Los Angeles Invitational in January 1962, but she trained for only ten days and lost to Jean Holmes. Not until her separation did Rudolph start training again in earnest. In early July, at the Los Angeles Coliseum, she defended her AAU title in the 100-yard dash. "Wonderful Wilma Does It Again," proclaimed the *Los Angeles Times*. In a late July rematch meet against the Soviet Union in Palo Alto, Rudolph won the 100-meter dash and anchored the winning 400-meter relay team. That August she joined an American track tour into Scandinavia and easily won her races.[58]

The 1964 Tokyo Olympics loomed ahead. One side of Rudolph was lured by the potential for more glory. The other side felt drawn to a private lifestyle and conventional womanhood. The marriage to Ward had failed to resolve her dilemma. She struggled to maintain her fitness. In January 1963 she lost at the Los Angeles Invitational. She then needed an emergency appendectomy, further hindering her training. "I think I'm getting too lazy," she said in March. "It's too much trouble starting back, getting in peak condition all over again. It's hard to say what I'll do."[59]

She remained indecisive as the State Department sent her on a goodwill tour through Senegal, Guinea, Ghana, Mali, and Upper Volta (now Burkina Faso) in April and May 1963. Upon her return she planned a long stay in Tennessee, "the most likely place I'll get my enthusiasm back." Instead she found Clarksville embroiled in racial turmoil. That spring's widely publicized demonstrations led by Dr. Martin Luther King Jr. and the Southern Christian Leadership Conference in Birmingham, Alabama, had sparked marches and sit-ins throughout the South. The same businesses that had once sponsored and honored Rudolph continued to exclude black people. On May 28 a group of 300 African Americans, including Rudolph, were turned away from a segregated drive-in restaurant. The next day the protestors encountered the locked doors on the restaurant and about 150 white youths heckling them. "I just can't believe it," said Rudolph. "Remember the reception I had here in 1960?"[60]

Rudolph's life was undergoing sea changes. On May 24 she officially divorced Ward. On May 27 she graduated from Tennessee State. Over the next two days, she participated in the Clarksville protest. Two months later, Rudolph remarried, this time to Robert Eldridge, her high school sweetheart and Yolanda's father. Once, Ed Rudolph had banned him from his home and Ed Temple had banned him from campus, but Eldridge had always had a special place in Wilma's heart. He had enrolled at Tennessee State and played on the basketball team. Only Ed Temple missed the huge, festive wedding celebration in Clarksville—he stubbornly maintained his disapproval of Eldridge, revealing some patriarchal sour grapes.[61]

This time, Rudolph's marriage effectively settled the question of her athletic future. She taught second grade at Cobb Elementary School, coached basketball and track at Burt High School, and, in May 1964, gave birth to her second daughter, whom she named Djauna. From her bed, with her baby, she watched fellow Tigerbelles Wyomia Tyus and Edith McGuire capture the 100- and 200-meter gold medals at the Tokyo Olympics. The next year she had her third child, Robert Jr. But as women's track grew popular in the 1960s, the media recognized Rudolph's legacy. "She was the first Negro girl athlete to be described as being 'beautiful' in the general-circulating daily press," wrote Doc Young. "She proved that a girl didn't require a face by Frankenstein to qualify for the world of track and field."[62]

Rudolph had hoped that her popularity would create opportunities for commercial endorsements and television jobs. But being a black woman constricted her marketability. She also felt frustrated teaching in her hometown, where the older teachers resisted new pedagogical ideas. So in 1966 she started working for the Job Corps, a government program run by the Office of Economic Opportunity. She served as athletic director for the Women's Job Corps Center in Poland Spring, Maine, and later transferred to a center in St. Louis. During the summer of 1967, when black ghettoes nationwide endured bloody and destructive riots, Rudolph served on a special sports advisory council. She and other professional athletes toured such cities as Cleveland, Detroit, and Baltimore to demonstrate their skills and encourage sports participation.[63]

But Rudolph grew restless at every stop in her career. She taught physical education at a junior high school in Michigan. She then moved to California, where she worked for both the Watts Community Action Committee and the Afro-American Cultural Center at UCLA. She won a brief moment in the spotlight in March 1969, when she accepted an invitation from the Italian newspaper *Il Tempo* to visit Rome and meet Pope Paul VI. The pro-communist daily *Paese Sera* published an article describing her as unemployed, a victim of racism, and so poor that she had pawned her gold medals. Rudolph refuted the charges in *Il Tempo*, but unfortunately that newspaper had pro-fascist sympathies. She had fallen victim to an Italian political newspaper war, exploited by communists and fascists alike.[64]

In the 1970s Rudolph continued to search for her niche. The German Olympic Committee hired her to help English-language television crews during the 1972 Munich Games. In 1973 she worked in Chicago for Mayor Richard Daley's Youth Foundation. In 1974 she moved to West Virginia and raised funds for a track Hall of Fame. She also raised a fourth child, a son named Xurry, and her oldest, Yolanda, followed her footsteps by entering Tennessee State on a track scholarship in 1976. But Rudolph was in debt, and she returned once again to Clarksville. In contrast, her old rival Jutta Heine was by this time a wealthy television personality in Germany. Peggy Fleming, the white gold-medal-winning U.S. figure skater from the 1968 Olympics, was a rich celebrity.[65]

The running craze of the mid- and late 1970s finally spurred Rudolph's post-track career. She toured the nation on the college lecture circuit, talking about self-discipline and hoping that the lessons of her athletic success could translate to all walks of life. She also won sponsorships for such businesses as a baking company, the movie studio 20th Century Fox, and the vitamin supplement Geritol. In 1977 Rudolph signed a contract with the state of Tennessee to promote in-state film production.[66]

By then, producer Bud Greenspan was bringing Rudolph's own life to the screen. Greenspan found her story rich in human drama: overcoming adversity, finding love, achieving ultimate triumph. He wrote, produced, and directed

Wilma, which starred Shirley Jo Finney and Cicely Tyson. The movie aired on NBC in December 1977 and earned excellent ratings. Rudolph also wrote a companion autobiography called *Wilma: The Story of Wilma Rudolph.* The movie's premiere party in Nashville attracted Tennessee's political elite, along with Ed Temple and Muhammad Ali. Rudolph received congratulatory calls from old friends and fellow athletes. "I didn't know my mama was a star," said seven-year-old Xurry.[67]

The mother of four was also the First Lady of American Track. Rudolph participated in track fundraisers, charity events, panel discussions, and celebrations of women's sports. Athletes flocked to her for advice. "Track people are selfish people—it's just you and the other guy out there," said four-time Olympic gold medal winner Evelyn Ashford. "But Wilma was generous." She lent perspectives that some male coaches never considered. She also criticized the hypocritical standards of "amateur" athletics for full-time track athletes, sparking a minor brouhaha in 1979. Her name was a touchstone of possibilities for women athletes, especially African Americans.[68]

Rudolph aged gracefully, maintaining her charm, fitness, and charisma. She also remained in the public eye. She wrote a children's book called *Wilma Rudolph on Track.* She garnered awards and attention, especially during the Olympiads. She also moved to Indianapolis in 1981 to start the Wilma Rudolph Foundation, a "three-tiered program to help young people in track" that provided coaching, academic assistance, and mentoring. It occupied Rudolph for much of the decade, though by the early 1990s she had returned to Tennessee, this time as vice president of Baptist Hospital in Nashville.[69]

Along the way she had divorced Eldridge, gone bankrupt, and lost several family members, including her advisor and brother Wesley. But she recovered financially and spiritually. On June 23, 1990, she turned fifty. Three hundred friends gathered to celebrate a woman who had known great difficulties and accomplished great things. "A sprinter's world is measured out in 10ths of a second, a mayfly's dance between the starter's gun and the tape," Alexander Wolff later wrote. "For Wilma Rudolph, the most elegant and revered woman sprinter of all, life was more of a distance race, an often hard road, well and courageously run."[70]

During the fall of 1994, Wilma Rudolph and Ed Temple started going for walks. They would wait until the early afternoon, when the sun was at its warmest, and then amble slowly around the "old track" at Tennessee State. Forty years earlier, Temple had started an athletic dynasty here, raking rocks off the cinder track by the pigpen. Now Rudolph traversed the oval with deliberation, holding onto Temple's arm, reminiscing about past glories. She had led the most remarkable of lives, surmounting a crippling handicap to become a champion athlete and an international icon. But she had always circled back to Tennessee, back to her family and her community and her mentor. Now, Wilma Rudolph was walking her life's anchor leg.[71]

Rudolph had been diagnosed with brain cancer that summer. Her condition quickly deteriorated. A blood clot in her leg ended her walks with the old coach. She died on the morning of November 12, 1994. She was only fifty-four years old.[72]

Her funeral revealed her exceptional legacy. After a memorial service at the Floyd Payne Campus Center on the Tennessee State campus, a motorcade carrying her four children, eight grandchildren, hundreds of nieces and nephews, and countless others—including track stars Jackie Joyner-Kersee, Florence Griffith Joyner, and Gail Devers—rolled northwest to Clarksville. Drivers pulled off Interstate 24 to let the procession pass, and some got out of their cars and laid their hands over their hearts. A wreath marked the exit for Wilma Rudolph Boulevard. When the cars passed an elementary school, the children, black and white alike, held signs and waved.[73]

Her inspirational story has been the subject of at least fifteen children's books. A life-size bronze statue in Clarksville, a residence hall at Tennessee State, a Congressional Gold Medal, and a United States postage stamp reflect Rudolph's honored place in local and national memory. She traveled a long and hard road, one filled with roadblocks for a poor, black, crippled girl from Clarksville, Tennessee. But Wilma Rudolph represents hope, the prospect of triumphing over racial bigotry, the possibility of overcoming gender prejudice, the courage to break the shackles of childhood disability. She lent the world her grace—her demeanor composed, her posture perfect, her long legs gliding, her style transcendent, her body and spirit running for freedom.[74]

NOTES

1. Alex Haley, "The Queen Who Earned Her Crown," *The Rotarian*, May 1961, 38; Wilma Rudolph, *Wilma: The Story of Wilma Rudolph* (New York: New American Library, 1977), 136. For a condensed version of *Rotarian* article, see Alex Haley, "The Girl Who Wouldn't Give Up," *Reader's Digest*, May 1961, 140–48.

2. *Nashville Tennessean*, September 6, 1960; Rudolph, *Wilma*, 17; Haley, "The Queen Who Earned Her Crown," 38–39; Allison Danzig, "Norton Runs Out of Passing Zone," *New York Times*, September 9, 1960; Ira Berkow, "Forever the Regal Champion," *New York Times*, November 13, 1994.

3. "World Speed Queen," *New York Times*, September 9, 1960; Barbara Heilman, "Wilma and Ed," *Sports Illustrated*, November 14, 1960, 48–49.

4. Rudolph, *Wilma*, 5–39.

5. Berkow, "Forever the Regal Champion"; *Tennessee State University Accent*, December 1994–January 1995; Haley, "The Queen Who Earned Her Crown," 39, 57.

6. Rudolph, *Wilma*, 40–57; "World Speed Queen."

7. Joan S. Hult, "The Story of Women's Athletics: Manipulating a Dream, 1890–1985," in *Women and Sport: Interdisciplinary Perspectives*, ed. D. Margaret Costa and Sharon R. Guthrie (Champaign, Ill.: Human Kinetics, 1994), 88–94.

8. Mary Jo Festle, *Playing Nice: Politics and Apologies in Women's Sports* (New York: Columbia University Press, 1996), 3–27; Helen Lenskyj, *Out of Bounds: Women, Sport and Sexuality* (Toronto: The Women's Press, 1986), 55–58; Donald J. Mrozek, "The 'Amazon' and the 'American Lady': Sexual Fears of Women Athletes," in *The New American Sport History: Recent Approaches and Perspectives*, ed. S. W. Pope, 198–214 (Urbana: University of Illinois Press, 1997).

9. Rudolph, *Wilma*, 50–51, 58–66; George Barker, "The Man Who REALLY Won the Olympics," *Nashville Tennessean Magazine*, October 23, 1960, 16.

10. Bobby L. Lovett and Linda T. Wynn, eds., *Profiles of African Americans in Tennessee* (Nashville: Local Conference on Afro-American Culture and History, 1996), 126–27; Heilman, "Wilma and Ed," 53; Ed Temple with B'Lou Carter, *Only the Pure in Heart Survive* (Nashville: Broadman Press, 1980), 19–20, 29–30.

11. Susan K. Cahn, *Coming on Strong: Gender and Sexuality in Twentieth-Century Women's Sport* (New York: The Free Press, 1994), 112–21; Rita Liberti, "'We Were Ladies, We Just Played Like Boys': African American Women and Competitive Basketball at Bennett College, 1928–42," in *The Sporting World of the Modern South*, ed. Patrick B. Miller, 153–74 (Urbana: University of Illinois Press, 2002); Pamela Grundy, *Learning to Win: Sports, Education, and Social Change in Twentieth-Century North Carolina* (Chapel Hill: University of North Carolina Press, 2001), 63–65, 136–52, 158–89; Jacqueline Jones, *Labor of Love, Labor of Sorrow: Black Women, Work, and the Family From Slavery to the Present* (New York: Basic Books, 1985), 79–231; Darlene Clark Hine and Kathleen Thompson, *A Shining Thread of Hope: The History of Black Women in America* (New York: Broadway Books, 1998), 165–265; Patrick B. Miller, "To 'Bring the Race Along Rapidly': Sport, Student Culture, and Educational Mission at Historically Black Colleges during the Interwar Years," in *The Sporting World of the Modern South*, 129–52. The AAU was a key governing body for amateur athletics.

12. Heilman, "Wilma and Ed," 50; Barker, "The Man Who REALLY Won the Olympics," 17; Haley, "The Queen Who Earned Her Crown," 57–58.

13. Temple, *Only the Pure in Heart Survive*, 46–49; uncited article dated October 9, 1963, vol. 4, Ed Temple Scrapbook Collection, Tennessee State University Special Collections (hereinafter Temple Scrapbook); *Nashville Tennessean*, December 21, 1977.

14. Haley, "The Queen Who Earned Her Crown," 58; Rudolph, *Wilma*, 67–79; "Tennesseean Wins 2 Girls Track Crowns," *Chicago Tribune*, August 19, 1956; *Nashville Banner*, June 29, 1957. On Jackie Robinson see Jules Tygiel, *Baseball's Great Experiment: Jackie Robinson and His Legacy* (New York: Oxford University Press, expanded ed., 1997); Arnold Rampersad, *Jackie Robinson: A Biography* (New York: Alfred A. Knopf, 1997). Although sport historians have considered the political effects of black male athletes such as Robinson, Joe Louis, Jack Johnson, and others, they have paid less attention to black female athletes, perhaps because few had national profiles. But the study of Wilma Rudolph suggests profound political effects for a female athlete's success. See Wayne Wilson, "Wilma Rudolph: The Making of an Olympic Icon," in *Out of the Shadows: A Biographical History of African American Athletes*, ed. David Wiggins, 207–22 (Fayetteville: University of Arkansas Press, 2006); Maureen Margaret Smith, "Identity and Citizenship: African American Athletes, Sport, and the Freedom Struggles of the 1960s" (Ph.D. diss., Ohio State University, 1999), 260–88.

15. Rudolph, *Wilma*, 80–85; "Earlene Brown Sets Mark in Discus, Shot Triumphs," *Los Angeles Times*, August 26, 1956.

16. Mark Dyreson, *Making the American Team: Sport, Culture, and the Olympic Experience* (Urbana: University of Illinois Press, 1998), 1–6; Douglas Hartman, *Race, Culture, and the Revolt of the Black Athlete* (Chicago: University of Chicago Press, 2003), 15–17; Allen Guttmann, *The Olympics: A History of the Modern Games* (Urbana: University of Illinois Press, 2002), 86–102; Kathryn Jay, *More Than Just a Game: Sports in American Life since 1945* (New York: Columbia University Press, 2004), 51–54. The Soviet Union had long refused to participate in the Olympics, but after World War II, Josef Stalin saw sport as an advertisement for worldwide communist superiority. In 1952 the IOC had sanctioned Soviet "amateurs" sponsored by the state. In 1956 it allowed the USSR to participate in Melbourne.

17. Allen Guttmann, *Games and Empires: Modern Sports and Cultural Imperialism* (New York: Columbia University Press, 1994), 129; Allen Guttmann, *Women's Sports: A History* (New York: Columbia University Press, 1991), 199–202; Festle, *Playing Nice*, 79–94; Lenskyj, *Out of Bounds*, 86–87; Jay, *More Than Just a Game*, 54–57.

18. *Baltimore Afro-American*, April 19, 1958; "Australia Bound," *Chicago Defender*, September 8, 1956; Bob Alden, "Tennessee State's Amazing Track Girls Work Their Way," *Washington Post and Times Herald*, August 30, 1956.

19. Mal Florence, "Rudolph's Not Fading Away," *Los Angeles Times*, July 25, 1984; *Nashville Banner*, November 14, 1994.

20. Wilfrid Smith, "Ron Delany Wins Record 1,500 Meters," *Chicago Tribune*, December 1, 1956; Ted Smits, "Morrow, U.S., Complete Olympic Track Rout," *Washington Post and Times Herald*, December 2, 1956.

21. Rudolph, *Wilma*, 100–108; untitled, *Chicago Defender*, January 12, 1957; "Tennessee Stars Crack Two Outdoor Marks," *Chicago Defender*, May 4, 1957; "Tennessee Girls Win 4th Tuskegee Title," *Chicago Defender*, May 11, 1957.

22. Rudolph, *Wilma*, 109–12.

23. Rudolph, *Wilma*, 113; Bob Alden, "Tennessee State's Amazing Track Girls Work Their Way," *Washington Post and Times Herald*, August 30, 1956; Haley, "The Queen Who Earned Her Crown," 58–60; *Nashville Banner*, November 14, 1994; Barker, "The Man Who REALLY Won the Olympics," 17.

24. Rudolph, *Wilma*, 113–17.

25. "Tennessee A. and I. Women Gain National Indoor Track Crown," *New York Times*, January 25, 1959; *Nashville Tennessean*, June 29, 1959; uncited article from 1959, Temple Scrapbook.

26. Joseph M. Sheehan, "U.S. Men Favored over Russians in 6 Events at Track Meeting Opening Today," *New York Times*, July 18, 1959; Joseph M. Sheehan, "U.S. Men Lead Soviet Union Team, 59–47, In Track," and Arthur Daley, "Meeting of the Powerhouses," both *New York Times*, July 19, 1959; Joseph M. Sheehan, "U.S. Men Beat Soviet in Track; Russian Women Are Victorious," *New York Times*, July 20, 1959; Joseph M. Sheehan, "Soviet's Performances Impress and Disturb U.S. Track Coaches," *New York Times*, July 21, 1959.

27. Arthur Daley, "Storm Finish," *New York Times*, July 20, 1959; *Nashville Tennessean*, September 3, 1959; "Pan-American Games Camera Highlights," *Chicago Defender*, September 12, 1959; Haley, "The Queen Who Earned Her Crown," 60–61; Heilman, "Wilma and Ed," 49.

28. "Wilma Rudolph Sets 2 Records," *New York Times*, April 17, 1960; *Nashville Banner*, May 25, 1960; "Rudolph Sets Track Marks," *Washington Post and Times Herald*, June 26, 1960.

29. "Tenn. State Runner Breaks World Mark," *Chicago Tribune*, July 10, 1960; "Chicago Girl Sets

Broad Jump Mark," *Chicago Tribune*, July 16, 1960; "American Woman Sets Sprint Mark," *New York Times*, July 11, 1960; Rudolph, *Wilma*, 120–21; source unknown, July 18, 1960, Temple Scrapbook.

30. Olga Fitokova Connolly, "Love Made Me an American," *Saturday Evening Post*, January 28, 1961, 15–17, 52–54; "Discus Title Goes to Mrs. Connolly," *New York Times*, July 11, 1960; "No Suffrage? 'U.S. Keeps Women's Track Hidden'—Olga," *Los Angeles Times*, July 19, 1960; Rudolph, *Wilma*, 120.

31. *Baltimore Afro-American*, September 10, 1960.

32. Rudolph, *Wilma*, 121–25; "AAU Politics Cause False Rumors," *Chicago Defender*, August 6, 1960; Earl S. Clanton III, "Morale Boosts Women's Squad," *Chicago Defender*, August 27, 1960.

33. Temple, *Only the Pure in Heart Survive*, 50, 82; Rudolph, *Wilma*, 126–28; Heilman, "Wilma and Ed," 49–50; Barker, "The Man Who REALLY Won the Olympics," 18; *Harrisburg (Pa.) Evening News*, August 25, 1960.

34. "Miss Rudolph Breaks Mark," *New York Times*, August 23, 1960; Rudolph, *Wilma*, 129–30; Barker, "The Man Who REALLY Won the Olympics," 18.

35. Rudolph, *Wilma*, 130–31; "Miss Rudolph Equals Mark in 100 Meters," *Chicago Tribune*, September 1, 1960; Leo H. Peterson, "Tennessee A&I Star Triumphs at Olympics," *Chicago Defender*, September 10, 1960; Barker, "The Man Who REALLY Won the Olympics," 18; undated article, *Nashville Banner*, Temple Scrapbook.

36. Paul Zimmerman, "Thomas Upset by Russian Jumpers," *Los Angeles Times*, September 2, 1960; *Nashville Banner*, September 3, 1960; Allison Danzig, "Americans Sweep Hurdles Medals," and Arthur Daley, "Considerable Improvement," *New York Times*, September 3, 1960.

37. Ed Temple, "Long Legs, Wide Smile, Big Heart," *Newsweek*, October 25, 1999, 58; Wilfrid Smith, "Six More U.S. Gold Medals; Gain on Russia," *Chicago Tribune*, September 3, 1960; Danzig, "Americans Sweep Hurdles"; Barker, "The Man Who REALLY Won the Olympics," 18; *Nashville Banner*, September 3, 1960; Peterson, "Tennessee A&I Star Triumphs."

38. "Girl Olympians Sentimental," *New York Times*, September 4, 1960; "Notes From Olympic Sidelines: U.S. Spectators Win Song Title," *New York Times*, September 6, 1960; Paul Zimmerman, "Yanks Sweep Hurdles; Wilma Victor," *Los Angeles Times*, September 6, 1960; source unknown, September 6, 1960, Temple Scrapbook. Along with her two golds, Didrikson also won a silver medal in 1932.

39. "World Speed Queen," *New York Times*, September 9, 1960; Paul Zimmerman, "U.S. Nabs 1,600-Meter, Fouls in 400," *Los Angeles Times*, September 9, 1960; Wilfrid Smith, "Russ Regain Gold Medal Lead," *Chicago Tribune*, September 9, 1960; *Nashville Banner*, September 9, 1960; *Philadelphia Inquirer*, September 9, 1960.

40. "Connolly, Norton Disgusted," *New York Times*, September 4, 1960; Allison Danzig, "Wilson and Sober Defend Athletes," *New York Times*, September 5, 1960; Allison Danzig, "Norton Runs Out of Passing Zone," *New York Times*, September 9, 1960; Paul Zimmerman, "U.S. Nabs 1,600-Meter, Fouls in 400," *Los Angeles Times*, September 9, 1960; Smith, "Russ Regain Gold Medal Lead"; source unknown, "Jesse Owens' Olympic Diary," December 1960, Temple Scrapbook; *Nashville Banner*, September 9, 1960.

41. "The Fastest Female," *Time*, September 19, 1960, 74; Joan Zyda, "Wilma Rudolph: Back on the Track," *Chicago Tribune*, December 18, 1977; "Olympian Quintessence," *Life*, September 19, 1960, 115; Arthur Daley, "Not According to Plan," *New York Times*, September 6, 1960; "Double Sprint Champion Hurries Only on Track," *New York Times*, September 9, 1960.

42. Ira Berkow, "Forever the Regal Champion," *New York Times*, November 13, 1994; Rudolph, *Wilma*, 137; Temple, *Only the Pure in Heart Survive*, 84; Haley, "The Queen Who Earned Her

Crown," 61; Wilfrid Smith, "Extinguish Olympic Flame as 100,000 See Final Parade," *Chicago Tribune*, September 12, 1960; *Clarksville Leaf-Chronicle*, September 10, 1960.

43. "World Wide Invitations Flood Wilma Rudolph," *Chicago Defender*, September 17, 1960; "Earlene Brown Sets Mark in Germany," *Chicago Defender*, October 1, 1960; "U.S. Wins Four Events," *New York Times*, September 16, 1960; "Wilma Rudolph Wins Bicycle," *Washington Post and Times Herald*, September 23, 1960; undated article, *Los Angeles Sentinel*, Wilma Rudolph Clippings File, Tennessee State University Special Collections; Joan Zyda, "Wilma Rudolph: Back on the Track," *Chicago Tribune*, December 18, 1977; Rudolph, *Wilma*, 138–40.

44. "Miss Rudolph Arrives," *New York Times*, September 26, 1960; Robert M. Lipsyte, "Wilma Rudolph Pauses Briefly For Medal, Visit and Plaudits," *New York Times*, September 27, 1960; "And to Complete the Report," *Chicago Tribune*, September 27, 1960; "Welcome, Champs," *Chicago Tribune*, September 29, 1960; Neil Milbert, "Wilma Rudolph Wins Race of Her Life," December 15, 1977; Joan Zyda, "Wilma Rudolph: Back on the Track," *Chicago Tribune*, December 18, 1977.

45. *Detroit Free Press*, September 28, 1960; Lee D. Jenkins, "U.S. Olympic Screams Leave Bad Taste," *Chicago Defender*, September 17, 1960; "Tenn. Cheers Olympic Stars," *Chicago Defender*, October 8, 1960; *Clarksville Leaf-Chronicle*, September 30, 1960.

46. Rudolph, *Wilma*, 141–45; *Clarksville Leaf-Chronicle*, September 28, 1960, October 5, 1960; Edward H. Brown Jr., "Clarksville," *Chicago Defender*, October 22, 1960; "Wilma's Home Town Win," *Life*, October 17, 1960, 110–15.

47. Temple, *Only the Pure in Heart Survive*, 84–85; Byron Roberts, "Miss Rudolph Continues to Set Fast Pace," *Washington Post and Times Herald*, October 31, 1960; "Rafer Johnson Wins AAU Sullivan Trophy," *Washington Post and Times Herald*, January 1, 1961; "Wilma Rudolph Victor in Voting," *New York Times*, December 25, 1961; "Miss Rudolph Gets Top Award," February 28, 1961; "1,030 Pay Tribute to Lena Horne, Oscar," and "W. Rudolph, Johnson Picked For Top Award," *Chicago Defender*, December 10, 1960; "Miss Rudolph Voted Woman Athlete of '60," *Chicago Tribune*, January 29, 1961; "Europe Salutes Wilma Rudolph," *Chicago Defender*, February 4, 1961; *The Meter*, November 17, 1994, May 20, 2000; A. S. "Doc" Young, *Negro Firsts in Sports* (Chicago: Johnson Publishing Company, Inc., 1963), 268–69; "Others Worthy of Honor," *Sports Illustrated*, January 9, 1961, 34.

48. Lester C. Lamon, *Blacks in Tennessee, 1791–1970* (Knoxville: University of Tennessee Press, 1971), 106–7; Henry Hampton and Steve Fayer, *Voices of Freedom: An Oral History of the Civil Rights Movement from the 1950s through the 1980s* (New York: Bantam Books, 1991), 53–72. Scholars of women in the civil rights movement have mostly concentrated their investigations on female political activists. See, for instance, Bettye Collier-Thomas and V. P. Franklin, eds., *Sisters in the Struggle: African American Women in the Civil Rights–Black Power Movement* (New York: New York University Press, 2001); Lynne Olsen, *Freedom's Daughters: The Unsung Heroines of the Civil Rights Movement from 1830 to 1970* (New York: Scribner, 2001); Belinda Robnett, *How Long? How Long? African-American Women in the Struggle for Civil Rights* (New York: Oxford University Press, 1997). The study of Wilma Rudolph suggests the potential for other investigations of the political ramifications of black female celebrities.

49. Barker, "The Man Who REALLY Won the Olympics," 18; Robert Hartmann, "Nixon Plane in Trouble," *Los Angeles Times*, September 14, 1960.

50. *The Meter*, March 1962; "President Is Host to Wilma Rudolph," *New York Times*, April 15, 1961; Rudolph, *Wilma*, 149–50.

51. Melinda M. Schwenk, "Negro Stars and the USIA's Portrait of Democracy," *Race, Gender, and Class* 8, no. 4 (2001): 127–28; "S. Africa's Race Plan Killed," *Chicago Defender*, February 4, 1961; Ralph Creger, "Ark. Author Answers Dixie Segregationist," *Chicago Defender*, April 8, 1961; "A.A.U.

Agrees to South Africa's 'Preferred Athlete List for Its Meets," *New York Times*, January 17, 1961; undated article in *Nashville Tennessean*, Temple Scrapbook.

52. Jeane Hoffman, "Speedy Wilma Rudolph Not Interested in Racing Men," *Los Angeles Times*, January 19, 1961; Doug Mauldin, "Male Supremacy Faces Big Test," *Los Angeles Times*, February 26, 1961; *Detroit News*, July 31, 1962; Robert L. Teague, "Everyone Has Wilma Rudolph on the Run," *New York Times*, February 4, 1961; "Wilma Rudolph 'Just Lazy,'" *Washington Post and Times Herald*, July 8, 1961; Young, *Negro Firsts in Sports*, 197 (italics in original).

53. "Wilma Rudolph: Not Spoiled by Success," *Sepia*, June 1961, 67; Jesse Owens, "Wilma Rudolph: Gazelle of the Track," *Saturday Evening Post*, October 1976, 44; *Tennessee State University Accent*, December 1994/January 1995; *The Meter*, November 17, 1994; Heilman, "Wilma and Ed," 50; "Man in Orbit," *Los Angeles Times*, June 1, 1962; "Tenn. Red Carpet for 2 Stars," *Chicago Defender*, September 17, 1960; uncited article dated January 28, 1961, Temple Scrapbook; "Everyone Has Wilma Rudolph on the Run," *New York Times*, February 4, 1961; John Steen, "Wilma Rudolph Earns Grant for Her College," *Washington Post and Times Herald*, April 14, 1961; "Wilma Rudolph 'Just Lazy,'" *Washington Post and Times Herald*, July 8, 1961.

54. James Murray, "A Big Night for Wilma," *Sports Illustrated*, January 30, 1961; "Girl on the Run," *Newsweek*, February 6, 1961, 54; "Storming the Citadel," *Time*, February 10, 1961, 57; "World, Two U.S. Records Fall in L.A.," *Chicago Tribune*, January 22, 1961; "Miss Rudolph Sets 2D Mark in 24 Hours," *Chicago Tribune*, February 19, 1961; Red Smith, "The Woman's Touch," *Washington Post and Times Herald*, February 2, 1961; *Detroit News*, July 31, 1962; uncited article dated January 23, 1961, Temple Scrapbook; "Wilma Wins, Collapses After 220 Loss," *Los Angeles Times*, March 12, 1961; Joseph M. Sheehan, "One World Record Set and Two Tied in Millrose Track at Garden," *New York Times*, February 4, 1961; "Wilma Rudolph Clips 220 Mark with 0:25 in Indoor Title Trials," *New York Times*, March 11, 1961; "Wilma Rudolph Is Ill," *New York Times*, March 14, 1961.

55. "Three Olympic Stars Eclipsed at Drake," *New York Times*, April 30, 1961; Arthur Daley, "Ready for Ivan," *New York Times*, June 27, 1961, July 4, 1961; "West German Women Rout Americans in Track; Men's Meet to Start Today," *New York Times*, July 18, 1961; Thomas Fitzpatrick, "Chicago Girls Win AAU Title," *Chicago Tribune*, July 3, 1961; "U.S. Sets Two Track Records," *Chicago Tribune*, July 16, 1961; "Miss Rudolph Sets World Dash Record," *Chicago Tribune*, July 20, 1961; uncited articles dated July 12, 1961 and July 13, 1961, Temple Scrapbook; "U.S. Track Men Rout British Team, 122 to 88," *Washington Post and Times Herald*, July 23, 1961; "U.S. Men Take 68–49 Lead over Poland in Track," *Washington Post and Times Herald*, July 30, 1961; "Beatty Upsets 1,500 Ace: U.S. Track Team Leads Poland, 8–3," *Los Angeles Times*, July 30, 1961.

56. "School Beckons Wilma," *Los Angeles Times*, August 4, 1961; "Wilma Rudolph Repeats as Top Female Athlete," *New York Times*, December 19, 1961; "Wilma Rudolph Gets Sullivan Sportsmanship Award," *New York Times*, February 26, 1962; *Nashville Banner*, June 27, 1963; *The Meter*, October 1–15, 1961; "Wilma Rudolph Wed to School Track Athlete," *Chicago Tribune*, November 29, 1961; "Wilma Voted Amateur of Year Award," *Chicago Tribune*, January 3, 1962.

57. "Wilma Rudolph Asks Divorce, Charges Cruelty," *Washington Post and Times Herald*, January 31, 1963; "Wilma's Plans for Tokyo Olympics Clouded by Illness and Divorce," *Washington Post and Times Herald*, February 21, 1963.

58. Mal Florence, "Jean Had Hunch She'd Beat Wilma," *Los Angeles Times*, January 21, 1962; Jim Murray, "Night at the Races," *Los Angeles Times*, January 22, 1962; Al Wolf, "U.S. Outlook Again Bleak for Meet With Russian Girls on July 21–22," *Los Angeles Times*, July 5, 1962; Al Wolf, "Wilma Rudolph Set to Try Comeback in AAU Track," *Los Angeles Times*, July 8, 1962; Al Wolf, "Wonderful Wilma Does It Again," *Los Angeles Times*, July 9, 1962; "Wilma Rudolph Starts Comeback This

Week," *Washington Post and Times Herald*, July 5, 1962; "81,000 See Russian Jump 7 Ft., 5 In.," *Chicago Tribune*, July 23, 1962; "Wilma Rudolph Ward Wins Dash in Oslo," *Chicago Tribune*, August 29, 1962; Joseph M. Sheehan, "Americans Figure to Win 14 Events," *New York Times*, July 21, 1962; "U.S. Wins 4 Track Events; Thomas Bows in High Jump," *New York Times*, August 24, 1962; "Miss Rudolph Heads Track Team for '62," *New York Times*, December 13, 1962.

59. Al Wolf, "Upsets Spice Indoor Track," *Los Angeles Times*, January 20, 1963; "Wilma Rudolph Out," *Washington Post and Times Herald*, February 6, 1963; "Wilma's Plans for Tokyo Olympics Clouded by Illness and Divorce," *Washington Post and Times Herald*, February 21, 1963; "Wilma May Skip Games," *Washington Post and Times Herald*, March 5, 1963.

60. "Wilma Rudolph Still Unsure on Olympics," *Washington Post and Times Herald*, April 16, 1963; "Wilma Rudolph Off to Senegal," *New York Times*, April 13, 1963; "Senegal in Salute to Wilma Rudolph," *New York Times*, April 14, 1963; "Wilma Rudolph to Tour Ghana," *New York Times*, April 24, 1963; "Wilma Rudolph in Upper Volta," *New York Times*, May 6, 1963; "Athlete in Protest," *New York Times*, May 30, 1963; "The Nation," *New York Times*, June 2, 1963; "Restaurant Bars Negro Feted in '60 With Parade," *Chicago Tribune*, May 31, 1963. On black athletes and State Department tours, see Damion Lamar Thomas, "'The Good Negroes': African-American Athletes and the Cultural Cold War, 1945–1968" (Ph.D. diss., University of California–Los Angeles, 2002).

61. "Wilma Gets Diploma," *Chicago Tribune*, May 28, 1963; Milbert, "Wilma Rudolph Wins Race of Her Life"; "Wilma Rudolph Weds Former Classmate," *Washington Post and Times Herald*, July 23, 1963; "Wilma Rudolph Is Married," *New York Times*, July 23, 1963; Rudolph, *Wilma*, 156–57.

62. "Wilma Rudolph, Expecting Baby, Out of Olympics," *Washington Post and Times Herald*, June 17, 1964; Bob Addie, "Sports for Women," *Washington Post and Times Herald*, December 8, 1967; uncited article dated January 16, 1964, Temple Scrapbook; Rudolph, *Wilma*, 158; *Nashville Tennessean*, October 4, 1964; "A Girl's Dream of Travel Can Come True on Running Track," *Los Angeles Times*, February 2, 1964; Al Wolf, "Lady Spikers on Upswing," *Los Angeles Times*, June 18, 1964; A. S. "Doc" Young, "Track for Girls Now 'In' (Barry Help Us)," *Chicago Defender*, August 22, 1964.

63. Joan Zyda, "Wilma Rudolph: Back on the Track," *Chicago Tribune*, December 18, 1967; Rudolph, *Wilma*, 158–61; "Miss Rudolph Trains 1100," *Washington Post and Times Herald*, April 19, 1966; Bob Addie, "Job Corps Enters Sports," *Washington Post and Times Herald*, June 15, 1967; "Olympian Irked by Track Rift," *Chicago Defender*, April 22, 1966; "Olympic Star Wilma Rudolph Joins Job Corps," *Chicago Defender*, December 3, 1966.

64. Rudolph, *Wilma*, 162–64; Alfred Friendly Jr., "Wilma Rudolph Denies Selling Medals," *New York Times*, March 26, 1969; "Pope Honors Miss Rudolph," *New York Times*, March 27, 1969; "The Newsmakers," *Los Angeles Times*, March 27, 1969; "Wilma Denies 'Broke' Stories," *Chicago Defender*, March 29, 1969; George Armstrong, "Gold Medals Weren't Sold, Says Wilma," *Washington Post and Times Herald*, March 30, 1969. Rudolph had sold three trophies from AP and UPI, which only became apparent in 1971, after a St. Louis housewife donated them to Tennessee State. See *Nashville Tennessean*, October 18, 1971.

65. "Lady in a Hurry," *Newsweek*, September 11, 1972, 60; "She Runs in Mother's Footsteps," *New York Times*, April 8, 1973; "Newsmakers," *Chicago Tribune*, February 17, 1973; "Track Scholarship for Star's Daughter," *Chicago Tribune*, May 26, 1976; *Nashville Tennessean*, July 21, 1974; William Gildea, "Blacks Find Olympic Gold No Ticket to Better Things," *Washington Post and Times Herald*, March 28, 1973; Rudolph, *Wilma*, 164–65.

66. William S. Lewis, "The World's Fastest Woman is a Whirlwind," *Encore American and Worldwide News*, November 27, 1978, 23–24; Milbert, "Wilma Rudolph Wins Race of Her Life"; "School Officials to Hear Athlete," *Los Angeles Times*, March 18, 1978; Mal Florence, "Rudolph's Not Fading

Away," *Los Angeles Times*, July 25, 1984; Frank Litsky, "Wilma Rudolph, Star of the 1960 Olympics, Dies at 54," *New York Times*, November 13, 1994; "Rudolph Film U.S. TV-Bound," *Washington Post*, December 3, 1975; *Nashville Banner*, September 27, 1977.

67. "Cicely Tyson Gets Role in TV Film on Wilma Rudolph," *Los Angeles Times*, April 23, 1977; "Shirley Jo Finney Gets Title Role in Wilma Rudolph TV Film," *Los Angeles Times*, July 12, 1977; John Hall, "Mr. Olympics," *Los Angeles Times*, January 20, 1978; Cecil Smith, "Sports as a Teaching Tool," *Los Angeles Times*, April 25, 1978; Bud Greenspan, "Real to Reel," *Los Angeles Times*, April 15, 1984; Charles Witbeck, "Shirley Jo Finney on the Run as 'Wilma,'" *Chicago Tribune*, December 18, 1977; Gary Deeb, "Greenspan, NBC Take Bold Step," *Chicago Tribune*, January 20, 1978; Gary Deeb, "Human Element Makes Bud Greenspan's Films Into Works of Art," *Los Angeles Times*, June 22, 1979; John J. O'Connor, "TV: Holidays," *New York Times*, December 20, 1977; Neil Amdur, "How TV Leans on Sports," *New York Times*, February 13, 1978; *Nashville Tennessean*, December 17, 1977.

68. "Wilma Rudolph Lends Grace to Reunion," *New York Times*, March 28, 1976; "Tennessee State Honors Coach with a New Track," *New York Times*, April 9, 1978; Evelyn Ashford, "In Her Tracks," *New York Times*, January 1, 1995; Jim Murray, "Games Girls Could Play," *Los Angeles Times*, November 1, 1973; Ted Green, "Women in Sports: The Movement Is REAL," *Los Angeles Times*, April 23, 1974; "Athletes of Today Remember Rudolph," *Los Angeles Times*, July 21, 1976; "38 of 60 Floats Win Awards," *Los Angeles Times*, January 2, 1979; "Fund-Raiser for Olympics on NBC," *Los Angeles Times*, April 21, 1979; "'No Payoffs, No Promises,' Says AAU," *Los Angeles Times*, July 30, 1979; Marie Hart, "SPORT: Women Sit in the Back of the Bus," *Chicago Tribune*, January 2, 1972; Edith Herman, "Ordinary People Keep the Women's Movement Running," *Chicago Tribune*, November 19, 1977; "Does USOC Pay Athletes?" *Chicago Tribune*, July 29, 1979; Don Pierson, "Amateurs in Name Only," *Chicago Tribune*, August 3, 1979; "King, Guthrie, Rudolph in Women's Hall of Fame," *Chicago Tribune*, September 17, 1980; "People," *Chicago Tribune*, April 23, 1981; Jody Homer, "Women's Sports Association Helps to Bridge Information Gap," *Chicago Tribune*, September 27, 1982; Kenneth Denlinger, "Now It Takes a Sermon," *Washington Post*, June 27, 1976.

69. "Good Healthy Livin'," *Essence*, January 1980, 81–82; Wilma Rudolph, *Wilma Rudolph on Track* (New York: Simon and Schuster, 1982); undated *Nashville Banner* article, Temple Scrapbook; "Rudolph, Young Honored," *Washington Post*, August 27, 1980; Charles S. Farrell, "Black Olympians Will Be Saluted," *Washington Post*, September 8, 1988; Mal Florence, "The Giants," *Los Angeles Times*, July 23, 1984; "Athletes Honored for Perseverance," *New York Times*, October 11, 1991; *Nashville Tennessean*, February 29, 1992, June 9, 1993.

70. Undated *Nashville Banner* article, Temple Scrapbook; "Fifty and Fabulous," *Ebony*, June 1992, 60–66; Alexander Wolff, "Fast Train from Clarksville," *Sports Illustrated*, November 21, 1994, 13.

71. *The Meter*, November 17, 1994.

72. Howie Evans, "Wilma Rudolph Is Battling Cancer," *New York Amsterdam News*, August 13, 1994; *The Meter*, November 17, 1994.

73. William C. Rhoden, "The End of a Winding Road," *New York Times*, November 19, 1994; *Nashville Tennessean*, January 11, 1994; Susan Reed, "Born to Win," *People*, November 28, 1994, 62.

74. Kathleen Krull and David Diaz, *Wilma Unlimited: How Wilma Rudolph Became the World's Fastest Human* (San Diego: Harcourt Brace, 1996); Tom Biracree, *Wilma Rudolph* (New York: Chelsea House, 1988); Victoria Sherrow and Larry Johnson, *Wilma Rudolph* (Minneapolis: Carolrhoda Books, 2000); Wayne R. Coffey, *Wilma Rudolph* (Woodbridge, Conn.: Blackbirch Press, 1993); Victoria Sherrow, *Wilma Rudolph: Olympic Champion* (New York: Chelsea House, 1995); Anne E. Schraff, *Wilma Rudolph: The Greatest Woman Sprinter in History* (Berkeley Heights, N.J.: Enslow Publishers, 2004); Jo Harper and Meryl Henderson, *Wilma Rudolph: Olympic Runner* (New York:

Aladdin Paperbacks, 2004); Linda Jacobs Altman, *Wilma Rudolph: Run for Glory* (St. Paul, Minn.: EMC Corp., 1975); Amy Ruth, *Wilma Rudolph* (Minneapolis: Lerner Publications, 2000); Alice K. Flanagan, *Wilma Rudolph: Athlete and Educator* (Chicago: Ferguson Publishing, 2000); Corinne J. Naden, *Wilma Rudolph* (Chicago: Raintree, 2004); David Conrad, *Stick to It: The Story of Wilma Rudolph* (Minneapolis: Compass Point Books, 2003); Eric Braun, *Wilma Rudolph* (Mankato, Minn.: Capstone Press, 2006); Ann Donegan Johnson and Steve Pileggi, *The Value of Overcoming Adversity: The Story of Wilma Rudolph* (Los Angeles: Value Tales, 1996); Lee Engfer, Cynthia Martin, and Anne Timmons, *Wilma Rudolph: Olympic Track Star* (Mankato, Minn.: Capstone Press, 2006); Jo Pitkin, *The Tennessee Tornado* (New York: Houghton Mifflin, 2004); *Jackson Advocate*, August 3–9, 1995; *Nashville Tennessean*, July 26, 2003, June 24, 2004, July 14 2004, June 20, 2005.

Jo Walker-Meador

(1930–)

The Country Music Association

DIANE PECKNOLD

In 1958 Jo Walker received a phone call from "D" Kilpatrick, manager of the Grand Ole Opry, asking whether she would be interested in working for a new trade organization in Nashville. The Country Music Association, Kilpatrick explained, had recently been formed to promote country music, to improve its image among broadcasters and help it compete with rock and roll for radio airtime, and to increase its audience. At the time, Walker-Meador later recalled, a position with the organization seemed like "a nothing job. The pay was practically nothing."[1] But when she met with the board, she reconsidered. "They were so sold on country music and they sold me," she told a reporter. "They believed so strongly in what they were doing. I figured if it went, I would be in on the ground floor."[2] She accepted a position as a "Gal Friday," handling correspondence, printing and mailing newsletters, working to raise funds to keep the fledgling organization afloat, and creating an administrative and promotional structure to advance the organization's goals.

The CMA did indeed "go," and in the process transformed country music from a marginal and much-denigrated regional style into a central component of the nation's popular music business. When Walker-Meador joined the organization in 1958, fewer than 110 of the more than 3,700 radio stations then operating played at least eight hours of country music a day.[3] By the time she retired from her position as executive director in 1991, country was the most popular radio format in America, with more than 2,500 stations reaching an audience estimated to be 20 million listeners larger than its closest competitor. Country radio stations commanded the largest local audiences in more than half of the nation's one hundred biggest cities—including Baltimore and

JO WALKER-MEADOR
1965. Courtesy of Country Music Hall of Fame and Museum.

Milwaukee—and their listeners were better educated and wealthier than those for any other genre.[4] In 1992 the genre's sales totaled nearly $1.5 billion a year, much of which was returned directly to Nashville's local recording industry.[5] As executive director of the Country Music Association for more than thirty years, Walker-Meador played a crucial role in this dramatic expansion and, by extension, in the "southernization" of American culture and, through the establishment of Nashville as a tourism and entertainment center, in the creation of a new southern urbanism.[6]

Scholars have variously interpreted the process of southernization as a shift of economic power from the industrial Northeast to the Sunbelt; as a demographic revolution that resulted from the largest internal migration in the nation's history; as a transformation of political style and values from liberalism to conservatism; and as a cultural renewal (or, as some would have it, degeneration) that produced some of the dominant popular expressions of the late twentieth century, from country and rock and roll to NASCAR and football.[7] While gender has played an important role in understanding southernization, most analyses have focused only on the travails of masculine working-class men. The distinct experiences of women and the role of regional definitions of femininity have received far less scrutiny.[8] Particularly in their examination of popular culture, historians have generally cast women merely as consumers or as objects of male frustration and insecurity. In his exploration of rock and roll's emergence as a cultural challenge to both racial segregation and gender conventions, for example, Pete Daniel notes that "women remained largely offstage as rock 'n' roll fans, consumers but not producers."[9] But he neglects the very active roles women played as fan club organizers and publicists, music executives, and songwriters. Elvis Presley's first national hit, "Heartbreak Hotel," was written by schoolteacher and songwriter Mae Boren Axton. Beginning in 1955 the head of the southern office for BMI, the performance rights licensing company that bankrolled much of the rock revolution, was a young woman named Frances Preston. She went on to become the company's president and chief executive officer in 1986, making her the head of the nation's largest performance rights organization. Thus, even in rock, where, as Daniel points out, they were less visible than in genres such as country, women actively shaped southern vernaculars into national mass culture.

Women have fared only slightly better in treatments of the economic and cultural significance of country music. While James Gregory offers Loretta Lynn as the embodiment of country music's origins in the southern diaspora rather than the South itself, he also suggests that "gender, or rather masculinity, [was] an inescapable theme, arguably *the* central theme of country music. . . . [E]ven the songs about mama and honky tonk angels (the usual female personae of the 1960s) almost always problematized the male and his life choices."[10] Thomas Sugrue agrees that the gender politics of southernization, and country music, focused primarily on challenged masculinity. Like the hardhat riots and other expressions of conservative working-class discontent, he argues, country music was "charged with new meanings in an era of shifting gender roles" and "shared much in common with pop music and rock in its challenges to authority and its appeal to insecure men (and sometimes women too)."[11] In such formulations, authors literally bracket the experiences and contributions of women, as well as changes and continuities in concepts of femininity.

This lacuna is all the more remarkable because both women and unique regional constructions of femininity were core components of the southernization process, and of the Sunbelt industrial development strategy that reconfigured the nation's economic and political landscape in the 1960s and 1970s. James Cobb has shown that, in their efforts to lure industries to the region, southern politicians and boosters frequently noted that industrial workers in the agrarian South could be had on the cheap because they were "wives, sons and daughters of farmers living on the farm," and therefore did not need to be paid a breadwinner's wage. In Georgia the apparel plants that represented the bulk of industrial growth in the state during the 1950s hired women in such disproportionate numbers that many men were relegated to "the status of a 'go-getter' who sat idle every day until five o'clock when his wife's work day ended and it was time to 'go get 'er.'" As northern companies relocated to the South, such gendered conceptions of work helped to justify low wages and to naturalize the region's fiercely antiunion politics and employment practices.[12]

More recently, Drew Whitelegg has argued that Delta Airlines, a key enterprise in the development of the modern South, relied on its female flight attendants to project a corporate image that traded on the rhetoric of family, femininity, and southern hospitality. Its "southern model" helped Delta minimize unionization, create a recognizable brand, and establish a position "at the forefront of the industry."[13] As late as the 1990s Nashville's Music Row continued to advance a similar familial conception of itself as a way of distinguishing its business community and the music it produced from New York and Los Angeles. As record labels' distant corporate headquarters, undergoing successive waves of consolidation, tried to centralize decisions about which artists to sign, how to produce their sounds and images, and how to promote them to audiences, Music Row serried ranks by emphasizing the intimate bonds of sociability, work, and neighborhood that characterized it as a music community. This familial vision grew at least in part from the extension of real family ties into the industry—where wives and daughters had traditionally taken on responsibilities in the running of country's business, as well as from the genre's particularly vibrant fan culture, composed primarily of women.[14]

Jo Walker-Meador's life and career exemplify many of the gendered dynamics of the developing southern service and entertainment industries, and they illuminate the experiences of women who participated in the massive midcentury rural-to-urban migration that shaped the lives of what Pete Daniel has called "the last generation of sharecroppers."[15] Walker-Meador's early experience on her parents' tobacco farm, the patterns of work and family that allowed her to move into the white-collar urban middle class, and the continuity of women's social networks from agrarian to urban contexts all provide insight into the ways gender influenced both the South's modernization and the southernization of American culture. As was the case for many of her contemporaries, Jo Walker-Meador's ability to assume a nontraditional role was based as much on continuities with traditional understandings of southern femininity as on conscious challenges to gender stereotypes.

Walker-Meador's story also sheds light on the particularly gendered history of the rise of country music, "the most conspicuous component of a Southernized national culture."[16] As executive director of the CMA, she helped to create and communicate a new perception of country music's cultural value, its commercial potential, and its audience. Much of that project focused on revising outsiders' images of the South and southern migrants. In contrast to the persistent hillbilly stereotype of wild men and lascivious women, the country industry consciously promoted a modern, middle-class image of business acumen and middle-class nuclear families for its music community.[17] While popular culture accounts of the southern migrants continued to imagine them as promiscuous, ignorant, violent, and destitute, the CMA's publicity campaigns domesticated its audience by touting the "country and western household," one guided by a male breadwinner of the blue-collar aristocracy. In this way, Walker-Meador's work reconstructed not only the cultural status of country music but also the national mythology of the region. And, because she emerged as the public face of the CMA, Walker-Meador herself became a powerful symbol of Music Row for outsiders, who often described her in terms that recalled the region's most famous, albeit fictional, business-savvy southern belle, Scarlett O'Hara. These responses suggested the ways in which national business interests and the public at large imagined southernness and southern industry, in part, through notions of gender and femininity during the second half of the twentieth century.

Josephine Edith Denning was born in 1924 in Robertson County, just a few miles south of the Kentucky border in Middle Tennessee. She was the sixth of eleven children born to Joseph and Maude Denning, both of whom had deep roots in the region. Like most of his neighbors, Joe Denning cultivated the dark-fired, heavy-leafed tobacco that gave the region its name: Black Patch. Black Patch farmers made the transition from mixed subsistence farming to intensive production of dark-fired tobacco for the international market by the 1880s.[18] By the time Denning and his wife and children worked their farm, the county was home to several of the largest tobacco plantations in the world, including Glenraven, an 865-acre farm that, at its height, functioned as a private town with its own post office, power plant, church, and school. Such concentrations of wealth were offset by a large population of tenant farmers, sharecroppers, and hired hands, black and white, who eked out a living through the hard physical labor required to produce tobacco.[19]

The Denning family fell somewhere in the middle of this hierarchy. Jo's father began adult life as a tenant farmer, but eventually he saved enough money to purchase his own land. Though this feat spared his family the worst hardships of the tobacco economy, the Dennings were always conscious of their precarious economic position. As in most tobacco-growing families, children's labor was essential to the family's welfare. "We did a lot of farm work," Jo later recalled. "We needed to and our father expected us to." Rather than buying one of the mechanical plant setters that became available around the turn of the century, for instance, Joe relied on his children to transplant seedlings from their early cultivation beds to the field where they would mature. Following a common division of labor by gender, Jo and her sisters would walk the field, dropping the young plants in orderly rows, while their brothers followed behind with a peg to dig holes and set the plants. Throughout the growing season, the children were also responsible for the difficult work of "suckering"—pulling new shoots from the maturing plants to preserve energy for the larger leaves—a task that involved long hours bending and stooping among the rows. When harvest time came, the children helped cut the leaves and hang them to cure in the tobacco barn.[20]

The work was difficult and dirty. "Tobacco is very staining and you'd get the gum under your fingernails and your hands would be stained. So we'd try to get that stain off by rubbing them on the concrete around the cistern," Jo remembered.[21] But she also credited her parents with teaching her the values of hard work and thrift that were essential to her success in the very different arena in which she ultimately made her career. Although she remembered her childhood as marked by poverty, like many southern farm women of her generation, she took pride in her family's ability to make do with very little, a virtue she summed up with an observation common among southern farm women of her generation, that the family never missed a meal.[22] "I can remember thinking when I was a child in the tobacco field, we didn't have a lot of things," she reflected. "We were poor but I don't think we ever thought about really being poor because we always had plenty to eat." Nonetheless, she determined even as a child that she wanted a more comfortable life and that she would pursue it through her own work. "But I always thought, 'Boy when I get grown and I go to work, I'm going to have all the candy I want to eat.'"[23]

Jo later attributed much of her professional success to her determination and her willingness to work hard, and connected these traits to her childhood experience on the farm. She also speculated that one of the qualities that made her attractive to the CMA's hiring committee was her "respect for superiors," and this, too, was likely shaped by growing up in Robertson County.[24] The Black Patch was characterized by close-knit communities and mutual aid networks. The Denning family attended church every Sunday at Orlinda Baptist Church, the only one in the area to offer weekly services. Church was a place to worship, develop a sense of community morality, and establish ties with neighbors, and Jo remained a staunch Christian throughout her life. The sense of community elaborated in church socializing was characterized by carefully observed rules of hierarchy and status. Robertson County was a place where a man like Felix Ewing, proprietor of Glenraven Plantation, expected and received the deference of those whom he considered his social inferiors.[25]

Community order and the clearly drawn distinctions of race, class, and gender on which it depended were generally sustained simply by observing rules of reciprocity, etiquette, and deferential manners. But it could also be enforced by violence when necessary. During the Black Patch War at the turn of the century, Ewing and other elite Robertson County growers led their less prosperous neighbors in establishing the Dark Tobacco District Planters' Protective Association of Kentucky and Tennessee (PPA). The association sought to force prices up by presenting a united front to tobacco buyers. Those who refused to join became targets of vigilante groups known as the tobacco night riders. The night riders whipped and beat farmers who would not join the PPA, scraped seedbeds and burned tobacco barns, and even seized tobacco market towns. Many in the region resisted the night riders, but many others viewed their activities as a legitimate form of community censure wielded for the common good.[26] Memories of the Black Patch War were rarely discussed openly by the time Jo was old enough to take notice, but the shared values of mutual aid and social hierarchy that fostered the violence were undoubtedly still in evidence.

The concept of mutual aid in evidence during the Black Patch War was obviously exclusionary and hierarchical, involving as it did violent reprisals against community members who did not submit to established authority. Though the violence of the Black Patch Wars was directed at both blacks and whites who did not join the PPA, in other circumstances and other locations, similar logics of exclusionary "mutual" aid and social hierarchy played an important role in the violent enforcement of racial segregation. But in Robertson County's stratified tobacco economy, racial hierarchy was cross-cut by class commonalities. Though public facilities such as schools and churches were segregated, work and social life often crossed the boundaries of race. Jo's family shared the difficult labor of tobacco farming with an African American family her father employed. She later recalled the relationship between the families as being one of mutual love and respect reinforced by the common experiences of communal work, collective meals, and, for the children, shared play and visits to neighbors of both races. The families maintained their ties for decades after the death of Jo's father and the end of the Walkers' farming enterprise.[27] As would be the case for her negotiations of gender restrictions, Jo did not challenge the racial hierarchy that structured community life in Robertson County, but found the spaces within it that allowed for different possibilities.

Growing up in Robertson County also gave Jo a direct personal connection to the southern diaspora the CMA would come to consider its most important audience during the 1960s. Between 1920 and 1960 the rural counties of the South and Midwest disgorged millions of rural-to-urban migrants, black and white, who reconfigured the social, political, and cultural landscape in their new communities and whose cultures were, in turn, reconfigured by urbanization. Country music became for many white migrants an affirmation of diasporic identity and helped construct a common white, working-class identity that could unite otherwise disparate experiences of region and class.[28]

Jo's parents' siblings and cousins joined the migration of southern uplanders to northern cities such as Detroit and Cincinnati and to nearer urban centers such as Louisville and Nashville. Like most migrants, her aunts and uncles maintained a strong sense of connection to their homeplaces and remained in close contact with their families. Joe and Maude frequently packed the children into the car for a drive to Michigan or Ohio, trips Jo remembered fondly. "You know, they had delis and bakeries and things that we didn't have around home, so it was a treat for me," she recalled of weeklong visits to the home of her mother's first cousin in Louisville.[29]

While in high school in Orlinda, Jo fastened on one of the most common paths away from agriculture for women: she made plans to become an English teacher and girls' basketball coach. She chose English because it was a way, not only to improve her own station in life, but to help her students improve theirs.

Jo always felt that she could have stayed in Robertson County if she chose, but she also knew that the path to a more comfortable life lay elsewhere, and that country ways and habits of speech would limit her possibilities. This was a lesson she learned in part from her middle-school grammar teacher. The teacher's efforts at "trying to get us little country kids to use proper grammar" proved a particular inspiration to Jo, who learned as she was working her way through college that the consequences for failing to learn "proper" speech were quite serious. Hiring committees at the companies where she worked, she later recalled, only considered candidates for entry-level white-collar jobs if they had shed their rural accents. Jo saw teaching as one way of helping the people in her community adapt to the modernization of the South. As she later remarked, her middle-school teacher "really made me want to teach in a country school and to try to help improve their status and acceptance in life."[30]

Teaching English was a way to help rural children shed some of the stigma Jo knew outsiders, even urban southerners, attached to the rural South. But it was also a way to remain involved with her real passion—basketball. Jo started playing basketball in grammar school, and the sport appealed to her natural inclinations toward competition and self-improvement. Like many towns throughout the rural South during the 1930s and early 1940s, Orlinda enthusiastically supported its girls' basketball team. "We were followed to tournaments," Jo recalled. "People would get a busload to go to follow the games. . . . The town really supported the team. And you know it brought recognition to the town and it brought recognition to us as individual players from our neighbors and friends in the community. We were kind of stars, you know."[31]

Participation in basketball was one way for young women to earn respect and recognition within their communities, and it provided them a socially sanctioned way to escape some of the restrictions imposed by gender roles, including those that required women to be self-effacing and noncompetitive.[32] Travel to games at other schools and to regional tournaments also offered players a chance to explore the wider world, an opportunity that Jo particularly valued. When she reflected on her life as an adult, she often attributed her persistence and drive to her early experience playing basketball. "That desire for liking a challenge stuck with me through the years. And I think it gave me some patience in achieving goals."[33]

Jo's early life in Robertson County was typical for a rural southern woman of her generation. She was deeply enmeshed within bonds of family, community, and social hierarchy, and she would never have described herself as someone who challenged gender conventions. Yet it was this very sense of social and geographical place that informed her remarkable achievements as a pioneering female executive in the country music industry. Pamela Grundy has suggested that the presence of "thoroughly modern" institutions like women's basketball should alert us to the transformative possibilities within "traditional" rural southern culture. Such institutions flourished at the margins of the dominant urban, middle-class culture that, while usually imagined as the standard of progressive modernity, frequently proved more restrictive than the "backward" rural culture against which it is often measured.[34] As Jo moved into adult life, into the city, and into the working world, she took with her the values and qualities that life in Robertson County had instilled—a keen sense of social hierarchy, power, and mutual aid; an understanding of the changing relationship between rural and urban in the modernizing South; and a sense of self-possession and determination that allowed her to aggressively pursue her goals within existing conventions of gender, race, and class. Jo's rural southern upbringing was not at odds with her later achievements in helping to develop the modern country music industry, but at the root of them.

Though her parents did everything they could to give Jo and her siblings opportunities, their constrained economic circumstances made it impossible to provide ten children with education beyond high school.[35] Jo knew she could not rely on financial support from her family, but kinship ties nonetheless provided a bridge from farm to urban life. When she graduated from high school, two of Jo's older sisters had already moved to Nashville to attend college, allaying any fears her parents might have had and providing models for living independently as young women in the big city. Her uncle helped her to get a wartime job in the salvage department at Vultee Aircraft Plant in Nashville, and her father's aunt offered her a room in her home in Old Hickory, about twelve miles outside of the city. Jo worked a full day, then attended evening classes at the Watkins Institute, where she studied business English and secretarial skills. "It was not an easy thing to do to work all day and then take the bus downtown and go to school for three hours and take the last bus out," she recalled, particularly because her classes ended only fifteen minutes before the last bus for Old Hickory departed. "I had to run all the way to the bus. If I missed the bus I was in trouble. I didn't have enough money to pay a hotel bill."[36]

Jo's experience of war work paralleled that of many women in defense industries during World War II. In the South, war work provided a critical source of economic support that allowed women, particularly poor white women, to establish themselves as independent.[37] Jo was only one of several women at Vultee who attended Watkins in the evening, using the unskilled work available at the plant as a gateway to white-collar work. Shopfloor friendships extended into social time; the camaraderie and sense of community established inside the plant eased the burdens of work and school. Some of the bonds she established at Vultee lasted throughout Jo's life. When she gave birth to her daughter in 1957, she named the baby Mary Michelle after her closest friend at Vultee, Mary McDaniel.[38]

The other women at Vultee helped Jo adjust not only to independent adulthood but to city life as well, providing guidance on the subtle distinctions between urban and rural mores about femininity. One of their more concerted efforts to convert Jo to cosmopolitan sophistication involved smoking. "Most of them lived there in Nashville. . . . Several of them smoked and they kept urging me to start smoking," she recalled. Though it was a tobacco-growing region, the customs of rural northern Tennessee reflected the gender conventions of the late nineteenth century, an era before the "New Woman" took up smoking. "I was brought up that it wasn't ladylike to smoke," Jo said, but her Vultee coworkers equated smoking with modernity and style, and made plain to Jo that the rules of appropriate behavior for women were different in Nashville. "It was kind of like, 'Get with modern-day things. Everyone smokes!'" she laughed.[39]

By the time she left Vultee, Jo had training in business English and secretarial skills, experience as secretary to the foreman of the salvage department, and a network of female friendships that she sustained throughout her life. Though she continued to pursue an undergraduate degree in English and physical education, taking several years of classes at Lambuth College in Jackson, Tennessee, and George Peabody College for Teachers in Nashville, she eventually decided that business was more to her liking than teaching. She held a series of secretarial and administrative positions, first for a Nashville stockbroker, then for a regional movie-theater chain and a shrimp packing and processing firm. In 1953 a friend and sorority sister named Betty Boles introduced Jo to Charles "Smokey" Walker, the manager of radio station WKDA, where Betty worked. The following year, Jo and Smokey were married. Smokey supported Jo's desire to have a career of her own, even to the point of agreeing to several months of weekly separations when the shrimp-packing company moved to Louisiana. Jo and Smokey both tired of the separations quickly, though, and despite the firm's attempts to keep her with an offer to purchase a radio station for Smokey to manage, neither wished to move. Jo sought employment closer to home, and found a position with the Ingram Barge Company.

Though Ingram Barge was in the process of transforming itself from a small regional carrier to one of the largest shipping firms in the country, Jo's position with the company offered few challenges. In 1956 a friend convinced her to become public relations manager to G. Edward Friar, the Democratic secretary of state under Governor Frank Clement. Jo's work for Friar was excellent training for the CMA position. She oversaw his campaign office alone, handling its finances, correspondence, and publicity as the only paid staff member. In the process she became familiar with many of the leading political figures in state and local politics—connections that would subsequently prove useful in her work with the CMA—and also with the process of politics generally. "Politics is part of living, I guess," Jo later reflected. "You're trying to win friends and influence people to your side, whether you're in a political campaign or whether you're promoting a type of music. You're approaching a lot of people with selling an idea, and I think the experiences were quite similar."[40]

The campaign required a full-time commitment from Jo, and she and Smokey agreed to delay their efforts to have children until the campaign was over; Friar's previous two managers had quit when they became pregnant, and he made it clear that he hoped the same would not be true of Jo. "Eddie said to me, 'Jo, try not to get pregnant till after the campaign.' So we then decided well, we would comply with that request," she recounted, "but somehow or other it didn't work out that way." Despite the pregnancy, unplanned but very joyfully welcomed, Jo continued to work for the Friar campaign. When her daughter, Michelle, was born, she took a few weeks off to recover, and then returned to work. In 1958, however, Friar withdrew from the gubernatorial race, and Jo decided she would like to spend some time at home with Michelle, who was then just a year old. But it was not long before the call from "D" Kilpatrick lured her back to work. Ironically, Jo had only a passing familiarity with country music. Despite their proximity to Nashville, Jo's family had not regularly listened to the Grand Ole Opry, and the closest she had ever gotten to seeing the show was standing under the windows in the alley one evening after she and some friends had arrived late to a sold-out house. Except for the all-day gospel sings she attended with her father and a brief course of piano lessons in her early twenties, she had no musical training, and would later describe herself as tone-deaf in interviews.[41]

The CMA position attracted Jo not because of her love of music, then, but because it offered a substantial business opportunity. Growing up in rural Robertson County had given Jo a keen sense of hierarchy and a notion of what powerful men could accomplish. As the CMA board explained the country music business and the new organization's structure and mission to her, she astutely evaluated the potential of the enterprise based on the prestige of those involved. Among them were some of the most prominent entrepreneurs in the business, in Nashville and beyond—Washington, D.C., broadcaster Connie B. Gay, Capitol Records executive Ken Nelson, BMI vice president Bob Burton, and Wesley Rose, president of Acuff-Rose Publishing, the cornerstone of Nashville's country music economy. "I really had no thoughts [about the industry], negative or positive, because I knew nothing about it. But I knew who some of these people were and what their influence was, and I knew that they were serious businessmen," she later remarked. "They were people with influence and clout."[42] Though their peers in the advertising and entertainment industries might have regarded them as unsophisticated because of their association with country music, the men who proposed the CMA had decades of successful experience in large corporations and government. Connie Gay owned his own lucrative broadcasting corporation in Washington, D.C., Ken Nelson had climbed the corporate ladder at Capitol Records, and Wesley Rose had several decades of experience at Standard Oil before joining his father at Acuff-Rose. Jo recognized that they brought with them not only a genuine interest in country music, but the business and political savvy to promote country as an industry.[43] In December 1958 she accepted the job and started work.

Although Jo was the first employee hired by the CMA, she accepted the position under the assumption that the board would soon hire a director to whom she would report, and that the director would be a man. "I think they had in mind from the beginning to hire a man. You know, that's the way it was in those days," she said. "I didn't think anything about that at all." Jo began work in December 1958 and was joined by the new executive director, Harry Stone, in February 1959. Stone was another powerful man, and an ideal candidate to inaugurate the public relations campaign the CMA had in mind. As station manager of WSM radio from 1932 to 1950, he had been a central figure in transforming the Grand Ole Opry show from a regional to a national phenomenon. By obtaining a berth for the Opry on NBC's Blue Network, securing national advertising sponsors, and blending regional authenticity with a nationally palatable vaudeville-variety style, Stone brought the show out from under the shadow of what was then the most popular country radio show in America, Chicago's *National Barn Dance*. He was well connected in broadcasting circles and in the local business community, and he had a reputation as an effective ambassador to the corporate interests the CMA hoped to reach.[44] Stone's salary requirements and financing expectations, however, were beyond the capacity of the CMA to support. Within a few months, it became clear to the board and the membership that they could not afford to keep an established executive as director of the organization. In November 1959 the board voted to release Stone, and he tendered his resignation. In the hope that the struggling organization could survive with a leaner staff the board made Jo Walker the sole full-time staff member and provided her, as one board member later described it, with "a little salary . . . just to watch things until we could find somebody. . . . And that's how she started. She was just going to hold things together until we could find somebody."[45]

As was the case for women in southern industry from textiles to chicken processing, Jo Walker-Meador's position with the CMA was available to her in part because, as a woman, she was relatively cheap labor in an underdeveloped industry. Moreover, she was equipped with pink-collar skills that few men possessed, and unlike Stone, she did not feel that the secretarial work vital to the organization's success was beneath her. "I could do a lot of the things that Harry could do and he couldn't do some of the things that had to be done in the office," she later observed. "We just didn't have the money to pay both of our salaries. Mine was a lot less, and, besides, I could type."[46]

Although Jo's new position changed her duties only slightly, she immediately brought to the post the organizational and political savvy she had developed over a decade of work in various corporate and political contexts, as well as a sense of personal responsibility for the well-being of the association. Her sensitivity to the CMA's precarious position and her instinct for politics became evident at the very next meeting of the board, in February 1960. Realizing that the association's treasury was nearly empty and that Stone's departure might have demoralized the membership, she asked to meet privately with the CMA's president, Connie B. Gay, the night before convening the full board. The organization had less than one thousand dollars, she warned him. If the meeting did not begin on a positive note, she feared the board might vote to dissolve the association. Gay followed her advice, and opened the morning meeting with a sunny monologue. If his recent cross-country trip was any indication, he said, country music was finally rebounding, gaining in popularity and airplay. Other board members added their own news of increased record sales and new country broadcast outlets. By the time the discussion turned to the pitiable financial condition of the organization, everyone agreed that their investment was beginning to pay off, and that they would throw the financial support of their institutions behind the CMA. Jo's shrewd forecasting of internal board politics had helped to avert disaster.[47]

Over the next two years, working only with part-time and volunteer staff, Jo helped the association's board members execute an ambitious research and public relations agenda. In addition to staffing board meetings and following up on decisions made there, she coordinated an increasingly complex schedule of events—an annual awards banquet that, by the late 1960s, grew into the nationally televised CMA Awards Show; a series of promotional live performances before advertising executives in major metropolitan centers; and a series of benefit concerts around the country, including showcases in Miami and Hollywood. She was also responsible for recruiting and maintaining contact with the membership, preparing a monthly newsletter that tracked country airplay, coordinating deejay requests for promotional albums, and generally spreading the word about the upswing in country music's popularity. When the board decided to conduct a survey of country radio airplay in 1961, they charged Jo personally with creating and sending the survey to every radio station in the United States and Canada, and with compiling and reporting the results.

As CMA director, Jo also established institutional continuity. CMA board officers served only one year in each position, and while officers frequently remained on the board in rotating capacities for more than one year at a time, only Jo could reliably coordinate long-term efforts. Thus, when the board voted in 1961 to establish a Country Music Hall of Fame, it was Jo who tracked the list of electors, prepared and mailed the ballots, monitored the electoral process, and counted the votes. It was she who commissioned the plaques, and she who coordinated the efforts of disparate board members involved in various stages of the massive capital campaign to build a museum that would house the plaques. Jo's roles as ambassador and public figurehead; secretary to the board; and executive liaison to the press, membership, and local politicians and businessmen were sometimes overwhelming. In one particularly memorable twenty-four-hour period in 1964, she represented the CMA at the Montgomery, Alabama, gala premier of a film about the life of Hank Williams; was driven back to Nashville to be dropped off at her office at 4:30 a.m. so she could prepare a memo for a meeting of the general membership the following afternoon; and then went directly to an 8:00 a.m. meeting with Mayor Beverly Briley to discuss the city's support for the new Hall of Fame building before attending the afternoon membership meeting.[48]

Though she considered herself someone with determination and ambition, Jo tended to use that drive in the service of the association rather than her own career. Like the board, Jo assumed for several years that her role would be to hold the association together until it was healthy enough to hire a new executive director. There were few female executive role models for either the board or Jo to look to for guidance. Several women had played important roles in the industry—the CMA board had included female officers from its inception—but women's work was often performed behind the scenes and without official titles or full salaries. As Jo learned more about the industry, she absorbed common wisdom about the importance of women's informal contributions, such as those of Mildred Acuff. "They always said it was Mildred Acuff, Roy's wife, who was instrumental in creating Acuff-Rose," she recalled as she reflected on the position of women in the industry when she joined the CMA. "Always what I had heard was that it was really Mildred and not Roy who had worked with Fred [Rose] to form Acuff-Rose. I don't know if Roy was more of the entertainer and

Mildred was more of a businesswoman and maybe she saw it as an investment." But such women served as role models by reputation only, and infrequently held publicly recognized roles. "When I came on the scene, [Mildred Acuff] was not a person that was in that office. She might have been in and out but she was not a person who held a position."[49]

One of the few prominent female executives in the business was Frances Preston, who had been hired to run BMI's Nashville office in 1958. Preston made it a point to get to know Jo, both so that BMI could support the association and because Preston believed in Jo's personal potential. When Preston joined the CMA board in 1960, Jo recalled, Preston encouraged her "to exert myself more and stand up for myself and just be more assertive and . . . let them know that I could do the work." But apparently it was Minnie Pearl who finally pointed out that perhaps the board should consider hiring Jo as their permanent executive director. Pearl "said to the board in a discussion about it, 'Well, why are we looking for someone else? Why don't we just make Jo the executive director? She's doing all the work anyway.' And everybody said 'Well, why not? We just hadn't thought about it in those terms.'" In November 1962 *Cashbox* reported that the outgoing board had promoted Jo to executive director "in order to give her added authority and to present an opportunity to carry her duties into new areas."[50]

Despite the paucity of prominent female executives, a network of women's work supported both Jo and the CMA. Until 1962 Walker-Meador remained the CMA's only full-time employee, and the organization's success depended on mobilizing volunteers to work; more often than not, these volunteers were women. "A couple of the board members' wives were good to come in and help me do some typing from time to time," she later remembered, "and Tex Ritter's band would come in and help me get out a mailing, fold and stuff things."[51] Even as late as 1964, when Jo had finally gotten a full-time secretary, she relied on a long-time friend who took two weeks off from her TVA job every year to run the CMA's booth at the annual convention. In later years, when the CMA was on firm enough financial footing to hire more paid staff, Jo's old friend Mary McDaniel, who then worked for an employment agency, recommended candidates to fill vacant positions. Jo's own work also relied on mobilizing family and friends to maintain the house and care for her daughter. In 1961, after Jo's father passed away, her mother moved in with Jo and Smokey and cared for Michelle. Particularly as Jo's responsibilities with the CMA became more time-consuming, her mother was a reassuring presence, as was Smokey's dedication to both his daughter and his mother-in-law. "He'd call her maybe two or three times during the day. . . . I'd get to work and get so absorbed in my work I didn't think about calling home."[52] Her mother's work at home allowed Jo to maintain both family and professional lives, and to focus wholeheartedly on the needs of the association. In a significant sense, then, the CMA's efforts represented an extension of southern women's traditional responsibilities for maintaining mutual aid networks and community cohesion.

In addition to bringing tremendous energy to her position, Jo made use of a well-honed understanding of the cultural politics of class and region. Though she never felt personally hindered by her rural southern background, it had made her intimately familiar with the stigma attached to rural culture and rural people, and to the southern migrants who moved from country to city. The desire to help rural schoolchildren overcome stereotypes about backwards, uneducated hillbillies had animated Jo's desire to become an English teacher, and she now found herself pursuing a parallel agenda in the CMA's campaign against disparaging images of country music and its audience.

The stigma attached to rural southern culture was more than just an affront to the sensibilities of those in the industry; it was also a significant business liability, and it was primarily for this reason that it became the focal point of much of Jo's publicity work for the CMA. The CMA could gain more extensive radio exposure for country music only by convincing potential advertising sponsors that the music would serve their marketing objectives by drawing an audience with significant purchasing power. As a result, the association's public relations campaign aimed particularly at revising the popular image of the southerners and southern migrants who made up the majority of the country audience. Rather than encouraging students not to fulfill hillbilly stereotypes through their speech, Jo now worked with the CMA to educate outsiders about the realities of rural modernization and southern migration. In performances for advertising executive groups, in press releases, in programming guidelines distributed by the association, and in personal correspondence with broadcasters, the association emphasized a single point—the country audience was made up of prosperous blue-collar workers, men and women who had, over the previous two decades, moved successfully from the farm into the urban workforce.[53] "The fans of our music elect the presidents, run the factories, grow the food, transport our goods, and in general manipulate the gears of this country every day," one CMA presentation told advertising executives in 1964.[54]

Country music celebrated its audience's working-class rural heritage, but it also ratified middle-class aspirations and modernity by invoking rural life primarily in a nostalgic mode. While the CMA marketing campaign emphasized the rural origins of the music's producers and consumers, it also narrated the way country's traditional core audience had successfully negotiated the transition to modern, middle-class urbanism. The CMA frequently quoted radio demographic research showing that its listeners were new arrivals to the city from the South and Midwest, but that they were also primarily successful blue-collar workers who owned their own cars and homes.[55] These, the association argued, were "the people who have a heritage of country music and find its fulfillment in their country music radio station."[56] Even if they stayed on the farm, country listeners were not isolated from modern culture. In one sales presentation, host Tex Ritter simultaneously satirized hillbilly stereotypes and remarked on the modernization of the rural audience by declaring, "There are no uninformed people any more. . . . There is a TV antenna on every outhouse." Even the doddering country grandmother "accepts the fact that they can send [men] to the moon for snapshots. The day of the haybales and horse collars is passé."[57]

Advice to programmers counseled them to treat the country audience as respectable, intelligent people, and also to recognize the seriousness of the country industry and the dignity of its participants.[58] In one programming seminar the CMA referred almost directly to the prejudices outsiders might have held against Jo and her school classmates when it responded to the hillbilly stereotype many on Music Row felt outside executives applied to the Nashville industry. "The industry has come a long way in recent years and no one can deny that C&W has grown up. We are not a group of raggedy, country boys and girls with missing front teeth. We have acquired status," the seminar leaders noted.[59] Country artists and entrepreneurs embodied rural southern modernization in CMA marketing materials. "The Country Singer who once gathered eggs and milked the cows is now a big butter and egg man. The Country song writer who once tended stock on daddy's farm is now consulting his broker regarding stock of another kind. The Country musician knows today that Dow Jones is not old Farmer Jones's city cousin!" one presentation to advertisers averred.[60]

Jo was well aware that country music was viewed as thoroughly déclassé, not only by northerners, but also by urban southerners. Even Nashville's elite resented the unsavory reputation they thought country music was bringing to the city they had fought to make "the Athens of the South." "The city fathers in those early days of CMA . . . they thought of us as more or less unwashed hillbillies out here on Music Row," as Jo later observed.[61] Jo took great pride in the country industry's growth and sophistication as an entertainment business, and she always embraced her own family and rural background. But that pride was tempered at times by her anxiety about outsiders' denigrating stereotypes of the rural southerners and migrants with whom country music was popularly associated. She recognized that, regardless of the hillbilly image's falsity, southerners in general and those in the country music business in particular had to take precautions to distance themselves from it nonetheless. When the CMA's request that the city post signs welcoming visitors to "Music City, USA" sparked controversy in 1962, Jo struggled with this contradiction. "I had mixed feelings about it," she recalled. "Naturally, I wanted them to put 'Music City, USA,' but . . . I also wanted people to think that Nashville was a center of culture and learning. . . . I guess I was thinking more at that time about the Yankees, or the northerners, thinking that we southerners didn't wear shoes, et cetera."[62]

While the CMA worked to convince entertainment executives in New York and Los Angeles that Nashville was populated by sophisticated modern businesspeople, it also emphasized its position as a uniquely southern center for music production. This was a vital component of the CMA's endeavors; executives in Nashville sought the acceptance of their counterparts elsewhere, but if the business were to be profitable for them, they also had to preserve Music Row's autonomy, its creative control and as much of the financial return as they could wrest from corporate headquarters. By making Nashville's southernness the basis of its commercial value, the CMA maximized the independence of local artists, executives, producers, and A&R men. Outside meddlers could never understand the mind of the South, this logic of regional exceptionalism implied, and therefore they had no authority to dictate country's content and form. This unique southernness was expressed in a variety of ways—by depicting modern studio recording sessions as informal, front-porch improvisations; by presenting the country industry as a close-knit family and emphasizing kinship ties within bands and businesses; and by offering a generous dose of congenial southern hospitality to visiting deejays, station managers, and businessmen at an annual fall convention held in Nashville.[63]

One way Jo communicated the message of the country industry's arrival as an important component of the entertainment field was through her own self-presentation as a polished, sophisticated businesswoman, and her functions as an executive and the public face of the CMA were supported by traditional southern conceptions of gender roles. She was an asset to the association not only because of her efficiency and drive, but also because, as a gracious, attractive woman, outsiders easily associated her with popular images of femininity that embodied both southernness and business acumen. Consciously or not, Jo's public persona became an integral part of the CMA's effort to establish an image of corporate respectability with a distinctly southern air. For many observers in the industry, Jo embodied the synthesis of southernness and commerce by calling to mind the most recognizable icon of white southern womanhood: Scarlett O'Hara.[64]

As Drew Gilpin Faust has argued, the character of Scarlett elaborated "the continuities as well as the contrasts" between southern belle and businesswoman, "between the Old South and the New."[65] Music trade papers routinely invoked these same tropes in their profiles of Jo. *Billboard* described her as a "lady who combines the softness and sensitivity of the Old South with the hard business realities of New York and Los Angeles."[66] Nashville's own music trade paper, *The Music Reporter*, likewise depicted Jo as a woman who combined "the cold calculating skills of an IBM machine, the southern charm of a plantation belle, and the shrewd cunning of a UN diplomat."[67] Profiles of the CMA often used similar descriptions of Jo to personify the qualities the association hoped to project to the industry. "Facts and figures . . . are but the surface extent of the CMA," one article opined in an effort to pin down the association's ineffable persuasive impact. "The organization and its director have become the symbol of Southern hospitality."[68] By molding their images of Jo to the template of Scarlett, the trades connected femininity, southernness, and business savvy in a particularly compelling way.

Jo's presence in the CMA also reinforced the familial imagery that dominated representations of the country industry. Newspapers and trade magazines emphasized her role as a mother, both in her personal and professional lives, and frequently depicted her as a homemaker despite her executive responsibilities. Headlines described her as a "country music matriarch" and the "den mother of country music," assessments she sometimes reinforced with her own commentary, as when she told one reporter, "If I ever left, it would be like parting with your child."[69] Most profiles included information about her home life, her daughter, and her husband. "Her family takes her job well," one article observed. "They don't feel they have lost a mother—they feel they have gained a celebrity."[70] Others more insistently emphasized an image of hospitality and home that might have struck readers as incongruous in descriptions of a male executive. A lifestyle feature in the *Nashville Banner* underscored the notion that Jo's duties with the CMA were not in conflict with her domestic responsibilities. Despite ten-hour workdays that left "little time for cooking much less entertaining," the article observed, Jo found a solution to her domestic difficulties in "a casual supper in front of the TV."[71] An article in *People* magazine similarly reconciled Jo's importance as an executive with a more traditional image of the cordial southern hostess by accompanying text about her influence and accomplishments with photos of her picking vegetables in her garden and having her hair set.[72]

In all of its work, the CMA thus negotiated between the positive and negative significations of southernness, rurality, and tradition, in part through its invocations of gendered and familial imagery. As the assimilation of Jo's public persona to Scarlett O'Hara suggests, however, race, or perhaps more appropriately its erasure, played a significant role in the image the CMA projected for the industry and its audience. From its inception as a commercial genre in the 1920s, record companies had insistently segregated country music as a white folk form, despite frequent borrowings and unacknowledged collaborations across the color line. But it was not until the 1960s that the music gained a reputation as being explicitly racist, in part because it played such a prominent role in the campaigns of segregationist George Wallace. As the civil rights movement and backlash against it gained momentum, the image of the poor white southerner as a racist redneck replaced the traditional hillbilly as the emblem of the region's backwardness.

Despite the political commitments of many of its artist members, the CMA itself generally avoided addressing race and racism directly. When it did, its position appeared to be moderately integrationist, and was driven primarily by marketing rather than social concerns. When Ray Charles's album *Modern Sounds in Country and Western Music* sold more than a million copies in 1962, the CMA enthusiastically cited it as proof that country was no longer limited to a niche market. "In one aspect of America's cultural life, integration has already taken place," one sales presentation announced to its audience in its discussion of *Modern Sounds*. "It is in evidence not as a regional phenomenon, but throughout all of North America, and as we check off the best selling and most programmed tunes today, we are impressed by a fact of both sociological and music import. The songs we hear are patently the creative products of many different social and racial groups." Such pronouncements worked both to emphasize country's growing market share and to distance the industry from the taint of southern racism, but for the most part, the CMA's politics of class and region elided race.[73]

Perhaps because the genre-based segregation that organized the popular music industry from the outset was largely naturalized by the 1960s, Jo never imagined country music as a form of sonic white flight from the increasing popularity of R&B and other black popular music. However, this possibility was clearly recognized by others in the industry, including Tandy Rice, a freelance publicity agent and future CMA president. Rice told a reporter in 1967 that country lyrics were "simple, and sincere, not about civil rights and such. . . . The lyrics are about what concerns everyday folks."[74] For her own part, Walker-Meador favored integration during the late 1950s and early 1960s, as did G. Edward Friar when she worked on his gubernatorial campaign, but she later recalled that the injustices the civil rights movement protested seemed entirely disconnected from her work at the CMA. Moreover, economic competition from soul music seemed irrelevant enough to the country market that she felt no conflict of interest in lending her time and expertise to the founders of the new Black Music Association (now the Black Entertainment and Music Association) as they worked to develop an infrastructure and marketing strategy.[75] Though country continued to be perceived as a potentially racist form because of its investment in whiteness-as-performance, Walker-Meador, reasonably or not, dismissed the perception, both in her thinking about her own values and in her marketing efforts for the CMA.

By the mid-1970s Jo Walker-Meador had built what many considered to be the most influential trade association in the music industry. The CMA had expanded from 200 members to 4,600, and its board numbered more than 40 officers and representatives. Jo had overseen the funding, construction, and early operations of the Country Music Hall of Fame and Museum, which quickly became one of the cornerstones of Nashville's music tourism industry and a pioneer in that field nationally.[76] In 1970 the mayor honored her with the Metronome Award, an annual recognition of the person who had done the most to advance Nashville's music industry. Two years later, she extended her role in developing Nashville's musical tourism through her vital part in establishing Fan Fair, an annual festival of concerts, autograph sessions, barbecues, and other fan activities. Developed to ease congestion at the industry's disk jockey convention each fall, Fan Fair was modeled in part on a country music festival held in Wembley, England. It soon became a ritual pilgrimage for many fans and an emblem of both country music's popularity and its down-home commercial style. By the late 1990s the festival drew more than a hundred thousand fans and contributed an estimated $10 million to the city's economy.[77]

In 1995 Jo was inducted into the Country Music Hall of Fame, taking her place among the artists and businesspeople most responsible for shaping the course of country music history. Though her association with country music was accidental, the role she played in developing the industry was intimately linked to her experiences as a woman growing up in the rural South at her particular historical moment, as one of thousands of women who took part in the migration from country to city and from farm to blue- and white-collar work at midcentury. Jo did not rebel against the limitations of traditional southern gender ideology, but instead located the spaces within them that allowed, perhaps even encouraged, her to transcend the fairly limited roles she was expected to fulfill. Indeed, as she assumed greater power within the country industry, the complex imagery of southern white womanhood proved to be an advantage both to her and to an organization that sought to project a particularly southern corporate style. The cultural politics of gender, class, and geography woven into

Jo's own identity profoundly shaped the transformation in perceptions of the country industry and its audience that she helped to forge, and the transition from a regional to a national country music culture she helped to navigate. As her plaque in the Hall of Fame suggests, "Jo Walker-Meador's success story is inseparable from that of CMA's as a trade organization."

NOTES

1. Jo Walker-Meador interview by Diane Pecknold, April 3, 2006, side 2, tape 1, audiotape in author's possession. Jo took her husband Charles "Smokey" Walker's name when she married him in 1954. Smokey was killed in a motorcycle accident in 1967, and she remained unmarried for a number of years, in part because the demands of her career left her little time for an independent social life. "I probably would have remarried before this if I had been a housewife," she told a *People* reporter in 1976. In 1981 she married Nashville businessman Robert Meador and took his name as a hyphenated suffix to the one under which she had become known professionally.

2. Nora Louise Krisch, "The Executive Director of the Country Music Association Isn't Musically Talented but She Knows What She Likes," *Houston Post*, January 12, 1971, 3.

3. "36 percent of U.S. AM Stations Carry C&W," *Billboard*, September 4, 1961, 2.

4. Maria Elizabeth Grabe, "Massification Revisited: Country Music and Demography," *Popular Music and Society* 21 (Winter 1997): 66; Bruce Feiler, "Gone Country," *New Republic*, February 5, 1996, 19.

5. Keith Negus, *Music Genres and Corporate Cultures* (New York: Routledge, 1999), 107; Don Cusic, "Country Green: The Money in Country Music," *South Atlantic Quarterly* 94 (Winter 1995), 235–36.

6. The term southernization originated with John Egerton's *The Americanization of Dixie: The Southernization of America* (New York: Harper's Magazine Press, 1974), which lamented the former more than it celebrated the latter, but concluded that "the North (that is to say, all of the non-Southern states) has lately shown itself to be more and more like the South in the political, racial, social and religious inclinations of its collective majority." For a discussion of Egerton's concept and the interrelation between notions of national homogenization, northern decline, and southern progress, see James C. Cobb, "An Epitaph for the North: Reflections on the Politics of Regional and National Identity at the Millennium," *Journal of Southern History* 66 (February 2000): 3–24.

7. For various conceptions of "southernization," see Egerton, *The Americanization of Dixie*; Kirkpatrick Sale, *Power Shift: The Rise of the Southern Rim and Its Challenge to the Eastern Establishment* (New York: Vintage, 1975); James N. Gregory, "Southernizing the American Working Class: Post-war Episodes of Regional and Class Transformation," *Labor History* 39, no. 2 (1998): 135–54; James N. Gregory, *The Southern Diaspora: How the Great Migrations of Black and White Southerners Transformed America* (Chapel Hill: University of North Carolina Press, 2005); Bruce J. Schulman, *The Seventies: The Great Shift in American Culture, Society, and Politics* (Cambridge: Da Capo, 2002 [2001]), 102–17; Bruce J. Schulman, *From Cotton Belt to Sunbelt* (New York: Oxford University Press, 1991).

8. For an example of efforts to redress this imbalance, see Catherine J. Curtis White, "Women in the Great Migration: Economic Activity of Black and White Southern-Born Female Migrants in 1920, 1940, and 1970," *Social Science History* 29, no. 3 (2005): 413–55.

9. Pete Daniel, *Lost Revolutions: The South in the 1950s* (Chapel Hill: University of North Carolina Press, 2000), 153.

10. Gregory, *Southern Diaspora*, 175–78; Gregory, "Southernizing the American Working Class," 151.

11. Thomas Sugrue, "The Incredible Disappearing Southerner?" *Labor History* 39, no. 2 (1998): 163–64.

12. James Cobb, *The Selling of the South: The Southern Crusade for Industrial Development, 1936–1980* (Baton Rouge: Louisiana State University Press, 1982), 112.

13. Drew Whitelegg, "From Smiles to Miles: Delta Airlines Flight Attendants and Southern Hospitality," *Southern Cultures* 11, no. 4 (2005): 7–27.

14. Negus, *Music Genres and Corporate Cultures*, 123–30.

15. Daniel, *Lost Revolutions*, 1.

16. Schulman, *The Seventies*, 254.

17. For an exploration of the gendered dynamics of the hillbilly stereotype in the twentieth century, see J. W. Williamson, *Hillbillyland: What the Movies Did to the Mountains and What the Mountains Did to the Movies* (Chapel Hill: University of North Carolina Press, 1995); and Anthony Harkins, *Hillbilly: A Cultural History of an American Icon* (New York: Oxford University Press, 2004).

18. Suzanne Marshall, *Violence in the Black Patch of Kentucky and Tennessee* (Columbia: University of Missouri Press, 1994).

19. Carroll Van West, "Glenraven Plantation," in *Tennessee Encyclopedia of History and Culture*, online edition, ed. Carroll Van West, http://tennesseeencyclopedia.net/imagegallery.php?EntryID=G021 (accessed March 31, 2008); Yolanda Reid, "Robertson County," ibid., http://tennesseeencyclopedia.net/imagegallery.php?EntryID=R041 (accessed March 31, 2008).

20. Walker-Meador interview by Pecknold, April 3, 2006, side 1, tape 1, audiotape in author's possession.

21. Ibid.

22. Lu Ann Jones, *Mama Learned Us to Work: Farm Women in the New South* (Chapel Hill: University of North Carolina Press, 2002), 5–6.

23. Walker-Meador interview by Pecknold, April 3, 2006, side 1, tape 1, audiotape in author's possession.

24. Walker-Meador interview by Pecknold, August 2, 1999, side 1, tape 1, audiotape in author's possession.

25. Marshall, *Violence in the Black Patch*, 106.

26. Ibid., 105–62.

27. Jo Walker-Meador, e-mail message to author, January 27, 2007.

28. Gregory, *The Southern Diaspora*; Chad Berry, *Southern Migrants, Northern Exiles* (Urbana: University of Illinois Press, 2000).

29. Walker-Meador interview by Pecknold, April 3, 2006, side 1, tape 1, audiotape in author's possession.

30. Ibid.

31. Walker-Meador interview by Pecknold, April 3, 2006, side 1, tape 1, audiotape in author's possession.

32. Pamela Grundy, "From Amazons to Glamazons: The Rise and Fall of North Carolina Women's Basketball," *Journal of American History* 87 (June 2000): 112–46.

33. Ibid.

34. Grundy, "From Amazons to Glamazons," 110. This observation is supported by a number of

essays exploring southern women's postwar political expression in Thomas H. Appleton and Angela Boswell, *Searching for Their Places: Women in the South across Four Centuries* (Columbia: University of Missouri Press, 2003).

35. One of Jo's siblings died in infancy.

36. Walker-Meador interview by Pecknold, April 3, 2006, side 1, tape 1, audiotape in author's possession.

37. Sherna Gluck, *Rosie the Riveter Revisited: Women, the War and Social Change* (Boston: Twayne, 1987); Mary Martha Thomas, *Riveting and Rationing in Dixie: Alabama Women and the Second World War* (Tuscaloosa: University of Alabama Press, 1987).

38. Walker-Meador interview by Pecknold, April 3, 2006, side 1, tape 1, audiotape in author's possession.

39. Walker-Meador interview by Pecknold, April 3, 2006, side 1, tape 1, audiotape in author's possession.

40. Walker-Meador interview by Pecknold, August 2, 1999, side 1, tape 1, audiotape in author's possession.

41. Jim Sparks and John Word, "Advantage Interviews: Jo Walker," *Advantage: The Nashville Business Magazine*, October 1980, 32.

42. Walker-Meador interview by Pecknold, August 2, 1999, side 1, tape 1, audiotape in author's possession; "There Was a Lot of Work to Be Done," *Radio & Records*, October 6, 1995, 65.

43. Diane Pecknold, "'I Wanna Play House': Configurations of Masculinity in the Nashville Sound Era," in *A Boy Named Sue: Gender and Country Music*, ed. Kristine M. McCusker and Diane Pecknold, 86–106 (Jackson: University Press of Mississippi, 2004).

44. Diane Pecknold, "The Selling Sound of Country Music: Class, Culture, and the Early Radio Marketing Strategy of the Country Music Association," in *Country Music Annual 2002*, ed. Charles K. Wolfe and James E. Akenson (Lexington: University Press of Kentucky, 2002), 54–81.

45. Joe Allison interview by Pecknold, March 26, 1999, side 2, tape 2, audiotape in author's possession.

46. Walker-Meador interview by Pecknold, August 2, 1999, side 1, tape 1, audiotape in author's possession; "Jo Walker, CMA's Lucky Accident," *Billboard*, March 18, 1978, CMA-8.

47. "Just Plain Jo Is a Dynamo," *Billboard*, October 28, 1967, 74; Walker-Meador interview by Pecknold, August 2, 1999, tape 1, side 2, audiotape in author's possession; *Close-Up*, February 26, 1960, 1.

48. Jo Walker-Meador interview by John Rumble, July 30, 1997, audiotape, side 2, tape 3, Country Music Foundation Oral History Collection (Country Music Hall of Fame and Museum Library, Nashville, Tenn.).

49. Walker-Meador interview by Pecknold, April 3, 2006, side 2, tape 1, audiotape in author's possession.

50. Walker-Meador interview by Rumble, July 30, 1997, side 1, tape 1; "Country Music Association Board Ups Jo Walker to Executive Director," *Cashbox*, November 24, 1962, unpag., Jo Walker vertical file (Country Music Hall of Fame and Museum Library).

51. Walker-Meador interview by Pecknold, April 3, 2006, side 2, tape 1, audiotape in author's possession.

52. Ibid.

53. For a discussion of southern migrants' success in the urban North, see Berry, *Southern Migrants, Northern Exiles*, and Gregory, *The Southern Diaspora*.

54. Joe Allison, "The Sound of Country Music, Presented for the Adcraft Club of Detroit on Fri-

day, April 17, 1964," 11, Country Music Association Sales and Marketing Programs (microfiche: fiche 1), Country Music Association Papers, Country Music Hall of Fame and Museum Library.

55. Joe Allison, "The Sound of Country Music, Presented for the Sales-Marketing Executives of Chicago, Monday, June 7, 1965," 17, Country Music Association Sales and Marketing Programs (microfiche: fiche 2), Country Music Association Papers.

56. Joe Allison, "The Sound of Country Music, Presented for the Adcraft Club of Detroit," 16.

57. Joe Allison, "The Sound of Country Music, Presented for the Sales-Marketing Executives of Chicago," 9–11.

58. "Sincerity No. 1 'Must' for C&W Show, Says CMA," *Music Reporter*, October 31, 1960, 26; Diane Pecknold, *The Selling Sound: The Rise of the Country Music Industry* (Durham: Duke University Press, 1997).

59. "Sincerity No. 1 'Must,'" 26.

60. Joe Allison, "The Sound of Country Music, Presented for the Adcraft Club of Detroit," 6.

61. Walker-Meador interview by Rumble, July 30, 1997, side 2, tape 2.

62. Walker-Meador interview by Rumble, July 30, 1997, side 1, tape 3.

63. Joli Jensen, *The Nashville Sound: Authenticity, Commercialization, and Country Music* (Nashville: Country Music Foundation and Vanderbilt University Press, 1998), 81–82; Pecknold, *Selling Sound.*

64. Tara McPherson, *Reconstructing Dixie* (Durham, N.C.: Duke University Press, 2003); Drew Gilpin Faust, "Clutching the Chains That Bind: Margaret Mitchell and *Gone with the Wind*," *Southern Cultures* 5 (Spring 1999): 6–20.

65. Faust, "Clutching the Ties That Bind," 12.

66. "Jo Walker, CMA's Lucky Accident," CMA-8.

67. Roger Schutt, "Den Mother of Country Music," *Music City News* 1 (November 1963): 5.

68. "CMA's Jo Walker the Ambassador of Country Sound," *Music Retailer*, June 1974, 13.

69. "Country Music Matriarch," *Lehighton Times News* 8 (October 1979): unpag., Jo Walker vertical file; Schutt, "Den Mother of Country Music"; Bill Hance, "Saw CMA Grow from 200 Members to 4,600," *Nashville Banner*, October 15, 1975, unpag., Jo Walker vertical file.

70. Schutt, "Den Mother of Country Music," 5; Pecknold, "'I Wanna Play House,'" 94–95.

71. Bernie Arnold, "Good Food, Good Television—That's Entertainment," *Nashville Banner*, October 5, 1977, 41.

72. "Host: She Can't Play an Instrument or Even Carry a Tune, but Jo Walker Is a Country Music 'Star,'" *People*, November 1976, 46–47.

73. Joe Allison, "CMA Sales Presentation to Canadian Radio and Television Executives Club, August 1963," Country Music Association Sales and Marketing Programs (microfiche: fiche 1). For a discussion of the conjunction between country's class and racial politics in the 1960s and 1970s, see Pecknold, *The Selling Sound.*

74. Donald Henahan, "Grand Old Nashville Sounds: They're Achangin'," *New York Times*, October 22, 1967, 82.

75. Jo Walker-Meador, e-mail message to author, January 27, 2007.

76. John Connell and Chris Gibson, *Sound Tracks: Popular Music, Identity, and Place* (New York: Routledge, 2003), 241–43.

77. Country Music Association, CMA Music Festival History, http://www.cmafest.com/2006/general/history.aspx (accessed May 10, 2006).

Bettye Berger
(1930–)

Transforming the Mainstream

LAURA HELPER-FERRIS

In 1965 Bettye Jo Berger landed a job as a booking agent with a firm in Memphis that counted all the hot local musicians as clients—Jerry Lee Lewis, Charlie Rich, the Bill Black Combo, Ace Cannon—as well as other well-known artists like Count Basie. The agency booked concerts at auditoriums and nightclubs all over the southern United States, and for a while Bettye handled the lucrative new college market. She was thirty-five years old, the only woman in the agency, and the only woman agent in town. But she soon had a falling-out with the proprietor, who wouldn't pay her the $1,800 he owed her because he maintained that was too much money for a woman to earn. She left and opened up her own booking agency. Piano player and singer Charlie Rich, also dissatisfied with the agency, became her first client, the one who made it possible for her to strike out on her own.[1]

Charlie Rich worked the fertile borderlands between rhythm and blues, jazz, country, and rock and roll. Most of the artists on her rapidly growing client list did so too. Soon she had local impresario Willie Mitchell, a trumpet player and bandleader, on her roster. The king of the live scene, he was also an increasingly influential producer at a local recording studio, Hi Records. Berger recalled: "And from then on . . . they started coming over. Very fast . . . we were busy, busy, busy. And it stayed that way for five or six years, while Memphis music was [booming]. . . . We had the Staple Singers, we had all the Stax artists. And it stayed busy in the colleges. We had the Bar-Kays, who were a very, very big group. . . . I was real proud of the agency, because we outdid [national agency] William Morris." Charlie Rich was white; most of the other artists were African

BETTYE BERGER

1971. Bettye Berger and Ivory Joe Hunter.

Press-Scimitar Photo/Special Collections/University of Memphis Libraries.

American. Bettye was a white woman. How did she forge such an unusual career in such segregated times?

Several aspects of her experience made Bettye's crossracial alliances possible. As she began her professional life, Memphis music and mass media reflected and confounded racial ideologies. A series of happy accidents and inspired choices dropped her into the Memphis musical scene and developed her considerable gifts. These circumstances included her postwar rural-to-urban migration, a history she shared with most Memphis musicians and a lot of their audience; stints in local radio, on an "all-girl" radio station, and on a rockabilly/blues station; and marriage to a Jewish nightclub owner, which put her in professional contact with both black musicians and the white audiences who wanted to hire them. These experiences and connections also defined her social position, casting her as something of an outsider in Memphis racial and class hierarchies. And as a professional woman, Bettye garnered both attention and sexism. In turn, her own struggles—with overt gender discrimination on the one hand, and inner anger and self-doubt on the other—gave her insight into the unfairness of racism, and empathy with African Americans.

Bettye's adventures seem worlds away from her quiet upbringing on her family's small farm just outside of Trenton, in Gibson County, about a hundred miles northeast of Memphis. Yet the seeds of her future life were there. The glamour of movies and records flavored traditional domesticity. Segregation separated people even as the same kinds of music moved them. The magic of radio and the allure of the city made other realms part of the peaceful farm.

Born in 1930, to farmers Arlie and Flossie Elliott, Bettye was the fourth of five girls, with two younger brothers coming along later. Extended family worked nearby farms. Her family's expectations about the girls' future were unspoken but powerful. "I would play with my cousins and we would pretend to be grownups," she recalled. "And we would play mothers and we'd get our dolls. And we would do what *our* mothers did. We would cook, and we would rock our babies. And that was sort of like, it was just a known fact that you'd marry and have a family, and take care of and cook for your husband—even if you have a cook you cook for your husband [laughter] and children and that's what you do." Bettye's mother certainly rocked babies and cooked for her husband and children. But domestic life on a farm during the Depression and World War II, in contrast to that in a postwar suburban house, also included work in the garden and fields. Children performed actual chores rather than playing at them. Thus domestic labor reached far outside the house, planting the idea that a woman was capable of a range of responsibilities and tasks. And during World War II, factory work supplanted farm work for many local women; the federal government located Milan Arsenal in a nearby town, "a bullet plant, that's what the folks called it."[2] Bettye remembers envying those women the comfort and freedom of pants.

Life included more than work. The family loved music, and like their neighbors they wove music and music making into everyday life. A primary place for music was the Baptist church, where everyone sang. Music was a part of playtime as well. The family had a record player for 78-r.p.m. records. She fondly recalled those times, "You had people over to your house if you had a party. And you played records, and you had lemonade, and that was what you would do on maybe a weekend, you know? And then you go to maybe a movie—that was always on a Saturday." The movies conveyed powerful images of romance, and (sometimes) female independence, set to swooning strings and hot and sweet jazz.

Bettye and her family also listened to music on the radio. She loved big band music on the Make Believe Ballroom and various live broadcasts. She learned to jitterbug by watching her older sisters practice in front of the radio (though she never accompanied them on their secret nighttime excursions to a local dance hall). Meanwhile, the whole family would listen every Saturday night to the Grand Ole Opry. Bettye's father, especially, liked its mixture of cornpone humor and folksy music.[3] On Sundays after church, the family listened to gospel music. The Elliotts' listening habits resembled those of most people in the region and throughout the country, black and white.

But it is likely that most of the radio music they heard was made by *white* musicians. For years radio programmers and sponsors ignored black audiences, even though many black Americans owned radios, and instead kept to the tried and proven formats of talk, drama, comedy, and sweet sounds made by white players. Nonetheless, black musicians made it onto the airwaves in a few specific ways. First, there were some who most listeners would not have identified as black; as historian Elijah Wald demonstrates, there were "quite a few blues specialists to be heard on hillbilly programs . . . [and fans] sometimes had difficulty sorting out radio players by race." Second, from the 1920s on, southern radio in particular let loose a certain amount of audibly black blues and religious music. During the Depression in the Delta, he notes, "Many radio singers . . . performed occasional blues numbers, and in some rural areas black string and jug ensembles lined up daily fifteen minute spots."[4] Third, white stations sometimes played the black pop sounds of Nat King Cole and Louis Jordan as well as the new black gospel of groups like the Dixie Hummingbirds. The rich mix of music, even with this relatively limited black programming, shaped listeners' musical understanding and offered them rare positive information about African Americans. On top of all the music offered by actual black people, radio broadcast a lot of music by white performers influenced by African American music, including the most popular groups like the Carter Family and Jimmie Rodgers.[5]

All of these crossovers were ironically the result of segregation; radio stations broadcast the same menu to *all* listeners because they assumed that those listeners were white. For the most part, black listeners of Bettye's generation (including many musicians) grew up with almost the same musical diet as she did. Even the Grand Ole Opry drew both black and white fans from all over the country, in part because it was what was on the radio. Audience experiences were not uniform, though. Black listeners would have had a better idea about who was black, and they would have come to all of this music with a wider knowledge of the genres that made it on the air. To pursue the example, the Grand Ole Opry drew on African American minstrel and vaudeville traditions that had already shaped decades of American culture, though it presented itself as a white hillbilly program. Black listeners were probably also more likely to seek out available black programming on other nights, as well.[6]

This mix of common experience and segregation mirrored everyday life in rural Tennessee. Local segregation isolated black communities and churches from white ones, and in these separate spaces people forged different musical genres. But sometimes the physical spaces were not so far apart. In Bettye's small West Tennessee town, the black church stood near white farms, including the Elliott land. The music flowed out across the brief distances to the little girl's ears, drawing her closer and encouraging her to break the social rules that kept her away: "Sometimes we would go, we would *sneak* (my cousins and I), and go to the country black church on Sunday night, and sit outside the window just to listen to them singing." Overhearing—both in person, as here, and via radio—was one of the most important ways that white people knew about black culture in general, whether they understood or misunderstood or only partly understood what they heard.

Bettye's contact with the black churchgoers themselves remained limited and contradictory. She actually knew and played with some of the kids who attended this church, but the rules were confusing: "Growing up, and living out in the country, we had some neighbors when I was like 10, and they had children [my age]—I had sisters older and younger than me—and we would play together sometimes. But on Sunday, somehow we knew not to. We went to different churches, and when we came home, we had a cousin, relatives came over, you know. . . . it was a day you did not go play with the blacks, because that was just the sort of thing you took for granted, didn't question it." The separate churches and the weekly social distance afterwards gave Bettye an unspoken sense that "the blacks" were different. Although white citizens framed segregation as somehow voluntary—"they" had "their own" churches—it was her own family's disapproval that meant that Bettye had to "sneak" to hear black church music. The congregants themselves would not have been unwelcoming.

Bettye moved to Memphis in 1947 when she was seventeen, intending to stay only for the summer while she worked at a soda fountain and lived with her sister. Memphis was the only city in the region. Standing at the juncture of three states (Mississippi, Arkansas, and Tennessee) Memphis featured the only bridge across the Mississippi for hundreds of miles. Its factories, river port, and stores drew both temporary and permanent rural migrants from across the region, and once in the city the newcomers maintained close ties with their families and churches back home in small towns and the countryside. Successive waves of migrants constituted the majority of the urban population. Rebounding after nineteenth-century epidemics, population increased at a high rate; from 1920 to 1930, according to a city planning report, the city grew from 160,000 to 250,000 people, and most of this growth came from rural migration. By 1950 the population had grown to almost 400,000, "an increase of 35 percent over that of 1940." The pharmacy housing Bettye's soda fountain stood at the heart of the Crosstown neighborhood, on Cleveland Street. Its theater, curb market, hamburger stand, carwash, grocery stores, bakeries, along with its towering Sears store and national catalog distribution center, represented a new downtown, or at least the forces that turned "downtown" into one among several business districts. Just a few years before, a study had found the traffic at the Cleveland intersections with Union and Poplar Avenues to be the city's most dangerous.[7]

Bettye found Memphis excitingly different from small-town Tennessee, from the crowds to the streetcars to the heightened pace. "My life was totally changed," she said later. But segregation was not so different. Later, she would identify her world as "white," but at the time, "that's just the way it was"—"white church, white restaurants, white theaters, everywhere we went was white only and I didn't think anything about it." Official policies and local practices restricted some public spaces to only white people (inside the main dining room of a restaurant, for example) while rendering any black presence in other public arenas socially invisible or at least inferior (streetcar passengers, street sweepers, pedestrians). The soda fountain where Bettye worked was called, of all things, the Whiteway Pharmacy, and it was as segregated as any other lunch counter.

But though Bettye didn't know it, black Memphians lived and worked all over her neighborhood. Black and white people lived literally next door to each other, as they did through many of the neighborhoods just east of downtown. It was also mixed by class and by land use, like those other neighborhoods. Working-class residents and small business owners included both black and white rural migrants, and a small but significant number of Italians, Greeks, Irish, and Eastern Europeans. The migrants flocked in to such older neighborhoods from surrounding areas at the same time that second- and third-generation immigrants moved eastwards into them from downtown.[8]

Regional radio carried only a few black voices in 1947. But even as a minor presence, black music formed a real and increasing part of local programming. Listeners in the Memphis region could pick up Sonny Boy Williamson's blues show from nearby Helena, in the Arkansas part of the Delta (B. B. King, then a tractor driver in Mississippi, timed his lunch breaks to that show's schedule). On Sundays several stations broadcast sermons and live gospel music from local black churches. Into the late 1940s WHBQ carried *Blues Time* for fifteen minutes every day, both sponsored and supplied with records by a Beale Street general store, A. Schwab's. Bettye does not remember hearing these shows, but along with a host of other white and black listeners across the eastern half of the country, she definitely listened to another show featuring rhythm and blues: "Through the week I would listen to my radio, and I would listen to the black music which was coming out of Nashville. . . . At night you could pick up more stations, and you could pick up [that music] loud and clear in the nighttime." Radio station WLAC was white owned and featured white disk jockeys, but at night they played music by black musicians—and at night their signal went clear across the western part of the state. Listeners could order their own copies of the records they heard, via mail order from the sponsor, Randy's Record Shop in Gallatin, about thirty miles northeast of Nashville.[9]

In 1949 this whole musical landscape went through a sea change, as local entrepreneurs discovered the African American market. First, radio engineer Sam Phillips drew up an FCC application to form a radio station that would feature all-black programming. His was a simultaneously commercial and moral vision to make "the Negro voice" audible to white and black listeners alike. But by the time he actually filed his application with the FCC, local station WDIA had had a mighty success with this format, minus the visionary component. Struggling to survive, WDIA station owner Bert Ferguson had started broadcasting niche music—hillbilly and "race" records—even hiring Nat D. Williams, a local black emcee and history teacher, as a disk jockey. We don't know how many white listeners this formatting attracted or alienated. But it garnered a tremendous response from the local black community. So Ferguson cut out the hillbilly music and hired more black deejays. It was the first radio station in the country with all-black programming and announcers. When WHBQ tried to compete, with an

R&B show featuring a dynamic white announcer, Dewey Phillips, it drew not only black listeners but an entirely new audience of white listeners passionate about this new danceable music. (Some new white listeners started tuning in to WDIA once they knew about the music, but most did not. They might have preferred Dewey's R&B to the black station's gospel and pop; they might have seen the station as they did black schools, as part of a separate culture.) A tiny radio station across the Mississippi, KWAM, also started programming both blues and country music. Later, Howlin' Wolf would have a radio show here. Phillips turned his attention to making records instead of broadcasting them, founding Sun Records and eventually recording a musician who was one of these white listeners, Elvis Presley.[10]

Working-class migrant and immigrant kids in neighborhoods like Crosstown were most likely to be the white listeners eagerly tuning in to these stations, possibly because they had already overheard a lot of black voices in everyday life. Yet radio, records, and mail order also made it possible for white listeners to listen to music from black musicians in part because these mass media transcended local segregation and, importantly, the actual bodies that segregation aimed to keep apart. Listeners could focus only on the music. Did this make white listeners radical, for so intimately engaging with black culture? Or conformist, for enjoying the music without engaging with the real people making it?

Bettye mostly missed out on this revolution as it was happening, because she focused her attention elsewhere between the late 1940s and 1955. At seventeen, her domestic expectations had remained the romantic, traditional visions of her childhood. And in that summer of 1947, through her sister, she met a handsome businessman who swept her off her feet. Otha Maddux was a little older than Bettye, a veteran of World War II, and already a successful dry cleaning entrepreneur. He took her out to the Silver Slipper on the edge of town, a supper club founded by a gambler and featuring live bands and dancing, and to downtown hotel ballrooms to dance to big bands. It was a heady jump into adulthood. After a whirlwind romance, they married. She was still a teenager, but she was far from the only one getting married so young. The average marriage age of American women was plummeting in this period of postwar domesticity. And soon enough, she had adult responsibilities along with the excitement: "We had three lovely children. And at that time my dream was to have a white house with a baby, pushing it in a basket, little stroller." Despite a local housing shortage, the family was able to get a small white house through the GI Bill. It was in Highland Heights, a white development in an eastern part of the city so recently rural that Otha had hunted there before the war, and so new that there was no phone service or sidewalks.[11]

But by the mid-1950s Bettye was frankly bored with life as a wife and mother. She wanted to go back to work while continuing to raise her daughters and son, and she even landed some gigs as a model. Her husband opposed her on this: "My husband resented me being, doing anything professionally. And so he just said, 'stop modeling or we will get divorced.' And I thought he was kidding but he wasn't and then—we got a divorce! And it was very shocking to me even. Because my family were devastated, because you didn't do that in those days. And so I knew that I had to hustle, and work." The couple had been married "eight wonderful years"; now they shared custody. This arrangement and Bettye's work would be sources of ongoing tension with her children.

At the same time, this is one of the amazing turns in Bettye's story, and the point where her life intersected with the emergent Memphis music industry. After her divorce, as the desire to work turned to necessity, Bettye thought big and called Sam Phillips. She didn't know him as Elvis's producer but as a local investor (he was an early important partner in the pioneering Holiday Inn chain) and, especially, as the founder of a new radio station featuring only female disk jockeys. She wanted Phillips to invest in a business idea she had that also capitalized on femininity.

Unlike many rural migrants and immigrants who started small businesses across the country in this period, and especially unlike women entering the business world, Bettye did not turn to her family for funding. Phillips shared her family's rural-to-urban move and sense of humor, but she had never met him before. And he was like no one else in the world. He was visionary to the point of hallucination, eccentric to the point of crazy. Although WDIA succeeded first at airing black voices, he did not give up on radio altogether. After Elvis hit big, he returned with the idea of featuring women's voices. Phillips may have felt a connection between the oppression of black and working-class musicians and the status of women—not only the unfairness people faced but also their creative responses and interesting perspectives. But his focus was on the sexy unusualness of women in a male domain. Or as Sam's partner Kemmons Wilson put it, "We got a lot of free publicity out of that because it was an 'All-Girl' station and we had sense enough to hire some good-looking girls."[12] They dubbed the station "WHER—one thousand beautiful watts."

Bettye approached Sam Phillips in 1956, after he had sold Elvis Presley's contract to RCA and after his radio station had begun to prove itself. She didn't know him at all, but she believed he would be responsive to her particular idea: "I wasn't calling about a job at the station, I wanted to open a business of my very own in the Peabody Hotel. [I wanted the store to] have very unusual designer clothes for men. And have models to be the salesgirls and give the man a martini when he walked in." Phillips ultimately declined to invest in her business, but he did offer a kind of investment in Bettye herself: "He *listened* to me. And you know no one listened to, I was barely a woman then, but no one listened! You're female, they're just not listening. So he listened, and that is something that I will always appreciate." Similarly, Elvis and other musicians later described how Phillips's patient, engaged listening had helped them find their voices in the studio.

Along with taking her seriously, Phillips also offered Bettye a job at WHER. He even took her over to introduce her to Dotty Abbott, the manager. "I'll never forget how huge this blue, iridescent blue Eldorado convertible was, with the top down, in 1957," she recalled. "And he drove me over to WHER and it was like walking into a fantasy land. Everything was pink and purple. And I loved the girls at that time that worked there. . . . So it was fun, it was like going to a party every day." It was also a challenge. Bettye's first job at the station was selling advertising, where she faced head-on the expectation that she be both professional and sexy:

> Today it might be quite different, but then it was, it was hard when you would go out to sell and you'd be sitting in an advertising agency. And everybody in there are TV salesmen and radio salesmen in their shirt and ties and you're the only woman in there with a briefcase. And they look at you like you were dead meat. But the head of the advertising agency would always be a southern gentleman and said let the lady come in first. They may not buy anything but the lady didn't have to wait as long. . . . And it was difficult to sell, because most every other station reached a broader audience. So they would also have felt this, say, you know, "Women? I'm going to put my product on the all-girl station? What would the guys think of that?"

Here, vividly, are the multiple sides of sexism. Sales representatives regarded a colleague as "dead meat" because she was a woman, but she got in first because the client, a southern gentleman, let ladies go first. Still, she carried into the office with her the question of whether women could be taken seriously. Ultimately the gamble worked, and the station became "very, very popular. . . . Because at that time there wasn't any women in radio to speak of at all. And we were getting a lot of attention from around the world."

What kind of music did WHER feature? Kemmons Wilson's mandate was clear: "Don't you play anything but love music, a man singing to a lady or a lady singing to a man." One of Bettye's fellow disc jockeys and the record librarian, Rena Franklin, remembered their playlist more specifically: "Mantovani came to Memphis, and I remember interviewing [him]. You tried to get music that went with your time of day. Being record librarian, that was my job, . . . to listen to all the music—Frank Sinatra, Ella Fitzgerald, June Christy. People sent us rock and roll music, of course, and we would get rid of it. And when I did the jazz program, I used Dave Brubek's 'Take Five.' And I think at that time, there certainly wasn't any other jazz program in Memphis."[13] Bettye says that Franklin's jazz show got a lot of black listeners: "They called to say we played the best jazz in town." The avoidance of rock and roll was no accident. Sam Phillips was, ironically, too identified with the new Memphis music, and he knew it: "Now, believe me, I love rock and roll. I loved it then and I love it now. But I knew the concept we had for this station, that we were not going to use any of my great rock and roll records! [laughs] This is how dedicated to the field we wanted to get in that station. There was a dearth, absolute dearth of album music. There was so much good music on the 12-inch LPs that was not being played, especially daytime radio."[14]

Bettye became a disk jockey herself after a while, playing some music she liked and some she didn't: "We played easy listening. . . . We played a lot of—I remember Frankie Laine, I didn't care for him that much but I did play 'Mule Train' a lot because the firemen at the station would call . . . and request that song. . . . I remember how I used to play that on Sunday afternoon and for a request. And we played—my favorites were people like Dinah Washington, Nat King Cole." Her favorite music on the station's playlist was made by African American musicians, although she herself did not identify them as such, nor did the station at the time.

When Bettye went on the air, she faced the same combination of opportunity and challenge that she had encountered as a sales rep. The novelty of the women disk jockeys' professionalism was apparently an endlessly fascinating feature and marketing ploy: "Woman [On-Air]: There's more to the job of girl announcer than what you hear from your radio. The girls pick their own music, run their own control board, plus looking after our remote control transmitter here at our studios. We have to take and log all transmitter readings every half hour as well as keep a program log." Their engineer, the sole male in the studio, managed to praise and damn them in the same breath: "Charlie Sullivan [On-Air]: The girls, for the most part, are really sweet, cooperative and hard workers. Of course, like all performers, some of the girls have their temperamental moments, but they wouldn't be good air personalities if they didn't try for perfection, which most of them do achieve."[15]

Later, Bettye acknowledged that the station gave them little training, and she was philosophical and funny about the qualification of being unqualified: "We messed up a lot, I mean we messed *up*, unbe*liev*able. . . . We had a lot of businesses who listened to us because we played the good music and they also wanted to hear our mess ups, our goofs. And then we got where we liked goofing a little bit and we'd do it on purpose. Like one particular time someone said, 'This is WHER, and now the news from a broad' [*laughter*]. . . . We took it in our stride and we knew we were new at it, and so we didn't allow that to [rattle us]." Most of their training came from this on-air experience. But whether it was the gimmick, the music, or the women's talents, WHER succeeded. Bettye became a public figure, not only appearing at parades and fairs and supermarket openings to represent the station but moonlighting as a model.

Even as the engineer dismissed the women as temperamental, "like all performers," Bettye found this work creative and satisfying, "what a performer feels." When programming her show, she paid some attention to what her listeners requested, and she also paid attention to the station's rules. She adopted her own personal method of deciding which records to play: "Oh, you would program your show to how your love affair was going at the time. If you were having—if everything was good, you played the love songs. And if everything was bad, you played the sad songs. And if you had seen your fella that day—there was one particular song I would play, 'Guess who I saw today?' And I'd play that [*laughing*]." Some influential male deejays in Memphis also programmed their shows according to their personal styles and individual tastes, while also courting listeners, taking requests, and working within their stations' mandated styles. Indeed, Memphis media was built on responding to new listeners: both the newly apparent black audience and the white teenagers who also liked R&B.

The most influential of these disk jockeys was Dewey Phillips, the crazy deejay still playing R&B over on WHBQ, another white station. Bettye was a bigger fan of Dewey's than of her own colleagues. She first heard black artists like Fats Domino, Solomon Burke, and Ivory Joe Hunter on Dewey's show, where he, as she put it, "took the Tony Bennetts and the pretty singers . . . off the charts." He was immensely popular with all kinds of listeners in Memphis. Bettye described how she would listen to his show in her car, but not always by herself and not necessarily when driving: "There were some fabulous drive-ins like the Fortunes Jungle Garden, and the Pig and Whistle. Everybody would drive up in their convertibles and turn Dewey on and order your onion rings and your cokes and have a, you know, a party there in the parking lot at the drive in." Yet although Dewey had been the first deejay in the country to put Elvis on the air, back in 1954, Bettye heard of Elvis only as he shot to national stardom in 1956.

She watched the girls in Ed Sullivan's TV studio audience screaming over Elvis, and she noticed the extensive media coverage of his popularity, but she herself thought he wasn't entirely clean: "I saw him in the motorcycle jackets, you know the pictures, and I thought that he was probably a motorcycle rider. In those day that wasn't very nice. With fingernails not too clean. And I kinda turned my nose up at it a little bit." Her reaction was similar to that of other white middle-class Memphians watching the show. Their reactions were more than simply personal. Memphis elites had long cast working-class, rural migrant, and immigrant whites, as well as blacks, as dirty, a threat to white purity. Bettye had not missed out on black and other new music during her married years simply because of her retreat into domesticity, but because that retreat was part of a middle-class whiteness literally separated from the city and its residents. But Elvis changed that world, as millions of white, middle-class suburban kids found his difference exciting and started to incorporate aspects of his style.

Like them, Bettye started to enjoy Elvis's music. Unlike most fans, though, she actually went on a date with him. In a novel, a date with Elvis might symbolize a heroine's brush with mythic sexual power, her introduction to a world of glamour, or even her entrée into black culture. But in reality, Bettye was almost too busy with her own exciting life to go out with Elvis. After one too many fights with management, she had quit WHER and started a show ("Tune Time with Tammy") on KWAM just across the river in Arkansas, where Johnny Cash once heard her play his record and came by the station to thank her.[16] She was also newly trying her hand at songwriting.

Bettye met Elvis in the fall of 1956, the year of his meteoric rise to national prominence, just after he had finished making his first movie, *Love Me Tender*. Disk jockey Dewey Phillips now had a TV show, and Bettye appeared on it to do a commercial for Honeysuckle Corn Meal. ("I had to take some corn sticks out [of the oven] on the camera and talk about [the corn meal])." Apparently Bettye caught Elvis's eye more than the cornmeal did: "When I got back to the station, the girls said, 'Elvis has called you.' And I was scared to death because I thought I was going to get fired because I had done a television commercial. Because . . . TV was a no-no, at that time. So, I thought they were, you know, just pulling my chain." But when Elvis called back, Bettye recognized his voice. He invited her to come over to his house that evening, but she hesitated—not because of him or her reputation or her work at the station, but because she had something else very important scheduled for that night. She had written a song ("Please Convince Me [That You Love Me]"), and a vocalist was going to record it at Sun Records. "So I told Elvis I couldn't make it," she recalled. "A couple of the girls fell on the floor, and he kind of laughed and he said, 'Well, you won't be there all night will you?' And I said, 'Oh no, we finish at 11:30.'" He persuaded her to meet him afterwards, not at Sun but at the radio station in the Hotel Chisca downtown, where Dewey Phillips broadcast his show until midnight. She recalled: "I was very tired. I had worked all day, I had gone to the station and I went in and got in a lounge chair and fell asleep. And I woke up and Elvis was standing over me with his entourage, and Dewey saying, 'Here is this birdbrain. All the women in the world would like to have a date with Presley and she's sleeping.' So I looked up and smiled and Elvis looked at me and smiled and he said, 'Do you like hamburgers?' And he pulled me up and gently hugged me and I said, 'Yes. I love hamburgers.' He said, 'With onions?' And I said, 'Yes.'" Bettye's initial impression of Elvis had been that he was "greasy," but ironically these hamburgers proved her wrong. She ended up terming him "a gentleman."

Although Elvis drew on a range of styles, including most notoriously black R&B, he did not lead fans to that music. So Bettye's introduction to local R&B did not come from him. A friend invited Bettye out to one popular nightclub, the Plantation Inn, but she balked, worrying that "it wasn't a nice place." Her hesitation connects with middle-class propriety: not only did the Plantation Inn feature black musicians, it was across the river in West Memphis, where gambling, liquor, strippers, and banned movies all found a venue. As with Elvis, personal contact soon enlightened her: "But I was all wrong, I mean it *was* [a nice place]. After I went the first time I enjoyed it immensely. And I went back just about every night that I could go." One of the big draws for her was the owners' son, who was just taking over the club himself. Bettye and Louis Jack Berger danced together, and sparks flew; they fell in love, and within a year they married.

Suddenly Bettye had moved across the river to a big house in the "nicer" part of West Memphis, Arkansas, with black domestic help. (She later had a fourth child, a son, with Berger.) And she was actually working at the club. She took money at the door ($2.50 a person), oversaw the cash register for the waiters, and monitored the customers for trouble. She also ended up looking after her husband's jukebox routes; he paid her by letting her keep the money for a "clothing allowance." She would collect the money from the boxes at the club, at his family's drive-in restaurant, and in other restaurants around West Memphis. Eventually, she helped restock the 45s that went on the jukeboxes: "I'd say, 'What do I buy?' And he'd say, 'Look in the charts, and see what's at the top ten, and get them, and then you listen to see what you like.' So I'd go over to Pop Tunes [in Memphis] and buy the records for the jukeboxes, for him, a lot. And I enjoyed that." Pop Tunes, an innovative local record store, sold records to jukebox operators and individuals alike. Store employees charted local sales and play. Like other jukebox operators, Bettye relied on the chart but supplemented its information with her own judgment. She had trained her ear by programming her radio show and writing songs. She honed it further by seeing from the jukebox counters whether listeners also liked her choices.[17]

Bettye also became aware of racial exclusion working at the Plantation Inn, where blacks could be waiters and singers but could never be customers, and where black musicians had to take their breaks in the kitchen or outside, since fraternizing with the white audience was out of the question. Louis Jack's family maintained a similar division at Pancho's, the Mexican restaurant that they ran next door, where Bettye sometimes worked as a hostess. Once she seated a black family, because she thought it was only fair that they should be able to eat there, but her in-laws would not let her do it again. As Jewish Memphians, and as entrepreneurs working with African Americans and Mexican Americans, the Bergers would have seemed almost black to other white Memphians. But to black people they certainly counted as white, and never more so than when they enforced the color line. It is possible that the black customers were testing the restaurant's policy as part of a pattern of explicit challenges to racial boundaries in public places. In 1958 protestors tried to enter the library, the art museum, and the zoo on "white-only" days; when officials blocked them, they filed suit in court.[18]

But as hostess at the club, Bettye got to know the black musicians. This time her in-between position led her to act as a go-between, a broker between the musicians and the fans. Over time, the white dancers wanted to bring the Plantation Inn sound back to their colleges around the region. Although a circuit of roadhouses and juke joints throughout the Mississippi and Arkansas Delta had supported country, blues, and now R&B musicians for some time, the colleges had booked only big bands or crooners. Now, at "Ole Miss, Arkansas State, and even the University of Arkansas, which is three hundred and something miles [away]," students wanted to hire the Plantation Inn musicians. At the same time, the musicians were interested in picking up extra money and gigs. Bettye became the broker between these interests, connecting the Plantation Inn musicians with the fraternities. Through them other dancers and musicians began to contact her as well. She even took some musicians into recording studios: she recorded William Bell of the PI's Del Rios in a small studio on Main Street, releasing the songs on Bet-T Records. She was the only woman among local booking agents, probably the only agent with a combination of radio and club experience, and the only one witnessing (and facilitating) the explosive growth of the new white college audience for rhythm and blues.[19]

Bettye's booking work grew out of the Bergers' extended family business network, and at first she helped bands informally while working more seriously at the club. But she and Louis Jack would soon divorce, acrimoniously. Without enough clients to support herself and her children, she again had to find work. She moved back to Memphis—renting an apartment in the suburb of Whitehaven, whose most famous resident was Elvis Presley—and returned to full-time work at WHER. She continued to moonlight as a booking agent because people kept calling her. She had built her own network, and, as with her jukebox and radio work, she knew local tastes, local styles, and the musicians who could match these.

In 1959 Plantation Inn musicians like the Veltones and the Del Rios started recording at a new local studio, Satellite Records—later renamed Stax Records, started by a white sister/brother team, Estelle Axton and Jim Stewart—in an old theater in a newly black neighborhood. When Rufus and Carla Thomas scored the label's first hit in 1960, an R&B track called "'Cause I Love You," they came to Bettye for help with booking.[20] Her artist William Bell signed with the label and scored a national hit with "You Don't Miss Your Water" in 1962. Stax went on to be the home of Otis Redding, Booker T. and the MGs, Sam and Dave, and other great soul acts. Its house band comprised Plantation Inn fans Booker T. and the MGs, two of them white, two black. Along with Willie Mitchell's Hi Records, it was the second flowering of Memphis music.

Bettye carried all this experience with her when she left WHER to work for Ray Brown's National Artists in 1965. At first she picked up Brown's extra clients, but soon she branched out into territory she already had made her own: "I asked him one day, 'Why don't you book colleges?' and he says, 'Why don't *you* book colleges?' So I went over to Arkansas State and called on them directly. And from then on I booked . . . all of their concerts." Booking involved a variety of activities beyond securing performance opportunities for artists and hiring musicians for venues. She helped artists get record deals, negotiated contracts, ran recording sessions, hired bands, produced singles and albums, organized club dates and tours, got artists and bands paid, did promo work for all of this, and handled taxes, accounting, and royalties. And all this time Bettye continued to write her own songs.[21]

So in 1966, when Bettye left National Artists to form her own agency, Continental Artists, she drew on the relationships she had nurtured since entering radio as well as all of her varied experiences in the music industry. Yet Bettye felt that, because she was a woman, she needed to bring a man into the business so that artists and venues would take her seriously. She hired and trained a male partner, and she was right: she got more business. As Stax grew, so did

Bettye's work with musicians, both black and white, including Booker T. and the MGs, the Bar-Kays, Johnny Taylor, the Temprees, Bobby Blue Bland, Don Bryant, Albert King, and Redbone. She found it was particularly fun to work and travel with women artists like Carla Thomas, Ann Peebles, and, later, Brenda Patterson. Her client Willie Mitchell had become a producer at Hi Records, which shared some musicians with Stax but featured a jazzier sound. Through Mitchell, Bettye signed Al Green and helped launch his astonishing career. Perhaps the high point of this era was a trip to Europe with the Stax artists, where she witnessed passionate European fans rapturously responding to her clients. She had come a long way from Trenton.

Meanwhile, Bettye had been forging ties in Nashville. Through Stax, she had come to book and then to manage Ivory Joe Hunter, a black pianist from Texas whose classic ballads appeared on pop, country, and R&B charts from the 1940s on. For years Hunter had dreamed of appearing on the Grand Ole Opry stage. Bettye landed that gig for him in 1972, and tapes of the event reveal that Opry stars and audiences alike received him with deep affection, respect, and knowledge of his music.[22]

But Bettye suffered devastating twin blows in 1974, losing not only her main account but her entire business. Ivory Joe Hunter, who had become her friend as well as her client, fell ill with cancer. A Houston doctor put him in a terrible nursing home, and Hunter's "lady friend" called Bettye for help. Through her network she got him a room at the cancer unit in Memphis's Methodist Hospital, but she couldn't afford the ambulance plane to get him from Houston to Memphis. On her way out of town to get Hunter out of the nursing home, she stopped by Graceland to ask Elvis's uncle Vester—"who knew Ivory Joe, of course"—to ask Elvis for help. The next thing she knew, she had a check from Elvis's foundation for the exact amount. To pay for Ivory Joe's ongoing care, she organized a benefit with the Grand Ole Opry featuring the amazing lineup of Tammy Wynette and George Jones, Isaac Hayes, and William Bell. It was a powerful expression of support from across the industry, with people weeping in the audience and a write-up in *Rolling Stone*. But Ivory Joe was very ill, and only a month later he died. Bettye came back to her office—only to find the Rolodex and all the money gone. Her partner had stolen her clients and her business.

This was a terrible time for Stax as well; the combined blows of Otis Redding's death in 1967, the assassination of Martin Luther King Jr. in 1968, and a bad distribution deal with Atlantic all sent the company spiraling into crisis and then bankruptcy.[23] The club scene was gone as well, because people didn't go out dancing like they once did. Of the whole music scene, only Hi Records was still going strong.

Bettye decided to move to Nashville to start over. By this time, a number of white Sun artists whose music had in the 1950s counted as black-inflected rock and roll or rockabilly now had hits on the white country charts—Jerry Lee Lewis, Charlie Rich, Johnny Cash. One of Sam Phillips's engineers, Jack Clement, had started his own Nashville studio. Ivory Joe Hunter left Bettye his music catalog, and she kept working as a songwriter. (She also spent several years caring for her brother, grievously injured in a car accident, and later for her dying mother.) Happily, she was less of a pioneer here: a number of women were already executives in the Nashville music industry, including Frances Preston (president of the local chapter of Broadcast Music International, the industry licensing organization) and Jo Walker-Meador (head of the Country Music Association). They became part of her extended network.

Like the Sun artists, Bettye had moved from soul back to country as the market changed and the Memphis music industry crashed. Two of her most important clients—Charlie Rich and Ivory Joe Hunter—were nationally famous singing piano players who combined black and white influences in their music and whose careers moved from R&B to country popularity. Their music and her work illuminate how blackness and whiteness were never as far apart as their images would imply.

As a songwriter, disk jockey, nightclub hostess, jukebox operator, booking agent, record producer, and manager, Bettye Berger bridged two eras in Memphis music: the rock and roll of the mid-1950s and the soul of the 1960s. In both eras local musicians gained regional and national prominence through the city's growing music industry, which in turn disseminated a wild mix of music that inspired fans to become musicians. Bettye was one of the handful of such audience members—and one of the only women—who became a professional behind the scenes instead. She was not actively part of the first flowering of Memphis music, but its successes created the conditions of possibility for her own. Amid contested local and national meanings of whiteness and blackness, the networks of the rock and roll era fostered Bettye's career; in turn, she built networks that helped usher in the soul epoch.

Entrepreneurs built the Memphis music industry by discovering and wooing new audiences. As a woman doing the wooing, Bettye had an unusual edge. But for all the doors that opened to her because of beauty or character or luck or love, there were many times people ignored or ridiculed Bettye and her work simply because she was a woman. She still struggles with deep anger, frustration, and self-doubt from these battles; she would have welcomed a feminist movement years before it came. Sometimes she has made this anger work for her, as when she left an established booking agency to form her own company.

She never rebelled against her upbringing or traditional ideas of femininity, but for better and for worse, she has never lived a mainstream life. Rather, her work has been an essential part of Memphis's transformation of the mainstream.

NOTES

1. Unless otherwise cited, all information about Bettye Berger and quotes from her are from interviews I conducted with her in Memphis August 5, 1994, August 2, 2006, and May 1, 2007.

2. See also the *Tennessee Encyclopedia*'s online entry about the Milan Arsenal: http://tennesseeencyclopedia.net/imagegallery.php?EntryID=M095 (accessed August 3, 2006).

3. Similarly, Carl Perkins's family, outside Jackson, Tennessee, would hold back on using the radio all week so they would have enough of the battery to be able to tune into the Opry (Interview by Charles McGovern and Pete Daniel, National Museum of American History, Smithsonian Institution, Memphis Rock and Soul project, 1995 [hereafter referred to as Memphis Rock and Soul]).

4. Elijah Wald, *Escaping the Delta: Robert Johnson and the Invention of the Blues* (New York: Amistad, 2004), 96.

5. Wald, *Escaping the Delta*. See also Philip H. Ennis, *The Seventh Stream: The Emergence of Rocknroll in American Popular Music* (Middletown, Conn.: Wesleyan University Press, 1992); and Louis Cantor, *Dewey and Elvis: The Life and Times of a Rock 'n' Roll Deejay* (Urbana: University of Illinois Press, 2005), for descriptions of radio programming before 1949. See Louis Cantor, *Wheelin' on Beale: How WDIA-Memphis Became the Nation's First All-Black Radio Station and Created the Sound That Changed America* (New York: Pharos Books, 1992), for a discussion of Mid-South and national advertisers' views of black consumers before and after Memphis radio station WDIA went on the air in 1949; Kathy M. Newman, "The Forgotten Fifteen Million: Black Radio, Radicalism, and the Construction of 'the Negro Market,'" for an overall account of radio sponsors' belated attention to black consumers (in *Communities of the Air: Radio Century, Radio Culture*, ed. Susan M. Squier, 109–33 [Durham, N.C.: Duke University Press, 2003]), and Jason Chambers, *Madison Avenue and the Color Line: African Americans in the Advertising Industry* (Philadelphia: University of Pennsylvania Press, 2007) for a discussion of the crucial role of black advertising men in the development of that market in the advertising business. In New York, white dancers Vernon and Irene Castle worked with black bandleader James Reese Europe to popularize black social dances among the white middle-class. See Katrina Hazzard-Gordon, *Jookin': The Rise of Social Dance Formations in African-American Culture* (New Brunswick, N.J.: Rutgers University Press, 1992).

6. Wald describes radio's cosmopolitan or democratic effect in *Escaping the Delta*: "Radio exposed blues players, and rural listeners in general, to other styles. It was a great leveler, allowing someone in a Delta cabin to listen to anything from hillbilly fiddling to opera. . . . It has become a cliché of jazz history that Louis Armstrong's favorite band was Guy Lombardo's Royal Canadians, and in the early 1960s Chris Strachwitz was horrified to find that most of the rural musicians he recorded for his Arhoolie roots label, from blues singers to Tex-Mex bands and Louisiana zydeco outfits, were enthusiastic fans of Lawrence Welk" (96). Memphis soul musician Rufus Thomas and his daughter, Carla Thomas, the singer, both enjoyed the Grand Ole Opry (Interview, Memphis Rock and Soul). See also these compilations and their liner notes for more examples of crossover listening: Various Artists, *From Where I Stand: The Black Experience In Country Music* (Burbank, Calif.: Warner Bros., 1998); and *Rhythm, Country, and Blues* (Nashville: MCA, 1994). For the black

Memphis roots of the Grand Ole Opry's founder, George Hay, see Larry Nager, *Memphis Beat: The Lives and Times of America's Musical Crossroads* (Darby, Pa.: Diane Publishing Company, 1995).

7. These official figures also state that the Memphis population "leapt up to 450,000 by 1955" (1966 Planning Report, Memphis Planning Commission). One among many "downtowns": Robert M. Fogelson, *Downtown: Its Rise and Fall, 1880–1950* (New Haven, Conn.: Yale University Press, 2003), 229. "Most dangerous" intersection: Robert Sigafoos, *Cotton Row to Beale Street: A Business History of Memphis* (Memphis: Memphis State University Press, 1980), 185. "The congestion was viewed as an indicator of business recovery" in the midst of the Depression.

8. U.S. Bureau of the Census, Sixteenth Census of the United States, Population and housing, statistics for census tracts, Memphis, Tenn., and adjacent area, 1940 (Washington, D.C.: U.S. Government Printing Office, 1942); U.S. Bureau of the Census, Seventeenth Census of the United States, Census tract statistics, Memphis, Tenn., 1950 (Washington, D.C.: U.S. Government Printing Office, 1942); interviews in Memphis with Budgie Linder (August 20, 1995) and Fred Frederickson (July 20, 1995); informal conversation with former neighborhood resident, June 2006.

9. B. B. King with David Ritz, *Blues All around Me: The Autobiography of B. B. King* (New York: Avon, 1996), 114. "Broadcast . . . from black churches": interview with Rev. Melvin Rodgers, Memphis, April 30, 1995. "*Blues Time*": Cantor, *Dewey and Elvis*, 60. "WLAC . . . Randy's Record Shop": almost every person I interviewed and every musician and music industry figure that Smithsonian curators interviewed for the Memphis Rock and Soul project mentioned WLAC's late night show, deejays, and sponsor with affection.

10. Charles McGovern discovered Phillips's FCC application (personal communication, December 1, 2005). On WDIA's origin, see Cantor, *Wheelin' on Beale*, Bert Ferguson, "WDIA: Memphis' Goodwill Station," in *Memphis 1948–1958*, ed. Liz Conway (Memphis: Memphis Brooks Museum of Art, 1986), 108–9. On Dewey Phillips, see Peter Guralnick, *Last Train to Memphis: The Rise of Elvis Presley* (Boston: Little, Brown, 1994); Dewey Phillips, *Red Hot and Blue* CD (Memphis: Memphis Archives, 1995); Cantor, *Dewey and Elvis*. For Howlin' Wolf on KWAM/KWEM, see James Segrest and Mark Hoffman, *Moanin' at Midnight: The Life and Times of Howlin' Wolf* (New York: Thunder's Mouth Press, 2005); Robert Gordon, *It Came from Memphis* (repr., New York: Atria, 2001); and Nager, *Memphis Beat*.

11. On the Silver Slipper, see "Slipper's Most Torrid Show—and No Applause," July 17, 1958, *Memphis Press-Scimitar*. Musicians played live music nearly everywhere Memphians went out: restaurants, bars, hotel lobbies, even movie theaters. There was a thriving black club scene, but at this point Bettye would have heard almost exclusively white musicians. See Roy C. Brewer, "Professional Musicians in Memphis (1900–1950): A Tradition of Compromise" (Ph.D. dissertation, University of Memphis, 1996). On postwar domesticity, see Rickie Solinger, *Wake Up, Little Susie: Single Pregnancy and Race before Roe v. Wade*, (Oxford: Routledge, 1994); and Stephanie Coontz, *The Way We Never Were: American Families and the Nostalgia Trap* (New York: Basic, 2000).

12. The Kitchen Sisters, Lost and Found Sound, "Golden Girls," *On the Media*, transcript at http://www.onthemedia.org/transcripts/transcripts_102805_girls.html (accessed August 3, 2006).

13. Ibid.

14. Ibid.

15. Ibid.

16. She was only the second woman disk jockey, and the first was also the station's receptionist.

17. Jukeboxes had ousted live musicians from restaurants; meanwhile, 45-r.p.m. singles had replaced 78s on jukeboxes and in homes (Brewer, "Professional Musicians in Memphis"; interview with jukebox operator George Sammons, Memphis Rock and Soul).

18. Historian Selma Lewis argues that while black Memphians faced discrimination, Jews could assimilate more easily and were eventually counted as white. Selma Lewis, *A Biblical People in the Bible Belt: The Jewish Community of Memphis, Tennessee, 1840s-1960s* (Macon, Ga.: Mercer University Press, 1998). See also Pete Daniel, *Lost Revolutions: The South in the 1950s* (Chapel Hill: University of North Carolina Press, 2000), for regional dynamics, and Karen Brodkin, *How Jews Became White Folks and What That Says About Race in America* (New Brunswick, N.J.: Rutgers University Press, 1999), for the national context. The Memphis newspapers, the *Press-Scimitar* and the *Commercial Appeal*, reported on protests against urban segregation, and on the lawsuits that Jessie Turner Sr., the head of the local NAACP, filed when public facilities denied access to black Memphians. These protests predated the 1960 sit-ins in Memphis and across the country. Black Memphians organized many other civil rights actions and informally protested discrimination in a variety of domains. Students from Memphis's LeMoyne-Owen College organized sit-ins at the downtown Woolworth's and at the main library in 1960, inspired by the Greensboro and Nashville sit-ins. By 1962 black Memphians had gained access to most of Memphis's public facilities, in part because city fathers wanted to head off the civil unrest they saw in other southern cities. See Laurie Green, *Battling the "Plantation Mentality": Memphis and the Black Freedom Struggle* (Chapel Hill: University of North Carolina Press, 2007); Michael Honey, *Black Workers Remember: An Oral History of Segregation, Unionism, and the Freedom Struggle* (Berkeley: University of California Press, 2002); Christopher Silver and John V. Moeser, *Separate City: Black Communities in the Urban South, 1940–1968* (Lexington: University of Kentucky Press, 1995); Beverly G. Bond and Janann Sherman, *Memphis in Black and White* (Mount Pleasant, S.C.: Arcadia, 2003); and Kenneth Goings, "'Unhidden' Transcripts: Memphis and African-American Agency, 1862–1920," in *The New African American Urban History*, ed. Kenneth W. Goings and Raymond A. Mohl, 146–66 (Thousand Oaks, Calif.: Sage, 1996).

19. Andrew Hamilton, "William Bell: 'Dangerous Lover,' co-written by Bell, b/w 'Heavenly Angel,' on Bet-T Records," http://www.allmusic.com (accessed August 1, 2006, confirmed by Bettye Berger, August 2, 2006). Other local booking agents had similarly varied experiences in the music industry. Nate Evans, a musician, also managed theaters and then got into booking. Evans, a Jewish entrepreneur, brought big-name black bands to the Malco movie theater at the intersection of Beale and Main and to the Handy Theater at the edge of the historically black Orange Mound neighborhood. Robert Henry, an African American promoter, owned a record store/pool hall on Beale Street, booking nationally famous black musicians into Beale clubs for black audiences (Cantor, *Dewey and Elvis*; and interview with Rev. Melvin Rodgers, 1995). He also worked with Nate Evans to set up the Midnight Rambles at Beale's Palace Theater, in which black musicians played for white audiences. Brewer, "Professional Musicians." Pop Tunes owner Joe Cuoghi, an Italian American, also capitalized on record store contacts (and jukebox routes) to book white and black musicians in local clubs. See Interview with John Novarese, Memphis Rock and Soul.

Black performances became an important part of white college experience in the 1950s and 1960s, inspiring some students to become musicians themselves. The black performers made good money on the college circuit, and some found this audience's welcome professionally satisfying. B. B. King's capture of the white college audience in the 1960s reinvigorated his career. But touring was hard under segregation, with few hotels or restaurants accepting black customers and, always, the threat of violence along the road. See King and Ritz, *Blues All around Me*; Daniel, *Lost Revolutions*; and Suzanne E. Smith, *Dancing in the Street: Motown and the Cultural Politics of Detroit* (Cambridge, Mass.: Harvard University Press, 2001).

20. Rob Bowman, *Soulsville, U.S.A.: The Story of Stax Records* (New York: Schirmer Books, 1997), 8.

21. She also briefly hosted a talk show on television in Jonesboro, Arkansas (an hour outside of Memphis and home of Arkansas State University), called "Open House with Bettye."

22. Ivory Joe Hunter's most famous song was "Since I Met You Baby," and it continued to cross genres across the decades: Hunter had a hit with it in the 1940s; Freddie Fender covered it in Spanish in the 1960s; and it was a hit again on the country charts for Sonny James in 1970, and again when both the original and the Fender versions appeared on the *Lone Star* soundtrack in the 1990s. Indeed, Sonny James's 1970 cover of "Since I Met You Baby" hit number 1 on the Billboard country charts, followed by his version of Hunter's "Empty Arms" which did the same.

23. For more details, see Bowman, *Soulsville USA*.

Jocelyn Dan Wurzburg

(1940–)

Feminist and Race Woman

GAIL S. MURRAY

In the summer of 1948 President Harry S. Truman struck hard at America's institutionalized racism when, by executive order, he simultaneously desegregated the military and forbade discriminatory hiring in the federal civil service. In the heart of the segregated South, a blond Jewish fourth-grader was engaged in her own struggle with the irrationality of racial segregation. She remembers earnestly asking her teacher, "If an [American] Indian came to Memphis, would he have to sit in the back of the bus?" Unable or unwilling to provide an answer, the teacher suggested the youngster write to ask the president of the United States. Months later, the little girl received her letter back, with stamps indicating it had been passed from the president's staff to the Department of Interior and then on to the Bureau of Indian Affairs. Enclosed was a pamphlet about Indian life and culture that made no mention of racial discrimination or second-class citizenship. At that point, the little girl in Memphis came to understand that "some questions, you just don't ask"; some topics were just not open for discussion.[1]

Thus began Jocelyn Dan Wurzburg's lifelong journey to deconstruct the southern mores of her white community, to become a voice for racial justice and women's rights, and to use the law to maximize opportunity for the disadvantaged. It was, however, a halting process. As a young Memphis housewife in the 1960s, Wurzburg exemplified her class, race, and gender privilege. Active in Jewish women's clubs and community activities while running a busy household that included a husband and three children, she enjoyed social status and economic advantages. Not until the assassination of Dr. Martin Luther King Jr. in 1968 did she revisit her childhood questions about race discrimination. She

JOCELYN DAN WURZBURG

2004. Courtesy of Jocelyn Dan Wurzburg.

then began to take what her social circle considered controversial stands against discrimination, for desegregation, and on equal employment opportunity. She founded and ran the Memphis Panel of American Women, which sent interracial teams to publicly discuss racial and religious prejudice (1968), and the Concerned Women of Memphis and Shelby County, a biracial activist group (1969). Her energy and leadership resulted in appointments to the Tennessee Human Development Commission, the State Advisory Committee to the U.S. Commission on Civil Rights, and the Tennessee Commission on the Status of Women. Years of Republican Party service garnered her a seat on the National Commission for the Observance of International Women's Year (1976). She drafted Tennessee's first antidiscrimination bill in employment and public accommodations (1979) and helped revise the Tennessee Family Law Code. She became Memphis's first professional mediator and founded the Mediation Association of Tennessee (1989). She has belonged to and served on the boards of most Memphis organizations concerned with racial or gender rights, and her leadership won awards from the city of Memphis, the Women of Achievement, and the National Conference of Christians and Jews. She has played an active role in numerous Jewish organizations, especially the national Social Action Committee of Reform Judaism. Now in her sixties, she continues to work as a professional mediator and actively promotes political candidates (both parties) and the Memphis Area Women's Council.

Wurzburg's trajectory from housewife to race activist to feminist is atypical in the South but not unprecedented. Female college students who came south during Freedom Summer, like Sara Evans, Mary King, and Casey Hayden, became sensitive to gender discrimination as they fought against embedded racism just as many nineteenth-century feminists had begun their public activism with abolition.[2] Even Wurzburg's roots in Reform Judaism did not predict a life of race activism, for Memphis Jews were well assimilated into the South's conservative social mores and racial etiquette. According to historian Debra Schultz, although a disproportionate number of Jewish women worked for civil rights, they did not "recall conscious Jewish identification during their time in the movement."[3] Memphis was not a destination for Freedom Summer workers, and Wurzburg had no contact with civil rights groups. Few Memphis Jews came from leftist or union backgrounds. Although Memphis rabbi James Wax played a visible role in seeking an end to the sanitation strike in 1968, his congregation did not embrace local black activism or unionism.[4] Jocelyn Wurzburg's initial racial activism developed within the context of secular white privilege; some years later her affiliation with the national Social Activism Committee of

Reform Judaism brought a sharper Jewish identity to her work. She often used her class, gender, and Republican Party connections to her advantage.

Jocelyn Dan was born in Memphis on August 3, 1940, to Rose Sternberger Heyman and Charles Lewis Dan. Her father was an Orthodox Lithuanian Jew, in the fourth generation to call Memphis home, and a sales agent for several small-town newspapers. Her mother's family came to Memphis from Germany via New Orleans before the Civil War and embraced Reform Judaism. Like many Jewish southerners, the Dan family identified themselves as secular Jews without being observant. "We did not light candles on Friday nights," Jocelyn later remarked, "and we always celebrated Christmas."[5] Her Jewish identity manifested itself in social prescriptions rather than in liberal activism: she did not date gentile boys, nor could she pledge a sorority at Southwestern (later Rhodes College) in Memphis, the Presbyterian college she attended. She married Richard Wurzburg (also from a fifth-generation Jewish family) after one year of college, and she earned a B.A. in sociology in 1965. She then moved into a life of suburban comfort, socializing with "the right people," joining various women's organizations in the synagogue and the community, putting her children into prestigious private schools. In retrospect, she referred to this period of her life as her "lady do-gooder" phase.[6]

Richard Wurzburg's employment in the family packaging business provided the family with a comfortable income, making regular household help and childcare available. Jocelyn did volunteer work for the Council of Jewish Women and with local Republicans to unseat Congressman Cliff Davis, a conservative Dixiecrat. Although she had grown up in a Democratic family, she was influenced by a conservative professor at Southwestern and her conservative, business-oriented in-laws. She embraced what she calls "Rockefeller Republicanism," fiscal conservatism tempered by social activism. She worked in numerous local elections, the Senate campaign of Howard Baker (1966), and Winfield Dunn's gubernatorial campaign in 1970. She enjoyed the social life of the Ridgeway Country Club and numerous civic organizations. Certainly there was an air of noblesse oblige about such activities, reminiscent of the work of nineteenth-century clubwomen. Although well educated, active in local politics, and abreast of world affairs, neither Jocelyn nor Richard Wurzburg worried about the city's endemic poverty, blatant racial discrimination, or struggling public schools.

Some of this changed for Jocelyn during the cataclysmic events of spring 1968, when Memphians confronted the intersections of race and class in a labor dispute between the city administration and its public works employees. The sanitation workers' strike, which lasted from February to April, was organized by a former garbage collector, T. O. Jones, who had long sought recognition by the American Federation of State, County, and Municipal Employees (AFSCME). Newly elected mayor Henry Loeb firmly believed that a public works strike was illegal (based on a legal injunction against a similar work action in 1966). Like most white Memphians, the Wurzburg family sympathized with management, not striking workers, and thus firmly supported Loeb. They blamed the strike on professional union organizers and East Coast outsiders, and the Memphis news media perpetuated this view.[7]

Jewish by birth, Loeb had joined the Episcopal Church with his wife, Mary. Neither Rabbi James Wax nor Dean William Dimmick of the Episcopal cathedral could persuade Loeb to meet with the strikers. Early in the strike, Loeb brought the Jewish international president of AFSCME, Jerry Wurf, to the local National Conference of Christians and Jews banquet. Loeb's arrival drew a standing ovation, dramatically illustrating to Wurf that the strikers could expect "little rebound sympathy from fellow Jews in Memphis." Unlike their East Coast brethren, Reform Jews in Memphis tended to be integrated into the conservative southern economic ethos.[8]

Strike supporters argued that institutionalized racism defined their labor opportunities and dictated their low pay. White men drove the sanitation trucks and received a full day's pay regardless of weather; black men dumped the cans, carried the garbage to the trucks, and were sent home unpaid whenever it rained. Strikers adopted the slogan "I am a Man" to emphasize that the strike was as much about human dignity as about low wages. Their supporters organized daily protest marches and evening rallies, collected food for the families of the strikers, and negotiated late payments on everything from rent to appliances. The Committee on the Move for Equality, made up of lay and clergy supporters working closely with union leadership, brought national spokespeople in, hoping to attract national press coverage and embarrass the city into a settlement. Bringing Dr. Martin Luther King Jr. represented their biggest coup.

While most white Memphians considered themselves racial moderates, nearly all supported the mayor in believing that the strike had nothing to do with civil rights. Desegregation of public facilities, parks, and restaurants had taken student and NAACP-led protests, but city leaders and white businessmen took credit for "peaceful" change. True, school desegregation was stymied in the courts, but no violent demonstrations had occurred on that front either. Thus whites persisted in seeing the strike as a labor dispute only. They did not want King to come, believing that his presence would enflame radicals and lead to violent confrontation. At best, they assumed that low wages were the consequence of supply and demand. At worst, they knew nothing about city-approved discrimination and the daily flagrant insults the workers endured.[9]

Dr. King's arrival on March 18 did little to assuage white fears of trouble. Speaking to over ten thousand supporters, he proposed a general work stoppage for all citizens and promised to lead it on March 22.[10] Snow postponed the march, but when King came back on March 28, he led thousands of strikers, supporters, and students up Beale Street and north toward City Hall. In the process, some unsupervised young marchers began to smash store windows with sticks. In the melee that followed, police violently moved in on all the marchers with clubs and tear gas. Scores of participants were beaten and gassed, including several prominent African American clergymen. Fearing widespread violence, city officials asked for the National Guard. In the following days, troops with armed weapons stood guard throughout the downtown area, but the daily marches persisted.[11] Jocelyn Wurzburg continued to support the mayor and sent him a personal letter saying so.

In the midst of planning the Poor People's Campaign, King's attempt to focus national attention on economic inequalities, he returned a third time to Memphis. King believed that the striking sanitation workers embodied the systemic racism and class discrimination that the dramatic march to Washington, D.C., was supposed to highlight. His assassination on April 4, the night before the Memphis march was to take place, brought Memphis's racial problems into high relief. African Americans blamed the city's white leadership for abetting the tragedy through its racialized labor policies.

Many local whites felt that their fears about the civil rights movement and Dr. King were justified as they viewed newscasts of riots and arson that raged across the country, though barely in Memphis. Other local whites were shocked and embarrassed that such a blatant act of racial violence could occur in their beloved city. One prominent white resident later recalled, "We believed we had a good start on integration here—that race relations were good. . . . And then when Dr. King was shot, many of us realized for the first time that the only black person we really knew was [one of our] servant[s.] Reality really hit us then."[12] Shocked and saddened by the assassination, many white Memphians wanted to do something to prove that Memphis was not a city of racial hatred. Many city leaders wanted to believe that, with a little tweaking, Memphis could achieve racial harmony.

A coalition of Memphis clergy, labor leaders, and concerned citizens organized by white businessman John T. Fisher planned an interracial rally on the Sunday following the assassination—a day President Johnson had declared a

"National Day of Mourning." Jocelyn Wurzburg attended, although she feared violence would break out. She still believed the strike itself was illegal, but felt she had a "civic duty to be present" to demonstrate that white Memphians "did not hate." Although the program featured African American and white speakers, including Catholic, Jewish, and Protestant clergy, many black leaders were too angry and discouraged to attend. After the city's intransigence on the strike, this gesture of reconciliation seemed too little, too late.[13] Wurzburg was particularly moved by one of the least heralded speakers—Mary Collier, a fifty-three-year-old black schoolteacher who spoke passionately about the black laborers she knew and the sacrifices they made to see that their children received a good education. She emphasized those human values that know no racial boundaries; she called for common cause between the races. It was hardly a revolutionary speech. But she managed to connect financial stability and the respect it commands with the realities of racialized underemployment in a gentle way that whites in the audience could hear.[14]

Wurzburg later invited Collier to speak to a group of Jewish friends who had not gone to the rally. By introducing them to an articulate, well-educated African American woman, she hoped to attack the conflation of race and class that so many southern whites assumed. Filling in for Collier, however, was an outspoken white professor who alienated the Jewish guests, for whom memories of the Holocaust were still vivid, by calling April 4 "the darkest day in the history of mankind." Wurzburg's friends and neighbors withdrew in shock, warning her not to support such radical civil rights business. She was disappointed by their lack of positive response, so she looked elsewhere for white women concerned about racial injustice.

Through local writer and activist Joan Beifuss, Wurzburg learned of a workshop called "Raising Children of Goodwill," in which participants investigated the roots of prejudice and its institutionalization. Some sixty Memphis women were attending this national program sponsored by the National Conference of Christians and Jews (NCCJ), with local support from Church Women United and B'nai B'rith. Mostly homemakers, both black and white, these women met once a week for all-day sessions featuring speakers and small group discussions. Wurzburg saw similarities between the goals of the Raising Children workshops and a presentation she had heard by the Little Rock Panel of American Women (PAW). She remarked on this to the head of the NCCJ, who immediately sought to bring PAW's founder and national director to Memphis to help with the city's healing process. Esther Brown, a white homemaker from Kansas, had worked for school integration in the early 1950s and had created the first PAW for a synagogue program. Its powerful resonance led her to offer the panel discussions in other venues, and soon other cities were copying the idea. Panelists hoped to change attitudes and assumptions by sharing their personal experiences of discrimination, be it ethnic, racial, or religious.[15] Brown flew to Memphis and worked with an initial group of twenty interested women, selected by Wurzburg and the NCCJ and including black and white, Protestant, Catholic, and Jewish women. Brown explained to them that the work of the panel was twofold; it re-educated and changed the women who participated in it, and it took the positive promise of attitudinal change into the community at large. She explained that minorities had done all they could to break down the barriers of discrimination; the rest of the work against discrimination rested with the most privileged, the group Brown called the "white majority."[16]

Wurzburg's PAW recruits spent the summer and fall of 1968 reading about racism, listening to invited experts, and participating in sensitivity training. At times their "gab-fests" went late into the night. In mock question-and-answer sessions, panelists who considered themselves totally free from prejudice often discovered some hidden ethnic assumptions. "One panelist came to the experience full of hostility," said Wurzburg, "and we had to learn where that rage came from and not take it personally." Those who could not handle the sometimes uncomfortable discussions, according to one former panelist, "were not invited to stay in the group."[17] Each panelist prepared a five-minute presentation in which she levied no blame, promoted no agenda, but simply described her own experience with prejudice—speaking not as an expert but as a homemaker or working mother. Each woman talked about how it felt to be seen as a member of a group rather than as an individual. They believed that America could have "unity without uniformity."[18]

When the group was ready to present the panel publicly, Wurzburg chose four women—a Catholic, a Jew, an African American, and a white Protestant—while she herself served as the moderator. She soon learned whose "chemistry" worked best with whom and who performed best in front of particular kinds of audiences. Panelists relied on family members or domestic workers for child-care in order to participate, sometimes presenting as many as three programs a week, although the privilege of class inherent in their volunteerism seems to have eluded them. Word-of-mouth brought invitations to speak to church auxiliaries, civic groups, and neighborhood associations. Most audiences were white since, as one former panelist remarked, "What we were saying was not news to other African Americans."[19]

Former PAW members still talk about the transformative experiences they had as panel members, the development of a sense of sisterhood, and the conviction that people *could* learn to let go of inherited prejudicial opinions. Members held social activities that sometimes included their husbands and children, believing that interracial parties served as "models" of the kind of Memphis community they hoped to promote. It was far from easy. A black panelist reported that she often felt that her words had little impact on white audiences and that friends criticized her for wasting her time with whites. Nonetheless, she felt "the time was right" to open such biracial dialogues. Her participation on the panel, though often frustrating, was "a calling" and part of her contribution to "the freedom struggle." Another participant later said, "That experience—I'll tell you—it made me a human being."[20] Wurzburg served as PAW's volunteer coordinator for six years.

The work of the panel and its message of tolerance brought the group to the attention of union and civil rights leaders as they prepared to challenge a one-year public works contract when it expired in 1969. Union members had had to settle for a mere ten-cents-an-hour raise plus a sick-leave policy when the strike was hastily settled after Dr. King's assassination. Inequities had not been resolved, but the city claimed they could not afford additional raises.[21] In an attempt to convince the white community that workers needed pay increases, Lester Rosen, chair of the Memphis Human Relations Commission, and Jessie Epps, local AFSCME organizer, decided to bring sympathetic women to the inner city to see the slum conditions in which the sanitation workers and their families lived. They hoped the Panel of American Women would promote this "home tour." But as Wurzburg pointed out, national PAW regulations prohibited her organization from taking sides in any municipal dispute. Instead, Wurzburg and a few friends telephoned individual women who they thought might be sympathetic—names gathered from years of networking with various women's organizations. Though Wurzburg herself was still not particularly sympathetic to unions per se, she did understand that race, limited employment opportunity, and substandard pay were inextricably linked. Over one hundred women responded to the telephone calls. They gathered at a local shopping center and boarded buses for the inner-city tour as union officials provided fact sheets about city employee salaries, living conditions, and the workers' lack of benefits. The union had carefully chosen the homes to visit and had prepared the residents for the type of questions that might be asked by their visitors—about salaries, heating bills, car payments, and other personal matters. When asked why city employees would allow their homes and families to be put on display, one of the former strikers remarked, "Sure, we didn't want them lookin' at us, but we was desperate. They had to see the conditions we lived under."[22]

This "home tour" brought an awareness of working-class poverty to a wide range of privileged women. Most were shocked to find that men who worked a full forty-hour week could afford only ramshackle houses in poor neighborhoods. One visitor noted, "[They] pay the same utility bills as I do [yet] I've got five tons of air-conditioning." Other women were embarrassed to have supported a mayor who condoned such "starvation wages" for city employees. The idea of well-to-do matrons traipsing through the homes of garbage collectors led to interviews with the Associated Press, *Time* magazine, and national TV networks.[23] Originally Epps and Rosen had invented the "home tour" so that the visitors would influence their husbands, and through them, the mayor and city council. However, the plight of the workers' families and the reality of racialized employment practices compelled these women to take direct action.

Tour participants chose a steering committee, which included Jocelyn Wurzburg, to draft a statement urging the city to come to terms with the union. The next day Diana Crump, a well-connected Episcopalian, read the statement to the city council subcommittee charged with employee wages. The council members' hostility and sarcasm shocked her. Noting that two of the other women on the steering committee were Catholic, one councilman suggested that the church could give up its tax-exempt status, thus providing the city with more income to pay the sanitation workers. Another councilman suggested that the women should begin their quest for justice by paying their domestic workers and yardmen higher salaries, implying that the women's concerns over low-wage workers were hypocritical at best. These wives of prominent business and professional men, and themselves volunteers in local political campaigns, were stunned by the Council's treatment. "We were so naïve," said Carol Blackburn. Talking to the council committee "was like talking to a brick wall." The reality of gender politics only strengthened the women's resolve, and they vowed to return for the full city council meeting.[24]

Wurzburg was not only outraged at the committee's badgering of the women, but also surprised at the "genteel" speech given by Crump, for the steering committee had crafted a stronger statement. Wurzburg and over two hundred others packed the council chambers the next day, and this time Wurzburg made the presentation herself. Her forceful and impassioned statement pointedly reminded the council members of the many ways these very women had worked on their campaigns, raised significant money for civic events, and created numerous social service programs. She offered this volunteer experience to the council to "attack poverty—here and now." The audience in the council chambers applauded enthusiastically, but the council members made no response at all. Instead, they moved to go directly into their regular business session. Furious, the women regrouped in the lobby, where one woman climbed some steps and shouted, "They didn't even thank us. Be assured—we are going to stay on the case!"[25]

Thus did a band of principally elite white women organize a new coalition for civic change. One of them, author Carol Lynn Yellin, later called this the "beginning of the feminist movement in Memphis," though their goals were less ideological than programmatic.[26] Calling themselves the Concerned Women of Memphis and Shelby County, the group recruited members from all the organizations, neighborhoods, and churches in which they had contacts. Because many had biracial experience on the Panel of American Women, they sought out African American colleagues to join in this fight. As one member noted, they brought together "a lot of women who cared deeply about what was going on and had no [other] way to express their feelings."[27] The Concerned Women issued an eleven-point "Call to Action for the City of Memphis" and then organized task forces to study and make recommendations to the city council. They organized task forces to address each of their eleven points, including affordable housing, access to health care and vocational training, establishment of free lunch programs in all city schools, creation of districts for school board elections (so African Americans might be elected), and a proposed minimum wage for domestic workers. Criticizing Memphis's reticence to participate in President Johnson's War on Poverty, they recommended that the city hire someone to coordinate federal grant applications and urged a state constitutional amendment to allow a city payroll tax, necessary to finance their proposed social services. They truly believed they "could end hunger, poverty, and racism in Memphis."[28]

The Concerned Women also sent telegrams to Mayor Loeb, council chairman Bob James, and union negotiator Jessie Epps stating that they would hold *all* of them "equally responsible" if the wage impasse with sanitation workers was not settled before the July 1 deadline. One reporter for the *Commercial Appeal* thought the Concerned Women represented "a formidable foe. . . . Many of them have money. All of them have affluent friends." The city did negotiate on all the union's demands before the deadline, averting a threatened second strike. City officials claimed the women's activities had nothing to do with their decisions. But years later, national AFSCME director Jerry Wurf told Wurzburg that he believed Concerned Women had made a major difference. In the settlement, city employees got an immediate eighteen-cents-an-hour increase, with the promise of full minimum wage salaries in one year. Workers also made gains in hazard and overtime pay, as well as work-related medical care benefits.[29]

But Wurzburg's heady sense of empowerment wilted when the media accounts of her two days before the city council brought sharp criticism from her husband and in-laws. In the interest of family harmony, Jocelyn gave up leadership of the group.[30] The gap grew between Jocelyn's developing social conscience and public persona and her husband's opposition to her activities.

Wurzburg joined several of the Concerned Women's task forces, including one that implemented a job application training program for low-skilled citizens, and she continued to direct the Panel of American Women. She also joined several organizations that most white Memphians found too radical, including the Urban League, the NAACP, and the Tennessee Council on Human Relations (TCHR). By 1972 she sat on the latter's subcommittee for employment and helped them bring training programs to the underemployed and the unemployed.[31]

The blight of racial prejudice and the heritage of Jim Crow were particularly evident in the painfully slow integration of Memphis City Schools. The NAACP filed *Northcross v. Board of Education of Memphis* in 1960 to force integration and lost, but won an appeal in 1962. However, plans developed by the school board failed to pass judicial oversight until 1966. School officials had no intention of sending white students to formerly all-black schools or of drawing neighborhood boundaries to include African Americans in majority-white schools. In 1972 Federal District Court judge Robert McCrae ordered the board to adopt a plan for faculty desegregation that would ensure that every school had at least 20 percent minority faculty. Continual white flight made attendance boundaries meaningless, so McCrae ordered busing to achieve integration.[32] As the city polarized into two antagonistic camps, the city schools asked the Panel of American Women to provide in-service training for teachers moving to minority schools. By compiling four different panels (twenty women) that made four presentations a day, Wurzburg was able to meet the school's demand.[33]

Meanwhile, African American teachers, students, and the NAACP led school boycotts on five consecutive Mondays in the fall of 1969. Dubbed "Black Mondays," these walkouts protested the composition of the school board from at-large districts, which guaranteed that any African American candidate could be outvoted.[34] A biracial coalition including Wurzburg lobbied state legislators for a bill that made five of the nine school board seats in Memphis district-specific. As a result, three African Americans won election to the school board in 1972. Not surprisingly, more and more white families fled to the "whiter" suburbs or enrolled their children in private schools. Judge McCrae ordered busing to achieve greater racial balance in the system. A group calling themselves Citizens Against Busing filed a class-action suit against the city, hoping to halt busing and thus make it impossible for many black families to enroll children anywhere except their all-black neighborhood schools.[35]

Indeed, mandatory busing of students produced even greater hostile reactions than the desegregation ruling itself, and white parents withdrew their children in alarming numbers before school began in the fall of 1972. The Memphis Better School Committee sought to bring academic innovations to the city schools and to stanch the decline of white students. Tensions mounted even within the Panel of American Women. Some members feared a dilution of academic standards if inner-city children "without preschool advantages" were bused to suburban elementary schools. Others felt that "private school parents" had abandoned racial justice when integration touched their own lives. Two white women enrolled their children in an all-black kindergarten at Caldwell Elementary to demonstrate their commitment to integration (and so that the program qualified for federal antipoverty funds). The fact that Wurzburg's three children had always attended private schools threw her commitment to desegregation into serious question. Other activists told her that despite her previous racial activism, she could not hold an office in the Memphis Better School Committee unless her children were in the public schools.[36] Again, Jocelyn bowed to family pressures and kept the children in private schools.

Though PAW members argued with one another over busing, they publicly presented a united commitment to making desegregation work. Under Wurzburg's direction, the panel submitted a grant to the federal Department of Health, Education, and Welfare (HEW) in 1973 to fund resource development for both teachers and students. The application required broad community sponsorship, so Wurzburg found herself drawing on years of community contacts with such organizations as the Urban League, parents' associations, and the Methodist General Board of Education. HEW approved the proposal and awarded the panel $10,000 from the Emergency School Assistance Program (ESAP), a program created to help local communities ease the traumas of desegregation. The grant took panel members directly into school classrooms, not only to share their own experiences, but also to help students share with one another their personal experiences of discrimination.[37] In June 1975 the panel secured federal funds to hold a one-day seminar for community leaders, hoping to shore up waning confidence in the public school system and stem white flight. The following year, PAW worked with faculty at Memphis State University to explore optional and alternative school models at a public forum.[38] Wurzburg remained in the background, as public school advocates distrusted her commitment.

Meanwhile, Wurzburg moved into fair employment advocacy. In 1971 her social and political activism garnered her an appointment from Governor Winfield Dunn (R) to the Tennessee Commission on Human Development (TCHD), a position she held through 1977. A few years before, the agency had begun to work closely with the Equal Employment Opportunity Commission (EEOC) to review hiring and employment practices in Tennessee. However, because of substantial resistance from the business community, combined with a cumbersome data-gathering strategy, they investigated only four out of twenty-nine complaints. Frustrated with this slow pace, the governor instructed Wurzburg and the other commissioners to turn their attention from private businesses to the backlog of citizen complaints against state agencies and government contractors. There, at least, state government could make a difference. Working closely with the TCHD's Memphis office, the commission heard thirty-seven complaints in 1975 and completed investigations of thirteen of those. The following year, the Memphis office was so successful in resolving disputes that it expanded its investigations to the Nashville area. In 1977, when Wurzburg became its secretary, the TCHD investigated 120 cases of racial discrimination in state employment practices.[39]

The commission had no enforcement power, and could only investigate, advise, and seek voluntary compliance. If the employer refused to change its practices, a complainant had no recourse but to sue under federal equal opportunity laws, a lengthy and complicated process. Wurzburg saw that this was at least part of the reason that employment discrimination could and did flourish in Tennessee.[40] Although she had no legal training or legislative experience and was closely identified with Republican politics, Wurzburg set about to draft equal employment legislation and present it to the state legislature for adoption. Her bill created a state agency to investigate and enforce nondiscrimination in employment and public accommodations. It would allow citizens to use "embarrassment and humiliation" as evidence of discrimination and give them the option of bypassing the state agency in order to sue privately. She worked closely with employment experts in Kentucky, the NAACP Legal Defense Fund, and the Lawyers' Committee against Discrimination Law, a Washington think tank. Other national organizations also expressed an interest in what she was doing because they thought Tennessee could become a model for other southern states without nondiscriminatory legislation.[41]

With the completed draft under her arm, Wurzburg went to Nashville to ask for the support of Senator Avon Williams, head of the state's legislative Black Caucus. Williams was not very receptive. "We've been trying to pass something like this for years," he growled. "Where were you when *my* bill came up?" "Probably playing golf at the country club," Wurzburg replied honestly. "But I'm here now. Would you take a look at my bill?" Still disdainful, Williams grabbed his Dictaphone and fired off a letter to William Robinson, head of the Lawyers' Committee against Discrimination Law. A few days later, Williams called Wurzburg to reverse his position. "Why didn't you tell me Bill Robinson had helped you write this bill?" Even with Williams's and the Black Caucus's support, the bill failed, and it continued to fail for six consecutive years. Finally passing in 1979 as an "add on" to a trucking weight bill, it became T.C.A. 4–2100 *et.seq.* In 1982 legislators amended the law to cover nondiscrimination in housing as well.[42]

Meanwhile, Wurzburg lobbied to parlay her activism, experience, and Republican connections into a presidential appointment during the Nixon administration. In particular, she sought a seat on the Equal Employment Opportunity Commission (EEOC). Reasoning that some legal knowledge would be helpful, she enrolled in Memphis State University's School of Law in 1974. At the age of thirty-four, with three children, numerous volunteer activities, and an active civic life, she found the transition to law school a difficult one. She thought she might only take classes for one year, but she eventually finished the degree in five years, graduating in 1979. Although she never was appointed to the EEOC, she did land a brief term on the advisory committee to EEOC chairman John Powell in 1975, working in his "kitchen cabinet."[43]

Moreover, from 1975 to 2000 Wurzburg served on Tennessee's State Advisory Committee to the United States Commission on Civil Rights (SAC-CCR). Congress had created the Commission on Civil Rights (CCR) to ensure compliance with the Civil Rights Act of 1957. Like the TCHR, it was a watchdog agency only, without enforcement authority.[44] The state advisory committees acted as the "eyes and ears" for the CCR at the state and local levels. However, as political appointees, their voices were certainly muted. The Tennessee SAC-CCR, headed by the Rev. Samuel "Billy" Kyles of Memphis, held hearings in various Tennessee cities, investigated complaints, and reported findings to the CCR's southern regional office in Atlanta. For example, the committee discovered that many Tennessee municipalities received federal funds for recreational activities and street improvements, but then discriminated against African American neighborhoods when they built the ballparks and paved the roads. They reported such violations of Title VI to the Justice Department. As presiding officer of SAC-CCR from 1993 to 1996, Wurzburg oversaw the investigation of numerous complaints, including several Tennessee church bombings.[45]

During the state and federal committee work, Jocelyn Wurzburg worried that Memphis's racial divide persisted. She wanted a visible tribute to Dr. Martin Luther King Jr. and his efforts on behalf of Memphis workers. She proposed that the city erect a memorial to Dr. King "at the corner of Main and Beale streets, where Black meets White," but knew that she would have to raise the funds herself. She lined up biracial support from the white activist Lucius Burch and an African American service organization, the Mallory Knights, and applied to the National Endowment of the Arts (NEA) for matching funds. As experience had taught her that federal agencies respond better with Congressional urging, she took an aide from Tennessee Republican senator William Brock's office with her to meet with NEA officials in Washington. The immediate response of the NEA was negative: "We don't do memorials." Wurzburg persisted, noting the symbolic impact of a King memorial in downtown Memphis. The NEA finally agreed to match local fundraising up to $25,000. She persuaded the Tennessee Council of Humanities to gather five well-known artists to judge proposed designs for the monument. Richard Hunt, an African American artist from Chicago, won the competition. His creation now stands just off the Main Street Mall in Memphis.[46]

Like many abolitionist foremothers, Wurzburg found her organizing efforts against racial discrimination heightened her awareness of discrimination against women as well. A feminist consciousness-raising class at the continuing education center of Southwestern College, her alma mater, as well as liberal national Republican women, inspired her emerging feminism. Thus when Governor Ray Blanton, a Republican, appointed her to the Tennessee Commission on the Status of Women, she welcomed the opportunity.[47]

President Kennedy had established the first national Commission on the Status of Women in 1961. In Tennessee, governors had appointed similar commissions beginning in 1963. Then in 1972 the state legislature mandated that a Commission on the Status of Women "study and highlight women's issues and make recommendations that would ensure women's participation as 'equal partners' with the state."[48] The commission issued a report in August 1975 based on a survey of 1,200 women's organizations. Of the 257 responses, only 18 percent of the organizations considered themselves "a part of the women's movement"; however, a majority favored the Equal Rights Amendment and supported legislation to prevent discrimination in the workplace. The report also identified a host of other gender discrimination concerns shared by women in Tennessee. For example, 95 percent believed women should serve on juries, and 87 percent believed Social Security and inheritance taxes discriminated against women. Despite these shared concerns, the commission bogged down under competing political agendas fueled by a resurgence of conservatism. Executive Director Carolyn Cowan resigned in 1977, and commissioners held information sessions and workshops across the state, attempting to reach more women and to refute the notion that the commission was somehow a "radical" organization.[49]

Meanwhile, in July 1976 President Gerald Ford tapped Wurzburg for a vacancy on the National Commission on the Observance of International Women's Year (IWY). Despite the fact that Congressman Ford had voted against the ERA, Wurzburg had high hopes that as president, he would become an advocate for women. His support in establishing a U.S. Commission of the IWY seemed to bear her out. Wurzburg was installed at a Rose Garden ceremony at the White House, joining such prominent commissioners as Congresswoman Bella Abzug, actress Jean Stapleton, publisher Gloria Steinem, actor Alan Alda, and activist Coretta Scott King.[50] Abzug garnered Congressional support for the U.S. Commission after the international IWY meeting in Mexico City called on each participating country to hold national conventions. Congress authorized the conference in conjunction with the nation's bicentennial; it was the first and only federally funded women's conference held in the United States and mandated that all states hold conventions to debate the IWY issues. They demanded that each state select a "religiously, ethnically, and economically diverse group of delegates" to the national meeting.[51]

Within months of Wurzburg's joining the US-IWY Commission, several members of the IWY staff along with state department personnel approached her with fears that delegates to the U.S. conference might discuss lesbian rights, an inflammatory issue among conservatives like Phyllis Schlafly and the Eagle Forum. Wurzburg's colleagues feared that debates over sexual preference rights would attract additional conservative attention, distort media coverage, and cut short discussion of other critical issues.[52] Wurzburg was sympathetic enough with these concerns that she helped draft a statement stating that homosexual rights were not germane to the discussion of discrimination against women per se. Rather, she contended, discrimination against gay men and lesbians represented a distinct and separate category, a different kind of civil rights violation. Her letter to the organizing committee urged the commission to enforce a ban at the state conventions on any discussions of "lesbianism, sexual preference, or alternative life styles."[53] While not ignorant of the reality of homophobia, she sought to remove one of the conservatives' "hot buttons" from the public debate at the national conference.

Yet Wurzburg never sent the letter. In another conversion moment like that which occurred after Dr. King's assassination, she came to appreciate the gay rights position. A lesbian delegate to Tennessee's state planning session in Knoxville pleaded with the organizers, "Don't leave us outside the pale. We have nowhere else to be heard." Although not articulated as a religious imperative, Wurzburg believes it was the Jewish history of exclusion that enabled her to hear and respond to this plea.[54]

The US-IWY Convention convened in Houston (although Wurzburg had submitted a bid for Memphis to be the host city) on November 18, 1977. Some twenty thousand delegates and guests, including Wurzburg (now a former member of the US-IWY Commission) and twenty-six Tennesseans elected at the state convention, attended.[55] Not all state delegations achieved the balance of "diverse racial, ethnic, and religious groups" that Congress had mandated. Some delegates charged election fraud at the state conventions. For example, the Mississippi delegation was all white.[56] A group of conservative delegates called the Citizen Review Committee investigated Tennessee's convention and charged that the coordinating committee was "not balanced in terms of points of view" as the law required, because only two members out of forty-six opposed the ERA. They also charged discriminatory registration practices and illegal voting for delegates. However, the Tennesseans were seated at the Houston meeting.[57] The debates on the Equal Rights Amendment, abortion, and gay rights were acrimonious, making the task of formulating a National Plan of Action nearly impossible. Nonetheless, the "Spirit of Houston" became a touchstone for Wurzburg.

In December 1979 Wurzburg completed her legal studies and joined the small Memphis firm of Williams, Benham and McDaniel. She wanted to handle employment cases, but the firm assigned her to what they euphemistically called "other problems"—collections and divorces. Even though she won her first five divorce cases, she found the process so contentious that she would go home sick to her stomach. "In divorce, I didn't think anybody [actually] won: the kids lost, both parties lost," she later recounted.[58] Her own marriage ended in 1982, the consequence of disparate views on women's place, civic activism, politics, and race. That same year, she left the law firm and opened her own practice handling mostly uncontested divorces. Two years later, she attended a workshop on mediation as an alternative to litigation; she immediately knew that the process of discussion and compromise suited her better than litigation. Wurzburg became the first professional mediator in Memphis. In 1995 she was selected to head the Family Section of the Memphis Bar Association, which also chose her for the newly established Alternative Dispute Resolution section head in 2002.[59]

Always self-identified as a secular Jew, Wurzburg found her religious identity through work on the Social Action Committee of Temple Israel, the Community Relations Council of the Memphis Jewish Federation, and the National Conference of Christians and Jews, receiving an award from them for her work on women's rights. At the national level, the Social Action Commission of Reform Judaism introduced her to a stimulating group of liberal thinking, socially conscious Jewish men and women whom she considered her "church home." She was instrumental in their moving the 1977 biennial convention to a state that had supported the ERA.[60]

Jocelyn Dan Wurzburg is not one to live life on the perimeter, looking in on the action. She has championed fairness, equity, and justice, and done so with subtlety, finesse, and good humor. When she found herself converted to the cause of African American low-wage city workers, she not only rallied to their cause but became an evangelist to bring others into the racial justice advocacy of the Panel of American Women and the Concerned Women of Memphis and Shelby County. She threw parties to bring people together across class, race, and political divisions. She raised money for causes she believed in, campaigned for candidates she thought would improve her city, drafted legislation to protect employee rights, and served on numerous state and national boards to advance social justice and women's rights. Wurzburg's activism was not shaped so much by ideological convictions or the claim of sisterhood across race and class divides as it was by her ability to find that middle ground where divergent interests could create social change. She energized scores of women who might otherwise not have taken up a cause, particularly privileged white women. Her lifelong commitments draw on the best that reform politics, social justice, equal rights, feminism, and Reform Judaism have to offer. From her fourth-grade question about the peculiarities of the color line to her lived experience as a white "race woman" and feminist, Jocelyn Wurzburg has combined privilege, networking skills, legal expertise, and charm to champion many underdog causes.

NOTES

1. Jocelyn Dan Wurzburg, interview with the author, August 24, 1999, transcript in the author's possession. Unless otherwise noted, biographical information and Wurzburg's views come from this initial interview.

2. Sara Evans, *Personal Politics: The Roots of Women's Liberation in the Civil Rights Movement and the New Left* (New York: Random House, 1979); Constance Curry, ed., *Deep in Our Hearts: Nine White Women in the Freedom Movement*, (Athens: University of Georgia Press, 2000); Julie Roy Jeffrey, *The Great Silent Army of Abolitionism: Ordinary Women in the Antislavery Movement,* (Chapel Hill: University of North Carolina Press, 1998); Nancy Isenberg, *Sex and Citizenship in Antebellum America* (Chapel Hill: University of North Carolina Press, 1998).

3. Debra Schultz, *Going South: Jewish Women in the Civil Rights Movement* (New York: NYU Press, 2001), 165.

4. For those Jews who were active in Memphis civil rights, see Selma S. Lewis, *A Biblical People in the Bible Belt: The Jewish Community of Memphis, Tennessee* (Macon, Ga.: Mercer University Press, 1998), 186–92, 196–200.

5. Author's telephone interview with Jocelyn Wurzburg, July 26, 2006.

6. Nicki Elrod, "Rights Record Catapults Her to National Panel," *Memphis Commercial Appeal,* July 6, 1976, A10.

7. For details of the Memphis Sanitation Workers Strike, see Joan Beifuss, *At the River I Stand: Memphis, the 1968 Strike, and Martin Luther King* (Memphis: B&W Books, 1985); Michael Honey, *Going Down Jericho Road: The Memphis Strike, Martin Luther King's Last Campaign* (New York: W. W. Norton, 2007); David Appleby, Allison Graham, and Steve Ross, producers, *At the River*

I Stand, DVD, California Newsreel, 1993; and Selma S. Lewis, "Social Religion and the Memphis Sanitation Strike," (Ph.D. dissertation: University of Memphis, 1988).

8. Taylor Branch, *At Canaan's Edge: America in the King Years, 1965–1968* (New York: Simon and Schuster, 2006), 697.

9. T. O. Jones interview, Memphis Sanitation Workers' Strike Collection, Special Collections, McWherter Library, University of Memphis (hereafter referred to as Strike Collection), C22, F111; James Lawson interview, Strike Collection, C22, F139; Ralph Jackson interview, Strike Collection, C21, F101; Velma Lois Jones, interview with the author, December 20, 1999; Honey, *Going Down Jericho Road*, 267, 316.

10. Beifuss, *At the River I Stand*, 193–96, 200–203; Honey, *Going Down Jericho Road*, 292–304. For information on those whites who did support the strikers, see Gail S. Murray, "White Privilege, Racial Justice: Women Activists in Memphis," in *Throwing Off the Cloak of Privilege*, ed. Gail S. Murray (Gainesville: University Press of Florida, 2004), 215–16.

11. Beifuss, *At the River I Stand*, 204, 217–33; Honey, *Going Down Jericho Road*, 346–56.

12. Peggy Jemison Bodine, telephone interview with the author, July 9, 2001.

13. Beifuss, *At the River I Stand*, 333–37.

14. Mary Collier Lawson, interview with the author, August 20, 1999.

15. Sara Alderman Murphy, *Breaking the Silence: Little Rock's Women's Emergency Committee to Open Our Schools, 1958–1963* (Fayetteville: University of Arkansas Press, 1997), 236–38.

16. Wurzburg interview, June 23, 2005.

17. Dorothy "Happy" Jones, interview with the author, August 5, 1999.

18. Wurzburg interviews, August 24, 1999, and June 23, 2005.

19. Modeane Thompson, interview with the author, August 17, 1999.

20. Quotes from Modeane Thompson and Happy Jones interviews. Wurzburg interviews August 24, 1999, and June 24, 2005; Anne Shafer interview with the author, August 17, 1999.

21. Beifuss, *At the River I Stand*, 345–48.

22. James Chisum, "Misery Tour Reaps Council Hearing," *Memphis Commercial Appeal*, June 15, 1969; quotation from Taylor Rogers, interview with the author, July 30, 1998.

23. Concerned Women of Memphis and Shelby County, unlabeled clipping in *Scrapbook*, Jocelyn Dan Wurzburg Collection, Mississippi Valley Special Collections, McWherter Library, University of Memphis (hereafter referred to as the JDW Collection).

24. Chisum, "Misery Tour"; "Women Urge: 'End Poverty in Memphis,'" *Memphis Press Scimitar*, June 17, 1969; "Embattled Women Backed by Blanchard; Meet Today," *Memphis Press Scimitar*, June 18, 1969; Wurzburg interviews.

25. James Chisum, "Tour Women Meet with Council Dound Call," *Memphis Commercial Appeal*, June 17, 1969.

26. Yellin quote from Wurzburg interview, June 24, 2005.

27. Annabelle Whittemore, interview with the author, November 19, 1999.

28. Jones interview; Concerned Women *Scrapbook*; William Street, "Ladies Place in Political Marketplace Awaits Outcome," *Memphis Commercial Appeal*, June 19, 1969.

29. Concerned Women *Scrapbook*; Street, "Ladies' Place"; F. Ray Marshall and Arvil Van Adams, "The Memphis Public Employees Strike," in *Racial Conflict and Negotiation*, ed. W. E. Charlmers and G. Cormick (Ann Arbor: University of Michigan Press, 1971), 104–5; Wurzburg interview June 24, 2005.

30. Jones interview.

31. Wurzburg to Bryant, October 21, 1970, and TCHR Newsletters, both in JDW Collection, Box 1, F20.

32. Floyd Montgomery Sharp, "The Desegregation of the Memphis City Schools under the Direction of Judge Robert Malcolm McCrae, Jr." (Ph. D. dissertation, University of Memphis, 1997), 64–203.

33. Wurzburg interviews; Shafer interview; Thompson interview.

34. "School Protest Talks to Resume," *Memphis Press Scimitar*, October 13, 1969; "674 Teachers and 65,000 Students Skip Classes at Memphis Schools," *Memphis Press Scimitar*, October 20, 1969; "Teachers Lead Out in 'Black Monday' March," *Memphis Tri-State Defender*, October 25, 1969; "March's Chants Fill Empty Stores," *Memphis Tri-State Defender*, November 2, 1969; Richard Lentz, "City to Seek Court Action on Walkouts after 1,995 Join 'Black Monday' Marches," *Memphis Tri-State Defender*, November 4; and Owen Cheek, "Thousands in March Here Demand Schools, Unions Share," *Memphis Tri-State Defender*, November 8, 1969.

35. Wurzburg interview, June 24, 2005; Sharp, "The Desegregation of the Memphis City Schools," 162–67, 185–92, 136–37; *Memphis Commercial Appeal*, September 27, 1972.

36. Wurzburg interview, June 24, 2005; Joyce Morrison interview with the author, October 5, 1999.

37. PAW papers, JDW Collection, Box 3, F5.

38. JDW Collection, Box 2, F20.

39. Ibid., Box 8, F2.

40. Wurzburg interview, June 24, 2005; Witherspoon, "Administrative Implementation," Appendix A, found in JDW Collection, Box 8, F2.

41. Wurzburg interview, February 8, 2005.

42. Wurzburg interview, June 24, 2005.

43. Ibid.

44. Steven F. Lawson, *Black Ballots: Voting Rights in the South, 1944–1969* (New York: Columbia University Press, 1976), 140, 149, 166, 199, 213–15.

45. Wurzburg interview, June 24, 2005; SAC papers in JDW Collection , Box 43, F17–21.

46. Wurzburg interview, June 24, 2005.

47. JDW Collection, Box 6.

48. "Commission," *Memphis Commercial Appeal*, January 25, 1978; "Tennessee Commission on the Status of Women," *Tennessee Encyclopedia of History and Culture*, http://tennesseeencyclopedia.net (accessed June 8, 2005).

49. Anne Gillenwater, "Discrimination of Women as Viewed by Tennessee Women's Organizations," typescript, JDW Collection, Box 21, F20; clippings, JDW Collection, Box 6.

50. Elrod, "Rights Record Catapults Her to National Panel"; JDW Collection, Box 6, F14.

51. "National Women's Conference, Houston," http://www.pbs.org/independentlens/sistersof77/conference.html (accessed June 14, 2005).

52. Conservatives had also attacked the U.S. Commission because of its support of the Equal Rights Amendment. JDW Collection, Box 6, F14.

53. Letter from Jocelyn Wurzburg to Ersa Poston, December 8, 1976, in the JDW Collection, Box 6, F19.

54. Wurzburg interview, June 24, 2005.

55. IWY Press release, JDW Collection, Box 6, F14. President Carter did not reappoint Wurzburg to the commission when he took office in 1977.

56. IWY Press Release, JDW Collection, Box 6, F14.

57. JDW Collection, Box 21, F27.

58. She also believes that her selective choices of law school courses did not prepare her well for the day-to-day demands of litigation. Mary Danelo, "Renaissance Woman," *Memphis Daily News*, May 31, 2002.

59. Wurzburg interview, June 24, 2005.

60. Wurzburg interviews February 8, 2005, and June 24, 2005.

Doris Bradshaw

(1954–)

Battling Environmental Racism

MELISSA CHECKER

Doris Bradshaw was born in Memphis, Tennessee, on September 7, 1954, four months after the Supreme Court decided *Brown v. Board of Education of Topeka, Kansas*, which ended legal public segregation in the United States. Long after the ink on the ruling had dried, however, black Memphians continued the struggle to overcome an entrenched system of racism and white privilege. Part of that system includes "environmental racism," or the unequal distribution of toxic waste and other environmental hazards in communities of color.[1] Doris Bradshaw devoted her early years to combating racial segregation and has spent her adult years fighting for environmental justice. Although her struggle is still unresolved, Bradshaw's temerity has raised awareness about Memphis's environmental disparities on local, state, national, and even international levels. Her story demonstrates how the spirit of survival and self-empowerment that began during slavery and Reconstruction transforms through the generations into civil rights and social justice activism. Indeed, Bradshaw's activism is a testament to the inequalities that stubbornly linger in the U.S. South. Her family history witnesses the protracted struggles of Tennessee's African Americans to combat those inequalities in various forms, on an everyday basis.

Bradshaw spent most of her life in a predominantly African American neighborhood surrounding the Memphis Defense Depot. Established in 1942 by the U.S. Army Corps of Engineers, the depot was at one time the largest military supply storehouse in the country.[2] Throughout the 1980s, ongoing investigations at the depot revealed that cleaners and solvents, petroleum products, pesticides, and metals had contaminated the groundwater around the site. As a result, the Environmental Protection Agency (EPA) placed the depot on its

DORIS BRADSHAW

2007. Courtesy of photographer, Melissa Checker.

"National Priorities List" in 1992, designating it one of the most polluted sites in the country and a high priority for federal cleanup. Bradshaw, who had integrated her Tennessee high school as a teenager and stood against racial discrimination in her Memphis workplace as a young adult, began to connect that contamination to the high incidence of rare diseases, especially rare cancers, that plagued her neighbors, most of whom were low-income African Americans. Had the depot, for decades a source of jobs and a community anchor, been poisoning its neighbors all along? As the people around her sickened and her suspicions grew, Bradshaw became painfully aware that she and most of her neighbors did not have the financial resources to move, and they had little choice but to stay. Steeped in a long family history of self-empowerment, Bradshaw drew on this legacy to launch an ongoing fight to obtain health care for neighborhood residents and former depot workers.

This battle linked her to the burgeoning national environmental justice movement, which opposes the widespread and disproportionate contamination of poor communities and communities of color in the United States.[3] Bradshaw soon moved to the forefront of that movement, tirelessly traveling across the continental United States, Alaska, Hawaii, and Puerto Rico to share her Memphis experiences with other local environmental justice activists and often with local, state, and national legislators. In less than a decade she won at least seven awards for her perseverance in environmental justice struggles. All the while, she never lost sight of her neighbors' needs, and she applied what she learned on her travels to the ongoing local struggle to find relief from the toxic conditions.

One of seven children born to hardworking parents, themselves children of former sharecroppers, Bradshaw was not formally trained in public policy studies or environmental science. Rather, her ability to engage in this battle is rooted in a five-generation family tree, each branch of which represents a line of people who were unwilling to be beaten by difficult circumstances, and who stood up in defense of themselves, their families, and other people facing injustice. Bradshaw's family stories and legends, most of which she learned from her great-grandmother Mary, strengthened her sense of purpose and resolve.

As Bradshaw explained, "And that's what I'm kind of like really, really proud of, myself—even though racism had always been an issue, we were told not to bow down to it, to stand up for what you believed. . . . There were many people in our family who got killed for doing that, for standing up."[4] Just as the environmental justice movement itself grew out of the civil rights movement, Bradshaw found in the lives of her foremothers and forefathers a legacy of self-empowerment and a struggle for justice in the face of racism in all its forms.

Indeed, the story of Bradshaw's activism begins long before she was born, with her great-great-grandmother, Julia Crawford. Born into slavery in the mid-1800s, Crawford's owner sold her away from her family at the age of eight to a plantation owner in southern Mississippi. Emancipation came soon after, though, and she married and started a family in a new era of nominal freedom. Crawford's husband left her while their children were still very young, however. Determined to support her family, she continued sharecropping even as a single mother. She imparted her toughness to her children, especially her daughter Mary (Doris Bradshaw's great-grandmother).

Although she "was a little fellow," according to Bradshaw, Mary was a "warrior." Helping her mother to support the family, Mary went to work at a young age doing wash for a white woman and had little opportunity to attend school. To make matters worse, according to Mary, every day the white woman's children would spit on her and call her names. Mary fought back. As Bradshaw retold Mary's story: "So one day the [white] lady said 'I'm going to hold [Mary] and I'm going to let y'all beat her' . . . and 'I closed my eyes with all my might and ran like a raging bull, and I ran up to that white lady and hit her and she flipped over.' After then they called her crazy Mary and they left her alone. . . . Mm-hmm, they was calling her crazy Mary but she wasn't crazy she just didn't believe in nobody doing anything to her or anyone, she was very protective of her kids and her family. She just wouldn't allow anyone to do anything out of place—no one would mess with her, no one." Mary married Enus Garrett when she was just thirteen and over time gave birth to seven children (tragically, the eldest son was killed at a young age, in an altercation with a white neighbor).

Together, the family struggled to survive as sharecroppers. The repressive sharecropping system, which came into wide use in the United States in the Reconstruction Era (1865–76), was not much better than slavery. But the Garretts, like many African American families, had initially acquired their *own* land during Reconstruction. Yet in the years that followed Reconstruction, hate groups such as the Ku Klux Klan forced families from their properties. Making matters worse, state governments found pseudo-legal reasons to revoke land claims and systematically denied or delayed loans to black farmers.[5] Thus, the majority of black Mississipians who remained in the agricultural sector after Reconstruction were sharecroppers or tenant farmers. For these Delta farmers, the 1920s were full of hardship for other reasons as well. The Great Mississippi Flood of 1927 destroyed vast acres of farmland, and the mechanization of cotton farming made competition for sharecropping fierce.

The Depression years (1929–39) also hit the South hard, especially African American southerners. Bradshaw remembered Mary telling her stories of how food from New Deal relief programs that was meant for sharecroppers was re-appropriated to white restaurants. Some of it, according to Mary, was left to rot rather than given to black people. "My grandmother said the catfish would grow so big [because] they'd throw that rotted food into one of the ponds or the lake or something." Mary and her neighbors cultivated small backyard farms to sustain themselves through the lean Depression years. Mary also learned how to use local plants and herbs as medicine, and she became a midwife.

Also in the 1930s, racial violence befell the family when two of Bradshaw's relatives were hanged in Mississippi on suspicion of, as Bradshaw put it, "doing something to a white woman."[6] Bradshaw pointed out the absurdity of such allegations: "Nobody in their right mind would do something to a white woman. But if they even back then looked at her a certain way . . ." In the same period, a white man shot and wounded one of Mary's sons. The extended family network pooled enough money to send him to St. Louis. But by then the family was exhausted and angry. According to Bradshaw, "all [the family] wanted to do was get the hell out of Mississippi, there was so much racism, so much oppression. . . . It was at a time where the racism was so bad people were getting killed and my great-grandfather thought someone was going to kill Mary because she never backed down from a fight." Mary and Enus's daughter, Susie (Bradshaw's grandmother), had gotten a job cleaning for a white woman in Memphis, and most of the family joined her there.

As the 1930s turned into the 1940s, Susie married and divorced, and then took a second husband, a man named Snookem Parker. Parker was drafted into World War II, and in addition to his soldier's wages, earned quite a bit of money gambling in Europe. He sent much of that money back to Susie and their new baby girl. Sending the money home turned out to be fortuitous: According to Bradshaw's grandparents, white officers informed black soldiers on the way back from the war that they would not be allowed to exchange European money once back in the United States and instructed them to throw the money overboard. Parker only "pretended to throw some of his away because he didn't trust them."

Susie herself diligently saved the money she received from her husband overseas until she had enough to buy two adjacent lots in south Memphis. Her mother, Mary, bought a third lot on the same stretch of land, not far from the burgeoning Memphis Defense Depot. Lumber was rationed during the war; for African Americans in Memphis, it was nearly impossible to obtain. But many African Americans working in the lumber and construction industries put aside scraps of wood and supplied their friends and neighbors with raw housing materials. Susie collected enough for her father, Enus, to build three houses on the three plots of land—one for him and his wife, one for Susie and Snookem

Parker, and one for their cousins. Although Snookem returned from the war quite ill with tuberculosis, he was able to recuperate under his own roof and on his own land, adjacent to his wife's kin. When he returned to factory work in Memphis, Susie could stay home and take care of the couple's only child, Pearl (Bradshaw's mother).

As she grew into a young woman in the late 1940s, Pearl was known for her beauty and her love of gospel music. Memphis was a hotbed of the new music, with nationally revered songwriters Lucie Campbell and Rev. Herbert Brewster active locally, and literally hundreds of quartets singing at churches and revivals throughout the region.[7] Bradshaw remembered, "My mom used to go to the church, and they would go and follow all the quartets singing. Back then that was the thing for teenagers." When she was about sixteen, Pearl met John Deberry, who was seven years her senior. She found John's face and spirit as attractive as his singing voice. Born in 1925, John came from a long line of ministers, all of whom were known for their community activism and social justice work. After a two-year courtship, John and Pearl married. John went into the army, serving in the Korean War. Upon his return, John enrolled in Owens College, a historically black junior college, to study law. To support the family, he worked two jobs, as a grave digger at Forest Hill Cemetery, and as a janitor cleaning office buildings. John also worked hard at fatherhood. He made sure he saw his children before bedtime and on Sundays, when he would also preach at various local churches. He scraped together enough of a living that Bradshaw's mother was able to stay home and raise six children.

Working multiple jobs to stay afloat has historically been a necessity for many African American families. Indeed, although the postwar "boom" led to prosperity and jobs for many white Americans, blacks benefited substantially less, especially in the South. Few good paying jobs were open to African Americans in a still-segregated 1950s Memphis, even for veterans with high school diplomas, and blacks were typically "last hired and first fired."[8] Those who did keep their manufacturing jobs worked under segregated circumstances (which among other things meant that blacks were relegated to the worst and lowest-paid jobs).[9] It is unsurprising, then, that in 1959 in Memphis, 70 percent of African Americans lived below the poverty line.[10]

One employer of both white and black Memphians was the defense depot, which by this time spread across 642 acres, creeping closer to the residences surrounding it. A military supply, storage, and maintenance facility, the depot employed 4,200 Memphis residents, who stored chemical warfare materials until 1961 (although the amount of chemical warfare–related hazardous materials dropped rapidly after World War II). Chemicals stored at the facility came primarily from national stockpiles of bauxite and fluorspar (nontoxic minerals used to make chemical agents). In addition, there was one reported instance in 1946 of leaking mustard bombs being taken to the depot's Dunn Field where they were drained and buried.[11] But for most of its operation, the depot seemed a benevolent presence, employing many residents.

Indeed, despite their dangerous neighbor and her family's economic struggles, Bradshaw remembers the early part of her childhood in the late 1950s quite fondly. The fourth of six children, she spent many nights next door to her parents, in her great-grandmother Mary's house, listening to stories of the old days and looking out for Mary, who was in the early stages of Alzheimer's disease. On the other side of Bradshaw's parents lived Susie and her third husband, Starling Hall. Two other cousins lived nearby in homes built by Enus, and a few streets over lived a third cousin. Altogether Enus built six houses for his kin, all within a mile of one another. Even more relatives passed through, knowing that if they fell on hard times, they could stay in one of the family's houses until they regained their footing. Bradshaw remembered, "Nobody was homeless unless they wanted to be, in our family. I remember whole families coming through, stay for months at a time, they'd use those houses to get on their feet." At this point in history, many African American families like the Bradshaws believed they were living out an American dream. Having saved enough money during the war for down payments on homes, they now had equity to pass down to future generations.[12]

However, Jim Crow laws restricted the location of these neighborhoods, and often they were located on swampland and/or near industrial sites, such as the Memphis Defense Depot.[13]

Even so, large lots of land enabled neighbors to grow vast gardens and share their bounty. According to Bradshaw, "everybody traded vegetables in the summer." Standing in her front yard, she remembered how it was: "Where that duplex is, that was open land. . . . the chicken coop was in our backyard. . . . We had fresh chickens all the time. . . . Everybody had their own garden. The biggest garden was where that duplex is . . . with every kind of vegetable you can imagine. We would walk out in the garden and pick up some tomatoes and eat them. There was always food. We never went hungry." She went on to muse, "I think I had the best of childhoods. Because we had the whole hill to run up and play, the fruit trees were plentiful. We had every type of fruit tree you could name in the backyard—peaches to pears to plums, blackberries. You know [with] all these types of fruits, they canned and they made pies and that was the good times. During the time of the ripening season, they always had big Sunday meals." Bradshaw also recalled playing with white children in her neighborhood. In fact, her grandparents were the first homeowners on the street, and white families came in and built around them. According to Bradshaw, neighbor relations remained cordial until the late 1950s when her neighbors moved to suburbs further east, possibly taking advantage of cheap mortgages and postwar home buying incentives not available to black Americans.

In the mid-twentieth century, racism was not only between whites and blacks, but also between African Americans. Bradshaw, who is dark skinned, was ostracized in her segregated elementary school for her darkness. Bradshaw recollected, "If you was a dark child most of the time you'd be poked fun of and teased. And the teachers was no better, they'd put you in the back of the class like you was retarded or something." Luckily for Bradshaw, what she faced in school was counteracted by her parents (and later, a kind and supportive teacher), who told her that she "could accomplish anything if [she] set her mind to it." Even so, young Bradshaw was fairly delighted to learn that her father had gotten a job in Alamo, Tennessee, the county seat of Crockett County. The summer before she began fourth grade, Doris and her family relocated to Alamo.

Her father's new job indicated that larger changes, for her family and the nation, were on the horizon. In the early 1960s the Kennedy administration made thousands of government jobs available to African Americans; John Deberry secured employment with the Government Services Administration (GSA) on the cusp of that trend. He soon received a promotion to manage a building in Alamo that housed a post office and another government office.

Moving to Alamo, eighty miles northeast of Memphis, challenged the Deberry family on a number of levels. As Bradshaw explained, "It was twenty years behind time. It was so far behind time and it was like the people didn't know nothing. It was just back woods. . . . The Klan was prevalent there. . . . It was really rough." One day, Bradshaw and her family were driving out in the country and got lost on a dirt road. They saw a sign depicting a little man with black face and white lips, running. The sign read, "Nigger run, and if you can't read, run anyway," Bradshaw said, "I never will forget that sign and I asked my mamma, 'where in the world are we?'"

Like so many veterans from World War II and Korea, John Deberry had returned from fighting for democracy abroad to a still-segregated South. In addition, rather than being rewarded for risking his life for his country, he found himself protecting his family from the kinds of dangerous racism depicted in the country road sign. The contradiction between saving democracy abroad and living under Jim Crow at home galvanized Deberry, as it did thousands of other black veterans across the country.[14] It was not long before Deberry and the rest of the family set about working to change Alamo. Bradshaw's mother volunteered for a local branch of the Equal Employment Opportunity Commission (EEOC), a U.S. agency created in 1964 to end discrimination based on race, color, religion, sex, or national origin in employment. She also worked to provide decent housing for rural residents living outside of Alamo. In addition to his job with the GSA, John became pastor of the Alamo Church of Christ. Now the entire family was in the spotlight, and soon, Alamo would never be the same.

As in many rural southern places, the black schools in Alamo opened for a month in the summer so that the students could use a month in the fall to pick cotton. This persisted even though cotton picking had significantly dwindled by the early 1960s. Bradshaw remembered, "Daddy thought that was the stupidest thing he had ever seen. . . . The black schools did it but the white schools didn't. So it was a double standard. My dad said he refused to let us go to a school like that." John started organizing the community and holding meetings. Eventually he formed an NAACP chapter in Alamo, and Pearl became its secretary. As Bradshaw saw it, her father was simply "bringing the town up to date."

Throughout the 1960s African Americans across the country were holding sit-ins, boycotting buses, and fighting for their rights as U.S. citizens. Although many of these battles were bloody, because he held a respected position in the community already, white people in the town gave John little trouble when he began organizing. He stepped up his efforts and launched an attack on the still-segregated school system, which in Alamo as elsewhere in Tennessee showed no signs of heeding the federal government's call to integrate "with all deliberate speed." Bradshaw recalled: "They [had been] saying nobody had registered at the school—the reason why they hadn't integrated was no one wanted to come there. So, they was going to make life hell for us, and they did, but it didn't work. . . . My parents they just taught us to fight back. Don't take anything don't let anyone treat you wrong. Don't let anybody mistreat you. If it's not funny don't laugh and if it doesn't itch don't scratch. . . . I didn't take anything off nobody. You couldn't spit on me or hit me without me fighting back. I was a fighter."

In 1968 John Deberry sent Doris and seven other black students to integrate Alamo High School. That first year for Bradshaw was a "year of misery," but the next year the school district started a busing program that brought more black students to the halls of Alamo High. Bolstered by this new influx, Bradshaw stepped into her parents' shoes: "We decided we would have black cheerleaders. We decided that if we were going to participate in all the sports, all the activities were going to be integrated. Things that they weren't used to doing, they had to do. There was going to be a black prom queen and also black queens on the court. Even if it means they have to have a white one and a black one. So we made a lot of waves."

Bradshaw became the youth president of the NAACP and focused on the cheerleading issue. For her it was emblematic of many inequities. While school sports teams were immediately integrated (and thanks to the black athletes, Alamo quickly started winning its games), African American students were denied access to most other school institutions. She continued: "In 1969, we went home and made cheerleading uniforms. About ten black girls, on our sewing machine. . . . And we trained that evening. For about a couple weeks we trained on what we were going to do. . . . We took one color of Alamo High and one color of Central [the high school from which the students had come], and blended. . . . So [the night of the game], the twelve of us got down on their floor, all the blacks got to that corner and we were the loudest thing in that gym. We cheered and cheered and they came and joined us. The [white] cheerleaders came and joined us and the kids kind of intermingled because they liked what we were doing." Infused with enthusiasm after her cheerleading success, Bradshaw next became the first black student in the band.

In the two years following Dr. Martin Luther King Jr.'s assassination, like hundreds of students around the country, Bradshaw ramped up her activism. She soon extended her organizing outside of the school's walls, leading a sit-in at Alamo's fanciest restaurant. The most important accomplishment of Bradshaw's high school years came in 1970, when she organized African American students to prevent one of their classmates, "one of the smartest kids in the school," from being sent to prison for a crime they believed he did not commit. The student was accused of rape, but Bradshaw and her peers were absolutely certain he was innocent. On the day of his trial, about a hundred black students, under Bradshaw's leadership, marched into the courthouse mimicking the Black Panthers by wearing black berets and armbands. She remembered, "The judge called my dad and said, 'Mr. Deberry your daughter is here with a hundred young people in the courtroom. Could you please come down here, we don't want a riot.' He said, 'well the kids are saying he didn't do it and they are there to make sure he gets a fair trial.'" Thanks in part to the esteem Alamo's leaders had for Deberry, the trial proceeded with the students' respectful but steadfast presence. At its end, the judge gave the young man over to Bradshaw's father for a year's probation. Today the young man is a doctor.

Bradshaw and her father thus managed to establish some concrete changes in the lives of Alamo's African Americans with little of the violence that accompanied such changes in other parts of the South. That is, until John challenged Alamo's sheriff. According to Doris, it was widely believed that the sheriff was corrupt. John alerted the FBI, and they launched an investigation that led to the sheriff's arrest. A few weeks later, Bradshaw remembers being in the living room with her family when a bullet shot through a window, barely missing them. "My father said, 'it is time to leave here, the family is in jeopardy. I'm not afraid but I refuse to let something happen to y'all.'" The family returned to Memphis.

On March 8, 1971, shortly after their return, something terrible did happen. Bradshaw's mother, sister, and foster brother were on their way to pick up Bradshaw and her sister when their car was hit by a drunk driver. All three died. Bradshaw recalled, "It changed our lives forever. . . . I didn't work in civil rights issues—I would participate in the marches, go to rallies but I wasn't a [leader] anymore. It took a lot out of fight out of us for a long time."

Living near but not in their old house on Mallory Street, and back among friends and family, the Deberrys struggled to move forward in their lives. Family matriarch Mary Garrett still lived in Memphis. With her Alzheimer's rapidly worsening, she now became Bradshaw's primary responsibility. This bond to her great-grandmother (and her grandmother Susie, who also still lived in Memphis) linked Bradshaw more directly with her family's distant past and with her grandmothers' strong spirit of defiance. Thus, although her mother's death "took the fight out" of her for a while, Doris continued to live in the midst of her family's inspiration.

Thanks to "white flight," Memphis was a more fully segregated city in the 1970s, and the depot neighborhood had become almost entirely African American. Most families were working to middle income, as this time was one of employment and wage opportunities for black workers. John Deberry, for instance, initially kept his job with the GSA. About a year later, he took a job with Federal Express, then a fledgling company that had just opened operations in Memphis. However, private industry was not for Deberry, and after only six months, he returned to work for the U.S. government. This time, John took a job with the postal service, where he stayed until his retirement a few decades later.

One afternoon, not long after her return to Memphis, Bradshaw acquainted herself with the family renting her old home. The oldest son, Kenneth Bradshaw, was a welder who had lived in Chicago and had protested the Vietnam War as well as segregation. "He was up-to-date on civil rights issues," remembered Bradshaw. Always dressing his tall, lean body in black slacks and a hat, Kenneth also "looked like a matador," Bradshaw smiled. However, she was only sixteen, and Kenneth was twenty-one. They remained friends for a year or so before they began dating, and in 1973, shortly after Bradshaw's high school graduation, they married. About a year later, and just before Mary's death in 1974, Bradshaw gave birth to their first child, Marquita.

For the first five years of her marriage, Bradshaw continued to put her activism on a back burner, devoting herself to raising children. Kenneth continued to work as a welder. But after the birth of their third child, the couple could no longer afford to be a single-income household, so Bradshaw landed a job at a bank. There, her past as a young activist caught back up with her. After receiving a promotion to the position of utility clerk, which had been a supervisory position, she was not given a corresponding raise. Bradshaw noticed that it was only African Americans who did not get raises when they were promoted—white employees always received them. Thanks to her mother's experience at the EEOC, Bradshaw knew exactly what to do: she filed a complaint with the agency.

While the EEOC was processing Bradshaw's complaint, the bank placed Bradshaw in the mailroom, where she had to lift heavy mailbags. One day, she "grabbed one of the mailbags to swing it and it popped my back. It ruptured two disks and broke three vertebrae." But, given the EEOC complaint, Bradshaw felt that she could not afford to miss work, lest her employer find an excuse to fire her.[15] When she finally went to the doctor, he recommended surgery and ordered her to stop working and request disability. Soon after, one of the Mallory Street houses became available, and the Bradshaws moved back in, both for financial reasons and to be closer to Susie, who still lived on the street.

A few years later, Bradshaw was at home one day when she received a notice from the nearby defense depot. The notice stated that investigations had found seventy-five waste disposal areas on depot land including arsenic, cadmium, chromium, lead, mercury, Polychlorinated Biphenyls (PCBs), chlordane, and chemical weapons residues.[16] Immediately, Bradshaw became gravely concerned for the health of her children (now numbering five), her husband, and her neighbors. She also realized that few Memphians were aware of the situation, and no one was organizing around it.

Although Memphis has the highest number of Superfund sites in Tennessee, few of its environmental groups have historically targeted toxics as a priority concern.[17] Thus, there were no "watchdog" groups that were monitoring the depot, or that were initially notified of its contamination. This prioritizing of ecological over urban concerns is typical of environmental groups across the United States, where environmentalism began as a white, middle-class movement more concerned with preservation and conservation than with urban issues.[18] At the same time, social justice and civil rights groups have historically focused on employment, education, and crime, rather than on clean air, water and soil. The environmental justice movement, which began in the mid-1980s, bridges social justice and environmentalism and calls attention to the fact that the environment is very much a priority for urban inhabitants, particularly people who are poor and people of color.

Since the beginning of the movement, numerous reports have shown that people of color find that their communities are more likely to host toxic waste sites than white neighborhoods. The most extensive of those studies, published in 2007 by the United Church of Christ, found that the proportion of people of color in neighborhoods hosting toxic sites was almost twice that of the proportion of those living in nonhost neighborhoods. Where facilities were clustered, people of color made up over a two-thirds majority. Ninety percent of states with facilities had disproportionately high percentages of people of color living in host neighborhoods.[19] Studies also showed that enforcement of environmental regulations depends significantly on an area's socioeconomic makeup—for example, penalties imposed on hazardous waste generators are five hundred times higher in places with white populations than in those with minority populations.[20] The reasons for this disproportion are multiple, and they include a legacy of housing segregation and differential access to economic and educational resources, as well as more direct acts of discrimination. Although environmental racism occurs nationwide, it is particularly pernicious in the South, due to its history of legalized segregation and lax environmental regulations. The Memphis Defense Depot is thus emblematic of environmental justice cases in many ways.

As Bradshaw read the information in the depot's letter she began to consider some of the oddities that seemed to go along with life in her neighborhood. For instance, the depot often incinerated its waste, and on many of the days that it did so, the neighborhood was a downright uncomfortable place to be. Bradshaw explained, "Some days [the smoke] would be so strong your eyes would water all day from being outside. Some summers, you'd have sores on you, if you'd get in the dew." She also remembered summer 1978, when she and her neighbors had seen a number of dogs inexplicably die. Perhaps most disturbing, after speaking to other residents, Bradshaw estimated that in the past year, nine women on Rozelle Street, just north of the depot, had been diagnosed with breast cancer. Doris Bradshaw's experiences are typical of many environmental justice leaders, who are often female and who come to environmental justice from a civil rights background. When these women begin to connect local illnesses to the facilities surrounding them, they draw on their civil rights backgrounds to take action.[21]

Without delay, Bradshaw called the number on the paper she received from the defense depot. "I put a message down, nobody respond, nobody called back, nobody let me know. I kept calling, calling. I never got any type of response from anybody. So I put the paper down, quit calling." Bradshaw soon became distracted by more unfortunate events. Her grandmother, Susie, suddenly became quite ill at the age of eighty-three. After several misdiagnoses, she was told she had bladder cancer and given just a few months to live. Bradshaw nursed her grandmother as the illness quickly overtook her body. In just a few weeks' time, she passed away. Bradshaw's entire neighborhood grieved for Susie, who had become a local icon, often inviting thirty or more guests to dinner on Sundays and generously sharing food from her bountiful garden.

After her grandmother's death, Bradshaw worked to get on with her life. One day, while she was cleaning Susie's room, she refound the paper from the depot. "I was cleaning up the room," she recalled, "so here comes the paper back in my hands. I called and called and called, no answer. No response from DOD [Department of Defense] and that was the only number I had to call." About a month later, in 1995, the Agency for Toxic Substances and Disease Registry (ATSDR) evaluated the possible public health impact of the site.[22] Upon completing that evaluation, they sent a letter to residents living around the area informing them of the EPA's findings, as well as their own assessment of the data, which contended that contamination at the site did not pose a health concern. More specifically, the ATSDR indicated, "contamination at the Depot does *not* pose a health concern to people living on or near the Depot, and it did not pose a health hazard in the past."[23]

But Bradshaw and her neighbors were not convinced—they knew people had grown extensive gardens, fished in nearby creeks, and played in ditches. They also knew that no one from the ATSDR had asked them about such behaviors. This rupture in communication and understanding between community members on one side, and policy makers and administrators on the other is a pernicious issue in environmental justice cases.[24] Often, the agencies testing toxic exposures do not investigate the degree to which community members historically or currently fish, garden, or do outside work around their homes. Bradshaw realized that if they wanted accurate reports, community members would have to raise their voices and fight for them.

She showed the ATSDR report down the street to the principal of Norris Elementary School, and from there, she decided to address it at the next PTA meeting. At the meeting, people living on the south and the north side of the depot revealed that they had received information about the contamination some time ago. These were middle-income areas, whereas the east and the west sides, which had only recently heard the news, were low-income areas. Moreover, the poorer neighborhood was 97 percent African American.[25] For Bradshaw and her neighbors, these racial and economic dynamics were no coincidence. They firmly believed that if theirs had been a white, middle- or upper-income neighborhood, the depot would have been more careful about its practices, relocated residents, or at least provided them with health care after discovering contamination.

Deciding to hold another meeting, Bradshaw and her neighbors distributed four thousand flyers. This time, over 350 residents crowded the Norris Elementary School cafeteria. After that there was no turning back. Bradshaw and her neighbors found themselves immersed in another civil rights battle. "It was just a whirlwind ride, and I tell you that," she chuckled. Meeting attendees formed the Defense Depot of Memphis Tennessee–Concerned Citizens Committee (DDMT-CCC), and placed Bradshaw at its helm. Soon, former depot workers who had long questioned the safety of depot procedures and who knew many coworkers who had died of cancer, or who had children with birth defects, approached DDMT-CCC. Armed with their personal experiences, the group contacted ATSDR and expressed their strong concerns about the health dangers the depot posed.

From its inception, one of DDMT-CCC's primary objectives has been to secure health care from some government agency—either ATSDR or DOD. Bradshaw explained, "All we wanted them to be was accountable. Put a little clinic there, pay for the people's medicine, and make the folks that were sick comfortable. That's all we wanted, and I don't think that was too much to ask for." In addition, Bradshaw and her group would not back down in their conviction that the ATSDR needed to revisit its study. As stated earlier, environmental justice organizations argue that agency studies are based on inadequate contact with communities, that they rely on inappropriate testing techniques and statistical methods that are unsuitable for small populations, and that they study the wrong types of illnesses.[26] Accordingly, Bradshaw has made it a central focus of her mission, both locally and nationally, to ensure that agency officials are made better aware of the cultural behaviors of low-income and minority communities.

In 1998 the ATSDR finally agreed to look again at the 1995 health assessment. But their second health document again reported that there were not enough recurring chemicals at the site to warrant action, and that those chemicals that did appear represented no apparent public health hazard from 1989 to the present for persons living around it. This time, the report *did* caution that the portion of Rozelle Street just west of Dunn Field (where the nine women were diagnosed with breast cancer) was a possible exception to this conclusion. Moreover, it stated that an increased chance of cancer could have existed for individuals and workers with daily exposure to polycyclic aromatic hydrocarbon (PAH)–contaminated soil from certain buildings, and that before 1989 the agency considered the public health hazard status of the depot area to be indeterminate.[27] Once again DDMT-CCC members disagreed with ATSDR's methodologies and scope of work. They contacted researchers at Howard University in Washington, D.C., who agreed to work in conjunction with the community to conduct a separate study of contaminants on the depot site.[28] Finally, after much agitation and activism, in 1998 the ATSDR agreed to provide a health clinic for depot residents and former employees. However, shortly after making that statement, the person responsible for it left the organization. Local politicians also routinely promised to help the group, but very few of those pledges came to fruition either. In 1998 depot officials placed Bradshaw on its Residents Advisory Board (RAB), a venue for community participation in depot clean-up efforts, but the board only served in an advisory capacity and had no real authority.

As they continued to fight for a solution to their contamination problems, Bradshaw and her neighbors increasingly realized that they were far from alone in their plight. Shortly after DDMT-CCC formed, they allied with the Memphis Peace and Justice Center, a local peace organization. While the Peace and Justice Center was not necessarily an environmental group, they connected Bradshaw to a program that trained southern communities to speak out against environmental injustice. Members of that movement formed the African American Environmental Justice Action Network (AAEJAN), of which Bradshaw became a board member.[29] From there, she was invited to participate in the Military Toxics Project (MTP), eventually taking a position on their board.[30] Bradshaw thus quickly became caught up in a growing network of grassroots environmental justice activists, meeting countless people in situations similar to hers. Through the MTP, she became a member of the Non-stockpile Core Group, which argues for the neutralization of chemical weapons, rather than their incineration, and makes recommendations to the DOD. She traveled to Alaska, Hawaii, and Puerto Rico, as well as across the mainland United States to attend training sessions, conferences, and protests. No matter where she went, she discovered that "where there was a [military] base, there were people suffering [from unusual or excessive illnesses]."

To reiterate, when DDMT-CCC began, the links between environmentalism and social justice were not clear to most Americans, let alone Tennesseans. All of her work earned Bradshaw notable recognition both at home and abroad. Thus, in bridging environmentalism and social justice, Bradshaw's actions have forged new and notable territory. For instance, she won the 1998 Memphis Women of Achievement Award, signaling the significance of her efforts to raise awareness of the links between toxic wastes and race. In 2002 Bradshaw won an award at the Second People of Color Environmental Justice Summit, and in 2003, she received a coveted Alston Bannerman fellowship, which provides sabbaticals for longtime activists. Both acknowledged Bradshaw's dedication to her cause. Also in 2002 Bradshaw was invited to attend the World Summit on Sustainable Development in Johannesburg, South Africa. Although she had to decline the invitation due to family obligations, her husband, Kenneth, and her daughter Marquita went in her stead. In all, over a ten-year period, Bradshaw received at least seven awards.

But in some ways, those awards were bittersweet as DDMT-CCC's battle became more urgent with each passing year. Ten years after founding the organization, Bradshaw found that many of its members had died. She realized that the most active people were those "that knew something was wrong and were suffering with cancer at that particular time." This urgency fueled DDMT-CCC's efforts and sustained their activism.

In 2004 that forbearance won the group another small victory. The DOD announced that they wanted to store hazardous waste on the site for forty-five days. The Tennessee Department of Environment and Conservation (TDEC) held a hearing about the matter, and Bradshaw organized enough community people to object that the state refused the permit. Following that success, Tennessee legislators appointed Bradshaw as chair of the Tennessee Environmental Justice Task Force. The Task Force represented a statewide effort to document conditions affecting communities of color that suffer from toxic contamination and to make recommendations for improving the role of TDEC in its relationships to contaminated communities.

Importantly, although Bradshaw's group had not yet won its war at the time of this book's publication, they took care to celebrate their victories along the way. Indeed, environmental justice activists find that recognition of small battles, and the perseverance required to fight them, is critical to nurturing a long-term movement. Moreover because environmental injustice stems from entrenched and interlocking systems of institutional racism, including legal and scientific institutions, it may take generations before the environmental justice movement sees substantial, definitive victories.[31]

For that reason, Bradshaw recognized the importance of changing Memphis's future by training a new generation of leaders. Like her grandmothers before her, Bradshaw planted the seeds of her temerity and courage in her children and the youth that surrounded her. For instance, in 1998 Marquita and some friends were discussing another friend who had recently been diagnosed with uterine cancer. A number of the girls mentioned that they had had cysts removed from ovaries and breasts. Alarmed, but with the examples of Bradshaw and her stories before them, Marquita, her sisters, Isis and Chelia, and her friends formed Youth Terminating Pollution (YTP), initially a spin-off of DDMT-CCC. Within a few years YTP became an independent organization, participating in hearings, outreach, and cultural exchanges with other youth who have been affected by military toxic dumpsites, and have held rallies and other events on environmental health issues. In 2000 a group of fourteen YTP members went to Washington, D.C., to meet with officials at the U.S. Department of Environmental Quality. In addition, they met with the Howard University researchers to discuss their plan for taking soil samples in their upcoming study.

Both DDMT-CCC and YTP took a broad view of environmental justice. They, like most environmental justice groups, defined the environment as "where we live, work, play and worship." Thus, for them environmental justice certainly meant finding adequate health care and relief from toxins. But it also meant working on the issues that prevent people from moving out of contaminated neighborhoods, such as unemployment, poor housing and schools, and crime.[32] Clean air, water, and soil, and affordable health care are then additions to a long list of resources historically denied to African Americans—the same resources for which Bradshaw and her parents and grandparents fought for decades. She may be tired of that fight, but the determination, perseverance, and self-determination that have defined her family for generations have also fortified Bradshaw and her children. As Bradshaw summed it up, "I think if your parents are the kind of people that tried to do right [by] a community, that's where you get this feeling that you got to do the right thing for your community and you've got to be a stand up type of person. . . . Even before I was even thought about, my mother and father and great-grandparents had a place in history where they fought against different things, they wasn't the type of people that people could run over them. They always believed in standing up for their rights, no matter the consequences."

Doris Bradshaw's ultimate contribution to Tennessee history is as yet undetermined. She continues her work on behalf of low-income people and people of color who continue to get the short, dirty end of the stick. Power structures that exclude them dictate where environmental hazards go and who lives in a clean and safe environment. Certainly, Bradshaw embodies a living history, one that exemplifies the transformation from self-empowerment and self-help to civil rights and now environmental justice activism. This long history teaches Bradshaw that she may not reap the rewards of her efforts in her own lifetime, but that they will come to fruition through the fortitude and empowerment of her daughters and her daughters' daughters. Frederick Douglass famously said,

"If there is no struggle, there is no progress."[33] Doris Bradshaw's story shows us the tenacity and strength of certain Tennessee women to continuously work to change the lives of current and future generations—indeed, without such resolve and protracted effort, change simply does not happen.

NOTES

1. See Robert Bullard, Paul Mohai, Robin Saha, and Beverly Wright, *Toxic Wastes and Race at Twenty, 1987–2007* (Cleveland: United Church of Christ, 2007), for information and definitions of environmental racism.

2. Vanessa Daniel, "Defense Depot of Memphis, Tennessee Concerned Citizens Committee," in *Community Activism at a Crossroads*, ed. Applied Research Center, 32–51 (Oakland, Calif.: Applied Research Center, 2002).

3. Although relatively new, there is a vast body of social science literature on the U.S. environmental justice movement. For a few examples, see Joni Adamson, Mei Mei Evans, and Rachel Stein, eds., *The Environmental Justice Reader: Politics, Poetics, and Pedagogy* (Tucson: University of Arizona Press, 2002); Bunyan Bryant, ed. *Environmental Justice: Issues, Policies and Solutions* (Washington, D.C.: Island Press, 1995); Robert Bullard, *Dumping in Dixie: Race, Class and Environmental Quality* (Boulder, Colo.: Westview Press, 2000); and Luke W. Cole and Sheila R. Foster, *From the Ground Up: Environmental Racism and the Rise of the Environmental Justice Movement* (New York: New York University Press, 2001).

4. All quotes from Doris Bradshaw derive from transcriptions of audiotaped interviews conducted by the author, which took place at several locations in Memphis, Tennessee, on January 27 and February 19, 2005.

5. An Associated Press (AP) survey found that in known cases, 406 black landowners were cheated out of, and forcibly removed from, more than 24,000 acres of farm and timberland—all of which is now owned by whites or corporations. See also Todd Lewan and Dolores Barclay, "Torn from the Land: Black Americans' Farmland Taken through Cheating, Intimidation, Even Murder," Electronic document. See http://www.ap.org/pages/whatsnew/how.html (2001). More recently, in 1997, the United States Department of Agriculture Civil Rights Action Team (CRAT) revealed that these activities continued well into the 1980s and early '90s. After settling a 1999 lawsuit the USDA has paid more than $630 million to farmers and former farmers who could document that they were unfairly denied loans. See http://www.oxfamamerica.org/advocacy/art4066.html.

6. Doris's husband, Kenneth, has written a book entitled *Quiet the Wind* telling the story of Mary's life and of her cousins' hangings.

7. Kip Lornell, *"Happy in the Service of the Lord": Afro-American Gospel Quartets in Memphis* (Urbana: University of Illinois Press, 1988).

8. Michael Honey, *Southern Black Labor and Black Civil Rights: Organizing Memphis Workers* (Urbana: University of Illinois Press, 1993), 221–22.

9. Importantly, in the 1950s and '60s, some factories began to unionize. See Michael Honey, *Black Workers Remember: An Oral History of Segregation, Unionism, and the Freedom Struggle* (Berkeley: University of California Press, 1999), 134.

10. Honey, *Southern Black Labor*, 288.

11. Superfund Site Assessment Branch Division of Health Assessment and Consultation Agency

for Toxic Substances and Disease Registry, "Public Health Assessment USA Defense Depot Memphis, Shelby County, Tennessee," http://www.atsdr.cdc.gov/HAC/PHA/memdef/mem_toc.html (accessed December 16, 1999).

12. See Melissa Checker, *Polluted Promises: Environmental Racism and the Search for Justice in a Southern Town* (New York: New York University Press, 2005), chaps. 3–4. See also Lance Freeman, "Black Homeownership: The Role of Temporal Changes and Residential Segregation at the End of the 20th Century," *Social Science Quarterly* 86, no. 2 (2005): 419.

13. See Checker, *Polluted Promises*, chap. 3. See also Roger Biles, "The Urban South in the Great Depression," *Journal of Southern History* 56, no. 1 (1993): 71–100.

14. A number of scholars have written about this contradiction. For some examples, see Beverly Bond and Janann Sherman, *Memphis in Black and White* (Charleston, S.C.: Arcadia, 2003), 133; Honey, *Southern Black Labor*; Checker, *Polluted Promises*; George Lipsitz, *A Life in the Struggle: Ivory Perry and the Culture of Opposition* (Philadelphia: Temple University Press, 1995 [1988]).

15. The results of the complaint remain confidential at the request of the parties involved.

16. Daniel, *Community Activism at a Crossroads*, 33.

17. Superfund sites are those designated by the U.S. EPA as the most toxic in the country; see http://www.scorecard.org (accessed June 7, 2007).

18. Checker *Polluted Promises*; Robert Gottlieb, *Forcing the Spring: The Transformation of the American Environmental Movement* (Washington, D.C.: Island, 1993).

19. Bullard et al., *Toxic Wastes and Race at Twenty.*

20. For a much more detailed discussion of these facts, and "environmental racism" defined, see Checker, *Polluted Promises.*

21. Checker, *Polluted Promises*; Gottlieb, *Forcing the Spring*; Andrea Simpson, "Who Hears Their Cry?: African American Women and the Fight for Environmental Justice in Memphis, Tennessee" in *The Environmental Justice Reader: Politics, Poetics, and Pedagogy*, ed. Joni Adamson, Mei Mei Evans, and Rachel Stein, 82–104 (Tucson: University of Arizona Press, 2002).

22. For more on the functions of the ATSDR, see http://www.atsdr.cdc.gov/about.html (accessed July 29, 2005).

23. Letter accessed through Superfund Site Assessment Branch Division of Health Assessment and Consultation Agency for Toxic Substances and Disease Registry, http://www.atsdr.cdc.gov/HAC/PHA/memdef/mem_toc.html (accessed April 1, 2008).

24. See Checker, *Polluted Promises*, and Checker, "'But I Know It's True': Environmental Risk Assessment, Justice and Anthropology," *Human Organization* 66, no. 2 (2007): 112–24.

25. Report accessed through Superfund Site Assessment Branch Division of Health Assessment and Consultation Agency for Toxic Substances and Disease Registry, available at: http://www.atsdr.cdc.gov/HAC/PHA/memdef/mem_toc.html (accessed April 1, 2008).

26. Simpson, "Who Hears Their Cry?" See also Checker, *Polluted Promises*, chap. 5.

27. Report accessed through Superfund Site Assessment Branch Division of Health Assessment and Consultation Agency for Toxic Substances and Disease Registry, http://www.atsdr.cdc.gov/HAC/PHA/memdef/mem_toc.html (accessed April 1, 2008).

28. Completed in 2003, that study revealed high levels of arsenic and heavy metals on depot land and called for more extensive testing outside the perimeter of depot property.

29. AAEJAN is a network of grassroots environmental justice groups throughout the South.

30. The Military Toxics Project is a national nonprofit network of neighborhood, veterans, Indigenous, peace, environmental, and other organizations representing people affected by military

contamination and pollution. For more information see: http://www.miltoxproj.org/ (accessed July 29, 2005).

31. See Checker, *Polluted Promises*, 96–97; Checker, "'But I Know It's True,'" 118–19.

32. Numerous studies of environmental justice describe this broad-based definition of the environment. For a few examples, see Melissa Checker, "It's in the Air: Redefining the Environment as a New Metaphor for Old Social Justice Struggles," *Human Organization* 61, no. 1 (2002): 94–105; and Patrick Novotny, "Where We Live, Work and Play: Reframing the Cultural Landscape of Environmentalism in the Environmental Justice Movement," *New Political Science* 23, no. 2 (1995): 61–78.

33. Frederick Douglass, "The Significance of Emancipation in the West Indies," Speech, Canandaigua, New York, August 3, 1857, found in *The Frederick Douglass Papers: Volume 3, Series One: Speeches, Debates, and Interviews, 1855–1863*, ed. John W. Blassingame (New Haven, Conn.: Yale University Press), 204.

Selected Bibliography

Adams, Jean, Margaret Kimball, and Jean Kimball. *Heroines of the Sky*. Garden City, N.Y.: Doubleday, Doran and Co., 1942.

Adamson, Joni, Mei Mei Evans, and Rachel Stein, eds. *The Environmental Justice Reader: Politics, Poetics, and Pedagogy*. Tucson: University of Arizona Press, 2002.

Baker, Jack D., and David Keith Hampton, eds. and annots., *Old Cherokee Families: Notes of Dr. Emmet Starr*. Vol. 1, *Letter Books A–F*. Oklahoma City: Baker Publishing, 1988.

Bestor, Arthur. *Backwoods Utopias: Sectarian and Owenite Phases of Communitarian Socialism in America, 1663–1829*. Philadelphia: University of Pennsylvania Press, 1950.

Bond, Beverly Greene. "'The Extent of the Law': Free Women of Color in Antebellum Memphis, Tennessee." In *Negotiating Boundaries of Southern Womanhood*, ed. Janet L. Coryell, Thomas H. Appleton Jr., Anastatia Sims, and Sandra Gioia Treadway, 7–26. Columbia: University of Missouri Press, 2000.

———. "'Till Fair Aurora Rise': African American Women in Memphis, Tennessee, 1840–1915." Ph.D. diss., University of Memphis, 1996.

Bowman, Rob. *Soulsville, U.S.A.: The Story of Stax Records*. New York: Schirmer Books, 1997.

Brandon, Edgar Ewing, ed. *Lafayette: Guest of the Nation*. Oxford, Ohio: Oxford Historical Press, 1950.

Brooks-Pazmany, Kathleen. *United States Women in Aviation, 1919–1929*. Washington, D.C.: Smithsonian Institution Press, 1991.

Bryant, Bunyan, ed. *Environmental Justice: Issues, Policies and Solutions*. Washington, D.C.: Island Press, 1995.

Bufwack, Mary A., and Robert K. Oermann. *Finding Her Voice: The Saga of Women in Country Music*. Nashville: Vanderbilt University Press and the Country Music Foundation Press, 1993, 2003.

Bullard, Robert. *Dumping in Dixie: Race, Class and Environmental Quality*. Boulder, Colo.: Westview Press, 2000.

Bullard, Robert, Paul Mohai, Robin Saha, and Beverly Wright. *Toxic Wastes and Race at Twenty, 1987–2007*. Cleveland: United Church of Christ, 2007.

Byerly, Victoria. *Hard Times Cotton Mill Girls: Personal Histories of Womanhood and Poverty in the South*. Ithaca, N.Y.: Cornell University Press, 1986.

Cantor, Louis. *Dewey and Elvis: The Life and Times of a Rock and Roll Deejay*. Urbana: University of Illinois Press, 2005.

Carby, Hazel V. "'In Body and Spirit': Representing Black Women Musicians." *Black Music Research Journal* 11, no. 2 (1991): 177–92.

Carriere, Marius, Jr. "Blacks in Pre–Civil War Memphis." *Tennessee Historical Quarterly* 48, no. 1 (1989): 3–14.

Checker, Melissa. *Polluted Promises: Environmental Racism and the Search for Justice in a Southern Town*. New York: New York University Press, 2005.

Cole, Luke W., and Sheila R. Foster. *From the Ground Up: Environmental Racism and the Rise of the Environmental Justice Movement*. New York: New York University Press, 2001.

Conway, Liz, ed. *Memphis 1948–1958*. Memphis: Memphis Brooks Museum of Art, 1986.

Corn, Joseph J. *The Winged Gospel: America's Romance with Aviation, 1900–1950*. New York: Oxford University Press, 1983.

Cotham, Perry C. *Toil, Turmoil and Triumph: A Portrait of the Tennessee Labor Movement*. Franklin, Tenn.: Hillsboro Press, 1995.

Cott, Nancy F. *The Grounding of Modern Feminism*. New Haven, Conn.: Yale University Press, 1989.

Cox, Brent Yanusdi. *Heart of the Eagle: Dragging Canoe and the Emergence of the Chickamauga Confederacy*. Milan, Tenn.: Chenanee Publishers, 1999.

Cumfer, Cynthia. *Separate Peoples, One Land: The Minds of Cherokees, Blacks, and Whites on the Tennessee Frontier*. Chapel Hill: University of North Carolina Press, 2007.

Curry, Constance, et al., eds. *Deep in Our Hearts: Nine White Women in the Freedom Movement*. Athens: University of Georgia Press, 2000.

Daniel, Pete. *Lost Revolutions: The South in the 1950s*. Chapel Hill: University of North Carolina Press, 2000.

Davis, Angela Y. *Blues Legacies and Black Feminism: Gertrude "Ma" Rainey, Bessie Smith, and Billie Holiday*. New York: Vintage Books, 1999.

Doyle, Don. *Nashville since the 1920s*. Knoxville: University of Tennessee Press, 1985.

Dunn, Durwood. "Apprenticeship and Indentured Servitude in Tennessee Before the Civil War." *West Tennessee Historical Society Papers* no. 36 (October 1982): 25–38.

Dykeman, Wilma. *The French Broad*. New York: Holt, Rinehart and Winston, 1955. Reprint, Newport, Tenn.: Wakestone Books, 1992.

———. "'The Past Is Never Dead. It's Not Even Past.'" In *Bloodroot: Reflections on Place by Appalachian Women Writers*, ed. Joyce Dyer, 105–10. Lexington: University Press of Kentucky, 1998.

———. *Roots and Branches*. Chapel Hill: North Caroliniana Society, Inc., and North Carolina Collection, 2001.

Dykeman, Wilma, and James Stokely. *Neither Black nor White*. New York: Holt, Rinehart, and Winston, Inc., 1957.

———. "Our Changing South: A Challenge." In *We Dissent*, ed. Hoke Norris, 3–13. New York: St. Martin's Press, 1962.

Earhart, Amelia. *The Fun of It*. Chicago: Academy Chicago Publishers, 1932.

Engelhardt, Elizabeth S. D. "Wilma Dykeman and the Women of Appalachia: The Ecology of Mid-Century Environmental Activism." *Women's Studies Quarterly* 29, no. 1 (2001): 155–69.

England, J. Merton. "The Free Negro in Ante-Bellum Tennessee." *Journal of Southern History* 9, no. 1 (1943): 37–58.

Evans, Sara. *Personal Politics: The Roots of Women's Liberation in the Civil Rights Movement and the New Left.* New York: Random House, 1979.

Festle, Mary Jo. *Playing Nice: Politics and Apologies in Women's Sports.* New York: Columbia University Press, 1996.

Finger, John R. *Tennessee Frontiers: Three Regions in Transition.* Bloomington: Indiana University Press, 2001.

Foreman, Carolyn Thomas. *Indian Women Chiefs.* Muskogee, Okla.: Hoffman Printing, 1954.

Fox, Pamela. "Recycled Trash: Gender and Authenticity in Country Music Autobiography." *American Quarterly* 50, no. 2 (1998): 234–66.

Giddings, Paula. *When and Where I Enter: The Impact of Black Women on Race and Sex in America.* New York: Amistad Press, 2007.

Gilbert, Amos. *Memoir of Frances Wright: The Pioneer Woman in the Cause of Human Rights.* Cincinnati: privately printed, 1855.

Glenn, Susan A. *Female Spectacle: The Theatrical Roots of Modern Feminism.* Cambridge, Mass.: Harvard University Press, 2000.

Goodstein, Anita Shafer. "A Rare Alliance: African American and White Women in the Tennessee Election of 1919 and 1920." *Journal of Southern History* 64, no. 2 (1968): 219–46.

Green, Laurie. *Battling the "Plantation Mentality": Memphis and the Black Freedom Struggle.* Chapel Hill: University of North Carolina Press, 2007.

Gruberg, Martin. *Women in American Politics: An Assessment and Sourcebook.* Oshkosh, Wis.: Academic Press, 1968.

Guttmann, Allen. *Women's Sports: A History.* New York: Columbia University Press, 1991.

Halberstam, David. *The Children.* New York: Random House, 1998.

Hall, Jacquelyn Dowd, James Leloudis, Robert Korstad, Mary Murphy, Lu Ann Jones, and Christopher B. Daly. *Like a Family: The Making of a Southern Cotton Mill World.* Chapel Hill: University of North Carolina Press, 1987.

Harlan, Louis R. "The Southern Education Board and the Race Issue in Public Education." *Journal of Southern History* 23, no. 2 (1957): 189–202.

Harrison, Cynthia. *Prelude to Feminism: Women's Organizations, the Federal Government and the Rise of the Women's Movement 1942 to 1968.* Ann Arbor, Mich.: University Microfilms, 1982.

Harrison, Daphne Duval. *Black Pearls: Blues Queens of the 1920's.* New Brunswick, N.J.: Rutgers University Press, 1988.

Hine, Darlene Clark, Elsa Barkley Brown, and Roslyn Terborg-Penn, eds. *Black Women in America: An Historical Encyclopedia*. Bloomington: Indiana University Press, 1994. S.v. "Diane Nash," by Jeanne Theodaris, 834–36.

Hine, Darlene Clark, and Kathleen Thompson. *A Shining Thread of Hope: The History of Black Women in America*. New York: Broadway Books, 1998.

Hodges, James A. *New Deal Labor Policy and the Southern Cotton Textile Industry, 1933–1941*. Knoxville: University of Tennessee Press, 1986.

Holt, Andrew David. *The Struggle for a State System of Public Schools in Tennessee, 1903–1913*. New York: Bureau of Publications, Teachers College, Columbia University, 1938.

Huehls, Betty Sparks. "Sue Shelton White: Lady Warrior." Ph.D. diss., University of Memphis, 2002.

———. "Sue Shelton White: The Making of a Radical." *West Tennessee Historical Society Papers* 48 (1994): 24–34.

Hunter, Alberta. *Chicago Living Legends: Alberta Hunter with Lovie Austin's Blues Serenaders*. Columbia Records, 1961.

Imes, William Lloyd. "The Legal Status of Free Negroes and Slaves in Tennessee." *Journal of Negro History* 4, no. 3 (1919): 254–72.

"Interview with Wilma Dykeman." *Appalachian Journal* 29, no. 4 (2002): 450.

Irons, Janet. *Testing the New Deal: The General Textile Strike of 1934 in the American South*. Urbana: University of Illinois Press, 2000.

Irwin, Inez Haynes. *Up Hill with Banners Flying*. Reprint, Penobscot, Maine: Traversity Press, 1964. (Originally published as *The Story of the Woman's Party*. New York: Harcourt, Brace, 1921.)

Jessen, Gene Nora. *The Powder Puff Derby of 1929*. Naperville, Ill.: Sourcebooks, 2002.

Jones, Beverly Washington. *Quest for Equality: The Life and Writings of Mary Eliza Church Terrell, 1863–1954*. Brooklyn: Carlson Publishing, 1990.

Jones, Jacqueline. *Labor of Love, Labor of Sorrow: Black Women, Work, and the Family from Slavery to the Present*. New York: Basic Books, 1985.

Kaledin, Eugenia. *Mothers and More: American Women in the 1950s*. Boston: Twayne Publishers, 1984.

Kibler, M. Allison. *Rank Ladies: Gender and Cultural Hierarchy in American Vaudeville*. Chapel Hill: University of North Carolina Press, 1999.

Lamon, Lester C. *Blacks in Tennessee, 1791–1970*. Knoxville: University of Tennessee Press, 1971.

Lebsock, Suzanne. *Free Women of Petersburg: Status and Culture in a Southern Town, 1784–1860*. New York: W. W. Norton, 1984.

Lewis, John, and Michael D'Orso. *Walking with the Wind: A Memoir of the Movement*. New York: Simon and Schuster, 1998.

Louis, James P. "Sue Shelton White and the Woman Suffrage Movement in Tennessee, 1913–20." *Tennessee Historical Quarterly* 22 (June 1963): 170–90.

Lovett, Bobby L. *The Civil Rights Movement in Tennessee: A Narrative*. Knoxville: University of Tennessee Press, 2005.

McCusker, Kristine, and Diane Pecknold, eds. *A Boy Named Sue: Gender and Country Music.* Jackson: University Press of Mississippi, 2004.

McWhorter, Diane. *Carry Me Home: Birmingham, Alabama: The Climactic Battle of the Civil Rights Revolution.* New York: Simon and Schuster, 2001.

Murphy, Sara Alderman. *Breaking the Silence: Little Rock's Women's Emergency Committee to Open Our Schools, 1958–1963.* Fayetteville: University of Arkansas Press, 1997.

Murray, Gail S. "White Privilege, Racial Justice: Women Activists in Memphis." In *Throwing Off the Cloak of Privilege: White Southern Women Activists in the Civil Rights Era,* ed. Gail S. Murray, 204–29. Gainesville: University Press of Florida, 2004.

Nash, Diane. "Inside the Sit-ins and the Freedom Rides: Testimony of a Southern Student." In *The New Negro,* ed. Mathew H. Ahmann, 45–60. Notre Dame, Ind.: Fides, 1961.

Oakes, Claudia. *United States Women in Aviation, 1930–1939.* Washington, D.C.: Smithsonian Institution Press, 1985.

Olsen, Lynne. *Freedom's Daughters: The Unsung Heroines of the Civil Rights Movement from 1830 to 1970.* New York: Scribner, 2001.

Owen, Robert. *The Life of Robert Owen Written by Himself.* 1857. Reprint, New York: A. M. Kelley, 1967.

Owen, Robert Dale. *Threading My Way.* 1874. Reprint, New York: A. M. Kelley, 1967.

Payne-Gaposchkin, Cecilia. "The Nashoba Plan for Removing the Evil of Slavery: Letters of Frances and Camilla Wright, 1820–1829." *Harvard Library Bulletin* 23 (July 1975): 221–51, (October 1975): 429–61.

Pearl, Minnie, with Joan Dew. *Minnie Pearl: An Autobiography.* New York: Simon and Schuster, 1980.

Pessen, Edward. *Jacksonian America: Society, Personality, and Politics.* Homewood, Ill.: Dorsey Press, 1969.

Planck, Charles E. *Women with Wings.* New York: Harper and Brothers, Inc., 1942.

Powledge, Fred. *Free At Last? The Civil Rights Movement and the People Who Made It.* Boston: Little Brown, 1991.

Ransby, Barbara. *Ella Baker and the Black Freedom Movement: A Radical Democratic Vision.* Chapel Hill: University of North Carolina Press, 2003.

Robnett, Belinda. *How Long? How Long? African-American Women in the Struggle for Civil Rights.* New York: Oxford University Press, 1997.

Rosen, Ruth. *The World Split Open: How the Modern Women's Movement Changed America.* New York: Viking Press, 2000.

Ross, Rosetta E. *Witnessing and Testifying: Black Women, Religion, and Civil Rights.* Minneapolis: Fortress Press, 2003.

Rudolph, Wilma. *Wilma: The Story of Wilma Rudolph.* New York: New American Library, 1977.

Rupp, Leila J., and Verta Taylor. *Survival in the Doldrums: The American Women's Rights Movement, 1945 to the 1960s.* New York: Oxford University Press, 1987.

Salmond, John A. *The General Textile Strike of 1934: From Maine to Alabama*. Columbia: University of Missouri Press, 2002.

Schultz, Debra. *Going South: Jewish Women in the Civil Rights Movement*. New York: New York University Press, 2001.

Scott, Anne Firor. *The Southern Lady: From Pedestal to Politics, 1830–1930*. Chicago: University of Chicago Press, 1970.

Silver, Christopher, and John V. Moeser. *The Separate City: Black Communities in the Urban South, 1940–1968*. Lexington: University Press of Kentucky, 1995.

Smith, Maureen Margaret. "Identity and Citizenship: African American Athletes, Sport, and the Freedom Struggles of the 1960s." Ph.D. diss., Ohio State University, 1999.

Stevens, Doris. *Jailed for Freedom*. New York: Liveright Publishing, 1920.

Tate, Jack B. "Sue White: An Appreciation." In *Women's Studies Manuscript Collections from the Schlesinger Library, Radcliffe College. Series 2, Women in National Politics*. Part A, "Democrats." Research Collections in Women's Studies. Edited by Anne Firor Scott and Randolph Boehm, microfilm reel 12. Bethesda, Md.: University Publications of America, 1992.

Taylor, A. Elizabeth. *The Woman Suffrage Movement in Tennessee*. New York: Bookman Associates, 1957.

Taylor, Frank C., and Gerald Cook. *Alberta Hunter: A Celebration in Blues*. New York: McGraw-Hill, 1987.

Terrell, Mary Church. *A Colored Woman in a White World*. New York: G. K. Hall and Co., 1980.

Thaden, Louise. *High, Wide and Frightened*. New York: Stackpole Sons, 1938.

Trollope, Frances. *Domestic Manners of the Americans*, 1832. Reprint, Gloucester, Mass.: Peter Smith, 1974.

Van Dyke, Roger R. "The Free Negro in Tennessee, 1790–1860." Ph.D. diss., Florida State University, 1972.

Ware, Susan. *Beyond Suffrage: Women in the New Deal*. Cambridge, Mass.: Harvard University Press, 1987.

Wheeler, Marjorie Spruill. *New Women of the New South: The Leaders of the Woman Suffrage Movement in the Southern States*. New York: Oxford University Press, 1993.

White, Deborah Gray. *Too Heavy A Load: Black Women in Defense of Themselves, 1894–1994*. New York: W. W. Norton, 1999.

White, Sue Shelton. "Mother's Daughter." In *These Modern Women: Autobiographical Essays from the Twenties*, ed. Elaine Showalter, 45–51. New York: The Feminist Press, 1979, 1989.

Wiggins, David, ed. *Out of the Shadows: A Biographical History of African American Athletes*. Fayetteville: University of Arkansas Press, 2006.

Wilkerson-Freeman, Sarah. "The Creation of a Subversive Feminist Dominion: Interracialist Social Workers and the Georgia New Deal." *Journal of Women's History* 32, no. 4 (2002): 132–54.

———. "Pauline Van de Graaf Orr (1861–1955): Feminist Education in Mississippi." In *Mississippi Women: Their Histories, Their Lives*, ed. Martha H. Swain, Elizabeth Anne Payne, and Marjorie Julian Spruill, 72–93. Athens: University of Georgia Press, 2003.

———. "The Second Battle for Woman Suffrage: Alabama White Women, the Poll Tax, and V. O. Key's Master Narrative of Southern Politics." *Journal of Southern History* 68, no. 2 (2002): 333–74.

———. "Stealth in the Political Arsenal of Southern Women." In *Southern Women at the Millennium: A Historical Perspective*, ed. Melissa Walker, Jeanette R. Dunn, and Joe P. Dunn, 42–82. Columbia: University of Missouri Press, 2003.

Williams, Emma Inman. *Historic Madison: The Story of Jackson and Madison County, Tennessee*. Jackson, Tenn.: Madison County Historical Society, 1946.

Contributors

BEVERLY GREENE BOND is an associate professor of history and director of African and African American Studies at the University of Memphis. She is the author, with Janann Sherman, of *Memphis in Black and White* (Arcadia Publishing, 2003) and *Images of America: Beale Street* (Arcadia Publishing, 2006). She also contributed essays to *Negotiating the Boundaries of Southern Womanhood: Dealing with the Powers That Be* (University of Missouri Press, 2000), *Trial and Triumph: Readings in Tennessee's African-American Past* (University of Tennessee Press, 2003), and *The Human Tradition: Portraits of African-American Life since 1865* (Scholarly Resources, 2003). She is currently working on another book on African-American women in Memphis between 1820 and 1905.

CAROLE BUCY is a professor of history at Volunteer State Community College. She received her Ph.D. from Vanderbilt University. She is revising her dissertation, "Exercising the Franchise, Building the Body Politic: The League of Women Voters, 1945–1964," for publication. She has recently written two elementary textbooks, *Tennessee through Time: The Early Years*, for fourth graders, and *Tennessee through Time: The Later Years*, for fifth graders (both Gibbs Smith, 2008). She was the founder of the Tennessee Women's History Project and has conducted teacher workshops on incorporating women's history.

MELISSA CHECKER is an assistant professor of urban studies at the City University of New York, Queens College. She is the author of *Polluted Promises: Environmental Racism and the Search for Justice in a Southern Town* (NYU Press, 2005) and coeditor, with Maggie Fishman, of *Local Actions: Cultural Activism, Power, and Public Life in the United States* (Columbia, 2004).

CYNTHIA CUMFER, J.D., Ph.D., was a visiting assistant professor of history and humanities at Reed College from 2002 to 2004 and has taught as an adjunct professor at Lewis and Clark Northwestern School of Law. She was corecipient of the Norris Hundley Jr. Prize from UCLA for her dissertation on the early Tennessee region. Her historical publications include articles in the *Journal of the Early Republic* and the *Oregon Law Review*. Her book, *Separate Peoples, One Land: The Minds of Cherokees, Blacks, and Whites on the Tennessee Frontier* (University of North Carolina Press, 2007), received the Tennessee History Book Award for 2007.

SARAH WILKERSON FREEMAN is associate professor of history at Arkansas State University in Jonesboro. She currently is at work on a study of southern women and the transformation of U.S. politics since the 1880s. Her publications include "The Creation of a Subversive Feminist Dominion: Interracialist Social Workers and the Georgia New Deal" (*Journal of Women's History*, 2002), "The Second Battle for Woman Suffrage: Alabama White Women, the Poll Tax, and V. O. Key's Master Narrative of Southern Politics" (*Journal of Southern History*, 2002), and "Stealth in the Political Arsenal of Southern Women: A Retrospective for the Millennium," in *Southern Women at the Millennium: A Historical Perspective*, ed. Melissa Walker, Jeanette R. Dunn, and Joe P. Dunn (Columbia: University of Missouri Press, 2003).

ARAM GOUDSOUZIAN is an assistant professor of history at the University of Memphis, where he teaches courses in African American history, American popular culture, and the modern United States. The author of *Sidney Poitier: Man, Actor, Icon* (North Carolina, 2004) and *The Hurricane of 1938* (Commonwealth Editions, 2004), he received his Ph.D. in history from Purdue University. He is currently writing a biography of basketball great Bill Russell.

LAURA HELPER-FERRIS earned her Ph.D. at Rice University and is an independent anthropologist. Her book on Memphis race relations and rock 'n' roll is under contract with Duke University Press. She also runs the Helper-Ferris Editorial Agency, offering developmental editing and publishing consultation to academic authors.

BETTY SPARKS HUEHLS is an independent scholar who received her Ph.D. from the University of Memphis. Her dissertation focused on Sue Shelton White. She has contributed articles to the *Tennessee Encyclopedia of History and Culture* and the *West Tennessee Historical Society Papers*.

CHERISSE JONES-BRANCH is an assistant professor of history at Arkansas State University in Jonesboro, where she teaches courses in African American and women's history. She is currently revising her dissertation, "Repairers of the Breach: Black and White Women and Racial Activism in South Carolina, 1940s–1960s," for publication with the University of Florida Press.

CONNIE L. LESTER is an assistant professor in the History Department at University of Central Florida in Orlando and the editor of the *Florida Historical Quarterly*. Her book, *Up From the Mudsills of Hell: The Farmers' Alliance, Populism, and Progressive Agriculture in Tennessee, 1870–1915*, was published by the University of Georgia Press in 2006. She served as associate editor for the *Tennessee Encyclopedia of History and Culture*, which was published by the Tennessee Historical Society in 1998.

KRISTINE M. MCCUSKER is an associate professor of history and director of Undergraduate Studies at Middle Tennessee State University. Her research interests are the Great Depression and World War II, mass media (especially country music), and gender. She is the editor, with Diane Pecknold, of *A Boy Named Sue: Gender and Country Music* (University Press of Mississippi, 2004), and has contributed work to *American Studies* and to *Southern Folklore*. Her book, *Lonesome Cowgirls and Honky Tonk Angels: The Women of Barn Dance Radio* (University of Illinois Press, 2008).

CELIA MORRIS received her Ph.D. from City University of New York. She is an independent scholar and author of *Storming the Statehouse: Running for Governor with Ann Richards and Dianne Feinstein* (Scribner's, 1992), *Fanny Wright: Rebel in America* (University of Illinois Press, 1992), *Bearing Witness: Sexual Harrassment and Beyond—Everywoman's Story* (Little, Brown, 1994), and *Finding Celia's Place* (Texas A&M University Press, 2000). She received the 1993 EMMA Award from the National Women's Political Caucus, was a co-winner of the 1985 Carr P. Collins Award for Distinguished Nonfiction from the Texas Institute of Letters, and was the Texas Women's Political Caucus's 1984 Woman of the Year. She has contributed essays and lectured extensively on women's historical and political roles.

GAIL S. MURRAY is an associate professor and chair of the Department of History at Rhodes College in Memphis. Her current work centers on biracial organizing in Memphis during the civil rights era. She recently edited *Throwing Off the Cloak of Privilege: White Southern Women Activists in the Civil Rights Era* (University Press of Florida, 2004), which includes her essay "White Privilege, Racial Justice: Women Activists in Memphis."

DIANE PECKNOLD is a visiting teaching scholar in the University of Louisville's Commonwealth Center for the Humanities and Society. She is also affiliated with the university's Department of Women's and Gender Studies and the Humanities Program. She is the editor, with Kristine McCusker, of *A Boy Named Sue: Gender and Country Music* (University Press of Mississippi, 2004), and has contributed articles to the *Encyclopedia of Recreation and Leisure in America* and the *Country Music Annual 2002*. Her current research explores the development of the country music industry during the 1950s and 1960s, the cultural meanings that fans and critics attached to the genre's commercialism during those years, how gender shaped male and female experiences of the industry's development, and how it contributed to the creation of a false dichotomy between fandom and professionalism.

MICHELLE R. SCOTT is an assistant professor in history and women's studies at the University of Maryland, Baltimore County. Her research and writing interests include African American history, United States social history, black women's history, and American musical culture. Her book *The Realm of a Blues Empress: Blues Culture and Bessie Smith in Black Chattanooga* is forthcoming from the University of Illinois Press, and she has contributed to the *Martin Luther King Jr. Papers Project* and *The Columbia Guide to African American History since 1939*. Professor Scott has been the recipient of a Mellon-Mays/Social Science Research Council Grant, a Ford Foundation Predoctoral Grant, a Smithsonian Institution Research Grant, and a Woodrow Wilson–Andrew W. Mellon Career Enhancement Postdoctoral Fellowship.

JANANN SHERMAN is the Olin Atkins Professor of History and chair of the History Department at the University of Memphis. Sherman received her Ph.D. from Rutgers University in 1993. Her particular areas of expertise are twentieth-century America, and women and American politics. Her publications include *The Perfect 36: Tennessee Delivers Woman Suffrage* (co-authored with Carol Lynn Yellin) (Serviceberry Press, 1998), *No Place for a Woman: A Life of Senator Margaret Chase Smith* (Rutgers University Press, 1999), *Conversations with Betty Friedan* (University Press of Mississippi, 2002), *Memphis in Black and White* (with Beverly Bond) (Arcadia Publishing, 2003), *Images of America: Beale Street* (with Beverly Bond) (Arcadia Publishing, 2006), and a forthcoming biography of Memphian and pioneer aviator Phoebe Fairgrave Omlie.

MELISSA WALKER, a native Tennessean, is associate professor of history at Converse College in Spartanburg, South Carolina. She grew up about fifty miles from Wilma Dykeman's home and read Dykeman's newspaper columns and books during her teenage years. Walker is the author, editor, or coeditor of five books on southern history including *Southern Farmers and Their Stories* (University Press of Kentucky, 2006) and *All We Knew Was to Farm* (Johns Hopkins University Press, 2000), winner of the Southern Association for Women Historians' Willie Lee Rose Prize.

LINDA T. WYNN is the assistant director for state programs with the Tennessee Historical Commission and on the faculty at Fisk University. Her publications include "Toward a More Perfect Democracy: The Struggle of African Americans in Fayette to Fulfill the Unfulfilled Right of Franchise" in *The History of African Americans in Tennessee: Trials and Triumphs* (University of Tennessee Press, 2002), and selections in the *Tennessee Encyclopedia of Culture and History* (Tennessee Historical Society), the *Encyclopedia of African American Business* (Greenwood Press, 2006), and *Notable Black American Men* vol. 2 (Thompson Gale, 2007). Wynn is editor of *Journey to Our Past: A Guide to African-American Markers in Tennessee* (Tennessee Historical Commission, 1999) and coeditor of *Profiles of African Americans in Tennessee* (Annual Local Conference on Afro-American Culture and History, 2006).

Index